MW00899326

CONTENTS

INTRODUCTION..12
APPETIZERS AND SIDE DISHES.........................14
1. Air Fried Green Tomatoes(2)........................14
2. Weekend Chicken Wings................................14
3. Garlic Lemon Roasted Chicken.....................14
4. Bok Choy And Butter Sauce(2)......................14
5. Hearty Eggplant Fries....................................14
6. Lemony Broccoli...14
7. Sausage Mushroom Caps(2)..........................14
8. Garlic And Parmesan Asparagus...................15
9. Preparation Time: 20 Minutes......................15
10. Ham And Cheese Grilled Sandwich.............15
11. Crispy Cinnamon Apple Chips....................15
12. Garlicky Roasted Chicken With Lemon......15
13. Homemade Prosciutto Wrapped Cheese Sticks 15
14. French Beans With Shallots & Almonds.............15
15. Green Beans..15
16. Molasses Cashew Delight..............................16
17. Roasted Brussels Sprouts.............................16
18. Balsamic Cabbage(2)....................................16
19. Simple Roasted Asparagus...........................16
20. Rice And Artichokes......................................16
21. Crunchy Parmesan Snack Mix.....................16
22. Garlic Roasted Asparagus............................16
23. Poached Fennel...17
24. Cherry Farro..17
25. Sweet Pickle Chips With Buttermilk...........17
26. Lemon-garlic Kale Salad...............................17
27. Pineapple Pork Ribs.....................................17
28. Sausage Mushroom Caps(3).........................17
29. Scallion & Cheese Sandwich........................17
30. Lemon Parmesan And Peas Risotto.............18
31. Baked Artichoke Hearts................................18
32. Baked Apple Sweet Potatoes........................18
33. Coriander Artichokes(1)...............................18
34. Simple Chicken Breasts................................18
35. Broiled Prosciutto-wrapped Pears..............18
36. Easy Parsnip Fries..18
37. Healthy Green Beans....................................19
38. Homemade Cheesy Sticks.............................19
39. Baked Italian Vegetables..............................19
40. Air Fry Garlic Baby Potatoes.......................19
41. Simple Baked Potatoes.................................19
42. Sweet Carrot Puree.......................................19
43. Butternut And Apple Mash..........................19
44. Lime Corn With Feta Cheese.......................20
45. Roasted Garlic Fries......................................20
46. Potato Croquettes...20
47. Charred Green Beans With Sesame Seeds....20
48. Cheesy Squash Casserole..............................20
49. Cauliflower Mash..21
50. Potato Chips With Creamy Lemon Dip.......21
51. Crispy Eggplant Slices..................................21
52. Classic Cauliflower Hash Browns................21
53. Mayo Potato Salad With Bacon....................21
54. Japanese Tempura Bowl................................21
55. Homemade Tortilla Chips.............................22
56. Baked Ratatouille..22
57. Simple Zucchini Crisps.................................22
58. Baked Sweet Potatoes...................................22
59. Chicken & Veggie Nuggets............................22
60. Cheese & Zucchini Cake With Yogurt..........22
61. Zucchini Spaghetti..23
62. Feta Lime Corn..23
63. Sesame Cabbage & Prawn Egg Roll Wraps..........23
64. Air Fry Broccoli Florets.................................23
65. Roasted Garlic(1)...23
66. Balsamic Cabbage(1).....................................23
67. Sesame Sticky Chicken Wings......................23
68. Butternut Squash Croquettes.......................24
69. Bbq Chicken Wings.......................................24
70. Mango Cashew Nuts......................................24
71. Green Beans And Mushrooms......................24
72. Pumpkin Fritters With Ham & Cheese........24
73. Herbed Polenta...25
74. Baked Asparagus...25
75. Cod Nuggets..25
76. Easy Home Fries(2).......................................25
77. Kale And Walnuts(2)......................................25
78. Perfect Crispy Potatoes................................25
79. Baked Turnip & Sweet Potato......................25
80. Parmesan Cabbage Wedges..........................26
81. Spicy Brussels Sprouts(2).............................26
82. Cheesy Crisps..26
83. Pineapple Spareribs......................................26
84. Stuffed Mushrooms With Rice & Cheese.....26
85. Simple Cauliflower Poppers.........................26
86. Garlic & Olive Oil Spring Vegetables...........27
87. Traditional Indian Kofta..............................27
88. Cinnamon-spiced Acorn Squash..................27
89. Broccoli Poppers...27
90. Buffalo Quesadillas.......................................28
91. Baked Lemon Broccoli..................................28
92. Grilled Sandwich With Ham & Cheese........28
93. Green Bean Casserole(3)...............................28
94. Classic French Fries......................................28
95. Broccoli Olives Tomatoes.............................28
96. Garlicky Potatoes..28
97. Sunday Calamari Rings.................................29
98. Chicken Wings In Alfredo Sauce.................29
99. Creamy Broccoli Casserole...........................29
100. Savory Curly Potatoes.................................29
101. Cheddar Cheese Cauliflower Casserole......29
102. Easy Broccoli Bread.....................................29
103. Cheesy Garlic Biscuits.................................29
104. Dijon Zucchini Patties.................................30
105. Jalapeno Bread..30
106. Crispy Onion Rings.....................................30

107. Baked Parmesan Zucchini 30
108. Buttered Broccoli With Parmesan 30
109. Parmesan Zucchini Chips 30
110. Cheddar & Prosciutto Strips 30
111. Pineapple & Mozzarella Tortillas 31
112. Rice Flour Bites 31
113. Parmesan Cauliflower 31
114. Savory Chicken Nuggets & Parmesan Cheese. 31
115. Buttered Corn 31
BREAKFAST RECIPES 32
116. Stylish Ham Omelet 32
117. Italian Sausage & Egg Taquitos 32
118. Easy French-style Apple Cake 32
119. Pea And Potato Samosas With Chutney 32
120. Hash Browns 33
121. Turkey Breakfast Sausage Patties 33
122. Grilled Cheese Sandwich 33
123. Mushroom Spinach Egg Muffins 33
124. Egg In A Hole 33
125. Hearty Sweet Potato Baked Oatmeal 34
126. Poppy Seed Muffins 34
127. Perfect Chicken Casserole 34
128. Parmesan Asparagus 34
129. Bacon And Cheddar Cheese Frittata 34
130. Smoked Sausage Breakfast Mix 34
131. Crunchy Asparagus With Cheese 35
132. Egg English Muffin With Bacon 35
133. Cinnamon Sweet Potato Chips 35
134. Sweet Berry Pastry 35
135. Smart Oven Jalapeño Popper Grilled Cheese
Recipe 35
136. Raspberries Oatmeal 35
137. Ham And Cheese Bagel Sandwiches 36
138. Cinnamon Streusel Bread 36
139. Milky Semolina Cutlets 36
140. Banana Coconut Muffins 36
141. Beans And Pork Mix 36
142. Cheesy Breakfast Casserole 36
143. Flavorful Pumpkin Bread 37
144. Honey Banana Pastry With Berries 37
145. Whole Wheat Carrot Bread 37
146. Classic Cheddar Cheese Omelet 37
147. Yogurt & Cream Cheese Zucchini Cakes 37
148. Ultimate Breakfast Burrito 37
149. Buttery Orange Toasts 38
150. Quick & Easy Granola 38
151. Meat Lover Omelet With Mozzarella 38
152. Basil Parmesan Bagel 38
153. Eggs In A Hole 38
154. Hashbrown Breakfast Casserole 38
155. Chicken Breakfast Sausages 38
156. Quick Cheddar Omelet 39
157. Cheddar Omelet With Soy Sauce 39
158. Caprese Sourdough Sandwich 39
159. Easy Egg Quiche 39
160. Healthy Baked Oatmeal 39
161. Tator Tots Casserole 39

162. Buttery Chocolate Toast 39
163. Coconut Brown Rice Porridge With Dates ... 40
164. Sweet Breakfast Casserole 40
165. Parsley Sausage Patties 40
166. Egg And Avocado Burrito 40
167. Fried Apple Lemon & Vanilla Turnovers 40
168. Fried Potatoes With Peppers And Onions 41
169. Chocolate Banana Bread 41
170. Baked Apple Breakfast Oats 41
171. Cheesy Artichoke-mushroom Frittata 41
172. Mixed Berry Dutch Baby Pancake 42
173. Spinach, Leek And Cheese Frittata 42
174. Nutritious Egg Breakfast Muffins 42
175. Vegetable Quiche 42
176. Crustless Breakfast Quiche 42
177. Smart Oven Baked Oatmeal Recipe 43
178. Apple Butter Pancake 43
179. Breakfast Sweet Potato Hash 43
180. Loaded Breakfast Potatoes 43
181. Eggs In Bell Pepper Rings 43
182. Healthy Squash 44
183. Zucchini Breakfast Casserole 44
184. Cheddar Eggs With Potatoes 44
185. Easy Zucchini Frittata 44
186. Veggies Breakfast Salad 44
187. Feta & Spinach Omelet With Mushrooms 44
188. Balsamic Chicken With Spinach & Kale 44
189. Berry Breakfast Oatmeal 45
190. Chives Salmon And Shrimp Bowls 45
191. Walnuts And Mango Oatmeal 45
192. Canadian Bacon Muffin Sandwiches 45
193. Vanilla Granola 45
194. Stuffed Poblanos 45
195. Spinach & Kale Balsamic Chicken 46
196. Banana And Oat Bread Pudding 46
197. Thai Style Omelette 46
198. Baked Breakfast Quiche 46
199. Crispy Ham Egg Cups 46
200. Spinach Egg Bites 46
201. Bacon And Egg Bread Cups 47
202. Salty Parsnip Patties 47
203. Baked Eggs 47
204. Cheesy Hash Brown Cups 47
205. Green Cottage Omelet 47
206. Turkey Sliders With Chive Mayo 47
207. Sausage Omelet 48
208. Breakfast Tater Tot Casserole 48
209. Simple Apple Crisp 48
210. Asparagus And Cheese Strata 48
211. Ricotta & Chorizo Corn Frittata 48
212. Veggie Frittata 49
213. Corn & Chorizo Frittata 49
214. Sweet Potato Chickpeas Hash 49
215. Easy Grilled Pork Chops With Sweet & Tangy
Mustard Glaze 49
216. Cinnamon French Toasts 49
217. Simply Bacon 50

218. Cheddar Cheese Hash Browns 50
219. Garlic And Cheese Bread Rolls 50
220. Cauliflower Hash Brown 50
221. Basil Prosciutto Crostini With Mozzarella 50
222. Potato Hash 50
223. Moist Orange Bread Loaf 50
224. Egg & Bacon Wraps With Salsa 51
225. Glazed Strawberry Toast 51
226. Zucchini Squash Pita Sandwiches Recipe 51
227. Peanut Butter Banana Bread 51
228. Creamy Parmesan & Ham Shirred Eggs 51
229. Breakfast Potatoes 52
230. Easy Cheesy Breakfast Casserole 52
LUNCH RECIPES 53
231. Juicy Turkey Burgers 53
232. Dijon And Swiss Croque Monsieur 53
233. Saucy Chicken With Leeks 53
234. Roasted Garlic(2) 53
235. Coconut Shrimp With Dip 53
236. Spanish Chicken Bake 54
237. Chicken Wings With Prawn Paste 54
238. Chicken Breast With Rosemary 54
239. Delightful Turkey Wings 54
240. Roasted Fennel, Ditalini, And Shrimp 54
241. Onion Omelet 55
242. Spicy Avocado Cauliflower Toast 55
243. Rosemary Lemon Chicken 55
244. Chicken With Veggies And Rice 55
245. Barbecue Air Fried Chicken 55
246. Tomato And Avocado 56
247. Chives Radishes 56
248. Parmesan Chicken Meatballs 56
249. Cheese-stuffed Meatballs 56
250. Ranch Chicken Wings 56
251. Duck Rolls 56
252. Tomato Frittata 57
253. Pecan Crunch Catfish And Asparagus 57
254. Turkey Legs 57
255. Parmesan-crusted Pork Loin 57
256. Baked Shrimp Scampi 57
257. Roasted Delicata Squash With Kale 57
258. Ground Chicken Meatballs 58
259. Roasted Mini Peppers 58
260. Spicy Egg And Ground Turkey Bake 58
261. Greek Lamb Meatballs 58
262. Pumpkin Pancakes 58
263. Balsamic Roasted Chicken 58
264. Oregano Chicken Breast 59
265. Lobster Tails 59
266. Ricotta Toasts With Salmon 59
267. Pork Stew 59
268. Skinny Black Bean Flautas 59
269. Sweet Potato And Parsnip Spiralized Latkes ..59
270. Cheddar & Cream Omelet 60
271. Lemon Pepper Turkey 60
272. Zucchini Stew 60
273. Sweet Potato Chips 60
274. Jicama Fries(1) 60
275. Vegetarian Philly Sandwich 60
276. Sweet Potato Rosti 60
277. Carrot And Beef Cocktail Balls 61
278. Coriander Potatoes 61
279. Herbed Radish Sauté(3) 61
280. Sweet & Sour Pork 61
281. Perfect Size French Fries 61
282. Easy Turkey Breasts With Basil 61
283. Squash And Zucchini Mini Pizza 62
284. Chicken Parmesan 62
285. Crispy Breaded Pork Chop 62
286. Philly Cheesesteak Egg Rolls 62
287. Air Fryer Beef Steak 62
288. Moroccan Pork Kebabs 63
289. Duck Breast With Figs 63
290. Delicious Chicken Burgers 63
291. Chicken Legs With Dilled Brussels Sprouts 63
292. Herb-roasted Turkey Breast 64
293. Bbq Chicken Breasts 64
294. Chicken Breasts With Chimichurri 64
295. Butter Fish With Sake And Miso 64
296. Orange Chicken Rice 64
297. Herbed Duck Legs 64
298. Chicken & Rice Casserole 65
299. Turkey And Almonds 65
300. Buttered Duck Breasts 65
301. Boneless Air Fryer Turkey Breasts 65
302. Simple Turkey Breast 65
303. Nutmeg Chicken Thighs 65
304. Glazed Lamb Chops 66
305. Air Fried Steak Sandwich 66
306. Okra Casserole 66
307. Roasted Beet Salad With Oranges & Beet Greens 66
308. Chicken Potato Bake 66
309. Chili Chicken Sliders 67
310. Lime And Mustard Marinated Chicken 67
311. Turkey Meatballs With Manchego Cheese 67
312. Easy Italian Meatballs 67
313. Beef Steaks With Beans 67
314. Spicy Green Crusted Chicken 68
315. Air Fryer Fish 68
316. Air Fryer Marinated Salmon 68
317. Kale And Pine Nuts 68
318. Buttermilk Brined Turkey Breast 68
319. Okra And Green Beans Stew 68
320. Beer Coated Duck Breast 68
321. Buttery Artichokes 69
322. Herb-roasted Chicken Tenders 69
323. Tomato Avocado Melt 69
324. Coriander Artichokes(3) 69
325. Roasted Grape And Goat Cheese Crostinis 69
326. Maple Chicken Thighs 69
327. Bok Choy And Butter Sauce(1) 70
328. Eggplant And Leeks Stew 70
329. Fried Chicken Tacos 70

330. Seven-layer Tostadas....................70
331. Turmeric Mushroom(3) 70
332. Deviled Chicken.........................71
333. Turkey-stuffed Peppers.................71
334. Rolled Salmon Sandwich................71
335. Zucchini And Cauliflower Stew.........71
336. Portobello Pesto Burgers..............71
337. Turkey And Mushroom Stew...............72
338. Easy Prosciutto Grilled Cheese 72
339. Spice-roasted Almonds.................72
340. Air Fried Sausages....................72
341. Chicken Caprese Sandwich..............72
342. Sweet Potato And Eggplant Mix 72
343. Turkey And Broccoli Stew..............72
344. Country Comfort Corn Bread............72
345. Basic Roasted Tofu....................73
DINNER RECIPES 74
346. Filet Mignon With Chili Peanut Sauce..74
347. Air Fryer Buffalo Mushroom Poppers ...74
348. Greek-style Monkfish With Vegetables..74
349. Lemon Garlic Shrimps...................74
350. Beef, Mushrooms And Noodles Dish 74
351. Coconut-crusted Haddock With Curried
Pumpkin Seeds 75
352. Morning Ham And Cheese Sandwich 75
353. Venetian Liver.........................75
354. Garlic Parmesan Shrimp.................75
355. Zingy Dilled Salmon....................75
356. Veggie Stuffed Bell Peppers...........75
357. Ham Rolls..............................76
358. Tasty Sausage Bacon Rolls.............76
359. Spicy Paprika Steak....................76
360. Coco Mug Cake..........................76
361. Spiced Salmon Kebabs 76
362. Salmon With Crisped Topped Crumbs.....77
363. Portuguese Bacalao Tapas..............77
364. Broccoli And Tomato Sauce.............77
365. Indian Meatballs With Lamb............77
366. Clam With Lemons On The Grill.........77
367. Spicy Cauliflower Rice................77
368. Rice And Tuna Puff....................78
369. Herbed Eggplant.......................78
370. Roasted Garlic Zucchini Rolls........78
371. Lobster Lasagna Maine Style..........78
372. Homemade Beef Stroganoff.............79
373. Beef Pieces With Tender Broccoli 79
374. Salmon Casserole......................79
375. Stuffed Okra..........................79
376. Roasted Butternut Squash With Brussels
Sprouts & Sweet Potato Noodles.............80
377. Pollock With Kalamata Olives And Capers....80
378. Fish Cakes With Horseradish Sauce 80
379. Lamb Skewers..........................80
380. Crumbly Oat Meatloaf..................80
381. One-pan Shrimp And Chorizo Mix Grill 81
382. Pesto & White Wine Salmon............81
383. Almond Asparagus......................81

384. Garlic Lamb Shank.....................81
385. Beef With Apples And Plums 81
386. Smoked Ham With Pears.................81
387. Marinated Cajun Beef..................81
388. Award Winning Breaded Chicken.........82
389. Chicken Lasagna With Eggplants........82
390. Korean Beef Bowl......................82
391. Stuffed Potatoes......................82
392. Oven-fried Herbed Chicken 82
393. Rich Meatloaf With Mustard And Peppers....83
394. Corned Beef With Carrots..............83
395. Chinese-style Spicy And Herby Beef....83
396. Salsa Stuffed Eggplants...............83
397. Air Fryer Roasted Broccoli...........83
398. Baked Veggie Egg Rolls...............84
399. Sage Beef.............................84
400. Healthy Mama Meatloaf................84
401. Cod With Avocado Mayo Sauce..........84
402. Italian Shrimp Scampi 84
403. Fennel & Tomato Chicken Paillard.....85
404. Grilled Halibut With Tomatoes And Hearts Of
Palm 85
405. Amazing Bacon And Potato Platter.....85
406. Turkey Wontons & Garlic-parmesan Sauce....85
407. Kale And Brussels Sprouts 85
408. Red Hot Chili Fish Curry............85
409. Pork Chops With Chicory Treviso......86
410. Garlic Butter Pork Chops............86
411. Bbq Pork Ribs........................86
412. Paprika Crab Burgers.................86
413. Grilled Chicken Tikka Masala.........86
414. Carrot Beef Cake.....................86
415. Fried Spicy Tofu.....................87
416. Scallops With Spinach 87
417. Cheesy Shrimp........................87
418. Crispy Scallops......................87
419. Breaded Shrimp With Lemon 87
420. Basil Tomatoes.......................87
421. Rigatoni With Roasted Broccoli & Chick Peas 88
422. Scallops With Capers Sauce...........88
423. Sirloin Steak With Cremini Mushroom Sauce.88
424. Chat Masala Grilled Snapper 88
425. Sesame Seeds Bok Choy...............88
426. Sage Sausages Balls.................88
427. Broccoli Stuffed Peppers............89
428. Irish Whisky Steak..................89
429. Beef Roast...........................89
430. Roasted Lamb.........................89
431. Cheese Zucchini Boats...............89
432. Asparagus Frittata..................89
433. Salmon Steak Grilled & Cilantro Garlic Sauce.90
434. Herbed Carrots.......................90
435. Lemongrass Pork Chops...............90
436. Traditional English Fish And Chips..90
437. Miso-glazed Salmon..................90
438. Steak With Cascabel-garlic Sauce....90
439. Prawn Burgers........................91

440. Green Beans And Lime Sauce 91
441. Baby Portabellas With Romano Cheese 91
442. Creole Beef Meatloaf 91
443. Cheese Breaded Pork 91
444. Artichoke Spinach Casserole 92
445. Lemon Duck Legs 92
446. Cajun Fish Fritters 92
447. Baked Egg And Veggies 92
448. Five Spice Pork 92
449. Okra With Green Beans 92
450. Creamy Breaded Shrimp 93
451. Tex-mex Chicken Quesadillas 93
452. Mozzarella & Olive Pizza Bagels 93
453. Tasty Grilled Red Mullet 93
454. Couscous Stuffed Tomatoes 93
455. Grilled Tasty Scallops 93
456. Lemony Green Beans 94
457. Bacon Pork Bites 94
458. Sautéed Green Beans 94
459. Smoked Sausage And Bacon Shashlik 94
460. Chargrilled Halibut Niçoise With Vegetables .. 94
FISH & SEAFOOD RECIPES **95**
461. Saucy Cod With Green Onions 95
462. Fried Calamari 95
463. Spicy Halibut 95
464. Panko-crusted Tilapia 95
465. Parmesan Tilapia Fillets 95
466. Fish Oregano Fingers 95
467. Old Bay Crab Cakes 96
468. Party Cod Nuggets 96
469. Lemon-garlic Butter Lobster 96
470. Salmon & Caper Cakes 96
471. Air Fried Haddock Filets 96
472. Rosemary Buttered Prawns 96
473. Sesame Seeds Coated Fish 96
474. Fish And Chips 97
475. Healthy Haddock 97
476. Old Bay Seasoned Scallops 97
477. Lemon-honey Snapper With Fruit 97
478. Lobster Tails With Lemon-garlic Sauce 97
479. Lemon Tilapia 97
480. Bacon Wrapped Shrimp 98
481. Fish Spicy Lemon Kebab 98
482. Lemony Tuna 98
483. Parsley Catfish Fillets 98
484. Breaded Calamari With Lemon 98
485. Easy Salmon Cakes 98
486. Spicy Lemon Cod 99
487. Baked Flounder Fillets 99
488. Baked Buttery Shrimp 99
489. Garlic Shrimp With Parsley 99
490. Caesar Shrimp Salad 99
491. Crispy Paprika Fish Fillets(2) 100
492. Pecan-crusted Catfish Fillets 100
493. Greek Cod With Asparagus 100
494. Garlic-butter Shrimp With Vegetables 100
495. Cilantro-lime Fried Shrimp 100

496. Tilapia Meunière With Vegetables 101
497. Squab Oregano Fingers 101
498. Oyster Club Sandwich 101
499. Garlic Butter Shrimp Scampi 102
500. Prawn French Cuisine Galette 102
501. Delightful Catfish Fillets 102
502. Prawn Grandma's Easy To Cook Wontons 102
503. Miso White Fish Fillets 102
504. Seafood Spring Rolls 102
505. Baked Garlic Tilapia 103
506. Tasty Tuna Loaf 103
507. Browned Shrimp Patties 103
508. Baked Tilapia With Garlic Aioli 103
509. Crab Cakes With Bell Peppers 103
510. Parmesan Fish Fillets 104
511. Scallops And Spring Veggies 104
512. Sweet & Spicy Lime Salmon 104
513. Harissa Shrimp 104
514. Chili Tuna Casserole 104
515. Basil Salmon With Tomatoes 105
516. Panko Crab Sticks With Mayo Sauce 105
517. Delicious Shrimp Casserole 105
518. Italian Salmon 105
519. Cajun Salmon With Lemon 105
520. Breaded Seafood 106
521. Lemon Butter Shrimp 106
522. Sweet Cajun Salmon 106
523. Parmesan-crusted Salmon Patties 106
524. Air Fryer Spicy Shrimp 106
525. Simple Lemon Salmon 106
526. Panko Catfish Nuggets 106
527. Blackened Tuna Steaks 107
528. Sweet And Savory Breaded Shrimp 107
529. Baked Tilapia 107
530. Mediterranean Sole 107
531. Spicy Catfish 108
532. Fried Cod Nuggets 108
533. Piri-piri King Prawns 108
534. Lobster Grandma's Easy To Cook Wontons .. 108
535. Breaded Fish Fillets 108
536. Shrimp And Cherry Tomato Kebabs 108
537. Teriyaki Salmon 109
538. Old Bay Shrimp 109
539. Coconut-crusted Prawns 109
540. Crispy Crab Legs 109
541. Easy Blackened Shrimp 109
542. Cajun Red Snapper 110
543. Crispy Salmon With Lemon-butter Sauce 110
544. Garlic-butter Catfish 110
545. Old Bay Tilapia Fillets 110
546. Roasted Nicoise Salad 110
547. Lemon Pepper White Fish Fillets 110
548. Roasted Halibut Steaks With Parsley 111
549. Italian Cod 111
550. Seafood Mac N Cheese 111
551. Easy Shrimp And Vegetable Paella 111
552. Quick Paella 112

553. Baked Garlic Paprika Halibut.............. 112
554. Basil White Fish.......................... 112
555. Easy Salmon Patties...................... 112
556. Honey Glazed Salmon..................... 112
557. Parmesan-crusted Hake With Garlic Sauce... 112
558. Fish Club Classic Sandwich............... 113
559. Tomato Garlic Shrimp.................... 113
560. Spiced Red Snapper...................... 113
561. Buttery Crab Legs........................ 113
562. Quick Tuna Patties....................... 113
563. Marinated Salmon........................ 113
564. Crispy Crab And Fish Cakes.............. 114
565. Air Fry Tuna Patties..................... 114
566. Grilled Soy Salmon Fillets............... 114
567. Moist & Juicy Baked Cod 114
568. Fired Shrimp With Mayonnaise Sauce 114
569. Crispy Fish Sticks........................ 115
570. Butter-wine Baked Salmon 115
571. Rosemary Garlic Shrimp.................. 115
572. Parmesan-crusted Halibut Fillets......... 115
573. Cheesy Tilapia Fillets.................... 115
574. Crusty Scallops.......................... 115
575. Spinach Scallops......................... 116
MEAT RECIPES..............................117
576. Bacon With Rosemary Potatoes.......... 117
577. Beef Rolls With Pesto & Spinach......... 117
578. Chicken Momo's Recipe.................. 117
579. Poultry Fried Baked Pastry.............. 117
580. Lush Salisbury Steak With Mushroom Gravy
.... 117
581. Pheasant Marinade Cutlet 118
582. Dry-rubbed Flat Iron Steak.............. 118
583. Bacon Ranch Chicken.................... 118
584. Meatballs(6)............................. 118
585. Pork Leg Roast With Candy Onions...... 118
586. Juicy Spicy Lemon Kebab................ 119
587. Ham Club Sandwich..................... 119
588. Spice-coated Steaks With Cucumber And Snap
Pea Salad 119
589. Perfect Beef Hash Brown Bake 120
590. Hot Chicken Wings...................... 120
591. Pineapple & Ginger Chicken Kabobs...... 120
592. Duck Liver Fries......................... 120
593. Pork Chops With Potatoes(2)............ 120
594. Provençal Chicken With Peppers......... 120
595. Bacon Wrapped Pork Tenderloin........ 121
596. Sweet Sticky Chicken Wings............. 121
597. Bacon-wrapped Sausage & Tomato Relish ... 121
598. Lamb Kofta.............................. 121
599. Meatballs(2)............................. 121
600. Classic Walliser Schnitzel 122
601. Pork Burger Cutlets With Fresh Coriander
Leaves 122
602. Festive Stuffed Pork Chops.............. 122
603. Honey Chicken Drumsticks.............. 122
604. Drumsticks With Barbecue-honeySauce........ 122
605. Spicy Pork Lettuce Wraps............... 122

606. Chicken Grandma's Easy To Cook
Wontons 123
607. Air Fryer Chicken Parmesan 123
608. Meatballs(10)............................ 123
609. Tasty Turkey Meatballs.................. 123
610. Honey & Garlic Chicken Thighs.......... 123
611. Juicy & Tender Pork Chops.............. 124
612. Juicy Pork Ribs Ole 124
613. Lamb Rack With Pistachio............... 124
614. Crispy Parmesan Escallops.............. 124
615. Steak Seared In Browned Butter......... 124
616. Mutton French Cuisine Galette.......... 125
617. Mutton Marinade Cutlet................. 125
618. Coconut Chicken Tenders................ 125
619. Beer Corned Beef With Carrots.......... 125
620. Honey Glazed Chicken Breasts.......... 125
621. Pork Schnitzel........................... 125
622. Pork Butt With Garlicky Coriander-parsley
Sauce 126
623. Mustardy Chicken....................... 126
624. Fried Chicken Tenderloins............... 126
625. Ranch Beef Patties....................... 126
626. Venison Tandoor......................... 126
627. Roasted Lamb Chops With Potatoes...... 127
628. Lamb Marinade Cutlet With Capsicum........... 127
629. Rosemary Pork Chops.................... 127
630. Herby Turkey Balls...................... 127
631. Simple Air Fried Chicken Wings......... 128
632. Herb Pork Tenderloin 128
633. Easy Pork Chops......................... 128
634. Mustard Chicken Tenders................ 128
635. Herb Turkey Tenderloin................. 128
636. Salsa Beef Meatballs..................... 128
637. Ritzy Chicken Roast..................... 128
638. Cayenne Turkey Breasts................. 129
639. Greek Chicken Breast.................... 129
640. Cripsy Crusted Pork Chops 129
641. Crispy Cajun Chicken Breast 129
642. Basil Mozzarella Chicken................ 129
643. Tasty Steak Tips 129
644. Chicken Wings With Chili-lime Sauce 129
645. Duck Breasts & Marmalade Balsamic Glaze.. 130
646. Popcorn Turkey.......................... 130
647. Garlic Butter Wings...................... 130
648. Thyme Turkey Nuggets.................. 130
649. Marinara Sauce Cheese Chicken......... 130
650. Balsamic Chicken With Mozzarella Cheese... 130
651. Rosemary Chicken Breasts............... 131
652. Tamarind Pork Chops With Green Beans 131
653. Baked Lemon Pepper Chicken........... 131
654. Baked Chicken Fritters................... 131
655. Chicken Thighs With Radish Slaw 131
656. Parmesan Chicken Fingers & Plum Sauce...... 132
657. Tender Baby Back Ribs................... 132
658. Meatballs(8)............................. 132
659. Lamb Skewered Momo's Recipe......... 132
660. Duck Oregano Fingers................... 132

661. Goat Cheese Meatballs 132
662. Sweet & Spicy Chicken 133
663. Honey And Wine Chicken Breasts 133
664. Chicken With Potatoes And Corn 133
665. Quail Chili 133
666. Braised Chicken With Hot Peppers 134
667. Savory Honey & Garlic Chicken 134
668. Air Fry Chicken Drumsticks 134
669. Balsamic Chicken Breast Roast 134
670. Pork Wellington 134
671. Beef Grandma's Easy To Cook Wontons 135
672. Duck Poppers 135
673. Fried Pork Scotch Egg 135
674. Golden Chicken Fries 135
675. Delicious Turkey Cutlets 136
676. Squab Cutlet 136
677. Chicken Rochambeau With Mushroom Sauce 136
678. Amazing Bacon & Potato Platter 136
679. Baked Chicken Noodle Casserole 137
680. Meatballs(12) 137
681. Tuscan Air Fried Veal Loin 137
682. Apricot-glazed Chicken Drumsticks 137
683. Zucchini Chicken Meatballs 137
684. Parmesan Chicken Cutlets 138
685. Juicy & Tender Chicken Breast 138
686. Barbecue Pork Club Sandwich & Mustard 138
687. Nice Goulash 138
688. Turkey Grandma's Easy To Cook Wontons ... 138
689. Flank Steak Fajitas 138
690. Cheese-encrusted Chicken Tenderloins With Peanuts 139
MEATLESS RECIPES 140
691. Spicy Thai-style Vegetables 140
692. Stuffed Mushrooms 140
693. Roasted Bell Peppers With Garlic 140
694. Vegetable Pie 140
695. Cheddar & Tempeh Stuffed Mushrooms 140
696. Mediterranean Baked Eggs With Spinach 141
697. Simple Ricotta & Spinach Balls 141
698. Cottage Cheese Flat Cakes 141
699. Teriyaki Tofu 141
700. Gorgonzola Cheese & Pumpkin Salad 141
701. Broccoli & Cheese Egg Ramekins 142
702. Air Fried Carrots, Yellow Squash & Zucchini 142
703. Mint French Cuisine Galette 142
704. Air Fried Kale Chips 142
705. Crispy Tofu Sticks 142
706. Green Chili Flat Cakes 142
707. Simple Ratatouille 143
708. Roasted Butternut Squash & Maple Syrup 143
709. Roasted Brussels Sprouts With Parmesan 143
710. Black Gram French Cuisine Galette 143
711. Potato Club Barbeque Sandwich 143
712. Cilantro Roasted Carrots With Cumin Seeds 144
713. Cheesy Rice And Olives Stuffed Peppers 144
714. Feta & Scallion Triangles 144

715. Roasted Carrots 144
716. Beetroot Chips 144
717. Amazing Macadamia Delight 144
718. Masala Potato Wedges 144
719. Balsamic Asparagus 145
720. Parsley Hearty Carrots 145
721. Rosemary Roasted Squash With Cheese 145
722. Amaranthus French Cuisine Galette 145
723. Mom's Blooming Buttery Onion 145
724. Parmesan Breaded Zucchini Chips 145
725. Lemony Wax Beans 146
726. Cinnamon Celery Roots 146
727. Korean Tempeh Steak With Broccoli 146
728. Yummy Chili Bean Burritos 146
729. Mushrooms Stuffed With Tempeh & Cheddar 146
730. Tomato & Feta Bites With Pine Nuts 146
731. Cheesy Broccoli Tots 147
732. Asparagus French Cuisine Galette 147
733. Nutmeg Broccoli With Eggs & Cheddar Cheese 147
734. Classic Baked Potatoes 147
735. Cottage Cheese Fingers 147
736. French Bean Toast 148
737. Asian-inspired Broccoli 148
738. Chili Cottage Cheese 148
739. Gherkins Flat Cakes 148
740. Bean, Salsa, And Cheese Tacos 148
741. Maple And Pecan Granola 149
742. Dill Baby Carrots With Honey 149
743. Cottage Cheese Pops 149
744. Lemony Brussels Sprouts And Tomatoes 149
745. Sweet-and-sour Brussels Sprouts 149
746. Potato Flat Cakes 149
747. Jalapeño Cheese Balls 150
748. Cottage Cheese Gnocchi's 150
749. Zucchini Crisps 150
750. Stuffed Peppers With Beans And Rice 150
751. Barbeque Corn Sandwich 151
752. Chili Veggie Skewers 151
753. Vegetable And Cheese Stuffed Tomatoes 151
754. Italian Baked Tofu 151
755. Cumin And Cayenne Spicy Sweet Potatoes ... 151
756. Cabbage Flat Cakes 152
757. Hearty Roasted Veggie Salad 152
758. Pizza 152
759. Cheese French Fries 152
760. Cottage Cheese French Cuisine Galette 152
761. Vegetable Spring Rolls 153
762. Cottage Cheese Best Homemade Croquette .. 153
763. Cauliflower Gnocchi's 153
764. Carrots & Shallots With Yogurt 153
765. Okra Spicy Lemon Kebab 153
766. Sweet And Spicy Broccoli 154
767. Stuffed Capsicum Baskets 154
768. Chinese Spring Rolls 154
769. Radish Flat Cakes 154

770. Zucchini Fried Baked Pastry 154
771. Cottage Cheese And Mushroom Mexican Burritos... 155
772. Ratatouille.. 155
773. Stuffed Portobello Mushrooms&Vegetables 155
774. Burger Cutlet.. 156
775. Cottage Cheese Best Homemade Croquette . 156
776. Zucchini Parmesan Crisps................................. 156
777. Cottage Cheese Spicy Lemon Kebab................ 156
778. Garlicky Sesame Carrots.................................. 156
779. Herbed Broccoli With Cheese........................... 157
780. Chickpea Fritters.. 157
781. Roasted Vegetables With Rice........................... 157
782. Panko Green Beans.. 157
783. Honey Chili Potatoes....................................... 157
784. Masala French Cuisine Galette.......................... 158
785. Cheese-walnut Stuffed Mushrooms................... 158
786. Mushroom Marinade Cutlet............................. 158
787. Asparagus Flat Cakes....................................... 158
788. Cheesy Cabbage Wedges.................................. 158
789. Masala Vegetable Skewers............................... 159
790. Cashew Cauliflower With Yogurt Sauce 159
791. Portobello Steaks.. 159
792. Spinach Enchiladas With Mozzarella................ 159
793. Asian Tofu "meatballs".................................... 159
794. Cabbage Fritters(1).. 160
795. Masala French Fries 160
796. Yam Spicy Lemon Kebab.................................. 160
797. Cheese & Vegetable Pizza................................ 160
798. Broccoli Momo's Recipe................................... 160
799. Cauliflower French Cuisine Galette 160
800. Garlicky Fennel Cabbage Steaks...................... 161
801. Vegan Meatloaf... 161
802. Parmesan Coated Green Beans......................... 161
803. Mushroom Pops.. 161
804. Potato Fries With Ketchup................................ 161
805. Palak French Cuisine Galette........................... 161
SNACKS AND DESSERTS RECIPES........................162
806. Baked Plums.. 162
807. Orange Citrus Blend 162
808. Autumn Walnut Crisp...................................... 162
809. Tasty Pumpkin Cookies.................................... 162
810. Coconut Chip Mixed Berry Crisp...................... 162
811. Yummy Scalloped Pineapple............................. 162
812. Vanilla And Oats Pudding................................ 162
813. Caramel Apple Cake.. 163
814. Avocado Bites... 163
815. Yogurt Pumpkin Bread..................................... 163
816. Spicy Cauliflower Florets................................. 163
817. Tapioca Pudding... 163
818. Perfectly Puffy Coconut Cookies 163
819. Eggless Brownies... 164
820. Tasty Jalapeno Poppers.................................... 164
821. Margherita Pizza.. 164
822. Tasty Potato Wedges.. 164
823. Chocolate Ramekins.. 164
824. Banana Butter Brownie.................................... 165

825. Mixed Berries With Pecan Streusel Topping 165
826. Delicious Jalapeno Poppers............................. 165
827. Pancetta And Asparagus With Fried Egg........ 165
828. Crispy Green Tomatoes With Horseradish.... 165
829. Fudgy Chocolate Brownies............................... 166
830. Cheesy Zucchini Tots....................................... 166
831. Vanilla Chocolate Chip Cookies........................ 166
832. Breaded Bananas With Chocolate Sauce........ 166
833. Garlic Edamame 166
834. Lemon Blackberries Cake(1)............................. 167
835. Cranberry Scones.. 167
836. Roasted Mixed Nuts... 167
837. Fried Bananas With Chocolate Sauce.............. 167
838. Mini Crab Cakes... 167
839. Berry Crumble With Lemon 168
840. Olive Garlic Puffs.. 168
841. Strawberries Stew... 168
842. Flavorful Coconut Cake................................... 168
843. Sausage And Mushroom Empanadas 168
844. Pita Bread Cheese Pizza.................................. 169
845. Chocolate Strawberry Cups.............................. 169
846. Shrimp Cheese Quiches................................... 169
847. Flavorful Crab Dip.. 169
848. Vanilla Brownies With Chocolate Chips 169
849. Arugula Artichoke Dip..................................... 169
850. Air Fryer Pepperoni Chips................................ 169
851. Lemon Cake Pudding With Blueberries........... 170
852. Raspberry-coco Desert.................................... 170
853. Raspberry Cream Rol-ups................................ 170
854. Famous New York Cheesecake......................... 170
855. Air Fried Chicken Wings.................................. 170
856. Healthy Lemon Tofu.. 171
857. Herbed Focaccia Bread................................... 171
858. Classic Pound Cake... 171
859. Chocolate Soufflé.. 171
860. Pork Taquitos 172
861. Zucchini Pancakes.. 172
862. Seafood Turnovers... 172
863. Almond Pecan Cookies..................................... 172
864. Preparation Time: 15 Minutes 172
865. Ultimate Chocolate And Coconut Pudding 172
866. Chocolate Pecan Pie.. 173
867. Perfect Chocolate Soufflé 173
868. Homemade Bbq Chicken Pizza......................... 173
869. Sweet Potato Croquettes.................................. 173
870. Ultimate Coconut Chocolate Cake.................... 173
871. Cookie Custards.. 174
872. Summer Citrus Sponge Cake 174
873. Delicious Lemon Bars...................................... 174
874. Tuna Melts With Scallions................................ 174
875. Moist Baked Donuts... 174
876. Almond Butter Cookies.................................... 174
877. Cheese And Ham Stuffed Baby Bella............... 175
878. Easy Egg Custard.. 175
879. Simple Strawberry Cobbler.............................. 175
880. Yogurt Cake(1).. 175
881. Easy Cheese Dip.. 175

882. Gooey Chocolate Fudge Cake 175
883. Strawberry Tart.................................... 175
884. Chocolate Cheesecake 176
885. Bbq Pulled Mushrooms......................... 176
886. Paprika Deviled Eggs 176
887. Bow Tie Pasta Chips 176
888. Air Fryer Mixed Nuts 176
889. Chestnuts Spinach Dip 177
890. Banana Brownies................................. 177
891. Sweet And Salty Snack Mix 177
892. Vanilla Soufflé...................................... 177
893. Mini Pancakes...................................... 177
894. Vanilla Almond Cookies........................ 178
895. Berry Tacos.. 178
896. Tofu Steaks 178
897. Date Bread 178
898. Delicious Raspberry Cobbler 178
899. Cheesy Beef Dip 178
900. Bacon Wrapped Brie 179
901. Banana Clafouti..................................... 179
902. Apple-peach Crumble With Honey.......... 179
903. Polenta Fries With Chili-lime Mayo 179
904. Shrimp And Artichoke Puffs 179
905. Almond Flour Blackberry Muffins............ 180
906. Baked Apple Slices 180
907. Jalapeno Spinach Dip 180
908. Peach-blueberry Tart 180
909. Oaty Chocolate Chip Cookies 180
910. Easy Almond Butter Pumpkin Spice Cookies 181
911. Easy Air Fryer Tofu................................. 181
912. Choco – Chip Muffins 181
913. Tasty Gingersnap Cookies 181
914. Jalapeno Pops 181
915. Mixed Berry Compote With Coconut Chips .. 181
916. Toasted Coco Flakes.............................. 182
917. Air Fryer Cabbage Chips 182
918. Moist Pound Cake 182
919. Almond Cherry Bars 182
920. Baked Yoghurt....................................... 182
OTHER FAVORITE RECIPES 183
921. Chocolate And Coconut Macaroons 183
922. Simple Air Fried Edamame 183
923. Hillbilly Broccoli Cheese Casserole 183
924. Banana Cake 183
925. Teriyaki Shrimp Skewers 183
926. Greek Frittata 184
927. Sweet Air Fried Pecans 184
928. Apple Fritters With Sugary Glaze 184
929. Baked Cherry Tomatoes With Basil.......... 184
930. Fast Cinnamon Toast 184
931. Dehydrated Vegetable Black Pepper Chips... 185
932. Salty Tortilla Chips................................. 185
933. Cinnamon Rolls With Cream Glaze 185
934. Enchilada Sauce.................................... 185
935. Shawarma Spice Mix 186
936. Chocolate Buttermilk Cake 186
937. Shrimp Spinach Frittata 186

938. Cheddar Jalapeño Cornbread............................ 186
939. Cheesy Green Bean Casserole 186
940. Ritzy Chicken And Vegetable Casserole.......... 187
941. Crunchy Green Tomatoes Slices 187
942. Arancini 187
943. Dehydrated Honey-rosemary Roasted Almonds
.... 187
944. Spicy Air Fried Old Bay Shrimp......................... 188
945. Asian Dipping Sauce.. 188
946. Cauliflower And Pumpkin Casserole 188
947. Herbed Cheddar Frittata.................................... 188
948. Ritzy Pimento & Almond Turkey Casserole.. 188
949. Sweet And Sour Peanuts 189
950. Garlicky Spiralized Zucchini And Squash....... 189
951. Parsnip Fries With Garlic-yogurt Dip............... 189
952. Kale Chips With Soy Sauce 189
953. Corn On The Cob With Mayonnaise 189
954. Sumptuous Beef And Bean Chili
Casserole 190
955. Simple Butter Cake.. 190
956. Supplì Al Telefono (risotto Croquettes).......... 190
957. Classic Churros 191
958. Oven Grits.. 191
959. Creamy Pork Gratin 191
960. Spanakopita.. 191
961. Lush Seafood Casserole 192
962. South Carolina Shrimp And Corn Bake 192
963. Shrimp With Sriracha And Worcestershire
Sauce 192
964. Buttery Knots With Parsley 193
965. Sausage And Colorful Peppers Casserole....... 193
966. Parmesan Cauliflower Fritters 193
967. Chicken Sausage And Broccoli Casserole....... 193
968. Chicken Divan.. 193
969. Southwest Seasoning 194
970. Dehydrated Crackers With Oats 194
971. Sweet Cinnamon Chickpeas 194
972. Broccoli, Carrot, And Tomato Quiche.............. 194
973. Simple Cheesy Shrimps....................................... 194
974. Air Fried Blistered Tomatoes 195
975. Chinese Pork And Mushroom Egg Rolls 195
976. Keto Cheese Quiche 195
977. Golden Salmon And Carrot Croquettes 196
978. Goat Cheese And Asparagus Frittata 196
979. Taco Beef And Chile Casserole 196
980. Pastrami Casserole.. 196
981. Chicken Ham Casserole....................................... 197
982. Kale Salad Sushi Rolls With Sriracha
Mayonnaise 197
983. Oven Baked Rice... 197
984. Air Fried Crispy Brussels Sprouts..................... 197
985. Traditional Latkes 197
986. Citrus Avocado Wedge Fries.............................. 198
987. Spinach And Chickpea Casserole...................... 198
988. Sumptuous Vegetable Frittata.......................... 198
989. Roasted Mushrooms... 198
990. Hot Wings... 199

991. Mediterranean Quiche 199
992. Potato Chips With Lemony Cream Dip............ 199
993. Caesar Salad Dressing 199
994. Crunchy And Beery Onion Rings..................... 199
995. Bartlett Pears With Lemony Ricotta................ 200
996. Garlicky Olive Stromboli 200

997. Butternut Squash With Hazelnuts 200
998. Lemony Shishito Peppers 200
999. Golden Nuggets.. 201
1000. Pão De Queijo.. 201
1001. Milky Pecan Tart.. 201

INTRODUCTION

The Instant Vortex Air Fryer Oven is a multi-use countertop appliance that prepares dishes by circulating super-heated air around the food, with little or no cooking oil, to achieve crunchy golden "air-fried" meals. It features an advanced microprocessor and 7-preset Smart Programs. With 1500 Watts of power, you will be able to cook anything fresh or frozen with a perfectly golden crispy outside and tender inside. There are six built-in programs, each with a default cooking time and temperature, that let you air fry, roast, broil, bake, reheat and dehydrate. You also have the option to adjust the time and temperature manually using the touchscreen controls on the LED display. One of this air fryer's most-exciting features is its rotisserie capacity. It's part of the roast setting, and it allows you to prepare a whole rotisserie-style chicken or roast beef in less than an hour. Activating the rotisserie rotate function is simple using the appropriate touchscreen control.

The Instant Vortex Air Fryer Oven reheats leftovers nicely, broils pork chops and asparagus and bakes potatoes. Another great feature is this appliance's dehydrate function. This is the one task that it doesn't perform quickly because dehydration happens at much lower temperatures. But don't worry—your patience will be rewarded in a few hours' time with perfectly dehydrated fruit chips and jerky. The oven reaches a maximum temperature of 400° F and has a 10-quart capacity, so it's great for preparing meals for larger families, but at 13 inches square, it doesn't take up a lot of counter space.

What does an air fryer do?

Air fryer ovens, which work more or less like convection ovens, are electrical appliances that can be used to cook meats and vegetables, prepare frozen foods and even bake desserts. Convection ovens work by using fans to circulate and evenly distribute hot air around the food. Air fryer ovens do the same thing, but because of their reduced size compared to full-size convection ovens, air circulates more quickly, resulting in a speedier cooking process. This gives foods that traditional texture and crispiness associated with deep frying. These appliances resemble countertop ovens. They have more space inside than traditional air fryers, which are equipped with only a basket or drawer. They also often include accessories. The Instant Oven comes with a drip tray, rotisserie basket, and rotisserie spit, lift and forks. With the two included vented cooking trays, you can cook two different foods at the same time.

What can you cook in an air fryer oven?

You can cook any type of fish, meat or vegetable in this appliance, and there's such a variety of functions that you can cook a number of foods more than one way. You can make desserts such as cookies, doughnuts and brownies, main dishes like meatloaf, lasagna and pizza, and healthy snacks such as kale chips. You'll love the ease with which you can make wings using the rotisserie basket. Frozen foods meant to be fried, including chicken nuggets and breaded cheese sticks, also turn out nicely, with a lot less fat than if they were fried in oil.

Does the Instant Vortex Air Fryer Oven offer health benefits?
Deep-frying foods may make them taste great, but this cooking method isn't known for being particularly good for you. Oil tends to be high in trans fats and calories, which are associated with a higher risk of high cholesterol, obesity and high blood pressure. With the Instant Vortex Plus Air Fryer Oven, you can use a much smaller quantity of oil to achieve the crunchy, crispy texture typical of deep-fried foods.

What are the pros and benefits of the Instant Vortex Plus?
In addition to this appliance's versatility and its capacity for preparing food in a healthy manner, cooking speed is one of its biggest pros. Preheating takes only a few minutes, and the actual cooking process happens in a fraction of the time compared to what it would take with other methods. Cleanup is a breeze with the Instant Oven, too. With an air fryer, you make less of a mess to begin with because you're using so little oil. The oven's accessories are dishwasher-safe, and the door can be removed for easy hand-washing. Last but not least, you can use appliances like the Instant Oven at any time of year. Conventional ovens always heat up the kitchen—maybe even the entire house—which means many people find it unthinkable to roast, bake or broil during the summer months. This air fryer is compact, and it works efficiently and quickly, resulting in a lot less heat inside the home. This makes it a practical, all-season appliance.

What are the cons of the Instant Oven?
The manual that accompanies this air fryer is thin and contains only a short table of suggested cooking times that doesn't provide much guidance. This consistently comes up in air fryer reviews as one of this appliance's top deficiencies. Users are left to figure out for themselves what quantities of foods to cook and for how long. The fact that chickens need to be trussed in order to rotate on the spit also isn't mentioned. Read enough air fryer reviews and you'll also see that some people aren't satisfied with the "fried" aspect of foods prepared in air fryers. The Instant Oven is no different in that respect. Food may lack that deep-fried flavor that traditional oil fryers deliver, so anyone looking for fried foods that look and taste greasy should choose alternative cooking methods. At 17 pounds, the Instant Oven also weighs too much to make it an appliance you keep in a cabinet and pull out whenever you need it. This means it will need a permanent home on a counter or island, something that may be an issue in houses with smaller kitchens.

APPETIZERS AND SIDE DISHES

1. Air Fried Green Tomatoes(2)

Servings: 4   Cooking Time: 8 Minutes
Ingredients:

2 medium green tomatoes	¼ cup blanched finely ground almond flour.
⅓ cup grated Parmesan cheese.	1 large egg.

Directions:
Slice tomatoes into ½-inch-thick slices. Take a medium bowl, whisk the egg. Take a large bowl, mix the almond flour and Parmesan.   Dip each tomato slice into the egg, then dredge in the almond flour mixture. Place the slices into the air fryer basket Adjust the temperature to 400 Degrees F and set the timer for 7 minutes. Flip the slices halfway through the cooking time. Serve immediately

2. Weekend Chicken Wings

Servings: 3   Cooking Time: 20 Minutes
Ingredients:

15 chicken wings	⅓ cup butter
⅓ cup chili sauce	½ tbsp vinegar

Directions:
Preheat Instant Vortex on AirFry function to 360 F. Season the wings with pepper and salt. Add them to the toaster oven. Press Start and cook for 15 minutes. Once ready, remove them to a bowl.   Melt the butter in a saucepan over low heat. Add in the vinegar and hot sauce. Stir and cook for 2-3 minutes. Turn the heat off. Pour the sauce over the chicken and toss to coat. Transfer the chicken to a serving platter. Serve with a side of celery strips and blue cheese dressing.

3. Garlic Lemon Roasted Chicken

Servings: 4   Cooking Time: 60 Minutes
Ingredients:

1 (3 ½ pounds) whole chicken	2 tbsp olive oil
Salt and black pepper to taste	1 lemon, cut into quarters
	5 garlic cloves

Directions:
Preheat Instant Vortex on Air Fry function to 360 F. Brush the chicken with olive oil and season with salt and pepper. Stuff with lemon and garlic cloves into the cavity.   Place the chicken breast-side down onto the Instant Vortex Air Fryer basket. Tuck the legs and wings tips under. Fit in the baking tray and cook for 45 minutes at 350 F on Bake function. Let rest for 5-6 minutes, then carve and serve.

4. Bok Choy And Butter Sauce(2)

Servings: 4   Cooking Time: 20 Minutes
Ingredients:

2 bok choy heads; trimmed and cut into strips	2 tbsp. chicken stock
1 tbsp. butter; melted	1 tsp. lemon juice
	1 tbsp. olive oil
	A pinch of salt and black pepper

Directions:
In a pan that fits your air fryer, mix all the ingredients, toss, introduce the pan in the air fryer and cook at 380°F for 15 minutes.   Divide between plates and serve as a side dish

5. Hearty Eggplant Fries

Servings: 2   Cooking Time: 20 Minutes
Ingredients:

1 eggplant, sliced	1 tsp soy sauce
1 tsp olive oil	Salt to taste

Directions:
Preheat Instant Vortex on AirFry function to 400 F. Make a marinade of olive oil, soy sauce, and salt and mix well in a bowl. Add in the eggplant and toss to coat.   Transfer them to the frying basket and place in the oven. Press Start and cook for 8 minutes. Serve drizzled with maple syrup.

6. Lemony Broccoli

Servings: 6   Cooking Time: 15 Minutes
Ingredients:

5 lemon slices	Salt and ground black pepper, to taste
1 head of broccoli, separated into florets	1 cup water

Directions:
Pour the water into the Instant Pot. Season the broccoli with salt and pepper to taste and add them to the instant pot, add the lemon slices and mix gently.   Cover the pan instantly and cook for 15 minutes. Relieve the pressure, divide the broccoli between the plates and serve.

7. Sausage Mushroom Caps(2)

Servings: 2   Cooking Time: 20 Minutes
Ingredients:

½ lb. Italian sausage	2 tbsp. blanched finely ground almond flour
6 large Portobello mushroom caps	
¼ cup grated Parmesan cheese.	1 tsp. minced fresh garlic
¼ cup chopped onion	

Directions:
Use a spoon to hollow out each mushroom cap, reserving scrapings.   In a medium skillet over medium heat, brown the sausage about 10 minutes or until fully cooked and no pink remains. Drain and then add reserved mushroom scrapings, onion, almond flour, Parmesan and garlic.   Gently fold ingredients together and continue cooking an additional minute, then remove from heat   Evenly spoon the mixture into mushroom caps and place the caps into a 6-inch round pan. Place pan into the air fryer basket   Adjust the temperature to 375 Degrees F and set the timer for 8 minutes. When

finished cooking, the tops will be browned and bubbling. Serve warm.

8. Garlic And Parmesan Asparagus

Servings: 4   Cooking Time: 8 Minutes
Ingredients:
- 1 cup water
- 3 garlic cloves, peeled and minced
- 1 bunch asparagus, trimmed
- 3 tablespoons Parmesan cheese, grated
- 3 tablespoons butter

Directions:
Place the water in the Instant Pot. Place the asparagus in aluminum foil, add the garlic and butter and seal the edges of the leaf.   Place in the pan, cover and cook for 8 minutes in the Manual setting. Relieve the pressure, arrange the asparagus on the plates, sprinkle with cheese and serve.

9. Preparation Time: 20 Minutes

Servings: 2   Cooking Time: 20 Minutes
Ingredients:
- 2 bell peppers, tops and seeds removed
- Salt and pepper, to taste
- 2/3 cup cream cheese
- 2 tablespoons mayonnaise
- 1 tablespoon fresh celery stalks, chopped

Directions:
Arrange the peppers in the lightly greased cooking basket. Cook in the preheated Air Fryer at 400 degrees F for 15 minutes, turning them over halfway through the cooking time.   Season with salt and pepper.   Then, in a mixing bowl, combine the cream cheese with the mayonnaise and chopped celery. Stuff the pepper with the cream cheese mixture and serve.

10. Ham And Cheese Grilled Sandwich

Servings: 2   Cooking Time: 15 Minutes
Ingredients:
- 4 slices bread
- ¼ cup butter
- 2 slices ham
- 2 slices cheese

Directions:
Preheat Instant Vortex on Air Fry function to 360 F. Place 2 bread slices on a flat surface. Spread butter on the exposed surfaces. Lay cheese and ham on two of the slices. Cover with the other 2 slices to form sandwiches. Place the sandwiches in the cooking basket and cook for 5 minutes on Bake function. For additional crispiness, set on Toast function for 2 minutes.

11. Crispy Cinnamon Apple Chips

Servings: 4   Cooking Time: 10 Minutes
Ingredients:
- 2 apples, cored and cut into thin slices
- Cooking spray
- 2 heaped teaspoons ground cinnamon

Directions:
Spritz the air fryer basket with cooking spray.   In a medium bowl, sprinkle the apple slices with the cinnamon. Toss until evenly coated. Spread the coated apple slices on the pan in a single layer. Put the air fryer basket on the baking pan and slide into Rack Position 2, select Air Fry, set temperature to 350ºF (180ºC) and set time to 10 minutes. After 5 minutes, remove from the oven. Stir the apple slices and return to the oven to continue cooking.   When cooking is complete, the slices should be until crispy. Remove from the oven and let rest for 5 minutes before serving.

12. Garlicky Roasted Chicken With Lemon

Servings: 4   Cooking Time: 60 Minutes
Ingredients:
- 1 whole chicken (around 3.5 lb)
- Salt and black pepper to taste
- 1 tbsp olive oil
- 1 lemon, cut into quarters
- 5 garlic cloves

Directions:
Rub the chicken with olive oil and season with salt and pepper. Stuff the cavity with lemon and garlic. Place chicken, breast-side down on a baking tray. Tuck the legs and wings tips under.   Select Bake function, adjust the temperature to 360 F, and press Start. Bake for 30 minutes, turn breast-side up, and bake it for another 15 minutes. Let rest for 5-6 minutes then carve.

13. Homemade Prosciutto Wrapped Cheese Sticks

Servings: 6   Cooking Time: 50 Minutes
Ingredients:
- 1 lb cheddar cheese
- 12 slices of prosciutto
- 1 cup flour
- 2 eggs, beaten
- 4 tbsp olive oil
- 1 cup breadcrumbs

Directions:
Cut the cheese into 6 equal sticks. Wrap each piece with 2 prosciutto slices. Place them in the freezer just enough to set. Preheat Instant Vortex on Air Fry function to 390 F. Dip the croquettes into flour first, then in eggs, and coat with breadcrumbs. Drizzle the basket with oil and fit in the baking tray. Cook for 10 minutes or until golden. Serve.

14. French Beans With Shallots & Almonds

Servings: 4   Cooking Time: 25 Minutes
Ingredients:
- 1 ½ pounds French beans
- 2 shallots, chopped
- 2 tbsp olive oil
- ½ cup almonds, toasted

Directions:
Preheat Instant Vortex on AirFry function to 400 F. Blanch the beans in boiling water for 5-6 minutes. Drain and mix with oil and shallots in a baking sheet. Cook for 10 minutes. Serve with almonds.

15. Green Beans

Servings: 4   Cooking Time: 20 Minutes
Ingredients:

6 cups green beans; trimmed
1 tbsp. hot paprika
2 tbsp. olive oil
A pinch of salt and black pepper

Directions:
Take a bowl and mix the green beans with the other ingredients, toss, put them in the air fryer's basket and cook at 370°F for 20 minutes   Divide between plates and serve as a side dish.

16. Molasses Cashew Delight

Servings: 4   Cooking Time: 20 Minutes
Ingredients:

3 cups cashews
3 tbsp liquid smoke
2 tsp salt
2 tbsp molasses

Directions:
Preheat Instant Vortex on Air Fry function to 360 F. In a bowl, add salt, liquid, molasses, and cashews; toss to coat thoroughly. Place the cashews in the frying baking tray and cook for 10 minutes, shaking every 5 minutes. Serve.

17. Roasted Brussels Sprouts

Servings: 6   Cooking Time: 30 Minutes
Ingredients:

1-1/2 pounds Brussels sprouts, ends trimmed and yellow leaves removed
1 teaspoon salt
3 tablespoons olive oil
1/2 teaspoon black pepper

Directions:
Start by preheating toaster oven to 400°F.   Toss Brussels sprouts in a large bowl, drizzle with olive oil, sprinkle with salt and pepper, then toss.   Roast for 30 minutes.

18. Balsamic Cabbage(2)

Servings: 4   Cooking Time: 20 Minutes
Ingredients:

6 cups red cabbage; shredded
4 garlic cloves; minced
1 tbsp. olive oil
1 tbsp. balsamic vinegar
Salt and black pepper to taste.

Directions:
In a pan that fits the air fryer, combine all the ingredients, toss, introduce the pan in the air fryer and cook at 380°F for 15 minutes   Divide between plates and serve as a side dish.

19. Simple Roasted Asparagus

Servings: 4   Cooking Time: 10 Minutes
Ingredients:

1 bunch asparagus
4 tablespoons olive oil
Salt and pepper to taste

Directions:
Start by preheating toaster oven to 425°F.   Wash the asparagus and cut off the bottom inch.   Toss the asparagus in olive oil and lay flat on a baking sheet.   Sprinkle salt and pepper over asparagus. Roast in the oven for 10 minutes.

20. Rice And Artichokes

Servings: 4   Cooking Time: 20 Minutes
Ingredients:

2 garlic cloves, peeled and crushed
1¼ cups chicken broth
1 tablespoon extra-virgin olive oil
5 ounces Arborio rice
1 tablespoon white wine
15 ounces canned artichoke hearts, chopped
16 ounces cream cheese
1 tablespoon grated Parmesan cheese
1½ tablespoons fresh thyme, chopped
Salt and ground black pepper, to taste
6 ounces graham cracker crumbs
1¼ cups water

Directions:
Put the Instant Pot in the sauté mode, add the oil, heat, add the rice and cook for 2 minutes. Add the garlic, mix and cook for 1 minute.   Transfer to a heat-resistant plate. Add the stock, crumbs, salt, pepper and wine, mix and cover the plate with aluminum foil.   Place the dish in the basket to cook the Instant Pot, add water, cover and cook for 8 minutes on rice. Release the pressure, remove the dish, uncover, add cream cheese, parmesan, artichoke hearts and thyme.   Mix well and serve.

21. Crunchy Parmesan Snack Mix

Servings: 6 Cups   Cooking Time: 6 Minutes
Ingredients:

2 cups oyster crackers
2 cups Chex rice
1 cup sesame sticks
8 tablespoons unsalted butter, melted
⅔ cup finely grated Parmesan cheese
1½ teaspoons granulated garlic
½ teaspoon kosher salt

Directions:
Toss together all the ingredients in a large bowl until well coated. Spread the mixture in the baking pan in an even layer.   Slide the baking pan into Rack Position 1, select Convection Bake, set temperature to 350°F (180°C) and set time to 6 minutes.   After 3 minutes, remove from the oven and stir the mixture. Return to the oven and continue cooking. When cooking is complete, the mixture should be lightly browned and fragrant. Let cool before serving.

22. Garlic Roasted Asparagus

Servings: 4   Cooking Time: 10 Minutes
Ingredients:

2 tablespoons olive oil
1 tablespoon balsamic vinegar
2 teaspoons minced garlic
1 pound (454 g) asparagus, woody ends trimmed
Salt and freshly ground black pepper, to taste

Directions:
In a large shallow bowl, toss the asparagus with the olive oil, balsamic vinegar, garlic, salt, and pepper until thoroughly coated. Put the asparagus in the air fryer basket.   Put the air fryer basket on the

baking pan and slide into Rack Position 2, select Roast, set temperature to 400ºF (205ºC), and set time to 10 minutes. Flip the asparagus with tongs halfway through the cooking time. When cooking is complete, the asparagus should be crispy. Remove from the oven and serve warm.

23. Poached Fennel

Servings: 3   Cooking Time: 6 Minutes
Ingredients:

Ground nutmeg	Salt, to taste
1 tablespoon white flour	2 big fennel bulbs, sliced
2 cups milk	2 tablespoons butter

Directions:
Put the Instant Pot in Saute mode, add the butter and melt. Add the fennel slices, mix and cook until lightly browned. Add the flour, salt, pepper, nutmeg and milk, mix, cover and cook in the manual for 6 minutes. Relieve the pressure, transfer the fennel to the dishes and serve.

24. Cherry Farro

Servings: 6   Cooking Time: 40 Minutes
Ingredients:

1 teaspoon lemon juice Salt, to taste	½ cup cherries, dried and chopped
1 tablespoon apple cider vinegar	1 tablespoon extra-virgin olive oil
1 cup whole grain faro	¼ cup green onions, chopped
2 cups cherries, pitted and cut into halves	10 mint leaves, chopped
3 cups water	

Directions:
Place the water in the Instant Pot, add the spelled rinse, stir, cover and cook in the Multigrain setting for 40 minutes. Relieve the pressure, drain the spelled, transfer it to a bowl and mix with salt, oil, lemon juice, vinegar, dried cherries, fresh cherries, green onions and mint. Mix well, divide between plates and serve.

25. Sweet Pickle Chips With Buttermilk

Servings: 3   Cooking Time: 20 Minutes
Ingredients:

36 sweet pickle chips	¼ cup cornmeal
1 cup buttermilk	Salt and black pepper to taste
3 tbsp smoked paprika	
2 cups flour	

Directions:
Preheat Instant Vortex on Air Fryer function to 400 F. In a bowl, mix flour, paprika, pepper, salt, cornmeal, and powder. Place pickles in buttermilk and set aside for 5 minutes. Dip the pickles in the spice mixture and place them in the greased air fryer basket. Fit in the baking tray and cook for 10 minutes. Serve warm.

26. Lemon-garlic Kale Salad

Servings: 8   Cooking Time: 10 Minutes
Ingredients:

2 cups sliced almonds	4 cloves crushed garlic
1/3 cup lemon juice	12 ounces kale, stems removed
1 teaspoon salt	
1-1/2 cups olive oil	

Directions:
Set toaster oven to toast and toast almonds for about 5 minutes. Combine lemon juice and salt in a small bowl, then add olive oil and garlic; mix well and set aside. Slice kale into thin ribbons; place in a bowl and sprinkle with almonds. Remove garlic from dressing, then add desired amount of dressing to kale and toss. Add additional dressing if necessary, and serve.

27. Pineapple Pork Ribs

Servings: 4   Cooking Time: 30 Minutes
Ingredients:

2 lb cut spareribs	2 cups water
7 oz salad dressing	Salt and black pepper to taste
1 (5-oz) can pineapple juice	

Directions:
Preheat your Instant Vortex to 390 F on Bake function. Sprinkle the ribs with salt and pepper and place them in a greased baking dish. Cook for 15 minutes. Prepare the sauce by combining the salad dressing and the pineapple juice. Serve the ribs drizzled with the sauce.

28. Sausage Mushroom Caps(3)

Servings: 2   Cooking Time: 8 Minutes
Ingredients:

½ lb. Italian sausage	2 tbsp. blanched finely ground almond flour
6 large Portobello mushroom caps	1 tsp. minced fresh garlic
¼ cup grated Parmesan cheese.	
¼ cup chopped onion	

Directions:
Use a spoon to hollow out each mushroom cap, reserving scrapings. In a medium skillet over medium heat, brown the sausage about 10 minutes or until fully cooked and no pink remains. Drain and then add reserved mushroom scrapings, onion, almond flour, Parmesan and garlic. Gently fold ingredients together and continue cooking an additional minute, then remove from heat Evenly spoon the mixture into mushroom caps and place the caps into a 6-inch round pan. Place pan into the air fryer basket Adjust the temperature to 375 Degrees F and set the timer for 8 minutes. When finished cooking, the tops will be browned and bubbling. Serve warm.

29. Scallion & Cheese Sandwich

Servings: 1   Cooking Time: 15 Minutes
Ingredients:

2 tbsp Parmesan cheese, shredded	1 tbsp butter
	2 slices bread

1 tsp fresh scallions, chopped   ¾ cup cheddar cheese

Directions:
Preheat Instant Vortex on AirFry function to 360 F. Lay the bread slices on a flat surface. Spread the exposed side with butter, followed by some cheddar cheese, and scallions. On the other slice, spread butter and then sprinkle the remaining cheddar cheese.   Bring the buttered sides together to form sandwich. Place the sandwich in baking tray and place in the oven. Press Start and cook for 10 minutes. Serve with berry sauce.

30. Lemon Parmesan And Peas Risotto

Servings: 6   Cooking Time: 17 Minutes
Ingredients:

2 tablespoons butter
1½ cup rice
1 yellow onion, peeled and chopped
1 tablespoon extra-virgin olive oil
1 teaspoon lemon zest, grated
3½ cups chicken stock

2 tablespoons lemon juice
2 tablespoons parsley, diced
2 tablespoons Parmesan cheese, finely grated
Salt and ground black pepper, to taste
1½ cup peas

Directions:
Put the Instant Pot in the sauté mode, add 1 tablespoon of butter and oil and heat them. Add the onion, mix and cook for 5 minutes.   Add the rice, mix and cook for another 3 minutes. Add 3 cups of broth and lemon juice, mix, cover and cook for 5 minutes on rice.   Release the pressure, put the Instant Pot in manual mode, add the peas and the rest of the broth, stir and cook for 2 minutes.   Add the cheese, parsley, remaining butter, lemon zest, salt and pepper to taste and mix. Divide between plates and serve.

31. Baked Artichoke Hearts

Servings: 6   Cooking Time: 25 Minutes
Ingredients:

15 oz frozen artichoke hearts, defrosted

1 tbsp olive oil
Pepper
Salt

Directions:
Fit the Instant Vortex oven with the rack in position Arrange artichoke hearts in baking pan and drizzle with olive oil. Season with pepper and salt.   Set to bake at 400 F for 30 minutes. After 5 minutes place the baking pan in the preheated oven.   Serve and enjoy.

32. Baked Apple Sweet Potatoes

Servings: 2   Cooking Time: 30 Minutes
Ingredients:

2 large sweet potatoes, diced
2 large green apples, diced

2 tsp cinnamon
2 tbsp maple syrup
1 tbsp olive oil

Directions:
Fit the Instant Vortex oven with the rack in position In a large bowl, add sweet potatoes, oil, cinnamon, and apples and toss well.   Spread sweet potatoes mixture in baking pan.   Set to bake at 400 F for 35 minutes. After 5 minutes place the baking pan in the preheated oven.   Drizzle with maple syrup and serve.

33. Coriander Artichokes(1)

Servings: 4   Cooking Time: 20 Minutes
Ingredients:

12 oz. artichoke hearts
1 tbsp. lemon juice
1 tsp. coriander, ground

½ tsp. cumin seeds
½ tsp. olive oil
Salt and black pepper to taste.

Directions:
In a pan that fits your air fryer, mix all the ingredients, toss, introduce the pan in the fryer and cook at 370°F for 15 minutes   Divide the mix between plates and serve as a side dish.

34. Simple Chicken Breasts

Servings: 4   Cooking Time: 30 Minutes
Ingredients:

4 boneless, skinless chicken breasts
1 tsp garlic powder

1 tsp salt and black pepper

Directions:
Spray the breasts and the Instant Vortex Air Fryer basket with cooking spray. Rub chicken with salt, garlic powder, and black pepper. Arrange the breasts on the basket. Fit in the baking pan and cook for 20 minutes at 360 F on Bake function until nice and crispy. Serve warm.

35. Broiled Prosciutto-wrapped Pears

Servings: 8   Cooking Time: 6 Minutes
Ingredients:

2 large, ripe Anjou pears
4 thin slices Parma prosciutto

2 teaspoons aged balsamic vinegar

Directions:
Peel the pears. Slice into 8 wedges and cut out the core from each wedge.   Cut the prosciutto into 8 long strips. Wrap each pear wedge with a strip of prosciutto. Place the wrapped pears in the air fryer basket.   Put the air fryer basket on the baking pan and slide into Rack Position 2, select Convection Broil, set temperature to High and set time to 6 minutes.   After 2 or 3 minutes, check the pears. The pears should be turned over if the prosciutto is beginning to crisp up and brown. Return to the oven and continue cooking.   When cooking is complete, remove from the oven. Drizzle the pears with the balsamic vinegar and serve warm.

36. Easy Parsnip Fries

Servings: 3   Cooking Time: 15 Minutes
Ingredients:

4 parsnips, sliced
1/4 cup flour
1/4 cup olive oil
1/4 cup water
A pinch of salt

Directions:
Preheat Instant Vortex on Air Fry function to 390 F. In a bowl, add the flour, olive oil, water, and parsnips; mix to coat. Line the fries in the greased Air Fryer basket and fit in the baking tray. Cook for 15 minutes. Serve with yogurt and garlic dip.

37. Healthy Green Beans

Servings: 2   Cooking Time: 10 Minutes
Ingredients:
8 oz green beans, trimmed and cut in half
1 tbsp tamari
1 tsp toasted sesame oil

Directions:
Fit the Instant Vortex oven with the rack in position 2.   Add all ingredients into the large bowl and toss well.   Transfer green beans in the air fryer basket then place an air fryer basket in the baking pan. Place a baking pan on the oven rack. Set to air fry at 400 F for 10 minutes.   Serve and enjoy.

38. Homemade Cheesy Sticks

Servings: 12   Cooking Time: 5 Minutes
Ingredients:
6 (6 oz) bread cheese
2 tbsp butter
2 cups panko crumbs

Directions:
Put the butter in a bowl and melt in the microwave for 2 minutes; set aside. With a knife, cut the cheese into equal-sized sticks. Brush each stick with butter and dip into panko crumbs. Arrange the sticks in a single layer in the basket. Fit in the baking tray and cook in the Instant Vortex at 390 F for 10 minutes on Air Fry function. Flip halfway through. Serve warm.

39. Baked Italian Vegetables

Servings: 6   Cooking Time: 30 Minutes
Ingredients:
1 eggplant, sliced
1 onion, sliced
1 potato, peel & cut into chunks
1 bell pepper, cut into strips
2 zucchini, sliced
2 tomatoes, quartered
5 fresh basil leaves, sliced
2 tsp Italian seasoning
2 tbsp olive oil
Pepper
Salt

Directions:
Fit the Instant Vortex oven with the rack in position Add all ingredients except basil leaves into the mixing bowl and toss well.   Transfer vegetable mixture on a prepared baking pan.   Set to bake at 400 F for 35 minutes. After 5 minutes place the baking dish in the preheated oven.   Garnish with basil leaves and serve.

40. Air Fry Garlic Baby Potatoes

Servings: 4   Cooking Time: 20 Minutes

Ingredients:
1 lb baby potatoes, cut into quarters
1/2 tsp granulated garlic
1 tbsp olive oil
1/2 tsp dried parsley
1/4 tsp salt

Directions:
Fit the Instant Vortex oven with the rack in position 2.   In a mixing bowl, toss baby potatoes with oil, garlic, parsley, and salt.   Transfer potatoes in air fryer basket then place air fryer basket in baking pan. Place a baking pan on the oven rack. Set to air fry at 350 F for 20 minutes.   Serve and enjoy.

41. Simple Baked Potatoes

Servings: 6   Cooking Time: 55 Minutes
Ingredients:
1 1/2 lbs baby potatoes
3 tbsp olive oil
Pepper
Salt

Directions:
Fit the Instant Vortex oven with the rack in position Add baby potatoes, salt, and water to a large pot and bring to boil over medium heat.   Cook potatoes until tender. Drain well and transfer to the skillet. Gently smash each potato using the back of a spoon. Drizzle potatoes with oil. Season with pepper and salt. Place potatoes in baking pan.   Set to bake at 450 F for 45 minutes. After 5 minutes place the baking pan in the preheated oven.   Serve and enjoy.

42. Sweet Carrot Puree

Servings: 4   Cooking Time: 5 Minutes
Ingredients:
Salt, to taste
1 teaspoon brown sugar
1½ pounds carrots, peeled and chopped
1 cup water
1 tablespoon butter, softened
1 tablespoon honey

Directions:
Place the carrots in the Instant Pot, add the water, cover and cook for 4 minutes in the Manual setting. Release the pressure naturally, drain the carrots and place them in a bowl.   Mix with an immersion blender, add the butter, salt and honey. Mix again, add the sugar on top and serve.

43. Butternut And Apple Mash

Servings: 4   Cooking Time: 15 Minutes
Ingredients:
1 butternut squash, peeled and cut into medium chunks
2 apples, cored and sliced
½ teaspoon apple pie spice
1 cup water
Salt, to taste
2 tablespoons butter, browned
1 yellow onion, thinly sliced

Directions:
Place the pieces of pumpkin, onion and apple in the steam basket of the Instant Pot, add the water to the Instant Pot, cover and cook for 8 minutes in manual setting.   Quickly release the pressure and transfer

the pumpkin, onion and apple to a bowl. Smash everything with a potato masher, add salt, apple pie spices and brown butter, mix well and serve hot.

44. Lime Corn With Feta Cheese

Servings: 2   Cooking Time: 20 Minutes

Ingredients:

2 ears of corn	½ cup feta cheese, grated
Juice of 1 lime	
1 tsp paprika	

Directions:
Preheat Instant Vortex on AirFry function to 370 F. Peel the corn and remove the silk. Place the corn in a baking pan and place in the oven. Press Start and cook for 15 minutes. When ready, remove, and drizzle the lime juice on top of each corn ear. Top with feta cheese and serve.

45. Roasted Garlic Fries

Servings: 1   Cooking Time: 30 Minutes

Ingredients:

Roasted Garlic:	Pepper
1 small head of garlic	Garlic Fries Topping:
2 teaspoons olive oil	1/4 cup minced
Baked Fries:	parsley
2 medium potatoes	1 teaspoon olive oil
2 teaspoons olive oil	1/8 teaspoon salt
Salt	2 cloves roasted garlic

Directions:
Start by preheating toaster oven to 425°F and lining a baking sheet with parchment paper.   Remove outer layer from garlic and chop off the top. Drizzle oil over the garlic, filling the top.   Cut your potatoes into fries and toss with oil, salt, and pepper. Place potatoes in a single layer on a greased baking sheet along with garlic head, and bake for 30 minutes, turning fries halfway through.   Remove two cloves of the garlic head, mince, and add parsley. Stir the garlic mixture with olive oil and salt. Drizzle over fries and serve.

46. Potato Croquettes

Servings: 4   Cooking Time: 8 Minutes

Ingredients:

2 medium Russet potatoes, peeled and cubed	1 egg yolk
	Pinch of ground nutmeg Salt and freshly ground black pepper, as needed
2 tablespoons all-purpose flour	
½ cup Parmesan cheese, grated	2 eggs
2 tablespoons chives, minced	½ cup breadcrumbs
	2 tablespoons vegetable oil

Directions:
In a pan of a boiling water, add the potatoes and cook for about 15 minutes.   Drain the potatoes well and transfer into a large bowl.   With a potato masher, mash the potatoes and set aside to cool completely.   In the bowl of mashed potatoes, add the flour, Parmesan cheese, egg yolk, chives, nutmeg, salt, and black pepper and mix until well combined.

Make small equal-sized balls from the mixture. Now, roll each ball into a cylinder shape.   In a shallow dish, crack the eggs and beat well.   In another dish, mix together the breadcrumbs, and oil. Dip the croquettes in egg mixture and then coat with the breadcrumbs mixture.   Press "Power Button" of Air Fry Oven and turn the dial to select the "Air Fry" mode.   Press the Time button and again turn the dial to set the cooking time to 8 minutes.   Now push the Temp button and rotate the dial to set the temperature at 390 degrees F.   Press "Start/Pause" button to start.   When the unit beeps to show that it is preheated, open the lid.   Arrange the croquettes in "Air Fry Basket" and insert in the oven. Serve warm.

47. Charred Green Beans With Sesame Seeds

Servings: 4   Cooking Time: 8 Minutes

Ingredients:

½ tablespoon Sriracha sauce	1 tablespoon reduced-sodium soy sauce or tamari
4 teaspoons toasted sesame oil, divided	½ tablespoon toasted sesame seeds
12 ounces (340 g) trimmed green beans	

Directions:
Whisk together the soy sauce, Sriracha sauce, and 1 teaspoon of sesame oil in a small bowl until smooth. Set aside.   Toss the green beans with the remaining sesame oil in a large bowl until evenly coated.   Place the green beans in the air fryer basket in a single layer.   Put the air fryer basket on the baking pan and slide into Rack Position 2, select Air Fry, set temperature to 375°F (190°C), and set time to 8 minutes.   Stir the green beans halfway through the cooking time.   When cooking is complete, the green beans should be lightly charred and tender. Remove from the oven to a platter. Pour the prepared sauce over the top of green beans and toss well. Serve sprinkled with the toasted sesame seeds.

48. Cheesy Squash Casserole

Servings: 6   Cooking Time: 30 Minutes

Ingredients:

2 lbs yellow summer squash, cut into chunks	3/4 cup cheddar cheese, shredded
	1/4 cup mayonnaise
1/2 cup liquid egg substitute	1/4 tsp salt

Directions:
Fit the Instant Vortex oven with the rack in position Add squash in a saucepan then pour enough water in a saucepan to cover the squash. Bring to boil. Turn heat to medium and cook for 10 minutes or until tender. Drain well.   In a large mixing bowl, combine together squash, egg substitute, mayonnaise, 1/2 cup cheese, and salt.   Transfer squash mixture into a greased baking dish.   Set to bake at 375 F for 35 minutes. After 5 minutes place the baking dish in the preheated oven.   Sprinkle remaining cheese on top.   Serve and enjoy.

49. Cauliflower Mash

Servings: 4   Cooking Time: 6 Minutes

Ingredients:

1½ cups water	1 tablespoon butter
½ teaspoon turmeric	Salt and ground black
1 cauliflower,	pepper, to taste
separated into florets	3 chives, diced

Directions:

Put water in the pot immediately, place the cabbage - flower in the basket for cooking, immediately cover the pot and cook 6 minutes to steam.   Release the pressure naturally for 2 minutes and quickly release the rest.   Transfer the cauliflower to a bowl and mash with a potato masher. Add salt, pepper, butter and saffron, mix, transfer to a blender and mix well. Serve with chives sprinkled on top.

50. Potato Chips With Creamy Lemon Dip

Servings: 3   Cooking Time: 25 Minutes

Ingredients:

3 large potatoes	3 tbsp olive oil.
1 cup sour cream	½ tsp lemon juice
2 scallions, white part minced	salt and black pepper

Directions:

Preheat Instant Vortex on AirFry function to 350 F. Cut the potatoes into thin slices; do not peel them. Brush them with olive oil and season with salt and pepper. Arrange on the frying basket.   Press Start on the oven and cook for 20-25 minutes. Season with salt and pepper. To prepare the dip, mix together the sour cream, olive oil, scallions, lemon juice, salt, and pepper.

51. Crispy Eggplant Slices

Servings: 4   Cooking Time: 8 Minutes

Ingredients:

1 medium eggplant, peeled and cut into ½-inch round slices	Salt, as required
	2 eggs, beaten
	1 cup Italian-style breadcrumbs
½ cup all-purpose flour	¼ cup olive oil

Directions:

In a colander, add the eggplant slices and sprinkle with salt. Set aside for about 45 minutes.   With paper towels, pat dry the eggplant slices.   In a shallow dish, place the flour.   Crack the eggs in a second dish and beat well.   In a third dish, mix together the oil, and breadcrumbs.   Coat each eggplant slice with flour, then dip into beaten eggs and finally, coat with the breadcrumbs mixture. Press "Power Button" of Air Fry Oven and turn the dial to select the "Air Fry" mode.   Press the Time button and again turn the dial to set the cooking time to 8 minutes.   Now push the Temp button and rotate the dial to set the temperature at 390 degrees F.   Press "Start/Pause" button to start. When the unit beeps to show that it is preheated, open the lid.   Arrange the eggplant slices in "Air Fry Basket" and insert in the oven.   Serve warm.

52. Classic Cauliflower Hash Browns

Servings: 2   Cooking Time: 20 Minutes

Ingredients:

2/3 pound cauliflower, peeled and grated	Sea salt and ground black pepper, to taste
	1/4 teaspoon ground allspice
2 eggs, whisked	
1/4 cup scallions, chopped	1/2 teaspoon cinnamon
1 teaspoon fresh garlic, minced	1 tablespoon peanut oil

Directions:

Boil cauliflower over medium-low heat until fork-tender, 5 to 7 minutes Drain the water; pat cauliflower dry with a kitchen towel.   Now, add the remaining ingredients; stir to combine well. Cook in the preheated Air Fryer at 395 degrees F for 20 minutes. Shake the basket once or twice. Serve with low-carb tomato sauce.

53. Mayo Potato Salad With Bacon

Servings: 4   Cooking Time: 15 Minutes

Ingredients:

1 lb potatoes, boiled and cubed	1 cup sour cream
	2 tbsp mayonnaise
4 oz bacon, chopped	Salt and black pepper
1 cup cheddar cheese, shredded	to taste
	1 tsp dried thyme

Directions:

Preheat Instant Vortex on AirFry function to 350 F. In a bowl, combine the potatoes, bacon, salt, pepper, and thyme. Transfer to a greased baking pan and place in the oven. Press Start and cook for about 10-12 minutes. Remove and stir in sour cream and mayonnaise to serve.

54. Japanese Tempura Bowl

Servings: 3   Cooking Time: 20 Minutes

Ingredients:

7 tablespoons whey protein isolate	3 tablespoons soda water
1 teaspoon baking powder	1 cup parmesan cheese, grated
Kosher salt and ground black pepper, to taste	1 onion, cut into rings
	1 bell pepper
	1 zucchini, cut into slices
1/2 teaspoon paprika	
1 teaspoon dashi granules	3 asparagus spears
2 eggs	2 tablespoons olive oil
1 tablespoon mirin	

Directions:

In a shallow bowl, mix the whey protein isolate, baking powder, salt, black pepper, paprika, dashi granules, eggs, mirin, and soda water.   In another shallow bowl, place grated parmesan cheese.   Dip the vegetables in tempura batter; lastly, roll over parmesan cheese to coat evenly. Drizzle each piece with olive oil.   Cook in the preheated Air Fryer at 400 degrees F for 10 minutes, shaking the basket halfway through the cooking time. Work in batches until the vegetables are crispy and golden brown.

55. Homemade Tortilla Chips

Servings: 4   Cooking Time: 55 Minutes

Ingredients:

Salt and black pepper to taste	1 cup flour
1 tbsp golden flaxseed meal	2 cups shredded Cheddar cheese

Directions:

Melt cheddar cheese in the microwave for 1 minute. Add flour, salt, flaxseed meal, and pepper. Mix well with a fork. On a board, place the dough and knead it with hands while warm until the ingredients are well combined. Divide the dough into 2 and with a rolling pin, roll them out flat into 2 rectangles. Use a pastry cutter to cut out triangle-shaped pieces. Line them in one layer on the Air Fryer basket and spray with cooking spray. Fit in the baking tray and cook for 10 minutes on Air Fry function at 400 F. Serve with a cheese dip.

56. Baked Ratatouille

Servings: 6   Cooking Time: 55 Minutes

Ingredients:

1 large eggplant, steamed and sliced	2 tbsp olive oil
1/4 tsp dried thyme	4 medium zucchini, sliced
2 bell pepper, sliced	1 tsp dried basil
4 tomatoes, sliced	1/2 tsp dried oregano

Directions:

Fit the Instant Vortex oven with the rack in position Add all vegetable slices to a large bowl and season with salt and drizzle with oil.   Layer vegetable slices into the greased baking dish.   Set to bake at 400 F for 60 minutes. After 5 minutes place the baking dish in the preheated oven.   Sprinkle with dried herbs.   Serve and enjoy.

57. Simple Zucchini Crisps

Servings: 4   Cooking Time: 14 Minutes

Ingredients:

2 zucchini, sliced into 1/4- to 1/2-inch-thick rounds (about 2 cups)	1/8 teaspoon sea salt
1/4 teaspoon garlic granules	Freshly ground black pepper, to taste (optional) Cooking spray

Directions:

Spritz the air fryer basket with cooking spray.   Put the zucchini rounds in the basket, spreading them out as much as possible. Top with a sprinkle of garlic granules, sea salt, and black pepper (if desired). Spritz the zucchini rounds with cooking spray. Put the air fryer basket on the baking pan and slide into Rack Position 2, select Roast, set temperature to 392°F (200°C), and set time to 14 minutes. Flip the zucchini rounds halfway through.   When cooking is complete, the zucchini rounds should be crisp-tender. Remove from the oven. Let them rest for 5 minutes and serve.

58. Baked Sweet Potatoes

Servings: 6   Cooking Time: 35 Minutes

Ingredients:

4 large sweet potatoes, peel and cut into cubes	2 tsp vinegar
	1/2 tsp paprika
	2 tbsp olive oil
8 sage leaves	1/2 tsp sea salt
1 tsp honey	

Directions:

Fit the Instant Vortex oven with the rack in position Add sweet potato, oil, sage, and salt in a baking dish and mix well.   Set to bake at 375 F for 40 minutes. After 5 minutes place the baking dish in the preheated oven.   Transfer roasted sweet potatoes into the large bowl and toss with honey, vinegar, and paprika.   Serve and enjoy.

59. Chicken & Veggie Nuggets

Servings: 4   Cooking Time: 10 Minutes

Ingredients:

1/2 of zucchini, roughly chopped	1 tablespoon onion powder
1/2 of carrot, roughly chopped	Salt and freshly ground black pepper, as needed
14 oz. chicken breast, cut into chunks	1 cup all-purpose flour
1/2 tablespoon mustard powder	2 tablespoons milk
1 tablespoon garlic powder	1 egg 1 cup panko breadcrumbs

Directions:

In a food processor, add the zucchini, and carrot and pulse until finely chopped.   Add the chicken, mustard powder, garlic powder, onion powder, salt, and black pepper and pulse until well combined. In a shallow dish, place the flour.   In a second dish, mix together the milk, and egg.   In a third dish, put the breadcrumbs.   Coat the nuggets with flour, then dip into egg mixture and finally, coat with the breadcrumbs.   Press "Power Button" of Air Fry Oven and turn the dial to select the "Air Fry" mode. Press the Time button and again turn the dial to set the cooking time to 10 minutes.   Now push the Temp button and rotate the dial to set the temperature at 390 degrees F.   Press "Start/Pause" button to start.   When the unit beeps to show that it is preheated, open the lid.   Arrange the nuggets in "Air Fry Basket" and insert in the oven.   Serve warm.

60. Cheese & Zucchini Cake With Yogurt

Servings: 4   Cooking Time: 20 Minutes

Ingredients:

1 1/2 cups flour	1 tbsp yogurt
1 tsp cinnamon	1/2 cup zucchini, shredded
3 eggs	
1 tsp baking powder	A pinch of salt
2 tbsp sugar	2 tbsp cream cheese, softened
1 cup milk	
2 tbsp butter, melted	

Directions:

In a bowl, whisk eggs with sugar, salt, cinnamon, cream cheese, flour, and baking powder. In another bowl, combine all of the liquid ingredients. Gently combine the dry and liquid mixtures. Stir in zucchini. Line the muffin tins with baking paper and pour in the batter. Arrange on a baking tray and place in the oven. Press Start and cook for 15 minutes. Serve chilled.

61. Zucchini Spaghetti

Servings: 4   Cooking Time: 20 Minutes
Ingredients:

1 lb. zucchinis, cut with a spiralizer	6 garlic cloves; minced
1 cup parmesan; grated	½ tsp. red pepper flakes
¼ cup parsley; chopped.	Salt and black pepper to taste.
¼ cup olive oil	

Directions:
In a pan that fits your air fryer, mix all the ingredients, toss, introduce in the fryer and cook at 370°F for 15 minutes   Divide between plates and serve as a side dish.

62. Feta Lime Corn

Servings: 2   Cooking Time: 20 Minutes
Ingredients:

2 ears of corn	2 tsp paprika
Juice of 2 small limes	4 oz feta cheese, grated

Directions:
Preheat Instant Vortex on Air Fry function to 370 F. Peel the corn and remove the silk. Place the corn in the baking pan and cook for 15 minutes. Squeeze the juice of 1 lime on top of each ear of corn. Top with feta cheese and serve.

63. Sesame Cabbage & Prawn Egg Roll Wraps

Servings: 4   Cooking Time: 25 Minutes
Ingredients:

2 tbsp vegetable oil	1 tbsp sugar
1-inch piece fresh ginger, grated	1 tbsp shredded Napa cabbage
1 tbsp minced garlic	1 tbsp sesame oil
1 carrot, cut into strips	8 cooked prawns, minced
¼ cup chicken broth	1 egg
2 tbsp soy sauce	8 egg roll wrappers

Directions:
Warm vegetable oil In a skillet over high heat and sauté ginger and garlic for 40 seconds until fragrant. Stir in carrot and cook for another 2 minutes. Pour in chicken broth, soy sauce, and sugar and bring to a boil. Add cabbage and let simmer until softened, for 4 minutes.   Remove the skillet from the heat and stir in sesame oil. Strain cabbage mixture and fold in minced prawns. Whisk an egg in a small bowl. Fill each egg roll wrapper with prawn mixture, arranging the mixture just below the center of the wrapper.   Fold the bottom part over the filling and tuck under. Fold in both sides and tightly roll up. Use the whisked egg to seal the wrapper. Place the rolls into the frying basket and spray with oil. Select

AirFry function, adjust the temperature to 380 F, and press Start. Cook for 12 minutes.

64. Air Fry Broccoli Florets

Servings: 2   Cooking Time: 10 Minutes
Ingredients:

1 lb broccoli florets	2 tbsp plain yogurt
1/2 tsp chili powder	1 tbsp chickpea flour
1/4 tsp turmeric	1/2 tsp salt

Directions:
Fit the Instant Vortex oven with the rack in position 2.   Add all ingredients to the bowl and toss well. Place marinated broccoli in a refrigerator for 15 minutes.   Place marinated broccoli in an air fryer basket then places an air fryer basket in a baking pan. Place a baking pan on the oven rack. Set to air fry at 390 F for 10 minutes.   Serve and enjoy.

65. Roasted Garlic(1)

Servings: 12 Cloves   Cooking Time: 20 Minutes
Ingredients:

1 medium head garlic	2 tsp. avocado oil

Directions:
Remove any hanging excess peel from the garlic but leave the cloves covered. Cut off ¼ of the head of garlic, exposing the tips of the cloves   Drizzle with avocado oil. Place the garlic head into a small sheet of aluminum foil, completely enclosing it. Place it into the air fryer basket. Adjust the temperature to 400 Degrees F and set the timer for 20 minutes. If your garlic head is a bit smaller, check it after 15 minutes   When done, garlic should be golden brown and very soft   To serve, cloves should pop out and easily be spread or sliced. Store in an airtight container in the refrigerator up to 5 days.   You may also freeze individual cloves on a baking sheet, then store together in a freezer-safe storage bag once frozen.

66. Balsamic Cabbage(1)

Servings: 4   Cooking Time: 20 Minutes
Ingredients:

6 cups red cabbage; shredded	1 tbsp. balsamic vinegar
4 garlic cloves; minced	Salt and black pepper to taste.
1 tbsp. olive oil	

Directions:
In a pan that fits the air fryer, combine all the ingredients, toss, introduce the pan in the air fryer and cook at 380°F for 15 minutes   Divide between plates and serve as a side dish.

67. Sesame Sticky Chicken Wings

Servings: 4   Cooking Time: 45 Minutes
Ingredients:

1 pound chicken wings	2 tbsp fresh garlic, minced
1 cup soy sauce, divided	1 tsp finely ground black pepper
½ cup brown sugar	2 tbsp cornstarch
½ cup apple cider	

vinegar
2 tbsp fresh ginger, minced

2 tbsp cold water
1 tsp sesame seeds

Directions:
In a bowl, add chicken wings and pour in a half cup of the soy sauce. Place in the fridge for 20 minutes. Then, drain and pat dry. Arrange the wings on the frying basket. Select AirFry function, adjust the temperature to 380 F, and press Start. Cook for 20-25 minutes at 380 F. Make sure you check them towards the end to avoid overcooking.   In a skillet and over medium heat, pour the remaining soy sauce, vinegar, sugar, ginger, garlic, and black pepper. Stir until sauce has reduced slightly, about 4 to 6 minutes.   Dissolve cornstarch in cold water and stir in the sauce. Cook until it thickens, about 2 minutes. Pour the sauce over the wings and sprinkle with sesame seeds to serve.

68. Butternut Squash Croquettes

Servings: 4   Cooking Time: 17 Minutes
Ingredients:

⅓ butternut squash, peeled and grated
⅓ cup all-purpose flour
2 eggs, whisked
4 cloves garlic, minced
1½ tablespoons olive oil

1 teaspoon fine sea salt
⅓ teaspoon freshly ground black pepper, or more to taste
⅓ teaspoon dried sage
A pinch of ground allspice

Directions:
Line the air fryer basket with parchment paper. Set aside.   In a mixing bowl, stir together all the ingredients until well combined.   Make the squash croquettes: Use a small cookie scoop to drop tablespoonfuls of the squash mixture onto a lightly floured surface and shape into balls with your hands. Transfer them to the basket.   Put the air fryer basket on the baking pan and slide into Rack Position 2, select Air Fry, set temperature to 345°F (174°C), and set time to 17 minutes.   When cooking is complete, the squash croquettes should be golden brown. Remove from the oven to a plate and serve warm.

69. Bbq Chicken Wings

Servings: 4   Cooking Time: 19 Minutes
Ingredients:

2 lbs. chicken wings
1 teaspoon smoked paprika
1 teaspoon garlic powder

1 teaspoon olive oil
Salt and ground black pepper, as required
¼ cup BBQ sauce

Directions:
In a large bowl combine chicken wings, smoked paprika, garlic powder, oil, salt, and pepper and mix well.   Press "Power Button" of Air Fry Oven and turn the dial to select the "Air Fry" mode.   Press the Time button and again turn the dial to set the cooking time to 19 minutes.   Now push the Temp button and rotate the dial to set the temperature at 360 degrees F.   Press "Start/Pause" button to start.   When the unit beeps to show that it is preheated, open the lid.   Arrange the chicken wings in "Air Fry Basket" and insert in the oven. After 12 minutes of cooking, flip the wings and coat with barbecue sauce evenly.   Serve immediately.

70. Mango Cashew Nuts

Servings: 2   Cooking Time: 25 Minutes
Ingredients:

1 cup Greek yogurt
2 tbsp mango powder
Salt and black pepper to taste

½ cup cashew nuts
1 tsp coriander powder
½ tsp masala powder

Directions:
Preheat Instant Vortex on Bake function to 360 F. In a bowl, mix all powders. Season with salt and pepper. Add cashews and toss to coat. Place in the oven and press Start. Cook for 15 minutes.

71. Green Beans And Mushrooms

Servings: 4   Cooking Time: 6 Minutes
Ingredients:

1 small yellow onion, peeled and chopped
6 ounces bacon, chopped
Salt and ground black pepper, to taste
Balsamic vinegar

1-pound fresh green beans, trimmed
1 garlic clove, peeled and minced
8 ounces mushrooms, sliced

Directions:
Place the beans in the Instant Pot, add water to cover them, cover the Instant Pot and cook for 3 minutes in manual configuration.   Release the pressure naturally, drain the beans and set aside. Place the Instant Pot in the sauté mode, add the bacon and sauté for 1 to 2 minutes, stirring constantly.   Add garlic and onion, mix and cook 2 minutes. Add the mushrooms, mix and cook until tender. Add the drain beans, salt, pepper and a pinch of vinegar, mix, remove from heat, divide between plates and serve.

72. Pumpkin Fritters With Ham & Cheese

Servings: 4   Cooking Time: 10 Minutes
Ingredients:

½ cup ham, chopped
1 cup dry pancake mix
2 tbsp canned puree pumpkin
1 oz cheddar, shredded

1 egg
½ tsp chili powder
3 tbsp of flour
½ cup beer
2 tbsp scallions, chopped

Directions:
Preheat Instant Vortex on AirFry function to 370 F. In a bowl, combine the pancake mix and chili powder. Mix in the egg, puree pumpkin, beer, cheddar cheese, ham, and scallions. Form balls and roll them in the flour. Arrange the balls into the basket. Press Start and cook for 12 minutes.

73. Herbed Polenta

Servings: 6   Cooking Time: 6 Minutes

Ingredients:

2 tablespoons extra virgin olive oil	Salt, to taste
2 teaspoons garlic, minced	1 bay leaf
4 cups vegetable stock	2 tablespoons fresh parsley, diced
½ cup yellow onion, peeled and chopped	2 teaspoons fresh oregano, diced
1 cup polenta	3 tablespoons fresh basil, diced
⅓ cup sundried tomatoes, chopped	1 teaspoon fresh rosemary, diced

Directions:

Put the Instant Pot in the sauté mode, add the oil and heat. Add the onion, mix and cook for 1 minute. Add the garlic, mix again and cook for 1 minute. Add the broth, salt, tomato, bay leaf, rosemary, oregano, half the basil, half the parsley and polenta. Without stirring, cover the Instant Pot and cook for 5 minutes and release the pressure naturally for 10 minutes.   Uncover the instant pot, discard the bay leaf, gently mix the polenta, add the rest of the parsley, basil and other salts, mix, divide between the dishes and serve.

74. Baked Asparagus

Servings: 4   Cooking Time: 15 Minutes

Ingredients:

30 asparagus spears, cut the ends	1 tbsp olive oil
1/2 tsp garlic powder	Pepper
	Salt

Directions:

Fit the Instant Vortex oven with the rack in position Add asparagus into the large bowl. Drizzle with oil. Sprinkle with garlic powder, pepper, and salt. Toss well.   Arrange asparagus in baking pan.   Set to bake at 400 F for 20 minutes. After 5 minutes place the baking pan in the preheated oven.   Serve and enjoy.

75. Cod Nuggets

Servings: 5   Cooking Time: 8 Minutes

Ingredients:

1 cup all-purpose flour	2 tablespoons olive oil
2 eggs	1 lb. cod, cut into 1x2
¾ cup breadcrumbs	½-inch strips
Pinch of salt	

Directions:

In a shallow dish, place the flour.   Crack the eggs in a second dish and beat well.   In a third dish, mix together the breadcrumbs, salt, and oil.   Coat the nuggets with flour, then dip into beaten eggs and finally, coat with the breadcrumbs.   Press "Power Button" of Air Fry Oven and turn the dial to select the "Air Fry" mode.   Press the Time button and again turn the dial to set the cooking time to 8 minutes.   Now push the Temp button and rotate the dial to set the temperature at 390 degrees F. Press "Start/Pause" button to start.   When the unit beeps to show that it is preheated, open the lid. Arrange the nuggets in "Air Fry Basket" and insert in the oven.   Serve warm.

76. Easy Home Fries(2)

Servings: 4   Cooking Time: 20 Minutes

Ingredients:

½ medium white onion; peeled and diced	1 tbsp. coconut oil; melted
1 medium green bell pepper; seeded and diced	½ tsp. pink Himalayan salt
1 medium jicama; peeled.	¼ tsp. ground black pepper

Directions:

Cut jicama into 1-inch cubes. Place into a large bowl and toss with coconut oil until coated. Sprinkle with pepper and salt. Place into the air fryer basket with peppers and onion.   Adjust the temperature to 400 Degrees F and set the timer for 10 minutes. Shake two or three times during cooking. Jicama will be tender and dark around edges. Serve immediately.

77. Kale And Walnuts(2)

Servings: 4   Cooking Time: 20 Minutes

Ingredients:

3 garlic cloves	½ cup almond milk
10 cups kale; roughly chopped.	1 tbsp. butter; melted
1/3 cup parmesan; grated	¼ tsp. nutmeg, ground
¼ cup walnuts; chopped.	Salt and black pepper to taste.

Directions:

In a pan that fits the air fryer, combine all the ingredients, toss, introduce the pan in the machine and cook at 360°F for 15 minutes   Divide between plates and serve.

78. Perfect Crispy Potatoes

Servings: 4   Cooking Time: 35 Minutes

Ingredients:

1 ½ pounds potatoes, halved	1 tbsp minced fresh rosemary
2 tbsp olive oil	Salt and black pepper to taste
3 garlic cloves, grated	

Directions:

In a bowl, mix potatoes, olive oil, garlic, rosemary, salt, and pepper until well-coated. Arrange the potatoes on the basket and fit in the baking tray. Cook at 360 F on Air Fry function for 25 minutes, shaking twice until crispy on the outside and tender on the inside. Serve.

79. Baked Turnip & Sweet Potato

Servings: 4   Cooking Time: 30 Minutes

Ingredients:

1 1/2 lbs sweet potato, sliced 1/4-inch thick	2 tbsp olive oil
	1 tbsp thyme, chopped

1 lb turnips, sliced 1/4-inch thick | 1 tsp paprika
1/4 tsp pepper
1/2 tsp sea salt

Directions:
Fit the Instant Vortex oven with the rack in position Add sliced sweet potatoes and turnips in a bowl and toss with seasoning and olive oil. Arrange sliced sweet potatoes and turnips in baking dish. Set to bake at 425 F for 35 minutes. After 5 minutes place the baking dish in the preheated oven. Garnish with thyme and serve.

80. Parmesan Cabbage Wedges

Servings: 4   Cooking Time: 30 Minutes
Ingredients:

½ head cabbage, cut into wedges
2 cup Parmesan cheese, grated

4 tbsp butter, melted
Salt and black pepper to taste
1 tsp smoked paprika

Directions:
Preheat Instant Vortex on AirFry function to 330 F. Line a baking sheet with parchment paper. Brush the cabbage wedges with butter and season with salt and pepper. Coat the cabbage with the Parmesan cheese and arrange on the baking sheet; sprinkle with paprika. Press Start and cook for 15 minutes. Flip the wedges over and cook for an additional 10 minutes. Serve with yogurt dip.

81. Spicy Brussels Sprouts(2)

Servings: 4   Cooking Time: 15 Minutes
Ingredients:

1 lb Brussels sprouts, cut in half
1 1/2 tbsp olive oil

1 tbsp gochujang
1/2 tsp salt

Directions:
Fit the Instant Vortex oven with the rack in position 2. In a large mixing bowl, mix together olive oil, gochujang, and salt. Add Brussels sprouts into the bowl and toss until well coated. Transfer Brussels sprouts in air fryer basket then place air fryer basket in baking pan. Place a baking pan on the oven rack. Set to air fry at 360 F for 20 minutes. Serve and enjoy.

82. Cheesy Crisps

Servings: 3   Cooking Time: 25 Minutes
Ingredients:

4 tbsp grated cheddar cheese + extra for rolling
1 cup flour + extra for kneading

¼ tsp chili powder
½ tsp baking powder
3 tsp butter
A pinch of salt

Directions:
In a bowl, add the cheddar cheese, flour, baking powder, chili powder, butter, and salt and mix until the mixture becomes crusty. Add some drops of water and mix well to get a dough. Remove the dough on a flat surface. Rub some extra flour in your palms and on the surface and knead the dough for a while. Using a rolling pin, roll the dough out into a thin sheet. With a pastry cutter, cut the dough

into your desired lings' shape. Add the cheese lings to the greased baking tray and cook for 8 minutes at 350 F on Air Fry function, flipping once halfway through. Serve.

83. Pineapple Spareribs

Servings: 4   Cooking Time: 35 Minutes
Ingredients:

2 lb cut spareribs
7 oz salad dressing
1 (5-oz) can pineapple juice

2 cups water
1 tsp garlic powder
Salt and black pepper

Directions:
Sprinkle the ribs with garlic powder, salt, and pepper. Arrange them on the frying basket. sprinkle with garlic salt. Select AirFry function, adjust the temperature to 400 F, and press Start. Cook for 20-25 minutes until golden brown. Prepare the sauce by combining the salad dressing and the pineapple juice. Serve the ribs drizzled with the sauce.

84. Stuffed Mushrooms With Rice & Cheese

Servings: 10   Cooking Time: 30 Minutes
Ingredients:

10 Swiss brown mushrooms
1 cup cooked brown rice
1 cup grated Grana Padano cheese

2 tbsp olive oil
1 tsp dried mixed herbs
Salt and black pepper to taste

Directions:
Brush mushrooms with oil and arrange onto the Instant Vortex Air Fryer baking tray. In a bowl, mix rice, Grana Padano cheese, herbs, salt, and pepper. Stuff the mushrooms with the mixture. Cook in the oven for 14 minutes at 360 F on Bake function until the cheese has melted. Serve.

85. Simple Cauliflower Poppers

Servings: 4   Cooking Time: 8 Minutes
Ingredients:

1 tablespoon olive oil
Salt and ground black pepper, as required

½ large head cauliflower, cut into bite-sized florets

Directions:
In a bowl, add all the ingredients and toss to coat well. Press "Power Button" of Air Fry Oven and turn the dial to select the "Air Fry" mode. Press the Time button and again turn the dial to set the cooking time to 8 minutes. Now push the Temp button and rotate the dial to set the temperature at 390 degrees F. Press "Start/Pause" button to start. When the unit beeps to show that it is preheated, open the lid. Arrange the cauliflower florets in "Air Fry Basket" and insert in the oven. Toss the cauliflower florets once halfway through. Serve warm.

86. Garlic & Olive Oil Spring Vegetables

Servings: 4   Cooking Time: 20 Minutes
Ingredients:

1 pound assorted spring vegetables (such as carrots, asparagus, radishes, spring onions, or sugar snap peas)	4 unpeeled garlic cloves 2 tablespoons olive oil Salt and pepper to taste

Directions:
Start by preheating toaster oven to 450°F. Combine vegetables, garlic, oil, salt, and pepper in a bowl and toss.   Roast for 20 minutes or until vegetables start to brown.

87. Traditional Indian Kofta

Servings: 4   Cooking Time: 20 Minutes
Ingredients:

Veggie Balls:	Sauce:
3/4-pound zucchini, grated and well drained	1/2 teaspoon cumin seeds
1/4-pound kohlrabi, grated and well drained	2 cloves garlic, roughly chopped
2 cloves garlic, minced	1 onion, chopped
1 tablespoon Garam masala	1 Kashmiri chili pepper, seeded and minced
1 cup paneer, crumbled	1 (1-inchpiece ginger, chopped
1/4 cup coconut flour	1 teaspoon paprika
1/2 teaspoon chili powder	1 teaspoon turmeric powder
Himalayan pink salt and ground black pepper, to taste	2 ripe tomatoes, pureed
1 tablespoon sesame oil	1/2 cup vegetable broth
	1/4 full fat coconut milk

Directions:
Start by preheating your Air Fryer to 360 degrees F. Thoroughly combine the zucchini, kohlrabi, garlic, Garam masala, paneer, coconut flour, chili powder, salt and ground black pepper.   Shape the vegetable mixture into small balls and arrange them in the lightly greased cooking basket.   Cook in the preheated Air Fryer at 360 degrees F for 15 minutes or until thoroughly cooked and crispy. Repeat the process until you run out of ingredients.   Heat the sesame oil in a saucepan over medium heat and add the cumin seeds. Once the cumin seeds turn brown, add the garlic, onions, chili pepper, and ginger. Sauté for 2 to 3 minutes.   Add the paprika, turmeric powder, tomatoes, and broth; let it simmer, covered, for 4 to 5 minutes, stirring occasionally. Add the coconut milk. Heat off; add the veggie balls and gently stir to combine.

88. Cinnamon-spiced Acorn Squash

Servings: 2   Cooking Time: 15 Minutes
Ingredients:

1 medium acorn squash, halved crosswise and deseeded	1 teaspoon light brown sugar Few dashes of ground cinnamon
1 teaspoon coconut oil	Few dashes of ground nutmeg

Directions:
On a clean work surface, rub the cut sides of the acorn squash with coconut oil. Scatter with the brown sugar, cinnamon, and nutmeg.   Put the squash halves in the air fryer basket, cut-side up. Put the air fryer basket on the baking pan and slide into Rack Position 2, select Air Fry, set temperature to 325°F (163°C), and set time to 15 minutes. When cooking is complete, the squash halves should be just tender when pierced in the center with a paring knife. Remove from the oven. Rest for 5 to 10 minutes and serve warm.   Parmesan Asparagus Fries   Prep time: 15 minutes | Cooking time: 6 minutes | Servings: 4   egg whites   1/4 cup water   1/4 cup plus 2 tablespoons grated Parmesan cheese, divided   3/4 cup panko bread crumbs   1/4 teaspoon salt   ounces (340 g) fresh asparagus spears, woody ends trimmed   Cooking spray   In a shallow dish, whisk together the egg whites and water until slightly foamy. In a separate shallow dish, thoroughly combine 1/4 cup of Parmesan cheese, bread crumbs, and salt.   Dip the asparagus in the egg white, then roll in the cheese mixture to coat well. Place the asparagus in the air fryer basket in a single layer, leaving space between each spear. Spritz the asparagus with cooking spray.   Put the air fryer basket on the baking pan and slide into Rack Position 2, select Air Fry, set temperature to 390°F (199°C), and set time to 6 minutes.   When cooking is complete, the asparagus should be golden brown and crisp. Remove from the oven. Sprinkle with the remaining 2 tablespoons of cheese and serve hot.

89. Broccoli Poppers

Servings: 4   Cooking Time: 10 Minutes
Ingredients:

2 tablespoons plain yogurt	1/4 teaspoon ground turmeric
1/2 teaspoon red chili powder	1 lb. broccoli, cut into small florets
1/4 teaspoon ground cumin	2 tablespoons chickpea flour
Salt, to taste	

Directions:
In a bowl, mix together the yogurt, and spices. Add the broccoli and coat with marinade generously. Refrigerate for about 20 minutes.   Press "Power Button" of Air Fry Oven and turn the dial to select the "Air Fry" mode.   Press the Time button and again turn the dial to set the cooking time to 10 minutes.   Now push the Temp button and rotate the dial to set the temperature at 400 degrees F. Press "Start/Pause" button to start.   When the unit beeps to show that it is preheated, open the lid. Arrange the broccoli florets in "Air Fry Basket" and insert in the oven.   Toss the broccoli florets once halfway through.   Serve warm.

90. Buffalo Quesadillas

Servings: 8   Cooking Time: 5 Minutes

Ingredients:

Nonstick cooking spray	½ cup green onions, sliced thin
2 cups chicken, cooked & chopped fine	8 flour tortillas, 8-inch diameter
½ cup Buffalo wing sauce	¼ cup blue cheese dressing
2 cups Monterey Jack cheese, grated	

Directions:

Lightly spray the baking pan with cooking spray. In a medium bowl, add chicken and wing sauce and toss to coat.   Place tortillas, one at a time on work surface. Spread ¼ of the chicken mixture over tortilla and sprinkle with cheese and onion. Top with a second tortilla and place on the baking pan.   Set oven to broil on 400°F for 8 minutes. After 5 minutes place baking pan in position 2. Cook quesadillas 2-3 minutes per side until toasted and cheese has melted.   Repeat with remaining ingredients.   Cut quesadillas in wedges and serve with blue cheese dressing or other dipping sauce.

91. Baked Lemon Broccoli

Servings: 4   Cooking Time: 20 Minutes

Ingredients:

1 1/2 lbs broccoli florets	2 garlic cloves, sliced
3 tbsp slivered almonds, toasted	1 tbsp fresh lemon juice
3 tbsp olive oil	

Directions:

Fit the Instant Vortex oven with the rack in position Add broccoli, pepper, salt, garlic, and oil in a large bowl and toss well.   Spread broccoli in baking dish. Set to bake at 425 F for 25 minutes. After 5 minutes place the baking dish in the preheated oven.   Add lemon juice and almonds over broccoli and toss well. Serve and enjoy.

92. Grilled Sandwich With Ham & Cheese

Servings: 2   Cooking Time: 15 Minutes

Ingredients:

4 bread slices	2 mozzarella cheese slices
¼ cup butter	
2 ham slices	

Directions:

Preheat Instant Vortex on AirFry function to 360 degrees F. Place 2 bread slices on a flat surface. Spread butter on the exposed surfaces. Lay cheese and ham on two of the slices.   Cover with the other 2 slices to form sandwiches. Place the sandwiches in the frying basket. Select Bake function, adjust the temperature to 380 F, and press Start. Cook for 5 minutes.

93. Green Bean Casserole(3)

Servings: 4   Cooking Time: 20 Minutes

Ingredients:

1 lb. fresh green beans, edges trimmed	¼ cup diced yellow onion
½ oz. pork rinds, finely ground	½ cup chopped white mushrooms
1 oz. full-fat cream cheese	½ cup chicken broth
½ cup heavy whipping cream.	4 tbsp. unsalted butter.
	¼ tsp. xanthan gum

Directions:

In a medium skillet over medium heat, melt the butter. Sauté the onion and mushrooms until they become soft and fragrant, about 3–5 minutes. Add the heavy whipping cream, cream cheese and broth to the pan. Whisk until smooth. Bring to a boil and then reduce to a simmer. Sprinkle the xanthan gum into the pan and remove from heat   Chop the green beans into 2-inch pieces and place into a 4-cup round baking dish. Pour the sauce mixture over them and stir until coated. Top the dish with ground pork rinds. Place into the air fryer basket   Adjust the temperature to 320 Degrees F and set the timer for 15 minutes. Top will be golden and green beans fork tender when fully cooked. Serve warm.

94. Classic French Fries

Servings: 6   Cooking Time: 35 Minutes

Ingredients:

6 medium russet potatoes	2 tbsp olive oil
	Salt to taste

Directions:

Preheat Instant Vortex on AirFry function to 360 F. Cut potatoes into ¼ by 3-inch pieces. Drizzle oil on the potatoes and toss to coat. Place the potatoes in the frying basket and place in the oven. Press Start and cook for 20-25 minutes. Season with salt and pepper and serve.

95. Broccoli Olives Tomatoes

Servings: 4   Cooking Time: 10 Minutes

Ingredients:

4 cups broccoli florets	1 tsp dried oregano
1/2 tsp lemon zest, grated	10 olives, pitted and sliced
2 garlic cloves, minced	1 tbsp fresh lemon juice
1 tbsp olive oil	1 cup cherry tomatoes
	1/4 tsp salt

Directions:

Fit the Instant Vortex oven with the rack in position Add broccoli, garlic, oil, tomatoes, and salt in a large bowl and toss well.   Spread broccoli mixture onto the baking pan.   Set to bake at 450 F for 15 minutes. After 5 minutes place the baking pan in the preheated oven.   Meanwhile, mix together oregano, olives, lemon juice, and lemon zest in a mixing bowl.   Add roasted vegetables to the bowl and toss well.   Serve and enjoy.

96. Garlicky Potatoes

Servings: 4   Cooking Time: 6 Minutes

Ingredients:

1 pound new potatoes, peeled and sliced thin	Salt and ground black pepper, to taste
1 cup water	2 garlic cloves, peeled and minced

1 tablespoon extra-virgin olive oil

¼ teaspoon dried rosemary

Directions:
Place the potatoes and water in the Instant Pot steamer basket, cover and cook for 4 minutes in manual mode. In a heat-resistant dish, mix the rosemary with olive oil and garlic, cover and microwave for 1 minute. Release the pressure from the Instant Pot, drain the potatoes and spread them over an upholstered pan. Add the oil, salt and pepper mixture, mix to cover, divide between the plates and serve.

97. Sunday Calamari Rings

Servings: 4   Cooking Time: 20 Minutes
Ingredients:
1 lb calamari (squid), cut in rings
¼ cup flour

2 large beaten eggs
1 cup breadcrumbs

Directions:
Coat the calamari rings with the flour and dip them in the eggs. Then, roll in the breadcrumbs. Refrigerate for 2 hours. Line them in the frying basket and spray with cooking spray. Select AirFry function, adjust the temperature to 380 F, and press Start. Cook for 14 minutes. Serve with garlic mayo and lemon wedges.

98. Chicken Wings In Alfredo Sauce

Servings: 4   Cooking Time: 30 Minutes
Ingredients:
1 ½ pounds chicken wings

Salt to taste
½ cup Alfredo sauce

Directions:
Preheat Instant Vortex on AirFry function to 390 F. Season the wings with salt. Arrange them on the frying basket without touching. Press Start and cook for 20-22 minutes until no longer pink in the center. Remove to a large bowl and coat well with the sauce. Serve.

99. Creamy Broccoli Casserole

Servings: 6   Cooking Time: 30 Minutes
Ingredients:
16 oz frozen broccoli florets, defrosted and drained
10.5 oz can cream of mushroom soup
1 cup cheddar cheese, shredded

1/2 tsp onion powder
1/3 cup almond milk
For topping:
1 tbsp butter, melted
1/2 cup cracker crumbs

Directions:
Fit the Instant Vortex oven with the rack in position Add all ingredients except topping ingredients into the 1.5-qt casserole dish. In a small bowl, mix together cracker crumbs and melted butter and sprinkle over the casserole dish mixture. Set to bake at 350 F for 35 minutes. After 5 minutes place the casserole dish in the preheated oven. Serve and enjoy.

100.   Savory Curly Potatoes

Servings: 2   Cooking Time: 20 Minutes
Ingredients:

2 potatoes, spiralized
1 tbsp extra-virgin olive oil

Salt and black pepper to taste
1 tsp paprika

Directions:
Preheat Instant Vortex on Air Fry function to 350 F. Place the potatoes in a bowl and coat with oil. Transfer them to the cooking basket and fit in the baking tray. Cook for 15 minutes, shaking once. Sprinkle with salt, pepper, and paprika and to serve.

101. Cheddar Cheese Cauliflower Casserole

Servings: 8   Cooking Time: 35 Minutes
Ingredients:
4 cups cauliflower florets
1 1/2 cups cheddar cheese, shredded
1 cup sour cream

4 bacon slices, cooked and crumbled
3 green onions, chopped

Directions:
Fit the Instant Vortex oven with the rack in position Boil water in a large pot. Add cauliflower in boiling water and cook for 8-10 minutes or until tender. Drain well. Transfer cauliflower in a large bowl. Add half bacon, half green onion, 1 cup cheese, and sour cream in cauliflower bowl and mix well. Transfer mixture into a greased baking dish and sprinkle with remaining cheese. Set to bake at 350 F for 30 minutes. After 5 minutes place the baking dish in the preheated oven. Garnish with remaining green onion and bacon. Serve and enjoy.

102.   Easy Broccoli Bread

Servings: 6   Cooking Time: 30 Minutes
Ingredients:
5 eggs, lightly beaten
3/4 cup broccoli florets, chopped
2 tsp baking powder

3 1/1 tbsp coconut flour
1 cup cheddar cheese, shredded

Directions:
Fit the Instant Vortex oven with the rack in position Add all ingredients into the bowl and mix well. Pour egg mixture into the greased loaf pan. Set to bake at 350 F for 35 minutes. After 5 minutes place the loaf pan in the preheated oven. Cut the loaf into the slices and serve.

103.   Cheesy Garlic Biscuits

Servings: 4   Cooking Time: 20 Minutes
Ingredients:
1 large egg.
1 scallion, sliced
¼ cup unsalted butter; melted and divided

½ cup shredded sharp Cheddar cheese.
⅓ cup coconut flour
½ tsp. baking powder.
½ tsp. garlic powder.

Directions:
Take a large bowl, mix coconut flour, baking powder and garlic powder. Stir in egg, half of the melted butter, Cheddar cheese and scallions. Pour the mixture into a 6-inch round baking pan. Place into the air fryer basket Adjust the temperature to 320 Degrees F and set the timer for 12 minutes To

serve, remove from pan and allow to fully cool. Slice into four pieces and pour remaining melted butter over each.

---

104. Dijon Zucchini Patties

Servings: 6   Cooking Time: 30 Minutes
Ingredients:

1 cup zucchini, shredded and squeeze out all liquid	1 egg, lightly beaten
2 tbsp onion, minced	1/2 tbsp Dijon mustard
1/4 tsp red pepper flakes	1/2 tbsp mayonnaise
1/4 cup parmesan cheese, grated	1/2 cup breadcrumbs
	Pepper
	Salt

Directions:
Fit the Instant Vortex oven with the rack in position Add all ingredients into the bowl and mix until well combined.   Make small patties from the zucchini mixture and place it in a parchment-lined baking pan.   Set to bake at 400 F for 35 minutes. After 5 minutes place the baking pan in the preheated oven. Serve and enjoy.

---

105. Jalapeno Bread

Servings: 10   Cooking Time: 50 Minutes
Ingredients:

3 cups all-purpose flour	1/4 cup butter, melted
8 oz cheddar cheese, shredded	1 1/2 cups buttermilk
1/2 tsp ground white pepper	3 jalapeno peppers, chopped
1 1/2 tbsp baking powder	2 tbsp sugar
	1 1/4 tsp salt

Directions:
Fit the Instant Vortex oven with the rack in position In a mixing bowl, mix flour, baking powder, sugar, white pepper, and salt.   Add jalapenos and cheese and stir to combine.   Whisk butter and buttermilk together and add to the flour mixture. Stir until just combined.   Pour batter into the greased 9*5-inch loaf pan.   Set to bake at 375 F for 55 minutes. After 5 minutes place the loaf pan in the preheated oven. Slice and serve.

---

106. Crispy Onion Rings

Servings: 4   Cooking Time: 30 Minutes
Ingredients:

2 sweet onions	1 package cornbread mix
2 cups buttermilk	1 tsp salt
2 cups pancake mix	
2 cups water	

Directions:
Preheat Instant Vortex on AirFry function to 370 F. Slice the onions into rings. Combine the pancake mix with the water. Line a baking sheet with parchment paper.   Dip the rings in the cornbread mixture first, and then in the pancake batter. Place half of the onion rings onto the sheet. Press Start and cook for 8 to 12 minutes, and repeat one more time. Serve with salsa rosa or garlic mayo.

---

107. Baked Parmesan Zucchini

Servings: 4   Cooking Time: 20 Minutes
Ingredients:

4 zucchinis	1/4 teaspoon garlic powder
1/2 cup grated parmesan	Salt and pepper to taste
1/2 teaspoon dried thyme	2 tablespoons olive oil
1/2 teaspoon dried oregano	2 tablespoons chopped fresh parsley leaves
1/2 teaspoon dried basil	

Directions:
Start by preheating the toaster oven to 350°F. Quarter the zucchini lengthwise.   Mix together parmesan, dried herbs, garlic powder, salt, and pepper.   Lay the zucchini flat-side up on a greased pan and drizzle with olive oil.   Pour the parmesan mix over the zucchini.   Bake for 15 minutes then switch the setting to broil for another 3 minutes.

---

108. Buttered Broccoli With Parmesan

Servings: 4   Cooking Time: 4 Minutes
Ingredients:

1 pound (454 g) broccoli florets	2 tablespoons olive oil
1 medium shallot, minced	2 teaspoons minced garlic
2 tablespoons unsalted butter, melted	¼ cup grated Parmesan cheese

Directions:
Combine the broccoli florets with the shallot, olive oil, butter, garlic, and Parmesan cheese in a medium bowl and toss until the broccoli florets are thoroughly coated.   Place the broccoli florets in the air fryer basket in a single layer.   Put the air fryer basket on the baking pan and slide into Rack Position 2, select Roast, set temperature to 360°F (182°C), and set time to 4 minutes.   When cooking is complete, the broccoli florets should be crisp-tender. Remove from the oven and serve warm.

---

109. Parmesan Zucchini Chips

Servings: 4   Cooking Time: 20 Minutes
Ingredients:

1 oz. pork rinds.	2 medium zucchini
½ cup grated Parmesan cheese.	1 large egg.

Directions:
Slice zucchini in ¼-inch-thick slices. Place between two layers of paper towels or a clean kitchen towel for 30 minutes to remove excess moisture   Place pork rinds into food processor and pulse until finely ground. Pour into medium bowl and mix with Parmesan   Beat egg in a small bowl.   Dip zucchini slices in egg and then in pork rind mixture, coating as completely as possible. Carefully place each slice into the air fryer basket in a single layer, working in batches as necessary.   Adjust temperature to 320 Degrees F and set the timer for 10 minutes. Flip chips halfway through the cooking time. Serve warm.

110.Cheddar & Prosciutto Strips

Servings: 6   Cooking Time: 50 Minutes
Ingredients:

1 lb cheddar cheese   2 eggs, beaten
12 prosciutto slices   4 tbsp olive oil
1 cup flour   1 cup breadcrumbs

Directions:
Cut the cheese into 6 equal pieces. Wrap each piece with 2 prosciutto slices. Place them in the freezer just enough to set, about 5 minutes; note that they mustn't be frozen.   Preheat Instant Vortex on AirFry function to 390 F. Dip the Strips into flour first, then in eggs, and coat with breadcrumbs. Place in the frying basket and drizzle with olive oil. Press Start and cook for 10 minutes or until golden brown. Serve with tomato dip.

111. Pineapple & Mozzarella Tortillas

Servings: 2   Cooking Time: 15 Minutes

Ingredients:

2 tortillas   8 mozzarella slices
8 ham slices   2 tbsp tomato sauce
8 thin pineapple slices   ½ tsp dried parsley

Directions:
Preheat Instant Vortex on Air Fry function to 330 F. Spread the tomato sauce onto the tortillas. Arrange 4 ham slices on each tortilla. Top the ham with the pineapple and sprinkle with mozzarella and parsley. Cook for 10 minutes and enjoy.

112. Rice Flour Bites

Servings: 4   Cooking Time: 12 Minutes

Ingredients:

6 tablespoons milk   ¾ cup rice flour
½ teaspoon vegetable oil   1 oz. Parmesan cheese, shredded

Directions:
In a bowl, add milk, flour, oil and cheese and mix until a smooth dough forms.   Make small equal-sized balls from the dough.   Press "Power Button" of Air Fry Oven and turn the dial to select the "Air Fry" mode.   Press the Time button and again turn the dial to set the cooking time to 12 minutes. Now push the Temp button and rotate the dial to set the temperature at 300 degrees F.   Press "Start/Pause" button to start.   When the unit beeps to show that it is preheated, open the lid. Arrange the balls in "Air Fry Basket" and insert in the oven.   Serve warm.

113. Parmesan Cauliflower

Servings: 5 Cups   Cooking Time: 15 Minutes

Ingredients:

8 cups small cauliflower florets (about 1¼ pounds / 567 g)   1 teaspoon garlic powder
3 tablespoons olive oil   ½ teaspoon salt
   ½ teaspoon turmeric
   ¼ cup shredded Parmesan cheese

Directions:
In a bowl, combine the cauliflower florets, olive oil, garlic powder, salt, and turmeric and toss to coat. Transfer to the air fryer basket.   Put the air fryer basket on the baking pan and slide into Rack Position 2, select Air Fry, set temperature to 390°F (199°C), and set time to 15 minutes.   After 5 minutes, remove from the oven and stir the cauliflower florets. Return to the oven and continue cooking.   After 6 minutes, remove from the oven and stir the cauliflower. Return to the oven and continue cooking for 4 minutes. The cauliflower florets should be crisp-tender.   When cooking is complete, remove from the oven to a plate. Sprinkle with the shredded Parmesan cheese and toss well. Serve warm.

114. Savory Chicken Nuggets With Parmesan Cheese

Servings: 4   Cooking Time: 25 Minutes

Ingredients:

1 lb chicken breasts, cubed   2 tbsp olive oil
Salt and black pepper to taste   2 tbsp panko breadcrumbs
5 tbsp plain breadcrumbs   2 tbsp grated Parmesan cheese

Directions:
Preheat Instant Vortex on Air Fry function to 380 F. Season the chicken with salt and pepper; set aside. In a bowl, mix the breadcrumbs with the Parmesan cheese.   Brush the chicken pieces with the olive oil, then dip into breadcrumb mixture, and transfer to the Air Fryer basket. Fit in the baking tray and lightly spray chicken with cooking spray. Cook for 10 minutes, flipping once halfway through until golden brown on the outside and no more pink on the inside. Serve warm.

115. Buttered Corn

Servings: 2   Cooking Time: 20 Minutes

Ingredients:

Salt and freshly ground black pepper, as needed   2 corn on the cob
   2 tablespoons butter, softened and divided

Directions:
Sprinkle the cobs evenly with salt and black pepper. Then, rub with 1 tablespoon of butter.   With 1 piece of foil, wrap each cob.   Press "Power Button" of Air Fry Oven and turn the dial to select the "Air Fry" mode.   Press the Time button and again turn the dial to set the cooking time to 20 minutes. Now push the Temp button and rotate the dial to set the temperature at 320 degrees F.   Press "Start/Pause" button to start.   When the unit beeps to show that it is preheated, open the lid. Arrange the cobs in "Air Fry Basket" and insert in the oven.   Serve warm.

116. Stylish Ham Omelet

Servings: 2   Cooking Time: 30 Minutes

Ingredients:

4 small tomatoes, chopped	2 tablespoons cheddar cheese
4 eggs	Salt and black pepper, to taste
2 ham slices	
1 onion, chopped	

Directions:

Preheat the Air fryer to 390F and grease an Air fryer pan. Place the tomatoes in the Air fryer pan and cook for about 10 minutes. Heat a nonstick skillet on medium heat and add onion and ham. Stir fry for about 5 minutes and transfer into the Air fryer pan. Whisk together eggs, salt and black pepper in a bowl and pour in the Air fryer pan. Set the Air fryer to 335F and cook for about 15 minutes. Dish out and serve warm.

117. Italian Sausage & Egg Taquitos

Servings: 4   Cooking Time: 15 Minutes

Ingredients:

3 eggs, scrambled	1 avocado, halved, pitted, peeled & chopped
6 oz. hot Italian sausage, cooked & crumbled	1 cup sharp cheddar cheese, grated
¼ cup sun dried tomatoes, drain & slice thin	12 corn tortillas, softened

Directions:

Line the baking pan with parchment paper. In a large bowl, place all ingredients and toss to mix. One at a time, place a tortilla on a cutting board and add some of the filling mixture. Start at one side and roll tortilla over filling. Place seam side down on prepared pan. Repeat with remaining tortillas and filling. Set to air fry at 425°F for 20 minutes. After 5 minutes, place the pan in position 2 of the oven and cook until taquitos are crisp and the cheese has melted. Serve immediately.

118. Easy French-style Apple Cake

Servings: 6   Cooking Time: 25 Minutes

Ingredients:

2 ¾ oz flour	3 tbsp cinnamon
5 tbsp sugar	2 whole apple, sliced
1 ¼ oz butter	

Directions:

Preheat Instant Vortex on Bake function to 360 F. In a bowl, mix 3 tbsp sugar, butter, and flour; form pastry using the batter. Roll out the pastry on a floured surface and transfer it to the basket. Arrange the apple slices atop. Cover apples with sugar and cinnamon and press Start. Cook cook for 20 minutes. Sprinkle with powdered sugar and mint and serve.

119. Pea And Potato Samosas With Chutney

Servings: 16 Samosas   Cooking Time: 22 Minutes

Ingredients:

Dough:

4 cups all-purpose flour, plus more for flouring the work surface	1 teaspoon turmeric
¼ cup plain yogurt	½ cup peas, thawed if frozen
½ cup cold unsalted butter, cut into cubes	2 cups mashed potatoes
2 teaspoons kosher salt	2 tablespoons yogurt
1 cup ice water	Cooking spray

Filling:

Chutney:

2 tablespoons vegetable oil	1 cup mint leaves, lightly packed
1 onion, diced	2 cups cilantro leaves, lightly packed
1½ teaspoons coriander	1 green chile pepper, deseeded and minced
1½ teaspoons cumin	½ cup minced onion
1 clove garlic, minced	Juice of 1 lime
1 teaspoon kosher salt	1 teaspoon granulated sugar
	1 teaspoon kosher salt
	2 tablespoons vegetable oil

Directions:

Put the flour, yogurt, butter, and salt in a food processor. Pulse to combine until grainy. Pour in the water and pulse until a smooth and firm dough forms. Transfer the dough on a clean and lightly floured working surface. Knead the dough and shape it into a ball. Cut in half and flatten the halves into 2 discs. Wrap them in plastic and let sit in refrigerator until ready to use. Meanwhile, make the filling: Heat the vegetable oil in a saucepan over medium heat. Add the onion and sauté for 5 minutes or until lightly browned. Add the coriander, cumin, garlic, turmeric, and salt and sauté for 2 minutes or until fragrant. Add the peas, potatoes, and yogurt and stir to combine well. Turn off the heat and allow to cool. Meanwhile, combine the ingredients for the chutney in a food processor. Pulse to mix well until glossy. Pour the chutney in a bowl and refrigerate until ready to use. Make the samosas: Remove the dough discs from the refrigerator and cut each disc into 8 parts. Shape each part into a ball, then roll the ball into a 6-inch circle. Cut the circle in half and roll each half into a cone. Scoop up 2 tablespoons of the filling into the cone, press the edges of the cone to seal and form into a triangle. Repeat with remaining dough and filling. Spritz the air fryer basket with cooking spray. Arrange the samosas in the pan and spritz with cooking spray. Put the air fryer basket on the baking pan and slide into Rack Position 2, select Air Fry, set temperature to 360°F (182°C) and set time to 15 minutes. Flip the samosas halfway through the cooking time. When cooked, the samosas will be golden brown and crispy. Serve the samosas with the chutney.

120. Hash Browns

Servings: 3   Cooking Time: 18 Minutes
Ingredients:

1 tsp flour	½ tsp Cajun seasoning
1 ½ pound potatoes peeled	
½ shallot	1 egg white
	½ tsp black pepper
	1 tsp coconut oil

Directions:
Keep the peeled potatoes in a bowl of water and mix them with Cajun seasoning as well as flour. Grate the potatoes and pour some cold water with a little salt to reduce the starch content. Set this mixture aside. Grate the shallot and set it aside, strain your potatoes using a fine strainer or cheesecloth. Ensure all the water has been strained out of the potatoes. Mix the ingredients in a bowl except the potatoes and ensure that they are well combined. Add the potatoes and mix them thoroughly. Form several patties.   Place your instant air fryer at 400 degrees Fahrenheit. Once the fryer indicates add food, add the patties on the pan. Flip every time the panel indicates turn food.   Serve while hot.

121. Turkey Breakfast Sausage Patties

Servings: 4   Cooking Time: 10 Minutes
Ingredients:

1 tablespoon chopped fresh thyme	½ teaspoon garlic powder
1 tablespoon chopped fresh sage	⅛ teaspoon crushed red pepper flakes
1¼ teaspoons kosher salt	⅛ teaspoon freshly ground black pepper
1 teaspoon chopped fennel seeds	1 pound (454 g) 93% lean ground turkey
¾ teaspoon smoked paprika	½ cup finely minced sweet apple (peeled)
½ teaspoon onion powder	

Directions:
Thoroughly combine the thyme, sage, salt, fennel seeds, paprika, onion powder, garlic powder, red pepper flakes, and black pepper in a medium bowl. Add the ground turkey and apple and stir until well incorporated. Divide the mixture into 8 equal portions and shape into patties with your hands, each about ¼ inch thick and 3 inches in diameter. Place the patties in the air fryer basket in a single layer.   Put the air fryer basket on the baking pan and slide into Rack Position 2, select Air Fry, set temperature to 400°F (205°C), and set time to 10 minutes.   Flip the patties halfway through the cooking time.   When cooking is complete, the patties should be nicely browned and cooked through. Remove from the oven to a plate and serve warm.

122. Grilled Cheese Sandwich

Servings: 1 Person   Cooking Time: 12 Minutes
Ingredients:

2 slices of bread	Tomatoes
2 pieces of bacon	Jack cheese
½ tsp of olive oil side	Peach preserves

Directions:
If you have left over bacon from air fried bacon recipe you can get two pieces. However, if you do not have any leftover bacon you can get two pieces and fry them at 200 degree Celsius.   Place olive oil on the side of the bread slices. Layer the rest of the ingredients on the non-oiled side following the following steps, peach preserves, tomatoes, jack cheese and cooked bacon.   Press down the bread to allow it to cook a little bit and peach side down too to allow the bread and the peel to spread evenly. Place the sandwich in an air fryer and cook it for 12 minutes   at 393 degrees Fahrenheit.   Serve once you are done.

123. Mushroom Spinach Egg Muffins

Servings: 12   Cooking Time: 20 Minutes
Ingredients:

12 eggs	1/2 cup fresh basil
1 cup mushrooms, diced	3/4 cup feta cheese, crumbled
1 cup spinach, chopped	Pepper
	Salt

Directions:
Fit the Instant Vortex oven with the rack in position Spray a muffin tray with cooking spray and set aside. In a bowl, whisk eggs with pepper and salt.   Add basil, mushrooms, spinach, and cheese and stir well. Pour egg mixture into the prepared muffin tray. Set to bake at 400 F for 25 minutes. After 5 minutes place the muffin tray in the preheated oven.   Serve and enjoy.

124. Egg In A Hole

Servings: 1   Cooking Time: 5 Minutes
Ingredients:

1 slice bread	1 egg
1 teaspoon butter, softened	1 tablespoon shredded Cheddar cheese
Salt and pepper, to taste	2 teaspoons diced ham

Directions:
On a flat work surface, cut a hole in the center of the bread slice with a 2½-inch-diameter biscuit cutter. Spread the butter evenly on each side of the bread slice and transfer to the baking pan.   Crack the egg into the hole and season as desired with salt and pepper. Scatter the shredded cheese and diced ham on top.   Slide the baking pan into Rack Position 1, select Convection Bake, set temperature to 330°F (166°C), and set time to 5 minutes.   When cooking is complete, the bread should be lightly browned and the egg should be set. Remove from the oven and serve hot.

125. Hearty Sweet Potato Baked Oatmeal

Servings: 6   Cooking Time: 30 Minutes

Ingredients:

1 egg, lightly beaten	1 tsp baking powder
1 tsp vanilla	1/4 tsp nutmeg
1 1/2 cups milk	2 tsp cinnamon
2 tbsp ground flax seed	1/3 cup maple syrup
1 cup sweet potato puree	2 cups old fashioned oats
	1/4 tsp salt

Directions:

Fit the Instant Vortex oven with the rack in position Spray an 8-inch square baking pan with cooking spray and set aside.   Add all ingredients except oats into the mixing bowl and mix until well combined.   Add oats and stir until just combined. Pour mixture into the prepared baking pan.   Set to bake at 350 F for 35 minutes. After 5 minutes place the baking pan in the preheated oven.   Serve and enjoy.

126. Poppy Seed Muffins

Servings: 12   Cooking Time: 20 Minutes

Ingredients:

3 tbsp poppy seeds	4/5 cup almond milk
1 tsp vanilla	1/4 tsp baking soda
8 tbsp maple syrup	2 tsp baking powder
2 tbsp lemon zest	1 1/4 cups flour
6 tbsp lemon juice	1 1/4 cups almond flour
1/4 cup butter, melted	Pinch of salt

Directions:

Fit the Instant Vortex oven with the rack in position Line 12-cups muffin tin with cupcake liners and set aside.   In a large bowl, mix together melted butter, milk, lemon zest, vanilla, lemon juice, poppy seeds, maple syrup, and almond flour.   Add flour, baking soda, and baking powder. Stir until well combined. Pour batter into the prepared muffin tin.   Set to bake at 350 F for 25 minutes, after 5 minutes, place the muffin tin in the oven.   Serve and enjoy.

127. Perfect Chicken Casserole

Servings: 8   Cooking Time: 30 Minutes

Ingredients:

1 cup mozzarella cheese, shredded	8 eggs
8 oz can crescent rolls	3/4 lb chicken breasts, cooked & shredded
1 1/2 cups basil pesto	Pepper
	Salt

Directions:

Fit the Instant Vortex oven with the rack in position Spray a 9*13-inch baking dish with cooking spray and set aside.   In a bowl, mix shredded chicken and pesto and set aside.   In a separate bowl, eggs, pepper, and salt.   Roll out the crescent roll into the prepared baking dish. Top with shredded chicken.   Pour egg mixture over chicken and top with shredded mozzarella cheese.   Set to bake at 350 F for 35 minutes. After 5 minutes place the baking dish in the preheated oven.   Serve and enjoy.

128. Parmesan Asparagus

Servings: 4   Cooking Time: 20 Minutes

Ingredients:

1 lb asparagus spears	1 cup breadcrumbs
1/4 cup flour	2 eggs, beaten
1/2 cup Parmesan cheese, grated	Salt and black pepper to taste

Directions:

Preheat Instant Vortex on AirFry function to 370 F. Combine breadcrumbs, Parmesan cheese, salt, and pepper in a bowl. Line a baking sheet with parchment paper.   Dip the spears into the flour first, then into the eggs, and finally coat with the crumb mixture. Arrange them on a baking tray and press Start. Bake for 8-10 minutes. Serve warm.

129. Bacon And Cheddar Cheese Frittata

Ingredients:

8 slices bacon, chopped	Coarse salt, freshly ground pepper, to taste
1/2 cup grated cheddar cheese	1/4 cup Romano cheese
12 large eggs	Dash of hot sauce
3 Tbsp milk	

Directions:

Preheat oven to 375°F.   Heat Instant Vortex oven and cook bacon over medium heat, stirring until crisp.   Set aside on a plate.   In a bowl, whisk eggs, milk, salt, pepper, cheeses and hot sauce. Add cooked bacon to egg mixture.   Pour eggs into Instant Vortex oven. When eggs are half set and edges begin to   pull away, place frittata in oven and bake for about 10 minutes, or until   center is no longer jiggly.   Cut into wedges inside pot or slide out onto serving plate.

130. Smoked Sausage Breakfast Mix

Servings: 4   Cooking Time: 30 Minutes

Ingredients:

1 and 1/2 pounds smoked sausage, diced and browned	4 and 1/2 cups water
	1 cup milk
A pinch of salt and black pepper	1/4 tsp. garlic powder
1 and 1/2 cups grits	1 and 1/2 tsp.s thyme, diced
16 ounces cheddar cheese, shredded	Cooking spray
	4 eggs, whisked

Directions:

Put the water in a pot, bring to a boil over medium heat, add grits, stir, cover, cook for 5 minutes and take off heat.   Add cheese, stir until it melts and mix with milk, thyme, salt, pepper, garlic powder and eggs and whisk really well.   Heat up your air fryer at 300 °F, grease with cooking spray and add browned sausage.   Add grits mix, spread and cook for 25 minutes.   Divide among plates and serve for breakfast.

131. Crunchy Asparagus With Cheese

Servings: 4   Cooking Time: 15 Minutes

Ingredients:

1 lb asparagus spears	1 cup breadcrumbs
¼ cup flour	2 eggs, beaten
½ cup Parmesan cheese, grated	Salt and black pepper to taste

Directions:

Preheat Instant Vortex on Air Fry function to 370 F. Combine the breadcrumbs and Parmesan cheese in a bowl. Season with salt and pepper.   Line a baking sheet with parchment paper. Dip the asparagus spears into the flour first, then into the eggs, and finally coat with crumbs.   Arrange them on the AirFryer Basket, fit in the baking sheet, and cook for about 8 to 10 minutes. Serve with melted butter, hollandaise sauce, or freshly squeezed lemon.

132. Egg English Muffin With Bacon

Servings: 1   Cooking Time: 10 Minutes

Ingredients:

1 egg	Salt and black pepper to taste
1 English muffin	
2 slices of bacon	

Directions:

Preheat Instant Vortex on Bake function to 395 F. Crack the egg into a ramekin. Place the muffin, egg and bacon in the oven. Cook for 9 minutes. Let cool slightly so you can assemble the sandwich.   Cut the muffin in half. Place the egg on one half and season with salt and pepper. Arrange the bacon on top. Top with the other muffin half.

133. Cinnamon Sweet Potato Chips

Servings: 6 To 8 Slices   Cooking Time: 8 Minutes

Ingredients:

2 tablespoons olive oil	1 small sweet potato, cut into ⅜ inch-thick slices
1 to 2 teaspoon ground cinnamon	

Directions:

Add the sweet potato slices and olive oil in a bowl and toss to coat. Fold in the cinnamon and stir to combine.   Lay the sweet potato slices in a single layer in the air fryer basket.   Put the air fryer basket on the baking pan and slide into Rack Position 2, select Air Fry, set temperature to 390°F (199°C), and set time to 8 minutes.   Stir the potato slices halfway through the cooking time.   When cooking is complete, the chips should be crisp. Remove the pan from the oven. Allow to cool for 5 minutes before serving.

134. Sweet Berry Pastry

Servings: 3   Cooking Time: 20 Minutes

Ingredients:

3 pastry dough sheets	¼ tsp vanilla extract
2 tbsp strawberries, mashed	2 cups cream cheese, softened
	1 tbsp honey

2 tbsp raspberries, mashed

Directions:

Preheat Instant Vortex oven on Bake function to 375 F. Spread the cream cheese on the dough sheets. In a bowl, combine berries, honey, and vanilla. Divide the mixture between the pastry sheets. Pinch the ends of the sheets to form puff. Place in the Instant Vortex oven and cook for 15 minutes.

135. Smart Oven Jalapeño Popper Grilled Cheese Recipe

Ingredients:

1 medium Jalapeño	2 teaspoons Honey
2 slices Whole Grain Bread	1 tablespoon Sliced Green Onions
2 teaspoons Mayonnaise	dash of Garlic Powder
1/2-ounce Shredded Mild Cheddar Cheese, (about 2 tablespoons)	1-ounce Shredded Monterey Jack Cheese, (about 1/4 cup)
1-ounce Cream Cheese, softened	1/4 cup Corn Flakes Cereal

Directions:

Cut jalapeño into 1/4-inch slices. If you want your Classic Sandwich less spicy, use a paring knife to remove the seeds and veins.   Adjust cooking rack to the top placement and select the BROIL setting. Place jalapeño slices on a baking sheet, and broil until they have softened and are just starting to brown, about 2 to 4 minutes. Remove pan and set aside.   Adjust the cooking rack to the bottom position. Place an empty sheet pan inside of the toaster oven, and preheat to 400°F on the BAKE setting.   Spread one side of each slice of bread with mayonnaise. Place the bread mayo-side-down on a cutting board.   In a small bowl, combine the cream cheese, green onion, and garlic powder. Spread each slice of bread with the mixture. Arrange jalapeño slices in an even layer on one slice and distribute the cheese evenly over both pieces of bread.   Carefully remove the pan and add the bread, mayo-side-down, to the pan. Return to the oven and bake until the bread is toasted and the cheese is melted and bubbly, about 6 to 7 minutes. Finishing Touches   Drizzle the honey over the jalapeño and sprinkle with corn flakes. Immediately top with the remaining cheesy bread slice.

136. Raspberries Oatmeal

Servings: 4   Cooking Time: 30 Minutes

Ingredients:

1 ½ cups coconut; shredded	2 tsp. stevia
½ cups raspberries	½ tsp. cinnamon powder
2 cups almond milk	Cooking spray
¼ tsp. nutmeg, ground	

Directions:

Grease the air fryer's pan with cooking spray, mix all the ingredients inside, cover and cook at 360°F for 15 minutes. Divide into bowls and serve

137. Ham And Cheese Bagel Sandwiches

Servings: 2   Cooking Time: 5 Minutes

Ingredients:

2 bagels
4 teaspoons honey mustard

4 slices cooked honey ham
4 slices Swiss cheese

Directions:

Start by preheating toaster oven to 400°F.   Spread honey mustard on each half of the bagel.   Add ham and cheese and close the bagel.   Bake the sandwich until the cheese is fully melted, approximately 5 minutes.

138.   Cinnamon Streusel Bread

Servings: 8   Cooking Time: 30 Minutes

Ingredients:

1 cup warm water
1 envelope yeast, quick rising
1/3 cup + 6 tsp milk, divided
1 egg
3 tbsp. sugar
3 ½ cups flour, divided

1 tbsp. + 2 tsp olive oil
1 tsp salt
2 tbsp. cinnamon
½ cup brown sugar
2 tbsp. butter, cold & cut in cubes
1 cup powdered sugar

Directions:

In a large bowl, add water and sprinkle yeast over top, stir to dissolve.   Stir in 1/3 cup milk, egg, and sugar until combined.   Add 2 cups flour and stir in until batter gets thick. With a wooden spoon, or mixer with dough hook attached, beat 100 strokes. Fold in oil and salt. Then stir in 1 ¼ cups flour until dough begins to come together.   Mix in cinnamon and transfer dough to a lightly floured work surface. Knead for 5 minutes then form into a ball.   Use remaining oil to grease a clean bowl and add dough. Cover and let rise 30 minutes.   Spray a 9-inch loaf pan with cooking spray.   After 30 minutes, punch dough down and divide into 8 equal pieces.   Place brown sugar in a shallow bowl and roll dough pieces in it, forming it into balls. Place in prepared pan and sprinkle remaining brown sugar over top.   In a small bowl, combine butter and ¼ cup flour until mixture resembles coarse crumbs. Sprinkle over top of bread.   Place rack in position 1 of the oven. Set to convection bake on 325°F and set timer for 35 minutes. After 5 minutes, add pan to the rack and bake 30 minutes or until golden brown.   Let cool in pan 10 minutes, then invert onto wire rack.   In a small bowl, whisk together powdered sugar and milk until smooth. Drizzle over warm bread and serve.

139.   Milky Semolina Cutlets

Servings: 2   Cooking Time: 15 | Minutes

Ingredients:

3 tablespoons of vegetable oil
1 cup of semolina
12 ounces of mixed

2 & 1/2 pounds of milk
1/2tsp. salt
1/2 tsp. black pepper, ground

vegetables (any of your choice), diced

Directions:

Pour the milk into a sauce pan and heat. Add the mixed vegetables and allow it to cook until they are soft for about 3 minutes.   Add the pepper and salt and then the semolina. Cook until the mixture thicken; this will take about 10 minutes.   Grease a flat plate with oil; spread the semolina mixture on it. Refrigerate for about 4 hours until it is firm.   Heat the air fryer to 350°F.   Remove from the refrigerator and cut into flat round shapes. Brush the cutlets with oil and place them into the air fryer. Cook for 10 minutes. Serve while hot with any sauce of your choice.

140.   Banana Coconut Muffins

Servings: 12   Cooking Time: 15 Minutes

Ingredients:

1 egg
3 ripe bananas, mashed
1/2 cup shredded coconut
2 cups all-purpose flour

2 tsp baking powder
1/2 tsp baking soda
1 cup of sugar
1 tsp vanilla
1/2 cup milk
1/2 cup applesauce
1/2 tsp salt

Directions:

Fit the Instant Vortex oven with the rack in position Line a 12-cup muffin tray with cupcake liners and set aside.   In a mixing bowl, whisk the egg with vanilla, milk, applesauce, and salt until well combined.   Add baking powder, baking soda, and sugar and mix well.   Add flour and mix until just combined.   Add shredded coconut and stir well. Pour mixture into the prepared muffin tray.   Set to bake at 350 F for 20 minutes. After 5 minutes place the muffin tray in the preheated oven.   Serve and enjoy.

141. Beans And Pork Mix

Servings: 4   Cooking Time: 20 Minutes

Ingredients:

1-pound pork stew meat, ground
1 tablespoon olive oil
1 cup canned kidney beans, drained and rinsed

1 red onion, chopped
1 teaspoon chili powder
Salt and black pepper to the taste
¼ teaspoon cumin, ground

Directions:

Heat up your air fryer at 360 degrees F, add the meat and the onion and cook for 5 minutes.   Add the beans and the rest of the ingredients, toss and cook for 15 minutes more.   Divide everything into bowls and serve for breakfast.

142.   Cheesy Breakfast Casserole

Servings: 4   Cooking Time: 16 Minutes

Ingredients:

6 slices bacon
6 eggs
Salt and pepper, to

½ cup chopped green bell pepper

taste
Cooking spray

½ cup chopped onion
¾ cup shredded Cheddar cheese

Directions:
Place the bacon in a skillet over medium-high heat and cook each side for about 4 minutes until evenly crisp. Remove from the heat to a paper towel-lined plate to drain. Crumble it into small pieces and set aside. Whisk the eggs with the salt and pepper in a medium bowl. Spritz the baking pan with cooking spray. Place the whisked eggs, crumbled bacon, green bell pepper, and onion in the prepared pan. Slide the baking pan into Rack Position 1, select Convection Bake, set temperature to 400°F (205°C) and set time to 8 minutes. After 6 minutes, remove the pan from the oven. Scatter the Cheddar cheese all over. Return the pan to the oven and continue to cook for another 2 minutes. When cooking is complete, let sit for 5 minutes and serve on plates.

143.	**Flavorful Pumpkin Bread**

Servings: 12   Cooking Time: 55 Minutes
Ingredients:

2 eggs
8 oz pumpkin puree
1 3/4 cups flour
1 1/2 cups sugar
1/3 cup water
1/2 cup vegetable oil
1/8 tsp ground ginger

1/4 tsp ground cloves
1/2 tsp ground nutmeg
1/2 tsp ground cinnamon
1 tsp baking soda
3/4 tsp salt

Directions:
Fit the Instant Vortex oven with the rack in position In a bowl, whisk eggs, sugar, water, oil, and pumpkin puree until combined. In a separate bowl, mix dry ingredients. Add dry ingredient mixture into the egg mixture and mix until well combined. Pour batter into the greased loaf pan. Set to bake at 350 F for 60 minutes, after 5 minutes, place the loaf pan in the oven. Slice and serve.

144.	**Honey Banana Pastry With Berries**

Servings: 2   Cooking Time: 15 Minutes
Ingredients:

3 bananas, sliced
2 puff pastry sheets, cut into thin strips

3 tbsp honey
Fresh berries to serve

Directions:
Preheat Instant Vortex on Bake function to 340 F. Place the banana slices into a baking dish. Cover with the pastry strips and top with honey. Cook for 12 minutes. Serve with berries.

145.	**Whole Wheat Carrot Bread**

Servings: 10   Cooking Time: 50 Minutes
Ingredients:

1 egg
3/4 cup whole wheat flour

1/2 cup brown sugar
1 tsp baking powder
1/2 tsp nutmeg

1 cup carrots, shredded
3/4 tsp vanilla
3/4 cup all-purpose flour

1 1/2 tsp cinnamon
3/4 cup yogurt
3 tbsp vegetable oil
1 tsp baking soda

Directions:
Fit the Instant Vortex oven with the rack in position In a large bowl, mix all dry ingredients and set aside. In a separate bowl, whisk the egg with vanilla, sugar, yogurt, and oil. Add carrots and fold well. Add dry ingredient mixture and stir until just combined. Pour mixture into the 9*5-inch greased loaf pan. Set to bake at 350 F for 55 minutes, after 5 minutes, place the loaf pan in the oven. Slice and serve.

146.	**Classic Cheddar Cheese Omelet**

Servings: 1   Cooking Time: 15 Minutes
Ingredients:

2 eggs, beaten
Black pepper to taste
1 cup cheddar cheese, shredded

1 whole onion, chopped
2 tbsp soy sauce

Directions:
Preheat Instant Vortex on Air Fry function to 340 F. In a bowl, mix the eggs with soy sauce, salt, and pepper. Stir in the onion and cheddar cheese. Pour the egg mixture in a greased baking pan and cook for 10-12 minutes. Serve and enjoy!

147.	**Yogurt & Cream Cheese Zucchini Cakes**

Servings: 4   Cooking Time: 20 Minutes
Ingredients:

1 ½ cups flour
1 tsp cinnamon
3 eggs
2 tsp baking powder
2 tbsp sugar
1 cup milk

2 tbsp butter, melted
1 tbsp yogurt
½ cup shredded zucchini
2 tbsp cream cheese

Directions:
In a bowl, whisk the eggs along with the sugar, salt, cinnamon, cream cheese, flour, and baking powder. In another bowl, combine all of the liquid ingredients. Gently combine the dry and liquid mixtures. Stir in zucchini. Line muffin tins with baking paper, and pour the batter inside them. Arrange on the Air Fryer tray and cook for 15-18 minutes on Bake function at 380 F. Serve chilled.

148.	**Ultimate Breakfast Burrito**

Servings: 8   Cooking Time: : 20 Minute
Ingredients:

16 ounces cooked bacon ends and pieces
16 eggs
1 tablespoon butter
8 hash brown squares

8 large soft flour tortillas
2 diced jalapeños
2 cups shredded sharp cheddar

Directions:
Place bacon on a baking sheet in toaster oven. Bake at 450°F until it reaches desired level of crispiness

and set aside.   Whisk together eggs in a bowl and set aside.   Melt butter into a sauce pan and mix in eggs until they are starting to cook but not fully hardened.   While eggs are cooking, microwave and cool hash brown squares.   Roll out tortillas and top them with hash browns, bacon, jalapeños, and cheese.   Wrap up the burritos and place them seam-down on a baking sheet.   Bake at 375°F for 15–20 minutes.

---

149.   Buttery Orange Toasts

Servings: 6   Cooking Time: 15 Minutes

Ingredients:

12 bread slices	1 stick butter
½ cup sugar	1 ½ tbsp cinnamon
1 ½ tbsp vanilla extract	2 oranges, zested

Directions:
Mix butter, sugar, and vanilla extract and microwave the mixture for 30 seconds until it melts. Add in orange zest. Spread the mixture onto bread slices. Lay the bread slices on the cooking basket and cook in the Instant Vortex oven for 5 minutes at 400 F on Toast function. Serve warm.

---

150.   Quick & Easy Granola

Servings: 4   Cooking Time: 8 Minutes

Ingredients:

2 cups oats	1/2 tsp cinnamon
2 tbsp chia seeds	1/4 cup honey
1 tsp vanilla	1/4 cup almond butter

Directions:
Fit the Instant Vortex oven with the rack in position In a bowl, mix the almond butter, honey, cinnamon, and vanilla.   Add oats and chia seeds and mix well. Transfer oats mixture onto the parchment-lined baking pan.   Place the baking pan in Instant Vortex oven and set to bake at 350 F for 8 minutes. Serve and enjoy.

---

151. Meat Lover Omelet With Mozzarella

Servings: 2   Cooking Time: 20 Minutes

Ingredients:

1 beef sausage, chopped	1 cup grated mozzarella cheese
4 slices prosciutto, chopped	4 eggs
3 oz salami, chopped	1 tbsp chopped onion
	1 tbsp ketchup

Directions:
Preheat Instant Vortex on Bake function to 350 F. Whisk the eggs with ketchup in a bowl. Stir in the onion. Brown the sausage in a greased pan over medium heat for 2 minutes.   Combine the egg mixture, mozzarella cheese, salami, and prosciutto. Pour the egg mixture over the sausage and give it a stir. Press Start and cook in the Instant Vortex for 15 minutes.

---

152.   Basil Parmesan Bagel

Servings: 1   Cooking Time: 6 Minutes

Ingredients:

2 tbsp butter, softened	1 tsp garlic powder
¼ tsp dried basil	Salt and black pepper to taste
1 tbsp Parmesan cheese, grated	1 bagel

Directions:
Preheat Instant Vortex on Bake function to 370 F. Cut the bagel in half. Combine the butter, Parmesan cheese, garlic, and basil in a small bowl. Season with salt and pepper. Spread the mixture onto the halved bagel. Place the bagel in the basket and press Start. Cook for 5-6 minutes.

---

153.   Eggs In A Hole

Servings: 1   Cooking Time: 7 Minutes

Ingredients:

2 eggs	Pepper and salt to taste
2 slices of bread	
2 tsp butter	

Directions:
Using a jar punch two holes in the middle of your bread slices. This is the area where you will place your eggs.   Preheat your fryer to 330-degree Fahrenheit for about 5 minutes. Spread a tablespoon of butter into the pan and then add bread from the slices.   Crack the eggs and place them at the center of the bread slices and lightly season them with salt and pepper.   Take out your slices and rebutter the pan with the remaining butter and fry the other part for 3 minutes.   Serve while hot.

---

154.   Hashbrown Breakfast Casserole

Servings: 8   Cooking Time: 50 Minutes

Ingredients:

3 cups shredded cauliflower	4 tbsp butter
1/2 cup mayonnaise	1 tbsp onion, minced
1 cup sour cream	1 cup cheddar cheese, shredded
1 tbsp bouillon powder	1/2 tsp pepper
	1 tsp salt

Directions:
Fit the Instant Vortex oven with the rack in position Set aside 1/3 cup shredded cheese.   In a bowl, add remaining ingredients and mix well.   Spread mixture into the greased 8*8-inch baking dish and sprinkle with remaining shredded cheese.   Set to bake at 350 F for 55 minutes. After 5 minutes place the baking dish in the preheated oven.   Serve and enjoy.

---

155. Chicken Breakfast Sausages

Servings: 8 Patties   Cooking Time: 10 Minutes

Ingredients:

1 Granny Smith apple, peeled and finely chopped	1/3 cup minced onion
2 tablespoons apple juice	3 tablespoons ground almonds
2 garlic cloves,	1/8 teaspoon freshly ground black pepper
	1 pound (454 g)

minced | ground chicken
1 egg white | breast

Directions:
Combine all the ingredients except the chicken in a medium mixing bowl and stir well.   Add the chicken breast to the apple mixture and mix with your hands until well incorporated.   Divide the mixture into 8 equal portions and shape into patties. Arrange the patties in the air fryer basket.   Put the air fryer basket on the baking pan and slide into Rack Position 2, select Air Fry, set temperature to 330°F (166°C) and set time to 10 minutes.   When done, a meat thermometer inserted in the center of the chicken should reach at least 165°F (74°C). Remove from the oven to a plate. Let the chicken cool for 5 minutes and serve warm.

156.	Quick Cheddar Omelet

Servings: 1   Cooking Time: 15 Minutes
Ingredients:

2 eggs, beaten | 1 whole onion,
1 cup cheddar cheese, | chopped
shredded | 2 tbsp soy sauce

Directions:
Preheat Instant Vortex on AirFry function to 340 F. Drizzle soy sauce over the chopped onions. Sauté the onions ina greased pan over medium heat for 5 minutes; turn off the heat.   In a bowl, mix the eggs with salt and pepper. Pour the egg mixture over onions and cook in the Instant Vortex for 6 minutes. Top with cheddar cheese and bake for 4 more minutes. Serve and enjoy!

157.	Cheddar Omelet With Soy Sauce

Servings: 1   Cooking Time: 15 Minutes
Ingredients:

2 eggs |
2 tbsp cheddar | ½ onion, sliced
cheese, grated | ¼ tsp pepper
1 tsp soy sauce | 1 tbsp olive oil

Directions:
Preheat Instant Vortex on Bake function to 350 F. Whisk the eggs along with the pepper and soy sauce. Place the onion in a greased baking dish and pour over the egg mixture. Press Start and cook for 12-14 minutes. Top with the grated cheddar cheese and serve sliced.

158.	Caprese Sourdough Sandwich

Servings: 2   Cooking Time: 25 Minutes
Ingredients:

4 sourdough bread | 1 tomato, sliced
slices | 2 mozzarella cheese
2 tbsp mayonnaise | slices
2 slices ham | Salt and black pepper
2 lettuce leaves | to taste

Directions:
On a clean board, lay the sourdough slices and spread with mayonnaise. Top 2 of the slices with ham, lettuce, tomato and mozzarella. Season with salt and pepper. Top with the remaining two slices to form two sandwiches. Spray with oil and transfer to the frying basket. Cook in the preheated Instant Vortex oven for 14 minutes at 340 F on Bake function.

159.	Easy Egg Quiche

Servings: 6   Cooking Time: 45 Minutes
Ingredients:

8 eggs | 6 oz cheddar cheese,
4 tbsp butter, melted | shredded
6 oz cream cheese |

Directions:
Fit the Instant Vortex oven with the rack in position Add eggs, cheese, butter, and cream cheese into the bowl and whisk until well combined.   Pour egg mixture into the greased pie dish.   Set to bake at 325 F for 50 minutes, after 5 minutes, place the pie dish in the oven.   Serve and enjoy.

160.	Healthy Baked Oatmeal

Servings: 6   Cooking Time: 20 Minutes
Ingredients:

1 egg | 1 1/2 cups milk
1/3 cup dried | 1 tsp baking powder
cranberries | 1/3 cup light brown
1 tsp vanilla | sugar
1 1/2 tsp cinnamon | 2 cups old fashioned
2 tbsp butter, melted | oats
1/2 cup applesauce | 1/4 tsp salt

Directions:
Fit the Instant Vortex oven with the rack in position Grease 8*8-inch baking dish and set aside.   In a bowl, mix egg, vanilla, butter, applesauce, baking powder, cinnamon, brown sugar, oats, and salt. Add milk and stir well.   Add cranberries and fold well.   Pour mixture into the prepared baking dish. Set to bake at 350 F for 25 minutes. After 5 minutes place the baking dish in the preheated oven. Serve and enjoy.

161.	Tator Tots Casserole

Servings: 8   Cooking Time: 30 Minutes
Ingredients:

8 eggs | 1/4 cup milk
28 oz tator tots | 1 lb breakfast
8 oz pepper jack | sausage, cooked
cheese, shredded | Pepper
2 green onions, sliced | Salt

Directions:
Fit the Instant Vortex oven with the rack in position Spray 13*9-inch baking pan with cooking spray and set aside.   In a bowl, whisk eggs with milk, pepper, and salt.   Layer sausage in a prepared baking pan then pour the egg mixture and sprinkle with half shredded cheese and green onions.   Add tator tots on top.   Set to bake at 400 F for 35 minutes. After 5 minutes place the baking pan in the preheated oven.   Top with remaining cheese and serve.

162.	Buttery Chocolate Toast

Servings: 1   Cooking Time: 5 Minutes
Ingredients:

Whole wheat bread slices
Coconut oil

Pure maple syrup
Cacao powder

Directions:
Toast the bread in toaster oven.   Spread coconut oil over the toast.   Drizzle maple syrup in lines over the toast.   Sprinkle cacao powder and serve.

163.   Coconut Brown Rice Porridge With Dates

Servings: 1 Or 2   Cooking Time: 23 Minutes
Ingredients:

½ cup cooked brown rice
1 cup canned coconut milk
¼ cup unsweetened shredded coconut
4 large Medjool dates, pitted and roughly chopped

¼ cup packed dark brown sugar
½ teaspoon kosher salt
¼ teaspoon ground cardamom
Heavy cream, for serving (optional)

Directions:
Place all the ingredients except the heavy cream in the baking pan and stir until blended.   Slide the baking pan into Rack Position 1, select Convection Bake, set temperature to 375°F (190°C) and set time to 23 minutes.   Stir the porridge halfway through the cooking time.   When cooked, the porridge will be thick and creamy.   Remove from the oven and ladle the porridge into bowls.   Serve hot with a drizzle of the cream, if desired.

164.   Sweet Breakfast Casserole

Servings: 4   Cooking Time: 30 Minutes
Ingredients:

3 tablespoons brown sugar
4 tablespoons margarine
2 tablespoons white sugar
1/2 tsp. cinnamon powder
1/2 cup flour
For the casserole:
2 eggs
2 tablespoons white sugar

2 and 1/2 cups white flour
1 tsp. baking soda
1 tsp. baking powder
2 eggs
1/2 cup milk
2 cups margarine milk
4 tablespoons margarine
Zest from 1 lemon, grated
1 and 2/3 cup blueberries

Directions:
In a bowl, mix eggs with 2 tablespoons white sugar, 2 and 1/2 cups white flour, baking powder, baking soda, 2 eggs, milk, margarine milk, 4 tablespoons margarine, lemon zest and blueberries, stir and pour into a pan that fits your air fryer.   In another bowls, mix 3 tablespoons brown sugar with 2 tablespoons white sugar, 4 tablespoons margarine, 1/2 cup flour and cinnamon, stir until you obtain a crumble and spread over blueberries mix.   Place in preheated air fryer and bake at 300 °F for 30 minutes.   Divide among plates and serve for breakfast.

165.   Parsley Sausage Patties

Servings: 4   Cooking Time: 20 Minutes
Ingredients:

1 lb ground Italian sausage
¼ cup breadcrumbs
1 tsp red pepper flakes

1 tsp dried parsley
Salt and black pepper to taste
¼ tsp garlic powder
1 egg, beaten

Directions:
Preheat Instant Vortex on Bake function to 350 F. Line a baking sheet with parchment paper. Combine all the ingredients in a large bowl.   Make patties out of the sausage mixture and arrange them on the baking sheet. Press Start. Cook for 15 minutes until golden.

166.   Egg And Avocado Burrito

Servings: 4   Cooking Time: 4 Minutes
Ingredients:

4 low-sodium whole-wheat flour tortillas
Filling:
1 hard-boiled egg, chopped
1 ripe avocado, peeled, pitted, and chopped
1 (1.2-ounce / 34-g) slice low-sodium, low-fat American cheese, torn into pieces

2 hard-boiled egg whites, chopped
1 red bell pepper, chopped
3 tablespoons low-sodium salsa, plus additional for serving (optional)
Special Equipment:
4 toothpicks (optional), soaked in water for at least 30 minutes

Directions:
Make the filling: Combine the egg, egg whites, avocado, red bell pepper, cheese, and salsa in a medium bowl and stir until blended.   Assemble the burritos: Arrange the tortillas on a clean work surface and place ¼ of the prepared filling in the middle of each tortilla, leaving about 1½-inch on each end unfilled. Fold in the opposite sides of each tortilla and roll up. Secure with toothpicks through the center, if needed.   Transfer the burritos to the air fryer basket.   Put the air fryer basket on the baking pan and slide into Rack Position 2, select Air Fry, set temperature to 390°F (199°C) and set time to 4 minutes.   When cooking is complete, the burritos should be crisp and golden brown.   Allow to cool for 5 minutes and serve with salsa, if desired.

167.Fried Apple Lemon & Vanilla Turnovers

Ingredients:

2 sheets frozen puff pastry (17-ounce/480g package), thawed (keep
3 medium Granny Smith apples, peeled and diced (about 3 cups)
2 tablespoons (30g)

cold until use)
1 teaspoon vanilla extract
1 teaspoon lemon juice
¾ teaspoon ground cinnamon
¼ teaspoon kosher salt

unsalted butter
L cup (70g) dark brown sugar

1 egg
1 tablespoon water
Turbinado sugar for sprinkling

Directions:
Combine filling ingredients in a medium saucepan and cook over medium heat, stirring occasionally, until apples are tender and syrup is thick, about 10 minutes. Transfer apple mixture to a plate and chill in the refrigerator until cool to the touch, about 20 minutes. Scramble egg and water in a small bowl. Place 1 sheet of puff pastry on a clean cutting board; reserve second sheet in the refrigerator. Divide pastry into 4 equal squares. Spoon 2 tablespoons apple mixture onto the center of each square. Brush the edges of each square with egg wash. Fold pastry diagonally over apple mixture and seal the edges with a fork. Place turnovers on a plate and refrigerate while preparing remaining turnovers. Repeat steps 4 to 6 with second sheet of puff pastry. Select AIRFRY/325°F (165°C)/SUPER CONVECTION/20 minutes and press START to preheat oven. Place turnovers on air fry rack. Brush tops with egg wash and sprinkle with turbinado sugar. Make 3 small slits in each turnover. Cook in rack position 4 until puffed and golden brown, about 20 minutes. Serve warm or at room temperature.

168.	Fried Potatoes With Peppers And Onions

Servings: 4   Cooking Time: 35 Minutes
Ingredients:

1 pound (454 g) red potatoes, cut into ½-inch dices
1 large red bell pepper, cut into ½-inch dices
1 large green bell pepper, cut into ½-inch dices
1 medium onion, cut into ½-inch dices

1½ tablespoons extra-virgin olive oil
1¼ teaspoons kosher salt
¾ teaspoon sweet paprika
¾ teaspoon garlic powder
Freshly ground black pepper, to taste

Directions:
Mix together the potatoes, bell peppers, onion, oil, salt, paprika, garlic powder, and black pepper in a large mixing and toss to coat. Transfer the potato mixture to the air fryer basket. Put the air fryer basket on the baking pan and slide into Rack Position 2, select Air Fry, set temperature to 350°F (180°C) and set time to 35 minutes. Stir the potato mixture three times during cooking. When done, the potatoes should be nicely browned. Remove from the oven to a plate and serve warm.

169.	Chocolate Banana Bread

Servings: 4   Cooking Time: 30 Minutes
Ingredients:

¼ cup cocoa powder
6 tablespoons plus 2 teaspoons all-purpose flour, divided
½ teaspoon kosher salt
¼ teaspoon baking soda
1½ ripe bananas
1 large egg, whisked
¼ cup vegetable oil

½ cup sugar
3 tablespoons buttermilk or plain yogurt (not Greek)
½ teaspoon vanilla extract
6 tablespoons chopped white chocolate
6 tablespoons chopped walnuts

Directions:
Mix together the cocoa powder, 6 tablespoons of the flour, salt, and baking soda in a medium bowl. Mash the bananas with a fork in another medium bowl until smooth. Fold in the egg, oil, sugar, buttermilk, and vanilla, and whisk until thoroughly combined. Add the wet mixture to the dry mixture and stir until well incorporated. Combine the white chocolate, walnuts, and the remaining 2 tablespoons of flour in a third bowl and toss to coat. Add this mixture to the batter and stir until well incorporated. Pour the batter into the baking pan and smooth the top with a spatula. Slide the baking pan into Rack Position 1, select Convection Bake, set temperature to 310°F (154°C) and set time to 30 minutes. When done, a toothpick inserted into the center of the bread should come out clean. Remove from the oven and allow to cool on a wire rack for 10 minutes before serving.

170.	Baked Apple Breakfast Oats

Servings: 1   Cooking Time: 15 Minutes
Ingredients:

1/3 cup vanilla Greek yogurt
1/3 cup rolled oats

1 apple
1 tablespoon peanut butter

Directions:
Preheat toaster oven to 400°F and set it on the warm setting. Cut apples into chunks approximately 1/2-inch-thick. Place apples in an oven-safe dish with some space between each chunk and sprinkle with cinnamon. Bake in the oven for 12 minutes. Combine yogurt and oats in a bowl. Remove the apples from the oven and combine with the yogurt. Top with peanut butter for a delicious and high-protein breakfast.

171.	Cheesy Artichoke-mushroom Frittata

Servings: 6   Cooking Time: 15 Minutes
Ingredients:

8 eggs
½ teaspoon kosher salt
¼ cup whole milk
¾ cup shredded Mozzarella cheese, divided
2 tablespoons unsalted butter, melted

1 cup coarsely chopped artichoke hearts
¼ cup chopped onion
½ cup mushrooms
¼ cup grated Parmesan cheese
¼ teaspoon freshly ground black pepper

Directions:
In a medium bowl, whisk together the eggs and salt. Let rest for a minute or two, then pour in the milk and whisk again. Stir in ½ cup of the Mozzarella cheese. Grease the baking pan with the butter. Stir in the artichoke hearts and onion and toss to coat with the butter. Slide the baking pan into Rack Position 2, select Roast, set temperature to 375°F (190°C) and set time to 12 minutes. After 5 minutes, remove from the oven. Spread the mushrooms over the vegetables. Pour the egg mixture on top. Stir gently just to distribute the vegetables evenly. Return the pan to the oven and continue cooking for 5 to 7 minutes, or until the edges are set. The center will still be quite liquid. Select Convection Broil, set temperature to Low and set time to 3 minutes. After 1 minute, remove the pan and sprinkle the remaining ¼ cup of the Mozzarella and Parmesan cheese over the frittata. Return the pan to the oven and continue cooking for 2 minutes. When cooking is complete, the cheese should be melted with the top completely set but not browned. Sprinkle the black pepper on top and serve.

172.Mixed Berry Dutch Baby Pancake

Servings: 4   Cooking Time: 14 Minutes
Ingredients:

1 tablespoon unsalted butter, at room temperature	1 teaspoon pure vanilla extract
1 egg	1 cup sliced fresh strawberries
2 egg whites	½ cup fresh raspberries
½ cup 2% milk	
½ cup whole-wheat pastry flour	½ cup fresh blueberries

Directions:
Grease the baking pan with the butter. Using a hand mixer, beat together the egg, egg whites, milk, pastry flour, and vanilla in a medium mixing bowl until well incorporated. Pour the batter into the pan. Slide the baking pan into Rack Position 1, select Convection Bake, set temperature to 330°F (166°C) and set time to 14 minutes. When cooked, the pancake should puff up in the center and the edges should be golden brown Allow the pancake to cool for 5 minutes and serve topped with the berries.

173.Spinach, Leek And Cheese Frittata

Servings: 2   Cooking Time: 22 Minutes
Ingredients:

4 large eggs	¼ cup halved grape tomatoes
4 ounces (113 g) baby bella mushrooms, chopped	1 tablespoon 2% milk
1 cup (1 ounce / 28-g) baby spinach, chopped	¼ teaspoon dried oregano
½ cup (2 ounces / 57-g) shredded Cheddar cheese	¼ teaspoon garlic powder
	½ teaspoon kosher

⅓ cup (from 1 large) chopped leek, white part only	salt
	Freshly ground black pepper, to taste
	Cooking spray

Directions:
Lightly spritz the baking pan with cooking spray. Whisk the eggs in a large bowl until frothy. Add the mushrooms, baby spinach, cheese, leek, tomatoes, milk, oregano, garlic powder, salt, and pepper and stir until well blended. Pour the mixture into the prepared baking pan. Slide the baking pan into Rack Position 1, select Convection Bake, set temperature to 300°F (150°C) and set time to 22 minutes. When cooked, the center will be puffed up and the top will be golden brown. Let the frittata cool for 5 minutes before slicing to serve.

174.Nutritious Egg Breakfast Muffins

Servings: 12   Cooking Time: 20 Minutes
Ingredients:

12 eggs	1/4 red bell pepper, diced
1/2 cup baby spinach, shredded	1/4 tsp garlic powder
1 cup cheddar cheese, shredded	1 cup ham, cooked and diced
1/4 cup mushrooms, diced & sautéed	3 tbsp onion, diced
	1/2 tsp seasoned salt

Directions:
Fit the Instant Vortex oven with the rack in position Spray a 12-cup muffin tray with cooking spray and set aside. In a large bowl, whisk eggs with garlic powder and salt. Add remaining ingredients and stir well. Pour egg mixture into the prepared muffin tray. Set to bake at 350 F for 25 minutes. After 5 minutes place the muffin tray in the preheated oven. Serve and enjoy.

175.Vegetable Quiche

Servings: 6   Cooking Time: 24 Minutes
Ingredients:

8 eggs	1 onion, chopped
cup coconut milk	1 cup Parmesan cheese, grated 1/2 tsp
1 cup tomatoes, chopped 1 cup	pepper
zucchini, chopped 1 tbsp butter	tsp salt

Directions:
Preheat the air fryer to 370 F. Melt butter in a pan over medium heat then add onion and sauté until onion lightly brown. Add tomatoes and zucchini to the pan and sauté for 4-5 minutes. Transfer cooked vegetables into the air fryer baking dish. Beat eggs with cheese, milk, pepper, and salt in a bowl. Pour egg mixture over vegetables in a baking dish. Place dish in the air fryer and cook for 24 minutes or until eggs are set. Slice and serve.

176.Crustless Breakfast Quiche

Servings: 4   Cooking Time: 10 Minutes
Ingredients:

6 eggs
1 cup cheddar cheese, shredded
1 shallot, sliced & sautéed

1/4 cup milk
3 bacon slices, sautéed & chopped
1/8 tsp pepper
1/8 tsp kosher salt

Directions:
Fit the Instant Vortex oven with the rack in position Spray an 8-inch baking dish with cooking spray and set aside.   In a bowl, whisk eggs with milk, pepper, and salt.   Add cheese, shallot, and bacon and stir well.   Pour egg mixture into the prepared baking dish.   Set to bake at 375 F for 15 minutes. After 5 minutes place the baking dish in the preheated oven. Serve and enjoy.

177. Smart Oven Baked Oatmeal Recipe

Ingredients:

1 small Ripe Banana, (6 inches long, abut 1/4 cup mashed)
1 tablespoon Flax Meal
1/2 cup Non-Dairy Milk, plus 2 tablespoons (like Almond Milk or Soy Milk)
1 cup Old Fashioned Rolled Oats
2 teaspoons Olive Oil

2 teaspoons Pure Maple Syrup
1/2 teaspoon Ground Cinnamon
1/2 teaspoon Pure Vanilla Extract
1/4 teaspoon Baking Powder
1/8 teaspoon Fine Sea Salt
1/4 cup Pecan Pieces, (1 ounce)

Directions:
Adjust the cooking rack to the bottom position and preheat toaster oven to 350°F on the BAKE setting. Grease a 7 x 5-inch toaster oven-safe baking dish. In a large bowl, add the banana and mash well. Stir in the flaxseed meal, maple syrup, olive oil, cinnamon, vanilla, baking powder, salt, milk, oats, and pecan pieces. Pour mixture into prepared baking dish.   Bake oatmeal until the middle is set and browned on the edges, about 25 to 35 minutes. (For softer scoop able oatmeal bake 25 to 30 minutes, for firm oatmeal bake 30 to 35 minutes.) Let sit at least 10 minutes before slicing and serving.

178.   Apple Butter Pancake

Ingredients:

1 tsp cinnamon
½ tsp ginger
3 large eggs, room temperature
¾ cup whole milk
¾ cup all-purpose flour
1 tsp almond extract
¼ tsp salt

2 Granny Smith apples, peeled, cored and sliced
1 Tbsp sugar
4 Tbsp butter, divided
2 tsp light brown sugar

Directions:
Preheat oven to 400°F.   Whisk together eggs, milk, flour, extract and salt.   Place sliced apples in a bowl with sugar, cinnamon and ginger.   Melt 2 Tbsp butter in heated Instant Vortex oven. Sprinkle brown sugar inside pot.   Add apples and cook until apples have softened. Transfer to plate.

Wipe out Instant Vortex oven and melt remaining 2 Tbsp butter.   When pot is very hot, add apples and pour batter. Bake for about 13-15 minutes.

179. Breakfast Sweet Potato Hash

Servings: 6   Cooking Time: 65 Minutes
Ingredients:

6 cups sweet potatoes, peeled and diced
1 tsp thyme
1 tsp onion powder
8 garlic cloves, minced

1 onion, diced
1/3 cup olive oil
1/2 tsp paprika
1 tbsp garlic powder
1/2 tsp pepper
2 tsp salt

Directions:
Fit the Instant Vortex oven with the rack in position Add sweet potatoes to a casserole dish and sprinkle with paprika, thyme, onion powder, garlic powder, pepper, and salt.   Drizzle oil over sweet potatoes and toss well.   Set to bake at 450 F for 60 minutes, after 5 minutes, place the casserole dish in the oven. Heat 1 tbsp of olive oil in a pan over medium heat. Add onion and garlic and sauté for 10 minutes. Add onion and garlic mixture to the sweet potatoes and mix well.   Serve and enjoy.

180.   Loaded Breakfast Potatoes

Servings: 3   Cooking Time: 20 Minutes
Ingredients:

3 gold potatoes, chopped
2 cloves garlic, diced fine
¼ tsp salt
¼ tsp pepper

½ tsp Old Bay seasoning
1 tbsp. olive oil
2 slices bacon, cook crisp & crumble
1 tbsp. maple syrup

Directions:
Place the baking pan in position 2 of the oven.   In a large bowl, add potatoes, garlic, and seasonings, toss to combine.   Drizzle oil over mixture and toss to coat.   Place potatoes in an even layer in the fryer basket and place on the baking pan.   Set oven to air fry at 400°F for 15 minutes. Cook until potatoes are nicely browned on the outside, and soft on the inside. Stir halfway through cooking time. Pour potatoes onto the baking pan, sprinkle with bacon and drizzle with syrup.   Place the pan in position 2 and set to broil at 400°F. Cook 1-2 minutes to caramelize the potatoes. Serve immediately.

181. Eggs In Bell Pepper Rings

Servings: 4   Cooking Time: 7 Minutes
Ingredients:

1 large red, yellow, or orange bell pepper, cut into four ¾-inch rings
4 eggs

Salt and freshly ground black pepper, to taste
2 teaspoons salsa
Cooking spray

Directions:
Coat the baking pan lightly with cooking spray. Put 4 bell pepper rings in the prepared baking pan. Crack one egg into each bell pepper ring and

sprinkle with salt and pepper. Top each egg with ½ teaspoon of salsa. Put the air fryer basket on the baking pan and slide into Rack Position 2, select Air Fry, set temperature to 350°F (180°C) and set time to 7 minutes. When done, the eggs should be cooked to your desired doneness. Remove the rings from the pan to a plate and serve warm.

182. Healthy Squash

Servings: 4   Cooking Time: 25 Minutes

Ingredients:

2 lbs yellow squash, cut into half-moons	¼ tsp pepper
1 tsp Italian seasoning	1 tbsp olive oil
	¼ tsp salt

Directions:
Add all ingredients into the large bowl and toss well. Preheat the air fryer to 400 F. Add squash mixture into the air fryer basket and cook for 10 minutes. Shake basket and cook for another 10 minutes. Shake once again and cook for 5 minutes more.

183. Zucchini Breakfast Casserole

Servings: 8   Cooking Time: 50 Minutes

Ingredients:

12 eggs	3 tbsp coconut flour
2 small zucchinis, shredded	1/4 cup coconut milk
1 lb ground sausage	1/4 tsp pepper
3 tomatoes, sliced	1/2 tsp salt

Directions:
Fit the Instant Vortex oven with the rack in position Cook sausage in a pan until lightly brown. Transfer sausage to a large mixing bowl. Add coconut flour, milk, eggs, zucchini, pepper, and salt. Stir well. Add eggs and whisk until well combined. Pour bowl mixture into the greased casserole dish and top with tomato slices. Set to bake at 350 F for 55 minutes, after 5 minutes, place the casserole dish in the oven. Serve and enjoy.

184. Cheddar Eggs With Potatoes

Servings: 3   Cooking Time: 24 Minutes

Ingredients:

3 potatoes, thinly sliced	2 eggs, beaten
2 oz cheddar cheese, shredded	1 tbsp all-purpose flour
	½ cup coconut cream

Directions:
Preheat Instant Vortex on AirFry function to 390 F. Place the potatoes the basket and press Start. Cook for 12 minutes. Mix the eggs, coconut cream, and flour until the cream mixture thickens. Remove the potatoes from the oven, line them in the ramekin and top with the cream mixture. Top with the cheddar cheese. Cook for 12 more minutes.

185. Easy Zucchini Frittata

Servings: 4   Cooking Time: 30 Minutes

Ingredients:

2 zucchinis, chopped and cooked	8 eggs
1 tbsp fresh parsley, chopped	1/2 tsp Italian seasoning
3 tbsp cheddar cheese, grated	Pepper
	Salt

Directions:
Fit the Instant Vortex oven with the rack in position In a bowl, whisk eggs with Italian seasoning, pepper, and salt. Add parsley, cheese, and zucchini and stir well. Pour egg mixture into the greased baking dish. Set to bake at 350 F for 35 minutes. After 5 minutes place the baking dish in the preheated oven. Serve and enjoy.

186. Veggies Breakfast Salad

Servings: 4   Cooking Time: 15 Minutes

Ingredients:

2 tablespoons olive oil	1 red onion, chopped
1 cup cherry tomatoes, halved	1 cup cheddar, shredded
1 zucchini, cubed	2 tablespoons chives, chopped
1 eggplant, cubed	Salt and black pepper to the taste
1 fennel bulb, shredded	8 eggs, whisked

Directions:
Add the oil to your air fryer, heat it up at 350 degrees F, add the onion and fennel and cook for 2 minutes. Add the tomatoes and the other ingredients except the cheese and toss. Sprinkle the cheese on top, cook the mix for 13 minutes more, divide into bowls and serve for breakfast.

187. Feta & Spinach Omelet With Mushrooms

Servings: 2   Cooking Time: 10 Minutes

Ingredients:

4 eggs, lightly beaten	3 oz feta cheese, crumbled
2 tbsp heavy cream	A handful of fresh parsley, chopped
2 cups spinach, chopped	Salt and black pepper to taste
1 cup mushrooms, chopped	

Directions:
In a bowl, whisk eggs and stir in spinach, mushrooms, feta, parsley, salt, and pepper. Pour into a greased baking pan and cook in the Instant Vortex oven for 12-14 minutes at 350 F on Bake function..

188. Balsamic Chicken With Spinach & Kale

Servings: 1   Cooking Time: 20 Minutes

Ingredients:

½ cup baby spinach	2 tbsp olive oil
½ cup romaine lettuce, shredded	1 tsp balsamic vinegar
3 large kale leaves, chopped	1 garlic clove, minced
	Salt and black pepper to taste

1 chicken breast, cut
into cubes

Directions:
Place the chicken, some olive oil, garlic, salt, and pepper in a bowl; toss to combine. Put on a lined baking dish and cook in the Instant Vortex for 14 minutes at 390F on Bake function.   Meanwhile, place the greens in a large bowl. Add the remaining olive oil and balsamic vinegar. Season with salt and pepper and toss to combine. Top with the sliced chicken and serve.

189.   Berry Breakfast Oatmeal

Servings: 4   Cooking Time: 20 Minutes
Ingredients:

1 egg	1/2 cup blackberries
2 cups old fashioned oats	1/2 cup strawberries, sliced
1 cup blueberries	1 1/2 tsp baking powder
1/4 cup maple syrup	
1 1/2 cups milk	1/2 tsp salt

Directions:
Fit the Instant Vortex oven with the rack in position In a bowl, mix together oats, salt, and baking powder. Add vanilla, egg, maple syrup, and milk and stir well. Add berries and fold well.   Pour mixture into the greased baking dish.   Set to bake at 375 F for 25 minutes. After 5 minutes place the baking dish in the preheated oven.   Serve and enjoy.

190.   Chives Salmon And Shrimp Bowls

Servings: 4   Cooking Time: 12 Minutes
Ingredients:

1 pound shrimp, peeled and deveined	2 teaspoons olive oil
	1 cup baby kale
½ pound salmon fillets, boneless and cubed	Salt and black pepper to the taste
	1 tablespoon chives, chopped
2 spring onions, chopped	

Directions:
Preheat the air fryer with the oil at 330 degrees F, add the shrimp, salmon and the other ingredients, toss gently and cook for 12 minutes.   Divide everything into bowls and serve.

191. Walnuts And Mango Oatmeal

Servings: 4   Cooking Time: 20 Minutes
Ingredients:

2 cups almond milk	1 cup mango, peeled and cubed
½ cup walnuts, chopped	3 tablespoons sugar
1 teaspoon vanilla extract	½ cup steel cut oats

Directions:
In your air fryer, combine the almond milk with the oats and the other ingredients, toss and cook at 360 degrees F for 20 minutes.   Divide the mix into bowls and serve for breakfast.

192.   Canadian Bacon Muffin Sandwiches

Servings: 4   Cooking Time: 8 Minutes
Ingredients:

4 English muffins, split	8 slices Canadian bacon
4 slices cheese	Cooking spray

Directions:
Make the sandwiches: Top each of 4 muffin halves with 2 slices of Canadian bacon, 1 slice of cheese, and finish with the remaining muffin half.   Put the sandwiches in the baking pan and spritz the tops with cooking spray.   Slide the baking pan into Rack Position 1, select Convection Bake, set temperature to 370ºF (188ºC), and set time to 8 minutes.   Flip the sandwiches halfway through the cooking time.   When cooking is complete, remove from the oven. Divide the sandwiches among four plates and serve warm.

193.   Vanilla Granola

Servings: 4   Cooking Time: 40 Minutes
Ingredients:

1 cup rolled oats	1 tablespoon coconut sugar
3 tablespoons maple syrup	
1 tablespoon sunflower oil	¼ teaspoon vanilla
	¼ teaspoon cinnamon
	¼ teaspoon sea salt

Directions:
Mix together the oats, maple syrup, sunflower oil, coconut sugar, vanilla, cinnamon, and sea salt in a medium bowl and stir to combine. Transfer the mixture to the baking pan.   Slide the baking pan into Rack Position 1, select Convection Bake, set temperature to 248ºF (120ºC) and set time to 40 minutes.   Stir the granola four times during cooking.   When cooking is complete, the granola will be mostly dry and lightly browned.   Let the granola stand for 5 to 10 minutes before serving.

194.   Stuffed Poblanos

Servings: 4   Cooking Time: 30 Minutes
Ingredients:

½ lb. spicy ground pork breakfast sausage	4 oz. full-fat cream cheese; softened.
4 large poblano peppers	¼ cup canned diced tomatoes and green chiles, drained
4 large eggs.	
½ cup full-fat sour cream.	8 tbsp. shredded pepper jack cheese

Directions:
In a medium skillet over medium heat, crumble and brown the ground sausage until no pink remains. Remove sausage and drain the fat from the pan. Crack eggs into the pan, scramble and cook until no longer runny   Place cooked sausage in a large bowl and fold in cream cheese. Mix in diced tomatoes and chiles. Gently fold in eggs   Cut a 4"–5" slit in the top of each poblano, removing the seeds

and white membrane with a small knife. Separate the filling into four and spoon carefully into each pepper. Top each with 2 tbsp. pepper jack cheese Place each pepper into the air fryer basket. Adjust the temperature to 350 Degrees F and set the timer for 15 minutes.   Peppers will be soft, and cheese will be browned when ready. Serve immediately with sour cream on top.

195. Spinach & Kale Balsamic Chicken

Servings: 1   Cooking Time: 20 Minutes

Ingredients:

½ cup baby spinach leaves	3 tbsp olive oil, divided
½ cup shredded romaine	1 tsp balsamic vinegar
3 large kale leaves, chopped	1 garlic clove, minced
4 oz chicken breasts, cut into cubes	Salt and black pepper to taste

Directions:
Place the chicken, 1 tbsp of olive oil, and garlic in a bowl. Season with salt and pepper and toss to combine. Put on a lined Air Fryer pan and cook for 14 minutes at 390 F on Bake function.   Place the greens in a large bowl. Add the remaining olive oil and balsamic vinegar. Season with salt and pepper and toss to combine. Top with the chicken and serve.

196. Banana And Oat Bread Pudding

Servings: 4   Cooking Time: 16 Minutes

Ingredients:

2 medium ripe bananas, mashed	½ cup low-fat milk
2 tablespoons maple syrup	1 teaspoon ground cinnamon
2 tablespoons peanut butter	2 slices whole-grain bread, cut into bite-sized cubes
1 teaspoon vanilla extract	¼ cup quick oats
	Cooking spray

Directions:
Spritz the baking pan lightly with cooking spray. Mix the bananas, milk, maple syrup, peanut butter, vanilla, and cinnamon in a large mixing bowl and stir until well incorporated.   Add the bread cubes to the banana mixture and stir until thoroughly coated. Fold in the oats and stir to combine. Transfer the mixture to the baking pan. Wrap the baking pan in aluminum foil.   Slide the baking pan into Rack Position 2, select Air Fry, set temperature to 350°F (180°C) and set time to 16 minutes.   After 10 minutes, remove the pan from the oven. Remove the foil. Return the pan to the oven and continue to cook for another 6 minutes. When done, the pudding should be set.   Let the pudding cool for 5 minutes before serving.

197. Thai Style Omelette

Servings: 2   Cooking Time: 10 Minutes

Ingredients:

3 & 1/2 oz minced Pancetta	1 cup onion, diced
2 Eggs	1 tablespoon fish salt

Directions:
Beat the eggs until it is light and fluffy. Preheat the Air fryer to 280°F.   In a bowl, add together all the ingredients. Pour the mixture into the air fryer tray. Remove after 10 minutes or once omelet is golden brown. Cut and serve.

198. Baked Breakfast Quiche

Servings: 6   Cooking Time: 45 Minutes

Ingredients:

6 eggs	1 cup tomatoes, chopped
1 cup milk	Pepper
1 cup cheddar cheese, grated	Salt

Directions:
Fit the Instant Vortex oven with the rack in position In a bowl, whisk eggs with cheese, milk, pepper, and salt. Stir in tomatoes.   Pour egg mixture into the greased pie dish.   Set to bake at 350 F for 50 minutes, after 5 minutes, place the pie dish in the oven.   Serve and enjoy.

199. Crispy Ham Egg Cups

Servings: 2   Cooking Time: 30 Minutes

Ingredients:

4 large eggs.	2 tbsp. diced red bell pepper.
4: 1-oz. slices deli ham	2 tbsp. diced white onion.
½ cup shredded medium Cheddar cheese.	2 tbsp. full-fat sour cream.
¼ cup diced green bell pepper.	

Directions:
Place one slice of ham on the bottom of four baking cups.   Take a large bowl, whisk eggs with sour cream. Stir in green pepper, red pepper and onion Pour the egg mixture into ham-lined baking cups. Top with Cheddar. Place cups into the air fryer basket. Adjust the temperature to 320 Degrees F and set the timer for 12 minutes or until the tops are browned. Serve warm.

200. Spinach Egg Bites

Servings: 12   Cooking Time: 20 Minutes

Ingredients:

8 eggs	1/4 cup almond milk
1/4 cup green onion, chopped	1 cup roasted red peppers, chopped
1 cup spinach, chopped	1/2 tsp salt

Directions:
Fit the Instant Vortex oven with the rack in position Spray 12-cups muffin tin with cooking spray and set aside.   In a bowl, whisk eggs with milk and salt. Add spinach, green onion, and red peppers to the egg mixture and stir to combine.   Pour egg mixture into the greased muffin tin.   Set to bake at

350 F for 25 minutes, after 5 minutes, place muffin tin in the oven.   Serve and enjoy.

201.   Bacon And Egg Bread Cups

Servings: 4   Cooking Time: 10 Minutes
Ingredients:

4 (3-by-4-inch) crusty rolls	3 strips precooked bacon, chopped
4 thin slices Gouda or Swiss cheese mini wedges	½ teaspoon dried thyme
5 eggs	Pinch salt
2 tablespoons heavy cream	Freshly ground black pepper, to taste

Directions:
On a clean work surface, cut the tops off the rolls. Using your fingers, remove the insides of the rolls to make bread cups, leaving a ½-inch shell. Place a slice of cheese onto each roll bottom.   Whisk together the eggs and heavy cream in a medium bowl until well combined. Fold in the bacon, thyme, salt, and pepper and stir well.   Scrape the egg mixture into the prepared bread cups. Place the bread cups in the baking pan.   Slide the baking pan into Rack Position 1, select Convection Bake, set temperature to 330°F (166°C) and set time to 10 minutes.   When cooked, the eggs should be cooked to your preference.   Serve warm.

202.   Salty Parsnip Patties

Servings: 2   Cooking Time: 20 Minutes
Ingredients:

1 large parsnip, grated	1 tbsp olive oil
3 eggs, beaten	1 cup flour
½ tsp garlic powder	Salt and black pepper to taste
¼ tsp nutmeg	

Directions:
In a bowl, combine flour, eggs, parsnip, nutmeg, and garlic powder. Season with salt and pepper. Form patties out of the mixture. Drizzle the AirFryer basket with olive oil and arrange the patties inside. Fit in the baking tray and cook for 15 minutes on Air Fry function at 360 F. Serve with garlic mayo.

203.   Baked Eggs

Servings: 4   Cooking Time: 15-20 | Minutes
Ingredients:

7 Oz. leg ham	1 lb baby spinach
4 eggs	1 tablespoon olive oil
4 tsps full cream milk	Salt and Pepper to taste
Margarine	

Directions:
Preheat the Air Fryer to 350°F. Layer four ramekins with margarine.   Equally divide the spinach and ham into the four ramekins. Break 1 egg into each and add a tsp. of milk. Spice with salt and pepper. Place into Air Fryer for about 15-20 minutes. For a runny yolk, cook for 15 minutes, for fully cooked; 20 minutes.

204.   Cheesy Hash Brown Cups

Servings: 6   Cooking Time: 9 Minutes
Ingredients:

4 eggs, beaten	1 cup diced ham
2¼ cups frozen hash browns, thawed	½ teaspoon Cajun seasoning
½ cup shredded Cheddar cheese	Cooking spray

Directions:
Lightly spritz a 12-cup muffin tin with cooking spray. Combine the beaten eggs, hash browns, diced ham, cheese, and Cajun seasoning in a medium bowl and stir until well blended.   Spoon a heaping 1½ tablespoons of egg mixture into each muffin cup. Put the muffin tin into Rack Position 1, select Convection Bake, set temperature to 350°F (180°C) and set time to 9 minutes.   When cooked, the muffins will be golden brown.   Allow to cool for 5 to 10 minutes on a wire rack and serve warm.

205.   Green Cottage Omelet

Servings: 1   Cooking Time: 20 Minutes
Ingredients:

3 eggs	3 tbsp kale, chopped
3 tbsp cottage cheese	Salt and black pepper
½ tbsp fresh parsley, chopped	to taste
	1 tsp olive oil

Directions:
Beat the eggs with a pinch of salt and black pepper in a bowl. Stir in the rest of the ingredients. Drizzle a baking pan with olive oil. Pour the pan into the Instant Vortex oven and press Start. Cook for 15 minutes on Bake function at 360 F until slightly golden and set. Serve warm.

206.   Turkey Sliders With Chive Mayo

Servings: 6   Cooking Time: 15 Minutes
Ingredients:

12 burger buns	Turkey Sliders:
Cooking spray	1 to 2 cloves garlic, minced
¾ pound (340 g) turkey, minced	Sea salt and ground black pepper, to taste
1 tablespoon oyster sauce	Chive Mayo:
¼ cup pickled jalapeno, chopped	1 tablespoon chives
2 tablespoons chopped scallions	1 cup mayonnaise
1 tablespoon chopped fresh cilantro	Zest of 1 lime
	1 teaspoon salt

Directions:
Spritz the air fryer basket with cooking spray. Combine the ingredients for the turkey sliders in a large bowl. Stir to mix well. Shape the mixture into 6 balls, then bash the balls into patties.   Arrange the patties in the pan and spritz with cooking spray. Put the air fryer basket on the baking pan and slide into Rack Position 2, select Air Fry, set temperature to 365°F (185°C) and set time to 15 minutes.   Flip the patties halfway through the cooking time. Meanwhile, combine the ingredients for the chive

mayo in a small bowl. Stir to mix well. When cooked, the patties will be well browned. Smear the patties with chive mayo, then assemble the patties between two buns to make the sliders. Serve immediately.

207. Sausage Omelet

Servings: 2   Cooking Time: 13 Minutes

Ingredients:

4 eggs	2 sausages, chopped
1 bacon slice, chopped	1 yellow onion, chopped

Directions:

In a bowl, crack the eggs and beat well. Add the remaining ingredients and gently, stir to combine. Place the mixture into a baking pan. Press "Power Button" of Air Fry Oven and turn the dial to select the "Air Fry" mode. Press the Time button and again turn the dial to set the cooking time to 13 minutes. Now push the Temp button and rotate the dial to set the temperature at 320 degrees F. Press "Start/Pause" button to start. When the unit beeps to show that it is preheated, open the lid. Arrange pan over the "Wire Rack" and insert in the oven. Cut into equal-sized wedges and serve hot.

208. Breakfast Tater Tot Casserole

Servings: 4   Cooking Time: 17 To 18 Minutes

Ingredients:

4 eggs	1 pound (454 g) frozen tater tots, thawed
1 cup milk	
Salt and pepper, to taste	
12 ounces (340 g) ground chicken sausage	¾ cup grated Cheddar cheese
	Cooking spray

Directions:

Whisk together the eggs and milk in a medium bowl. Season with salt and pepper to taste and stir until mixed. Set aside. Place a skillet over medium-high heat and spritz with cooking spray. Place the ground sausage in the skillet and break it into smaller pieces with a spatula or spoon. Cook for 3 to 4 minutes until the sausage starts to brown, stirring occasionally. Remove from heat and set aside. Coat the baking pan with cooking spray. Arrange the tater tots in the baking pan. Slide the baking pan into Rack Position 1, select Convection Bake, set temperature to 400°F (205°C) and set time to 14 minutes. After 6 minutes, remove the pan from the oven. Stir the tater tots and add the egg mixture and cooked sausage. Return the pan to the oven and continue cooking. After 6 minutes, remove the pan from the oven. Scatter the cheese on top of the tater tots. Return the pan to the oven and continue to cook for another 2 minutes. When done, the cheese should be bubbly and melted. Let the mixture cool for 5 minutes and serve warm.

209. Simple Apple Crisp

Servings: 8   Cooking Time: 35 Minutes

Ingredients:

4 medium apples, peel & slice	For topping:
1 tsp cinnamon	1/2 cup brown sugar
4 tbsp sugar	3/4 cup all-purpose flour
1/3 cup butter, melted	3/4 cup rolled oats

Directions:

Fit the Instant Vortex oven with the rack in position Add sliced apples, cinnamon, and sugar in a greased 9-inch baking dish and mix well. In a bowl, mix oats, brown sugar, and flour. Add melted butter and mix well. Sprinkle oat mixture over sliced apples. Set to bake at 375 F for 40 minutes. After 5 minutes place the baking dish in the preheated oven. Serve and enjoy.

210. Asparagus And Cheese Strata

Servings: 4   Cooking Time: 17 Minutes

Ingredients:

6 asparagus spears, cut into 2-inch pieces	4 eggs
1 tablespoon water	2 tablespoons chopped flat-leaf parsley
2 slices whole-wheat bread, cut into ½-inch cubes	½ cup grated Havarti or Swiss cheese
3 tablespoons whole milk	Pinch salt
	Freshly ground black pepper, to taste
	Cooking spray

Directions:

Add the asparagus spears and 1 tablespoon of water in the baking pan. Slide the baking pan into Rack Position 1, select Convection Bake, set temperature to 330°F (166°C) and set time to 4 minutes. When cooking is complete, the asparagus spears will be crisp-tender. Remove the asparagus from the pan and drain on paper towels. Spritz the pan with cooking spray. Place the bread and asparagus in the pan. Whisk together the eggs and milk in a medium mixing bowl until creamy. Fold in the parsley, cheese, salt, and pepper and stir to combine. Pour this mixture into the baking pan. Select Bake and set time to 13 minutes. Put the pan back to the oven. When done, the eggs will be set and the top will be lightly browned. Let cool for 5 minutes before slicing and serving.

211. Ricotta & Chorizo Corn Frittata

Servings: 2   Cooking Time: 12 Minutes

Ingredients:

4 eggs, beaten	1 tbsp chopped parsley
1 large potato, boiled and cubed	½ chorizo, sliced
½ cup frozen corn	1 tbsp olive oil
½ cup ricotta cheese, crumbled	Salt and black pepper to taste

Directions:

Preheat Instant Vortex on Bake function to 330 F. Cook the chorizo in a greased skillet over medium heat for 3 minutes; transfer to a baking dish. Mix the eggs, salt, and pepper in a bowl. Stir in the remaining ingredients. Pour the mixture over the chorizo and press Start. Cook for 25 minutes.

212. Veggie Frittata

Servings: 4   Cooking Time: 12 Minutes

Ingredients:

½ cup chopped red bell pepper	1 egg
⅓ cup grated carrot	6 egg whites
⅓ cup minced onion	⅓ cup 2% milk
1 teaspoon olive oil	1 tablespoon shredded Parmesan cheese

Directions:

Mix together the red bell pepper, carrot, onion, and olive oil in the baking pan and stir to combine. Slide the baking pan into Rack Position 1, select Convection Bake, set temperature to 350°F (180°C) and set time to 12 minutes.   After 3 minutes, remove the pan from the oven. Stir the vegetables. Return the pan to the oven and continue cooking. Meantime, whisk together the egg, egg whites, and milk in a medium bowl until creamy.   After 3 minutes, remove the pan from the oven. Pour the egg mixture over the top and scatter with the Parmesan cheese. Return the pan to the oven and continue cooking for additional 6 minutes.   When cooking is complete, the eggs will be set and the top will be golden around the edges.   Allow the frittata to cool for 5 minutes before slicing and serving.

213. Corn & Chorizo Frittata

Servings: 2   Cooking Time: 20 Minutes

Ingredients:

4 eggs	1 tbsp fresh parsley, chopped
1 large potato, boiled and cubed	½ chorizo, sliced
½ cup frozen corn	1 tbsp olive oil
½ cup feta cheese, crumbled	Salt and black pepper to taste

Directions:

Preheat Instant Vortex on Air Fry function to 375 F. Heat the olive oil in a skillet over medium heat and cook the chorizo cook for 3 minutes. Beat the eggs with salt and pepper in a bowl. Stir in chorizo and the remaining ingredients. Pour the mixture into the baking pan of Instant Vortex oven and cook for 10-15 minutes on Bake function. Serve sliced.

214. Sweet Potato Chickpeas Hash

Servings: 4   Cooking Time: 30 Minutes

Ingredients:

14.5 oz can chickpeas, drained	1 bell pepper, chopped
1 tsp paprika	1 onion, diced
1 tsp garlic powder	1/2 tsp ground black pepper
1 sweet potato, peeled and cubed	1 tsp salt
1 tbsp olive oil	

Directions:

Fit the Instant Vortex oven with the rack in position Spread sweet potato, chickpeas, bell pepper, and onion in a baking pan.   Drizzle with oil and season with paprika, garlic powder, pepper, and salt. Stir well.   Set to bake at 390 F for 35 minutes, after 5 minutes, place the baking pan in the oven.

215. Easy Grilled Pork Chops With Sweet & Tangy Mustard Glaze

Servings: 4   Cooking Time: 45 Minutes

Ingredients:

For the glace 1 ½ tsp cider	2 bay leaves
1 tsp Dijon mustard	2 tsp of salt
2 tsp brown sugar for the brine	2 cloves smashed
3 cups light brown	1 ½ cups of ice cubes
	4 boneless pork chops

Directions:

Make the glaze by placing all the ingredients in a small bowl and set them aside.   Brine your pork by placing it inside water with bay leaves, brown sugar, and garlic and heat it on medium heat. Cover and bring the mixture to boil. Uncover and stir it until the sugar is completely dissolved in the mixture. Add ice cubes to cool into it is slightly warm to the touch.   Once it is cooled submerge the pork chops and set aside for 15 minutes. Prepare your grill. Put the instant vortex fryer on GRILL mode and wait for it to attain the desired temperature. once it has attained 400 degree Celsius then it is time to add your pork chops. Usually the appliance will be indicated 'add food'.   Remove the pork chops from the salt mixture and pat them with paper towels. Place them on the grill and cover. Do not remove until they are well cooked. Once the instant fryer indicates TURN FOOD. flip your food and glaze it twice before allowing it to cook some more. Transfer the pork to a clean cutting board once the appliance has indicated end. Serve while hot.

216. Cinnamon French Toasts

Servings: 2   Cooking Time: 5 Minutes

Ingredients:

2 eggs	2 teaspoons olive oil
¼ cup whole milk	1/8 teaspoon ground cinnamon
3 tablespoons sugar	4 bread slices
1/8 teaspoon vanilla extract	

Directions:

In a large bowl, mix together all the ingredients except bread slices.   Coat the bread slices with egg mixture evenly.   Press "Power Button" of Air Fry Oven and turn the dial to select the "Air Fry" mode. Press the Time button and again turn the dial to set the cooking time to 6 minutes.   Now push the Temp button and rotate the dial to set the temperature at 390 degrees F.   Press "Start/Pause" button to start.   When the unit beeps to show that it is preheated, open the lid and lightly, grease the sheet pan.   Arrange the bread slices into "Air Fry Basket" and insert in the oven.   Flip the bread slices once halfway through.   Serve warm.

217. Simply Bacon

Servings: 1 Person   Cooking Time: 10 Minutes
Ingredients:
4 pieces of bacon
Directions:
Place the bacon strips on the instant vortex air fryer. Cook for 10 minutes   at 200 degrees Celsius. Check when it browns and shows to be ready. Serve.

218.   Cheddar Cheese Hash Browns

Servings: 4   Cooking Time: 20 Minutes
Ingredients:

4 russet potatoes, peeled, grated	½ cup grated cheddar cheese
1 brown onion, chopped	1 egg, lightly beaten
3 garlic cloves, chopped	Salt and black pepper
	3 tbsp finely thyme sprigs

Directions:
In a bowl, mix potatoes, onion, garlic, cheese, egg, salt, black pepper, and thyme. Spray the fryer tray with cooking spray. Press the hash brown mixture into the tray.   Cook in the Instant Vortex oven for 12-16 minutes at 400 F on Bake function. Shake once halfway through cooking until the hash browns are golden and crispy. Serve.

219.   Garlic And Cheese Bread Rolls

Servings: 2   Cooking Time: 5 Minutes
Ingredients:

8 tablespoons of grated cheese	Garlic bread spice mix
6 tsp.s of melted margarine	2 bread rolls

Directions:
Slice the bread rolls from top in a crisscross pattern but not cut through at the bottom.   Put all the cheese into the slits and brush the tops of the bread rolls with melted margarine. Sprinkle the garlic mix on the rolls.   Heat the air fryer to 350°F. Place the rolls into the basket and cook until cheese is melted for about 5 minutes.

220.   Cauliflower Hash Brown

Servings: 4   Cooking Time: 10 Minutes
Ingredients:

2 cups cauliflower, finely grated, soaked and drained	2 teaspoons chili flakes
2 tablespoons xanthan gum	1 teaspoon garlic
Salt, to taste	1 teaspoon onion powder
Pepper powder, to taste	2 teaspoons vegetable oil

Directions:
Preheat the Air fryer to 300-degree F and grease an Air fryer basket with oil.   Heat vegetable oil in a nonstick pan and add cauliflower.   Sauté for about 4 minutes and dish out the cauliflower in a plate. Mix the cauliflower with xanthum gum, salt, chili flakes, garlic and onion powder.   Mix well and refrigerate the hash for about 20 minutes.   Place the hash in the Air fryer basket and cook for about 10 minutes.   Flip the hash after cooking halfway through and dish out to serve warm.

221.   Basil Prosciutto Crostini With Mozzarella

Servings: 1   Cooking Time: 7 Minutes
Ingredients:

½ cup tomatoes, chopped	3 prosciutto slices, chopped
3 oz mozzarella cheese, chopped	1 tsp dried basil
1 tbsp olive oil	6 small slices of French bread

Directions:
Preheat Instant Vortex on Toast function to 350 F. Place in the bread slices and toast them for 5 minutes. Top the bread with tomatoes, prosciutto, and mozzarella. Sprinkle with basil. Drizzle with olive oil. Return to oven and cook for 1 more minute, enough to become melty and warm.

222.   Potato Hash

Servings: 2   Cooking Time: 25 Minutes
Ingredients:

5 big potatoes	½ green pepper
1 medium onion	½ tsp savory
2 eggs	½ tsp black pepper
½ tsp of thyme	2 tsp duck fat

Directions:
Melt the duck fat in the fryer for 2 minutes   and then peal your onion then dice it. Add to the fryer, wash and seed the green pepper to add a sumptuous taste. Cook for 5 minutes.   Wash your potatoes and peel them according to your taste and preference. Dice the potatoes into small cubes and add to the fryer along with the seasonings set the timer to 20 minutes   and allow it to cook.   Spray a nonstick pan with cooking spray and grind some pepper before adding it in. let the pepper heat for a minute before adding your egg. Cook until the egg becomes solid. Take the pan out and set it aside. Chop up the eggs.   Add the egg to the potato mixture once the timer runs out.

223.   Moist Orange Bread Loaf

Servings: 10   Cooking Time: 50 Minutes
Ingredients:

4 eggs	2 tsp baking powder
4 oz butter, softened	2 cups all-purpose flour
1 cup of orange juice	
1 orange zest, grated	1 tsp vanilla
1 cup of sugar	

Directions:
Fit the Instant Vortex oven with the rack in position In a large bowl, whisk eggs and sugar until creamy. Whisk in vanilla, butter, orange juice, and orange zest.   Add flour and baking powder and mix until combined.   Pour batter into the greased 9*5-inch loaf pan.   Set to bake at 350 F for 55 minutes, after

5 minutes, place the loaf pan in the oven. Slice and serve.

224. Egg & Bacon Wraps With Salsa

Servings: 3   Cooking Time: 15 Minutes

Ingredients:

3 tortillas
2 previously scrambled eggs
3 slices bacon, cut into strips

3 tbsp salsa
3 tbsp cream cheese
1 cup Pepper Jack cheese, grated

Directions:
Preheat Instant Vortex on AirFry function to 390 F. Spread 1 tbsp of cream cheese onto each tortilla. Divide the eggs and bacon between the tortillas evenly. Top with salsa and sprinkle some grated cheese over. Roll up the tortillas and press Start. Cook for 10 minutes. Serve.

225. Glazed Strawberry Toast

Servings: 4 Toasts   Cooking Time: 8 Minutes

Ingredients:

4 slices bread, ½-inch thick
1 teaspoon sugar

1 cup sliced strawberries
Cooking spray

Directions:
On a clean work surface, lay the bread slices and spritz one side of each slice of bread with cooking spray.   Place the bread slices in the air fryer basket, sprayed side down. Top with the strawberries and a sprinkle of sugar.   Put the air fryer basket on the baking pan and slide into Rack Position 2, select Air Fry, set temperature to 375°F (190°C), and set time to 8 minutes.   When cooking is complete, the toast should be well browned on each side. Remove from the oven to a plate and serve.

226. Zucchini Squash Pita Sandwiches Recipe

Ingredients:

1 small Zucchini Squash, (5-6 ounces)
Salt and Pepper, to taste
2 Whole Wheat Pitas
1/2 cup Hummus
1/2 cup Diced Red Bell Pepper, (about half a large pepper)
1/2 cup Chopped Red Onion, (about 1/4 a large onion)

1 1/2 cups Fresh Spinach, (2 handfuls)
2 teaspoons Olive Oil
1/4 teaspoon Dried Oregano
1/4 teaspoon Dried Thyme
1/4 teaspoon Garlic Powder
2 tablespoons Crumbled Feta Cheese, (about 1 ounce)

Directions:
Adjust the cooking rack to the lowest placement and preheat toaster oven to 425°F on the BAKE setting. While the oven preheats, quarter the zucchini lengthwise and then cut into 1/2-inch thick pieces. Cut the bell pepper and onion into 1-inch thick pieces.   Add the vegetables to a roasting pan. Drizzle with oil and sprinkle over the oregano, garlic powder, and salt and pepper, to taste. Toss to combine.   Roast vegetables for 10 minutes. Carefully remove the pan and stir. Return pan to oven and continue cooking until the vegetables have softened and started to brown, about 5 minutes more. Remove from the toaster oven and set aside. Reduce the temperature to 375°F and warm the pitas by placing them directly on the cooking rack for 1 to 2 minutes.   Spread warm pitas with hummus. Layer with spinach, roasted vegetables, and crumbled feta.

227. Peanut Butter Banana Bread

Servings: 6   Cooking Time: 40 Minutes

Ingredients:

1 cup plus 1 tablespoon all-purpose flour
1¼ teaspoons baking powder
1 large egg
2 medium ripe bananas, peeled and mashed
¾ cup walnuts, roughly chopped

¼ teaspoon salt
1/3 cup granulated sugar
¼ cup canola oil
2 tablespoons creamy peanut butter
2 tablespoons sour cream
1 teaspoon vanilla extract

Directions:
Preheat the Air fryer to 330F and grease a nonstick baking dish.   Mix together the flour, baking powder and salt in a bowl.   Whisk together egg with sugar, canola oil, sour cream, peanut butter and vanilla extract in a bowl.   Stir in the bananas and beat until well combined.   Now, add the flour mixture and fold in the walnuts gently.   Mix until combined and transfer the mixture evenly into the prepared baking dish.   Arrange the baking dish in an Air fryer basket and cook for about 40 minutes. Remove from the Air fryer and place onto a wire rack to cool.   Cut the bread into desired size slices and serve.

228. Creamy Parmesan & Ham Shirred Eggs

Servings: 2   Cooking Time: 20 Minutes

Ingredients:

2 tsp butter
4 eggs, divided
2 tbsp heavy cream
3 tbsp Parmesan cheese, shredded

4 slices of ham
¼ tsp paprika
¾ tsp salt
¼ tsp pepper
2 tsp chopped chives

Directions:
Preheat Instant Vortex on Bake function to 320 F. Grease a pie pan with the butter. Arrange the ham slices on the bottom of the pan to cover it completely. Whisk one egg along with the heavy cream, salt, and pepper in a bowl.   Pour the mixture over the ham slices. Crack the other eggs over the ham. Sprinkle with Parmesan cheese. Cook for 14 minutes. Season with paprika, garnish with chives, and serve.

229.   Breakfast Potatoes

Servings: 4   Cooking Time: 35 Minutes

Ingredients:

2 lbs potatoes, scrubbed and cut into 1/2-inch cubes	1 tbsp olive oil
	1/2 tsp sweet paprika
	Pepper
1 tsp garlic powder	Salt

Directions:

Fit the Instant Vortex oven with the rack in position Place potato cubes on the parchment-lined baking pan.   Drizzle with oil and season with paprika, garlic powder, pepper, and salt. Toss potatoes well. Set to bake at 425 F for 40 minutes, after 5 minutes, place the baking pan in the oven.   Serve and enjoy.

230.   Easy Cheesy Breakfast Casserole

Servings: 8   Cooking Time: 30 Minutes

Ingredients:

6 eggs, lightly beaten	2 cups cheddar cheese, shredded
8 oz can crescent rolls	1 lb breakfast sausage, cooked

Directions:

Fit the Instant Vortex oven with the rack in position Spray a 9*13-inch baking dish with cooking spray and set aside.   Spread crescent rolls in the bottom of the prepared baking dish and top with sausage, egg, and cheese.   Set to bake at 350 F for 35 minutes. After 5 minutes place the baking dish in the preheated oven.   Serve and enjoy.

Lunch Recipes

231. Juicy Turkey Burgers

Servings: 8   Cooking Time: 25 Minutes

Ingredients:

1 lb ground turkey 85% lean / 15% fat	2 tsp Worcestershire Sauce
¼ cup unsweetened apple sauce	1 tsp minced garlic
½ onion grated	¼ cup plain breadcrumbs
1 Tbsp ranch seasoning	Salt and pepper to taste

Directions:

Combine the onion, ground turkey, unsweetened apple sauce, minced garlic, breadcrumbs, ranch seasoning, Worchestire sauce, and salt and pepper. Mix them with your hands until well combined. Form 4 equally sized hamburger patties with them. Place these burgers in the refrigerator for about 30 minutes to have them firm up a bit.   While preparing for cooking, select the Air Fry option. Set the temperature of 360°F and the cook time as required. Press start to begin preheating.   Once the preheating temperature is reached, place the burgers on the tray in the Air fryer basket, making sure they don't overlap or touch. Cook on for 15 minutes   flipping halfway through.

232. Dijon And Swiss Croque Monsieur

Servings: 2   Cooking Time: 13 Minutes

Ingredients:

4 slices white bread	1/2 cup whole milk
2 tablespoons unsalted butter	1/4 teaspoon freshly ground black pepper
1 tablespoon all-purpose flour	1/8 teaspoon salt
3/4 cups shredded Swiss cheese	1 tablespoon Dijon mustard
	4 slices ham

Directions:

Start by cutting crusts off bread and placing them on a pan lined with parchment paper.   Melt 1 tablespoon of butter in a sauce pan, then dab the top sides of each piece of bread with butter.   Toast bread inoven for 3-5 minutes until each piece is golden brown.   Melt the second tablespoon of butter in the sauce pan and add the flour, mix together until they form a paste.   Add the milk and continue to mix until the sauce begins to thicken. Remove from heat and mix in 1 tablespoon of Swiss cheese, salt, and pepper; continue stirring until cheese is melted.   Flip the bread over in the pan so the untoasted side is facing up.   Set two slices aside and spread Dijon on the other two slices. Add ham and sprinkle 1/4 cup Swiss over each piece. Broil for about 3 minutes.   Top the sandwiches off with the other slices of bread, soft-side down.   Top with sauce and sprinkle with remaining Swiss. Toast for another 5 minutes or until the cheese is golden brown.   Serve immediately.

233. Saucy Chicken With Leeks

Servings: 6   Cooking Time: 10 Minutes

Ingredients:

2 large-sized tomatoes, chopped	2 leeks, sliced
3 cloves garlic, minced	½ teaspoon smoked cayenne pepper
½ teaspoon dried oregano	2 tablespoons olive oil
6 chicken legs, boneless and skinless	A freshly ground nutmeg

Directions:

In a mixing dish, thoroughly combine all ingredients, minus the leeks. Place in the refrigerator and let it marinate overnight.   Lay the leeks onto the bottom of an Air Fryer cooking basket. Top with the chicken legs.   Roast chicken legs at 375 degrees F for 18 minutes, turning halfway through. Serve with hoisin sauce.

234. Roasted Garlic(2)

Servings: 12 Cloves   Cooking Time: 12 Minutes

Ingredients:

1 medium head garlic	2 tsp. avocado oil

Directions:

Remove any hanging excess peel from the garlic but leave the cloves covered. Cut off ¼ of the head of garlic, exposing the tips of the cloves   Drizzle with avocado oil. Place the garlic head into a small sheet of aluminum foil, completely enclosing it. Place it into the air fryer basket. Adjust the temperature to 400 Degrees F and set the timer for 20 minutes. If your garlic head is a bit smaller, check it after 15 minutes   When done, garlic should be golden brown and very soft   To serve, cloves should pop out and easily be spread or sliced. Store in an airtight container in the refrigerator up to 5 days.   You may also freeze individual cloves on a baking sheet, then store together in a freezer-safe storage bag once frozen.

235. Coconut Shrimp With Dip

Servings: 4   Cooking Time: 9 Minutes

Ingredients:

1 lb large raw shrimp peeled and deveined with tail on	¼ tsp black pepper
2 eggs beaten	½ cup All-Purpose Flour
¼ cup Panko Breadcrumbs	½ cup unsweetened shredded coconut
1 tsp salt	Oil for spraying

Directions:

Clean and dry the shrimp. Set it aside.   Take 3 bowls. Put flour in the first bowl. Beat eggs in the second bowl. Mix coconut, breadcrumbs, salt, and black pepper in the third bowl.   Select the Air Fry option and adjust the temperature to 390°F. Push start and preheating will start.   Dip each shrimp in flour followed by the egg and then coconut mixture, ensuring shrimp is covered on all sides during each dip. Once the preheating is done, place shrimp in a single layer on greased tray in the basket of the Instant Pot Duo Crisp Air Fryer. Spray the shrimp with oil lightly, and then close the Air Fryer basket lid. Cook for around 4 minutes. After 4 minutes open the Air Fryer basket lid and flip the shrimp over. Respray the shrimp with oil, close the Air Fryer basket lid, and cook for five more minutes. Remove shrimp from the basket and serve with Thai Sweet Chili Sauce.

236. Spanish Chicken Bake

Servings: 4   Cooking Time: 25 Minutes

Ingredients:

½ onion, quartered	1/8 cup chorizo
½ red onion, quartered	4 chicken thighs, boneless
½ lb. potatoes, quartered	¼ teaspoon dried oregano
4 garlic cloves	
4 tomatoes, quartered	½ green bell pepper, julienned
¼ teaspoon paprika powder	Salt
	Black pepper

Directions:
Toss chicken, veggies, and all the Ingredients: in a baking tray. Press "Power Button" of Air Fry Oven and turn the dial to select the "Bake" mode. Press the Time button and again turn the dial to set the cooking time to 25 minutes. Now push the Temp button and rotate the dial to set the temperature at 425 degrees F. Once preheated, place the baking pan inside and close its lid. Serve warm.

237. Chicken Wings With Prawn Paste

Servings: 6   Cooking Time: 8 Minutes

Ingredients:

Corn flour, as required	1½ teaspoons sugar
2 pounds mid-joint chicken wings	2 teaspoons sesame oil
2 tablespoons prawn paste	1 teaspoon Shaoxing wine
4 tablespoons olive oil	2 teaspoons fresh ginger juice

Directions:
Preheat the Air fryer to 360 degree F and grease an Air fryer basket. Mix all the ingredients in a bowl except wings and corn flour. Rub the chicken wings generously with marinade and refrigerate overnight. Coat the chicken wings evenly with corn flour and keep aside. Set the Air fryer to 390 degree F and arrange the chicken wings in the Air fryer basket. Cook for about 8 minutes and dish out to serve hot.

238. Chicken Breast With Rosemary

Servings: 4   Cooking Time: 60 Minutes

Ingredients:

4 bone-in chicken breast halves	1/4 teaspoon pepper
3 tablespoons softened butter	1 tablespoon rosemary
1/2 teaspoon salt	1 tablespoon extra-virgin olive oil

Directions:
Start by preheating toaster oven to 400°F. Mix butter, salt, pepper, and rosemary in a bowl. Coat chicken with the butter mixture and place in a shallow pan. Drizzle oil over chicken and roast for 25 minutes. Flip chicken and roast for another 20 minutes. Flip chicken one more time and roast for a final 15 minutes.

239. Delightful Turkey Wings

Servings: 4   Cooking Time: 26 Minutes

Ingredients:

2 pounds turkey wings	3 tablespoons olive oil
4 tablespoons chicken rub	

Directions:
Preheat the Air fryer to 380 degree F and grease an Air fryer basket. Mix the turkey wings, chicken rub, and olive oil in a bowl until well combined. Arrange the turkey wings into the Air fryer basket and cook for about 26 minutes, flipping once in between. Dish out the turkey wings in a platter and serve hot.

240. Roasted Fennel, Ditalini, And Shrimp

Servings: 4   Cooking Time: 30 Minutes

Ingredients:

1 pound extra large, thawed, tail-on shrimp	1 teaspoon salt
	2 tablespoons olive oil
1 teaspoon fennel seeds	1/2 teaspoon freshly ground black pepper
1 fennel bulb, halved and sliced crosswise	Grated zest of 1 lemon
4 garlic cloves, chopped	1/2 pound whole wheat ditalini

Directions:
Start by preheating toaster oven to 450°F. Toast the seeds in a medium pan over medium heat for about 5 minutes, then toss with shrimp. Add water and 1/2 teaspoon salt to the pan and bring the mixture to a boil. Reduce heat and simmer for 30 minutes. Combine fennel, garlic, oil, pepper, and remaining salt in a roasting pan. Roast for 20 minutes, then add shrimp mixture and roast for another 5 minutes or until shrimp are cooked. While the fennel is roasting, cook pasta per the directions on the package, drain, and set aside. Remove the shrimp mixture and mix in pasta, roast for another 5 minutes.

241. Onion Omelet

Servings: 2   Cooking Time: 15 Minutes

Ingredients:

4 eggs
¼ teaspoon low-sodium soy sauce
Ground black pepper, as required
1 teaspoon butter
1 medium yellow onion, sliced
¼ cup Cheddar cheese, grated

Directions:

In a skillet, melt the butter over medium heat and cook the onion and cook for about 8-10 minutes. Remove from the heat and set aside to cool slightly. Meanwhile, in a bowl, add the eggs, soy sauce and black pepper and beat well.   Add the cooked onion and gently, stir to combine.   Place the zucchini mixture into a small baking pan.   Press "Power Button" of Air Fry Oven and turn the dial to select the "Air Fry" mode.   Press the Time button and again turn the dial to set the cooking time to 5 minutes.   Now push the Temp button and rotate the dial to set the temperature at 355 degrees F. Press "Start/Pause" button to start.   When the unit beeps to show that it is preheated, open the lid. Arrange pan over the "Wire Rack" and insert in the oven.   Cut the omelet into 2 portions and serve hot.

242. Spicy Avocado Cauliflower Toast

Servings: 2   Cooking Time: 15 Minutes

Ingredients:

1/2 large head of cauliflower, leaves removed
3 1/4 teaspoons olive oil
1 small jalapeño
1 tablespoon chopped cilantro leaves
2 slices whole grain bread
1 medium avocado
Salt and pepper
5 radishes
1 green onion
2 teaspoons hot sauce
1 lime

Directions:

Start by preheating toaster oven to 450°F.   Cut cauliflower into thick pieces, about 3/4-inches-thick, and slice jalapeño into thin slices.   Place cauliflower and jalapeño in a bowl and mix together with 2 teaspoons olive oil.   Add salt and pepper to taste and mix for another minute.   Coat a pan with another teaspoon of olive oil, then lay the cauliflower mixture flat across the pan.   Cook for 20 minutes, flipping in the last 5 minutes.   Reduce heat to toast.   Sprinkle cilantro over the mix while it is still warm, and set aside.   Brush bread with remaining oil and toast until golden brown, about 5 minutes.   Dice onion and radish.   Mash avocado in a bowl, then spread on toast and sprinkle salt and pepper to taste.   Put cauliflower mix on toast and cover with onion and radish. Drizzle with hot sauce and serve with a lime wedge.

243. Rosemary Lemon Chicken

Servings: 8   Cooking Time: 45 Minutes

Ingredients:

4-lb. chicken, cut into pieces
2 large garlic cloves, minced
Salt and black pepper, to taste
Flour for dredging 3 tablespoons olive oil
1 large onion, sliced
Peel of ½ lemon
1 1/2 teaspoons rosemary leaves
1 tablespoon honey
1/4 cup lemon juice
1 cup chicken broth

Directions:

Dredges the chicken through the flour then place in the baking pan.   Whisk broth with the rest of the Ingredients: in a bowl.   Pour this mixture over the dredged chicken in the pan.   Press "Power Button" of Air Fry Oven and turn the dial to select the "Bake" mode.   Press the Time button and again turn the dial to set the cooking time to 45 minutes.   Now push the Temp button and rotate the dial to set the temperature at 400 degrees F.   Once preheated, place the baking pan inside and close its lid.   Baste the chicken with its sauce every 15 minutes.   Serve warm.

244. Chicken With Veggies And Rice

Servings: 3   Cooking Time: 20 Minutes

Ingredients:

3 cups cold boiled white rice
1 cup cooked chicken, diced
½ cup frozen carrots
½ cup frozen peas
½ cup onion, chopped
6 tablespoons soy sauce
1 tablespoon vegetable oil

Directions:

Preheat the Air fryer to 360 degree F and grease a 7" nonstick pan.   Mix the rice, soy sauce, and vegetable oil in a bowl.   Stir in the remaining ingredients and mix until well combined. Transfer the rice mixture into the pan and place in the Air fryer.   Cook for about 20 minutes and dish out to serve immediately.

245. Barbecue Air Fried Chicken

Servings: 10   Cooking Time: 26 Minutes

Ingredients:

1 teaspoon Liquid Smoke
2 cloves Fresh Garlic smashed
1/2 cup Apple Cider Vinegar
1 Tablespoon Kosher Salt
1 Tablespoon Freshly Ground Black Pepper
2 teaspoons Garlic Powder
3 pounds Chuck Roast well-marbled with intramuscular fat
1.5 cups Barbecue Sauce
1/4 cup Light Brown Sugar + more for sprinkling
2 Tablespoons Honey optional and in place of 2 TBL sugar

Directions:

Add meat to the Instant Pot Duo Crisp Air Fryer Basket, spreading out the meat.   Select the option Air Fry.   Close the Air Fryer lid and cook at 300 degrees F for 8 minutes. Pause the Air Fryer and flip meat over after 4 minutes.   Remove the lid and baste with more barbecue sauce and sprinkle with a little brown sugar.   Again Close the Air Fryer lid and set the temperature at 400°F for 9 minutes. Watch meat though the lid and flip it over after 5 minutes.

---

246. Tomato And Avocado

Servings: 4   Cooking Time: 12 Minutes

Ingredients:

½ lb. cherry tomatoes; halved

2 avocados, pitted; peeled and cubed

1 ¼ cup lettuce; torn

1/3 cup coconut cream

A pinch of salt and black pepper

Cooking spray

Directions:

Grease the air fryer with cooking spray, combine the tomatoes with avocados, salt, pepper and the cream and cook at 350°F for 5 minutes shaking once   In a salad bowl, mix the lettuce with the tomatoes and avocado mix, toss and serve.

---

247. Chives Radishes

Servings: 4   Cooking Time: 12 Minutes

Ingredients:

20 radishes; halved

2 tbsp. olive oil

1 tbsp. garlic; minced

1 tsp. chives; chopped.

Salt and black pepper to taste.

Directions:

In your air fryer's pan, combine all the ingredients and toss.   Introduce the pan in the machine and cook at 370°F for 15 minutes   Divide between plates and serve as a side dish.

---

248. Parmesan Chicken Meatballs

Servings: 4   Cooking Time: 12 Minutes

Ingredients:

1-lb. ground chicken

1 large egg, beaten

½ cup Parmesan cheese, grated

½ cup pork rinds, ground

1 teaspoon garlic powder

1 teaspoon paprika

1 teaspoon kosher salt

½ teaspoon pepper

Crust:

½ cup pork rinds, ground

Directions:

Toss all the meatball Ingredients: in a bowl and mix well.   Make small meatballs out this mixture and roll them in the pork rinds.   Place the coated meatballs in the air fryer basket.   Press "Power Button" of Air Fry Oven and turn the dial to select the "Bake" mode.   Press the Time button and again turn the dial to set the cooking time to 12 minutes.   Now push the Temp button and rotate the dial to set the temperature at 400 degrees F. Once preheated, place the air fryer basket inside and close its lid.   Serve warm.

---

249. Cheese-stuffed Meatballs

Servings: 4   Cooking Time: 10 Minutes

Ingredients:

⅓ cup soft bread crumbs

3 tablespoons milk

Freshly ground black pepper

1-pound 95 percent

1 tablespoon ketchup

1 egg

½ teaspoon dried marjoram

Pinch salt

lean ground beef

20 ½-inch cubes of cheese

Olive oil for misting

Directions:

Preparing the ingredients. In a large bowl, combine the bread crumbs, milk, ketchup, egg, marjoram, salt, and pepper, and mix well. Add the ground beef and mix gently but thoroughly with your hands. Form the mixture into 20 meatballs. Shape each meatball around a cheese cube. Mist the meatballs with olive oil and put into the instant crisp air fryer basket.   Air frying. Close air fryer lid. Bake for 10 to 13 minutes or until the meatballs register 165°f on a meat thermometer.

---

250. Ranch Chicken Wings

Servings: 3   Cooking Time: 10 Minutes

Ingredients:

1/4 cup almond meal

2 tablespoons butter, melted

6 tablespoons parmesan cheese, preferably freshly grated

1/4 cup flaxseed meal

1 tablespoon Ranch seasoning mix

2 tablespoons oyster sauce

6 chicken wings, bone-in

Directions:

Start by preheating your Air Fryer to 370 degrees F. In a resealable bag, place the almond meal, flaxseed meal, butter, parmesan, Ranch seasoning mix, andoyster sauce. Add the chicken wings and shake to coat on all sides.   Arrange the chicken wings in the Air Fryer basket. Spritz the chicken wings with a nonstick cooking spray.   Cook for 11 minutes. Turn them over and cook an additional 11 minutes. Serve warm with your favorite dipping sauce, if desired. Enjoy!

---

251. Duck Rolls

Servings: 3   Cooking Time: 40 Minutes

Ingredients:

1 pound duck breast fillet, each cut into 2 pieces

3 tablespoons fresh parsley, finely chopped

1 small red onion, finely chopped

1 garlic clove, crushed

1½ teaspoons ground cumin

1 teaspoon ground cinnamon

½ teaspoon red chili powder

Salt, to taste

2 tablespoons olive oil

Directions:

Preheat the Air fryer to 355 degree F and grease an Air fryer basket.   Mix the garlic, parsley, onion, spices, and 1 tablespoon of olive oil in a bowl. Make a slit in each duck piece horizontally and coat with onion mixture.   Roll each duck piece tightly and transfer into the Air fryer basket.   Cook for about 40 minutes and cut into desired size slices to serve.

252. Tomato Frittata

Servings: 2   Cooking Time: 30 Minutes

Ingredients:

4 eggs	½ cup milk
¼ cup onion, chopped	1 cup Gouda cheese, shredded
½ cup tomatoes, chopped	Salt, as required

Directions:

In a small baking pan, add all the ingredients and mix well.   Press "Power Button" of Air Fry Oven and turn the dial to select the "Air Fry" mode. Press the Time button and again turn the dial to set the cooking time to 30 minutes.   Now push the Temp button and rotate the dial to set the temperature at 340 degrees F.   Press "Start/Pause" button to start.   When the unit beeps to show that it is preheated, open the lid.   Arrange the baking pan over the "Wire Rack" and insert in the oven. Cut into 2 wedges and serve.

253. Pecan Crunch Catfish And Asparagus

Servings: 4   Cooking Time: 12 Minutes

Ingredients:

1 cup whole wheat panko breadcrumbs	3 teaspoons chopped fresh thyme
1/4 cup chopped pecans	Salt and pepper to taste
1-1/2 tablespoons extra-virgin olive oil, plus more for the pan	1-1/4 pounds asparagus
1 tablespoon honey	4 (5- to 6-ounce each) catfish filets

Directions:

Start by preheating toaster oven to 425°F. Combine breadcrumbs, pecans, 2 teaspoons thyme, 1 tablespoon oil, salt, pepper and 2 tablespoons water.   In another bowl combine asparagus, the rest of the thyme, honey, salt, and pepper.   Spread the asparagus in a flat layer on a baking sheet. Sprinkle a quarter of the breadcrumb mixture over the asparagus.   Lay the catfish over the asparagus and press the rest of the breadcrumb mixture into each piece. Roast for 12 minutes.

254. Turkey Legs

Servings: 2   Cooking Time: 40 Minutes

Ingredients:

2 large turkey legs	1 tsp season salt
1 1/2 tsp smoked paprika	½ tsp garlic powder
1 tsp brown sugar	oil for spraying avocado, canola, etc.

Directions:

Mix the smoked paprika, brown sugar, seasoned salt, garlic powder thoroughly.   Wash and pat dry the turkey legs.   Rub the made seasoning mixture all over the turkey legs making sure to get under the skin also.   While preparing for cooking, select the Air Fry option. Press start to begin preheating. Once the preheating temperature is reached, place the turkey legs on the tray in the Instant Pot Duo Crisp Air Fryer basket. Lightly spray them with oil.

Air Fry the turkey legs on 400°F for 20 minutes. Then, open the Air Fryer lid and flip the turkey legs and lightly spray with oil. Close the Instant Pot Duo Crisp Air Fryer lid and cook for 20 more minutes. Remove and Enjoy.

255. Parmesan-crusted Pork Loin

Servings: 4   Cooking Time: 20 Minutes

Ingredients:

1 pound pork loin	1 teaspoon salt
1/2 tablespoon garlic powder	2 tablespoons parmesan cheese
1/2 tablespoon onion powder	1 tablespoon olive oil

Directions:

Start by preheating toaster oven to 475°F.   Place pan in the oven and let it heat while the oven preheats.   Mix all ingredients in a shallow dish and roll the pork loin until it is fully coated. Remove pan and sear the pork in the pan on each side.   Once seared, bake pork in the pan for 20 minutes.

256. Baked Shrimp Scampi

Servings: 4   Cooking Time: 10 Minutes

Ingredients:

1 lb large shrimp	1/2 tsp salt
8 tbsp butter	1/4 tsp cayenne pepper
1 tbsp minced garlic (use 2 for extra garlic flavor)	1/4 tsp paprika
	1/2 tsp onion powder
1/4 cup white wine or cooking sherry	3/4 cup bread crumbs

Directions:

Take a bowl and mix the bread crumbs with dry seasonings.   On the stovetop (or in the Instant Pot on saute), melt the butter with the garlic and the white wine.   Remove from heat and add shrimp and the bread crumb mix.   Transfer the mix to a casserole dish.   Choose the Bake operation and add food to the Instant Pot Duo Crisp Air Fryer. Close the lid and Bake at 350°F for 10 minutes or until they are browned.   Serve and enjoy.

257. Roasted Delicata Squash With Kale

Servings: 2   Cooking Time: 10 Minutes

Ingredients:

1 medium delicata squash	2 tablespoons olive oil
1 bunch kale	Salt and pepper
1 clove garlic	

Directions:

Start by preheating toaster oven to 425°F.   Clean squash and cut off each end. Cut in half and remove the seeds. Quarter the halves.   Toss the squash in 1 tablespoon of olive oil.   Place the squash on a greased baking sheet and roast for 25 minutes, turning halfway through.   Rinse kale and remove stems. Chop garlic.   Heat the leftover oil in a medium skillet and add kale and salt to taste.

Sauté the kale until it darkens, then mix in the garlic. Cook for another minute then remove from heat and add 2 tablespoons of water. Remove squash from oven and lay it on top of the garlic kale. Top with salt and pepper to taste and serve.

258. Ground Chicken Meatballs

Servings: 4   Cooking Time: 10 Minutes

Ingredients:

1-lb. ground chicken	1/2 teaspoon garlic
1/3 cup panko	powder
1 teaspoon salt	1 teaspoon thyme
2 teaspoons chives	1 egg

Directions:

Toss all the meatball Ingredients: in a bowl and mix well. Make small meatballs out this mixture and place them in the air fryer basket. Press "Power Button" of Air Fry Oven and turn the dial to select the "Air Fry" mode. Press the Time button and again turn the dial to set the cooking time to 10 minutes. Now push the Temp button and rotate the dial to set the temperature at 350 degrees F. Once preheated, place the air fryer basket inside and close its lid. Serve warm.

259. Roasted Mini Peppers

Servings: 6   Cooking Time: 15 Minutes

Ingredients:

1 bag mini bell peppers	Salt and pepper to taste
Cooking spray	

Directions:

Start by preheating toaster oven to 400°F. Wash and dry the peppers, then place flat on a baking sheet. Spray peppers with cooking spray and sprinkle with salt and pepper. Roast for 15 minutes.

260. Spicy Egg And Ground Turkey Bake

Servings: 6   Cooking Time: 10 Minutes

Ingredients:

1½ pounds ground turkey	2 tablespoons sesame oil
6 whole eggs, well beaten	2 leeks, chopped
1/3 teaspoon smoked paprika	3 cloves garlic, finely minced
2 egg whites, beaten	1 teaspoon ground black pepper
Tabasco sauce, for drizzling	1/2 teaspoon sea salt

Directions:

Warm the oil in a pan over moderate heat; then, sweat the leeks and garlic until tender; stir periodically. Next, grease 6 oven safe ramekins with pan spray. Divide the sautéed mixture among six ramekins. In a bowl, beat the eggs and egg whites using a wire whisk. Stir in the smoked paprika, salt and black pepper; whisk until everything is thoroughly combined. Divide the egg mixture among the ramekins. Air-fry

approximately 22 minutes at 345 degrees F. Drizzle Tabasco sauce over each portion and serve.

261. Greek Lamb Meatballs

Servings: 12   Cooking Time: 12 Minutes

Ingredients:

1 pound ground lamb	½ teaspoon salt
½ cup breadcrumbs	
¼ cup milk	½ teaspoon black pepper
2 egg yolks	
1 teaspoon ground coriander	1 lemon, juiced and zested
1 teaspoon ground cumin	¼ cup fresh parsley, chopped
3 garlic cloves, minced	½ cup crumbled feta cheese
1 teaspoon dried oregano	Olive oil, for shaping
	Tzatziki, for dipping

Directions:

Combine all ingredients except olive oil in a large mixing bowl and mix until fully incorporated. Form 12 meatballs, about 2 ounces each. Use olive oil on your hands so they don't stick to the meatballs. Set aside. Select the Broil function on the COSORI Air Fryer Toaster Oven, set time to 12 minutes, then press Start/Cancel to preheat. Place the meatballs on the food tray, then insert the tray at top position in the preheated air fryer toaster oven. Press Start/Cancel. Take out the meatballs when done and serve with a side of tzatziki.

262. Pumpkin Pancakes

Servings: 4   Cooking Time: 12 Minutes

Ingredients:

3 tablespoons pumpkin filling	1 square puff pastry
	1 small egg, beaten

Directions:

Roll out a square of puff pastry and layer it with pumpkin pie filling, leaving about ¼-inch space around the edges. Cut it up into 8 equal sized square pieces and coat the edges with beaten egg. Press "Power Button" of Air Fry Oven and turn the dial to select the "Air Fry" mode. Press the Time button and again turn the dial to set the cooking time to 12 minutes. Now push the Temp button and rotate the dial to set the temperature at 355 degrees F. Press "Start/Pause" button to start. When the unit beeps to show that it is preheated, open the lid. Arrange the squares into a greased "Sheet Pan" and insert in the oven. Serve warm.

263. Balsamic Roasted Chicken

Servings: 4   Cooking Time: 1 Hour

Ingredients:

1/2 cup balsamic vinegar	1 teaspoon salt
	1 teaspoon pepper
1/4 cup Dijon mustard	4 bone-in, skin-on chicken thighs
1/3 cup olive oil	4 bone-in, skin-on chicken drumsticks
Juice and zest from 1	

lemon
3 minced garlic cloves

1 tablespoon chopped parsley

Directions:
Mix vinegar, lemon juice, mustard, olive oil, garlic, salt, and pepper in a bowl, then pour into a sauce pan. Roll chicken pieces in the pan, then cover and marinate for at least 2 hours, but up to 24 hours. Preheat the toaster oven to 400°F and place the chicken on a fresh baking sheet, reserving the marinade for later. Roast the chicken for 50 minutes. Remove the chicken and cover it with foil to keep it warm. Place the marinade in the toaster oven for about 5 minutes until it simmers down and begins to thicken. Pour marinade over chicken and sprinkle with parsley and lemon zest.

264.	Oregano Chicken Breast

Servings: 6   Cooking Time: 25 Minutes
Ingredients:

2 lbs. chicken breasts, minced	1 teaspoon garlic powder
1 tablespoon avocado oil	1 teaspoon oregano
1 teaspoon smoked paprika	1/2 teaspoon salt
	Black pepper, to taste

Directions:
Toss all the meatball Ingredients: in a bowl and mix well. Make small meatballs out this mixture and place them in the air fryer basket. Press "Power Button" of Air Fry Oven and turn the dial to select the "Air Fry" mode. Press the Time button and again turn the dial to set the cooking time to 25 minutes. Now push the Temp button and rotate the dial to set the temperature at 375 degrees F. Once preheated, place the air fryer basket inside and close its lid. Serve warm.

265.	Lobster Tails

Servings: 2   Cooking Time: 8 Minutes
Ingredients:

2 6oz lobster tails	1 tsp chopped chives
1 tsp salt	1 Tbsp minced garlic
2 Tbsp unsalted butter melted	1 tsp lemon juice

Directions:
Combine butter, garlic, salt, chives, and lemon juice to prepare butter mixture. Butterfly lobster tails by cutting through shell followed by removing the meat and resting it on top of the shell. Place them on the tray in the Instant Pot Duo Crisp Air Fryer basket and spread butter over the top of lobster meat. Close the Air Fryer lid, select the Air Fry option and cook on 380°F for 4 minutes. Open the Air Fryer lid and spread more butter on top, cook for extra 2-4 minutes until done.

266.	Ricotta Toasts With Salmon

Servings: 2   Cooking Time: 4 Minutes
Ingredients:

4 bread slices	1 teaspoon lemon zest
1 garlic clove, minced	Freshly ground black
8 oz. ricotta cheese	

pepper, to taste
4 oz. smoked salmon

Directions:
In a food processor, add the garlic, ricotta, lemon zest and black pepper and pulse until smooth. Spread ricotta mixture over each bread slices evenly. Press "Power Button" of Air Fry Oven and turn the dial to select the "Air Fry" mode. Press the Time button and again turn the dial to set the cooking time to 4 minutes. Now push the Temp button and rotate the dial to set the temperature at 355 degrees F. Press "Start/Pause" button to start. When the unit beeps to show that it is preheated, open the lid and lightly, grease the sheet pan. Arrange the bread slices into "Air Fry Basket" and insert in the oven. Top with salmon and serve.

267.	Pork Stew

Servings: 4   Cooking Time: 12 Minutes
Ingredients:

2 lb. pork stew meat; cubed	½ tsp. smoked paprika
1 eggplant; cubed	Salt and black pepper to taste.
½ cup beef stock	
2 zucchinis; cubed	A handful cilantro; chopped.

Directions:
In a pan that fits your air fryer, mix all the ingredients, toss, introduce in your air fryer and cook at 370°F for 30 minutes   Divide into bowls and serve right away.

268.	Skinny Black Bean Flautas

Servings: 10   Cooking Time: 25 Minutes
Ingredients:

2 (15-ounce) cans black beans	2 teaspoons taco seasoning
1 cup shredded cheddar	10 (8-inch) whole wheat flour tortillas
1 (4-ounce) can diced green chilies	Olive oil

Directions:
Start by preheating toaster oven to 350°F. Drain black beans and mash in a medium bowl with a fork. Mix in cheese, chilies, and taco seasoning until all ingredients are thoroughly combined. Evenly spread the mixture over each tortilla and wrap tightly. Brush each side lightly with olive oil and place on a baking sheet. Bake for 12 minutes, turn, and bake for another 13 minutes.

269.	Sweet Potato And Parsnip Spiralized Latkes

Servings: 12   Cooking Time: 20 Minutes
Ingredients:

1 medium sweet potato	1/2 teaspoon garlic powder
1 large parsnip	1/2 teaspoon sea salt
4 cups water	1/2 teaspoon ground pepper
1 egg + 1 egg white	
2 scallions	

Directions:

Start by spiralizing the sweet potato and parsnip and chopping the scallions, reserving only the green parts. Preheat toaster oven to 425°F. Bring 4 cups of water to a boil. Place all of your noodles in a colander and pour the boiling water over the top, draining well. Let the noodles cool, then grab handfuls and place them in a paper towel; squeeze to remove as much liquid as possible. In a large bowl, beat egg and egg white together. Add noodles, scallions, garlic powder, salt, and pepper, mix well. Prepare a baking sheet; scoop out 1/4 cup of mixture at a time and place on sheet. Slightly press down each scoop with your hands, then bake for 20 minutes, flipping halfway through.

270. Cheddar & Cream Omelet

Servings: 2   Cooking Time: 8 Minutes
Ingredients:

4 eggs	¼ cup cream
Salt and ground black pepper, as required	¼ cup Cheddar cheese, grated

Directions:
In a bowl, add the eggs, cream, salt, and black pepper and beat well. Place the egg mixture into a small baking pan. Press "Power Button" of Air Fry Oven and turn the dial to select the "Air Fry" mode. Press the Time button and again turn the dial to set the cooking time to 8 minutes. Now push the Temp button and rotate the dial to set the temperature at 350 degrees F. Press "Start/Pause" button to start. When the unit beeps to show that it is preheated, open the lid. Arrange pan over the "Wire Rack" and insert in the oven. After 4 minutes, sprinkle the omelet with cheese evenly. Cut the omelet into 2 portions and serve hot. Cut into equal-sized wedges and serve hot.

271. Lemon Pepper Turkey

Servings: 6   Cooking Time: 45 Minutes
Ingredients:

3 lbs. turkey breast	1 teaspoon lemon pepper
2 tablespoons oil	
1 tablespoon Worcestershire sauce	1/2 teaspoon salt

Directions:
Whisk everything in a bowl and coat the turkey liberally. Place the turkey in the Air fryer basket. Press "Power Button" of Air Fry Oven and turn the dial to select the "Air Fry" mode. Press the Time button and again turn the dial to set the cooking time to 45 minutes. Now push the Temp button and rotate the dial to set the temperature at 375 degrees F. Once preheated, place the air fryer basket inside and close its lid. Serve warm.

272. Zucchini Stew

Servings: 4   Cooking Time: 12 Minutes
Ingredients:

8 zucchinis, roughly cubed	1 tbsp. olive oil
¼ cup tomato sauce	¼ tsp. rosemary; dried

½ tsp. basil; chopped.	Salt and black pepper to taste.

Directions:
Grease a pan that fits your air fryer with the oil, add all the ingredients, toss, introduce the pan in the fryer and cook at 350°F for 12 minutes Divide into bowls and serve.

273. Sweet Potato Chips

Servings: 2   Cooking Time: 40 Minutes
Ingredients:

2 sweet potatoes	Olive oil
Salt and pepper to taste	Cinnamon

Directions:
Start by preheating toaster oven to 400°F. Cut off each end of potato and discard. Cut potatoes into 1/2-inch slices. Brush a pan with olive oil and lay potato slices flat on the pan. Bake for 20 minutes, then flip and bake for another 20.

274. Jicama Fries(1)

Servings: 4   Cooking Time: 12 Minutes
Ingredients:

1 small jicama; peeled.	¼ tsp. ground black pepper
¼ tsp. onion powder.	
¾tsp. chili powder	¼ tsp. garlic powder.

Directions:
Cut jicama into matchstick-sized pieces. Place pieces into a small bowl and sprinkle with remaining ingredients. Place the fries into the air fryer basket Adjust the temperature to 350 Degrees F and set the timer for 20 minutes. Toss the basket two or three times during cooking. Serve warm.

275. Vegetarian Philly Sandwich

Servings: 2   Cooking Time: 20 Minutes
Ingredients:

2 tablespoons olive oil	1 green bell pepper, thinly sliced
8 ounces sliced portabello mushrooms	1 red bell pepper, thinly sliced
1 vidalia onion, thinly sliced	4 slices 2% provolone cheese
Salt and pepper	4 rolls

Directions:
Preheat toaster oven to 475°F. Heat the oil in a medium sauce pan over medium heat. Sauté mushrooms about 5 minutes, then add the onions and peppers and sauté another 10 minutes. Slice rolls lengthwise and divide the vegetables into each roll. Add the cheese and toast until the rolls start to brown and the cheese melts.

276. Sweet Potato Rosti

Servings: 2   Cooking Time: 15 Minutes
Ingredients:

½ lb. sweet potatoes, peeled, grated and squeezed	1 tablespoon fresh parsley, chopped finely

Salt and ground black pepper, as required | 2 tablespoons sour cream

Directions:
In a large bowl, mix together the grated sweet potato, parsley, salt, and black pepper. Press "Power Button" of Air Fry Oven and turn the dial to select the "Air Fry" mode. Press the Time button and again turn the dial to set the cooking time to 15 minutes. Now push the Temp button and rotate the dial to set the temperature at 355 degrees F. Press "Start/Pause" button to start. When the unit beeps to show that it is preheated, open the lid and lightly, grease the sheet pan. Arrange the sweet potato mixture into the "Sheet Pan" and shape it into an even circle. Insert the "Sheet Pan" in the oven. Cut the potato rosti into wedges. Top with the sour cream and serve immediately.

277. Carrot And Beef Cocktail Balls

Servings: 10   Cooking Time: 20 Minutes
Ingredients:

1-pound ground beef	1 teaspoon dried
2 carrots	oregano
1 red onion, peeled and chopped	1 egg
	3/4 cup breadcrumbs
2 cloves garlic	1/2 teaspoon salt
1/2 teaspoon dried rosemary, crushed	1/2 teaspoon black pepper, or to taste
1/2 teaspoon dried basil	1 cup plain flour

Directions:
Preparing the ingredients. Place ground beef in a large bowl. In a food processor, pulse the carrot, onion and garlic; transfer the vegetable mixture to a large-sized bowl. Then, add the rosemary, basil, oregano, egg, breadcrumbs, salt, and black pepper. Shape the mixture into even balls; refrigerate for about 30 minutes. Roll the balls into the flour. Air frying. Close air fryer lid. Then, air-fry the balls at 350 degrees f for about 20 minutes, turning occasionally; work with batches. Serve with toothpicks.

278. Coriander Potatoes

Servings: 4   Cooking Time: 25 Minutes
Ingredients:

Salt and black pepper to the taste	1 pound gold potatoes, peeled and cut into wedges
1 tablespoon tomato sauce	1 teaspoon chili powder
2 tablespoons coriander, chopped	1 tablespoon olive oil
½ teaspoon garlic powder	

Directions:
In a bowl, combine the potatoes with the tomato sauce and the other Ingredients:, toss, and transfer to the air fryer's basket. Cook at 370 degrees F for 25 minutes, divide between plates and serve as a side dish.

279. Herbed Radish Sauté(3)

Servings: 4   Cooking Time: 12 Minutes
Ingredients:

2 bunches red radishes; halved	2 tbsp. balsamic vinegar
2 tbsp. parsley; chopped.	Salt and black pepper to taste.
1 tbsp. olive oil	

Directions:
Take a bowl and mix the radishes with the remaining ingredients except the parsley, toss and put them in your air fryer's basket. Cook at 400°F for 15 minutes, divide between plates, sprinkle the parsley on top and serve as a side dish

280. Sweet & Sour Pork

Servings: 4   Cooking Time: 27 Minutes
Ingredients:

2 pounds Pork cut into chunks	1/4 teaspoon Freshly Ground Black Pepper
2 large Eggs	1/16 teaspoon Chinese Five Spice
1 teaspoon Pure Sesame Oil (optional)	3 Tablespoons Canola Oil
1 cup Potato Starch (or cornstarch)	Oil Mister
1/2 teaspoon Sea Salt	

Directions:
In a mixing bowl, combine salt, potato starch, Chinese Five Spice, and peppers. In another bowl, beat the eggs & add sesame oil. Then dredge the pieces of Pork into the Potato Starch and remove the excess. Then dip each piece into the egg mixture, shake off excess, and then back into the Potato Starch mixture. Place pork pieces into the Instant Pot Duo Crisp Air Fryer Basket after spray the pork with oil. Close the Air Fryer lid and cook at 340°F for approximately 8 to12 minutes (or until pork is cooked), shaking the basket a couple of times for evenly distribution.

281. Perfect Size French Fries

Servings: 1   Cooking Time: 30 Minutes
Ingredients:

1 medium potato	Salt and pepper to taste
1 tablespoon olive oil	

Directions:
Start by preheating your oven to 425°F. Clean the potato and cut it into fries or wedges. Place fries in a bowl of cold water to rinse. Lay the fries on a thick sheet of paper towels and pat dry. Toss in a bowl with oil, salt, and pepper. Bake for 30 minutes.

282. Easy Turkey Breasts With Basil

Servings: 4   Cooking Time: 10 Minutes
Ingredients:

2 pounds turkey breasts, bone-in skin-on	2 tablespoons olive oil
Coarse sea salt and	1 teaspoon fresh basil leaves, chopped

ground black pepper, to taste   2 tablespoons lemon zest, grated

Directions:
Rub olive oil on all sides of the turkey breasts; sprinkle with salt, pepper, basil, and lemon zest. Place the turkey breasts skin side up on a parchment-lined cooking basket.   Cook in the preheated Air Fryer at 330 degrees F for 30 minutes. Now, turn them over and cook an additional 28 minutes.   Serve with lemon wedges, if desired.

283.	Squash And Zucchini Mini Pizza

Servings: 4   Cooking Time: 15 Minutes
Ingredients:

1 pizza crust	1 yellow summer
1/2 cup parmesan	squash
cheese	Olive oil
4 tablespoons	Salt and pepper
oregano	
1 zucchini	

Directions:
Start by preheating toaster oven to 350°F.   If you are using homemade crust, roll out 8 mini portions; if crust is store-bought, use a cookie cutter to cut out the portions.   Sprinkle parmesan and oregano equally on each piece. Layer the zucchini and squash in a circle – one on top of the other – around the entire circle.   Brush with olive oil and sprinkle salt and pepper to taste.   Bake for 15 minutes and serve.

284.	Chicken Parmesan

Servings: 4   Cooking Time: 10 Minutes
Ingredients:

2 (6-oz. boneless, skinless chicken breasts	1 oz. pork rinds, crushed
1 cup low-carb, no-sugar-added pasta sauce.	½ cup grated Parmesan cheese, divided.
1 cup shredded mozzarella cheese, divided.	4 tbsp. full-fat mayonnaise, divided.
	½ tsp. garlic powder.
	¼ tsp. dried oregano.
	½ tsp. dried parsley.

Directions:
Slice each chicken breast in half lengthwise and lb. out to 3/4-inch thickness. Sprinkle with garlic powder, oregano and parsley   Spread 1 tbsp. mayonnaise on top of each piece of chicken, then sprinkle ¼ cup mozzarella on each piece.   In a small bowl, mix the crushed pork rinds and Parmesan. Sprinkle the mixture on top of mozzarella Pour sauce into 6-inch round baking pan and place chicken on top. Place pan into the air fryer basket. Adjust the temperature to 320 Degrees F and set the timer for 25 minutes   Cheese will be browned and internal temperature of the chicken will be at least 165 Degrees F when fully cooked. Serve warm.

285.	Crispy Breaded Pork Chop

Servings: 6   Cooking Time: 12 Minutes
Ingredients:

olive oil spray	1 large egg, beaten
6 3/4-inch thick center-cut boneless pork chops, fat trimmed (5 oz each)	2 tbsp grated parmesan cheese
	1 1/4 tsp sweet paprika
kosher salt	1/2 tsp garlic powder
1/2 cup panko crumbs, check labels for GF	1/2 tsp onion powder
	1/4 tsp chili powder
1/3 cup crushed cornflakes crumbs	1/8 tsp black pepper

Directions:
Preheat the Instant Pot Duo Crisp Air Fryer for 12 minutes at 400°F.   On both sides, season pork chops with half teaspoon kosher salt.   Then combine cornflake crumbs, panko, parmesan cheese, 3/4 tsp kosher salt, garlic powder, paprika, onion powder, chili powder, and black pepper in a large bowl.   Place the egg beat in another bowl. Dip the pork in the egg & then crumb mixture.   When the air fryer is ready, place 3 of the chops into the Instant Pot Duo Crisp Air Fryer Basket and spritz the top with oil.   Close the Air Fryer lid and cook for 12 minutes turning halfway, spritzing both sides with oil.   Set aside and repeat with the remaining.

286.	Philly Cheesesteak Egg Rolls

Servings: 4-5   Cooking Time: 20 Minutes
Ingredients:

1 egg	1 pound thinly slice
1 tablespoon milk	roast beef
2 tablespoons olive oil	8 ounces shredded pepper jack cheese
1 small red onion	8 ounces shredded provolone cheese
1 small red bell pepper	8-10 egg roll skins
1 small green bell pepper	Salt and pepper

Directions:
Start by preheating toaster oven to 425°F.   Mix together egg and milk in a shallow bowl and set aside for later use.   Chop onions and bell peppers into small pieces.   Heat the oil in a medium sauce pan and add the onions and peppers.   Cook onions and peppers for 2–3 minutes until softened.   Add roast beef to the pan and sauté for another 5 minutes. Add salt and pepper to taste.   Add cheese and mix together until melted.   Remove from heat and drain liquid from pan.   Roll the egg roll skins flat. Add equal parts of the mix to each egg roll and roll them up per the instructions on the package. Brush each egg roll with the egg mixture.   Line a pan with parchment paper and lay egg rolls seam-side down with a gap between each roll.   Bake for 20–25 minutes, depending on your preference of egg roll crispness.

287.	Air Fryer Beef Steak

Servings: 4   Cooking Time: 15 Minutes

Ingredients:

1 tbsp. Olive oil	2 pounds of ribeye
Pepper and salt	steak

Directions:

Preparing the ingredients. Season meat on both sides with pepper and salt. Rub all sides of meat with olive oil. Preheat instant crisp air fryer to 356 degrees and spritz with olive oil. Air frying. Close air fryer lid. Set temperature to 356°f, and set time to 7 minutes. Cook steak 7 minutes. Flip and cook an additional 6 minutes. Let meat sit 2-5 minutes to rest. Slice and serve with salad.

288. Moroccan Pork Kebabs

Servings: 4   Cooking Time: 45 Minutes

Ingredients:

1/4 cup orange juice	3/4 teaspoon black
1 tablespoon tomato	pepper
paste	1-1/2 pounds
1 clove chopped garlic	boneless pork loin
1 tablespoon ground	1 small eggplant
cumin	1 small red onion
1/8 teaspoon ground	Pita bread (optional)
cinnamon	1/2 small cucumber
4 tablespoons olive	2 tablespoons
oil	chopped fresh mint
1-1/2 teaspoons salt	Wooden skewers

Directions:

Start by placing wooden skewers in water to soak. Cut pork loin and eggplant into 1- to 1-1/2-inch chunks. Preheat toaster oven to 425°F. Cut cucumber and onions into pieces and chop the mint. In a large bowl, combine the orange juice, tomato paste, garlic, cumin, cinnamon, 2 tablespoons of oil, 1 teaspoon of salt, and 1/2 teaspoon of pepper. Add the pork to this mixture and refrigerate for at least 30 minutes, but up to 8 hours. Mix together vegetables, remaining oil, and salt and pepper. Skewer the vegetables and bake for 20 minutes. Add the pork to the skewers and bake for an additional 25 minutes. Remove ingredients from skewers and sprinkle with mint; serve with flatbread if using.

289. Duck Breast With Figs

Servings: 2   Cooking Time: 45 Minutes

Ingredients:

1 pound boneless	2 tablespoons lemon
duck breast	juice
6 fresh figs, halved	3 tablespoons brown
1 tablespoon fresh	sugar
thyme, chopped	1 teaspoon olive oil
2 cups fresh	Salt and black
pomegranate juice	pepper, as required

Directions:

Preheat the Air fryer to 400 degree F and grease an Air fryer basket. Put the pomegranate juice, lemon juice, and brown sugar in a medium saucepan over medium heat. Bring to a boil and simmer on low heat for about 25 minutes. Season the duck breasts generously with salt and black pepper. Arrange the duck breasts into the Air fryer basket, skin side up and cook for about 14 minutes, flipping once in between. Dish out the duck breasts onto a cutting board for about 10 minutes. Meanwhile, put the figs, olive oil, salt, and black pepper in a bowl until well mixed. Set the Air fryer to 400 degree F and arrange the figs into the Air fryer basket. Cook for about 5 more minutes and dish out in a platter. Put the duck breast with the roasted figs and drizzle with warm pomegranate juice mixture. Garnish with fresh thyme and serve warm.

290. Delicious Chicken Burgers

Servings: 4   Cooking Time: 30 Minutes

Ingredients:

4 boneless, skinless	½ teaspoon paprika
chicken breasts	¼ teaspoon dried
1¾ ounces plain flour	tarragon
2 eggs	¼ teaspoon dried
4 hamburger buns,	oregano
split and toasted	1 teaspoon dried
4 mozzarella cheese	garlic
slices	1 teaspoon chicken
1 teaspoon mustard	seasoning
powder	½ teaspoon cayenne
1 teaspoon	pepper
Worcestershire sauce	Salt and black
¼ teaspoon dried	pepper, as required
parsley	

Directions:

Preheat the Air fryer to 355 degree F and grease an Air fryer basket. Put the chicken breasts, mustard, paprika, Worcestershire sauce, salt, and black pepper in a food processor and pulse until minced. Make 4 equal-sized patties from the mixture. Place the flour in a shallow bowl and whisk the egg in a second bowl. Combine dried herbs and spices in a third bowl. Coat each chicken patty with flour, dip into whisked egg and then coat with breadcrumb mixture. Arrange the chicken patties into the Air fryer basket in a single layer and cook for about 30 minutes, flipping once in between. Place half bun in a plate, layer with lettuce leaf, patty and cheese slice. Cover with bun top and dish out to serve warm.

291. Chicken Legs With Dilled Brussels Sprouts

Servings: 2   Cooking Time: 10 Minutes

Ingredients:

2 chicken legs	1/2 teaspoon paprika
1/2 teaspoon kosher	1/2 pound Brussels
salt	sprouts
1/2 teaspoon black	1 teaspoon dill, fresh
pepper	or dried

Directions:

Start by preheating your Air Fryer to 370 degrees F. Now, season your chicken with paprika, salt, and pepper. Transfer the chicken legs to the cooking basket. Cook for 10 minutes. Flip the chicken legs and cook an additional 10 minutes. Reserve. Add the Brussels sprouts to the cooking basket; sprinkle with dill. Cook at 380 degrees F for 15 minutes, shaking the basket halfway through.   Serve with the reserved chicken legs.

292.   Herb-roasted Turkey Breast

Servings: 8   Cooking Time: 60 Minutes
Ingredients:

3 lb turkey breast	2 tsp kosher salt
Rub Ingredients:	1 tsp pepper
2 tbsp olive oil	1 tsp dried rosemary
2 tbsp lemon juice	1 tsp dried thyme
1 tbsp minced Garlic	1 tsp ground sage
2 tsp ground mustard	

Directions:
Take a small bowl and thoroughly combine the Rub Ingredients: in it. Rub this on the outside of the turkey breast and under any loose skin.   Place the coated turkey breast keeping skin side up on a cooking tray.   Place the drip pan at the bottom of the cooking chamber of the Instant Pot Duo Crisp Air Fryer. Select Air Fry option, post this, adjust the temperature to 360°F and the time to one hour, then touch start.   When preheated, add the food to the cooking tray in the lowest position. Close the lid for cooking.   When the Air Fry program is complete, check to make sure that the thickest portion of the meat reads at least 160°F, remove the turkey and let it rest for 10 minutes before slicing and serving.

293.   Bbq Chicken Breasts

Servings: 4   Cooking Time: 15 Minutes
Ingredients:

4 boneless skinless chicken breast about 6 oz each	1-2 Tbsp bbq seasoning

Directions:
Cover both sides of chicken breast with the BBQ seasoning. Cover and marinate the in the refrigerator for 45 minutes.   Choose the Air Fry option and set the temperature to 400°F. Push start and let it preheat for 5 minutes.   Upon preheating, place the chicken breast in the Instant Pot Duo Crisp Air Fryer basket, making sure they do not overlap. Spray with oil.   Cook for 13-14 minutes flipping halfway.   Remove chicken when the chicken reaches an internal temperature of 160°F. Place on a plate and allow to rest for 5 minutes before slicing.

294.   Chicken Breasts With Chimichurri

Servings: 1   Cooking Time: 35 Minutes
Ingredients:

1 chicken breast, bone-in, skin-on	Chimichurri
1/2 bunch fresh cilantro	1 teaspoon salt
1/4 bunch fresh parsley	1/2 teaspoon garlic powder
1/2 shallot, peeled, cut in quarters	1/2 teaspoon cumin ground
1/2 tablespoon paprika ground	1/2 tablespoon canola oil
1/2 tablespoon chili	Chimichurri
	2 tablespoons olive

powder	oil
1/2 tablespoon fennel ground	4 garlic cloves, peeled
1/2 teaspoon black pepper, ground	Zest and juice of 1 lemon
1/2 teaspoon onion powder	1 teaspoon kosher salt

Directions:
Preheat the Air fryer to 300 degree F and grease an Air fryer basket.   Combine all the spices in a suitable bowl and season the chicken with it. Sprinkle with canola oil and arrange the chicken in the Air fryer basket.   Cook for about 35 minutes and dish out in a platter.   Put all the ingredients in the blender and blend until smooth.   Serve the chicken with chimichurri sauce.

295.   Butter Fish With Sake And Miso

Servings: 4   Cooking Time: 11 Minutes
Ingredients:

4 (7-ounce) pieces of butter fish	1/3 cup mirin
1/3 cup sake	2/3 cup sugar
	1 cup white miso

Directions:
Start by combining sake, mirin, and sugar in a sauce pan and bring to a boil.   Allow to boil for 5 minutes, then reduce heat and simmer for another 10 minutes.   Remove from heat completely and mix in miso.   Marinate the fish in the mixture for as long as possible, up to 3 days if possible. Preheat toaster oven to 450°F and bake fish for 8 minutes.   Switch your setting to Broil and broil another 2-3 minutes, until the sauce is caramelized.

296.   Orange Chicken Rice

Servings: 4   Cooking Time: 55 Minutes
Ingredients:

3 tablespoons olive oil	Salt to taste
1 medium onion, chopped	4 (6-oz.) boneless, skinless chicken thighs
1 3/4 cups chicken broth	Black pepper, to taste
1 cup brown basmati rice	2 tablespoons fresh mint, chopped
Zest and juice of 2 oranges	2 tablespoons pine nuts, toasted

Directions:
Spread the rice in a casserole dish and place the chicken on top.   Toss the rest of the Ingredients: in a bowl and liberally pour over the chicken. Press "Power Button" of Air Fry Oven and turn the dial to select the "Bake" mode.   Press the Time button and again turn the dial to set the cooking time to 55 minutes.   Now push the Temp button and rotate the dial to set the temperature at 350 degrees F.   Once preheated, place the casserole dish inside and close its lid.   Serve warm.

297.   Herbed Duck Legs

Servings: 2   Cooking Time: 30 Minutes

Ingredients:

½ tablespoon fresh thyme, chopped	2 duck legs
½ tablespoon fresh parsley, chopped	1 teaspoon five spice powder
1 garlic clove, minced	Salt and black pepper, as required

Directions:
Preheat the Air fryer to 340 degree F and grease an Air fryer basket. Mix the garlic, herbs, five spice powder, salt, and black pepper in a bowl. Rub the duck legs with garlic mixture generously and arrange into the Air fryer basket. Cook for about 25 minutes and set the Air fryer to 390 degree F. Cook for 5 more minutes and dish out to serve hot.

298. Chicken & Rice Casserole

Servings: 6   Cooking Time: 40 Minutes

Ingredients:

2 lbs. bone-in chicken thighs	1 teaspoon hot Hungarian paprika
Salt and black pepper	2 tablespoons tomato paste
1 teaspoon olive oil	2 cups chicken broth
5 cloves garlic, chopped	3 cups brown rice, thawed
2 large onions, chopped	2 tablespoons parsley, chopped
2 large red bell peppers, chopped	6 tablespoons sour cream
1 tablespoon sweet Hungarian paprika	

Directions:
Mix broth, tomato paste, and all the spices in a bowl. Add chicken and mix well to coat. Spread the rice in a casserole dish and add chicken along with its marinade. Top the casserole with the rest of the Ingredients:. Press "Power Button" of Air Fry Oven and turn the dial to select the "Bake" mode. Press the Time button and again turn the dial to set the cooking time to 40 minutes. Now push the Temp button and rotate the dial to set the temperature at 350 degrees F. Once preheated, place the baking pan inside and close its lid. Serve warm.

299. Turkey And Almonds

Servings: 2   Cooking Time: 10 Minutes

Ingredients:

1 big turkey breast, skinless; boneless and halved	2 shallots; chopped
	1 tbsp. sweet paprika
1/3 cup almonds; chopped	2 tbsp. olive oil
	Salt and black pepper to taste.

Directions:
In a pan that fits the air fryer, combine the turkey with all the other ingredients, toss. Put the pan in the machine and cook at 370°F for 25 minutes Divide everything between plates and serve.

300. Buttered Duck Breasts

Servings: 4   Cooking Time: 22 Minutes

Ingredients:

2: 12-ounces duck breasts	3 tablespoons unsalted butter, melted
Salt and ground black pepper, as required	¼ teaspoon star anise powder
½ teaspoon dried thyme, crushed	

Directions:
Preheat the Air fryer to 390 degree F and grease an Air fryer basket. Season the duck breasts generously with salt and black pepper. Arrange the duck breasts into the prepared Air fryer basket and cook for about 10 minutes. Dish out the duck breasts and drizzle with melted butter. Season with thyme and star anise powder and place the duck breasts again into the Air fryer basket. Cook for about 12 more minutes and dish out to serve warm.

301. Boneless Air Fryer Turkey Breasts

Servings: 4   Cooking Time: 50 Minutes

Ingredients:

3 lb boneless breast	1 tsp salt
¼ cup mayonnaise	½ tsp garlic powder
2 tsp poultry seasoning	¼ tsp black pepper

Directions:
Choose the Air Fry option on the Instant Pot Duo Crisp Air fryer. Set the temperature to 360°F and push start. The preheating will start. Season your boneless turkey breast with mayonnaise, poultry seasoning, salt, garlic powder, and black pepper. Once preheated, Air Fry the turkey breasts on 360°F for 1 hour, turning every 15 minutes or until internal temperature has reached a temperature of 165°F.

302. Simple Turkey Breast

Servings: 10   Cooking Time: 40 Minutes

Ingredients:

1: 8-pounds bone-in turkey breast	2 tablespoons olive oil
Salt and black pepper, as required	

Directions:
Preheat the Air fryer to 360 degree F and grease an Air fryer basket. Season the turkey breast with salt and black pepper and drizzle with oil. Arrange the turkey breast into the Air Fryer basket, skin side down and cook for about 20 minutes. Flip the side and cook for another 20 minutes. Dish out in a platter and cut into desired size slices to serve.

303. Nutmeg Chicken Thighs

Servings: 4   Cooking Time: 10 Minutes

Ingredients:

2 lb. chicken thighs	A pinch of salt and black pepper
2 tbsp. olive oil	
½ tsp. nutmeg, ground	

Directions:

Season the chicken thighs with salt and pepper and rub with the rest of the ingredients   Put the chicken thighs in air fryer's basket, cook at 360°F for 15 minutes on each side, divide between plates and serve.

304.   Glazed Lamb Chops

Servings: 4   Cooking Time: 15 Minutes

Ingredients:

1 tablespoon Dijon mustard	½ teaspoon olive oil
½ tablespoon fresh lime juice	Salt and ground black pepper, as required
1 teaspoon honey	4 (4-ounce) lamb loin chops

Directions:

In a black pepper large bowl, mix together the mustard, lemon juice, oil, honey, salt, and black pepper.   Add the chops and coat with the mixture generously.   Place the chops onto the greased "Sheet Pan".   Press "Power Button" of Ninja Foodi Digital Air Fry Oven and turn the dial to select the "Air Bake" mode.   Press the Time button and again turn the dial to set the cooking time to 15 minutes.   Now push the Temp button and rotate the dial to set the temperature at 390 degrees F. Press "Start/Pause" button to start.   When the unit beeps to show that it is preheated, open the lid. Insert the "Sheet Pan" in oven.   Flip the chops once halfway through.   Serve hot.

305.   Air Fried Steak Sandwich

Servings: 4   Cooking Time: 16 Minutes

Ingredients:

Large hoagie bun, sliced in half	1 tablespoon of fresh bleu cheese, crumbled
6 ounces of sirloin or flank steak, sliced into bite-sized pieces	8 medium-sized cherry tomatoes, sliced in half
½ tablespoon of mustard powder	1 cup of fresh arugula, rinsed and patted dry
½ tablespoon of soy sauce	

Directions:

Preparing the ingredients. In a small mixing bowl, combine the soy sauce and onion powder; stir with a fork until thoroughly combined.   Lay the raw steak strips in the soy-mustard mixture, and fully immerse each piece to marinate.   Set the instant crisp air fryer to 320 degrees for 10 minutes. Arrange the soy-mustard marinated steak pieces on a piece of tin foil, flat and not overlapping, and set the tin foil on one side of the instant crisp air fryer basket. The foil should not take up more than half of the surface.   Lay the hoagie-bun halves, crusty-side up and soft-side down, on the other half of the air-fryer.   Air frying. Close air fryer lid.   After 10 minutes, the instant crisp air fryer will shut off; the hoagie buns should be starting to crisp and the steak will have begun to cook.   Carefully, flip the hoagie buns so they are now crusty-side down and soft-side up; crumble a layer of the bleu cheese on each hoagie half.   With a long spoon, gently stir the marinated

steak in the foil to ensure even coverage.   Set the instant crisp air fryer to 360 degrees for 6 minutes. After 6 minutes, when the fryer shuts off, the bleu cheese will be perfectly melted over the toasted bread, and the steak will be juicy on the inside and crispy on the outside.   Remove the cheesy hoagie halves first, using tongs, and set on a serving plate; then cover one side with the steak, and top with the cherry-tomato halves and the arugula. Close with the other cheesy hoagie-half, slice into two pieces, and enjoy.

306.   Okra Casserole

Servings: 4   Cooking Time: 12 Minutes

Ingredients:

2 red bell peppers; cubed	¼ cup tomato puree
2 tomatoes; chopped.	1 tbsp. cilantro; chopped.
3 garlic cloves; minced	1 tsp. olive oil
3 cups okra	2 tsp. coriander, ground
½ cup cheddar; shredded	Salt and black pepper to taste.

Directions:

Grease a heat proof dish that fits your air fryer with the oil, add all the ingredients except the cilantro and the cheese and toss them really gently Sprinkle the cheese and the cilantro on top, introduce the dish in the fryer and cook at 390°F for 20 minutes.   Divide between plates and serve for lunch.

307.   Roasted Beet Salad With Oranges & Beet Greens

Servings: 6   Cooking Time: 1-1/2 Hours

Ingredients:

6 medium beets with beet greens attached	1/4 cup extra-virgin olive oil
2 large oranges	2 garlic cloves, minced
1 small sweet onion, cut into wedges	1/2 teaspoon grated orange peel
1/3 cup red wine vinegar	

Directions:

Start by preheating toaster oven to 400°F.   Trim leaves from beets and chop, then set aside.   Pierce beets with a fork and place in a roasting pan. Roast beets for 1-1/2 hours.   Allow beets to cool, peel, then cut into 8 wedges and put into a bowl. Place beet greens in a sauce pan and cover with just enough water to cover. Heat until water boils, then immediately remove from heat.   Drain greens and press to remove liquid from greens, then add to beet bowl.   Remove peel and pith from orange and segment, adding each segment to the bowl.   Add onion to beet mixture. In a separate bowl mix together vinegar, oil, garlic and orange peel. Combine both bowls and toss, sprinkle with salt and pepper.   Let stand for an hour before serving.

308.   Chicken Potato Bake

Servings: 4   Cooking Time: 25 Minutes

Ingredients:

- 4 potatoes, diced
- 1 tablespoon garlic, minced
- 1.5 tablespoons olive oil
- 1/8 teaspoon salt
- 1/8 teaspoon pepper
- 1.5 lbs. boneless skinless chicken
- 3/4 cup mozzarella cheese, shredded
- parsley chopped

Directions:

Toss chicken and potatoes with all the spices and oil in a baking pan. Drizzle the cheese on top of the chicken and potato. Press "Power Button" of Air Fry Oven and turn the dial to select the "Bake" mode. Press the Time button and again turn the dial to set the cooking time to 25 minutes. Now push the Temp button and rotate the dial to set the temperature at 375 degrees F. Once preheated, place the baking pan inside and close its lid. Serve warm.

309. Chili Chicken Sliders

Servings: 4   Cooking Time: 10 Minutes

Ingredients:

- 1/3 teaspoon paprika
- 1/3 cup scallions, peeled and chopped
- 3 cloves garlic, peeled and minced
- 1 teaspoon ground black pepper, or to taste
- 1/2 teaspoon fresh basil, minced
- 1 ½ cups chicken, minced
- 1 ½ tablespoons coconut aminos
- 1/2 teaspoon grated fresh ginger
- 1/2 tablespoon chili sauce
- 1 teaspoon salt

Directions:

Thoroughly combine all ingredients in a mixing dish. Then, form into 4 patties. Cook in the preheated Air Fryer for 18 minutes at 355 degrees F. Garnish with toppings of choice.

310. Lime And Mustard Marinated Chicken

Servings: 4   Cooking Time: 10 Minutes

Ingredients:

- 1/2 teaspoon stone-ground mustard
- 1/2 teaspoon minced fresh oregano
- 1teaspoon freshly cracked mixed peppercorns
- 1/3 cup freshly squeezed lime juice
- 2 small-sized chicken breasts, skin-on
- 1 teaspoon kosher salt

Directions:

Preheat your Air Fryer to 345 degrees F. Toss all of the above ingredients in a medium-sized mixing dish; allow it to marinate overnight. Cook in the preheated Air Fryer for 26 minutes.

311. Turkey Meatballs With Manchego Cheese

Servings: 4   Cooking Time: 10 Minutes

Ingredients:

- 1 pound ground turkey
- 1/2 pound ground
- 2 tablespoons yellow onions, finely chopped
- pork
- 1 egg, well beaten
- 1 teaspoon dried basil
- 1 teaspoon dried rosemary
- 1/4 cup Manchego cheese, grated
- 1 teaspoon fresh garlic, finely chopped
- Sea salt and ground black pepper, to taste

Directions:

In a mixing bowl, combine all the ingredients until everything is well incorporated. Shape the mixture into 1-inch balls. Cook the meatballs in the preheated Air Fryer at 380 degrees for 7 minutes. Shake halfway through the cooking time. Work in batches. Serve with your favorite pasta.

312. Easy Italian Meatballs

Servings: 4   Cooking Time: 13 Minutes

Ingredients:

- 2-lb. lean ground turkey
- ¼ cup onion, minced
- 2 cloves garlic, minced
- 2 tablespoons parsley, chopped
- 2 eggs
- 1½ cup parmesan cheese, grated
- ½ teaspoon red pepper flakes
- ½ teaspoon Italian seasoning Salt and black pepper to taste

Directions:

Toss all the meatball Ingredients: in a bowl and mix well. Make small meatballs out this mixture and place them in the air fryer basket. Press "Power Button" of Air Fry Oven and turn the dial to select the "Air Fry" mode. Press the Time button and again turn the dial to set the cooking time to 13 minutes. Now push the Temp button and rotate the dial to set the temperature at 350 degrees F. Once preheated, place the air fryer basket inside and close its lid. Flip the meatballs when cooked halfway through. Serve warm.

313. Beef Steaks With Beans

Servings: 4   Cooking Time: 10 Minutes

Ingredients:

- 4 beef steaks, trim the fat and cut into strips
- 1 cup green onions, chopped
- 2 cloves garlic, minced
- 1 red bell pepper, seeded and thinly sliced
- 1 can tomatoes, crushed
- 1 can cannellini beans
- 3/4 cup beef broth
- 1/4 teaspoon dried basil
- 1/2 teaspoon cayenne pepper
- 1/2 teaspoon sea salt
- 1/4 teaspoon ground black pepper, or to taste

Directions:

Preparing the ingredients. Add the steaks, green onions and garlic to the instant crisp air fryer basket. Air frying. Close air fryer lid. Cook at 390 degrees f for 10 minutes, working in batches. Stir in the remaining ingredients and cook for an additional 5 minutes.

314. Spicy Green Crusted Chicken

Servings: 6   Cooking Time: 40 Minutes

Ingredients:

6 eggs, beaten	6 teaspoons oregano
6 teaspoons parsley	Salt and freshly
4 teaspoons thyme	ground black pepper,
1 pound chicken	to taste
pieces	4 teaspoons paprika

Directions:

Preheat the Air fryer to 360 degree F and grease an Air fryer basket.   Whisk eggs in a bowl and mix all the ingredients in another bowl except chicken pieces.   Dip the chicken in eggs and then coat generously with the dry mixture.   Arrange half of the chicken pieces in the Air fryer basket and cook for about 20 minutes.   Repeat with the remaining mixture and dish out to serve hot.

315. Air Fryer Fish

Servings: 4   Cooking Time: 17 Minutes

Ingredients:

4-6 Whiting Fish fillets cut in half	¼ cup flour
Oil to mist	2 tsp old bay
Fish Seasoning	1 ½ tsp salt
¾ cup very fine cornmeal	1 tsp paprika
	½ tsp garlic powder
	½ tsp black pepper

Directions:

Put the Ingredients: for fish seasoning in a Ziplock bag and shake it well. Set aside.   Rinse and pat dry the fish fillets with paper towels. Make sure that they still are damp.   Place the fish fillets in a ziplock bag and shake until they are completely covered with seasoning.   Place the fillets on a baking rack to let any excess flour to fall off.   Grease the bottom of the Instant Pot Duo Crisp Air Fryer basket tray and place the fillets on the tray. Close the lid, select the Air Fry option and cook filets on 400°F for 10 minutes.   Open the Air Fryer lid and spray the fish with oil on the side facing up before flipping it over, ensure that the fish is fully coated. Flip and cook another side of the fish for 7 minutes. Remove the fish and serve.

316. Air Fryer Marinated Salmon

Servings: 4   Cooking Time: 12 Minutes

Ingredients:

4 salmon fillets or 1 1lb fillet cut into 4 pieces	6 Tbsps Soy Sauce
	¼ cup Dijon Mustard
1 Tbsp brown sugar	1 Green onions finely chopped
½ Tbsp Minced Garlic	

Directions:

Take a bowl and whisk together soy sauce, dijon mustard, brown sugar, and minced garlic. Pour this mixture over salmon fillets, making sure that all the fillets are covered. Refrigerate and marinate for 20-30 minutes.   Remove salmon fillets from marinade and place them in greased or lined on the tray in the Instant Pot Duo Crisp Air Fryer basket, close the lid.   Select the Air Fry option and Air Fry for around 12 minutes at 400°F.   Remove from Instant Pot Duo Crisp Air Fryer and top with chopped green onions.

317. Kale And Pine Nuts

Servings: 4   Cooking Time: 12 Minutes

Ingredients:

10 cups kale; torn	1 tbsp. lemon juice
1/3 cup pine nuts	2 tbsp. olive oil
2 tbsp. lemon zest; grated	Salt and black pepper to taste.

Directions:

In a pan that fits the air fryer, combine all the ingredients, toss, introduce the pan in the machine and cook at 380°F for 15 minutes   Divide between plates and serve as a side dish.

318. Buttermilk Brined Turkey Breast

Servings: 8   Cooking Time: 20 Minutes

Ingredients:

¾ cup brine from a can of olives	2 fresh thyme sprigs
	1 fresh rosemary
3½ pounds boneless, skinless turkey breast	sprig
	½ cup buttermilk

Directions:

Preheat the Air fryer to 350 degree F and grease an Air fryer basket.   Mix olive brine and buttermilk in a bowl until well combined.   Place the turkey breast, buttermilk mixture and herb sprigs in a resealable plastic bag.   Seal the bag and refrigerate for about 12 hours.   Remove the turkey breast from bag and arrange the turkey breast into the Air fryer basket.   Cook for about 20 minutes, flipping once in between.   Dish out the turkey breast onto a cutting board and cut into desired size slices to serve.

319. Okra And Green Beans Stew

Servings: 4   Cooking Time: 12 Minutes

Ingredients:

1 lb. green beans; halved	3 tbsp. tomato sauce
	1 tbsp. thyme; chopped.
4 garlic cloves; minced	Salt and black pepper to taste.
1 cup okra	

Directions:

In a pan that fits your air fryer, mix all the ingredients, toss, introduce the pan in the air fryer and cook at 370°F for 15 minutes   Divide the stew into bowls and serve.

320. Beer Coated Duck Breast

Servings: 2   Cooking Time: 20 Minutes

Ingredients:

1 tablespoon fresh thyme, chopped	6 cherry tomatoes
	1 teaspoon mustard
1 cup beer	Salt and ground black
1: 10½-ouncesduck	pepper, as required

breast
1 tablespoon olive oil
1 tablespoon balsamic vinegar

Directions:
Preheat the Air fryer to 390 degree F and grease an Air fryer basket. Mix the olive oil, mustard, thyme, beer, salt, and black pepper in a bowl. Coat the duck breasts generously with marinade and refrigerate, covered for about 4 hours. Cover the duck breasts and arrange into the Air fryer basket. Cook for about 15 minutes and remove the foil from breast. Set the Air fryer to 355 degree F and place the duck breast and tomatoes into the Air Fryer basket. Cook for about 5 minutes and dish out the duck breasts and cherry tomatoes. Drizzle with vinegar and serve immediately.

321. Buttery Artichokes

Servings: 4   Cooking Time: 20 Minutes
Ingredients:

4 artichokes, trimmed and halved	4 tablespoons butter, melted
3 garlic cloves, minced	¼ teaspoon cumin, ground
1 tablespoon olive oil	1 tablespoon lemon zest, grated
Salt and black pepper to the taste	

Directions:
In a bowl, combine the artichokes with the oil, garlic and the other Ingredients:, toss well and transfer them to the air fryer's basket. Cook for 20 minutes at 370 degrees F, divide between plates and serve as a side dish.

322. Herb-roasted Chicken Tenders

Servings: 2   Cooking Time: 10 Minutes
Ingredients:

7 ounces chicken tenders	1/2 teaspoon Herbes de Provence
1 tablespoon olive oil	2 tablespoons Dijon mustard
1 tablespoon honey	Salt and pepper

Directions:
Start by preheating toaster oven to 450°F. Brush bottom of pan with 1/2 tablespoon olive oil. Season the chicken with herbs, salt, and pepper. Place the chicken in a single flat layer in the pan and drizzle the remaining olive oil over it. Bake for about 10 minutes. While the chicken is baking, mix together the mustard and honey for a tasty condiment.

323. Tomato Avocado Melt

Servings: 2   Cooking Time: 4 Minutes
Ingredients:

4 slices of bread	1 small Roma tomato
1-2 tablespoons mayonnaise	1/2 avocado
Cayenne pepper	8 slices of cheese of your choice

Directions:
Start by slicing avocado and tomato and set aside. Spread mayonnaise on the bread. Sprinkle cayenne pepper over the mayo to taste. Layer tomato and avocado on top of cayenne pepper. Top with cheese and put on greased baking sheet. Broil on high for 2–4 minutes, until the cheese is melted and bread is toasted.

324. Coriander Artichokes(3)

Servings: 4   Cooking Time: 12 Minutes
Ingredients:

12 oz. artichoke hearts	½ tsp. cumin seeds
1 tbsp. lemon juice	½ tsp. olive oil
1 tsp. coriander, ground	Salt and black pepper to taste.

Directions:
In a pan that fits your air fryer, mix all the ingredients, toss, introduce the pan in the fryer and cook at 370°F for 15 minutes   Divide the mix between plates and serve as a side dish.

325. Roasted Grape And Goat Cheese Crostinis

Servings: 10   Cooking Time: 5 Minutes
Ingredients:

1 pound seedless red grapes	1 rustic French baguette
1 teaspoon chopped rosemary	2 tablespoons unsalted butter
4 tablespoons olive oil	8 ounces goat cheese
1 cup sliced shallots	1 tablespoon honey

Directions:
Start by preheating toaster oven to 400°F. Toss grapes, rosemary, and 1 tablespoon of olive oil in a large bowl. Transfer to a roasting pan and roast for 20 minutes. Remove the pan from the oven and set aside to cool. Slice the baguette into 1/2-inch-thick pieces. Brush each slice with olive oil and place on baking sheet. Bake for 8 minutes, then remove from oven and set aside. In a medium skillet add butter and one tablespoon of olive oil. Add shallots and sauté for about 10 minutes. Mix goat cheese and honey in a medium bowl, then add contents of shallot pan and mix thoroughly. Spread shallot mixture onto baguette, top with grapes, and serve.

326. Maple Chicken Thighs

Servings: 4   Cooking Time: 30 Minutes
Ingredients:

4 large chicken thighs, bone-in	1 clove minced garlic
2 tablespoons French mustard	1/2 teaspoon dried marjoram
2 tablespoons Dijon mustard	2 tablespoons maple syrup

Directions:
Mix chicken with everything in a bowl and coat it well. Place the chicken along with its marinade in the baking pan. Press "Power Button" of Air Fry Oven and turn the dial to select the "Bake" mode. Press the Time button and again turn the dial to set

the cooking time to 30 minutes. Now push the Temp button and rotate the dial to set the temperature at 370 degrees F. Once preheated, place the baking pan inside and close its lid. Serve warm.

327. Bok Choy And Butter Sauce(1)

Servings: 4   Cooking Time: 12 Minutes

Ingredients:

2 bok choy heads; trimmed and cut into strips	2 tbsp. chicken stock
	1 tsp. lemon juice
	1 tbsp. olive oil
1 tbsp. butter; melted	A pinch of salt and black pepper

Directions:

In a pan that fits your air fryer, mix all the ingredients, toss, introduce the pan in the air fryer and cook at 380°F for 15 minutes. Divide between plates and serve as a side dish

328. Eggplant And Leeks Stew

Servings: 4   Cooking Time: 12 Minutes

Ingredients:

2 big eggplants, roughly cubed	3 leeks; sliced
	2 tbsp. olive oil
½ bunch cilantro; chopped.	1 tbsp. hot sauce
	1 tbsp. sweet paprika
1 cup veggie stock	1 tbsp. tomato puree
2 garlic cloves; minced	Salt and black pepper to taste.

Directions:

In a pan that fits the air fryer, mix all the ingredients, toss, introduce in the fryer and cook at 380°F for 20 minutes   Divide the stew into bowls and serve for lunch.

329. Fried Chicken Tacos

Servings: 4   Cooking Time: 10 Minutes

Ingredients:

Chicken	Coleslaw
1 lb. chicken tenders or breast chopped into 2-inch pieces	¼ tsp red pepper flakes
1 tsp garlic powder	2 cups coleslaw mix
½ tsp onion powder	1 Tbsp brown sugar
1 large egg	½ tsp salt
1 ½ tsp salt	2 Tbsp apple cider vinegar
1 tsp paprika	
3 Tbsp buttermilk	1 Tbsp water
¾ cup All-purpose flour	Spicy Mayo
	½ tsp salt
3 Tbsp corn starch	
½ tsp black pepper	¼ cup mayonnaise
½ tsp cayenne pepper	1 tsp garlic powder
oil for spraying	2 Tbsp hot sauce
	1 Tbsp buttermilk
	Tortilla wrappers

Directions:

Take a large bowl and mix together coleslaw mix, water, brown sugar, salt, apple cider vinegar, and red pepper flakes. Set aside. Take another small bowl and combine mayonnaise, hot sauce, buttermilk, garlic powder, and salt. Set this mixture aside. Select the Instant Pot Duo Crisp Air Fryer option, adjust the temperature to 360°F and push start. Preheating will start. Create a clear station by placing two large flat pans side by side. Whisk together egg and buttermilk with salt and pepper in one of them. In the second, whisk flour, corn starch, black pepper, garlic powder, onion powder, salt, paprika, and cayenne pepper. Cut the chicken tenders into 1-inch pieces. Season all pieces with a little salt and pepper. Once the Instant Pot Duo Crisp Air Fryer is preheated, remove the tray and lightly spray it with oil. Coat your chicken with egg mixture while shaking off any excess egg, followed by the flour mixture, and place it on the tray and tray in the basket, making sure your chicken pieces don't overlap. Close the Air Fryer lid, and cook on 360°F for 10 minutes while flipping and spraying halfway through cooking. Once the chicken is done, remove and place chicken into warmed tortilla shells. Top with coleslaw and spicy mayonnaise.

330. Seven-layer Tostadas

Servings: 6   Cooking Time: 5 Minutes

Ingredients:

1 (16-ounce) can refried pinto beans	1-1/2 cups guacamole
	1/2 cup thinly sliced green onions
1 cup light sour cream	
1/2 teaspoon taco seasoning	1/2 cup sliced black olives
1 cup shredded Mexican cheese blend	6-8 whole wheat flour tortillas small enough to fit in your oven
1 cup chopped tomatoes	Olive oil

Directions:

Start by placing baking sheet into toaster oven while preheating it to 450°F. Remove pan and drizzle with olive oil. Place tortillas on pan and cook in oven until they are crisp, turn at least once, this should take about 5 minutes or less. In a medium bowl, mash refried beans to break apart any chunks, then microwave for 2 1/2 minutes. Stir taco seasoning into the sour cream. Chop vegetables and halve olives. Top tortillas with ingredients in this order: refried beans, guacamole, sour cream, shredded cheese, tomatoes, onions, and olives.

331. Turmeric Mushroom(3)

Servings: 4   Cooking Time: 12 Minutes

Ingredients:

1 lb. brown mushrooms	1 tsp. olive oil
4 garlic cloves; minced	½ tsp. turmeric powder
¼ tsp. cinnamon powder	Salt and black pepper to taste.

Directions:

In a bowl, combine all the ingredients and toss. Put the mushrooms in your air fryer's basket and cook at 370°F for 15 minutes   Divide the mix between plates and serve as a side dish.

332. Deviled Chicken

Servings: 8   Cooking Time: 40 Minutes

Ingredients:

2 tablespoons butter	3/4 cup Parmesan,
2 cloves garlic,	freshly grated
chopped	1/4 cup chives,
1 cup Dijon mustard	chopped
1/2 teaspoon cayenne	2 teaspoons paprika
pepper	8 small bone-in
1 1/2 cups panko	chicken thighs, skin
breadcrumbs	removed

Directions:

Toss the chicken thighs with crumbs, cheese, chives, butter, and spices in a bowl and mix well to coat. Transfer the chicken along with its spice mix to a baking pan.   Press "Power Button" of Air Fry Oven and turn the dial to select the "Air Fry" mode. Press the Time button and again turn the dial to set the cooking time to 40 minutes.   Now push the Temp button and rotate the dial to set the temperature at 350 degrees F.   Once preheated, place the baking pan inside and close its lid.   Serve warm.

333. Turkey-stuffed Peppers

Servings: 6   Cooking Time: 35 Minutes

Ingredients:

1 pound lean ground	1/3 onion, minced
turkey	1/2 teaspoon salt
1 tablespoon olive oil	Pepper to taste
2 cloves garlic,	3 large red bell
minced	peppers
1 tablespoon cilantro	1 cup chicken broth
(optional)	1/4 cup tomato sauce
1 teaspoon garlic	1-1/2 cups cooked
powder	brown rice
1 teaspoon cumin	1/4 cup shredded
powder	cheddar
	6 green onions

Directions:

Start by preheating toaster oven to 400°F.   Heat a skillet on medium heat.   Add olive oil to the skillet, then mix in onion and garlic.   Sauté for about 5 minutes, or until the onion starts to look opaque. Add the turkey to the skillet and season with cumin, garlic powder, salt, and pepper.   Brown the meat until thoroughly cooked, then mix in chicken broth and tomato sauce.   Reduce heat and simmer for about 5 minutes, stirring occasionally.   Add the brown rice and continue stirring until it is evenly spread through the mix.   Cut the bell peppers lengthwise down the middle and remove all of the seeds.   Grease a pan or line it with parchment paper and lay all peppers in the pan with the outside facing down.   Spoon the meat mixture evenly into each pepper and use the back of the spoon to level. Bake for 30 minutes.   Remove pan from oven and sprinkle cheddar over each pepper, then put it back in for another 3 minutes, or until the cheese is melted.   While the cheese melts, dice the green onions. Remove pan from oven and sprinkle onions over each pepper and serve.

334. Rolled Salmon Sandwich

Servings: 1   Cooking Time: 5 Minutes

Ingredients:

1 piece of flatbread	Pinch of salt
1 salmon filet	1/2 teaspoon thyme
1 tablespoon green	1/2 teaspoon sesame
onion, chopped	seeds
1/4 teaspoon dried	1/4 English cucumber
sumac	1 tablespoon yogurt

Directions:

Start by peeling and chopping the cucumber. Cut the salmon at a 45-degree angle into 4 slices and lay them flat on the flatbread.   Sprinkle salmon with salt to taste. Sprinkle onions, thyme, sumac, and sesame seeds evenly over the salmon.   Broil the salmon for at least 3 minutes, but longer if you want a more well-done fish.   While you broil your salmon, mix together the yogurt and cucumber. Remove your flatbread from the toaster oven and put it on a plate, then spoon the yogurt mix over the salmon.   Fold the sides of the flatbread in and roll it up for a gourmet lunch that you can take on the go.

335. Zucchini And Cauliflower Stew

Servings: 4   Cooking Time: 12 Minutes

Ingredients:

1 cauliflower head,	2 green onions;
florets separated	chopped.
1 ½ cups zucchinis;	1 tbsp. balsamic
sliced	vinegar
1 handful parsley	1 tbsp. olive oil
leaves; chopped.	Salt and black pepper
½ cup tomato puree	to taste.

Directions:

In a pan that fits your air fryer, mix the zucchinis with the rest of the ingredients except the parsley, toss, introduce the pan in the air fryer and cook at 380°F for 20 minutes   Divide into bowls and serve for lunch with parsley sprinkled on top.

336. Portobello Pesto Burgers

Servings: 4   Cooking Time: 26 Minutes

Ingredients:

4 portobello	1 large ripe tomato
mushrooms	1 log fresh goat
1/4 cup sundried	cheese
tomato pesto	8 large fresh basil
4 whole-grain	leaves
hamburger buns	

Directions:

Start by preheating toaster oven to 425°F.   Place mushrooms on a pan, round sides facing up.   Bake for 14 minutes.   Pull out tray, flip the mushrooms and spread 1 tablespoon of pesto on each piece. Return to oven and bake for another 10 minutes. Remove the mushrooms and toast the buns for 2 minutes.   Remove the buns and build the burger by placing tomatoes, mushroom, 2 slices of cheese, and a sprinkle of basil, then topping with the top bun.

337. Turkey And Mushroom Stew

Servings: 4   Cooking Time: 12 Minutes

Ingredients:

½ lb. brown mushrooms; sliced	¼ cup tomato sauce
1 turkey breast, skinless, boneless; cubed and browned	1 tbsp. parsley; chopped.
	Salt and black pepper to taste.

Directions:

In a pan that fits your air fryer, mix the turkey with the mushrooms, salt, pepper and tomato sauce, toss, introduce in the fryer and cook at 350°F for 25 minutes   Divide into bowls and serve for lunch with parsley sprinkled on top.

338. Easy Prosciutto Grilled Cheese

Servings: 1   Cooking Time: 5 Minutes

Ingredients:

2 slices muenster cheese	2 slices white bread
Four thinly-shaved pieces of prosciutto	1 tablespoon sweet and spicy pickles

Directions:

Set toaster oven to the Toast setting.   Place one slice of cheese on each piece of bread.   Put prosciutto on one slice and pickles on the other. Transfer to a baking sheet and toast for 4 minutes or until the cheese is melted.   Combine the sides, cut, and serve.

339. Spice-roasted Almonds

Servings: 32   Cooking Time: 10 Minutes

Ingredients:

1 tablespoon chili powder	1/2 teaspoon ground coriander
1 tablespoon olive oil	1/4 teaspoon ground cinnamon
1/2 teaspoon salt	1/4 teaspoon black pepper
1/2 teaspoon ground cumin	2 cups whole almonds

Directions:

Start by preheating toaster oven to 350°F.   Mix olive oil, chili powder, coriander, cinnamon, cumin, salt, and pepper.   Add almonds and toss together. Transfer to a baking pan and bake for 10 minutes.

340. Air Fried Sausages

Servings: 6   Cooking Time: 13 Minutes

Ingredients:

6 sausage	olive oil spray

Directions:

Pour 5 cup of water into Instant Pot Duo Crisp Air Fryer. Place air fryer basket inside the pot, spray inside with nonstick spray and put sausage links inside.   Close the Air Fryer lid and steam for about 5 minutes.   Remove the lid once done. Spray links with olive oil and close air crisp lid.   Set to air crisp at 400°F for 8 min flipping halfway through so both sides get browned.

341. Chicken Caprese Sandwich

Servings: 2   Cooking Time: 3 Minutes

Ingredients:

2 leftover chicken breasts, or pre-cooked breaded chicken	4 slices of whole grain bread
1 large ripe tomato	1/4 cup olive oil
4 ounces mozzarella cheese slices	1/3 cup fresh basil leaves
	Salt and pepper to taste

Directions:

Start by slicing tomatoes into thin slices.   Layer tomatoes then cheese over two slices of bread and place on a greased baking sheet.   Toast in the toaster oven for about 2 minutes or until the cheese is melted.   Heat chicken while the cheese melts. Remove from oven, sprinkle with basil, and add chicken.   Drizzle with oil and add salt and pepper. Top with other slice of bread and serve.

342. Sweet Potato And Eggplant Mix

Servings: 4   Cooking Time: 20 Minutes

Ingredients:

2 sweet potatoes, peeled and cut into medium wedges	4 garlic cloves, minced
2 eggplants, roughly cubed	1 teaspoon nutmeg, ground
1 tablespoon avocado oil	Salt and black pepper to the taste
Juice of 1 lemon	1 tablespoon rosemary, chopped

Directions:

In your air fryer, combine the potatoes with the eggplants and the other Ingredients:, toss and cook at 370 degrees F for 20 minutes.   Divide the mix between plates and serve as a side dish.

343. Turkey And Broccoli Stew

Servings: 4   Cooking Time: 12 Minutes

Ingredients:

1 broccoli head, florets separated	1 tbsp. parsley; chopped.
1 turkey breast, skinless; boneless and cubed	1 tbsp. olive oil
1 cup tomato sauce	Salt and black pepper to taste.

Directions:

In a baking dish that fits your air fryer, mix the turkey with the rest of the ingredients except the parsley, toss, introduce the dish in the fryer, bake at 380°F for 25 minutes   Divide into bowls, sprinkle the parsley on top and serve.

344. Country Comfort Corn Bread

Servings: 12   Cooking Time: 20 Minutes

Ingredients:

1 cup yellow cornmeal	2 teaspoons baking powder
1-1/2 cups oatmeal	1 cup milk
1/4 teaspoon salt	

| 1/4 cup granulated | 1 large egg |
| sugar | 1/2 cup applesauce |

Directions:
Start by blending oatmeal into a fine powder. Preheat toaster oven to 400°F. Mix oatmeal, cornmeal, salt, sugar, and baking powder, and stir to blend. Add milk, egg, and applesauce, and mix well. Pour into a pan and bake for 20 minutes.

---

345. Basic Roasted Tofu

Servings: 4   Cooking Time: 45 Minutes

Ingredients:

1 or more (16-ounce)	1 tablespoon soy
containers extra-firm	sauce
tofu	1 tablespoon rice
1 tablespoon sesame	vinegar
oil	1 tablespoon water

Directions:

Start by drying the tofu: first pat dry with paper towels, then lay on another set of paper towels or a dish towel. Put a plate on top of the tofu then put something heavy on the plate (like a large can of vegetables). Leave it there for at least 20 minutes. While tofu is being pressed, whip up marinade by combining oil, soy sauce, vinegar, and water in a bowl and set aside. Cut the tofu into squares or sticks. Place the tofu in the marinade for at least 30 minutes. Preheat toaster oven to 350°F. Line a pan with parchment paper and add as many pieces of tofu as you can, giving each piece adequate space. Bake 20–45 minutes; tofu is done when the outside edges look golden brown. Time will vary depending on tofu size and shape.

Dinner Recipes

346. Filet Mignon With Chili Peanut Sauce

Servings: 4   Cooking Time: 20 Minutes

Ingredients:

2 pounds filet mignon, sliced into bite-sized strips	1 tablespoon ginger-garlic paste
1 tablespoon oyster sauce	1 teaspoon chili powder
2 tablespoons sesame oil	1/4 cup peanut butter
2 tablespoons tamari sauce	2 tablespoons lime juice
1 tablespoon mustard	1 teaspoon red pepper flakes
	2 tablespoons water

Directions:

Place the beef strips, oyster sauce, sesame oil, tamari sauce, ginger-garlic paste, mustard, and chili powder in a large ceramic dish.   Cover and allow it to marinate for 2 hours in your refrigerator. Cook in the preheated Air Fryer at 400 degrees F for 18 minutes, shaking the basket occasionally.   Mix the peanut butter with lime juice, red pepper flakes, and water. Spoon the sauce onto the air fried beef strips and serve warm.

347. Air Fryer Buffalo Mushroom Poppers

Servings: 8   Cooking Time: 50 Minutes

Ingredients:

1 pound fresh whole button mushrooms	Cooking spray
1/2 teaspoon kosher salt	2 large eggs, lightly beaten
3 tablespoons 1/3-less-fat cream cheese,	1/4 cup buffalo-style hot sauce
1/4 cup all-purpose flour	2 tablespoons chopped fresh chives
Softened 1 jalapeño chile, seeded and minced	1/2 cup low-fat buttermilk
1/4 teaspoon black pepper	1/2 cup plain fat-free yogurt
1 cup panko breadcrumbs	2 ounces blue cheese, crumbled (about 1/2 cup)
	3 tablespoons apple cider vinegar

Directions:

Remove stems from mushroom caps, chop stems and set caps aside. Stir together chopped mushroom stems, cream cheese, jalapeño, salt, and pepper. Stuff about 1 teaspoon of the mixture into each mushroom cap, rounding the filling to form a smooth ball.   Place panko in a bowl, place flour in a second bowl, and eggs in a third Coat mushrooms in flour, dip in egg mixture, and dredge in panko, pressing to adhere. Spray mushrooms well with cooking spray.   Place half of the mushrooms in air fryer basket, and cook for 20 minutes at 350°F. Transfer cooked mushrooms to a large bowl. Drizzle buffalo sauce over mushrooms; toss to coat then sprinkle with chives.   Stir buttermilk, yogurt, blue cheese, and cider vinegar in a small bowl. Serve mushroom poppers with blue cheese sauce.

348. Greek-style Monkfish With Vegetables

Servings: 2   Cooking Time: 20 Minutes

Ingredients:

2 teaspoons olive oil	2 monkfish fillets
1 cup celery, sliced	2 tablespoons lime juice
2 bell peppers, sliced	Coarse salt and ground black pepper, to taste
1 teaspoon dried thyme	1 teaspoon cayenne pepper
1/2 teaspoon dried marjoram	1/2 cup Kalamata olives, pitted and sliced
1/2 teaspoon dried rosemary	
1 tablespoon soy sauce	

Directions:

In a nonstick skillet, heat the olive oil for 1 minute. Once hot, sauté the celery and peppers until tender, about 4 minutes. Sprinkle with thyme, marjoram, and rosemary and set aside.   Toss the fish fillets with the soy sauce, lime juice, salt, black pepper, and cayenne pepper. Place the fish fillets in a lightly greased cooking basket and bake at 390 degrees F for 8 minutes.   Turn them over, add the olives, and cook an additional 4 minutes. Serve with the sautéed vegetables on the side.

349. Lemon Garlic Shrimps

Servings: 2   Cooking Time: 8 Minutes

Ingredients:

1½ tablespoons fresh lemon juice	¾ pound medium shrimp, peeled and deveined
1 tablespoon olive oil	
1 teaspoon lemon pepper	¼ teaspoon paprika
	¼ teaspoon garlic powder

Directions:

Preheat the Air fryer to 400 degree F and grease an Air fryer basket.   Mix lemon juice, olive oil, lemon pepper, paprika and garlic powder in a large bowl. Stir in the shrimp and toss until well combined. Arrange shrimp into the Air fryer basket in a single layer and cook for about 8 minutes.   Dish out the shrimp in serving plates and serve warm.

350. Beef, Mushrooms And Noodles Dish

Servings: 5   Cooking Time: 35 Minutes

Ingredients:

1½ pounds beef steak	2 cups mushrooms, sliced
1 package egg noodles, cooked	1 whole onion, chopped
1 ounce dry onion soup mix	

1 can (15 oz cream mushroom soup

½ cup beef broth
3 garlic cloves, minced?

Directions:
Preheat your Air Fryer to 360 F. Drizzle onion soup mix all over the meat. In a mixing bowl, mix the sauce, garlic cloves, beef broth, chopped onion, sliced mushrooms and mushroom soup. Top the meat with the prepared sauce mixture. Place the prepared meat in the air fryer's cooking basket and cook for 25 minutes. Serve with cooked egg noodles.

351. Coconut-crusted Haddock With Curried Pumpkin Seeds

Servings: 4   Cooking Time: 10 Minutes
Ingredients:

2 teaspoons canola oil
2 teaspoons honey
1 teaspoon curry powder
1/4 teaspoon ground cinnamon
1 teaspoon salt
1 cup pumpkin seeds
1-1/2 pounds haddock or cod filets

1/2 cup roughly grated unsweetened coconut
3/4 cups panko-style bread crumbs
2 tablespoons butter, melted
3 tablespoons apricot fruit spread
1 tablespoon lime juice

Directions:
Start by preheating toaster oven to 350°F.   In a medium bowl, mix honey, oil, curry powder, 1/2 teaspoon salt, and cinnamon.   Add pumpkin seeds to the bowl and toss to coat, then lay flat on a baking sheet.   Toast for 14 minutes, then transfer to a bowl to cool.   Increase the oven temperature to 450°F.   Brush a baking sheet with oil and lay filets flat.   In another medium mixing bowl, mix together bread crumbs, butter, and remaining salt. In a small bowl mash together apricot spread and lime juice.   Brush each filet with apricot mixture, then press bread crumb mixture onto each piece. Bake for 10 minutes.   Transfer to a plate and top with pumpkin seeds to serve.

352. Morning Ham And Cheese Sandwich

Servings: 4   Cooking Time: 15 Minutes
Ingredients:

8 slices whole wheat bread
4 slices cheese

4 slices lean pork ham
8 slices tomato

Directions:
Preheat your air fryer to 360 f. Lay four slices of bread on a flat surface. Spread the slices with cheese, tomato, turkey and ham. Cover with the remaining slices to form sandwiches. Add the sandwiches to the air fryer cooking basket and cook for 10 minutes.

353. Venetian Liver

Servings: 6   Cooking Time: 15-30;
Ingredients:

500g veal liver
2 white onions
100g of water

2 tbsp vinegar
Salt and pepper to taste

Directions:
Chop the onion and put it inside the pan with the water. Set the air fryer to 1800C and cook for 20 minutes.   Add the liver cut into small pieces and vinegar, close the lid, and cook for an additional 10 minutes.   Add salt and pepper.

354. Garlic Parmesan Shrimp

Servings: 2   Cooking Time: 10 Minutes
Ingredients:

1 pound shrimp, deveined and peeled
½ cup parmesan cheese, grated
¼ cup cilantro, diced
1 tablespoon olive oil

1 teaspoon salt
1 teaspoon fresh cracked pepper
1 tablespoon lemon juice
6 garlic cloves, diced

Directions:
Preheat the Air fryer to 350 degree F and grease an Air fryer basket.   Drizzle shrimp with olive oil and lemon juice and season with garlic, salt and cracked pepper.   Cover the bowl with plastic wrap and refrigerate for about 3 hours.   Stir in the parmesan cheese and cilantro to the bowl and transfer to the Air fryer basket.   Cook for about 10 minutes and serve immediately.

355. Zingy Dilled Salmon

Servings: 2   Cooking Time: 20 Minutes
Ingredients:

2 salmon steaks
Coarse sea salt, to taste
1/4 teaspoon freshly ground black pepper, or more to taste
1 tablespoon sesame oil
Zest of 1 lemon

1 tablespoon fresh lemon juice
1 teaspoon garlic, minced
1/2 teaspoon smoked cayenne pepper
1/2 teaspoon dried dill

Directions:
Preheat your Air Fryer to 380 degrees F. Pat dry the salmon steaks with a kitchen towel.   In a ceramic dish, combine the remaining ingredients until everything is well whisked.   Add the salmon steaks to the ceramic dish and let them sit in the refrigerator for 1 hour. Now, place the salmon steaks in the cooking basket. Reserve the marinade. Cook for 12 minutes, flipping halfway through the cooking time.   Meanwhile, cook the marinade in a small sauté pan over a moderate flame. Cook until the sauce has thickened.   Pour the sauce over the steaks and serve.

356. Veggie Stuffed Bell Peppers

Servings: 6   Cooking Time: 25 Minutes
Ingredients:

1 carrot, peeled and finely chopped
1 potato, peeled and finely chopped

6 large bell peppers, tops and seeds removed
2 garlic cloves,

½ cup fresh peas, shelled
1/3 cup cheddar cheese, grated
minced
Salt and black pepper, to taste

Directions:
Preheat the Air fryer to 350F and grease an Air fryer basket. Mix vegetables, garlic, salt and black pepper in a bowl. Stuff the vegetable mixture in each bell pepper and arrange in the Air fryer pan. Cook for about 20 minutes and top with cheddar cheese. Cook for about 5 more minutes and dish out to serve warm.

---

357. Ham Rolls

Servings: 4   Cooking Time: 15 Minutes

Ingredients:

12-ounce refrigerated pizza crust, rolled into ¼ inch thickness
1/3 pound cooked ham, sliced
¾ cup Mozzarella cheese, shredded
3 cups Colby cheese, shredded
3-ounce roasted red bell peppers
1 tablespoon olive oil

Directions:
Preheat the Air fryer to 360 degree F and grease an Air fryer basket. Arrange the ham, cheeses and roasted peppers over one side of dough and fold to seal. Brush the dough evenly with olive oil and cook for about 15 minutes, flipping twice in between. Dish out in a platter and serve warm.

---

358. Tasty Sausage Bacon Rolls

Servings: 4   Cooking Time: 1 Hour 44 Minutes

Ingredients:

Sausage:
8 bacon strips
8 pork sausages
Relish:
8 large tomatoes
1 clove garlic, peeled
1 small onion, peeled
3 tbsp chopped parsley
A pinch of salt
A pinch of pepper
2 tbsp sugar
1 tsp smoked paprika
1 tbsp white wine vinegar

Directions:
Start with the relish; add the tomatoes, garlic, and onion in a food processor. Blitz them for 10 seconds until the mixture is pulpy. Pour the pulp into a saucepan, add the vinegar, salt, pepper, and place it over medium heat. Bring to simmer for 10 minutes; add the paprika and sugar. Stir with a spoon and simmer for 10 minutes until pulpy and thick. Turn off the heat, transfer the relish to a bowl and chill it for an hour. In 30 minutes after putting the relish in the refrigerator, move on to the sausages. Wrap each sausage with a bacon strip neatly and stick in a bamboo skewer at the end of the sausage to secure the bacon ends. Open the Air Fryer, place 3 to 4 wrapped sausages in the fryer basket and cook for 12 minutes at 350 F. Ensure that the bacon is golden and crispy before removing them. Repeat the cooking process for the remaining wrapped sausages. Remove the relish from the refrigerator. Serve the sausages and relish with turnip mash.

---

359. Spicy Paprika Steak

Servings: 2   Cooking Time: 20 Minutes

Ingredients:

1/2 Ancho chili pepper, soaked in hot water before using
2 teaspoons smoked paprika
1 1/2 tablespoons olive oil
1 tablespoon brandy
2 beef steaks
Kosher salt, to taste
1 teaspoon ground allspice
3 cloves garlic, sliced

Directions:
Sprinkle the beef steaks with salt, paprika, and allspice. Add the steak to a baking dish that fits your fryer. Scatter the sliced garlic over the top. Now, drizzle it with brandy and olive oil; spread minced Ancho chili pepper over the top. Bake at 385 degrees F for 14 minutes, turning halfway through. Serve warm.

---

360. Coco Mug Cake

Servings: 1   Cooking Time: 20 Minutes

Ingredients:

1 large egg.
2 tbsp. granular erythritol.
2 tbsp. coconut flour.
2 tbsp. heavy whipping cream.
¼ tsp. baking powder.
¼ tsp. vanilla extract.

Directions:
In a 4-inch ramekin, whisk egg, then add remaining ingredients. Stir until smooth. Place into the air fryer basket. Adjust the temperature to 300 Degrees F and set the timer for 25 minutes. When done a toothpick should come out clean. Enjoy right out of the ramekin with a spoon. Serve warm.

---

361. Spiced Salmon Kebabs

Servings: 3   Cooking Time: 15 Minutes

Ingredients:

2 tablespoons chopped fresh oregano
2 teaspoons sesame seeds
1 teaspoon ground cumin
Salt and pepper to taste
1 ½ pounds salmon fillets
2 tablespoons olive oil
2 lemons, sliced into rounds

Directions:
Place the instant pot air fryer lid on and preheat the instant pot at 390 degrees F. Place the grill pan accessory in the instant pot. Create dry rub by combining the oregano, sesame seeds, cumin, salt, and pepper. Rub the salmon fillets with the dry rub and brush with oil. Place on the grill pan, close the air fryer lid and grill the salmon for 15 minutes. Serve with lemon slices once cooked.

362. Salmon With Crisped Topped Crumbs

Servings: 2   Cooking Time: 15 Minutes

Ingredients:

1-1/2 cups soft bread crumbs	1 teaspoon grated lemon zest
2 tablespoons minced fresh parsley	1/4 teaspoon lemon-pepper seasoning
1 tablespoon minced fresh thyme or 1 teaspoon dried thyme	1/4 teaspoon paprika
	1 tablespoon butter, melted
2 garlic cloves, minced	2 salmon fillets (6 ounces each)
1/2 teaspoon salt	

Directions:

In a medium bowl mix well bread crumbs, fresh parsley thyme, garlic, lemon zest, salt, lemon-pepper seasoning, and paprika.   Place the instant pot air fryer lid on, lightly grease baking pan of the instant pot with cooking spray. Add salmon fillet with skin side down. Evenly sprinkle crumbs on tops of salmon and place the baking pan in the instant pot. Close the air fryer lid and cook at 390F for 10 minutes.   Let it rest for 5 minutes.   Serve and enjoy.

363. Portuguese Bacalao Tapas

Servings: 4   Cooking Time: 26 Minutes

Ingredients:

1-pound codfish fillet, chopped	2 tablespoon butter
	1/4 cup olive oil
2 Yukon Gold potatoes, peeled and diced	3/4 teaspoon red pepper flakes
	freshly ground black pepper to taste
1 yellow onion, thinly sliced	
1 clove garlic, chopped, divided	2 hard-cooked eggs, chopped
1/4 cup chopped fresh parsley, divided	5 pitted green olives
	5 pitted black olives

Directions:

Place the instant pot air fryer lid on, lightly grease baking pan of the instant pot with cooking spray. Add butter and place the baking pan in the instant pot.   Close the air fryer lid and melt butter at 360F. Stir in onions and cook for 6 minutes until caramelized.   Stir in black pepper, red pepper flakes, half of the parsley, garlic, olive oil, diced potatoes, and chopped fish. For 10 minutes, cook on 360F. Halfway through cooking time, stir well to mix.   Cook for 10 minutes at 390F until tops are lightly browned.   Garnish with remaining parsley, eggs, black and green olives.   Serve and enjoy with chips.

364. Broccoli And Tomato Sauce

Servings: 4   Cooking Time: 7 Minutes

Ingredients:

1 broccoli head, florets separated	1 tbsp. olive oil
1/4 cup scallions;	1 tbsp. sweet paprika
	Salt and black pepper to taste.
chopped	
1/2 cup tomato sauce	

Directions:

In a pan that fits the air fryer, combine the broccoli with the rest of the Ingredients: toss.   Put the pan in the fryer and cook at 380°F for 15 minutes Divide between plates and serve.

365. Indian Meatballs With Lamb

Servings: 8   Cooking Time: 14 Minutes

Ingredients:

1 garlic clove	1/4 tablespoon turmeric
1 tablespoon butter	
4 oz chive stems	
1/3 teaspoon cayenne pepper	1/4 teaspoon bay leaf
	1 teaspoon salt
1 teaspoon ground coriander	1-pound ground lamb
	1 egg
	1 teaspoon ground black pepper

Directions:

Peel the garlic clove and mince it   Combine the minced garlic with the ground lamb.   Then sprinkle the meat mixture with the turmeric, cayenne pepper, ground coriander, bay leaf, salt, and ground black pepper.   Beat the egg in the forcemeat.   Then grate the chives and add them in the lamb forcemeat too.   Mix it up to make the smooth mass.   Then preheat the air fryer to 400 F. Put the butter in the air fryer basket tray and melt it. Then make the meatballs from the lamb mixture and place them in the air fryer basket tray.   Cook the dish for 14 minutes.   Stir the meatballs twice during the cooking.   Serve the cooked meatballs immediately.   Enjoy!

366. Clam With Lemons On The Grill

Servings: 6   Cooking Time: 6 Minutes

Ingredients:

4 pounds littleneck clams	1 teaspoon crushed red pepper flakes
Salt and pepper to taste	5 tablespoons olive oil
1 clove of garlic, minced	1 loaf crusty bread, halved
1/2 cup parsley, chopped	1/2 cup Parmesan cheese, grated

Directions:

Place the instant pot air fryer lid on and preheat the instant pot at 390 degrees F.   Place the grill pan accessory in the instant pot.   Place the clams on the grill pan, close the air fryer lid and cook for 6 minutes.   Once the clams have opened, take them out and extract the meat.   Transfer the meat into a bowl and season with salt and pepper.   Stir in the garlic, parsley, red pepper flakes, and olive oil. Serve on top of bread and sprinkle with Parmesan cheese.

367. Spicy Cauliflower Rice

Servings: 2   Cooking Time: 22 Minutes

Ingredients:

1 cauliflower head, cut into florets 1/2 tsp cumin	1 zucchini, trimmed and cut into cubes
1/2 tsp chili powder	1/2 tsp paprika
6 onion spring, chopped 2 jalapenos, chopped	1/2 tsp garlic powder
4 tbsp olive oil	1/2 tsp cayenne pepper 1/2 tsp pepper
	1/2 tsp salt

Directions:

Preheat the air fryer to 370 F.   Add cauliflower florets into the food processor and process until it looks like rice.   Transfer cauliflower rice into the air fryer baking pan and drizzle with half oil. Place pan in the air fryer and cook for 12 minutes, stir halfway through.   Heat remaining oil in a small pan over medium heat.   Add zucchini and cook for 5-8 minutes.   Add onion and jalapenos and cook for 5 minutes.   Add spices and stir well. Set aside.   Add cauliflower rice in the zucchini mixture and stir well.   Serve and enjoy.

368.   Rice And Tuna Puff

Servings: 6   Cooking Time: 60 Minutes

Ingredients:

2/3 cup uncooked white rice	1 1/2 cups milk
1 1/3 cups water	2 egg yolks
1/3 cup butter	1 (12 ounces) can tuna, undrained
1/4 cup all-purpose flour	2 tablespoons grated onion
1 teaspoon salt	1 tablespoon lemon juice
1/4 teaspoon ground black pepper	2 egg whites

Directions:

In a saucepan, bring water to a boil. Stir in rice, cover, and cook on low heat until liquid is fully absorbed, around 20 minutes.   In another saucepan over medium heat, melt butter. Stir in pepper, salt, and flour. Cook for 2 minutes, whisking constantly and slowly adding milk. Continue cooking and stirring until thickened.   In a medium bowl, whisk egg yolks. Slowly whisk in half of the thickened milk mixture. Add to a pan of remaining milk and continue cooking and stirring for 2 more minutes. Stir in lemon juice, onion, tuna, and rice.   Place the instant pot air fryer lid on, lightly grease baking pan of the instant pot with cooking spray. And transfer rice mixture into it. Beat egg whites until stiff peak forms. Slowly fold into rice mixture.   Cover pan with foil, place the baking pan in the instant pot and close the air fryer lid.   Cook at 360F for 20 minutes.   Cook for 15 minutes at 390F until tops are lightly browned and the middle has set.   Serve and enjoy.

369.   Herbed Eggplant

Servings: 2   Cooking Time: 15 Minutes

Ingredients:

1 large eggplant, cubed	1/2 teaspoon garlic powder
1/2 teaspoon dried marjoram, crushed	Salt and black

1/2 teaspoon dried oregano, crushed	pepper, to taste
1/2 teaspoon dried thyme, crushed	Olive oil cooking spray

Directions:

Preheat the Air fryer to 390 degree F and grease an Air fryer basket.   Mix herbs, garlic powder, salt, and black pepper in a bowl.   Spray the eggplant cubes with cooking spray and rub with the herb mixture.   Arrange the eggplant cubes in the Air fryer basket and cook for about 15 minutes, flipping twice in between.   Dish out onto serving plates and serve hot.

370.   Roasted Garlic Zucchini Rolls

Servings: 4   Cooking Time: 20 Minutes

Ingredients:

2 medium zucchinis	1/4 cup heavy cream
1/2 cup full-fat ricotta cheese	2 tbsp. unsalted butter.
1/4 white onion; peeled. And diced	2 tbsp. vegetable broth.
2 cups spinach; chopped	1/2 tsp. finely minced roasted garlic
1/2 cup sliced baby portobello mushrooms	1/4 tsp. dried oregano.
3/4 cup shredded mozzarella cheese, divided.	1/8 tsp. xanthan gum
	1/4 tsp. salt
	1/2 tsp. garlic powder.

Directions:

Using a mandoline or sharp knife, slice zucchini into long strips lengthwise. Place strips between paper towels to absorb moisture. Set aside   In a medium saucepan over medium heat, melt butter. Add onion and sauté until fragrant. Add garlic and sauté 30 seconds.   Pour in heavy cream, broth and xanthan gum. Turn off heat and whisk mixture until it begins to thicken, about 3 minutes.   Take a medium bowl, add ricotta, salt, garlic powder and oregano and mix well. Fold in spinach, mushrooms and 1/2 cup mozzarella   Pour half of the sauce into a 6-inch round baking pan. To assemble the rolls, place two strips of zucchini on a work surface. Spoon 2 tbsp. of ricotta mixture onto the slices and roll up. Place seam side down on top of sauce. Repeat with remaining ingredients   Pour remaining sauce over the rolls and sprinkle with remaining mozzarella. Cover with foil and place into the air fryer basket. Adjust the temperature to 350 Degrees F and set the timer for 20 minutes. In the last 5 minutes, remove the foil to brown the cheese. Serve immediately.

371.Lobster Lasagna Maine Style

Servings: 6   Cooking Time: 50 Minutes

Ingredients:

1/2 (15 ounces) container ricotta cheese	1 egg
	1 tablespoon chopped fresh parsley
1 cup shredded Cheddar cheese	1/2 teaspoon freshly ground black pepper

1/2 cup shredded mozzarella cheese
1/2 cup grated Parmesan cheese
1/2 medium onion, minced
1-1/2 teaspoons minced garlic

1 (16 ounces) jar Alfredo pasta sauce
8 no-boil lasagna noodles
1 pound cooked and cubed lobster meat
5-ounce package baby spinach leaves

Directions:
Mix well half of Parmesan, half of the mozzarella, half of cheddar, egg, and ricotta cheese in a medium bowl. Stir in pepper, parsley, garlic, and onion. Place the instant pot air fryer lid on, lightly grease baking pan of the instant pot with cooking spray. On the bottom of the pan, spread ½ of the Alfredo sauce, top with a single layer of lasagna noodles. Followed by 1/3 of lobster meat, 1/3 of ricotta cheese mixture, 1/3 of spinach. Repeat layering process until all ingredients are used up. Sprinkle remaining cheese on top. Shake pan to settle lasagna and burst bubbles. Cover pan with foil and place the baking pan in the instant pot. Close the air fryer lid and cook at 360F for 30 minutes Remove foil and cook for 10 minutes at 390F until tops are lightly browned. Let it stand for 10 minutes. Serve and enjoy.

372. Homemade Beef Stroganoff

Servings: 3   Cooking Time: 20 Minutes
Ingredients:

1 pound thin steak
4 tbsp butter
1 whole onion, chopped
1 cup sour cream

8 oz mushrooms, sliced
4 cups beef broth
16 oz egg noodles, cooked

Directions:
Preheat your Air Fryer to 400 F. Using a microwave proof bowl, melt butter in a microwave oven. In a mixing bowl, mix the melted butter, sliced mushrooms, cream, onion, and beef broth. Pour the mixture over steak and set aside for 10 minutes. Place the marinated beef in your fryer's cooking basket, and cook for 10 minutes. Serve with cooked egg noodles and enjoy!

373. Beef Pieces With Tender Broccoli

Servings: 4   Cooking Time: 13 Minutes
Ingredients:

6 oz. broccoli
10 oz. beef brisket
4 oz chive stems
1 teaspoon paprika
1/3 cup water
1 teaspoon olive oil

1 teaspoon butter
1 tablespoon flax seeds
½ teaspoon chili flakes

Directions:
Cut the beef brisket into the medium/convenient pieces.   Sprinkle the beef pieces with the paprika and chili flakes.   Mix the meat up with the help of the hands.   Then preheat the air fryer to 360 F. Spray the air fryer basket tray with the olive oil. Put the beef pieces in the air fryer basket tray and cook the meat for 7 minutes.   Stir it once during the cooking.   Meanwhile, separate the broccoli into the florets.   When the time is over – add the broccoli florets in the air fryer basket tray. Sprinkle the ingredients with the flax seeds and butter.   Add water.   Dice the chives and add them in the air fryer basket tray too.   Stir it gently using the wooden spatula.   Then cook the dish at 265 F for 6 minutes more.   When the broccoli is tender – the dish is cooked.   Serve the dish little bit chilled.   Enjoy!

374. Salmon Casserole

Servings: 8   Cooking Time: 12 Minutes
Ingredients:

7 oz Cheddar cheese, shredded
½ cup cream
1-pound salmon fillet
1 tablespoon dried dill
1 teaspoon dried parsley
1 teaspoon salt
1 teaspoon ground coriander

½ teaspoon ground black pepper
2 green pepper, chopped
4 oz chive stems, diced
7 oz bok choy, chopped
1 tablespoon olive oil

Directions:
Sprinkle the salmon fillet with the dried dill, dried parsley, ground coriander, and ground black pepper. Massage the salmon fillet gently and leave it for 5 minutes to make the fish soaks the spices. Meanwhile, sprinkle the air fryer casserole tray with the olive oil inside.   After this, cut the salmon fillet into the cubes.   Separate the salmon cubes into 2 parts.   Then place the first part of the salmon cubes in the casserole tray.   Sprinkle the fish with the chopped bok choy, diced chives, and chopped green pepper.   After this, place the second part of the salmon cubes over the vegetables.   Then sprinkle the casserole with the shredded cheese and heavy cream.   Preheat the air fryer to 380 F. Cook the salmon casserole for 12 minutes.   When the dish is cooked – it will have acrunchy light brown crust.   Serve it and enjoy!

375. Stuffed Okra

Servings: 2   Cooking Time: 12 Minutes
Ingredients:

8 ounces large okra
¼ cup chickpea flour
¼ of onion, chopped
2 tablespoons coconut, grated freshly
1 teaspoon garam masala powder

½ teaspoon ground turmeric
½ teaspoon red chili powder
½ teaspoon ground cumin
Salt, to taste

Directions:
Preheat the Air fryer to 390F and grease an Air fryer basket.   Mix the flour, onion, grated coconut, and spices in a bowl and toss to coat well.   Stuff the flour mixture into okra and arrange into the Air fryer basket.   Cook for about 12 minutes and dish out in a serving plate.

376. Roasted Butternut Squash With Brussels Sprouts & Sweet Potato Noodles

Servings: 2   Cooking Time: 15 Minutes

Ingredients:

Squash:	2 cloves garlic
3 cups chopped butternut squash	A small pinch red pepper flakes
2 teaspoons extra light olive oil	1 tablespoon extra light olive oil
1/8 teaspoon sea salt	1 teaspoon sesame oil
Veggies:	1 teaspoon onion powder
5-6 Brussels sprouts	1 teaspoon garlic powder
5 fresh shiitake mushrooms	1/4 teaspoon sea salt
1/2 teaspoon black sesame seeds	Noodles:
1/2 teaspoon white sesame seeds	1 bundle sweet potato vermicelli
A few sprinkles ground pepper	2-3 teaspoons low-sodium soy sauce

Directions:

Start by soaking potato vermicelli in water for at least 2 hours.   Preheat toaster oven to 375°F. Place squash on a baking sheet with edges, then drizzle with olive oil and sprinkle with salt and pepper. Mix together well on pan.   Bake the squash for 30 minutes, mixing and flipping half way through.   Remove the stems from the mushrooms and chop the Brussels sprouts.   Chop garlic and mix the veggies.   Drizzle sesame and olive oil over the mixture, then add garlic powder, onion powder, sesame seeds, red pepper flakes, salt, and pepper. Bake veggie mix for 15 minutes.   While the veggies bake, put noodles in a small sauce pan and add just enough water to cover.   Bring water to a rolling boil and boil noodles for about 8 minutes.   Drain noodles and combine with squash and veggies in a large bowl.   Drizzle with soy sauce, sprinkle with sesame seeds, and serve.

377. Pollock With Kalamata Olives And Capers

Servings: 3   Cooking Time: 20 Minutes

Ingredients:

2 tablespoons olive oil	2 ripe tomatoes, diced
1 red onion, sliced	12 Kalamata olives, pitted and chopped
2 cloves garlic, chopped	2 tablespoons capers
1 Florina pepper, deveined and minced	1 teaspoon oregano
3 pollock fillets,skinless	1 teaspoon rosemary
	Sea salt, to taste
	1/2 cup white wine

Directions:

Start by preheating your Air Fryer to 360 degrees F. Heat the oil in a baking pan. Once hot, sauté the onion, garlic, and pepper for 2 to 3 minutes or until fragrant.   Add the fish fillets to the baking pan. Top with the tomatoes, olives, and capers. Sprinkle with the oregano, rosemary, and salt. Pour in white wine and transfer to the cooking basket.   Turn the

temperature to 395 degrees F and bake for 10 minutes. Taste for seasoning and serve on individual plates, garnished with some extra Mediterranean herbs if desired. Enjoy!

378. Fish Cakes With Horseradish Sauce

Servings: 4   Cooking Time: 20 Minutes

Ingredients:

Halibut Cakes:	2 garlic cloves, minced
1 pound halibut	
2 tablespoons olive oil	1 cup Romano cheese, grated
1/2 teaspoon cayenne pepper	1 egg, whisked
1/4 teaspoon black pepper	1 tablespoon Worcestershire sauce
Salt, to taste	Mayo Sauce:
2 tablespoons cilantro, chopped	1 teaspoon horseradish, grated
1 shallot, chopped	1/2 cup mayonnaise

Directions:

Start by preheating your Air Fryer to 380 degrees F. Spritz the Air Fryer basket with cooking oil.   Mix all ingredients for the halibut cakes in a bowl; knead with your hands until everything is well incorporated.   Shape the mixture into equally sized patties. Transfer your patties to the Air Fryer basket. Cook the fish patties for 10 minutes, turning them over halfway through.   Mix the horseradish and mayonnaise. Serve the halibut cakes with the horseradish mayo.

379. Lamb Skewers

Servings: 4   Cooking Time: 20 Minutes

Ingredients:

2 lb. lamb meat; cubed	2 tbsp. lemon juice
2 red bell peppers; cut into medium pieces	1 tbsp. red vinegar
	1 tbsp. garlic; minced
1/4 cup olive oil	1/2 tsp. rosemary; dried
1 tbsp. oregano; dried	A pinch of salt and black pepper

Directions:

Take a bowl and mix all the ingredients and toss them well.   Thread the lamb and bell peppers on skewers, place them in your air fryer's basket and cook at 380°F for 10 minutes on each side. Divide between plates and serve with a side salad

380. Crumbly Oat Meatloaf

Servings: 8   Cooking Time: 60 Minutes

Ingredients:

2 lbs. ground beef	1 tablespoon Worcestershire sauce
1 cup of salsa	
3/4 cup Quaker Oats	Salt and black pepper to taste
1/2 cup chopped onion	
1 large egg, beaten	

Directions:

Thoroughly mix ground beef with salsa, oats, onion, egg, and all the ingredients in a bowl.   Grease a meatloaf pan with oil or butter and spread the minced beef in the pan. Press "Power Button" of Air Fry Oven and turn the dial to select the "Bake" mode. Press the Time button and again turn the dial to set the cooking time to 60 minutes. Now push the Temp button and rotate the dial to set the temperature at 350 degrees F. Once preheated, place the beef baking pan in the oven and close its lid. Slice and serve.

381.   One-pan Shrimp And Chorizo Mix Grill

Servings: 4   Cooking Time: 15 Minutes

Ingredients:

1 ½ pounds large shrimps, peeled and deveined	6 links fresh chorizo sausage
Salt and pepper to taste	2 bunches asparagus spears, trimmed
	Lime wedges

Directions:
Place the instant pot air fryer lid on and preheat the instant pot at 390 degrees F. Place the grill pan accessory in the instant pot. Season the shrimps with salt and pepper to taste. Set aside. Place the chorizo on the grill pan and the sausage. Place the asparagus on top. Close the air fryer lid and grill for 15 minutes. Serve with lime wedges.

382.   Pesto & White Wine Salmon

Servings: 4   Cooking Time: 10 Minutes

Ingredients:

1-1/4 pounds salmon filet	2 tablespoons white wine
2 tablespoons pesto	1 lemon

Directions:
Cut the salmon into 4 pieces and place on a greased baking sheet. Slice the lemon into quarters and squeeze 1 quarter over each piece of salmon. Drizzle wine over salmon and set aside to marinate while preheating the toaster oven on broil. Spread pesto over each piece of salmon. Broil for at least 10 minutes, or until the fish is cooked to desired doneness and the pesto is browned.

383.   Almond Asparagus

Servings: 3   Cooking Time: 6 Minutes

Ingredients:

1 pound asparagus	2 tablespoons balsamic vinegar
1/3 cup almonds, sliced	Salt and black pepper, to taste
2 tablespoons olive oil	

Directions:
Preheat the Air fryer to 400F and grease an Air fryer basket. Mix asparagus, oil, vinegar, salt, and black pepper in a bowl and toss to coat well. Arrange asparagus into the Air fryer basket and sprinkle with the almond slices. Cook for about 6 minutes and dish out to serve hot.

384.   Garlic Lamb Shank

Servings: 5   Cooking Time: 24 Minutes

Ingredients:

2 tablespoon garlic, peeled	17 oz. lamb shanks
1 teaspoon kosher salt	½ cup chicken stock
1 tablespoon dried parsley	1 teaspoon butter
4 oz chive stems, chopped	1 teaspoon dried rosemary
	1 teaspoon nutmeg
	½ teaspoon ground black pepper

Directions:
Chop the garlic roughly. Make the cuts in the lamb shank and fill the cuts with the chopped garlic. Then sprinkle the lamb shank with the kosher salt, dried parsley, dried rosemary, nutmeg, and ground black pepper. Stir the spices on the lamb shank gently. Then put the butter and chicken stock in the air fryer basket tray. Preheat the air fryer to 380 F. Put the chives in the air fryer basket tray. Add the lamb shank and cook the meat for 24 minutes. When the lamb shank is cooked – transfer it to the serving plate and sprinkle with the remaining liquid from the cooked meat. Enjoy!

385.   Beef With Apples And Plums

Servings: 4   Cooking Time: 30 Minutes

Ingredients:

2pounds beef stew meat, cubed	2tablespoons butter, melted
1cup apples, cored and cubed	Salt and black pepper to the taste
1cup plums, pitted and halved	1tablespoon chives, chopped
½ cup red wine	

Directions:
In the air fryer's pan, mix the beef with the apples and the other ingredients, toss, put the pan in the machine and cook at 390 degrees F for 30 minutes. Divide the mix between plates and serve right away.

386.   Smoked Ham With Pears

Servings: 2   Cooking Time: 30 Minutes

Ingredients:

15 oz pears, halved	1 tbsp apple cider vinegar
8 pound smoked ham	1 tsp black pepper
1 ½ cups brown sugar	1 tsp vanilla extract
¾ tbsp allspice	

Directions:
Preheat your air fryer to 330 f. In a bowl, mix pears, brown sugar, cider vinegar, vanilla extract, pepper, and allspice. Place the mixture in a frying pan and fry for 2-3 minutes. Pour the mixture over ham. Add the ham to the air fryer cooking basket and cook for 15 minutes. Serve ham with hot sauce, to enjoy!

387.   Marinated Cajun Beef

Servings: 2   Cooking Time: 20 Minutes

Ingredients:

2 tablespoons Cajun seasoning, crushed	1/3 cup beef broth
1/2 teaspoon garlic	1/3 teaspoon cayenne pepper

powder
3/4 pound beef tenderloins
½ tablespoon pear cider vinegar

1 ½ tablespoon olive oil
1/2 teaspoon freshly ground black pepper
1 teaspoon salt

Directions:
Firstly, coat the beef tenderloins with salt, cayenne pepper, and black pepper.   Mix the remaining items in a medium-sized bowl; let the meat marinate for 40 minutes in this mixture.   Roast the beef for about 22 minutes at 385 degrees F, turning it halfway through the cooking time.

388. Award Winning Breaded Chicken

Servings: 4   Cooking Time: 20 Minutes
Ingredients:

1 1/2 tsp.s olive oil
1 tsp. red pepper flakes, crushed 1/3 tsp. chicken bouillon granules 1/3 tsp. shallot powder
1 1/2 tablespoons tamari soy sauce 1/3 tsp. cumin powder

1½ tablespoons mayo 1 tsp. kosher salt
For the chicken:
2 beaten eggs
Breadcrumbs
1½ chicken breasts, boneless and skinless
1 ½ tablespoons plain flour

Directions:
Margarine fly the chicken breasts, and then, marinate them for at least 55 minutes. Coat the chicken with plain flour; then, coat with the beaten eggs; finally, roll them in the breadcrumbs. Lightly grease the cooking basket. Air-fry the breaded chicken at 345 °F for 12 minutes, flipping them halfway.

389. Chicken Lasagna With Eggplants

Servings: 10   Cooking Time: 17 Minutes
Ingredients:

6 oz Cheddar cheese, shredded
7 oz Parmesan cheese, shredded
2 eggplants
1-pound ground chicken
1 teaspoon paprika

1 teaspoon salt
½ teaspoon cayenne pepper
½ cup heavy cream
2 teaspoon butter
4 oz chive stems, diced

Directions:
Take the air fryer basket tray and spread it with the butter.   Then peel the eggplants and slice them. Separate the sliced eggplants into 3 parts. Combine the ground chicken with the paprika, salt, cayenne pepper, and diced chives.   Mix the mixture up.   Separate the ground chicken mixture into 2 parts.   Make the layer of the first part of the sliced eggplant in the air fryer basket tray.   Then make the layer of the ground chicken mixture. After this, sprinkle the ground chicken layer with the half of the shredded Cheddar cheese,   Then cover the cheese with the second part of the sliced eggplant.   The next step is to make the layer of the ground chicken and all shredded Cheddar cheese, Cover the cheese layer with the last part of the sliced eggplants.   Then sprinkle the eggplants with shredded Parmesan cheese.   Pour the heavy cream and add butter.   Preheat the air fryer to 365 F.   Cook the lasagna for 17 minutes.   When the time is over – let the lasagna chill gently.   Serve it!

390. Korean Beef Bowl

Servings: 4   Cooking Time: 18 Minutes
Ingredients:

1 tablespoon minced garlic
1 teaspoon ground ginger
4 oz chive stems, chopped
2 tablespoon apple cider vinegar
1 teaspoon olive oil

1 teaspoon stevia extract
1 tablespoon flax seeds
1 teaspoon olive oil
1-pound ground beef
4 tablespoon chicken stock

Directions:
Sprinkle the ground beef with the apple cider vinegar and stir the meat with the help of the spoon. After this, sprinkle the ground beef with the ground ginger, minced garlic, and olive oil.   Mix it up. Preheat the air fryer to 370 F.   Put the ground beef in the air fryer basket tray and cook it for 8 minutes. After this, stir the ground beef carefully and sprinkle with the chopped chives, flax seeds, olive oil, and chicken stock.   Mix the dish up and cook it for 10 minutes more.   When the time is over – stir the dish carefully.   Serve Korean beef bowl immediately.   Enjoy!

391. Stuffed Potatoes

Servings: 4   Cooking Time: 31 Minutes
Ingredients:

4 potatoes, peeled
½ of brown onion, chopped
2 tablespoons chives, chopped

1 tablespoon butter
½ cup Parmesan cheese, grated
3 tablespoons canola oil

Directions:
Preheat the Air fryer to 390F and grease an Air fryer basket.   Coat the potatoes with canola oil and arrange into the Air fryer basket.   Cook for about 20 minutes and transfer into a platter.   Cut each potato in half and scoop out the flesh from each half. Heat butter in a frying pan over medium heat and add onions.   Sauté for about 5 minutes and dish out in a bowl.   Mix the onions with the potato flesh, chives, and half of cheese.   Stir well and stuff the potato halves evenly with the onion potato mixture. Top with the remaining cheese and arrange the potato halves into the Air fryer basket.   Cook for about 6 minutes and dish out to serve warm.

392. Oven-fried Herbed Chicken

Servings: 2   Cooking Time: 15 Minutes
Ingredients:

1/2 cup buttermilk
2 cloves garlic, minced
1-1/2 teaspoons salt
1 tablespoon oil
1/2 pound boneless, skinless chicken breasts
1 cup rolled oats
1/2 teaspoon red pepper flakes
1/2 cup grated parmesan cheese
1/4 cup fresh basil leaves or rosemary needles
Olive oil spray

Directions:
Mix together buttermilk, oil, 1/2 teaspoon salt, and garlic in a shallow bowl. Roll chicken in buttermilk and refrigerate in bowl overnight. Preheat your toaster oven to 425°F. Mix together the oats, red pepper, salt, parmesan, and basil, and mix roughly to break up oats. Place the mixture on a plate. Remove the chicken from the buttermilk mixture and let any excess drip off. Roll the chicken in the oat mixture and transfer to a baking sheet lightly coated with olive oil spray. Spray the chicken with oil spray and bake for 15 minutes.

393. Rich Meatloaf With Mustard And Peppers

Servings: 5   Cooking Time: 20 Minutes
Ingredients:

1 pound beef, ground
1/2 pound veal, ground
1 egg
4 tablespoons vegetable juice
1/2 cup pork rinds
2 bell peppers, chopped
2 garlic cloves, minced
2 tablespoons tomato paste
1 onion, chopped
2 tablespoons soy sauce
1 (1-ounce package ranch dressing mix
Sea salt, to taste
1/2 teaspoon ground black pepper, to taste
7 ounces tomato puree
1 tablespoon Dijon mustard

Directions:
Start by preheating your Air Fryer to 330 degrees F. In a mixing bowl, thoroughly combine the ground beef, veal, egg, vegetable juice, pork rinds, bell peppers, onion, garlic, tomato paste, soy sauce, ranch dressing mix, salt, and ground black pepper. Mix until everything is well incorporated and press into a lightly greased meatloaf pan. Cook approximately 25 minutes in the preheated Air Fryer. Whisk the tomato puree with the mustard and spread the topping over the top of your meatloaf. Continue to cook 2 minutes more. Let it stand on a cooling rack for 6 minutes before slicing and serving. Enjoy!

394. Corned Beef With Carrots

Servings: 3   Cooking Time: 35 Minutes
Ingredients:

1 tbsp beef spice
1 whole onion, chopped
4 carrots, chopped
12 oz bottle beer
1½ cups chicken broth
4 pounds corned beef

Directions:
Preheat your air fryer to 380 f. Cover beef with beer and set aside for 20 minutes. Place carrots, onion and beef in a pot and heat over high heat. Add in broth and bring to a boil. Drain boiled meat and veggies; set aside. Top with beef spice. Place the meat and veggies in your air fryer's cooking basket and cook for 30 minutes.

395. Chinese-style Spicy And Herby Beef

Servings: 4   Cooking Time: 20 Minutes
Ingredients:

1 pound flank steak, cut into small pieces
1 teaspoon fresh sage leaves, minced
1/3 cup olive oil
3 teaspoons sesame oil
3 tablespoons Shaoxing wine
2 tablespoons tamari
1 teaspoon hot sauce
1/8 teaspoon xanthum gum
1 teaspoon seasoned salt
3 cloves garlic, minced
1 teaspoon fresh rosemary leaves, finely minced
1/2 teaspoon freshly cracked black pepper

Directions:
Warm the oil in a sauté pan over a moderate heat. Now, sauté the garlic until just tender and fragrant. Now, add the remaining ingredients. Toss to coat well. Then, roast for about 18 minutes at 345 degrees F. Check doneness and serve warm.

396. Salsa Stuffed Eggplants

Servings: 2   Cooking Time: 25 Minutes
Ingredients:

1 large eggplant
8 cherry tomatoes, quartered
½ tablespoon fresh parsley
2 teaspoons olive oil, divided
2 teaspoons fresh lemon juice, divided
2 tablespoons tomato salsa
Salt and black pepper, as required

Directions:
Preheat the Air fryer to 390 degree F and grease an Air fryer basket. Arrange the eggplant into the Air fryer basket and cook for about 15 minutes. Cut the eggplant in half lengthwise and drizzle evenly with one teaspoon of oil. Set the Air fryer to 355 degree F and arrange the eggplant into the Air fryer basket, cut-side up. Cook for another 10 minutes and dish out in a bowl. Scoop out the flesh from the eggplant and transfer into a bowl. Stir in the tomatoes, salsa, parsley, salt, black pepper, remaining oil, and lemon juice. Squeeze lemon juice on the eggplant halves and stuff with the salsa mixture to serve.

397. Air Fryer Roasted Broccoli

Servings: 4   Cooking Time: 10 Minutes
Ingredients:

1 tsp. herbes de provence seasoning
1 tablespoon olive oil
Salt and pepper to taste

(optional)
4 cups fresh broccoli
Directions:
Drizzle or spray broccoli with olive and sprinkle seasoning throughout   Spray air fryer basket with cooking oil, place broccoli and cook for 5-8 minutes on 360F   Open air fryer and examine broccoli after 5 minutes because different fryer brands cook at different rates.

---

398.   Baked Veggie Egg Rolls

Servings: 2   Cooking Time: 20 Minutes
Ingredients:

1/2 tablespoon olive or vegetable oil	2 scallions
2 cups thinly-sliced chard	1/2 tablespoon fresh ginger
1/4 cup grated carrot	1/2 tablespoon soy sauce
1/2 cup chopped pea pods	6 egg roll wrappers
3 shiitake mushrooms	Olive oil spray for cookie sheet and egg rolls
2 medium cloves garlic	

Directions:
Start by mincing mushrooms, garlic, and ginger and slicing scallions.   Heat oil on medium heat in a medium skillet and char peas, carrots, scallions, and mushrooms.   Cook 3 minutes, then add ginger. Stir in soy sauce and remove from heat.   Preheat toaster oven to 400°F and spray cookie sheet. Spoon even portions of vegetable mix over each egg roll wrapper, and wrap them up.   Place egg rolls on cookie sheet and spray with olive oil. Bake for 20 minutes until egg roll shells are browned.

---

399.   Sage Beef

Servings: 4   Cooking Time: 30 Minutes
Ingredients:

2pounds beef stew meat, cubed	½ tablespoon garlic powder
1tablespoon sage, chopped	1teaspoon Italian seasoning
2tablespoons butter, melted	Salt and black pepper to the taste
½ teaspoon coriander, ground	

Directions:
In the air fryer's pan, mix the beef with the sage, melted butter and the other ingredients, introduce the pan in the fryer and cook at 360 degrees F for 30 minutes.   Divide everything between plates and serve.

---

400.   Healthy Mama Meatloaf

Servings: 8   Cooking Time: 40 Minutes
Ingredients:

1 tablespoon olive oil	1-lb. ground beef
1 green bell pepper, diced	2 large eggs
1/2 cup diced sweet onion	3/4 cup shredded carrot
	3/4 cup shredded

1/2 teaspoon minced garlic	zucchini
1 cup whole wheat bread crumbs	salt and ground black pepper to taste
	1/4 cup ketchup, or to taste

Directions:
Thoroughly mix ground beef with egg, onion, garlic, crumbs, and all the ingredients in a bowl.   Grease a meatloaf pan with oil or butter and spread the minced beef in the pan.   Press "Power Button" of Air Fry Oven and turn the dial to select the "Bake" mode.   Press the Time button and again turn the dial to set the cooking time to 40 minutes.   Now push the Temp button and rotate the dial to set the temperature at 375 degrees F.   Once preheated, place the beef baking pan in the oven and close its lid.   Slice and serve.

---

401.   Cod With Avocado Mayo Sauce

Servings: 2   Cooking Time: 20 Minutes
Ingredients:

2 cod fish fillets	2 teaspoons olive oil
1 egg	1 teaspoon lemon juice
Sea salt, to taste	
1/2 avocado, peeled, pitted, and mashed	1 garlic clove, minced
1 tablespoon mayonnaise	1/4 teaspoon black pepper
3 tablespoons sour cream	1/4 teaspoon salt
1/2 teaspoon yellow mustard	1/4 teaspoon hot pepper sauce

Directions:
Start by preheating your Air Fryer to 360 degrees F. Spritz the Air Fryer basket with cooking oil.   Pat dry the fish fillets with a kitchen towel. Beat the egg in a shallow bowl. Add in the salt and olive oil. Dip the fish into the egg mixture, making sure to coat thoroughly. Cook in the preheated Air Fryer approximately 12 minutes.   Meanwhile, make the avocado sauce by mixing the remaining ingredients in a bowl. Place in your refrigerator until ready to serve.   Serve the fish fillets with chilled avocado sauce on the side.

---

402.   Italian Shrimp Scampi

Servings: 4   Cooking Time: 20 Minutes
Ingredients:

2 egg whites	1/2 cup coconut flour
1 cup Parmigiano-Reggiano, grated	1 teaspoon garlic powder
1/2 teaspoon celery seeds	1/2 teaspoon dried rosemary
1/2 teaspoon porcini powder	1/2 teaspoon sea salt
1/2 teaspoon onion powder	1/2 teaspoon ground black pepper
	1 ½ pounds shrimp, deveined

Directions:
Whisk the egg with coconut flour and Parmigiano-Reggiano. Add in seasonings and mix to combine

well. Dip your shrimp in the batter. Roll until they are covered on all sides. Cook in the preheated Air Fryer at 390 degrees F for 5 to 7 minutes or until golden brown. Work in batches. Serve with lemon wedges if desired.

403. Fennel & Tomato Chicken Paillard

Servings: 1   Cooking Time: 12 Minutes
Ingredients:

1/4 cup olive oil	1/4 cup sliced
1 boneless skinless	mushrooms
chicken breast	2 tablespoons sliced
Salt and pepper	black olives
1 garlic clove, thinly	1-1/2 teaspoons
sliced	capers
1 small diced Roma	2 sprigs fresh thyme
tomato	1 tablespoon chopped
1/2 fennel bulb,	fresh parsley
shaved	

Directions:
Start by pounding the chicken until it is about 1/2-inch thick.   Preheat the toaster oven to 400°F and brush the bottom of a baking pan with olive oil. Sprinkle salt and pepper on both sides of the chicken and place it in the baking pan.   In a bowl, mix together all other ingredients, including the remaining olive oil.   Spoon mixture over chicken and bake for 12 minutes.

404. Grilled Halibut With Tomatoes And Hearts Of Palm

Servings: 4   Cooking Time: 15 Minutes
Ingredients:

4 halibut fillets	2 tablespoons oil
Juice from 1 lemon	½ cup hearts of
Salt and pepper to	palm, rinse and
taste	drained
	1 cup cherry tomatoes

Directions:
Place the instant pot air fryer lid on and preheat the instant pot at 390 degrees F.   Place the grill pan accessory in the instant pot.   Season the halibut fillets with lemon juice, salt, and pepper. Brush with oil.   Place the fish on the grill pan.   Arrange the hearts of palms and cherry tomatoes on the side and sprinkle with more salt and pepper.   Close the air fryer lid and cook for 15 minutes.

405. Amazing Bacon And Potato Platter

Servings: 4   Cooking Time: 40 Minutes
Ingredients:

6 garlic cloves,	4 potatoes, halved
squashed	2 sprigs rosemary
4 streaky cut rashers	1 tbsp olive oil
bacon	

Directions:
Preheat your air fryer to 392 f. In a mixing bowl, mix garlic, bacon, potatoes and rosemary; toss in oil.

Place the mixture in your air fryer's cooking basket and roast for 25-30 minutes. Serve and enjoy!

406. Turkey Wontons With Garlic-parmesan Sauce

Servings: 8   Cooking Time: 20 Minutes
Ingredients:

8 ounces cooked	1/3 cup cream cheese,
turkey breasts,	room temperature 8
shredded 16 wonton	ounces Asiago cheese,
wrappers	shredded
1½ tablespoons	1 tsp. garlic powder
margarine, melted	Fine sea salt and
3 tablespoons	freshly ground black
Parmesan cheese,	pepper, to taste
grated	

Directions:
In a small-sized bowl, mix the margarine, Parmesan, garlic powder, salt, and black pepper; give it a good stir.   Lightly grease a mini muffin pan; lay 1 wonton wrapper in each mini muffin cup. Fill each cup with the cream cheese and turkey mixture. Air-fry for 8 minutes at 335 °F. Immediately top with Asiago cheese and serve warm.

407. Kale And Brussels Sprouts

Servings: 8   Cooking Time: 7 Minutes
Ingredients:

1 lb. Brussels sprouts,	2 cups kale, torn
trimmed	1 tbsp. olive oil
3 oz. mozzarella,	Salt and black pepper
shredded	to taste.

Directions:
In a pan that fits the air fryer, combine all the Ingredients: except the mozzarella and toss.   Put the pan in the air fryer and cook at 380°F for 15 minutes   Divide between plates, sprinkle the cheese on top and serve.

408. Red Hot Chili Fish Curry

Servings: 4   Cooking Time: 20 Minutes
Ingredients:

2 tablespoons	1 cup coconut milk
sunflower oil	Salt and white
1 pound fish, chopped	pepper, to taste
2 red chilies, chopped	1/2 teaspoon
1 tablespoon	fenugreek seeds
coriander powder	1 shallot, minced
1 teaspoon red curry	1 garlic clove, minced
paste	1 ripe tomato, pureed

Directions:
Preheat your Air Fryer to 380 degrees F; brush the cooking basket with 1 tablespoon of sunflower oil. Cook your fish for 10 minutes on both sides. Transfer to the baking pan that is previously greased with the remaining tablespoon of sunflower oil. Add the remaining ingredients and reduce the heat to 350 degrees F. Continue to cook an additional 10 to 12 minutes or until everything is heated through. Enjoy!

409. Pork Chops With Chicory Treviso

Servings: 2   Cooking Time: 0-15;
Ingredients:

4 pork chops	1 chicory stalk
40g butter	Salt to taste
Flour to taste	

Directions:
Cut the chicory into small pieces. Place the butter and chicory in pieces on the basket of the air fryer previously preheated at 1800C and brown for 2 min. Add the previously floured and salted pork slices (directly over the chicory), simmer for 6 minutes turning them over after 3 minutes.   Remove the slices and place them on a serving plate, covering them with the rest of the red chicory juice collected at the bottom of the basket.

410. Garlic Butter Pork Chops

Servings: 4   Cooking Time: 8 Minutes
Ingredients:

4 pork chops	2 teaspoons parsley
1 tablespoon coconut butter	2 teaspoons garlic, grated
1 tablespoon coconut oil	Salt and black pepper, to taste

Directions:
Preheat the Air fryer to 350 degree F and grease an Air fryer basket.   Mix all the seasonings, coconut oil, garlic, butter, and parsley in a bowl and coat the pork chops with it.   Cover the chops with foil and refrigerate to marinate for about 1 hour.   Remove the foil and arrange the chops in the Air fryer basket. Cook for about 8 minutes and dish out in a bowl to serve warm.

411. Bbq Pork Ribs

Servings: 2 To 3   Cooking Time: 5 Hrs 30 Minutes
Ingredients:

1 lb pork ribs	1 tsp oregano
1 tsp soy sauce	3 tbsp barbecue sauce
Salt and black pepper to taste	2 cloves garlic, minced
1 tbsp + 1 tbsp maple syrup	1 tbsp cayenne pepper
	1 tsp sesame oil

Directions:
Put the chops on a chopping board and use a knife to cut them into smaller pieces of desired sizes. Put them in a mixing bowl, add the soy sauce, salt, pepper, oregano, one tablespoon of maple syrup, barbecue sauce, garlic, cayenne pepper, and sesame oil. Mix well and place the pork in the fridge to marinate in the spices for 5 hours.   Preheat the Air Fryer to 350 F. Open the Air Fryer and place the ribs in the fryer basket. Slide the fryer basket in and cook for 15 minutes. Open the Air fryer, turn the ribs using tongs, apply the remaining maple syrup with a brush, close the Air Fryer, and continue cooking for 10 minutes.

412. Paprika Crab Burgers

Servings: 3   Cooking Time: 20 Minutes
Ingredients:

2 eggs, beaten	1 shallot, chopped
2 garlic cloves, crushed	10 ounces crab meat
1 tablespoon olive oil	1 teaspoon smoked paprika
1 teaspoon yellow mustard	1/2 teaspoon ground black pepper
1 teaspoon fresh cilantro, chopped	Sea salt, to taste
	3/4 cup parmesan cheese

Directions:
In a mixing bowl, thoroughly combine the eggs, shallot, garlic, olive oil, mustard, cilantro, crab meat, paprika, black pepper, and salt. Mix until well combined.   Shape the mixture into 6 patties. Roll the crab patties over grated parmesan cheese, coating well on all sides. Place in your refrigerator for 2 hours.   Spritz the crab patties with cooking oil on both sides. Cook in the preheated Air Fryer at 360 degrees F for 14 minutes. Serve on dinner rolls if desired.

413. Grilled Chicken Tikka Masala

Servings: 4   Cooking Time: 20 Minutes
Ingredients:

1 tsp. Tikka Masala 1 tsp. fine sea salt	2 heaping tsps. whole grain mustard
2 tsps. coriander, ground 2 tablespoon olive oil	2 tsp.s onion powder
	1½ tablespoons cider vinegar Basmati rice, steamed
2 large-sized chicken breasts, skinless and halved lengthwise	1/3 tsp. red pepper flakes, crushed

Directions:
Preheat the air fryer to 335 °For 4 minutes.   Toss your chicken together with the other ingredients, minus basmati rice. Let it stand at least 3 hours. Cook for 25 minutes in your air fryer; check for doneness because the time depending on the size of the piece of chicken.   Serve immediately over warm basmati rice. Enjoy!

414. Carrot Beef Cake

Servings: 10   Cooking Time: 60 Minutes
Ingredients:

3 eggs, beaten	2 cups shredded carrots
1/2 cup almond milk	2 lbs. lean ground beef
1-oz. onion soup mix	1/2-lb. ground pork
1 cup dry bread crumbs	

Directions:
Thoroughly mix ground beef with carrots and all other ingredients in a bowl.   Grease a meatloaf pan with oil or butter and spread the minced beef in the pan.   Press "Power Button" of Air Fry Oven and turn the dial to select the "Bake" mode.   Press the Time button and again turn the dial to set the cooking time to 60 minutes.   Now push the Temp button and rotate the dial to set the temperature at 350 degrees F.   Once preheated, place the beef

baking pan in the oven and close its lid.   Slice and serve.

415. Fried Spicy Tofu

Servings: 4   Cooking Time: 20 Minutes
Ingredients:

16 ounces firm tofu, pressed and cubed
1 tablespoon vegan oyster sauce
1 tablespoon tamari sauce
1 teaspoon cider vinegar
1 teaspoon pure maple syrup
1 teaspoon sriracha
1/2 teaspoon shallot powder
1/2 teaspoon porcini powder
1 teaspoon garlic powder
1 tablespoon sesame oil
2 tablespoons golden flaxseed meal

Directions:
Toss the tofu with the oyster sauce, tamari sauce, vinegar,maple syrup, sriracha, shallot powder, porcini powder, garlic powder, and sesame oil. Let it marinate for 30 minutes.   Toss the marinated tofu with the flaxseed meal.   Cook at 360 degrees F for 10 minutes; turn them over and cook for 12 minutes more.

416. Scallops With Spinach

Servings: 2   Cooking Time: 10 Minutes
Ingredients:

1: 12-ouncespackage frozen spinach, thawed and drained
8 jumbo sea scallops
Olive oil cooking spray
1 tablespoon fresh basil, chopped
Salt and ground black pepper, as required
¾ cup heavy whipping cream
1 tablespoon tomato paste
1 teaspoon garlic, minced

Directions:
Preheat the Air fryer to 350 degree F and grease an Air fryer pan.   Season the scallops evenly with salt and black pepper.   Mix cream, tomato paste, garlic, basil, salt, and black pepper in a bowl. Place spinach at the bottom of the Air fryer pan, followed by seasoned scallops and top with the cream mixture.   Transfer into the Air fryer and cook for about 10 minutes.   Dish out in a platter and serve hot.

417.Cheesy Shrimp

Servings: 4   Cooking Time: 20 Minutes
Ingredients:

2/3 cup Parmesan cheese, grated
2 pounds shrimp, peeled and deveined
4 garlic cloves, minced
2 tablespoons olive oil
1 teaspoon dried basil
½ teaspoon dried oregano
1 teaspoon onion powder
½ teaspoon red pepper flakes, crushed
Ground black pepper, as required

2 tablespoons fresh lemon juice

Directions:
Preheat the Air fryer to 350 degree F and grease an Air fryer basket.   Mix Parmesan cheese, garlic, olive oil, herbs, and spices in a large bowl. Arrange half of the shrimp into the Air fryer basket in a single layer and cook for about 10 minutes. Dish out the shrimps onto serving plates and drizzle with lemon juice to serve hot.

418. Crispy Scallops

Servings: 4   Cooking Time: 6 Minutes
Ingredients:

18 sea scallops, cleaned and patted very dry
1/8 cup all-purpose flour
1 tablespoon 2% milk
½ egg
¼ cup cornflakes, crushed
½ teaspoon paprika
Salt and black pepper, as required

Directions:
Preheat the Air fryer to 400 degree F and grease an Air fryer basket.   Mix flour, paprika, salt, and black pepper in a bowl.   Whisk egg with milk in another bowl and place the cornflakes in a third bowl.   Coat each scallop with the flour mixture, dip into the egg mixture and finally, dredge in the cornflakes.   Arrange scallops in the Air fryer basket and cook for about 6 minutes.   Dish out the scallops in a platter and serve hot.

419. Breaded Shrimp With Lemon

Servings: 3   Cooking Time: 14 Minutes
Ingredients:

½ cup plain flour
2 egg whites
1 cup breadcrumbs
1 pound large shrimp, peeled and deveined
Salt and ground black pepper, as required
¼ teaspoon lemon zest
¼ teaspoon cayenne pepper
¼ teaspoon red pepper flakes, crushed
2 tablespoons vegetable oil

Directions:
Preheat the Air fryer to 400 degree F and grease an Air fryer basket.   Mix flour, salt, and black pepper in a shallow bowl.   Whisk the egg whites in a second bowl and mix the breadcrumbs, lime zest and spices in a third bowl.   Coat each shrimp with the flour, dip into egg whites and finally, dredge in the breadcrumbs.   Drizzle the shrimp evenly with olive oil and arrange half of the coated shrimps into the Air fryer basket.   Cook for about 7 minutes and dish out the coated shrimps onto serving plates. Repeat with the remaining mixture and serve hot.

420. Basil Tomatoes

Servings: 2   Cooking Time: 10 Minutes
Ingredients:

1 tablespoon fresh basil, chopped
Olive oil cooking spray

2 tomatoes, halved
Salt and black pepper, as required

Directions:
Preheat the Air fryer to 320 degree F and grease an Air fryer basket. Spray the tomato halves evenly with olive oil cooking spray and season with salt, black pepper and basil. Arrange the tomato halves into the Air fryer basket, cut sides up. Cook for about 10 minutes and dish out onto serving plates.

421. Rigatoni With Roasted Broccoli And Chick Peas

Servings: 4   Cooking Time: 10 Minutes
Ingredients:
1 can anchovies packed in oil
4 cloves garlic, chopped
1 can chickpeas
1 chicken bouillon cube

1 pound broccoli, cut into small florets
1/2 pound whole wheat rigatoni
1/2 cup grated Romano cheese

Directions:
Drain and chop anchovies (set aside oil for later use), and cut broccoli into small florets. Preheat toaster oven to 450°F. In a shallow sauce pan, sauté anchovies in their oil, with garlic, until the garlic browns. Drain the chickpeas, saving the canned liquid. Add the chickpea liquid and bouillon to the anchovies, stir until bouillon dissolves. Pour anchovy mix into a roasting pan and add broccoli and chickpeas. Roast for 20 minutes. While the veggies roast, cook rigatoni per package directions; drain the pasta, saving one cup of water. Add the pasta to the anchovy mix and roast for another 10 minutes. Add reserved water, stirring in a little at a time until the pasta reaches the desired consistency. Top with Romano and serve.

422. Scallops With Capers Sauce

Servings: 2   Cooking Time: 6 Minutes
Ingredients:
10: 1-ouncesea scallops, cleaned and patted very dry
2 teaspoons capers, finely chopped
Salt and ground black pepper, as required
¼ cup extra-virgin olive oil

2 tablespoons fresh parsley, finely chopped
1 teaspoon fresh lemon zest, finely grated
½ teaspoon garlic, finely chopped

Directions:
Preheat the Air fryer to 390 degree F and grease an Air fryer basket. Season the scallops evenly with salt and black pepper. Arrange the scallops in the Air fryer basket and cook for about 6 minutes. Mix parsley, capers, olive oil, lemon zest and garlic in a bowl. Dish out the scallops in a platter and top with capers sauce.

423. Sirloin Steak With Cremini Mushroom Sauce

Servings: 5   Cooking Time: 20 Minutes
Ingredients:
2 tablespoons butter
2 pounds sirloin, cut into four pieces
Salt and cracked black pepper, to taste
1 teaspoon cayenne pepper
1/2 teaspoon dried rosemary

1/2 teaspoon dried dill
1/4 teaspoon dried thyme
1 pound Cremini mushrooms, sliced
1 cup sour cream
1 teaspoon mustard
1/2 teaspoon curry powder

Directions:
Start by preheating your Air Fryer to 396 degrees F. Grease a baking pan with butter. Add the sirloin, salt, black pepper, cayenne pepper, rosemary, dill, and thyme to the baking pan. Cook for 9 minutes. Next, stir in the mushrooms, sour cream, mustard, and curry powder. Continue to cook another 5 minutes or until everything is heated through. Spoon onto individual serving plates.

424. Chat Masala Grilled Snapper

Servings: 5   Cooking Time: 25 Minutes
Ingredients:
2 ½ pounds whole fish
Salt to taste
3 tablespoons fresh lime juice

1/3 cup chat masala
5 tablespoons olive oil

Directions:
Place the instant pot air fryer lid on and preheat the instant pot at 390 degrees F. Place the grill pan accessory in the instant pot. Season the fish with salt, chat masala and lime juice. Brush with oil Place the fish on a foil basket and place it inside the grill. Close the air fryer lid and cook for 25 minutes.

425. Sesame Seeds Bok Choy

Servings: 4   Cooking Time: 6 Minutes
Ingredients:
4 bunches baby bok choy, bottoms removed and leaves separated
1 teaspoon sesame seeds

Olive oil cooking spray
1 teaspoon garlic powder

Directions:
Preheat the Air fryer to 325F and grease an Air fryer basket. Arrange the bok choy leaves into the Air fryer basket and spray with the cooking spray. Sprinkle with garlic powder and cook for about 6 minutes, shaking twice in between. Dish out in the bok choy onto serving plates and serve garnished with sesame seeds.

426. Sage Sausages Balls

Servings: 4   Cooking Time: 20 Minutes

Ingredients:

3 ½ oz sausages, sliced	1 cup onion, chopped
Salt and black pepper to taste	3 tbsp breadcrumbs
	½ tsp garlic puree
	1 tsp sage

Directions:

Preheat your air fryer to 340 f. In a bowl, mix onions, sausage meat, sage, garlic puree, salt and pepper. Add breadcrumbs to a plate. Form balls using the mixture and roll them in breadcrumbs. Add onion balls in your air fryer's cooking basket and cook for 15 minutes. Serve and enjoy!

427. Broccoli Stuffed Peppers

Servings: 2   Cooking Time: 40 Minutes

Ingredients:

4 eggs	1 tsp dried thyme
1/2 cup cheddar cheese, grated	1/4 cup feta cheese, crumbled 1/2 cup broccoli, cooked
2 bell peppers, cut in half and remove seeds 1/2 tsp garlic powder	1/4 tsp pepper 1/2 tsp salt

Directions:

Preheat the air fryer to 325 F.   Stuff feta and broccoli into the bell peppers halved.   Beat egg in a bowl with seasoning and pour egg mixture into the pepper halved over feta and broccoli.   Place bell pepper halved into the air fryer basket and cook for 35-40 minutes.   Top with grated cheddar cheese and cook until cheese melted.   Serve and enjoy.

428. Irish Whisky Steak

Servings: 6   Cooking Time: 20 Minutes

Ingredients:

2 pounds sirloin steaks	2 garlic cloves, thinly sliced
1 ½ tablespoons tamari sauce	2 tablespoons Irish whiskey
1/3 teaspoon cayenne pepper	2 tablespoons olive oil
1/3 teaspoon ground ginger	Fine sea salt, to taste

Directions:

Firstly, add all the ingredients, minus the olive oil and the steak, to a resealable plastic bag.   Throw in the steak and let it marinate for a couple of hours. After that, drizzle the sirloin steaks with 2 tablespoons olive oil.   Roast for approximately 22 minutes at 395 degrees F, turning it halfway through the time.

429. Beef Roast

Servings: 4   **Ingredients:**

1 tbsp. smoked paprika	2 lbs. beef roast
3 tbsp. garlic; minced	3 tbsp. olive oil
	Salt and black pepper to taste

Directions:

In a bowl, combine all the ingredients and coat the roast well.   Place the roast in your air fryer and cook at 390°F for 55 minutes. Slice the roast, divide it between plates and serve with a side salad

430. Roasted Lamb

Servings: 4   Cooking Time: 1 Hour 30 Minutes

Ingredients:

2½ pounds half lamb leg roast, slits carved	2 garlic cloves, sliced into smaller slithers
1 tablespoon dried rosemary	Cracked Himalayan rock salt and cracked peppercorns, to taste
1 tablespoon olive oil	

Directions:

Preheat the Air fryer to 400 degree F and grease an Air fryer basket.   Insert the garlic slithers in the slits and brush with rosemary, oil, salt, and black pepper.   Arrange the lamb in the Air fryer basket and cook for about 15 minutes.   Set the Air fryer to 350 degree F on the Roast mode and cook for 1 hour and 15 minutes.   Dish out the lamb chops and serve hot.

431. Cheese Zucchini Boats

Servings: 2   Cooking Time: 20 Minutes

Ingredients:

2 medium zucchinis	2 tbsp. grated vegetarian Parmesan cheese
¼ cup full-fat ricotta cheese	
¼ cup shredded mozzarella cheese	1 tbsp. avocado oil
¼ cup low-carb, no-sugar-added pasta sauce.	¼ tsp. garlic powder.
	½ tsp. dried parsley.
	¼ tsp. dried oregano.

Directions:

Cut off 1-inch from the top and bottom of each zucchini.   Slice zucchini in half lengthwise and use a spoon to scoop out a bit of the inside, making room for filling. Brush with oil and spoon 2 tbsp. pasta sauce into each shell   Take a medium bowl, mix ricotta, mozzarella, oregano, garlic powder and parsley   Spoon the mixture into each zucchini shell. Place stuffed zucchini shells into the air fryer basket.   Adjust the temperature to 350 Degrees F and set the timer for 20 minutes   To remove from the fryer basket, use tongs or a spatula and carefully lift out. Top with Parmesan. Serve immediately.

432. Asparagus Frittata

Servings: 4   Cooking Time: 10 Minutes

Ingredients:

6 eggs	2 tsp butter, melted
3 mushrooms, sliced	1 cup mozzarella cheese, shredded 1 tsp pepper
10 asparagus, chopped 1/4 cup half and half	1 tsp salt

Directions:

Toss mushrooms and asparagus with melted butter and add into the air fryer basket.   Cook mushrooms and asparagus at 350 F for 5 minutes. Shake basket twice.   Meanwhile, in a bowl, whisk together eggs, half and half, pepper, and salt. Transfer cook mushrooms and asparagus into the air fryer baking dish.   Pour egg mixture over mushrooms and asparagus. Place dish in the air fryer and cook at 350 F for 5 minutes or until eggs are set. Slice and serve.

---

433. Salmon Steak Grilled With Cilantro Garlic Sauce

Servings: 2   Cooking Time: 15 Minutes

Ingredients:

2 salmon steaks	2 cloves of garlic, minced
Salt and pepper to taste	1 cup cilantro leaves
2 tablespoons vegetable oil	½ cup Greek yogurt
	1 teaspoon honey

Directions:
Place the instant pot air fryer lid on and preheat the instant pot at 390 degrees F. Place the grill pan accessory in the instant pot. Season the salmon steaks with salt and pepper. Brush with oil. Place on the grill pan, close the air fryer lid and grill for 15 minutes and make sure to flip halfway through the cooking time. In a food processor, mix the garlic, cilantro leaves, yogurt, and honey. Season with salt and pepper to taste. Pulse until smooth. Serve the salmon steaks with the cilantro sauce.

---

434. Herbed Carrots

Servings: 8   Cooking Time: 14 Minutes

Ingredients:

2 tablespoons olive oil	6 large carrots, peeled and sliced lengthwise
½ tablespoon fresh oregano, chopped	2 tablespoons olive oil, divided
½ tablespoon fresh parsley, chopped	½ cup fat-free Italian dressing
Salt and black pepper, to taste	Salt, to taste

Directions:
Preheat the Air fryer to 360-degree F and grease an Air fryer basket. Mix the carrot slices and olive oil in a bowl and toss to coat well. Arrange the carrot slices in the Air fryer basket and cook for about 12 minutes. Dish out the carrot slices onto serving plates and sprinkle with herbs, salt and black pepper. Transfer into the Air fryer basket and cook for 2 more minutes. Dish out and serve hot.

---

435. Lemongrass Pork Chops

Servings: 3   Cooking Time: 2 Hrs 20 Minutes

Ingredients:

3 slices pork chops	2 shallots, chopped
2 garlic cloves, minced	2 tbsp olive oil
1 ½ tbsp sugar	1 ¼ tsp soy sauce
4 stalks lemongrass, trimmed and chopped	1 ¼ tsp fish sauce
	1 ½ tsp black pepper

Directions:
In a bowl, add the garlic, sugar, lemongrass, shallots, olive oil, soy sauce, fish sauce, and black pepper; mix well. Add the pork chops, coat them with the mixture and allow to marinate for around 2 hours to

get nice and savory. Preheat the Air Fryer to 400 F. Cooking in 2 to 3 batches, remove and shake each pork chop from the marinade and place it in the fryer basket. Cook it for 7 minutes. Turn the pork chops with kitchen tongs and cook further for 5 minutes. Remove the chops and serve with a side of sautéed asparagus.

---

436. Traditional English Fish And Chips

Servings: 4   Cooking Time: 17 Minutes

Ingredients:

1 3/4 pounds potatoes	8 sprigs fresh thyme
4 tablespoons olive oil	4 (6-ounce) pieces cod
1-1/4 teaspoons kosher salt	1 lemon
1-1/4 teaspoons black pepper	1 clove garlic
	2 tablespoons capers

Directions:
Start by preheating toaster oven to 450°F. Cut potatoes into 1-inch chunks. Place potatoes, 2 tablespoons oil, salt, and thyme in a baking tray and toss to combine. Spread in a flat layer and bake for 30 minutes. Wrap mixture in foil to keep warm. Wipe tray with a paper towel and then lay cod in the tray. Slice the lemon and top cod with lemon, salt, pepper, and thyme. Drizzle rest of the oil over the cod and bake for 12 minutes. Place cod and potatoes on separate pans and bake together for an additional 5 minutes. Combine and serve.

---

437. Miso-glazed Salmon

Servings: 4   Cooking Time: 5 Minutes

Ingredients:

1/4 cup red or white miso	2 tablespoons vegetable oil
1/3 cup sake	1/4 cup sugar
1 tablespoon soy sauce	4 skinless salmon filets

Directions:
In a shallow bowl, mix together the miso, sake, oil, soy sauce, and sugar. Toss the salmon in the mixture until thoroughly coated on all sides. Preheat your toaster oven to "high" on broil mode. Place salmon in a broiling pan and broil until the top is well charred—about 5 minutes.

---

438. Steak With Cascabel-garlic Sauce

Servings: 4   Cooking Time: 20 Minutes

Ingredients:

2 teaspoons brown mustard	2 teaspoons cumin seeds
2 tablespoons mayonnaise	3 cloves garlic, pressed
1 ½ pounds beef flank steak, trimmed and cubed	Pink peppercorns to taste, freshly cracked
2 teaspoons minced	1 teaspoon fine table salt

cascabel
½ cup scallions, finely chopped
1/3 cup Crème fraîche
1/3 teaspoon black pepper, preferably freshly ground

Directions:
Firstly, fry the cumin seeds just about 1 minute or until they pop.   After that, season your beef flank steak with fine table salt, black pepper and the fried cumin seeds; arrange the seasoned beef cubes on the bottom of your baking dish that fits in the air fryer. Throw in the minced cascabel, garlic, and scallions; air-fry approximately 8 minutes at 390 degrees F. Once the beef cubes start to tender, add your favorite mayo, Crème fraîche, freshly cracked pink peppercorns and mustard; air-fry 7 minutes longer. Serve over hot wild rice.

439.   Prawn Burgers

Servings: 2   Cooking Time: 6 Minutes
Ingredients:

½ cup prawns, peeled, deveined and finely chopped
½ cup breadcrumbs
2-3 tablespoons onion, finely chopped
3 cups fresh baby greens
½ teaspoon ginger, minced

½ teaspoon garlic, minced
½ teaspoon red chili powder
½ teaspoon ground cumin
¼ teaspoon ground turmeric
Salt and ground black pepper, as required

Directions:
Preheat the Air fryer to 390 degree F and grease an Air fryer basket.   Mix the prawns, breadcrumbs, onion, ginger, garlic, and spices in a bowl.   Make small-sized patties from the mixture and transfer to the Air fryer basket.   Cook for about 6 minutes and dish out in a platter.   Serve immediately warm alongside the baby greens.

440.   Green Beans And Lime Sauce

Servings: 4   Cooking Time: 20 Minutes
Ingredients:

1 lb. green beans, trimmed
2 tbsp. ghee; melted
1 tbsp. lime juice

1 tsp. chili powder
A pinch of salt and black pepper

Directions:
Take a bowl and mix the ghee with the rest of the ingredients except the green beans and whisk really well.   Mix the green beans with the lime sauce, toss   Put them in your air fryer's basket and cook at 400°F for 8 minutes. Serve right away.

441.   Baby Portabellas With Romano Cheese

Servings: 4   Cooking Time: 20 Minutes
Ingredients:

1 pound baby portabellas

1/2 teaspoon shallot powder

1/2 cup almond meal
2 eggs
2 tablespoons milk
1 cup Romano cheese, grated
Sea salt and ground black pepper

1 teaspoon garlic powder
1/2 teaspoon cumin powder
1/2 teaspoon cayenne pepper

Directions:
Pat the mushrooms dry with a paper towel.   To begin, set up your breading station. Place the almond meal in a shallow dish. In a separate dish, whisk the eggs with milk.   Finally, place grated Romano cheese and seasonings in the third dish. Start by dredging the baby portabellas in the almond meal mixture; then, dip them into the egg wash. Press the baby portabellas into Romano cheese, coating evenly.   Spritz the Air Fryer basket with cooking oil. Add the baby portabellas and cook at 400 degrees F for 6 minutes, flipping them halfway through the cooking time.

442.   Creole Beef Meatloaf

Servings: 6   Cooking Time: 15 Minutes
Ingredients:

1 lb. ground beef
1/2 tablespoon butter
1 red bell pepper diced
1/3 cup red onion diced
1/3 cup cilantro diced
1/3 cup zucchini diced

1 tablespoon creole seasoning
1/2 teaspoon turmeric
1/2 teaspoon cumin
1/2 teaspoon coriander
2 garlic cloves minced
Salt and black pepper to taste

Directions:
Mix the beef minced with all the meatball ingredients in a bowl.   Make small meatballs out of this mixture and place them in the Air fryer basket. Press "Power Button" of Air Fry Oven and turn the dial to select the "Air Fry" mode.   Press the Time button and again turn the dial to set the cooking time to 15 minutes.   Now push the Temp button and rotate the dial to set the temperature at 370 degrees F.   Once preheated, place the Air fryer basket in the oven and close its lid.   Slice and serve warm.

443.   Cheese Breaded Pork

Servings: 6   Cooking Time: 15 Minutes
Ingredients:

6 pork chops
6 tbsp seasoned breadcrumbs
2 tbsp parmesan cheese, grated

1 tbsp melted butter
½ cup mozzarella cheese, shredded
1 tbsp marinara sauce

Directions:
Preheat your air fryer to 390 f. Grease the cooking basket with cooking spray. In a small bowl, mix breadcrumbs and parmesan cheese. In another microwave proof bowl, add butter and melt in the microwave.   Brush the pork with butter and dredge into the breadcrumbs. Add pork to the cooking basket and cook for 6 minutes. Turnover

and top with marinara sauce and shredded mozzarella; cook for 3 more minutes

444. Artichoke Spinach Casserole

Servings: 4   Cooking Time: 20 Minutes

Ingredients:

⅓cup full-fat mayonnaise	2 cups fresh spinach; chopped
oz. full-fat cream cheese; softened.	2 cups cauliflower florets; chopped
¼ cup diced yellow onion	1 cup artichoke hearts; chopped
⅓cup full-fat sour cream.	1 tbsp. salted butter; melted.
¼ cup chopped pickled jalapeños.	

Directions:

Take a large bowl, mix butter, onion, cream cheese, mayonnaise and sour cream. Fold in jalapeños, spinach, cauliflower and artichokes.   Pour the mixture into a 4-cup round baking dish. Cover with foil and place into the air fryer basket   Adjust the temperature to 370 Degrees F and set the timer for 15 minutes. In the last 2 minutes of cooking, remove the foil to brown the top. Serve warm.

445. Lemon Duck Legs

Servings: 6   Cooking Time: 25 Minutes

Ingredients:

1 lemon	
2-pound duck legs	½ teaspoon dried rosemary
1 teaspoon ground coriander	1 tablespoon olive oil
1 teaspoon ground nutmeg	1 teaspoon stevia extract
1 teaspoon kosher salt	¼ teaspoon sage

Directions:

Squeeze the juice from the lemon and grate the zest. Combine the lemon juice and lemon zest together in the big mixing bowl.   Add the ground coriander, ground nutmeg, kosher salt, dried rosemary, and sage.   Sprinkle the liquid with the olive oil and stevia extract.   Whisk it carefully and put the duck legs there.   Stir the duck legs and leave them for 15 minutes to marinate.   Meanwhile, preheat the air fryer to 380 F.   Put the marinated duck legs in the air fryer and cook them for 25 minutes.   Turn the duck legs into another side after 15 minutes of cooking.   When the duck legs are cooked – let them cool little.   Serve and enjoy!

446. Cajun Fish Fritters

Servings: 4   Cooking Time: 20 Minutes

Ingredients:

2 catfish fillets	3 ounces butter
1 cup parmesan cheese	1/2 cup buttermilk
1 teaspoon baking powder	1 teaspoon Cajun seasoning
1 teaspoon baking soda	1 cup Swiss cheese, shredded

Directions:

Bring a pot of salted water to a boil. Boil the fish fillets for 5 minutes or until it is opaque. Flake the fish into small pieces.   Mix the remaining ingredients in a bowl; add the fish and mix until well combined. Shape the fish mixture into 12 patties. Cook in the preheated Air Fryer at 380 degrees F for 15 minutes. Work in batches. Enjoy!

447. Baked Egg And Veggies

Servings: 2   Cooking Time: 20 Minutes

Ingredients:

1 cup fresh spinach; chopped	1 medium Roma tomato; diced
1 small zucchini, sliced lengthwise and quartered	2 large eggs.
	2 tbsp. salted butter
½ medium green bell pepper; seeded and diced	¼ tsp. garlic powder.
	¼ tsp. onion powder.
	½ tsp. dried basil
	¼ tsp. dried oregano.

Directions:

Grease two (4-inchramekins with 1 tbsp. butter each. Take a large bowl, toss zucchini, bell pepper, spinach and tomatoes. Divide the mixture in two and place half in each ramekin.   Crack an egg on top of each ramekin and sprinkle with onion powder, garlic powder, basil and oregano. Place into the air fryer basket. Adjust the temperature to 330 Degrees F and set the timer for 10 minutes. Serve immediately.

448. Five Spice Pork

Servings: 4   Cooking Time: 20 Minutes

Ingredients:

1-pound pork belly	2 tablespoons swerve
2 tablespoons dark soy sauce	2 teaspoons ginger, minced
1 tablespoon Shaoxing: cooking wine	1 tablespoon hoisin sauce
2 teaspoons garlic, minced	1 teaspoon Chinese Five Spice

Directions:

Preheat the Air fryer to 390 degree F and grease an Air fryer basket.   Mix all the ingredients in a bowl and place in the Ziplock bag.   Seal the bag, shake it well and refrigerate to marinate for about 1 hour. Remove the pork from the bag and arrange it in the Air fryer basket.   Cook for about 15 minutes and dish out in a bowl to serve warm.

449. Okra With Green Beans

Servings: 2   Cooking Time: 20 Minutes

Ingredients:

½, 10-ouncesbag frozen cut okra	½, 10-ouncesbag frozen cut green beans
¼ cup nutritional yeast	
3 tablespoons balsamic vinegar	Salt and black pepper, to taste

Directions:

92

Preheat the Air fryer to 400F and grease an Air fryer basket. Mix the okra, green beans, nutritional yeast, vinegar, salt, and black pepper in a bowl and toss to coat well. Arrange the okra mixture into the Air fryer basket and cook for about 20 minutes. Dish out in a serving dish and serve hot.

450. Creamy Breaded Shrimp

Servings: 3   Cooking Time: 20 Minutes
Ingredients:

¼ cup all-purpose flour	½ cup mayonnaise
1 cup panko breadcrumbs	¼ cup sweet chili sauce
1 pound shrimp, peeled and deveined	1 tablespoon Sriracha sauce

Directions:
Preheat the Air fryer to 400-degree F and grease an Air fryer basket. Place flour in a shallow bowl and mix the mayonnaise, chili sauce, and Sriracha sauce in another bowl. Place the breadcrumbs in a third bowl. Coat each shrimp with the flour, dip into mayonnaise mixture and finally, dredge in the breadcrumbs. Arrange half of the coated shrimps into the Air fryer basket and cook for about 10 minutes. Dish out the coated shrimps onto serving plates and repeat with the remaining mixture.

451. Tex-mex Chicken Quesadillas

Servings: 4   Cooking Time: 10 Minutes
Ingredients:

2 green onions	1/4 cup fresh cilantro leaves
2 cups shredded skinless rotisserie chicken meat	4 burrito-size flour tortillas
1-1/2 cups shredded Monterey Jack cheese	1/2 cup reduced-fat sour cream
1 pickled jalapeño	

Directions:
Start by preheating toaster oven to 425°F. Thinly slice the green onions and break apart. Mix together chicken, cheese, jalapeño, and onions in a bowl, then evenly divide mixture onto one half of each tortilla. Fold opposite half over mixture and place quesadillas onto a baking sheet. Bake for 10 minutes. Cut in halves or quarters and serve with sour cream.

452. Mozzarella & Olive Pizza Bagels

Servings: 4   Cooking Time: 10 Minutes
Ingredients:

1/4 cup marinara sauce	2 whole wheat bagels
1/4 teaspoon Italian seasoning	1/4 cup chopped green pepper
1/8 teaspoon red pepper flakes	3 tablespoons sliced black olives
3/4 cup shredded low-moisture mozzarella cheese	Fresh basil
	1 teaspoon parmesan cheese

Directions:
Start by preheating toaster oven to 375°F and lining a pan with parchment paper. Cut bagels in half and lay on pan with inside facing up. Spread sauce over each half. Sprinkle red pepper flakes and 2 tablespoons of mozzarella over each half. Top each half with olives and peppers and then top with another tablespoon of mozzarella. Bake for 8 minutes, then switch to broil setting and broil for another 2 minutes. Top with basil and parmesan and serve.

453. Tasty Grilled Red Mullet

Servings: 8   Cooking Time: 15 Minutes
Ingredients:

8 whole red mullets, gutted and scales removed	Salt and pepper to taste
Juice from 1 lemon	1 tablespoon olive oil

Directions:
Place the instant pot air fryer lid on and preheat the instant pot at 390 degrees F. Place the grill pan accessory in the instant pot. Season the red mullet with salt, pepper, and lemon juice. Place red mullets on the grill pan and brush with olive oil. Close the air fryer lid and grill for 15 minutes.

454. Couscous Stuffed Tomatoes

Servings: 4   Cooking Time: 25 Minutes
Ingredients:

4 tomatoes, tops and seeds removed	1½ cups couscous
1 parsnip, peeled and finely chopped	1 teaspoon olive oil
1 cup mushrooms, chopped	1 garlic clove, minced
	1 tablespoon mirin sauce

Directions:
Preheat the Air fryer to 355 degree F and grease an Air fryer basket. Heat olive oil in a skillet on low heat and add parsnips, mushrooms and garlic. Cook for about 5 minutes and stir in the mirin sauce and couscous. Stuff the couscous mixture into the tomatoes and arrange into the Air fryer basket. Cook for about 20 minutes and dish out to serve warm.

455. Grilled Tasty Scallops

Servings: 2   Cooking Time: 10 Minutes
Ingredients:

1 pound sea scallops, cleaned and patted dry	1 tablespoon dried oregano
Salt and pepper to taste	1 tablespoon ground coriander
3 dried chilies	1 tablespoon ground fennel
2 tablespoon dried thyme	2 teaspoons chipotle pepper

Directions:
Place the instant pot air fryer lid on and preheat the instant pot at 390 degrees F. Place the grill pan accessory in the instant pot. Mix all ingredients in

a bowl.   Dump the scallops on the grill pan, close the air fryer lid and cook for 10 minutes.

456.   Lemony Green Beans

Servings: 3   Cooking Time: 12 Minutes

Ingredients:

1 pound green beans, trimmed and halved	1 tablespoon fresh lemon juice
1 teaspoon butter, melted	¼ teaspoon garlic powder

Directions:

Preheat the Air fryer to 400F and grease an Air fryer basket.   Mix all the ingredients in a bowl and toss to coat well.   Arrange the green beans into the Air fryer basket and cook for about 12 minutes.   Dish out in a serving plate and serve hot.

457.   Bacon Pork Bites

Servings: 6   Cooking Time: 14 Minutes

Ingredients:

1-pound pork brisket	½ teaspoon red pepper
6 oz. bacon, sliced	
1 teaspoon salt	1 teaspoon olive oil
1 teaspoon turmeric	1 tablespoon apple cider vinegar

Directions:

Cut the pork brisket into the medium bites.   Then put the pork bites in the big mixing bowl. Sprinkle the meat with the turmeric, salt, red pepper, and apple cider vinegar.   Mix the pork bites carefully and leave them for 10 minutes to marinate. Then wrap the pork bites in the sliced bacon. Secure the pork bites with the toothpicks. Preheat the air fryer to 370 F.   Put the prepared bacon pork bites on the air fryer tray.   Cook the pork bites for 8 minutes.   After this, turn the pork bites into another side.   Cook the dish for 6 minutes more.   When the bacon pork bites are cooked – let them in the air fryer for 2 minutes. Then transfer the dish to the serving plate.   Enjoy!

458.   Sautéed Green Beans

Servings: 2   Cooking Time: 10 Minutes

Ingredients:

8 ounces fresh green beans, trimmed and cut in half	1 teaspoon sesame oil
	1 tablespoon soy sauce

Directions:

Preheat the Air fryer to 390F and grease an Air fryer basket.   Mix green beans, soy sauce, and sesame oil in a bowl and toss to coat well.   Arrange green beans into the Air fryer basket and cook for about 10 minutes, tossing once in between.   Dish out onto serving plates and serve hot.

459.   Smoked Sausage And Bacon Shashlik

Servings: 4   Cooking Time: 20 Minutes

Ingredients:

1 pound smoked Polish beef sausage, sliced	1 tablespoon mustard
	2 bell peppers, sliced
1 tablespoon olive oil	Salt and ground black pepper, to taste
2 tablespoons Worcestershire sauce	

Directions:

Toss the sausage with the mustard, olive, and Worcestershire sauce. Thread sausage and peppers onto skewers.   Sprinkle with salt and black pepper. Cook in the preheated Air Fryer at 360 degrees Ffor 11 minutes. Brush the skewers with the reserved marinade.

460.   Chargrilled Halibut Niçoise With Vegetables

Servings: 6   Cooking Time: 15 Minutes

Ingredients:

1 ½ pounds halibut fillets	4 cups torn lettuce leaves
Salt and pepper to taste	1 cup cherry tomatoes, halved
2 tablespoons olive oil	4 large hard-boiled eggs, peeled and sliced
2 pounds mixed vegetables	

Directions:

Place the instant pot air fryer lid on and preheat the instant pot at 390 degrees F.   Place the grill pan accessory in the instant pot.   Rub the halibut with salt and pepper. Brush the fish with oil.   Place on the grill.   Surround the fish fillet with the mixed vegetables, close the air fryer lid and grill for 15 minutes.   Assemble the salad by serving the fish fillet with mixed grilled vegetables, lettuce, cherry tomatoes, and hard-boiled eggs.

Fish & Seafood Recipes

461. Saucy Cod With Green Onions

Servings: 4   Cooking Time: 20 Minutes

Ingredients:

4 cod fillets	5 slices of ginger,
2 tbsp fresh cilantro,	chopped
chopped	5 tbsp soy sauce
Salt to taste	3 tbsp oil
4 green onions,	5 rock sugar cubes
chopped	

Directions:

Preheat Instant Vortex on AirFry function to 390 F. Season the cod with salt and coriander and drizzle with some olive oil. Place the fish fillet in the basket and press Start. Cook for 15 minutes.   Heat the remaining olive oil in a skillet over medium heat and sauté green onions and ginger for 3 minutes. Add in the remaining ingredients and 1 cup of water. Bring to a boil and cook for 5 minutes until the sauce thickens. Pour the sauce over the fish and serve.

462. Fried Calamari

Servings: 6-8   Cooking Time: 7 Minutes

Ingredients:

½ tsp. salt	
½ tsp. Old Bay	½ C. semolina flour
seasoning	
1/3 C. plain cornmeal	½ C. almond flour
	5-6 C. olive oil
	1 ½ pounds baby squid

Directions:

Preparing the Ingredients. Rinse squid in cold water and slice tentacles, keeping just ¼-inch of the hood in one piece.   Combine 1-2 pinches of pepper, salt, Old Bay seasoning, cornmeal, and both flours together. Dredge squid pieces into flour mixture and place into the Instant Vortex air fryer oven.   Air Frying. Spray liberally with olive oil. Cook 15 minutes at 345 degrees till coating turns a golden brown.

463. Spicy Halibut

Servings: 4   Cooking Time: 12 Minutes

Ingredients:

1 lb halibut fillets	1/4 cup olive oil
1/2 tsp chili powder	1/4 tsp garlic powder
1/2 tsp smoked	Pepper
paprika	Salt

Directions:

Fit the Instant Vortex oven with the rack in position Place halibut fillets in a baking dish.   In a small bowl, mix oil, garlic powder, paprika, pepper, chili powder, and salt.   Brush fish fillets with oil mixture.   Set to bake at 425 F for 17 minutes. After 5 minutes place the baking dish in the preheated oven.   Serve and enjoy.

464. Panko-crusted Tilapia

Servings: 3   Cooking Time: 10 Minutes

Ingredients:

2 tsp. Italian	1/3 C. egg whites
seasoning	1/3 C. almond flour
2 tsp. lemon pepper	3 tilapia fillets
1/3 C. panko	Olive oil
breadcrumbs	

Directions:

Preparing the Ingredients. Place panko, egg whites, and flour into separate bowls. Mix lemon pepper and Italian seasoning in with breadcrumbs.   Pat tilapia fillets dry. Dredge in flour, then egg, then breadcrumb mixture.   Air Frying. Add to the Oven rack/basket and spray lightly with olive oil. Place the Rack on the middle-shelf of the Instant Vortex air fryer oven.   Cook 10-11 minutes at 400 degrees, making sure to flip halfway through cooking.

465. Parmesan Tilapia Fillets

Servings: 4   Cooking Time: 15 Minutes

Ingredients:

¾ cup Parmesan	1 tsp paprika
cheese, grated	
1 tbsp olive oil	¼ tsp garlic powder
1 tbsp fresh parsley,	¼ tsp salt
chopped	4 tilapia fillets

Directions:

Preheat Instant Vortex on AirFry function to 350 F. In a bowl, mix parsley, Parmesan cheese, garlic, salt, and paprika. Coat in the tilapia fillets and place them in a lined baking sheet. Drizzle with the olive oil press Start. Cook cook for 8-10 minutes until golden. Serve warm.

466. Fish Oregano Fingers

Ingredients:

½ lb. firm white fish fillet cut into Oregano Fingers	3 tbsp. lemon juice
	2 tsp salt
1 tbsp. lemon juice	1 ½ tsp pepper powder
2 cups of dry breadcrumbs	1 tsp red chili flakes or to taste
1 cup oil for frying	3 eggs
1 ½ tbsp. ginger-garlic paste	5 tbsp. corn flour
	2 tsp tomato ketchup

Directions:

Rub a little lemon juice on the Oregano Fingers and set aside. Wash the fish after an hour and pat dry. Make the marinade and transfer the Oregano Fingers into the marinade. Leave them on a plate to dry for fifteen minutes. Now cover the Oregano Fingers with the crumbs and set aside to dry for fifteen minutes.   Pre heat the Instant Vortex oven at 160 degrees Fahrenheit for 5 minutes or so. Keep the fish in the fry basket now and close it properly. Let the Oregano Fingers cook at the same temperature for another 25 minutes. In between the cooking process, toss the fish once in a while to avoid burning the food. Serve either with tomato ketchup or chili sauce. Mint sauce also works well with the fish.

---

467.   Old Bay Crab Cakes

Servings: 4   Cooking Time: 20 Minutes

Ingredients:

2 slices dried bread, crusts removed	Small amount of milk
1 tablespoon mayonnaise	1 tablespoon parsley flakes
1 tablespoon Worcestershire sauce	1 teaspoon Old Bay® Seasoning
1 tablespoon baking powder	1/4 teaspoon salt
	1 egg
	1 pound lump crabmeat

Directions:
Preparing the Ingredients. Crush your bread over a large bowl until it is broken down into small pieces. Add milk and stir until bread crumbs are moistened. Mix in mayo and Worcestershire sauce. Add remaining ingredients and mix well. Shape into 4 patties.   Air Frying. Cook at 360 degrees for 20 minutes, flip half way through.

---

468.   Party Cod Nuggets

Servings: 4   Cooking Time: 25 Minutes

Ingredients:

1 ¼ lb cod fillets, cut into 4 chunks each	1 cup cornflakes
½ cup flour	1 tbsp olive oil
1 egg	Salt and black pepper to taste

Directions:
Place the oil and cornflakes in a food processor and process until crumbed. Season the fish chunks with salt and pepper. In a bowl, beat the egg with 1 tbsp of water.   Dredge the chunks in flour first, then dip in the egg, and finally coat with cornflakes. Arrange on a lined sheet and press Start. Cook on AirFry function at 350 F for 15 minutes until crispy. Serve.

---

469.   Lemon-garlic Butter Lobster

Servings: 2   Cooking Time: 15 Minutes

Ingredients:

4 oz lobster tails	Salt and black pepper to taste
1 tsp garlic, minced	½ tbsp lemon Juice
1 tbsp butter	

Directions:
Add all the ingredients to a food processor except for lobster and blend well. Wash lobster and halve using a meat knife; clean the skin of the lobster and cover with the marinade.   Preheat your Instant Vortex to 380 F on Air Fry function. Place the lobster in the cooking basket and fit in the baking tray; cook for 10 minutes. Serve with fresh herbs.

---

470.   Salmon & Caper Cakes

Servings: 2   Cooking Time: 15 Minutes + Chilling Time

Ingredients:

8 oz salmon, cooked	1 tbsp fresh parsley, chopped
1 ½ oz potatoes, mashed	Zest of 1 lemon
A handful of capers	1 ¾ oz plain flour

Directions:
Carefully flake the salmon. In a bowl, mix the salmon, zest, capers, dill, and mashed potatoes. Form small cakes from the mixture and dust them with flour; refrigerate for 60 minutes. Preheat Instant Vortex to 350 F. Press Start and cook the cakes for 10 minutes on AirFry function. Serve chilled.

---

471. Air Fried Haddock Filets

Servings: 8   Cooking Time: 20 Minutes

Ingredients:

Nonstick cooking spray	1 cup cornflakes, crushed
2 egg whites	2 lbs. haddock fillets, cut in 8 pieces
½ tsp dill	
½ tsp pepper	

Directions:
Place baking pan in position 2 of the oven. Lightly spray fryer basket with cooking spray.   In a shallow bowl, whisk together egg whites, dill, and pepper.   Place crushed cornflakes in a separate shallow dish.   Dip fish in egg mixture, then cornflakes, coating completely. Place in fryer basket. Place basket on the baking pan and set oven to air fryer on 400°F. Cook 18-20 minutes, turning over halfway through, until fish flakes easily with a fork. Serve.

---

472.   Rosemary Buttered Prawns

Servings: 2   Cooking Time: 15 Minutes + Marinating Time

Ingredients:

8 large prawns	½ tbsp melted butter
1 rosemary sprig, chopped	Salt and black pepper to taste

Directions:
Combine butter, rosemary, salt, and pepper in a bowl. Add in the prawns and mix to coat. Cover the bowl and refrigerate for 1 hour.   Preheat Instant Vortex on Air Fry function to 350 F Remove the prawns from the fridge and place them in the basket. Fit in the baking tray and cook for 10 minutes, flipping once. Serve.

---

473.   Sesame Seeds Coated Fish

Servings: 5   Cooking Time: 8 Minutes

Ingredients:

3 tablespoons plain flour	Pinch of salt
2 eggs	Pinch of black pepper
½ cup sesame seeds, toasted	3 tablespoons olive oil
½ cup breadcrumbs	5 frozen fish fillets (white fish of your choice)
1/8 teaspoon dried rosemary, crushed	

Directions:
Preparing the Ingredients. In a shallow dish, place flour. In a second shallow dish, beat the eggs. In a third shallow dish, add remaining ingredients except fish fillets and mix till a crumbly mixture forms. Coat the fillets with flour and shake off the excess flour. Next, dip the fillets in the egg. Then coat the fillets with sesame seeds mixture generously. Preheat the Instant Vortex air fryer oven to 390 degrees F. Air Frying. Line an Air fryer rack/basket with a piece of foil. Arrange the fillets into prepared basket. Cook for about 14 minutes, flipping once after 10 minutes.

474. Fish And Chips

Servings: 4   Cooking Time: 20 Minutes

Ingredients:

4 (4-ounce) fish fillets	¾ cup crushed
Pinch salt	potato chips
Freshly ground black	2 tablespoons olive
pepper	oil, divided
½ teaspoon dried	1 russet potatoes,
thyme	peeled and cut into
1 egg white	strips

Directions:
Preparing the Ingredients. Pat the fish fillets dry and sprinkle with salt, pepper, and thyme. Set aside. In a shallow bowl, beat the egg white until foamy. In another bowl, combine the potato chips and 1 tablespoon of olive oil and mix until combined. Dip the fish fillets into the egg white, then into the crushed potato chip mixture to coat. Toss the fresh potato strips with the remaining 1 tablespoon olive oil. Air Frying. Use your separator to divide the Oven rack/basket in half, then fry the chips and fish. The chips will take about 20 minutes; the fish will take about 10 to 12 minutes to cook.

475. Healthy Haddock

Servings: 2   Cooking Time: 25 Minutes

Ingredients:

1 lb haddock fillets	1/4 cup onion, diced
1/4 cup parsley,	1 tsp ginger, grated
chopped	3/4 cup soy sauce
1 lemon juice	Pepper
1/4 cup brown sugar	Salt

Directions:
Fit the Instant Vortex oven with the rack in position Add fish fillets and remaining ingredients into the large bowl and coat well and place in the refrigerator for 1 hour. Place marinated fish fillets into the baking dish. Set to bake at 325 F for 30 minutes. After 5 minutes place the baking dish in the preheated oven. Serve and enjoy.

476. Old Bay Seasoned Scallops

Servings: 4   Cooking Time: 4 Minutes

Ingredients:

1 lb sea scallops	2 tbsp butter, melted
1/2 tsp garlic powder	1/2 tsp old bay
1/2 cup crushed	seasoning
crackers	

Directions:
Fit the Instant Vortex oven with the rack in position 2.   In a shallow dish, mix crushed crackers, garlic powder, and old bay seasoning.   Add melted butter in a separate shallow dish.   Dip scallops in melted butter and coat with crushed crackers. Place coated scallops in air fryer basket then place air fryer basket in baking pan.   Place a baking pan on the oven rack. Set to air fry at 390 F for 4 minutes. Serve and enjoy.

477. Lemon-honey Snapper With Fruit

Servings: 4   Cooking Time: 12 Minutes

Ingredients:

4 (4-ounce / 113-g)	1 cup red grapes
red snapper fillets	1 tablespoon freshly
2 teaspoons olive oil	squeezed lemon juice
3 plums, halved and	1 tablespoon honey
pitted	½ teaspoon dried
3 nectarines, halved	thyme
and pitted	

Directions:
Arrange the red snapper fillets in the air fryer basket and drizzle the olive oil over the top.   Put the air fryer basket on the baking pan and slide into Rack Position 2, select Air Fry, set temperature to 390°F (199°C), and set time to 12 minutes.   After 4 minutes, remove from the oven. Top the fillets with the plums and nectarines. Scatter the red grapes all over the fillets. Drizzle with the lemon juice and honey and sprinkle the thyme on top. Return the pan to the oven and continue cooking for 8 minutes, or until the fish is flaky.   When cooking is complete, remove from the oven and serve warm.

478. Lobster Tails With Lemon-garlic Sauce

Servings: 4   Cooking Time: 15 Minutes

Ingredients:

1 lb lobster tails	Salt and black pepper
1 garlic clove, minced	to taste
1 tbsp butter	½ tbsp lemon Juice

Directions:
Add all the ingredients to a food processor, except for lobster and blend well. Wash lobster and halve using meat knife; clean the skin of the lobster and cover with the marinade.   Preheat your Instant Vortex to 380 F. Place the lobster in the cooking basket and press Start. Cook for 10 minutes on AirFry function. Serve with fresh herbs.

479. Lemon Tilapia

Servings: 4   Cooking Time: 12 Minutes

Ingredients:

1 tablespoon olive oil	1 teaspoon minced
1 tablespoon lemon	garlic
juice	½ teaspoon chili
4 tilapia fillets	powder

Directions:

Line the baking pan with parchment paper. In a shallow bowl, stir together the olive oil, lemon juice, garlic, and chili powder to make a marinade. Put the tilapia fillets in the bowl, turning to coat evenly. Place the fillets in the baking pan in a single layer. Put the air fryer basket on the baking pan and slide into Rack Position 2, select Air Fry, set temperature to 375ºF (190ºC), and set time to 12 minutes. When cooked, the fish will flake apart with a fork. Remove from the oven to a plate and serve hot.

480. Bacon Wrapped Shrimp

Servings: 4   Cooking Time: 5 Minutes
Ingredients:
1¼ pound tiger shrimp, peeled and deveined	1 pound bacon

Directions:
Preparing the Ingredients. Wrap each shrimp with a slice of bacon. Refrigerate for about 20 minutes. Preheat the Instant Vortex air fryer oven to 390 degrees F. Air Frying. Arrange the shrimp in the Oven rack/basket. Place the Rack on the middle-shelf of the Instant Vortex air fryer oven. Cook for about 5-7 minutes.

481. Fish Spicy Lemon Kebab

Ingredients:
1 lb. boneless fish roughly chopped	4 tbsp. chopped coriander
3 onions chopped	3 tbsp. cream
5 green chilies- roughly chopped	2 tbsp. coriander powder
1 ½ tbsp. ginger paste	4 tbsp. fresh mint chopped
1 ½ tsp garlic paste	3 tbsp. chopped capsicum
1 ½ tsp salt	3 eggs
3 tsp lemon juice	2 ½ tbsp. white sesame seeds
2 tsp garam masala	

Directions:
Take all the ingredients mentioned under the first heading and mix them in a bowl. Grind them thoroughly to make a smooth paste. Take the eggs in a different bowl and beat them. Add a pinch of salt and leave them aside. Take a flat plate and in it mix the sesame seeds and breadcrumbs. Mold the fish mixture into small balls and flatten them into round and flat kebabs. Dip these kebabs in the egg and salt mixture and then in the mixture of breadcrumbs and sesame seeds. Leave these kebabs in the fridge for an hour or so to set. Pre heat the Instant Vortex oven at 160 degrees Fahrenheit for around 5 minutes. Place the kebabs in the basket and let them cook for another 25 minutes at the same temperature. Turn the kebabs over in between the cooking process to get a uniform cook. Serve the kebabs with mint sauce.

482. Lemony Tuna

Servings: 4   Cooking Time: 10 Minutes
Ingredients:

2 (6-ounce) cans water packed plain tuna	½ cup breadcrumbs
2 teaspoons Dijon mustard	1 egg
	Chefman of hot sauce
1 tablespoon fresh lime juice	3 tablespoons canola oil
2 tablespoons fresh parsley, chopped	Salt and freshly ground black pepper, to taste

Directions:
Preparing the Ingredients. Drain most of the liquid from the canned tuna. In a bowl, add the fish, mustard, crumbs, citrus juice, parsley, and hot sauce and mix till well combined. Add a little canola oil if it seems too dry. Add egg, salt and stir to combine. Make the patties from tuna mixture. Refrigerate the tuna patties for about 2 hours. Air Frying. Preheat the air fryer oven to 355 degrees F. Cook for about 10-12 minutes.

483. Parsley Catfish Fillets

Servings: 4   Cooking Time: 25 Minutes
Ingredients:
4 catfish fillets, rinsed and dried	1 tbsp olive oil
¼ cup seasoned fish fry	1 tbsp fresh parsley, chopped

Directions:
Add seasoned fish fry and fillets in a large Ziploc bag; massage well to coat. Place the fillets in the Instant Vortex basket and cook for 14-16 minutes at 360 F on AirFry function. Top with parsley.

484. Breaded Calamari With Lemon

Servings: 4   Cooking Time: 12 Minutes
Ingredients:
2 large eggs	1 pound (454 g) calamari rings
2 garlic cloves, minced	Cooking spray
½ cup cornstarch	1 lemon, sliced
1 cup bread crumbs	

Directions:
In a small bowl, whisk the eggs with minced garlic. Place the cornstarch and bread crumbs into separate shallow dishes. Dredge the calamari rings in the cornstarch, then dip in the egg mixture, shaking off any excess, finally roll them in the bread crumbs to coat well. Let the calamari rings sit for 10 minutes in the refrigerator. Spritz the air fryer basket with cooking spray. Transfer the calamari rings to the pan. Put the air fryer basket on the baking pan and slide into Rack Position 2, select Air Fry, set temperature to 390ºF (199ºC), and set time to 12 minutes. Stir the calamari rings once halfway through the cooking time. When cooking is complete, remove from the oven. Serve the calamari rings with the lemon slices sprinkled on top.

485. Easy Salmon Cakes

Servings: 2   Cooking Time: 15 Minutes + Cooling Time

Ingredients:

8 oz salmon, cooked	A handful of parsley, chopped
1 ½ oz potatoes, mashed	Zest of 1 lemon
A handful of capers	1 ¾ oz plain flour

Directions:
Carefully flake the salmon in a bowl. Stir in zest, capers, dill, and mashed potatoes. Shape the mixture into cakes and dust them with flour. Place in the fridge for 60 minutes.   Preheat your Instant Vortex to 350 F on Air Fry function. Remove the cakes from the fridges and arrange them on the greased basket. Fit in the baking tray and cook for 10 minutes, shaing once halfway through. Serve chilled.

486.   Spicy Lemon Cod

Servings: 2   Cooking Time: 10 Minutes
Ingredients:

1 lb cod fillets	1 tbsp fresh lemon juice
1/4 tsp chili powder	1/8 tsp cayenne pepper
1 tbsp fresh parsley, chopped	1/4 tsp salt
1 1/2 tbsp olive oil	

Directions:
Fit the Instant Vortex oven with the rack in position Arrange fish fillets in a baking dish. Drizzle with oil and lemon juice.   Sprinkle with chili powder, salt, and cayenne pepper.   Set to bake at 400 F for 15 minutes. After 5 minutes place the baking dish in the preheated oven.   Garnish with parsley and serve.

487.   Baked Flounder Fillets

Servings: 2   Cooking Time: 12 Minutes
Ingredients:

2 flounder fillets, patted dry	½ teaspoon coarse sea salt
1 egg	½ teaspoon lemon pepper
½ teaspoon Worcestershire sauce	¼ teaspoon chili powder
¼ cup almond flour	Cooking spray
¼ cup coconut flour	

Directions:
In a shallow bowl, beat together the egg with Worcestershire sauce until well incorporated.   In another bowl, thoroughly combine the almond flour, coconut flour, sea salt, lemon pepper, and chili powder.   Dredge the fillets in the egg mixture, shaking off any excess, then roll in the flour mixture to coat well.   Spritz the baking pan with cooking spray. Place the fillets in the pan.   Slide the baking pan into Rack Position 1, select Convection Bake, set temperature to 390°F (199°C), and set time to 12 minutes.   After 7 minutes, remove from the oven and flip the fillets and spray with cooking spray. Return the pan to the oven and continue cooking for 5 minutes, or until the fish is flaky.   When cooking is complete, remove from the oven and serve warm.

488.   Baked Buttery Shrimp

Servings: 4   Cooking Time: 15 Minutes

Ingredients:

1 lb shrimp, peel & deveined	4 tsp cayenne pepper
2 tsp garlic powder	1/2 cup butter, melted
2 tsp dry mustard	2 tsp onion powder
2 tsp cumin	1 tsp dried oregano
2 tsp paprika	1 tsp dried thyme
2 tsp black pepper	3 tsp salt

Directions:
Fit the Instant Vortex oven with the rack in position Add shrimp, butter, and remaining ingredients into the mixing bowl and toss well.   Transfer shrimp mixture into the baking pan.   Set to bake at 400 F for 20 minutes. After 5 minutes place the baking pan in the preheated oven.   Serve and enjoy.

489.   Garlic Shrimp With Parsley

Servings: 4   Cooking Time: 5 Minutes
Ingredients:

18 shrimp, shelled and deveined	1 teaspoon onion powder
2 garlic cloves, peeled and minced	1 teaspoon lemon-pepper seasoning
2 tablespoons extra-virgin olive oil	½ teaspoon hot paprika
2 tablespoons freshly squeezed lemon juice	½ teaspoon salt
½ cup fresh parsley, coarsely chopped	¼ teaspoon cumin powder

Directions:
Toss all the ingredients in a mixing bowl until the shrimp are well coated.   Cover and allow to marinate in the refrigerator for 30 minutes. When ready, transfer the shrimp to the air fryer basket.   Put the air fryer basket on the baking pan and slide into Rack Position 2, select Air Fry, set temperature to 400°F (205°C), and set time to 5 minutes.   When cooking is complete, the shrimp should be pink on the outside and opaque in the center. Remove from the oven and serve warm.

490.   Caesar Shrimp Salad

Servings: 4   Cooking Time: 15 Minutes
Ingredients:

½ baguette, cut into 1-inch cubes (about 2½ cups)	4 tablespoons extra-virgin olive oil, divided
¼ teaspoon granulated garlic	¾ cup Caesar dressing, divided
¼ teaspoon kosher salt	1 pound (454 g) medium shrimp, peeled and deveined
2 romaine lettuce hearts, cut in half lengthwise and ends trimmed	2 ounces (57 g) Parmesan cheese, coarsely grated

Directions:
Make the croutons: Put the bread cubes in a medium bowl and drizzle 3 tablespoons of olive oil over top. Season with granulated garlic and salt and toss to coat. Transfer to the air fryer basket in a single layer. Put the air fryer basket on the baking pan and slide into Rack Position 2, select Air Fry, set temperature

to 400°F (205°C), and set time to 4 minutes. Toss the croutons halfway through the cooking time. When done, remove from the oven and set aside. Brush 2 tablespoons of Caesar dressing on the cut side of the lettuce. Set aside.   Toss the shrimp with the ¼ cup of Caesar dressing in a large bowl until well coated. Set aside.   Coat the baking pan with the remaining 1 tablespoon of olive oil. Arrange the romaine halves on the coated pan, cut side down. Brush the tops with the remaining 2 tablespoons of Caesar dressing.   Slide the baking pan into Rack Position 2, select Roast, set temperature to 375°F (190°C), and set time to 10 minutes.   After 5 minutes, remove from the oven and flip the romaine halves. Spoon the shrimp around the lettuce. Return the pan to the oven and continue cooking.   When done, remove from the oven. If they are not quite cooked through, roast for another 1 minute.   On each of four plates, put a romaine half. Divide the shrimp among the plates and top with croutons and grated Parmesan cheese. Serve immediately.

491.   Crispy Paprika Fish Fillets(2)

Servings: 4   Cooking Time: 15 Minutes

Ingredients:

1/2 cup seasoned breadcrumbs	1/2 teaspoon ground black pepper
1 tablespoon balsamic vinegar	1 teaspoon celery seed
1/2 teaspoon seasoned salt	2 fish fillets, halved
1 teaspoon paprika	1 egg, beaten

Directions:
Preparing the Ingredients. Add the breadcrumbs, vinegar, salt, paprika, ground black pepper, and celery seeds to your food processor. Process for about 30 seconds.   Coat the fish fillets with the beaten egg; then, coat them with the breadcrumbs mixture.   Air Frying. Cook at 350 degrees F for about 15 minutes.

492.   Pecan-crusted Catfish Fillets

Servings: 4   Cooking Time: 12 Minutes

Ingredients:

1 teaspoon fine sea salt	½ cup pecan meal
¼ teaspoon ground black pepper	Avocado oil spray For Garnish (Optional):
4 (4-ounce / 113-g) catfish fillets	Fresh oregano Pecan halves

Directions:
Spray the air fryer basket with avocado oil spray. Combine the pecan meal, sea salt, and black pepper in a large bowl. Dredge each catfish fillet in the meal mixture, turning until well coated. Spritz the fillets with avocado oil spray, then transfer to the basket. Put the air fryer basket on the baking pan and slide into Rack Position 2, select Air Fry, set temperature to 375°F (190°C), and set time to 12 minutes.   Flip the fillets halfway through the cooking time. When cooking is complete, the fish should be cooked through and no longer translucent. Remove from

the oven and sprinkle the oregano sprigs and pecan halves on top for garnish, if desired. Serve immediately.

493.   Greek Cod With Asparagus

Servings: 2   Cooking Time: 20 Minutes

Ingredients:

1 lb cod, cut into 4 pieces	1/2 tsp red chili flakes
8 asparagus spears	1/2 cup olives, chopped
1 leek, sliced	2 tbsp olive oil
1 onion, quartered	1/4 tsp pepper
2 tomatoes, halved	1/4 tsp salt
1/2 tsp oregano	

Directions:
Fit the Instant Vortex oven with the rack in position Arrange fish pieces, olives, asparagus, leek, onion, and tomatoes in a baking dish.   Season with oregano, chili flakes, pepper, and salt and drizzle with olive oil.   Set to bake at 400 F for 25 minutes. After 5 minutes place the baking dish in the preheated oven.   Serve and enjoy.

494.   Garlic-butter Shrimp With Vegetables

Servings: 4   Cooking Time: 15 Minutes

Ingredients:

1 pound (454 g) small red potatoes, halved	1 (12- to 13-ounce / 340- to 369-g) package kielbasa or other smoked sausages
2 ears corn, shucked and cut into rounds, 1 to 1½ inches thick	
2 tablespoons Old Bay or similar seasoning	3 garlic cloves, minced
½ cup unsalted butter, melted	1 pound (454 g) medium shrimp, peeled and deveined

Directions:
Place the potatoes and corn in a large bowl.   Stir together the butter and Old Bay seasoning in a small bowl. Drizzle half the butter mixture over the potatoes and corn, tossing to coat. Spread out the vegetables in the baking pan.   Slide the baking pan into Rack Position 2, select Roast, set temperature to 350°F (180°C), and set time to 15 minutes.   Meanwhile, cut the sausages into 2-inch lengths, then cut each piece in half lengthwise. Put the sausages and shrimp in a medium bowl and set aside.   Add the garlic to the bowl of remaining butter mixture and stir well.   After 10 minutes, remove the pan and pour the vegetables into the large bowl. Drizzle with the garlic butter and toss until well coated. Arrange the vegetables, sausages, and shrimp in the pan.   Return to the oven and continue cooking. After 5 minutes, check the shrimp for doneness. The shrimp should be pink and opaque. If they are not quite cooked through, roast for an additional 1 minute.   When done, remove from the oven and serve on a plate.

495.   Cilantro-lime Fried Shrimp

Servings: 4   Cooking Time: 10 Minutes

Ingredients:

1 pound raw shrimp, peeled and deveined with tails on or off (see Prep tip)
½ cup chopped fresh cilantro
Juice of 1 lime
1 egg
½ cup all-purpose flour
¾ cup bread crumbs
Salt
Pepper
Cooking oil
½ cup cocktail sauce (optional)

Directions:
Preparing the Ingredients. Place the shrimp in a plastic bag and add the cilantro and lime juice. Seal the bag. Shake to combine. Marinate in the refrigerator for 30 minutes.   In a small bowl, beat the egg. In another small bowl, place the flour. Place the bread crumbs in a third small bowl, and season with salt and pepper to taste.   Spray the air fryer rack/basket with cooking oil.   Remove the shrimp from the plastic bag. Dip each in the flour, then the egg, and then the bread crumbs.   Air Frying. Place the shrimp in the Instant Vortex air fryer oven. It is okay to stack them. Spray the shrimp with cooking oil. Cook for 4 minutes.   Open the air fryer oven and flip the shrimp. I recommend flipping individually instead of shaking to keep the breading intact. Cook for an additional 4 minutes, or until crisp.   Cool before serving. Serve with cocktail sauce if desired.

496.   Tilapia Meunière With Vegetables

Servings: 4   Cooking Time: 20 Minutes
Ingredients:

10 ounces (283 g) Yukon Gold potatoes, sliced ¼-inch thick
5 tablespoons unsalted butter, melted, divided
1 teaspoon kosher salt, divided
4 (8-ounce / 227-g) tilapia fillets
½ pound (227 g) green beans, trimmed
Juice of 1 lemon
2 tablespoons chopped fresh parsley, for garnish

Directions:
In a large bowl, drizzle the potatoes with 2 tablespoons of melted butter and ¼ teaspoon of kosher salt. Transfer the potatoes to the baking pan. Slide the baking pan into Rack Position 2, select Roast, set temperature to 375ºF (190ºC), and set time to 20 minutes.   Meanwhile, season both sides of the fillets with ½ teaspoon of kosher salt. Put the green beans in the medium bowl and sprinkle with the remaining ¼ teaspoon of kosher salt and 1 tablespoon of butter, tossing to coat. After 10 minutes, remove from the oven and push the potatoes to one side. Put the fillets in the middle of the pan and add the green beans on the other side. Drizzle the remaining 2 tablespoons of butter over the fillets. Return the pan to the oven and continue cooking, or until the fish flakes easily with a fork and the green beans are crisp-tender.   When cooked, remove from the oven. Drizzle the lemon juice over the fillets and sprinkle the parsley on top for garnish. Serve hot.

497.   Squab Oregano Fingers

Ingredients:

½ lb. squab Oregano Fingers
2 cups of dry breadcrumbs
1 cup oil for frying
1 ½ tbsp. ginger-garlic paste
3 tbsp. lemon juice
2 tsp salt
1 ½ tsp pepper powder
1 tsp red chili flakes or to taste
3 eggs
5 tbsp. corn flour
2 tsp tomato ketchup

Directions:
Make the marinade and transfer the Oregano Fingers into the marinade. Leave them on a plate to dry for fifteen minutes. Now cover the Oregano Fingers with the crumbs and set aside to dry for fifteen minutes.   Pre heat the Instant Vortex oven at 160 degrees Fahrenheit for 5 minutes or so. Keep the fish in the fry basket now and close it properly. Let the Oregano Fingers cook at the same temperature for another 25 minutes. In between the cooking process, toss the fish once in a while to avoid burning the food. Serve either with tomato ketchup or chili sauce. Mint sauce also works well with the fish.

498.   Oyster Club Sandwich

Ingredients:

2 slices of white bread
1 tbsp. softened butter
½ lb. shelled oyster
1 small capsicum
For Barbeque Sauce:
¼ tbsp. Worcestershire sauce
½ flake garlic crushed
½ tsp. olive oil
¼ cup chopped onion
¼ tsp. mustard powder
1 tbsp. tomato ketchup
½ tbsp. sugar
¼ tbsp. red chili sauce
½ cup water.
A pinch of salt and black pepper to taste

Directions:
Take the slices of bread and remove the edges. Now cut the slices horizontally. Cook the ingredients for the sauce and wait till it thickens. Now, add the oyster to the sauce and stir till it obtains the flavors. Roast the capsicum and peel the skin off. Cut the capsicum into slices. Mix the ingredients together and apply it to the bread slices. Pre-heat the Instant Vortex oven for 5 minutes at 300 Fahrenheit. Open the basket of the Fryer and place the prepared Classic Sandwiches in it such that no two Classic Sandwiches are touching each other. Now keep the fryer at 250 degrees for around 15 minutes.   Turn the Classic Sandwiches in between the cooking process to cook both slices. Serve the Classic Sandwiches with tomato ketchup or mint sauce.

499. Garlic Butter Shrimp Scampi

Servings: 4   Cooking Time: 8 Minutes

Ingredients:

Sauce:
¼ cup unsalted butter
2 tablespoons fish stock or chicken broth
2 cloves garlic, minced
2 tablespoons chopped fresh basil leaves
1 tablespoon chopped fresh parsley, plus more for garnish

1 tablespoon lemon juice
1 teaspoon red pepper flakes
Shrimp:
1 pound (454 g) large shrimp, peeled and deveined, tails removed
Fresh basil sprigs, for garnish

Directions:

Put all the ingredients for the sauce in the baking pan and stir to incorporate.   Put the air fryer basket on the baking pan and slide into Rack Position 2, select Air Fry, set temperature to 350°F (180°C), and set time to 8 minutes. After 3 minutes, remove from the oven and add the shrimp to the baking pan, flipping to coat in the sauce. Return to the oven and continue cooking for 5 minutes until the shrimp are pink and opaque. Stir the shrimp twice during cooking.   When cooking is complete, remove from the oven. Serve garnished with the parsley and basil sprigs.

500.   Prawn French Cuisine Galette

Ingredients:

2 tbsp. garam masala
1 lb. minced prawn
3 tsp ginger finely chopped
1-2 tbsp. fresh coriander leaves

2 or 3 green chilies finely chopped
1 ½ tbsp. lemon juice
Salt and pepper to taste

Directions:

Mix the ingredients in a clean bowl.   Mold this mixture into round and flat French Cuisine Galettes. Wet the French Cuisine Galettes slightly with water. Pre heat the Instant Vortex oven at 160 degrees Fahrenheit for 5 minutes. Place the French Cuisine Galettes in the fry basket and let them cook for another 25 minutes at the same temperature. Keep rolling them over to get a uniform cook. Serve either with mint sauce or ketchup.

501.   Delightful Catfish Fillets

Servings: 4   Cooking Time: 25 Minutes

Ingredients:

4 catfish fillets
¼ cup seasoned fish fry

1 tbsp olive oil
1 tbsp parsley, chopped

Directions:

Add seasoned fish fry and catfish fillets in a large Ziploc bag and massage well to coat. Place the fillets in your Instant Vortex Air Fryer basket and fit in the baking tray; cook for 10 minutes at 360 F on Air Fry

function. Flip the fish and cook for 2-3 more minutes. Top with parsley and serve.

502.   Prawn Grandma's Easy To Cook Wontons

Ingredients:

1 ½ cup all-purpose flour
½ tsp. salt
5 tbsp. water
2 cups minced prawn

2 tbsp. oil
2 tsp. ginger-garlic paste
2 tsp. soya sauce
2 tsp. vinegar

Directions:

Squeeze the dough and cover it with plastic wrap and set aside. Next, cook the ingredients for the filling and try to ensure that the prawn is covered well with the sauce. Roll the dough and place the filling in the center.   Now, wrap the dough to cover the filling and pinch the edges together. Pre heat the Instant Vortex oven at 200° F for 5 minutes. Place the wontons in the fry basket and close it. Let them cook at the same temperature for another 20 minutes. Recommended sides are chili sauce or ketchup.

503.   Miso White Fish Fillets

Servings: 2   Cooking Time: 10 Minutes

Ingredients:

2 cod fish fillets
2 tbsp brown sugar
2 tbsp miso

1 tbsp garlic, chopped

Directions:

Fit the Instant Vortex oven with the rack in position 2.   Add all ingredients to the zip-lock bag and marinate fish in the refrigerator overnight.   Place marinated fish fillets in the air fryer basket then place an air fryer basket in the baking pan.   Place a baking pan on the oven rack. Set to air fry at 350 F for 10 minutes.   Serve and enjoy.

504.   Seafood Spring Rolls

Servings: 4   Cooking Time: 20 Minutes

Ingredients:

1 tablespoon olive oil
2 teaspoons minced garlic
1 cup matchstick cut carrots
2 (4-ounce / 113-g) cans tiny shrimp, drained

2 cups finely sliced cabbage
4 teaspoons soy sauce
Salt and freshly ground black pepper, to taste
16 square spring roll wrappers
Cooking spray

Directions:

Spray the air fryer basket with cooking spray. Set aside.   Heat the olive oil in a medium skillet over medium heat until it shimmers.   Add the garlic to the skillet and cook for 30 seconds. Stir in the cabbage and carrots and sauté for about 5 minutes, stirring occasionally, or until the vegetables are lightly tender.   Fold in the shrimp and soy sauce and sprinkle with salt and pepper, then stir to combine. Sauté for another 2 minutes, or until the moisture is evaporated. Remove from the heat and set aside to cool. Put a spring roll wrapper on a work surface and spoon 1 tablespoon of the shrimp mixture onto the lower end of the wrapper. Roll the wrapper away from you halfway, and then fold in the right and left sides, like an envelope. Continue to roll to the very end, using a little water to seal the edge. Repeat with the remaining wrappers and filling. Place the spring rolls in the air fryer basket in a single layer, leaving space between each spring roll. Mist them lightly with cooking spray. Put the air fryer basket on the baking pan and slide into Rack Position 2, select Air Fry, set temperature to 375°F (190°C), and set time to 10 minutes. Flip the rolls halfway through the cooking time. When cooking is complete, the spring rolls will be heated through and start to brown. If necessary, continue cooking for 5 minutes more. Remove from the oven and cool for a few minutes before serving.

---

505. Baked Garlic Tilapia

Servings: 4   Cooking Time: 15 Minutes

Ingredients:

1 lb tilapia fillets	2 tbsp dried parsley
2 tbsp garlic, minced	Pepper
2 tbsp olive oil	Salt

Directions:
Fit the Instant Vortex oven with the rack in position Place fish fillets in a baking dish. Drizzle with oil and season with pepper and salt. Sprinkle garlic and parsley over fish fillets. Set to bake at 400 F for 20 minutes. After 5 minutes place the baking dish in the preheated oven. Serve and enjoy.

---

506. Tasty Tuna Loaf

Servings: 6   Cooking Time: 40 Minutes

Ingredients:

Nonstick cooking spray	¼ cup milk
12 oz. can chunk white tuna in water, drain & flake	½ tsp fresh lemon juice
¾ cup bread crumbs	½ tsp dill
1 onion, chopped fine	1 tbsp. fresh parsley, chopped
2 eggs, beaten	½ tsp salt
	½ tsp pepper

Directions:
Place rack in position 1 of the oven. Spray a 9-inch loaf pan with cooking spray. In a large bowl, combine all ingredients until thoroughly mixed. Spread evenly in prepared pan. Set oven to bake on 350°F for 45 minutes. After 5 minutes, place the pan in the oven and cook 40 minutes, or until top is golden brown. Slice and serve.

---

507. Browned Shrimp Patties

Servings: 4   Cooking Time: 12 Minutes

Ingredients:

½ pound (227 g) raw shrimp, shelled, deveined, and chopped finely	2 teaspoons Worcestershire sauce
	½ teaspoon salt

2 cups cooked sushi rice	½ teaspoon garlic powder
¼ cup chopped red bell pepper	½ teaspoon Old Bay seasoning
¼ cup chopped celery	½ cup plain bread crumbs
¼ cup chopped green onion	Cooking spray

Directions:
Put all the ingredients except the bread crumbs and oil in a large bowl and stir to incorporate. Scoop out the shrimp mixture and shape into 8 equal-sized patties with your hands, no more than ½-inch thick. Roll the patties in the bread crumbs on a plate and spray both sides with cooking spray. Place the patties in the air fryer basket. Put the air fryer basket on the baking pan and slide into Rack Position 2, select Air Fry, set temperature to 390°F (199°C), and set time to 12 minutes. Flip the patties halfway through the cooking time. When cooking is complete, the outside should be crispy brown. Divide the patties among four plates and serve warm.

---

508. Baked Tilapia With Garlic Aioli

Servings: 4   Cooking Time: 15 Minutes

Ingredients:

Tilapia:	1 teaspoon paprika
4 tilapia fillets	Garlic Aioli:
1 tablespoon extra-virgin olive oil	2 garlic cloves, minced
1 teaspoon garlic powder	1 tablespoon mayonnaise
1 teaspoon dried basil	Juice of ½ lemon
A pinch of lemon-pepper seasoning	1 teaspoon extra-virgin olive oil
	Salt and pepper, to taste

Directions:
On a clean work surface, brush both sides of each fillet with the olive oil. Sprinkle with the garlic powder, paprika, basil, and lemon-pepper seasoning. Place the fillets in the baking pan. Slide the baking pan into Rack Position 1, select Convection Bake, set temperature to 400°F (205°C), and set time to 15 minutes. Flip the fillets halfway through. Meanwhile, make the garlic aioli: Whisk together the garlic, mayo, lemon juice, olive oil, salt, and pepper in a small bowl until smooth. When cooking is complete, the fish should flake apart with a fork and no longer translucent in the center. Remove the fish from the oven and serve with the garlic aioli on the side.

---

509. Crab Cakes With Bell Peppers

Servings: 4   Cooking Time: 10 Minutes

Ingredients:

8 ounces (227 g) jumbo lump crab meat	¼ cup diced red bell pepper
1 egg, beaten	¼ cup mayonnaise

Juice of ½ lemon
⅓ cup bread crumbs
¼ cup diced green
bell pepper

1 tablespoon Old Bay
seasoning
1 teaspoon flour
Cooking spray

Directions:
Make the crab cakes: Place all the ingredients except the flour and oil in a large bowl and stir until well incorporated.   Divide the crab mixture into four equal portions and shape each portion into a patty with your hands. Top each patty with a sprinkle of ¼ teaspoon of flour.   Arrange the crab cakes in the air fryer basket and spritz them with cooking spray.   Put the air fryer basket on the baking pan and slide into Rack Position 2, select Air Fry, set temperature to 375°F (190°C), and set time to 10 minutes.   Flip the crab cakes halfway through. When cooking is complete, the cakes should be cooked through. Remove from the oven and divide the crab cakes among four plates and serve.

510.	**Parmesan Fish Fillets**

Servings: 4   Cooking Time: 17 Minutes
Ingredients:

⅓ cup grated
Parmesan cheese
½ teaspoon fennel
seed
½ teaspoon tarragon
⅓ teaspoon mixed
peppercorns

2 eggs, beaten
4 (4-ounce / 113-g)
fish fillets, halved
2 tablespoons dry
white wine
1 teaspoon seasoned
salt

Directions:
Place the grated Parmesan cheese, fennel seed, tarragon, and mixed peppercorns in a food processor and pulse for about 20 seconds until well combined. Transfer the cheese mixture to a shallow dish.   Place the beaten eggs in another shallow dish.   Drizzle the dry white wine over the top of fish fillets. Dredge each fillet in the beaten eggs on both sides, shaking off any excess, then roll them in the cheese mixture until fully coated. Season with the salt.   Arrange the fillets in the air fryer basket. Put the air fryer basket on the baking pan and slide into Rack Position 2, select Air Fry, set temperature to 345°F (174°C), and set time to 17 minutes.   Flip the fillets once halfway through the cooking time. When cooking is complete, the fish should be cooked through no longer translucent. Remove from the oven and cool for 5 minutes before serving.

511.	**Scallops And Spring Veggies**

Servings: 4   Cooking Time: 8 Minutes
Ingredients:

½ pound asparagus
ends trimmed, cut
into 2-inch pieces
1 cup sugar snap peas
1 pound sea scallops
1 tablespoon lemon
juice

2 teaspoons olive oil
½ teaspoon dried
thyme
Pinch salt
Freshly ground black
pepper

Directions:
Preparing the Ingredients. Place the asparagus and sugar snap peas in the Oven rack/basket. Place the Rack on the middle-shelf of the Instant Vortex air fryer oven.   Air Frying. Cook for 2 to 3 minutes or until the vegetables are just starting to get tender. Meanwhile, check the scallops for a small muscle attached to the side, and pull it off and discard.   In a medium bowl, toss the scallops with the lemon juice, olive oil, thyme, salt, and pepper. Place into the Oven rack/basket on top of the vegetables. Place the Rack on the middle-shelf of the Instant Vortex air fryer oven.   Air Frying.   Steam for 5 to 7 minutes. Until the scallops are just firm, and the vegetables are tender. Serve immediately.

512.	**Sweet & Spicy Lime Salmon**

Servings: 6   Cooking Time: 15 Minutes
Ingredients:

1 1/2 lbs salmon
fillets
3 tbsp brown sugar
2 tbsp fresh lime juice
1/3 cup olive oil

1/2 tsp red pepper
flakes
2 garlic cloves,
minced
Pepper
Salt

Directions:
Fit the Instant Vortex oven with the rack in position Place salmon on a prepared baking sheet and season with pepper and salt.   In a small bowl, whisk oil, red pepper flakes, garlic, brown sugar, and lime juice. Pour oil mixture over salmon.   Set to bake at 350 F for 20 minutes. After 5 minutes place the baking dish in the preheated oven.   Serve and enjoy.

513.	**Harissa Shrimp**

Servings: 4   Cooking Time: 15 Minutes
Ingredients:

1 ¼ lb tiger shrimp
½ tsp old bay
seasoning

¼ tsp harissa
powder
Salt to taste
1 tbsp olive oil

Directions:
Preheat your Instant Vortex oven to 390 F on AirFry function. In a bowl, mix the ingredients. Place the mixture in the cooking basket and cook for 5 minutes. Serve with a drizzle of lemon juice.

514.	**Chili Tuna Casserole**

Servings: 4   Cooking Time: 16 Minutes
Ingredients:

½ tablespoon sesame
oil
⅓ cup yellow onions,
chopped
½ bell pepper,
deveined and
chopped
2 cups canned tuna,
chopped
½ chili pepper,
deveined and finely
minced

Cooking spray
5 eggs, beaten
1½ tablespoons sour
cream
⅓ teaspoon dried
basil
⅓ teaspoon dried
oregano
Fine sea salt and
ground black pepper,
to taste

Directions:
Heat the sesame oil in a nonstick skillet over medium heat until it shimmers.   Add the onions

and bell pepper and sauté for 4 minutes, stirring occasionally, or until tender.   Add the canned tuna and keep stirring until the tuna is heated through.   Meanwhile, coat the baking pan lightly with cooking spray.   Transfer the tuna mixture to the baking pan, along with the beaten eggs, chili pepper, sour cream, basil, and oregano. Stir to combine well. Season with sea salt and black pepper. Slide the baking pan into Rack Position 1, select Convection Bake, set temperature to 325°F (160°C), and set time to 12 minutes.   When cooking is complete, the eggs should be completely set and the top lightly browned. Remove from the oven and serve on a plate.

515. Basil Salmon With Tomatoes

Servings: 4   Cooking Time: 15 Minutes

Ingredients:

4 (6-ounce / 170-g) salmon fillets, patted dry	1 teaspoon kosher salt, divided
2 pints cherry or grape tomatoes, halved if large, divided	2 garlic cloves, minced
	1 small red bell pepper, deseeded and chopped
3 tablespoons extra-virgin olive oil, divided	2 tablespoons chopped fresh basil, divided

Directions:

Season both sides of the salmon with ½ teaspoon of kosher salt.   Put about half of the tomatoes in a large bowl, along with the remaining ½ teaspoon of kosher salt, 2 tablespoons of olive oil, garlic, bell pepper, and 1 tablespoon of basil. Toss to coat and then transfer to the baking pan.   Arrange the salmon fillets in the pan, skin-side down. Brush them with the remaining 1 tablespoon of olive oil. Slide the baking pan into Rack Position 2, select Roast, set temperature to 375°F (190°C), and set time to 15 minutes.   After 7 minutes, remove the pan and fold in the remaining tomatoes. Return the pan to the oven and continue cooking.   When cooked, remove from the oven. Serve sprinkled with the remaining 1 tablespoon of basil.

516. Panko Crab Sticks With Mayo Sauce

Servings: 4   Cooking Time: 12 Minutes

Ingredients:

Crab Sticks:	1 cup flour
2 eggs	Cooking spray
⅓ cup panko bread crumbs	Mayo Sauce:
1 tablespoon old bay seasoning	½ cup mayonnaise
1 pound (454 g) crab sticks	1 lime, juiced
	2 garlic cloves, minced

Directions:

In a bowl, beat the eggs. In a shallow bowl, place the flour. In another shallow bowl, thoroughly combine the panko bread crumbs and old bay seasoning. Dredge the crab sticks in the flour, shaking off any excess, then in the beaten eggs, finally press them in the bread crumb mixture to coat well.   Arrange the crab sticks in the air fryer basket and spray with cooking spray.   Put the air fryer basket on the baking pan and slide into Rack Position 2, select Air Fry, set temperature to 390°F (199°C), and set time to 12 minutes.   Flip the crab sticks halfway through the cooking time.   Meanwhile, make the sauce by whisking together the mayo, lime juice, and garlic in a small bowl.   When cooking is complete, remove from the oven. Serve the crab sticks with the mayo sauce on the side.

517. Delicious Shrimp Casserole

Servings: 10   Cooking Time: 30 Minutes

Ingredients:

1 lb shrimp, peeled & tail off	2 tsp onion powder
2 tsp old bay seasoning	10.5 oz can cream of mushroom soup
2 cups cheddar cheese, shredded	12 oz long-grain rice
	1 tsp salt

Directions:

Fit the Instant Vortex oven with the rack in position Cook rice according to the packet instructions. Add shrimp into the boiling water and cook for 4 minutes or until cooked. Drain shrimp.   In a bowl, mix rice, shrimp, and remaining ingredients and pour into the greased 13*9-inch casserole dish. Set to bake at 350 F for 35 minutes. After 5 minutes place the casserole dish in the preheated oven. Serve and enjoy.

518.   Italian Salmon

Servings: 4   Cooking Time: 20 Minutes

Ingredients:

1 3/4 lbs salmon fillet	1/4 cup olives, pitted and chopped
1/4 cup sun-dried tomatoes, drained	1/3 cup basil pesto
1 tbsp fresh dill, chopped	1/3 cup artichoke hearts
1/4 cup capers	1 tsp paprika
	1/4 tsp salt

Directions:

Fit the Instant Vortex oven with the rack in position Arrange salmon fillet in a baking pan and season with paprika and salt.   Pour remaining ingredients on top of salmon.   Set to bake at 400 F for 25 minutes. After 5 minutes place the baking pan in the preheated oven.   Serve and enjoy.

519.   Cajun Salmon With Lemon

Servings: 1   Cooking Time: 10 Minutes

Ingredients:

1 salmon fillet	Juice of ½ lemon
¼ tsp brown sugar	2 lemon wedges
1 tbsp cajun seasoning	1 tbsp fresh parsley, chopped

Directions:

Preheat Instant Vortex on Bake function to 350 F. Combine sugar and lemon and coat in the salmon. Sprinkle with the Cajun seasoning as well. Place a parchment paper on a baking tray and press Start.

Cook for 14-16 minutes. Serve with lemon wedges and chopped parsley.

520. Breaded Seafood

Servings: 4   Cooking Time: 15 Minutes
Ingredients:

1 lb scallops, mussels, fish fillets, prawns, shrimp	Salt and black pepper to taste
2 eggs, lightly beaten	1 cup breadcrumbs mixed with zest of 1 lemon

Directions:
Dip the seafood pieces into the eggs and season with salt and black pepper. Coat in the crumbs and spray with cooking spray. Arrange them on the frying basket and press Start. Cook for 10 minutes at 400 F on AirFry function. Serve with lemon wedges.

521. Lemon Butter Shrimp

Servings: 4   Cooking Time: 12 Minutes
Ingredients:

1 1/4 lbs shrimp, peeled & deveined	2 tbsp fresh lemon juice
2 tbsp fresh parsley, chopped	1/4 cup butter
1 tbsp garlic, minced	Pepper
	Salt

Directions:
Fit the Instant Vortex oven with the rack in position Add shrimp into the baking dish.   Melt butter in a pan over low heat. Add garlic and sauté for 30 seconds. Stir in lemon juice.   Pour melted butter mixture over shrimp. Season with pepper and salt. Set to bake at 350 F for 17 minutes. After 5 minutes place the baking dish in the preheated oven. Garnish with parsley and serve.

522. Sweet Cajun Salmon

Servings: 1   Cooking Time: 10 Minutes
Ingredients:

1 salmon fillet	Juice of ½ lemon
¼ tsp brown sugar	2 lemon wedges
1 tbsp cajun seasoning	1 tbsp chopped parsley

Directions:
Preheat Instant Vortex on Bake function to 350 F. Combine sugar and lemon juice; coat the salmon with this mixture. Coat with the Cajun seasoning as well. Place a parchment paper on a baking tray and cook the fish in your Instant Vortex for 10 minutes. Serve with lemon wedges and parsley.

523. Parmesan-crusted Salmon Patties

Servings: 4   Cooking Time: 13 Minutes
Ingredients:

1 pound (454 g) salmon, chopped into ½-inch pieces	1½ tablespoons milk
2 tablespoons coconut flour	½ teaspoon chipotle powder
2 tablespoons grated	½ teaspoon dried

Parmesan cheese
½ white onion, peeled and finely chopped
½ teaspoon butter, at room temperature

parsley flakes
⅓ teaspoon ground black pepper
⅓ teaspoon smoked cayenne pepper
1 teaspoon fine sea salt

Directions:
Put all the ingredients for the salmon patties in a bowl and stir to combine well.   Scoop out 2 tablespoons of the salmon mixture and shape into a patty with your palm, about ½ inch thick. Repeat until all the mixture is used. Transfer to the refrigerator for about 2 hours until firm.   When ready, arrange the salmon patties in the baking pan. Slide the baking pan into Rack Position 1, select Convection Bake, set temperature to 395°F (202°C), and set time to 13 minutes.   Flip the patties halfway through the cooking time.   When cooking is complete, the patties should be golden brown. Remove from the oven and cool for 5 minutes before serving.

524. Air Fryer Spicy Shrimp

Servings: 4   Cooking Time: 6 Minutes
Ingredients:

1 lb shrimp, peeled and deveined	2 tsp paprika
1/4 tsp chili powder	1/4 tsp cayenne
1 tsp dried oregano	2 tbsp olive oil
1 tsp garlic powder	Pepper
1 tsp onion powder	Salt

Directions:
Fit the Instant Vortex oven with the rack in position 2.   In a bowl, toss shrimp with remaining ingredients.   Add shrimp to the air fryer basket then place an air fryer basket in the baking pan. Place a baking pan on the oven rack. Set to air fry at 400 F for 6 minutes.   Serve and enjoy.

525. Simple Lemon Salmon

Servings: 2   Cooking Time: 20 Minutes
Ingredients:

2 salmon fillets	Zest of a lemon
Salt to taste	

Directions:
Spray the fillets with olive oil and rub them with salt and lemon zest. Line baking paper in a baking dish. Cook the fillets in your Instant Vortex for 10 minutes at 360 F on Air Fry, turning once.

526. Panko Catfish Nuggets

Servings: 4   Cooking Time: 7 To 8 Minutes
Ingredients:

2 medium catfish fillets, cut into chunks (approximately 1 × 2 inch)	2 tablespoons skim milk
	½ cup cornstarch
Salt and pepper, to	1 cup panko bread crumbs
	Cooking spray

taste

2 eggs

Directions:

In a medium bowl, season the fish chunks with salt and pepper to taste. In a small bowl, beat together the eggs with milk until well combined. Place the cornstarch and bread crumbs into separate shallow dishes. Dredge the fish chunks one at a time in the cornstarch, coating well on both sides, then dip in the egg mixture, shaking off any excess, finally press well into the bread crumbs. Spritz the fish chunks with cooking spray. Arrange the fish chunks in the air fryer basket in a single layer. Put the air fryer basket on the baking pan and slide into Rack Position 2, select Air Fry, set temperature to 390°F (199°C), and set time to 8 minutes. Flip the fish chunks halfway through the cooking time. When cooking is complete, they should be no longer translucent in the center and golden brown. Remove the fish chunks from the oven to a plate. Serve warm.

---

527. Blackened Tuna Steaks

Ingredients:

2 Tbsp canola oil	1 Tbsp ground
4 (8-oz) tuna steaks,	cinnamon
preferably sushi-	1 Tbsp nutmeg
grade	1 Tbsp ground cloves
Blackening Spice:	1 tsp coriander
½ cup freshly ground	1 tsp cumin
black pepper	1 tsp cayenne pepper
2 Tbsp kosher salt	½ tsp celery salt
1 Tbsp cardamom	

Directions:

First prepare the blackening spice by combining all the spices. Preheat Instant Vortex oven. Place oil inside the pot and wait until smoking. Sprinkle blackening mixture on top of both sides of tuna steaks (about -2 Tbsp of blackening spice, depending on how spicy you want your steaks). Add tuna into Instant Vortex oven and cook about 3 minutes each side. The tuna should be browned on the outside and rare on the inside.

---

528. Sweet And Savory Breaded Shrimp

Servings: 2   Cooking Time: 20 Minutes

Ingredients:

½ pound of fresh shrimp, peeled from their shells and rinsed	2 raw eggs
	½ teaspoon of turmeric powder
½ cup of breadcrumbs (we like Panko, but any brand or home recipe will do)	½ teaspoon of red chili powder
	½ teaspoon of cumin powder
½ white onion, peeled and rinsed and finely chopped	½ teaspoon of black pepper powder
1 teaspoon of ginger-garlic paste	½ teaspoon of dry mango powder
	Pinch of salt

Directions:

Preparing the Ingredients. Cover the basket of the Instant Vortex air fryer oven with a lining of tin foil, leaving the edges uncovered to allow air to circulate through the basket. Preheat the Instant Vortex air fryer oven to 350 degrees. In a large mixing bowl, beat the eggs until fluffy and until the yolks and whites are fully combined. Dunk all the shrimp in the egg mixture, fully submerging. In a separate mixing bowl, combine the bread crumbs with all the dry ingredients until evenly blended. One by one, coat the egg-covered shrimp in the mixed dry ingredients so that fully covered, and place on the foil-lined air-fryer basket. Air Frying. Set the air-fryer timer to 20 minutes. Halfway through the cooking time, shake the handle of the air-fryer so that the breaded shrimp jostles inside and fry-coverage is even. After 20 minutes, when the fryer shuts off, the shrimp will be perfectly cooked and their breaded crust golden-brown and delicious! Using tongs, remove from the air fryer oven and set on a serving dish to cool.

---

529. Baked Tilapia

Servings: 4   Cooking Time: 10 Minutes

Ingredients:

1 1/4 lbs tilapia fillets	1/2 tsp oregano
2 tsp onion powder	1/2 tsp chili powder
2 tbsp olive oil	2 tbsp sweet paprika
1/2 tsp garlic powder	1 tsp pepper
1/2 tsp dried thyme	1/2 tsp salt

Directions:

Fit the Instant Vortex oven with the rack in position Brush fish fillets with oil and place in baking dish. Mix together spices and sprinkle over the fish fillets. Set to bake at 425 F for 15 minutes. After 5 minutes place the baking dish in the preheated oven. Serve and enjoy.

---

530. Mediterranean Sole

Servings: 6   Cooking Time: 20 Minutes

Ingredients:

Nonstick cooking spray	2 tbsp. fresh parsley, chopped fine
2 tbsp. olive oil	1 tsp oregano
8 scallions, sliced thin	1 tsp pepper
2 cloves garlic, diced fine	2 lbs. sole, cut in 6 pieces
4 tomatoes, chopped	4 oz. feta cheese, crumbled
½ cup dry white wine	

Directions:

Place the rack in position 1 of the oven. Spray an 8x11-inch baking dish with cooking spray. Heat the oil in a medium skillet over medium heat. Add scallions and garlic and cook until tender, stirring frequently. Add the tomatoes, wine, parsley, oregano, and pepper. Stir to mix. Simmer for 5 minutes, or until sauce thickens. Remove from heat. Pour half the sauce on the bottom of the prepared dish. Lay fish on top then pour remaining sauce over the top. Sprinkle with feta. Set the oven to bake on 400°F for 25 minutes. After 5 minutes, place the baking dish on the rack and cook 15-18 minutes or until fish flakes easily with a fork. Serve immediately.

531. Spicy Catfish

Servings: 4   Cooking Time: 15 Minutes

Ingredients:

1 lb catfish fillets, cut 1/2-inch thick	2 tsp onion powder
1 tsp crushed red pepper	1/2 tsp ground cumin
1 tbsp dried oregano, crushed	1/2 tsp chili powder Pepper
	Salt

Directions:
Fit the Instant Vortex oven with the rack in position In a small bowl, mix cumin, chili powder, crushed red pepper, onion powder, oregano, pepper, and salt. Rub fish fillets with the spice mixture and place in baking dish.   Set to bake at 350 F for 20 minutes. After 5 minutes place the baking dish in the preheated oven.   Serve and enjoy.

532. Fried Cod Nuggets

Servings: 4   Cooking Time: 25 Minutes

Ingredients:

1 1/4 lb cod fillets, cut into 4 to 6 chunks each	1 cup cornflakes
1/2 cup flour	1 tbsp olive oil
1 egg	Salt and black pepper to taste

Directions:
Place the olive oil and cornflakes in a food processor and process until crumbed. Season the fish chunks with salt and pepper. In a bowl, beat the egg along with 1 tbsp of water. Dredge the chunks in flour first, then dip in the egg, and finally coat with cornflakes. Arrange the fish pieces on a lined sheet and cook in your Instant Vortex on Air Fry at 350 F for 15 minutes until crispy.

533. Piri-piri King Prawns

Servings: 2   Cooking Time: 8 Minutes

Ingredients:

12 king prawns, rinsed	1 teaspoon garlic paste
1 tablespoon coconut oil	1 teaspoon curry powder
Salt and ground black pepper, to taste	1/2 teaspoon piri piri powder
1 teaspoon onion powder	1/2 teaspoon cumin powder

Directions:
Combine all the ingredients in a large bowl and toss until the prawns are completely coated. Place the prawns in the air fryer basket.   Put the air fryer basket on the baking pan and slide into Rack Position 2, select Air Fry, set temperature to 360°F (182°C), and set time to 8 minutes.   Flip the prawns halfway through the cooking time.   When cooking is complete, the prawns will turn pink. Remove from the oven and serve hot.

534. Lobster Grandma's Easy To Cook Wontons

Ingredients:

1 1/2 cup all-purpose flour	2 tbsp. oil
1/2 tsp. salt	2 tsp. ginger-garlic paste
5 tbsp. water	2 tsp. soya sauce
For filling:	2 tsp. vinegar
2 cups minced lobster	

Directions:
Squeeze the dough and cover it with plastic wrap and set aside. Next, cook the ingredients for the filling and try to ensure that the lobster is covered well with the sauce.   Roll the dough and place the filling in the center. Now, wrap the dough to cover the filling and pinch the edges together.   Pre heat the Instant Vortex oven at 200° F for 5 minutes. Place the wontons in the fry basket and close it. Let them cook at the same temperature for another 20 minutes. Recommended sides are chili sauce or ketchup.

535. Breaded Fish Fillets

Servings: 4   Cooking Time: 7 Minutes

Ingredients:

1 pound (454 g) fish fillets	Cooking spray
	Crumb Coating:
1 tablespoon coarse brown mustard	3/4 cup panko bread crumbs
1 teaspoon Worcestershire sauce	1/4 cup stone-ground cornmeal
1/2 teaspoon hot sauce	
Salt, to taste	1/4 teaspoon salt

Directions:
On your cutting board, cut the fish fillets crosswise into slices, about 1 inch wide.   In a small bowl, stir together the mustard, Worcestershire sauce, and hot sauce to make a paste and rub this paste on all sides of the fillets. Season with salt to taste.   In a shallow bowl, thoroughly combine all the ingredients for the crumb coating and spread them on a sheet of wax paper.   Roll the fish fillets in the crumb mixture until thickly coated. Spritz all sides of the fish with cooking spray, then arrange them in the air fryer basket in a single layer.   Put the air fryer basket on the baking pan and slide into Rack Position 2, select Air Fry, set temperature to 400°F (205°C), and set time to 7 minutes.   When cooking is complete, the fish should flake apart with a fork. Remove from the oven and serve warm.

536. Shrimp And Cherry Tomato Kebabs

Servings: 4   Cooking Time: 5 Minutes

Ingredients:

1 1/2 pounds (680 g) jumbo shrimp, cleaned, shelled and deveined	1 teaspoon dried parsley flakes
1 pound (454 g) cherry tomatoes	1/2 teaspoon dried basil
	1/2 teaspoon dried

2 tablespoons butter, melted
1 tablespoons Sriracha sauce
Sea salt and ground black pepper, to taste
oregano
½ teaspoon mustard seeds
½ teaspoon marjoram
Special Equipment:
4 to 6 wooden skewers, soaked in water for 30 minutes

Directions:
Put all the ingredients in a large bowl and toss to coat well.   Make the kebabs: Thread, alternating jumbo shrimp and cherry tomatoes, onto the wooden skewers. Place the kebabs in the air fryer basket.   Put the air fryer basket on the baking pan and slide into Rack Position 2, select Air Fry, set temperature to 400°F (205°C), and set time to 5 minutes.   When cooking is complete, the shrimp should be pink and the cherry tomatoes should be softened. Remove from the oven. Let the shrimp and cherry tomato kebabs cool for 5 minutes and serve hot.

537.   Teriyaki Salmon

Servings: 4   Cooking Time: 15 Minutes
Ingredients:

4 (6-ounce / 170-g) skinless salmon fillets
4 heads baby bok choy, root ends trimmed off and cut in half lengthwise through the root
¾ cup Teriyaki sauce, divided
1 teaspoon sesame oil
1 tablespoon vegetable oil
1 tablespoon toasted sesame seeds

Directions:
Set aside ¼ cup of Teriyaki sauce and pour the remaining sauce into a resealable plastic bag. Put the salmon into the bag and seal, squeezing as much air out as possible. Allow the salmon to marinate for at least 10 minutes.   Arrange the bok choy halves in the baking pan. Drizzle the oils over the vegetables, tossing to coat. Drizzle about 1 tablespoon of the reserved Teriyaki sauce over the bok choy, then push them to the sides of the pan. Put the salmon fillets in the middle of the pan. Slide the baking pan into Rack Position 2, select Roast, set temperature to 375°F (190°C), and set time to 15 minutes.   When done, remove the pan and brush the salmon with the remaining Teriyaki sauce. Serve garnished with the sesame seeds.

538.   Old Bay Shrimp

Servings: 4   Cooking Time: 10 Minutes
Ingredients:

1 lb jumbo shrimp
Salt to taste
¼ tsp old bay seasoning
⅓ tsp smoked paprika
¼ tsp chili powder
1 tbsp olive oil

Directions:
Preheat Instant Vortex on AirFry function to 390 F. In a bowl, add the shrimp, paprika, oil, salt, old bay seasoning, and chili powder; mix well. Place the shrimp in the oven and cook for 5 minutes.

539.   Coconut-crusted Prawns

Servings: 4   Cooking Time: 8 Minutes
Ingredients:

12 prawns, cleaned and deveined
1 teaspoon fresh lemon juice
½ teaspoon cumin powder
Salt and ground black pepper, to taste
1 medium egg
⅓ cup beer
½ cup flour, divided
1 tablespoon curry powder
1 teaspoon baking powder
½ teaspoon grated fresh ginger
1 cup flaked coconut

Directions:
In a large bowl, toss the prawns with the lemon juice, cumin powder, salt, and pepper until well coated. Set aside.   In a shallow bowl, whisk together the egg, beer, ¼ cup of flour, curry powder, baking powder, and ginger until combined.   In a separate shallow bowl, put the remaining ¼ cup of flour, and on a plate, place the flaked coconut.   Dip the prawns in the flour, then in the egg mixture, finally roll in the flaked coconut to coat well. Transfer the prawns to a baking sheet.   Put the air fryer basket on the baking pan and slide into Rack Position 2, select Air Fry, set temperature to 350°F (180°C), and set time to 8 minutes.   After 5 minutes, remove from the oven and flip the prawns. Return to the oven and continue cooking for 3 minutes more. When cooking is complete, remove from the oven and serve warm.

540.   Crispy Crab Legs

Servings: 4   Cooking Time: 15 Minutes
Ingredients:

3 pounds crab legs
½ cup butter, melted

Directions:
Preheat Instant Vortex on Air Fry function to 380 F. Cover the crab legs with salted water and let them stay for a few minutes. Drain, pat them dry, and place the legs in the basket. Fit in the baking tray and brush with some butter; cook for 10 minutes, flipping once. Drizzle with the remaining butter and serve.

541.   Easy Blackened Shrimp

Servings: 6   Cooking Time: 10 Minutes
Ingredients:

1 lb shrimp, deveined
1 tbsp olive oil
1/4 tsp pepper
2 tsp blackened seasoning
1/4 tsp salt

Directions:
Fit the Instant Vortex oven with the rack in position Toss shrimp with oil, pepper, blackened seasoning, and salt.   Transfer shrimp into the baking pan. Set to bake at 400 F for 15 minutes. After 5 minutes place the baking pan in the preheated oven.   Serve and enjoy.

542. Cajun Red Snapper

Servings: 2   Cooking Time: 12 Minutes

Ingredients:

8 oz red snapper fillets	1/4 cup breadcrumbs
2 tbsp parmesan cheese, grated	1/4 tsp Worcestershire sauce
1/2 tsp Cajun seasoning	1 garlic clove, minced
	1/4 cup butter

Directions:

Fit the Instant Vortex oven with the rack in position Melt butter in a pan over low heat. Add Cajun seasoning, garlic, and Worcestershire sauce into the melted butter and stir well.   Brush fish fillets with melted butter and place into the baking dish.   Mix together parmesan cheese and breadcrumbs and sprinkle over fish fillets.   Set to bake at 400 F for 17 minutes. After 5 minutes place the baking dish in the preheated oven.   Serve and enjoy.

543. Crispy Salmon With Lemon-butter Sauce

Ingredients:

4 (4-6-oz) salmon fillets, patted dry	2 Tbsp olive oil
Salt and pepper, to taste	2 Tbsp fresh lemon juice
1 large garlic clove, minced	1 lemon zested
1/3 cup dry white wine	3 Tbsp unsalted butter, diced
	2 Tbsp chopped fresh dill

Directions:

Place Instant Vortex oven over medium heat. Sprinkle salt and pepper on salmon fillets and add 1 Tbsp oil to the pan.   Add salmon flesh side down and cook 3-4 minutes. Flip the salmon and cook an additional 3 minutes on skin side. Transfer to a plate. Wipe out Instant Vortex oven and add remaining Tbsp olive oil over medium heat.   Add garlic and saute for 1 minute.   Pour in white wine and lemon juice. Stir for one minute.   Add lemon zest and continue stirring until slightly reduced.   Reduce heat to low and add cubed butter, stirring after each addition.   Sprinkle in fresh dill and stir all together.   Season with salt and pepper and pour sauce over salmon fillets.

544. Garlic-butter Catfish

Servings: 2   Cooking Time: 20 Minutes

Ingredients:

2 catfish fillets	2 tbsp butter, melted
2 tsp blackening seasoning	1 garlic clove, mashed
Juice of 1 lime	2 tbsp cilantro

Directions:

In a bowl, blend in garlic, lime juice, cilantro, and butter. Pour half of the mixture over the fillets and sprinkle with blackening seasoning. Place the fillets in the basket and fit in the baking tray; cook for 15 minutes at 360 F on Air Fry function. Serve the fish with remaining sauce.

545. Old Bay Tilapia Fillets

Servings: 4   Cooking Time: 15 Minutes

Ingredients:

1 pound tilapia fillets	2 tbsp canola oil
1 tbsp old bay seasoning	2 tbsp lemon pepper
	Salt to taste
	2-3 butter buds

Directions:

Preheat your Instant Vortex oven to 400 F on Bake function. Drizzle tilapia fillets with canola oil. In a bowl, mix salt, lemon pepper, butter buds, and seasoning; spread on the fish. Place the fillet on the basket and fit in the baking tray. Cook for 10 minutes, flipping once until tender and crispy.

546. Roasted Nicoise Salad

Servings: 4   Cooking Time: 15 Minutes

Ingredients:

10 ounces (283 g) small red potatoes, quartered	8 tablespoons extra-virgin olive oil, divided
1 teaspoon kosher salt, divided	1 (9-ounce / 255-g) bag spring greens, washed and dried if needed
1/2 pound (227 g) green beans, trimmed	
1 pint cherry tomatoes	2 (5-ounce / 142-g) cans oil-packed tuna, drained
1 teaspoon Dijon mustard	2 hard-cooked eggs, peeled and quartered
3 tablespoons red wine vinegar	1/3 cup kalamata olives, pitted
Freshly ground black pepper, to taste	

Directions:

In a large bowl, drizzle the potatoes with 1 tablespoon of olive oil and season with 1/4 teaspoon of kosher salt. Transfer to the baking pan.   Slide the baking pan into Rack Position 2, select Roast, set temperature to 375°F (190°C), and set time to 15 minutes.   Meanwhile, in a mixing bowl, toss the green beans and cherry tomatoes with 1 tablespoon of olive oil and 1/4 teaspoon of kosher salt until evenly coated.   After 10 minutes, remove the pan and fold in the green beans and cherry tomatoes. Return the pan to the oven and continue cooking. Meanwhile, make the vinaigrette by whisking together the remaining 6 tablespoons of olive oil, mustard, vinegar, the remaining 1/2 teaspoon of kosher salt, and black pepper in a small bowl. Set aside.   When done, remove from the oven. Allow the vegetables to cool for 5 minutes.   Spread out the spring greens on a plate and spoon the tuna into the center of the greens. Arrange the potatoes, green beans, cheery tomatoes, and eggs around the tuna. Serve drizzled with the vinaigrette and scattered with the olives.

547. Lemon Pepper White Fish Fillets

Servings: 2   Cooking Time: 12 Minutes

Ingredients:

12 oz white fish fillets
Pepper

1/2 tsp lemon pepper
seasoning
Salt

Directions:
Fit the Instant Vortex oven with the rack in position 2. Spray fish fillets with cooking spray and season with lemon pepper seasoning, pepper, and salt. Place fish fillets in the air fryer basket then place an air fryer basket in the baking pan. Place a baking pan on the oven rack. Set to air fry at 360 F for 12 minutes. Serve and enjoy.

548. Roasted Halibut Steaks With Parsley

Servings: 4   Cooking Time: 10 Minutes
Ingredients:

1 pound (454 g)
halibut steaks
¼ cup vegetable oil
2½ tablespoons
Worcester sauce
2 tablespoons
vermouth
1 tablespoon freshly
squeezed lemon juice

2 tablespoons honey
1 tablespoon fresh
parsley leaves,
coarsely chopped
Salt and pepper, to
taste
1 teaspoon dried basil

Directions:
Put all the ingredients in a large mixing dish and gently stir until the fish is coated evenly. Transfer the fish to the air fryer basket. Put the air fryer basket on the baking pan and slide into Rack Position 2, select Roast, set temperature to 390°F (199°C), and set time to 10 minutes. Flip the fish halfway through cooking time. When cooking is complete, the fish should reach an internal temperature of at least 145°F (63°C) on a meat thermometer. Remove from the oven and let the fish cool for 5 minutes before serving.

549. Italian Cod

Servings: 4   Cooking Time: 20 Minutes
Ingredients:

1/4 cup olives, sliced
1 lb cherry tomatoes,
halved
2 garlic cloves,
crushed
1 small onion,
chopped

1 1/2 lbs cod fillet
1 tbsp olive oil
1/4 cup of water
1 tsp Italian
seasoning
Pepper
Salt

Directions:
Fit the Instant Vortex oven with the rack in position Place fish fillets, olives, tomatoes, garlic, and onion in a baking dish. Drizzle with oil. Sprinkle with Italian seasoning, pepper, and salt. Pour water into the dish. Set to bake at 400 F for 25 minutes. After 5 minutes place the baking dish in the preheated oven. Serve and enjoy.

550. Seafood Mac N Cheese

Servings: 8   Cooking Time: 30 Minutes
Ingredients:

Nonstick cooking
spray

3 cups milk
1/8 tsp nutmeg

16 oz. macaroni
7 tbsp. butter, divided
¾ lb. medium
shrimp, peel, devein,
& cut in ½-inch
pieces
½ cup Italian panko
bread crumbs
1 cup onion, chopped
fine
1 ½ tsp garlic, diced
fine
1/3 cup flour

½ tsp Old Bay
seasoning
1 tsp salt
¾ tsp pepper
1 1/3 cup Parmesan
cheese, grated
1 1/3 cup Swiss
cheese, grated
1 1/3 cup sharp
cheddar cheese,
grated
½ lb. lump crab
meat, cooked

Directions:
Place wire rack in position 1 of the oven. Spray a 7x11-inch baking dish with cooking spray. Cook macaroni according to package directions, shortening cooking time by 2 minutes. Drain and rinse with cold water. Melt 1 tablespoon butter in a large skillet over med-high heat. Add shrimp and cook, stirring, until they turn pink. Remove from heat. Melt remaining butter in a large saucepan over medium heat. Once melted, transfer 2 tablespoons to a small bowl and mix in bread crumbs. Add onions and garlic to saucepan and cook, stirring, until they soften. Whisk in flour and cook 1 minute, until smooth. Whisk in milk until there are no lumps. Bring to a boil, reduce heat and simmer until thickened, whisking constantly. Whisk in seasonings. Stir in cheese until melted and smooth. Fold in macaroni and seafood. Transfer to prepared dish. Sprinkle bread crumb mixture evenly over top. Set oven to bake on 400°F for 25 minutes. After 5 minutes, place dish on the rack and bake 20 minutes, until topping is golden brown and sauce is bubbly. Let cool 5 minutes before serving.

551. Easy Shrimp And Vegetable Paella

Servings: 4   Cooking Time: 16 Minutes
Ingredients:

1 (10-ounce / 284-g)
package frozen
cooked rice, thawed
1 (6-ounce / 170-g)
jar artichoke hearts,
drained and chopped
½ teaspoon dried
thyme

¼ cup vegetable
broth
½ teaspoon turmeric
1 cup frozen cooked
small shrimp
½ cup frozen baby
peas
1 tomato, diced

Directions:
Mix together the cooked rice, chopped artichoke hearts, vegetable broth, thyme, and turmeric in the baking pan and stir to combine. Slide the baking pan into Rack Position 1, select Convection Bake, set temperature to 340°F (171°C), and set time to 16 minutes. After 9 minutes, remove from the oven and add the shrimp, baby peas, and diced tomato to the baking pan. Mix well. Return the pan to the oven and continue cooking for 7 minutes more, or until the shrimp are done and the paella is bubbling.

When cooking is complete, remove from the oven. Cool for 5 minutes before serving.

552. Quick Paella

Servings: 4   Cooking Time: 15 Minutes

Ingredients:

1 (10-ounce) package frozen cooked rice, thawed	½ teaspoon dried thyme
1 (6-ounce) jar artichoke hearts, drained and chopped	1 cup frozen cooked small shrimp
¼ cup vegetable broth	½ cup frozen baby peas
½ teaspoon turmeric	1 tomato, diced

Directions:

Preparing the Ingredients. In a 6-by-6-by-2-inch pan, combine the rice, artichoke hearts, vegetable broth, turmeric, and thyme, and stir gently. Air Frying. Place in the Instant Vortex air fryer oven and bake for 8 to 9 minutes or until the rice is hot. Remove from the air fryer oven and gently stir in the shrimp, peas, and tomato. Cook for 5 to 8 minutes or until the shrimp and peas are hot and the paella is bubbling.

553. Baked Garlic Paprika Halibut

Servings: 4   Cooking Time: 12 Minutes

Ingredients:

1 lb halibut fillets	1/4 tsp garlic powder
1/2 tsp smoked paprika	Pepper
1/4 cup olive oil	Salt

Directions:

Fit the Instant Vortex oven with the rack in position Place fish fillets in a baking dish.   In a small bowl, mix together oil, garlic powder, paprika, pepper, and salt.   Brush fish fillets with oil mixture.   Set to bake at 425 F for 17 minutes. After 5 minutes place the baking dish in the preheated oven.   Serve and enjoy.

554. Basil White Fish

Servings: 4   Cooking Time: 20 Minutes

Ingredients:

2 tbsp fresh basil, chopped	Salt and black pepper to taste
2 garlic cloves, minced	2 tbsp pine nuts
1 tbsp Parmesan cheese, grated	4 white fish fillets
	2 tbsp olive oil

Directions:

Preheat Instant Vortex on AirFry function to 350 F. Season the fillets with salt and pepper and place in the basket. Drizzle with some olive oil and press Start. Cook for 12-14 minutes. In a bowl, mix basil, remaining olive oil, pine nuts, garlic, and Parmesan cheese and spread on the fish. Serve.

555. Easy Salmon Patties

Servings: 6 Patties   Cooking Time: 11 Minutes

Ingredients:

1 (14.75-ounce / 418-g) can Alaskan pink salmon, drained and bones removed	2 scallions, diced
	1 teaspoon garlic powder
½ cup bread crumbs	Salt and pepper, to taste
1 egg, whisked	Cooking spray

Directions:

Stir together the salmon, bread crumbs, whisked egg, scallions, garlic powder, salt, and pepper in a large bowl until well incorporated.   Divide the salmon mixture into six equal portions and form each into a patty with your hands.   Arrange the salmon patties in the air fryer basket and spritz them with cooking spray.   Put the air fryer basket on the baking pan and slide into Rack Position 2, select Air Fry, set temperature to 400°F (205°C), and set time to 10 minutes.   Flip the patties once halfway through.   When cooking is complete, the patties should be golden brown and cooked through. Remove the patties from the oven and serve on a plate.

556. Honey Glazed Salmon

Servings: 4   Cooking Time: 8 Minutes

Ingredients:

4 salmon fillets	Pepper
2 tsp soy sauce	Salt
1 tbsp honey	

Directions:

Fit the Instant Vortex oven with the rack in position 2.   Brush salmon with soy sauce and season with pepper and salt.   Place salmon in the air fryer basket then place an air fryer basket in the baking pan.   Place a baking pan on the oven rack. Set to air fry at 375 F for 8 minutes.   Brush salmon with honey and serve.

557. Parmesan-crusted Hake With Garlic Sauce

Servings: 3   Cooking Time: 10 Minutes

Ingredients:

Fish:	3 hake fillets, patted dry
6 tablespoons mayonnaise	Nonstick cooking spray
1 tablespoon fresh lime juice	Garlic Sauce:
1 teaspoon Dijon mustard	¼ cup plain Greek yogurt
1 cup grated Parmesan cheese	2 tablespoons olive oil
Salt, to taste	2 cloves garlic, minced
¼ teaspoon ground black pepper, or more to taste	½ teaspoon minced tarragon leaves

Directions:

Mix the mayo, lime juice, and mustard in a shallow bowl and whisk to combine. In another shallow bowl, stir together the grated Parmesan cheese, salt, and pepper.   Dredge each fillet in the mayo mixture, then roll them in the cheese mixture until they are evenly coated on both sides.   Spray the air fryer basket with nonstick cooking spray. Place the fillets in the pan. Put the air fryer basket on the baking pan and slide into Rack Position 2, select Air Fry, set temperature to 395ºF (202ºC), and set time to 10 minutes. Flip the fillets halfway through the cooking time. Meanwhile, in a small bowl, whisk all the ingredients for the sauce until well incorporated. When cooking is complete, the fish should flake apart with a fork. Remove the fillets from the oven and serve warm alongside the sauce.

558. Fish Club Classic Sandwich

Ingredients:

2 slices of white bread	½ tsp. olive oil
1 tbsp. softened butter	¼ cup chopped onion
1 tin tuna	¼ tsp. mustard powder
1 small capsicum	
For Barbeque Sauce:	½ tbsp. sugar
¼ tbsp. Worcestershire sauce	¼ tbsp. red chili sauce
½ flake garlic crushed	1 tbsp. tomato ketchup
	½ cup water.
	A pinch of salt and black pepper to taste

Directions:
Take the slices of bread and remove the edges. Now cut the slices horizontally. Cook the ingredients for the sauce and wait till it thickens. Now, add the fish to the sauce and stir till it obtains the flavors. Roast the capsicum and peel the skin off. Cut the capsicum into slices. Mix the ingredients together and apply it to the bread slices. Pre-heat the Instant Vortex oven for 5 minutes at 300 Fahrenheit. Open the basket of the Fryer and place the prepared Classic Sandwiches in it such that no two Classic Sandwiches are touching each other. Now keep the fryer at 250 degrees for around 15 minutes. Turn the Classic Sandwiches in between the cooking process to cook both slices. Serve the Classic Sandwiches with tomato ketchup or mint sauce.

559. Tomato Garlic Shrimp

Servings: 4   Cooking Time: 25 Minutes
Ingredients:

1 lb shrimp, peeled	1 tbsp olive oil
1 tbsp garlic, sliced	Pepper
2 cups cherry tomatoes	Salt

Directions:
Fit the Instant Vortex oven with the rack in position Add shrimp, oil, garlic, tomatoes, pepper, and salt into the large bowl and toss well. Transfer shrimp mixture into the baking dish. Set to bake at 400 F for 30 minutes. After 5 minutes place the baking dish in the preheated oven. Serve and enjoy.

560. Spiced Red Snapper

Servings: 4   Cooking Time: 10 Minutes

Ingredients:

1 teaspoon olive oil	¼ teaspoon thyme
1½ teaspoons black pepper	4 (4-ounce / 113-g) red snapper fillets, skin on
¼ teaspoon garlic powder	4 thin slices lemon
⅛ teaspoon cayenne pepper	Nonstick cooking spray

Directions:
Spritz the baking pan with nonstick cooking spray. In a small bowl, stir together the olive oil, black pepper, garlic powder, thyme, and cayenne pepper. Rub the mixture all over the fillets until completely coated. Lay the fillets, skin-side down, in the baking pan and top each fillet with a slice of lemon. Slide the baking pan into Rack Position 1, select Convection Bake, set temperature to 390ºF (199ºC), and set time to 10 minutes. Flip the fillets halfway through the cooking time. When cooking is complete, the fish should be cooked through. Let the fish cool for 5 minutes and serve.

561. Buttery Crab Legs

Servings: 4   Cooking Time: 15 Minutes
Ingredients:

3 pounds crab legs	1 cup butter, melted

Directions:
Preheat Instant Vortex on AirFry function to 380 F. Dip the crab legs in salted water and let stay for a few minutes. Drain, pat dry, and place the legs in the basket and press Start. Cook for 10 minutes. Pour the butter over crab legs and serve.

562. Quick Tuna Patties

Servings: 10   Cooking Time: 10 Minutes
Ingredients:

15 oz can tuna, drained and flaked	1/2 tsp dried mixed herbs
3 tbsp parmesan cheese, grated	1/2 tsp garlic powder
1/2 cup breadcrumbs	2 tbsp onion, minced
1 tbsp lemon juice	1 celery stalk, chopped
2 eggs, lightly beaten	Pepper
	Salt

Directions:
Fit the Instant Vortex oven with the rack in position 2. Add all ingredients into the mixing bowl and mix until well combined. Make patties from mixture and place in the air fryer basket then place the air fryer basket in the baking pan. Place a baking pan on the oven rack. Set to air fry at 360 F for 10 minutes. Serve and enjoy.

563. Marinated Salmon

Servings: 2   Cooking Time: 10 Minutes
Ingredients:

2 salmon fillets, skinless and boneless	2 garlic cloves, minced
For marinade:	2 tbsp mirin
2 tbsp scallions, minced	2 tbsp soy sauce
1 tbsp ginger, grated	1 tbsp olive oil

Directions:
Fit the Instant Vortex oven with the rack in position 2. Add all marinade ingredients into the zip-lock bag and mix well. Add salmon in the bag. The sealed bag shakes well and places it in the fridge for 30 minutes. Arrange marinated salmon fillets in an air fryer basket then place an air fryer basket in the baking pan. Place a baking pan on the oven rack. Set to air fry at 360 F for 10 minutes. Serve and enjoy.

564. Crispy Crab And Fish Cakes

Servings: 4   Cooking Time: 12 Minutes

Ingredients:

8 ounces (227 g) imitation crab meat	¾ cup crushed saltine cracker crumbs
4 ounces (113 g) leftover cooked fish (such as cod, pollock, or haddock)	2 teaspoons dried parsley flakes
2 tablespoons minced celery	1 teaspoon prepared yellow mustard
2 tablespoons minced green onion	½ teaspoon garlic powder
2 tablespoons light mayonnaise	½ teaspoon dried dill weed, crushed
1 tablespoon plus 2 teaspoons Worcestershire sauce	½ teaspoon Old Bay seasoning
	½ cup panko bread crumbs
	Cooking spray

Directions:
Pulse the crab meat and fish in a food processor until finely chopped. Transfer the meat mixture to a large bowl, along with the celery, green onion, mayo, Worcestershire sauce, cracker crumbs, parsley flakes, mustard, garlic powder, dill weed, and Old Bay seasoning. Stir to mix well. Scoop out the meat mixture and form into 8 equal-sized patties with your hands. Place the panko bread crumbs on a plate. Roll the patties in the bread crumbs until they are evenly coated on both sides. Put the patties in the baking pan and spritz them with cooking spray. Slide the baking pan into Rack Position 1, select Convection Bake, set temperature to 390°F (199°C), and set time to 12 minutes. Flip the patties halfway through the cooking time. When cooking is complete, they should be golden brown and cooked through. Remove the pan from the oven. Divide the patties among four plates and serve.

565. Air Fry Tuna Patties

Servings: 4   Cooking Time: 6 Minutes

Ingredients:

1 egg, lightly beaten	1 tbsp mustard
8 oz can tuna, drained	1/4 tsp garlic powder
1/4 cup breadcrumbs	Pepper
	Salt

Directions:
Fit the Instant Vortex oven with the rack in position 2. Add all ingredients into the large bowl and mix until well combined. Make four equal shapes of patties from the mixture and place in the air fryer basket then place an air fryer basket in the baking pan. Place a baking pan on the oven rack. Set to air fry at 400 F for 6 minutes. Serve and enjoy.

566. Grilled Soy Salmon Fillets

Servings: 4   Cooking Time: 8 Minutes

Ingredients:

4 salmon fillets	1 tablespoon fresh lemon juice
1/4 teaspoon ground black pepper	1/2 cup soy sauce
1/2 teaspoon cayenne pepper	1/2 cup water
1/2 teaspoon salt	1 tablespoon honey
1 teaspoon onion powder	2 tablespoons extra-virgin olive oil

Directions:
Preparing the Ingredients. Firstly, pat the salmon fillets dry using kitchen towels. Season the salmon with black pepper, cayenne pepper, salt, and onion powder. To make the marinade, combine together the lemon juice, soy sauce, water, honey, and olive oil. Marinate the salmon for at least 2 hours in your refrigerator. Arrange the fish fillets on a grill basket in your Instant Vortex air fryer oven. Air Frying. Bake at 330 degrees for 8 to 9 minutes, or until salmon fillets are easily flaked with a fork. Work with batches and serve warm.

567. Moist & Juicy Baked Cod

Servings: 2   Cooking Time: 10 Minutes

Ingredients:

1 lb cod fillets	1 tbsp fresh lemon juice
1 1/2 tbsp olive oil	1/4 tsp salt
3 dashes cayenne pepper	

Directions:
Fit the Instant Vortex oven with the rack in position Place fish fillets in a baking pan. Drizzle with oil and lemon juice and sprinkle with cayenne pepper and salt. Set to bake at 400 F for 15 minutes. After 5 minutes place the baking pan in the preheated oven. Serve and enjoy.

568. Fired Shrimp With Mayonnaise Sauce

Servings: 4   Cooking Time: 7 Minutes

Ingredients:

Shrimp	Sauce:
12 jumbo shrimp	1 teaspoon grated lemon rind
½ teaspoon garlic salt	1 teaspoon Dijon mustard
¼ teaspoon freshly cracked mixed peppercorns	1 teaspoon chipotle powder
4 tablespoons mayonnaise	½ teaspoon cumin powder

Directions:
In a medium bowl, season the shrimp with garlic salt and cracked mixed peppercorns. Place the shrimp in the air fryer basket. Put the air fryer

basket on the baking pan and slide into Rack Position 2, select Air Fry, set temperature to 395°F (202°C), and set time to 7 minutes. After 5 minutes, remove from the oven and flip the shrimp. Return to the oven and continue cooking for 2 minutes more, or until they are pink and no longer opaque. Meanwhile, stir together all the ingredients for the sauce in a small bowl until well mixed. When cooking is complete, remove the shrimp from the oven and serve alongside the sauce.

569. Crispy Fish Sticks

Servings: 8   Cooking Time: 6 Minutes
Ingredients:

8 ounces (227 g) fish fillets (pollock or cod), cut into ½ × 3 inches strips Cooking spray	Salt, to taste (optional) ½ cup plain bread crumbs

Directions:
Season the fish strips with salt to taste, if desired. Place the bread crumbs on a plate, then roll the fish in the bread crumbs until well coated. Spray all sides of the fish with cooking spray. Transfer to the air fryer basket in a single layer. Put the air fryer basket on the baking pan and slide into Rack Position 2, select Air Fry, set temperature to 400°F (205°C), and set time to 6 minutes. When cooked, the fish sticks should be golden brown and crispy. Remove from the oven to a plate and serve hot.

570. Butter-wine Baked Salmon

Servings: 4   Cooking Time: 10 Minutes
Ingredients:

4 tablespoons butter, melted	1 tablespoon lime juice
2 cloves garlic, minced	1 teaspoon smoked paprika
Sea salt and ground black pepper, to taste	½ teaspoon onion powder
¼ cup dry white wine	4 salmon steaks Cooking spray

Directions:
Place all the ingredients except the salmon and oil in a shallow dish and stir to mix well. Add the salmon steaks, turning to coat well on both sides. Transfer the salmon to the refrigerator to marinate for 30 minutes. When ready, put the salmon steaks in the air fryer basket, discarding any excess marinade. Spray the salmon steaks with cooking spray. Put the air fryer basket on the baking pan and slide into Rack Position 2, select Air Fry, set temperature to 360°F (182°C), and set time to 10 minutes. Flip the salmon steaks halfway through. When cooking is complete, remove from the oven and divide the salmon steaks among four plates. Serve warm.

571. Rosemary Garlic Shrimp

Servings: 4   Cooking Time: 10 Minutes
Ingredients:

1 lb shrimp, peeled and deveined	1/2 tbsp fresh rosemary, chopped
2 garlic cloves, minced	Pepper
1 tbsp olive oil	Salt

Directions:
Fit the Instant Vortex oven with the rack in position Add shrimp and remaining ingredients in a large bowl and toss well. Pour shrimp mixture into the baking dish. Set to bake at 400 F for 15 minutes. After 5 minutes place the baking dish in the preheated oven. Serve and enjoy.

572. Parmesan-crusted Halibut Fillets

Servings: 4   Cooking Time: 10 Minutes
Ingredients:

2 medium-sized halibut fillets	Kosher salt and freshly cracked mixed peppercorns, to taste
Dash of tabasco sauce	2 eggs
1 teaspoon curry powder	1½ tablespoons olive oil
½ teaspoon ground coriander	½ cup grated Parmesan cheese
½ teaspoon hot paprika	

Directions:
On a clean work surface, drizzle the halibut fillets with the tabasco sauce. Sprinkle with the curry powder, coriander, hot paprika, salt, and cracked mixed peppercorns. Set aside. In a shallow bowl, beat the eggs until frothy. In another shallow bowl, combine the olive oil and Parmesan cheese. One at a time, dredge the halibut fillets in the beaten eggs, shaking off any excess, then roll them over the Parmesan cheese until evenly coated. Arrange the halibut fillets in the air fryer basket in a single layer. Put the air fryer basket on the baking pan and slide into Rack Position 2, select Roast, set temperature to 365°F (185°C), and set time to 10 minutes. When cooking is complete, the fish should be golden brown and crisp. Cool for 5 minutes before serving.

573. Cheesy Tilapia Fillets

Servings: 4   Cooking Time: 15 Minutes
Ingredients:

¾ cup grated Parmesan cheese	1 tbsp chopped parsley
1 tbsp olive oil	¼ tsp garlic powder
2 tsp paprika	4 tilapia fillets

Directions:
Preheat Instant Vortex on Air Fry function to 350 F. Mix parsley, Parmesan cheese, garlic, and paprika in a bowl. Brush the olive oil over the fillets and then coat with the Parmesan mixture. Place the tilapia onto a lined baking sheet and cook for 8-10 minutes, turning once. Serve.

574. Crusty Scallops

Servings: 4   Cooking Time: 20 Minutes
Ingredients:

12 fresh scallops	3 tbsp flour
Salt and black pepper	1 egg, lightly beaten
to taste	1 cup breadcrumbs

Directions:
Coat the scallops with flour. Dip into the egg, then into the breadcrumbs. Arrange them on the frying basket and spray with cooking spray. Cook for 12 minutes at 360 F on AirFry function.

---

575.   Spinach Scallops

Servings: 2   Cooking Time: 10 Minutes

Ingredients:

8 sea scallops	12 oz frozen spinach,
1 tbsp fresh basil,	thawed and drained
chopped	1 tsp garlic, minced

| 1 tbsp tomato paste | 1/2 tsp pepper |
| 3/4 cup heavy cream | 1/2 tsp salt |

Directions:
Fit the Instant Vortex oven with the rack in position Layer spinach in the baking dish.   Spray scallops with cooking spray and season with pepper and salt. Place scallops on top of spinach.   In a small bowl, mix garlic, basil, tomato paste, whipping cream, pepper, and salt and pour over scallops and spinach. Set to bake at 350 F for 15 minutes. After 5 minutes place the baking dish in the preheated oven. Serve and enjoy.

Meat Recipes

576. Bacon With Rosemary Potatoes

Servings: 4   Cooking Time: 40 Minutes

Ingredients:

2 garlic cloves, minced	2 lb potatoes, halved
4 bacon slices, chopped	1 tbsp fresh rosemary, chopped
	2 tbsp olive oil

Directions:

In a mixing bowl, mix garlic, bacon, olive oil, and rosemary; toss in potatoes. Place the mixture in a baking dish Roast in the preheated Instant Vortex for 25-30 minutes at 400 F on AirFry function.

577. Beef Rolls With Pesto & Spinach

Servings: 4   Cooking Time: 30 Minutes

Ingredients:

2 pounds beef steaks, sliced	3 tbsp pesto
Salt and black pepper to taste	¾ cup spinach, chopped
6 slices mozzarella cheese	3 oz bell pepper, deseeded and sliced

Directions:

Top the meat with pesto, mozzarella cheese, spinach, and bell pepper. Roll up the slices and secure using a toothpick. Season with salt and pepper. Place the slices in the basket and fit in the baking tray; cook for 15 minutes on Air Fry function at 400 F, turning once. Serve immediately!

578. Chicken Momo's Recipe

Ingredients:

1 ½ cup all-purpose flour	2 tbsp. oil
½ tsp. salt	2 tsp. ginger-garlic paste
5 tbsp. water	2 tsp. soya sauce
2 cups minced chicken	2 tsp. vinegar

Directions:

Squeeze the dough and cover it with plastic wrap and set aside. Next, cook the ingredients for the filling and try to ensure that the beef is covered well with the sauce.   Roll the dough and cut it into a square. Place the filling in the center. Now, wrap the dough to cover the filling and pinch the edges together. Pre heat the Instant Vortex oven at 200° F for 5 minutes. Place the wontons in the fry basket and close it. Let them cook at the same temperature for another 20 minutes. Recommended sides are chili sauce or ketchup.

579. Poultry Fried Baked Pastry

Ingredients:

1 or 2 green chilies that are finely	½ tsp. cumin
	Water to knead the
chopped or mashed	dough
1 tsp. coarsely crushed coriander	1 lb. mixed minced poultry (squab, chicken, duck, pheasant, turkey)
1 dry red chili broken into pieces	¼ cup boiled peas
A small amount of salt (to taste)	1 tsp. powdered ginger
2 tbsp. unsalted butter	½ tsp. dried mango powder
1 ½ cup all-purpose flour	½ tsp. red chili power.
A pinch of salt to taste	1-2 tbsp. coriander.

Directions:

You will first need to make the outer covering. In a large bowl, add the flour, butter and enough water to knead it into dough that is stiff. Transfer this to a container and leave it to rest for five minutes. Place a pan on medium flame and add the oil. Roast the mustard seeds and once roasted, add the coriander seeds and the chopped dry red chilies. Add all the dry ingredients for the filling and mix the ingredients well. Add a little water and continue to stir the ingredients. Make small balls out of the dough and roll them out.   Cut the rolled-out dough into halves and apply a little water on the edges to help you fold the halves into a cone. Add the filling to the cone and close up the samosa. Pre-heat the Instant Vortex oven for around 5 to 6 minutes at 300 Fahrenheit. Place all the samosas in the fry basket and close the basket properly. Keep the Instant Vortex oven at 200 degrees for another 20 to 25 minutes.   Around the halfway point, open the basket and turn the samosas over for uniform cooking. After this, fry at 250 degrees for around 10 minutes in order to give them the desired golden-brown color. Serve hot. Recommended sides are tamarind or mint sauce.

580. Lush Salisbury Steak With Mushroom Gravy

Servings: 2   Cooking Time: 33 Minutes

Ingredients:

For the Mushroom Gravy:	1 tablespoon dry mustard
¾ cup sliced button mushrooms	2 tablespoons tomato paste
¼ cup thinly sliced onions	¼ teaspoon garlic powder
¼ cup unsalted butter, melted	½ teaspoon onion powder
½ teaspoon fine sea salt	½ teaspoon fine sea salt
¼ cup beef broth	
For the Steaks:	¼ teaspoon ground black pepper
½ pound (227 g) ground beef (85% lean)	Chopped fresh thyme leaves, for garnish

Directions:
Toss the mushrooms and onions with butter in the baking pan to coat well, then sprinkle with salt. Slide the baking pan into Rack Position 1, select Convection Bake, set temperature to 390°F (199°C) and set time to 8 minutes. Stir the mixture halfway through the cooking. When cooking is complete, the mushrooms should be tender. Pour the broth in the baking pan and set time to 10 more minutes to make the gravy. Meanwhile, combine all the ingredients for the steaks, except for the thyme leaves, in a large bowl. Stir to mix well. Shape the mixture into two oval steaks. Arrange the steaks over the gravy and set time to 15 minutes. When cooking is complete, the patties should be browned. Flip the steaks halfway through. Transfer the steaks onto a plate and pour the gravy over. Sprinkle with fresh thyme and serve immediately.

581. Pheasant Marinade Cutlet

Ingredients:

2 cups sliced pheasant	For the filling:
1 big capsicum (Cut this capsicum into big cubes)	2 cup fresh green coriander
	½ cup mint leaves
1 onion (Cut it into quarters. Now separate the layers carefully.)	4 tsp. fennel
	2 tbsp. ginger-garlic paste
	1 small onion
5 tbsp. gram flour	6-7 flakes garlic (optional)
A pinch of salt to taste	Salt to taste
	3 tbsp. lemon juice

Directions:
You will first need to make the sauce. Add the ingredients to a blender and make a thick paste. Slit the pieces of pheasant and stuff half the paste into the cavity obtained. Take the remaining paste and add it to the gram flour and salt. Toss the pieces of pheasant in this mixture and set aside. Apply a little bit of the mixture on the capsicum and onion. Place these on a stick along with the pheasant pieces. Pre heat the Instant Vortex oven at 290 Fahrenheit for around 5 minutes. Open the basket. Arrange the satay sticks properly. Close the basket. Keep the sticks with the mutton at 180 degrees for around half an hour while the sticks with the vegetables are to be kept at the same temperature for only 7 minutes. Turn the sticks in between so that one side does not get burnt and also to provide a uniform cook.

582. Dry-rubbed Flat Iron Steak

Ingredients:

1 tsp coarse salt	½ tsp thyme
1 tsp paprika	
1 tsp cumin	¼ tsp black pepper
1 tsp garlic powder	4 (6-oz) flat iron steaks
1 tsp onion powder	
½ tsp coriander	2 Tbsp olive oil

Directions:

Combine first eight ingredients in a small bowl. Rub the seasonings onto the steaks and drizzle with 2 Tbsp olive oil. Heat Instant Vortex oven over medium heat. Place steaks into Instant Vortex oven and sear for 3 minutes on each side. Cook for an additional 3 minutes for medium-rare. Let meat rest for 10 minutes before slicing.

583. Bacon Ranch Chicken

Servings: 6   Cooking Time: 45 Minutes
Ingredients:

2 lbs chicken breasts	4 oz cream cheese
1 packet dry ranch dressing mix	1 cup sour cream
	12 oz broccoli, steam
2 cups cheddar cheese, shredded	1 lb bacon, cooked & chopped
1 tsp garlic powder	

Directions:
Fit the Instant Vortex oven with the rack in position Place chicken breasts and broccoli into the greased baking pan. Mix together sour cream, cream cheese, garlic powder, bacon, and ranch dressing mix and pour over chicken and broccoli. Sprinkle cheddar cheese on top of chicken and broccoli mixture. Set to bake at 350 F for 50 minutes. After 5 minutes place the baking pan in the preheated oven. Serve and enjoy.

584. Meatballs(6)

Servings: 8   Cooking Time: 25 Minutes
Ingredients:

3 eggs	1/2 cup fresh parsley, minced
2 lbs ground beef	
2 tsp cumin	1 tsp cinnamon
5 garlic cloves, minced	2 tsp dried oregano
	1 tsp pepper
1 onion, grated	2 tsp salt
1 cup breadcrumbs	

Directions:
Fit the Instant Vortex oven with the rack in position Add all ingredients into the large mixing bowl and mix until well combined. Make small meatballs from mixture and place in baking pan. Set to bake at 400 F for 30 minutes. After 5 minutes place the baking pan in the preheated oven. Serve and enjoy.

585. Pork Leg Roast With Candy Onions

Servings: 4   Cooking Time: 52 Minutes
Ingredients:

2 teaspoons sesame oil	1 thyme sprig, chopped
1 teaspoon dried sage, crushed	2 pounds (907 g) pork leg roast, scored
1 teaspoon cayenne pepper	½ pound (227 g) candy onions, sliced
1 rosemary sprig, chopped	4 cloves garlic, finely chopped
Sea salt and ground black pepper, to taste	2 chili peppers, minced

Directions:

118

In a mixing bowl, combine the sesame oil, sage, cayenne pepper, rosemary, thyme, salt and black pepper until well mixed. In another bowl, place the pork leg and brush with the seasoning mixture. Place the seasoned pork leg in the baking pan. Put the baking pan into Rack Position 2, select Air Fry, set temperature to 400°F (205°C) and set time to 40 minutes. After 20 minutes, remove from the oven. Flip the pork leg. Return the pan to the oven and continue cooking. After another 20 minutes, add the candy onions, garlic, and chili peppers to the pan and air fry for another 12 minutes. When cooking is complete, the pork leg should be browned. Transfer the pork leg to a plate. Let cool for 5 minutes and slice. Spread the juices left in the pan over the pork and serve warm with the candy onions.

586. Juicy Spicy Lemon Kebab

Ingredients:

2 tsp. garam masala	3 onions chopped
4 tbsp. chopped coriander	5 green chilies-roughly chopped
3 tbsp. cream	1 ½ tbsp. ginger paste
2 tbsp. coriander powder	
4 tbsp. fresh mint (chopped)	1 ½ tsp. garlic paste
3 tbsp. chopped capsicum	1 ½ tsp. salt
2 lb. chicken breasts cubed	3 tsp. lemon juice
	2 tbsp. peanut flour
	3 eggs

Directions:
Mix the dry ingredients in a bowl. Make the mixture into a smooth paste and coat the chicken cubes with the mixture. Beat the eggs in a bowl and add a little salt to them. Dip the cubes in the egg mixture and coat them with sesame seeds and leave them in the refrigerator for an hour. Pre heat the Instant Vortex oven at 290 Fahrenheit for around 5 minutes. Place the kebabs in the basket and let them cook for another 25 minutes at the same temperature. Turn the kebabs over in between the cooking process to get a uniform cook. Serve the kebabs with mint sauce.

587. Ham Club Sandwich

Ingredients:

2 slices of white bread	½ tsp. olive oil
1 tbsp. softened butter	¼ tsp. mustard powder
1 lb. ham (Sliced)	
1 small capsicum	¼ cup chopped onion
For Barbeque Sauce:	
¼ tbsp. Worcestershire sauce	½ tbsp. sugar
½ flake garlic crushed	1 tbsp. tomato ketchup
	¼ tbsp. red chili sauce
	½ cup water.
	A pinch of salt and black pepper to taste

Directions:
Take the slices of bread and remove the edges. Now cut the slices horizontally. Cook the ingredients for the sauce and wait till it thickens. Now, add the ham slices to the sauce and stir till it obtains the flavors. Roast the capsicum and peel the skin off. Cut the capsicum into slices. Mix the ingredients together and apply it to the bread slices. Pre-heat the Instant Vortex oven for 5 minutes at 300 Fahrenheit. Open the basket of the Fryer and place the prepared Classic Sandwiches in it such that no two Classic Sandwiches are touching each other. Now keep the fryer at 250 degrees for around 15 minutes. Turn the Classic Sandwiches in between the cooking process to cook both slices. Serve the Classic Sandwiches with tomato ketchup or mint sauce.

588. Spice-coated Steaks With Cucumber And Snap Pea Salad

Servings: 4   Cooking Time: 15 Minutes

Ingredients:

1 (1½-pound / 680-g) boneless top sirloin steak, trimmed and halved crosswise	⅛ teaspoon ground cinnamon
	3 tablespoons mayonnaise
1½ teaspoons chili powder	1½ tablespoons white wine vinegar
1½ teaspoons ground cumin	1 tablespoon minced fresh dill
¾ teaspoon ground coriander	1 small garlic clove, minced
⅛ teaspoon cayenne pepper	8 ounces (227 g) sugar snap peas, strings removed and cut in half on bias
1¼ teaspoons plus ⅛ teaspoon salt, divided	
½ teaspoon plus ⅛ teaspoon ground black pepper, divided	½ English cucumber, halved lengthwise and sliced thin
1 teaspoon plus 1½ tablespoons extra-virgin olive oil, divided	2 radishes, trimmed, halved and sliced thin
	2 cups baby arugula

Directions:
In a bowl, mix chili powder, cumin, coriander, cayenne pepper, cinnamon, 1¼ teaspoons salt and ½ teaspoon pepper until well combined. Add the steaks to another bowl and pat dry with paper towels. Brush with 1 teaspoon oil and transfer to the bowl of spice mixture. Roll over to coat thoroughly. Arrange the coated steaks in the basket, spaced evenly apart. Put the air fryer basket on the baking pan and slide into Rack Position 2, select Air Fry, set temperature to 400°F (205°C) and set time to 15 minutes. Flip the steak halfway through to ensure even cooking. When cooking is complete, an instant-read thermometer inserted in the thickest part of the meat should register at least 145°F (63°C). Transfer the steaks to a clean work surface and wrap with aluminum foil. Let stand while preparing salad. Make the salad: In a large bowl, stir together 1½ tablespoons olive oil, mayonnaise, vinegar, dill, garlic, ⅛ teaspoon salt,

and ⅛ teaspoon pepper. Add snap peas, cucumber, radishes and arugula. Toss to blend well.   Slice the steaks and serve with the salad.

---

589.   Perfect Beef Hash Brown Bake

Servings: 4   Cooking Time: 40 Minutes

Ingredients:

1 lb ground beef	30 oz frozen
2 cups cheddar cheese, shredded	shredded hash browns
1 cup milk	1 tsp garlic powder
10 oz can cream of mushroom soup	1 tbsp onion, minced
	Pepper
	Salt

Directions:

Fit the Instant Vortex oven with the rack in position In a pan, brown ground beef with garlic powder, onion, pepper, and salt. Drain.   In a bowl, mix meat, shredded cheese, milk, soup, and hash browns. Pour meat mixture into the greased 9*13-inch baking dish.   Set to bake at 350 F for 45 minutes. After 5 minutes place the baking dish in the preheated oven.   Serve and enjoy.

---

590.   Hot Chicken Wings

Servings: 2   Cooking Time: 20 Minutes + Chilling Time

Ingredients:

8 chicken wings	2 tbsp hot curry paste
1 tbsp water	½ tbsp baking powder
2 tbsp potato starch	

Directions:

Combine hot curry paste and water in a small bowl. Add in the wings toss to coat. Cover the bowl with plastic wrap and refrigerate for 30 minutes. Preheat Instant Vortex on Air Fry function to 370 degrees. In a bowl, mix the baking powder with potato starch. Remove the wings from the fridge and dip them in the starch mixture.   Place on a lined baking dish and cook in your Instant Vortex for 7 minutes. Flip over and cook for 5 minutes.

---

591.   Pineapple & Ginger Chicken Kabobs

Servings: 2   Cooking Time: 20 Minutes

Ingredients:

2 chicken breasts, cut into 2-inch pieces	1 tbsp fresh ginger, grated
½ cup soy sauce	4 scallions, chopped
½ cup pineapple juice	2 tbsp toasted sesame seeds
¼ cup sesame oil	A pinch of black pepper
4 cloves garlic, chopped	

Directions:

In a bowl, toss to coat all the ingredients except the chicken. Let sit for 10 minutes.   Preheat your Instant Vortex oven on Air Fry function to 390 F. Remove the chicken pieces and pat them dry using paper towels. Thread the chicken pieces onto skewers and trim any fat. Place in the AirFryer

---

basket and fit in the baking tray. Cook for 7-10 minutes, flipping once. Serve.

---

592.   Duck Liver Fries

Ingredients:

A pinch of salt to taste	For the garnish: ingredients for the
1 tbsp. lemon juice	marinade:
1 cup melted cheddar cheese	1 tbsp. olive oil
1 lb. duck liver (Cut in to long Oregano Fingers)	1 tsp. mixed herbs
	½ tsp. red chili flakes

Directions:

Take all the ingredients mentioned under the heading "For the marinade" and mix them well. Cook the duck liver Oregano Fingers and soak them in the marinade.   Pre heat the Instant Vortex oven for around 5 minutes at 300 Fahrenheit. Take out the basket of the fryer and place the chicken Oregano Fingers in them. Close the basket.   Now keep the fryer at 220 Fahrenheit for 20 or 25 minutes. In between the process, toss the fries twice or thrice so that they get cooked properly. Towards the end of the cooking process (the last 2 minutes or so), sprinkle the cut coriander leaves on the fries. Add the melted cheddar cheese over the fries and serve hot.

---

593.   Pork Chops With Potatoes(2)

Servings: 6   Cooking Time: 25 Minutes

Ingredients:

6 pork chops	1 lb baby potatoes, quartered
1 oz dried Italian dressing	Pepper
1/4 cup olive oil	Salt
1 onion, chopped	

Directions:

Fit the Instant Vortex oven with the rack in position Brush pork chops with oil and season with pepper and salt.   Place pork chops into the baking dish. Toss potatoes, onion, and Italian dressing in a bowl and place potatoes and onion around the pork chops in baking dish.   Set to bake at 425 F for 30 minutes. After 5 minutes place the baking dish in the preheated oven.   Serve and enjoy.

---

594.   Provençal Chicken With Peppers

Servings: 2   Cooking Time: 20 Minutes

Ingredients:

2 chicken tenders	1 tbsp butter, softened
Salt and black pepper to taste	2 mini red peppers, sliced
½ tsp herbs de Provence	1 onion, sliced

Directions:

Preheat Instant Vortex on AirFry function to 390 F. Lay a foil on a flat surface. Place the chicken, red peppers, and onion on the foil, sprinkle with herbs de Provence and brush with butter. Season with salt and black pepper. Wrap the foil around the breasts.

Place the wrapped chicken in the basket and press Start; cook for 12 minutes. Remove and carefully unwrap. Serve with the sauce extract and veggies.

595. Bacon Wrapped Pork Tenderloin

Servings: 4   Cooking Time: 15 Minutes

Ingredients:

Pork:	Apple Gravy:
1-2 tbsp. Dijon mustard	1 tbsp. almond flour
3-4 strips of bacon	2 tbsp. ghee
1 pork tenderloin	1 chopped onion
½ - 1 tsp. Dijon mustard	2-3 Granny Smith apples
	1 C. vegetable broth

Directions:
Preparing the Ingredients. Spread Dijon mustard all over tenderloin and wrap the meat with strips of bacon.   Air Frying. Place into the Instant Vortex air fryer oven, set temperature to 360°F, and set time to 15 minutes and cook 10-15 minutes at 360 degrees. Use a meat thermometer to check for doneness.   To make sauce, heat ghee in a pan and add shallots. Cook 1-2 minutes.   Then add apples, cooking 3-5 minutes until softened.   Add flour and ghee to make a roux. Add broth and mustard, stirring well to combine.   When the sauce starts to bubble, add 1 cup of sautéed apples, cooking till sauce thickens.   Once pork tenderloin I cook, allow to sit 5-10 minutes to rest before slicing. Serve topped with apple gravy.

596. Sweet Sticky Chicken Wings

Servings: 4   Cooking Time: 20 Minutes

Ingredients:

16 chicken wings	4 garlic cloves, minced
¼ cup butter	
¼ cup honey	¾ cup potato starch
½ tbsp salt	

Directions:
Preheat Instant Vortex on AirFry function to 370 F. Coat the wings with potato starch and place them in a greased baking dish. Press Start and cook for 5 minutes. Whisk the rest of the ingredients in a bowl. Pour the sauce over the wings and cook for another 10 minutes. Serve warm.

597. Bacon-wrapped Sausage With Tomato Relish

Servings: 4   Cooking Time: 32 Minutes

Ingredients:

8 pork sausages	1 small onion, peeled
8 bacon strips	3 tablespoons chopped parsley
Relish:	
8 large tomatoes, chopped	1 teaspoon smoked paprika
1 clove garlic, peeled	2 tablespoons sugar
1 tablespoon white wine vinegar	Salt and ground black pepper, to taste

Directions:
Purée the tomatoes, onion, and garlic in a food processor until well mixed and smooth.   Pour the purée in a saucepan and drizzle with white wine vinegar. Sprinkle with salt and ground black pepper. Simmer over medium heat for 10 minutes.   Add the parsley, paprika, and sugar to the saucepan and cook for 10 more minutes or until it has a thick consistency. Keep stirring during the cooking. Refrigerate for an hour to chill.   Wrap the sausage with bacon strips and secure with toothpicks, then place them in the basket.   Put the air fryer basket on the baking pan and slide into Rack Position 2, select Air Fry, set temperature to 350°F (180°C) and set time to 12 minutes.   Flip the bacon-wrapped sausage halfway through.   When cooking is complete, the bacon should be crispy and browned. Transfer the bacon-wrapped sausage on a plate and baste with the relish or just serve with the relish alongside.

598. Lamb Kofta

Servings: 4   Cooking Time: 10 Minutes

Ingredients:

1 pound (454 g) ground lamb	1 teaspoon garlic powder
1 tablespoon ras el hanout (North African spice)	1 teaspoon cumin
	2 tablespoons mint, chopped
½ teaspoon ground coriander	Salt and ground black pepper, to taste
1 teaspoon onion powder	Special Equipment:
	4 bamboo skewers

Directions:
Combine the ground lamb, ras el hanout, coriander, onion powder, garlic powder, cumin, mint, salt, and ground black pepper in a large bowl. Stir to mix well. Transfer the mixture into sausage molds and sit the bamboo skewers in the mixture. Refrigerate for 15 minutes.   Spritz the air fryer basket with cooking spray. Place the lamb skewers in the pan and spritz with cooking spray.   Put the air fryer basket on the baking pan and slide into Rack Position 2, select Air Fry, set temperature to 380°F (193°C) and set time to 10 minutes.   Flip the lamb skewers halfway through.   When cooking is complete, the lamb should be well browned.   Serve immediately.

599. Meatballs(2)

Servings: 4   Cooking Time: 15 Minutes

Ingredients:

1 lb ground lamb	1 tbsp garlic, minced
1 tsp onion powder	1 tsp ground cumin
1 tsp ground coriander	Pepper
	Salt

Directions:
Fit the Instant Vortex oven with the rack in position Add all ingredients into the mixing bowl and mix until well combined.   Make small balls from the meat mixture and place them into the baking pan. Set to bake at 400 F for 20 minutes. After 5 minutes place the baking pan in the preheated oven.   Serve and enjoy.

600. Classic Walliser Schnitzel

Servings: 2   Cooking Time: 14 Minutes

Ingredients:

½ cup pork rinds
½ tablespoon fresh parsley
½ teaspoon fennel seed
½ teaspoon mustard
⅓ tablespoon cider vinegar

1 teaspoon garlic salt
⅓ teaspoon ground black pepper
2 eggs
2 pork schnitzel, halved
Cooking spray

Directions:

Spritz the air fryer basket with cooking spray.   Put the pork rinds, parsley, fennel seeds, and mustard in a food processor. Pour in the vinegar and sprinkle with salt and ground black pepper. Pulse until well combined and smooth.   Pour the pork rind mixture in a large bowl. Whisk the eggs in a separate bowl.   Dunk the pork schnitzel in the whisked eggs, then dunk in the pork rind mixture to coat well. Shake the excess off.   Arrange the schnitzel in the pan and spritz with cooking spray.   Put the air fryer basket on the baking pan and slide into Rack Position 2, select Air Fry, set temperature to 350°F (180°C) and set time to 14 minutes.   After 7 minutes, remove from the oven. Flip the schnitzel. Return to the oven and continue cooking.   When cooking is complete, the schnitzel should be golden and crispy.   Serve immediately.

601. Pork Burger Cutlets With Fresh Coriander Leaves

Ingredients:

½ lb. pork (Make sure that you mince the pork fine)
½ cup breadcrumbs
½ cup of boiled peas
¼ tsp. cumin powder
A pinch of salt to taste
¼ tsp. ginger finely chopped

1 green chili finely chopped
1 tsp. lemon juice
1 tbsp. fresh coriander leaves. Chop them finely
¼ tsp. red chili powder
¼ tsp. dried mango powder

Directions:

Take a container and into it pour all the masalas, onions, green chilies, peas, coriander leaves, lemon juice, and ginger and 1-2 tbsp. breadcrumbs. Add the minced pork as well. Mix all the ingredients well. Mold the mixture into round Cutlets. Press them gently. Now roll them out carefully. Pre heat the Instant Vortex oven at 250 Fahrenheit for 5 minutes. Open the basket of the Fryer and arrange the Cutlets in the basket. Close it carefully. Keep the fryer at 150 degrees for around 10 or 12 minutes. In between the cooking process, turn the Cutlets over to get a uniform cook. Serve hot with mint sauce.

602. Festive Stuffed Pork Chops

Servings: 4   Cooking Time: 40 Minutes

Ingredients:

4 pork chops
Salt and black pepper to taste
4 cups stuffing mix
2 tbsp olive oil

4 garlic cloves, minced
2 tbsp fresh sage leaves, chopped

Directions:

Cut a hole in pork chops and fill chops with stuffing mix. In a bowl, mix sage, garlic, oil, salt, and pepper. Rub the chops with the marinade and let sit for 10 minutes.   Preheat Instant Vortex on Bake function to 380 F. Put the chops in a baking tray and place in the oven. Press Start and cook for 25 minutes. Serve and enjoy!

603. Honey Chicken Drumsticks

Servings: 2   Cooking Time: 20 Minutes + Marinating Time

Ingredients:

2 chicken drumsticks, skin removed
2 tbsp olive oil

2 tbsp honey
½ tbsp garlic puree

Directions:

Mix all the ingredients in a bowl. Allow to marinate for 30 minutes. Place the chicken in the basket and press Start. Cook for 15 minutes at 400 F on AirFry function. Serve warm.

604. Drumsticks With Barbecue-honey Sauce

Servings: 5   Cooking Time: 18 Minutes

Ingredients:

1 tablespoon olive oil
10 chicken drumsticks
Chicken seasoning or rub, to taste

Salt and ground black pepper, to taste
1 cup barbecue sauce
¼ cup honey

Directions:

Grease the basket with olive oil.   Rub the chicken drumsticks with chicken seasoning or rub, salt and ground black pepper on a clean work surface. Arrange the chicken drumsticks in the basket. Put the air fryer basket on the baking pan and slide into Rack Position 2, select Air Fry, set temperature to 390°F (199°C) and set time to 18 minutes.   Flip the drumsticks halfway through.   When cooking is complete, the drumsticks should be lightly browned. Meanwhile, combine the barbecue sauce and honey in a small bowl. Stir to mix well.   Remove the drumsticks from the oven and baste with the sauce mixture to serve.

605. Spicy Pork Lettuce Wraps

Servings: 4   Cooking Time: 12 Minutes

Ingredients:

1 (1-pound / 454-g) medium pork tenderloin, silver skin and external fat trimmed
⅔ cup soy sauce, divided
1 teaspoon cornstarch

½ large red bell pepper, deseeded and chopped
2 scallions, chopped, white and green parts separated
1 head butter lettuce

1 medium jalapeño, deseeded and minced
1 can diced water chestnuts
½ cup roasted, chopped almonds
¼ cup coarsely chopped cilantro

Directions:
Cut the tenderloin into ¼-inch slices and place them in the baking pan. Baste with about 3 tablespoons of soy sauce. Stir the cornstarch into the remaining sauce and set aside.   Slide the baking pan into Rack Position 2, select Roast, set temperature to 375°F (190°C), and set time to 12 minutes.   After 5 minutes, remove from the oven. Place the pork slices on a cutting board. Place the jalapeño, water chestnuts, red pepper, and the white parts of the scallions in the baking pan and pour the remaining sauce over. Stir to coat the vegetables with the sauce. Return the pan to the oven and continue cooking. While the vegetables cook, chop the pork into small pieces. Separate the lettuce leaves, discarding any tough outer leaves and setting aside the small inner leaves for another use. You'll want 12 to 18 leaves, depending on size and your appetites.   After 5 minutes, remove from the oven. Add the pork to the vegetables, stirring to combine. Return the pan to the oven and continue cooking for the remaining 2 minutes until the pork is warmed back up and the sauce has reduced slightly.   When cooking is complete, remove from the oven. Place the pork and vegetables in a medium serving bowl and stir in half the green parts of the scallions. To serve, spoon some pork and vegetables into each of the lettuce leaves. Top with the remaining scallion greens and garnish with the nuts and cilantro.

606.   Chicken Grandma's Easy To Cook Wontons

Ingredients:
1 ½ cup all-purpose flour
2 tsp. ginger-garlic paste
2 tsp. soya sauce
½ tsp. salt
5 tbsp. water
2 cups minced chicken
2 tbsp. oil
2 tsp. vinegar

Directions:
Squeeze the dough and cover it with plastic wrap and set aside. Next, cook the ingredients for the filling and try to ensure that the chicken is covered well with the sauce.   Roll the dough and place the filling in the center. Now, wrap the dough to cover the filling and pinch the edges together.   Pre heat the Instant Vortex oven at 200° F for 5 minutes. Place the wontons in the fry basket and close it. Let them cook at the same temperature for another 20 minutes. Recommended sides are chili sauce or ketchup.

607.   Air Fryer Chicken Parmesan

Servings: 4   Cooking Time: 9 Minutes
Ingredients:
½ C. keto marinara
6 tbsp. mozzarella
1 tbsp. melted ghee
6 tbsp. gluten-free

cheese
2 tbsp. grated parmesan cheese
seasoned breadcrumbs
1   8-ounce chicken breasts

Directions:
Preparing the Ingredients. Ensure air fryer oven is preheated to 360 degrees. Spray the basket with olive oil.   Mix parmesan cheese and breadcrumbs together. Melt ghee.   Brush melted ghee onto the chicken and dip into breadcrumb mixture.   Place coated chicken in the air fryer oven and top with olive oil.   Air Frying. Set temperature to 360°F, and set time to 6 minutes. Cook 2 breasts for 6 minutes and top each breast with a tablespoon of sauce and 1½ tablespoons of mozzarella cheese. Cook another 3 minutes to melt cheese.   Keep cooked pieces warm as you repeat the process with remaining breasts.

608.   Meatballs(10)

Servings: 6   Cooking Time: 20 Minutes
Ingredients:
2 lbs ground chicken
1/2 cup parmesan cheese, grated
1 cup breadcrumbs
1 egg, lightly beaten
1 tbsp fresh parsley, chopped
1 tsp Italian seasoning
1 tsp garlic, minced
2 tbsp olive oil
Pepper
Salt

Directions:
Fit the Instant Vortex oven with the rack in position Add all ingredients into the bowl and mix until well combined.   Make small balls from meat mixture and place in baking pan.   Set to bake at 400 F for 25 minutes. After 5 minutes place the baking pan in the preheated oven.   Serve and enjoy.

609.   Tasty Turkey Meatballs

Servings: 6   Cooking Time: 25 Minutes
Ingredients:
2 eggs
2 lbs ground turkey
1/2 cup breadcrumbs
1 tsp cumin
1 tsp oregano
1 tsp fresh mint, chopped
1/2 tsp pepper
1/2 cup parsley, chopped
1/2 cup onion, minced
1 tbsp garlic, minced
1/2 tsp pepper
1 tsp salt

Directions:
Fit the Instant Vortex oven with the rack in position Add all ingredients into the mixing bowl and mix until well combined.   Make small balls from meat mixture and place onto the parchment-lined baking pan.   Set to bake at 375 F for 30 minutes. After 5 minutes place the baking pan in the preheated oven. Serve and enjoy.

610.   Honey & Garlic Chicken Thighs

Servings: 4   Cooking Time: 30 Minutes
Ingredients:

4 thighs, skin-on
3 tbsp honey
2 tbsp Dijon mustard

½ tbsp garlic powder
Salt and black pepper to taste

Directions:
In a bowl, mix honey, mustard, garlic, salt, and black pepper. Coat the thighs in the mixture and arrange them on the greased basket. Fit in the baking tray and cook for 16 minutes at 400 F on Air Fry function, turning once halfway through. Serve warm.

611. Juicy & Tender Pork Chops

Servings: 4   Cooking Time: 15 Minutes
Ingredients:

4 pork chops, boneless
1 tsp onion powder
1 tsp smoked paprika

1/4 cup olive oil
1 tsp pepper
2 tsp salt

Directions:
Fit the Instant Vortex oven with the rack in position Brush pork chops with oil and season with onion powder, paprika, pepper, and salt.   Place pork chops in a baking pan.   Set to bake at 400 F for 20 minutes. After 5 minutes place the baking pan in the preheated oven.   Serve and enjoy.

612.   Juicy Pork Ribs Ole

Servings: 4   Cooking Time: 25 Minutes
Ingredients:

1 rack of pork ribs
1/2 cup low-fat milk
1 tablespoon envelope taco seasoning mix
1/2 teaspoon ground black pepper

1 can tomato sauce
1 teaspoon seasoned salt
1 tablespoon cornstarch
1 teaspoon canola oil

Directions:
Preparing the Ingredients. Place all ingredients in a mixing dish; let them marinate for 1 hour.   Air Frying.   Cook the marinated ribs approximately 25 minutes at 390 degrees F   Work with batches. Enjoy .

613.   Lamb Rack With Pistachio

Servings: 2   Cooking Time: 20 Minutes
Ingredients:

½ cup finely chopped pistachios
1 teaspoon chopped fresh rosemary
3 tablespoons panko bread crumbs
Salt and freshly ground black pepper, to taste

2 teaspoons chopped fresh oregano
1 tablespoon olive oil
1 lamb rack, bones fat trimmed and frenched
1 tablespoon Dijon mustard

Directions:
Put the pistachios, rosemary, bread crumbs, oregano, olive oil, salt, and black pepper in a food processor. Pulse to combine until smooth.   Rub the lamb rack with salt and black pepper on a clean work surface, then place it in the basket.   Put the air fryer basket on the baking pan and slide into Rack Position 2, select Air Fry, set temperature to 380°F (193°C) and set time to 12 minutes.   Flip

the lamb halfway through.   When cooking is complete, the lamb should be lightly browned. Transfer the lamb on a plate and brush with Dijon mustard on the fat side, then sprinkle with the pistachios mixture over the lamb rack to coat well. Put the lamb rack back to the oven and air fry for 8 more minutes or until the internal temperature of the rack reaches at least 145°F (63°C).   Remove the lamb rack from the oven with tongs and allow to cool for 5 minutes before slicing to serve.

614.   Crispy Parmesan Escallops

Servings: 4   Cooking Time: 20 Minutes
Ingredients:

4 skinless chicken breasts
1 cup panko breadcrumbs
1 cup flour

¼ cup Parmesan cheese, grated
3 fresh sage leaves, chopped
2 eggs, beaten

Directions:
Place the chicken breasts between 2 sheets of cling film and beat well using a rolling pin to a ¼-inch thickness. In a bowl, mix Parmesan cheese, sage, and breadcrumbs.   Dip the chicken into the flour and then into the eggs. Finally, dredge into the breadcrumbs mixture. Transfer to the basket and cook in the Instant Vortex for 14 minutes at 350 F on AirFry mode.

615.   Steak Seared In Browned Butter

Ingredients:

2 (1-lb) steaks, 1 inch thick
1 Tbsp extra-virgin olive oil
3 Tbsp unsalted butter, divided
2 fresh rosemary sprigs

1 lb. Yukon gold potatoes, sliced about ½-inch thick
Salt and freshly ground black pepper, to taste
½ cup beef broth

Directions:
Let the steaks rest at room temperature for 30 minutes.   In Instant Vortex oven over medium-high heat, heat the oil and 1 Tbsp of butter.   Add the potatoes and rosemary and cook for 5 minutes, until fork tender. Season with salt and pepper. Remove from the pot and set aside.   Season the steak with salt and pepper. Add the steak to Instant Vortex oven over high heat and cook for 5 minutes on each side for medium-rare, or longer if desired. Remove the steaks and let them rest on a cutting board.   Melt the remaining 2 Tbsp of butter over medium heat, stirring often. Add the broth when the butter starts to brown. Keep stirring and scraping up the browned bits using a wooden spoon.   Add the potatoes to the pan and heat through, about 5 minutes. Cut the steaks in half, spoon the potatoes and browned butter over each steak, and serve.

616. Mutton French Cuisine Galette

Ingredients:

2 tbsp. garam masala	2 or 3 green chilies
1 lb. minced mutton	finely chopped
3 tsp ginger finely	1 ½ tbsp. lemon
chopped	juice
1-2 tbsp. fresh	Salt and pepper to
coriander leaves	taste

Directions:
Mix the ingredients in a clean bowl. Mold this mixture into round and flat French Cuisine Galettes. Wet the French Cuisine Galettes slightly with water. Pre heat the Instant Vortex oven at 160 degrees Fahrenheit for 5 minutes. Place the French Cuisine Galettes in the fry basket and let them cook for another 25 minutes at the same temperature. Keep rolling them over to get a uniform cook. Serve either with mint sauce or ketchup.

617. Mutton Marinade Cutlet

Ingredients:

2 cups sliced mutton	6-7 flakes garlic
1 big capsicum (Cut	(optional)
this capsicum into big	Salt to taste
cubes)	5 tbsp. gram flour
2 tbsp. ginger-garlic	A pinch of salt to
paste	taste
1 small onion	2 cup fresh green
1 onion (Cut it into	coriander
quarters. Now	½ cup mint leaves
separate the layers	4 tsp. fennel
carefully.)	3 tbsp. lemon juice

Directions:
You will first need to make the sauce. Add the ingredients to a blender and make a thick paste. Slit the pieces of mutton and stuff half the paste into the cavity obtained. Take the remaining paste and add it to the gram flour and salt. Toss the pieces of mutton in this mixture and set aside. Apply a little bit of the mixture on the capsicum and onion. Place these on a stick along with the mutton pieces. Pre heat the Instant Vortex oven at 290 Fahrenheit for around 5 minutes. Open the basket. Arrange the satay sticks properly. Close the basket. Keep the sticks with the mutton at 180 degrees for around half an hour while the sticks with the vegetables are to be kept at the same temperature for only 7 minutes. Turn the sticks in between so that one side does not get burnt and also to provide a uniform cook.

618. Coconut Chicken Tenders

Servings: 4   Cooking Time: 20 Minutes
Ingredients:

1 lb chicken breast,	1/2 tsp garlic powder
skinless, boneless &	1/2 tsp cayenne
cut into strips	pepper
1 egg, lightly beaten	1 tsp paprika
1/4 cup shredded	1/4 tsp black pepper
coconut	1/2 tsp sea salt
1/2 cup almond meal	

Directions:
Fit the Instant Vortex oven with the rack in position In a shallow dish, mix almond meal, shredded coconut, paprika, cayenne pepper, garlic powder, pepper, and salt.   In a separate bowl, whisk the egg.   Dip each chicken strip in egg then coat with almond meal mixture,   Place coat chicken strips in a parchment-lined baking pan.   Set to bake at 400 F for 25 minutes. After 5 minutes place the baking pan in the preheated oven.   Serve and enjoy.

619. Beer Corned Beef With Carrots

Servings: 4   Cooking Time: 35 Minutes
Ingredients:

1 tbsp beef spice	12 oz bottle beer
1 white onion,	1 ½ cups chicken
chopped	broth
2 carrots, chopped	4 pounds corned beef

Directions:
Cover beef with beer and let sit in the fridge for 30 minutes. Transfer to a pot over medium heat and add in chicken broth, carrots, and onion. Bring to a boil and simmer for 10 minutes. Drain boiled meat and veggies and place them in a baking dish. Sprinkle with beef spice. Select Bake function, adjust the temperature to 400 F, and press Start. Cook for 30 minutes.

620. Honey Glazed Chicken Breasts

Servings: 4   Cooking Time: 10 Minutes
Ingredients:

4 (4-ounce / 113-g)	2 tablespoons soy
boneless, skinless	sauce
chicken breasts	2 teaspoons grated
Chicken seasoning or	fresh ginger
rub, to taste	2 garlic cloves,
Salt and ground black	minced
pepper, to taste	Cooking spray
¼ cup honey	

Directions:
Spritz the air fryer basket with cooking spray. Rub the chicken breasts with chicken seasoning, salt, and black pepper on a clean work surface. Arrange the chicken breasts in the basket and spritz with cooking spray.   Put the air fryer basket on the baking pan and slide into Rack Position 2, select Air Fry, set temperature to 400°F (205°C) and set time to 10 minutes.   Flip the chicken breasts halfway through.   When cooking is complete, the internal temperature of the thickest part of the chicken should reach at least 165°F (74°C).   Meanwhile, combine the honey, soy sauce, ginger, and garlic in a saucepan and heat over medium-high heat for 3 minutes or until thickened. Stir constantly. Remove the chicken from the oven and serve with the honey glaze.

621. Pork Schnitzel

Servings: 10   Cooking Time: 30 Minutes
Ingredients:

10 pork cutlets
1 tsp salt
1 tsp pepper
1 cup flour
2 eggs
1 cup Panko bread crumbs
Nonstick cooking spray

Directions:
Place each cutlet between plastic wrap and pound to ¼-inch thick. Sprinkle both sides with salt and pepper. Place the flour in a shallow dish. In a separate shallow dish, beat the eggs. Place the bread crumbs in another shallow dish. Place the baking pan in position 2 of the oven. Spray the fryer basket with cooking spray. Dip each cutlet first in flour, then egg, then coat with bread crumbs. Place in basket in a single layer, these will need to be cooked in batches. Place basket on the pan and set oven to air fry on 375°F for 10 minutes. Cook each cutlet 3-4 minutes per side, or until nicely browned. Repeat with remaining cutlets. Serve immediately.

622. Pork Butt With Garlicky Coriander-parsley Sauce

Servings: 4   Cooking Time: 30 Minutes
Ingredients:
1 teaspoon golden flaxseeds meal
1 egg white, well whisked
1 tablespoon soy sauce
1 teaspoon lemon juice, preferably freshly squeezed
1 pound (454 g) pork butt, cut into pieces 2-inches long
Garlicky Coriander-Parsley Sauce:
1 tablespoon olive oil
Salt and ground black pepper, to taste
3 garlic cloves, minced
⅓ cup fresh coriander leaves
⅓ cup fresh parsley leaves
1 teaspoon lemon juice
½ tablespoon salt
⅓ cup extra-virgin olive oil

Directions:
Combine the flaxseeds meal, egg white, soy sauce, lemon juice, salt, black pepper, and olive oil in a large bowl. Dunk the pork strips in and press to submerge. Wrap the bowl in plastic and refrigerate to marinate for at least an hour. Arrange the marinated pork strips in the basket. Put the air fryer basket on the baking pan and slide into Rack Position 2, select Air Fry, set temperature to 380°F (193°C) and set time to 30 minutes. After 15 minutes, remove from the oven. Flip the pork. Return to the oven and continue cooking. When cooking is complete, the pork should be well browned. Meanwhile, combine the ingredients for the sauce in a small bowl. Stir to mix well. Arrange the bowl in the refrigerator to chill until ready to serve. Serve the air fried pork strips with the chilled sauce.

623. Mustardy Chicken

Servings: 4   Cooking Time: 20 Minutes
Ingredients:
1 tsp garlic powder
4 chicken breasts, sliced
1 tbsp fresh thyme, chopped
½ cup dry white wine
Salt and black pepper to taste
½ cup Dijon mustard
2 cups breadcrumbs
1 tbsp lemon zest
2 tbsp olive oil

Directions:
In a bowl, mix garlic, breadcrumbs, olive oil, lemon zest, salt, and pepper. In another bowl, mix mustard and wine. Dip the chicken slices in the wine mixture and then coat in the crumb mixture. Place the prepared chicken in the greased basket and fit in the baking tray; cook for 15 minutes at 350 F on Air Fry function, shaking once until golden brown. Serve.

624. Fried Chicken Tenderloins

Servings: 4   Cooking Time: 15 Minutes
Ingredients:
8 chicken tenderloins
2 tbsp butter, softened
2 oz breadcrumbs
1 large egg, whisked

Directions:
Preheat Instant Vortex on Air Fry function to 380 F. Combine butter and breadcrumbs in a bowl. Keep mixing and stirring until the mixture gets crumbly. Dip the chicken in the egg, then in the crumb mix. Place in the greased basket and fit in the baking tray; cook for 10 minutes, flipping once until crispy. Set on Broil function for crispier taste. Serve.

625. Ranch Beef Patties

Servings: 4   Cooking Time: 12 Minutes
Ingredients:
1 lb ground beef
1/2 tsp onion powder
1/2 tsp garlic powder
2 tsp dried parsley
1/8 tsp dried dill
1/2 tsp paprika
1/2 tsp dried dill
Pepper
Salt

Directions:
Fit the Instant Vortex oven with the rack in position 2. Line the air fryer basket with parchment paper. Add all ingredients into the large bowl and mix until well combined. Make four even shape patties from the meat mixture and place in the air fryer basket then place an air fryer basket in the baking pan. Place a baking pan on the oven rack. Set to air fry at 350 F for 12 minutes. Serve and enjoy.

626. Venison Tandoor

Ingredients:
2 cups sliced venison
1 big capsicum (Cut this capsicum into big cubes)
1 onion (Cut it into quarters. Now separate the layers carefully.)
5 tbsp. gram flour
A pinch of salt to
2 cup fresh green coriander
½ cup mint leaves
4 tsp. fennel
2 tbsp. ginger-garlic paste
1 small onion
6-7 flakes garlic (optional)

taste

For the filling:

Salt to taste

3 tbsp. lemon juice

Directions:

You will first need to make the sauce. Add the ingredients to a blender and make a thick paste. Slit the pieces of venison and stuff half the paste into the cavity obtained. Take the remaining paste and add it to the gram flour and salt.   Toss the pieces of venison in this mixture and set aside. Apply a little bit of the mixture on the capsicum and onion. Place these on a stick along with the venison pieces. Pre heat the Instant Vortex oven at 290 Fahrenheit for around 5 minutes.   Open the basket. Arrange the satay sticks properly. Close the basket. Keep the sticks with the venison at 180 degrees for around half an hour while the sticks with the vegetables are to be kept at the same temperature for only 7 minutes. Turn the sticks in between so that one side does not get burnt and also to provide a uniform cook.

627.	Roasted Lamb Chops With Potatoes

Servings: 4   Cooking Time: 20 Minutes

Ingredients:

8 (½-inch thick) lamb loin chops (about 2 pounds / 907 g)	2 garlic cloves, minced or smashed
2 teaspoons kosher salt or 1 teaspoon fine salt, divided	1 teaspoon curry powder
¾ cup plain whole milk yogurt	1 teaspoon smoked paprika
1 tablespoon freshly grated ginger (1- or 2-inch piece) or 1 teaspoon ground ginger	½ teaspoon cayenne pepper
	12 ounces (340 g) small red potatoes, quartered
	Cooking spray

Directions:

Sprinkle the lamb chops on both sides with 1 teaspoon of kosher salt and set aside.   Meanwhile, make the marinade by stirring together the yogurt, garlic, ginger, curry powder, paprika, cayenne pepper, and remaining 1 teaspoon of kosher salt in a large bowl.   Transfer 2 tablespoons of the marinade to a resealable plastic bag, leaving those 2 tablespoons in the bowl. Place the lamb chops in the bag. Squeeze out as much air as possible and squish the bag around so that the chops are well coated with the marinade. Set aside.   Add the potatoes to the bowl and toss until well coated. Spritz the air fryer basket with cooking spray. Arrange the potatoes in the basket.   Put the air fryer basket on the baking pan and slide into Rack Position 2, select Roast, set temperature to 375°F (190°C), and set time to 10 minutes.   Once cooking is complete, remove from the oven.   Remove the chops from the marinade, draining off all but a thin coat. Return them to the baking pan.   Select Convection Broil, set the temperature to High, and set the time for 10 minutes. After 5 minutes, remove from the oven and turn over the chops and potatoes. Return to the oven and

continue cooking until the lamb read 145°F (63°C) on a meat thermometer. If you want it more well done, continue cooking for another few minutes. Serve warm.

628.	Lamb Marinade Cutlet With Capsicum

Ingredients:

2 cups sliced lamb	6-7 flakes garlic (optional)
1 big capsicum (Cut this capsicum into big cubes)	Salt to taste
2 cup fresh green coriander	1 onion (Cut it into quarters. Now separate the layers carefully.)
½ cup mint leaves	
4 tsp. fennel	5 tbsp. gram flour
2 tbsp. ginger-garlic paste	A pinch of salt to taste
1 small onion	3 tbsp. lemon juice

Directions:

You will first need to make the sauce. Add the ingredients to a blender and make a thick paste. Slit the pieces of lamb and stuff half the paste into the cavity obtained. Take the remaining paste and add it to the gram flour and salt. Toss the pieces of lamb in this mixture and set aside. Apply a little bit of the mixture on the capsicum and onion.   Place these on a stick along with the lamb pieces. Pre heat the Instant Vortex oven at 290 Fahrenheit for around 5 minutes. Open the basket. Arrange the satay sticks properly. Close the basket.   Keep the sticks with the lamb at 180 degrees for around half an hour while the sticks with the vegetables are to be kept at the same temperature for only 7 minutes.   Turn the sticks in between so that one side does not get burnt and also to provide a uniform cook.

629.	Rosemary Pork Chops

Servings: 4   Cooking Time: 30 Minutes

Ingredients:

4 pork chops, boneless	4 garlic cloves, minced
1 tsp dried rosemary, crushed	1 tbsp fresh rosemary, chopped
1/4 tsp pepper	1/4 tsp salt

Directions:

Fit the Instant Vortex oven with the rack in position Season pork chops with pepper and salt and set aside.   In a small bowl, mix together garlic and rosemary and rub over pork chops.   Place pork chops in a baking pan.   Set to bake at 425 F for 35 minutes. After 5 minutes place the baking pan in the preheated oven.   Serve and enjoy.

630.	Herby Turkey Balls

Servings: 2   Cooking Time: 20 Minutes

Ingredients:

½ lb ground turkey	½ tbsp dried parsley
1 egg, beaten	Salt and black pepper to taste
1 cup breadcrumbs	
1 tbsp dried thyme	

Directions:

Preheat Instant Vortex on AirFry function to 350 F. In a bowl, place ground turkey, thyme, parsley, salt, and pepper. Mix well and shape the mixture into balls. Dip in breadcrumbs, then in the egg, and finally in the breadcrumbs again. Place the nuggets in the basket and cook for 15 minutes.

631. Simple Air Fried Chicken Wings

Servings: 4   Cooking Time: 15 Minutes
Ingredients:

1 tablespoon olive oil	1 teaspoon garlic
8 whole chicken	powder
wings	Freshly ground black
Chicken seasoning or	pepper, to taste
rub, to taste	

Directions:
Grease the basket with olive oil.   On a clean work surface, rub the chicken wings with chicken seasoning and rub, garlic powder, and ground black pepper.   Arrange the well-coated chicken wings in the basket.   Put the air fryer basket on the baking pan and slide into Rack Position 2, select Air Fry, set temperature to 400°F (205°C) and set time to 15 minutes.   Flip the chicken wings halfway through. When cooking is complete, the internal temperature of the chicken wings should reach at least 165°F (74°C).   Remove the chicken wings from the oven. Serve immediately.

632. Herb Pork Tenderloin

Servings: 4   Cooking Time: 35 Minutes
Ingredients:

1 lb pork tenderloin	1 tbsp olive oil
1/2 tbsp dried	Pepper
rosemary	Salt
1/2 tsp dried thyme	

Directions:
Fit the Instant Vortex oven with the rack in position Mix rosemary, thyme, oil, pepper, and salt and rub over pork tenderloin.   Place pork tenderloin in baking pan.   Set to bake at 400 F for 40 minutes. After 5 minutes place the baking pan in the preheated oven.   Slice and serve.

633. Easy Pork Chops

Servings: 2   Cooking Time: 25 Minutes
Ingredients:

2 pork chops	Pepper
2 tsp brown sugar	Salt
1 tsp smoked paprika	

Directions:
Fit the Instant Vortex oven with the rack in position Mix smoked paprika, brown sugar, pepper, and salt and rub all over pork chops.   Place pork chops in a baking pan.   Set to bake at 325 F for 30 minutes. After 5 minutes place the baking pan in the preheated oven.   Serve and enjoy.

634. Mustard Chicken Tenders

Servings: 4   Cooking Time: 20 Minutes
Ingredients:

1/2 C. coconut flour	2 beaten eggs
1 tbsp. spicy brown	1 pound of chicken
mustard	tenders

Directions:
Preparing the Ingredients. Season tenders with pepper and salt.   Place a thin layer of mustard onto tenders and then dredge in flour and dip in egg. Air Frying. Add to the Instant Vortex air fryer oven, set temperature to 390°F, and set time to 20 minutes.

635. Herb Turkey Tenderloin

Servings: 4   Cooking Time: 40 Minutes
Ingredients:

24 oz turkey	1 tbsp dried sage
tenderloin	Pepper
1 tbsp dried rosemary	Salt

Directions:
Fit the Instant Vortex oven with the rack in position Rub turkey tenderloin with rosemary, sage, pepper, and salt.   Place turkey tenderloin into the baking pan.   Set to bake at 350 F for 45 minutes. After 5 minutes place the baking pan in the preheated oven. Slice and serve.

636. Salsa Beef Meatballs

Servings: 4   Cooking Time: 10 Minutes
Ingredients:

1 pound (454 g)	1 clove garlic, minced
ground beef (85%	1/2 teaspoon ground
lean)	cumin
1/2 cup salsa	1 teaspoon fine sea
1/4 cup diced green or	salt
red bell peppers	Lime wedges, for
1 large egg, beaten	serving
1/4 cup chopped	Cooking spray
onions	
1/2 teaspoon chili	
powder	

Directions:
Spritz the air fryer basket with cooking spray. Combine all the ingredients in a large bowl. Stir to mix well.   Divide and shape the mixture into 1-inch balls. Arrange the balls in the pan and spritz with cooking spray.   Put the air fryer basket on the baking pan and slide into Rack Position 2, select Air Fry, set temperature to 350°F (180°C) and set time to 10 minutes.   Flip the balls with tongs halfway through.   When cooking is complete, the balls should be well browned.   Transfer the balls on a plate and squeeze the lime wedges over before serving.

637. Ritzy Chicken Roast

Servings: 6   Cooking Time: 1 Hour
Ingredients:

1 teaspoon Italian	1 teaspoon salt
seasoning	2 tablespoons olive
1/2 teaspoon garlic	oil
powder	1 (3-pound / 1.4-kg)
1/2 teaspoon paprika	whole chicken, giblets
1/2 teaspoon freshly	

ground black pepper
1/2 teaspoon onion
powder

removed, pat dry
Cooking spray

Directions:
Spritz the air fryer basket with cooking spray. In a small bowl, mix the Italian seasoning, garlic powder, paprika, salt, pepper, and onion powder. Brush the chicken with the olive oil and rub it with the seasoning mixture. Tie the chicken legs with butcher's twine. Place the chicken in the basket, breast side down. Put the air fryer basket on the baking pan and slide into Rack Position 2, select Air Fry, set the temperature to 350ºF (180ºC) and set the time to an hour. After 30 minutes, remove from the oven. Flip the chicken over and baste it with any drippings collected in the bottom drawer of the oven. Return to the oven and continue cooking. When cooking is complete, a thermometer inserted into the thickest part of the thigh should reach at least 165ºF (74ºC). Let the chicken rest for 10 minutes before carving and serving.

638. Cayenne Turkey Breasts

Servings: 4   Cooking Time: 25 Minutes
Ingredients:

1 lb turkey breast,
boneless and skinless
2 cups panko
breadcrumbs

Cayenne pepper and
salt to taste
1 stick butter, melted

Directions:
Preheat Instant Vortex on AirFry function to 350 F. In a bowl, mix breadcrumbs, cayenne pepper, and salt. Brush the butter onto the turkey and coat with the breadcrumbs. Cook for 15 minutes.

639. Greek Chicken Breast

Servings: 4   Cooking Time: 25 Minutes
Ingredients:

4 chicken breasts,
skinless & boneless
1 tbsp olive oil
For rub:
1 tsp oregano
1 tsp thyme

1 tsp parsley
1 tsp onion powder
1 tsp basil
Pepper
Salt

Directions:
Fit the Instant Vortex oven with the rack in position 2. Brush chicken with olive oil. In a small bowl, mix together all rub ingredients and rub all over the chicken breasts. Place chicken into the air fryer basket then places the air fryer basket in the baking pan. Place a baking pan on the oven rack. Set to air fry at 390 F for 25 minutes. Serve and enjoy.

640. Cripsy Crusted Pork Chops

Servings: 4   Cooking Time: 40 Minutes
Ingredients:

4 pork chops,
boneless
1 cup parmesan
cheese
1 tbsp olive oil
1 tsp garlic powder

1 cup breadcrumbs
1/2 tsp Italian
seasoning
Pepper
Salt

Directions:
Fit the Instant Vortex oven with the rack in position In a shallow dish, mix breadcrumbs, parmesan cheese, Italian seasoning, garlic powder, pepper, and salt. Brush pork chops with oil and coat with breadcrumb mixture. Place coated pork chops in a baking pan. Set to bake at 350 F for 45 minutes. After 5 minutes place the baking pan in the preheated oven. Serve and enjoy.

641. Crispy Cajun Chicken Breast

Servings: 2   Cooking Time: 25 Minutes
Ingredients:

2 chicken breasts
3/4 cup breadcrumbs
1 tsp garlic powder
1 tsp paprika

1 tsp Cajun seasoning
2 tbsp mayonnaise
1/2 tsp pepper
1/2 tsp salt

Directions:
Fit the Instant Vortex oven with the rack in position In a shallow dish, mix breadcrumbs, Cajun seasoning, paprika, garlic powder, pepper, and salt. Brush chicken with mayonnaise and coat with breadcrumbs. Place coated chicken breasts into the baking pan. Set to bake at 425 F for 30 minutes. After 5 minutes place the baking pan in the preheated oven. Serve and enjoy.

642. Basil Mozzarella Chicken

Servings: 4   Cooking Time: 25 Minutes
Ingredients:

4 chicken breasts,
cubed
4 basil leaves
1/4 cup balsamic
vinegar

4 slices tomato
1 tbsp butter
4 slices mozzarella
cheese

Directions:
Heat butter and balsamic vinegar in a pan over medium heat. Pour over the chicken. Place the chicken in a baking pan and cook for 20 minutes at 400 F on Bake function. Top with cheese, and Bake for 1 minute until the cheese melts. Cover with basil and tomato slices and serve.

643. Tasty Steak Tips

Servings: 4   Cooking Time: 5 Minutes
Ingredients:

1 lb steak, cut into
cubes
1 tsp olive oil
1/4 tsp garlic powder

1 tsp Montreal steak
seasoning
Pepper
Salt

Directions:
Fit the Instant Vortex oven with the rack in position 2. In a bowl, add steak cubes and remaining ingredients and toss well. Add marinated steak cubes to the air fryer basket then place an air fryer basket in the baking pan. Place a baking pan on the oven rack. Set to air fry at 400 F for 5 minutes. Serve and enjoy.

644. Chicken Wings With Chili-lime Sauce

Servings: 2   Cooking Time: 25 Minutes

Ingredients:

10 chicken wings
2 tbsp hot chili sauce

½ tbsp lime juice
Salt and black pepper to taste

Directions:

Preheat Instant Vortex on AirFry function to 350 F. Mix lime juice and chili sauce. Toss in the chicken wings. Transfer them to the basket and press Start. Cook for 25 minutes. Serve.

---

645. Duck Breasts With Marmalade Balsamic Glaze

Servings: 4   Cooking Time: 13 Minutes

Ingredients:

4 (6-ounce / 170-g) skin-on duck breasts
1 teaspoon salt
¼ cup orange marmalade

1 tablespoon white balsamic vinegar
¾ teaspoon ground black pepper

Directions:

Cut 10 slits into the skin of the duck breasts, then sprinkle with salt on both sides.   Place the breasts in the air fryer basket, skin side up.   Put the air fryer basket on the baking pan and slide into Rack Position 2, select Air Fry, set temperature to 400°F (205°C) and set time to 10 minutes.   Meanwhile, combine the remaining ingredients in a small bowl. Stir to mix well.   When cooking is complete, brush the duck skin with the marmalade mixture. Flip the breast and air fry for 3 more minutes or until the skin is crispy and the breast is well browned. Serve immediately.

---

646. Popcorn Turkey

Servings: 4   Cooking Time: 10 Minutes

Ingredients:

Nonstick cooking spray
1 cup flour
2 eggs
2 tbsp. Cajun seasoning

½ cup milk
2 cups bread crumbs
1 large turkey breast, cut in 1-inch pieces

Directions:

Place the baking pan in position 2 of the oven. Lightly spray the fryer basket with cooking spray. In a large bowl, whisk together flour, eggs, milk, and seasoning.   Place bread crumbs in a shallow dish. Add the turkey to the batter and stir to coat. Roll each piece of turkey in the bread crumbs and place them in the fryer basket, these may need to be cooked in batches. Spray them lightly with cooking spray.   Place the basket in the oven and set to air fry on 375°F for 10 minutes. Cook turkey nuggets until crisp and golden brown, turning over halfway through cooking time. Serve with your favorite dipping sauce.

---

647. Garlic Butter Wings

Servings: 4   Cooking Time: 25 Minutes

Ingredients:

1 lb chicken wings
1 tsp garlic powder

1/2 tsp salt
For sauce:

1/4 tsp pepper
1/2 tsp Italian seasoning

1 tbsp butter, melted
1/8 tsp garlic powder

Directions:

Fit the Instant Vortex oven with the rack in position 2.   In a large bowl, toss chicken wings with Italian seasoning, garlic powder, pepper, and salt. Arrange chicken wings in the air fryer basket then place an air fryer basket in the baking pan.   Place a baking pan on the oven rack. Set to air fry at 390 F for 25 minutes.   In a bowl, mix melted butter and garlic powder.   Add chicken wings and toss until well coated.   Serve and enjoy.

---

648. Thyme Turkey Nuggets

Servings: 2   Cooking Time: 20 Minutes

Ingredients:

8 oz turkey breast
1 egg, beaten
1 cup breadcrumbs

½ tsp dried thyme
Salt and black pepper to taste

Directions:

Preheat Instant Vortex on Air Fry function to 350 F. Pulse the turkey in a food processor and transfer to a bowl. Stir in thyme, salt, and pepper.   Form nugget-sized balls out of turkey mixture and dip in breadcrumbs, then in egg, and finally in the breadcrumbs again. Place the nuggets on a greased AirFryer basket and fit in the baking tray. Cook for 10 minutes, shaking once until golden brown. Serve warm.

---

649. Marinara Sauce Cheese Chicken

Servings: 2   Cooking Time: 25 Minutes

Ingredients:

2 chicken breasts, sliced
1 egg, beaten
½ cup breadcrumbs
A pinch of salt and black pepper

2 tbsp tomato sauce
2 tbsp Romano cheese, grated
2 slices mozzarella cheese

Directions:

Dip the breasts into the egg, then into the crumbs, and arrange in the basket. Fit in the baking tray and cook for 5 minutes at 400 F on Air Fry function. Turn and top with tomato sauce, Romano and mozzarella cheeses. Cook for 5 more minutes until the cheese is melted. Serve.

---

650. Balsamic Chicken With Mozzarella Cheese

Servings: 4   Cooking Time: 25 Minutes

Ingredients:

4 chicken breasts, cubed
4 fresh basil leaves
¼ cup balsamic vinegar

2 tomatoes, chopped
1 tbsp butter, melted
4 mozzarella cheese, grated

Directions:

In a bowl, mix butter and balsamic vinegar. Add in the chicken and toss to coat. Transfer to a baking tray and press Start. Cook for 20 minutes at 400 F on AirFry function. Top with mozzarella cheese and Bake until the cheese melts. Top with basil and tomatoes and serve.

651.   Rosemary Chicken Breasts

Servings: 2   Cooking Time: 15minutes
Ingredients:

2 chicken breasts	½ cup dried
Salt and black pepper to taste	rosemary
	1 tbsp butter, melted

Directions:
Preheat Instant Vortex on Air Fry function to 390 F. Lay a foil on a flat surface. Place the breasts on the foil, sprinkle with rosemary, tarragon, salt, and pepper and and drizzle the butter.   Wrap the foil around the breasts. Place the wrapped chicken in the AirFryer basket and fit in the baking tray; cook for 12 minutes. Remove and carefully unwrap. Serve with the sauce extract and steamed veggies.

652.   Tamarind Pork Chops With Green Beans

Servings: 4   Cooking Time: 30 Minutes + Marinating Time
Ingredients:

2 tbsp tamarind paste	1 tbsp olive oil
½ lb green beans, trimmed	2 tbsp molasses
1 tbsp garlic, minced	4 tbsp southwest seasoning
½ cup green mole sauce	2 tbsp ketchup
3 tbsp corn syrup	4 pork chops

Directions:
In a bowl, mix all the ingredients, except for potatoes, pork chops, and mole sauce. Add in 2 tbsp of water. Let the pork chops marinate in the mixture for 30 minutes.   Place pork chops in the basket and fit in the baking tray; cook for 25 minutes on Air Fry function at 350 F. Blanch the green beans in salted water in a pot over medium heat for 2-3 minutes until tender. Drain and season with salt and pepper. Serve the pork with green beans and mole sauce.

653.   Baked Lemon Pepper Chicken

Servings: 4   Cooking Time: 35 Minutes
Ingredients:

4 chicken thighs	2 tbsp fresh lemon
1 tsp garlic powder	juice
1/2 tsp onion powder	1/2 tsp paprika
1 tbsp lemon pepper seasoning	2 tbsp olive oil
	1 tsp salt

Directions:
Fit the Instant Vortex oven with the rack in position Add chicken in the mixing bowl.   Pour lemon juice and olive oil over chicken and coat well.   Mix lemon pepper seasoning, paprika, Italian seasoning, onion powder, garlic powder, and salt and rub all over the chicken thighs.   Place chicken in baking pan.   Set to bake at 400 F for 40 minutes. After 5 minutes place the baking pan in the preheated oven. Serve and enjoy.

654.   Baked Chicken Fritters

Servings: 4   Cooking Time: 25 Minutes
Ingredients:

1 lb ground chicken	1/2 cup shallots,
1 cup breadcrumbs	chopped
1 egg, lightly beaten	2 cups broccoli,
1 garlic clove, minced	chopped
1 1/2 cup mozzarella cheese, shredded	Pepper
	Salt

Directions:
Fit the Instant Vortex oven with the rack in position Add all ingredients into the bowl and mix until well combined.   Make small patties and place them in a parchment-lined baking pan.   Set to bake at 390 F for 30 minutes. After 5 minutes place the baking pan in the preheated oven.   Serve and enjoy.

655.   Chicken Thighs With Radish Slaw

Servings: 4   Cooking Time: 27 Minutes
Ingredients:

4 bone-in, skin-on chicken thighs	3 cups shredded cabbage
1½ teaspoon kosher salt, divided	½ small red onion, thinly sliced
1 tablespoon smoked paprika	4 large radishes, julienned
½ teaspoon granulated garlic	3 tablespoons red wine vinegar
½ teaspoon dried oregano	2 tablespoons olive oil
¼ teaspoon freshly ground black pepper	Cooking spray

Directions:
Salt the chicken thighs on both sides with 1 teaspoon of kosher salt. In a small bowl, combine the paprika, garlic, oregano, and black pepper. Sprinkle half this mixture over the skin sides of the thighs. Spritz the baking pan with cooking spray and place the thighs skin-side down in the pan. Sprinkle the remaining spice mixture over the other sides of the chicken pieces.   Slide the baking pan into Rack Position 2, select Roast, set temperature to 375°F (190°C), and set time to 27 minutes.   After 10 minutes, remove from the oven and turn over the chicken thighs. Return to the oven and continue cooking.   While the chicken cooks, place the cabbage, onion, and radishes in a large bowl. Sprinkle with the remaining kosher salt, vinegar, and olive oil. Toss to coat. After another 9 to 10 minutes, remove from the oven and place the chicken thighs on a cutting board. Place the cabbage mixture in the pan and toss with the chicken fat and spices.   Spread the cabbage in an even layer on the pan and place the chicken on it, skin-side up. Return the pan to the oven and continue cooking. Roast for another 7 to 8 minutes. When cooking is complete, the cabbage is just becoming tender. Remove from the oven. Taste and adjust the seasoning if necessary. Serve.

656. Parmesan Chicken Fingers With Plum Sauce

Servings: 2   Cooking Time: 20 Minutes

Ingredients:

2 chicken breasts, cut in strips	1 egg white
3 tbsp Parmesan cheese, grated	2 tbsp plum sauce, optional
¼ tbsp fresh chives, chopped	½ tbsp fresh thyme, chopped
⅓ cup breadcrumbs	½ tbsp black pepper
	1 tbsp water

Directions:

Preheat Instant Vortex on Air Fry function to 360 F. Mix the chives, Parmesan cheese, thyme, pepper and breadcrumbs. In another bowl, whisk the egg white and mix with the water. Dip the chicken strips into the egg mixture and then in the breadcrumb mixture. Place the strips in the greased basket and fit in the baking tray. Cook for 10 minutes, flipping once. Serve with plum sauce.

657. Tender Baby Back Ribs

Servings: 4   Cooking Time: 45 Minutes

Ingredients:

1 rack baby back ribs, separated in 2-3 rib sections	3 tbsp. white wine
	2 tbsp. olive oil
1 tsp salt	1 tsp lemon juice
1 tsp pepper	¼ tsp paprika
2 cloves garlic, crushed	1 tsp soy sauce
1 bay leaf	2 thyme stems
	Nonstick cooking spray

Directions:

In a large bowl, combine all ingredients, except ribs, and mix well.   Add ribs and turn to coat all sides. Let marinate at room temperature 30 minutes. Lightly spray fryer basket with cooking spray. Place baking pan in position 1 of the oven.   Add ribs to basket, in a single layer, and place on baking pan. Set oven to air fry on 360°F for 45 minutes. Baste ribs with marinade and turn a few times while cooking. Serve immediately.

658. Meatballs(8)

Servings: 4   Cooking Time: 10 Minutes

Ingredients:

1 egg, lightly beaten	1/2 cup cheddar cheese, shredded
1 lb ground beef	
1/4 cup onion, chopped	1/4 cup cilantro, chopped
2 tbsp taco seasoning	Pepper
1 tbsp garlic, minced	Salt

Directions:

Fit the Instant Vortex oven with the rack in position 2.   Line the air fryer basket with parchment paper. Add ground beef and remaining ingredients into the large bowl and mix until well combined.   Make small meatballs from meat mixture and place in the air fryer basket then place an air fryer basket in the baking pan.   Place a baking pan on the oven rack.

Set to air fry at 400 F for 10 minutes.   Serve and enjoy.

659. Lamb Skewered Momo's Recipe

Ingredients:

2 cups minced lamb	5 tbsp. water
2 tbsp. oil	2 tsp. ginger-garlic paste
1 ½ cup all-purpose flour	
½ tsp. salt	2 tsp. soya sauce
	2 tsp. vinegar

Directions:

Squeeze the dough and cover it with plastic wrap and set aside. Next, cook the ingredients for the filling and try to ensure that the lamb is covered well with the sauce. Roll the dough and cut it into a square. Place the filling in the center.   Now, wrap the dough to cover the filling and pinch the edges together. Pre heat the Instant Vortex oven at 200° F for 5 minutes. Place the wontons in the fry basket and close it. Let them cook at the same temperature for another 20 minutes. Recommended sides are chili sauce or ketchup.

660. Duck Oregano Fingers

Ingredients:

2 tsp. salt	2 cup dry breadcrumbs
1 tsp. pepper powder	
1 tsp. red chili powder	2 tsp. oregano
6 tbsp. corn flour	2 tsp. red chili flakes
1 lb. boneless duck (Cut into Oregano Fingers)	1 ½ tbsp. ginger-garlic paste
	4 tbsp. lemon juice
	4 eggs

Directions:

Mix all the ingredients for the marinade and put the duck Oregano Fingers inside and let it rest overnight. Mix the breadcrumbs, oregano and red chili flakes well and place the marinated Oregano Fingers on this mixture. Cover it with plastic wrap and leave it till right before you serve to cook.   Pre heat the Instant Vortex oven at 160 degrees Fahrenheit for 5 minutes. Place the Oregano Fingers in the fry basket and close it. Let them cook at the same temperature for another 15 minutes or so. Toss the Oregano Fingers well so that they are cooked uniformly.

661. Goat Cheese Meatballs

Servings: 8   Cooking Time: 12 Minutes

Ingredients:

1 lb ground beef	1 tbsp Worcestershire sauce
1 lb ground pork	
2 eggs, lightly beaten	1/2 cup goat cheese, crumbled
1/4 cup fresh parsley, chopped	
	1/2 cup breadcrumbs
1 tbsp garlic, minced	Pepper
1 onion, chopped	Salt

Directions:

Fit the Instant Vortex oven with the rack in position 2.   Line the air fryer basket with parchment paper. Add all ingredients into a large bowl and mix until well combined.   Make small balls from meat mixture and place in the air fryer basket then place an air fryer basket in the baking pan. Place a baking pan on the oven rack. Set to air fry at 400 F for 12 minutes. Serve and enjoy.

---

662. Sweet & Spicy Chicken

Servings: 6   Cooking Time: 30 Minutes

Ingredients:

6 chicken breasts, skinless, boneless, cut in 1-inch pieces
1 cup corn starch
2 cups water
1 cup ketchup
½ cup brown sugar
1 tbsp. sesame oil
3 tbsp. soy sauce
2 tbsp. black sesame seeds
2 tbsp. white sesame seeds
½ tsp red pepper flakes
½ tsp garlic powder
2 tbsp. green onion, chopped

Directions:

Place baking pan in position 2. Lightly spray fryer basket with cooking spray.   Place the cornstarch in a large bowl. Add chicken and toss to coat chicken thoroughly.   Working in batches, place chicken in a single layer in the basket and place on baking pan. Set oven to air fryer on 350°F for 10 minutes. Stir the chicken halfway through cooking time. Transfer chicken to baking sheet.   In a large skillet over medium heat, whisk together remaining ingredients, except green onion. Bring to a boil, stirring occasionally. Cook until sauce has thickened, about 3-5 minutes.   Add chicken and stir to coat. Cook another 3-5 minutes, stirring frequently. Serve garnished with green onions.

---

663. Honey And Wine Chicken Breasts

Servings: 4   Cooking Time: 15 Minutes

Ingredients:

2 chicken breasts, rinsed and halved
1 tablespoon melted butter
1/2 teaspoon freshly ground pepper, or to taste
1 teaspoon paprika
3/4 teaspoon sea salt, or to taste
1 teaspoon dried rosemary
2 tablespoons dry white wine
1 tablespoon honey

Directions:

Preparing the Ingredients. Firstly, pat the chicken breasts dry. Lightly coat them with the melted butter. Then, add the remaining ingredients.   Air Frying. Transfer them to the air fryer rack/basket; bake about 15 minutes at 330 degrees F. Serve warm and enjoy

---

664. Chicken With Potatoes And Corn

Servings: 4   Cooking Time: 25 Minutes

Ingredients:

4 bone-in, skin-on chicken thighs
2 teaspoons kosher salt, divided
½ cup butter, melted, divided
3 ears corn, shucked
1 cup Bisquick baking mix
1 pound (454 g) small red potatoes, quartered
and cut into rounds 1- to 1½-inches thick
⅓ cup heavy whipping cream
½ teaspoon freshly ground black pepper

Directions:

Sprinkle the chicken on all sides with 1 teaspoon of kosher salt. Place the baking mix in a shallow dish. Brush the thighs on all sides with ¼ cup of butter, then dredge them in the baking mix, coating them all on sides. Place the chicken in the center of the baking pan.   Place the potatoes in a large bowl with 2 tablespoons of butter and toss to coat. Place them on one side of the chicken on the pan.   Place the corn in a medium bowl and drizzle with the remaining butter. Sprinkle with ¼ teaspoon of kosher salt and toss to coat. Place on the pan on the other side of the chicken.   Slide the baking pan into Rack Position 2, select Roast, set temperature to 375°F (190°C), and set time to 25 minutes. After 20 minutes, remove from the oven and put the potatoes back to the bowl. Return the pan to oven and continue cooking.   As the chicken continues cooking, add the cream, black pepper, and remaining kosher salt to the potatoes. Lightly mash the potatoes with a potato masher.   When cooking is complete, the corn should be tender and the chicken cooked through, reading 165°F (74°C) on a meat thermometer. Remove from the oven. Serve the chicken with the smashed potatoes and corn on the side.

---

665. Quail Chili

Ingredients:

1 lb. quail (Cut into cubes)
2 ½ tsp. ginger-garlic paste
1 tsp. red chili sauce
2 tbsp. tomato ketchup
2 tsp. soya sauce
1-2 tbsp. honey
¼ tsp. Ajinomoto
¼ tsp. salt
¼ tsp. red chili powder/black pepper
A few drops of edible orange food coloring
2 tbsp. olive oil
1 ½ tsp. ginger garlic paste
½ tbsp. red chili sauce
1-2 tsp. red chili flakes

Directions:

Mix all the ingredients for the marinade and put the quail cubes inside and let it rest overnight.   Mix the breadcrumbs, oregano and red chili flakes well and place the marinated Oregano Fingers on this mixture. Cover it with plastic wrap and leave it till right before you serve to cook.   Pre heat the Instant Vortex oven at 160 degrees Fahrenheit for 5 minutes. Place the Oregano Fingers in the fry basket and close it. Let them cook at the same temperature for another 15 minutes or so. Toss the Oregano Fingers well so that they are cooked uniformly.

666. Braised Chicken With Hot Peppers

Servings: 4   Cooking Time: 27 Minutes

Ingredients:

1½ teaspoon kosher salt, divided
1 link sweet Italian sausage (about 4 ounces / 113 g), whole
8 ounces (227 g) miniature bell peppers, halved and deseeded
1 small onion, thinly sliced
2 garlic cloves, minced

4 bone-in, skin-on chicken thighs (about 1½ pounds / 680 g)
1 tablespoon olive oil
4 hot pickled cherry peppers, deseeded and quartered, along with 2 tablespoons pickling liquid from the jar
¼ cup chicken stock
Cooking spray

Directions:

Salt the chicken thighs on both sides with 1 teaspoon of kosher salt. Spritz the baking pan with cooking spray and place the thighs skin-side down on the pan. Add the sausage.   Slide the baking pan into Rack Position 2, select Roast, set temperature to 375°F (190°C), and set time to 27 minutes.   While the chicken and sausage cook, place the bell peppers, onion, and garlic in a large bowl. Sprinkle with the remaining kosher salt and add the olive oil. Toss to coat.   After 10 minutes, remove from the oven and flip the chicken thighs and sausage. Add the pepper mixture to the pan. Return the pan to the oven and continue cooking.   After another 10 minutes, remove from the oven and add the pickled peppers, pickling liquid, and stock. Stir the pickled peppers into the peppers and onion. Return the pan to the oven and continue cooking.   When cooking is complete, the peppers and onion should be soft and the chicken should read 165°F (74°C) on a meat thermometer. Remove from the oven. Slice the sausage into thin pieces and stir it into the pepper mixture. Spoon the peppers over four plates. Top with a chicken thigh.

667. Savory Honey & Garlic Chicken

Servings: 2   Cooking Time: 20 Minutes + Marinating Time

Ingredients:

2 chicken drumsticks, skin removed
2 tbsp olive oil

2 tbsp honey
½ tbsp garlic, minced

Directions:

Add garlic, olive oil, and honey to a sealable zip bag. Add chicken and toss to coat; set aside for 30 minutes. Add the coated chicken to the basket and fit in the baking sheet; cook for 15 minutes at 400 F on Air Fry function, flipping once. Serve and enjoy!

668. Air Fry Chicken Drumsticks

Servings: 6   Cooking Time: 25 Minutes

Ingredients:

6 chicken drumsticks
1/2 tsp garlic powder
2 tbsp olive oil
1/2 tsp ground cumin

3/4 tsp paprika
Pepper
Salt

Directions:

Fit the Instant Vortex oven with the rack in position 2.   Add chicken drumsticks and olive oil in a large bowl and toss well.   Sprinkle garlic powder, paprika, cumin, pepper, and salt over chicken drumsticks and toss until well coated.   Place chicken drumsticks in the air fryer basket then place an air fryer basket in the baking pan.   Place a baking pan on the oven rack. Set to air fry at 400 F for 25 minutes.   Serve and enjoy.

669. Balsamic Chicken Breast Roast

Servings: 2   Cooking Time: 40 Minutes

Ingredients:

¼ cup balsamic vinegar
2 teaspoons dried oregano
2 garlic cloves, minced
1 tablespoon olive oil

⅛ teaspoon salt
½ teaspoon freshly ground black pepper
2 (4-ounce / 113-g) boneless, skinless, chicken-breast halves
Cooking spray

Directions:

In a small bowl, add the vinegar, oregano, garlic, olive oil, salt, and pepper. Mix to combine.   Put the chicken in a resealable plastic bag. Pour the vinegar mixture in the bag with the chicken, seal the bag, and shake to coat the chicken. Refrigerate for 30 minutes to marinate.   Spritz the baking pan with cooking spray. Put the chicken in the prepared baking pan and pour the marinade over the chicken. Slide the baking pan into Rack Position 1, select Convection Bake, set temperature to 400°F (205°C) and set time to 40 minutes.   After 20 minutes, remove the pan from the oven. Flip the chicken. Return the pan to the oven and continue cooking. When cooking is complete, the internal temperature of the chicken should registers at least 165°F (74°C). Let sit for 5 minutes, then serve.

670. Pork Wellington

Servings: 6   Cooking Time: 30 Minutes

Ingredients:

1 ½ lb. pork tenderloin
½ tsp salt
½ tsp pepper
1 tsp thyme
1 sheet puff pastry
4 oz. prosciutto, sliced thin

1 tbsp. Dijon mustard
1 tbsp. olive oil
1 tbsp. butter
8 oz. mushrooms, chopped
1 shallot, chopped
1 egg, beaten

Directions:

Season tenderloin with salt, pepper, and thyme on all sides.   On parchment covered work surface, roll out pastry as long as the tenderloin and wide enough to cover it completely.   Lay the prosciutto across the pastry to cover it and spread with mustard. Melt butter and oil in a large skillet over high heat.

Add mushrooms and shallot and cook 5-10 minutes, until golden brown. Remove from pan. Add tenderloin to the skillet and brown on all sides. Spread mushrooms over mustard and add pork. Roll up to completely cover tenderloin. Use beaten egg to seal the edge. Set oven to bake on 425°F for 35 minutes. Line baking pan with parchment paper and place pork on it, seam side down. Brush top with remaining egg. After oven preheats 5 minutes, place pan in position 1 and cook 30 or until puffed and golden brown. Remove from oven and let rest 5 minutes before slicing and serving.

671. Beef Grandma's Easy To Cook Wontons

Ingredients:

beef steak	2 tsp. soya sauce
2 tbsp. oil	½ tsp. salt
2 tsp. ginger-garlic paste	5 tbsp. water
1 ½ cup all-purpose flour	For filling:
	2 cups minced
	2 tsp. vinegar

Directions:
Squeeze the dough and cover it with plastic wrap and set aside. Next, cook the ingredients for the filling and try to ensure that the beef is covered well with the sauce. Roll the dough and place the filling in the center. Now, wrap the dough to cover the filling and pinch the edges together. Pre heat the Instant Vortex oven at 200° F for 5 minutes. Place the wontons in the fry basket and close it. Let them cook at the same temperature for another 20 minutes. Recommended sides are chili sauce or ketchup.

672. Duck Poppers

Ingredients:

½ cup hung curd	1 ½ tsp. garlic paste
1 tsp. lemon juice	Salt and pepper to taste
1 tsp. red chili flakes	1 tsp. dry oregano
1 cup cubed duck	1 tsp. dry basil

Directions:
Add the ingredients into a separate bowl and mix them well to get a consistent mixture. Dip the duck pieces in the above mixture and leave them aside for some time. Pre heat the Instant Vortex oven at 180° C for around 5 minutes. Place the coated duck pieces in the fry basket and close it properly. Let them cook at the same temperature for 20 more minutes. Keep turning them over in the basket so that they arc cooked properly. Serve with tomato ketchup.

673. Fried Pork Scotch Egg

Servings: 2   Cooking Time: 25 Minutes
Ingredients:

3 soft-boiled eggs, peeled	2 teaspoons of garlic powder
8 ounces of raw minced pork, or	Pinch of salt and pepper
sausage outside the casings	1 cup of breadcrumbs (Panko, but other brands are fine, or home-made bread crumbs work too)
2 teaspoons of ground rosemary	
2 raw eggs	

Directions:
Preparing the Ingredients. Cover the basket of the Instant Vortex air fryer oven with a lining of tin foil, leaving the edges uncovered to allow air to circulate through the basket. Preheat the air fryer oven to 350 degrees. In a mixing bowl, combine the raw pork with the rosemary, garlic powder, salt, and pepper. This will probably be easiest to do with your masher or bare hands (though make sure to wash thoroughly after handling raw meat!); combine until all the spices are evenly spread throughout the meat. Divide the meat mixture into three equal portions in the mixing bowl, and form each into balls with your hands. Lay a large sheet of plastic wrap on the countertop, and flatten one of the balls of meat on top of it, to form a wide, flat meat-circle. Place one of the peeled soft-boiled eggs in the center of the meat-circle and then, using the ends of the plastic wrap, pull the meat-circle so that it is fully covering and surrounding the soft-boiled egg. Tighten and shape the plastic wrap covering the meat so that if forms a ball, and make sure not to squeeze too hard lest you squish the soft-boiled egg at the center of the ball! Set aside. Repeat steps 5-7 with the other two soft-boiled eggs and portions of meat-mixture. In a separate mixing bowl, beat the two raw eggs until fluffy and until the yolks and whites are fully combined. One by one, remove the plastic wrap and dunk the pork-covered balls into the raw egg, and then roll them in the bread crumbs, covering fully and generously. Place each of the bread-crumb covered meat-wrapped balls onto the foil-lined surface of the air fryer oven. Three of them should fit nicely, without touching. Air Frying. Set the Instant Vortex air fryer oven timer to 25 minutes. About halfway through the cooking time, shake the handle of the air-fryer vigorously, so that the scotch eggs inside roll around and ensure full coverage. After 25 minutes, the air fryer oven will shut off, and the scotch eggs should be perfect – the meat fully cooked, the egg-yolks still runny on the inside, and the outsides crispy and golden-brown. Using tongs, place them on serving plates, slice in half, and enjoy

674. Golden Chicken Fries

Servings: 4 To 6   Cooking Time: 6 Minutes
Ingredients:

1 pound (454 g) chicken tenders, cut into about ½-inch-wide strips	2 eggs
	Cooking spray
	Seasonings:
Salt, to taste	½ teaspoon garlic powder
¼ cup all-purpose flour	1 tablespoon chili powder
¾ cup panko bread crumbs	½ teaspoon onion powder
¾ cup crushed	

organic nacho cheese
tortilla chips

1 teaspoon ground
cumin

Directions:
Stir together all seasonings in a small bowl and set aside.   Sprinkle the chicken with salt. Place strips in a large bowl and sprinkle with 1 tablespoon of the seasoning mix. Stir well to distribute seasonings. Add flour to chicken and stir well to coat all sides. Beat eggs in a separate bowl.   In a shallow dish, combine the panko, crushed chips, and the remaining 2 teaspoons of seasoning mix.   Dip chicken strips in eggs, then roll in crumbs. Mist with oil or cooking spray. Arrange the chicken strips in a single layer in the basket.   Put the air fryer basket on the baking pan and slide into Rack Position 2, select Air Fry, set the temperature to 400°F (205°C) and set the time to 6 minutes.   After 4 minutes, remove from the oven. Flip the strips with tongs. Return to the oven and continue cooking.   When cooking is complete, the chicken should be crispy and its juices should be run clear.   Allow to cool under room temperature before serving.

---

675.   Delicious Turkey Cutlets

Servings: 4   Cooking Time: 25 Minutes
Ingredients:

1 egg	1/4 cup parmesan cheese, grated
1 1/2 lbs turkey cutlets	1/2 cup almond flour
1/2 tsp garlic powder	1/4 tsp pepper
1/2 tsp onion powder	1/2 tsp salt
1/2 tsp dried parsley	

Directions:
Fit the Instant Vortex oven with the rack in position Add egg in a small bowl and whisk well.   In a shallow dish, mix almond flour, parmesan cheese, parsley, onion powder, garlic powder, pepper, and salt.   Dip turkey cutlet into the egg and coat with almond flour mixture.   Place coated turkey cutlets into the baking pan.   Set to bake at 350 F for 30 minutes. After 5 minutes place the baking pan in the preheated oven.   Serve and enjoy.

---

676.   Squab Cutlet

Ingredients:

2 lb. boneless squab cut into slices	4 tsp. tandoori masala
1st Marinade:	2 tbsp. dry fenugreek leaves
3 tbsp. vinegar or lemon juice	1 tsp. black salt
2 or 3 tsp. paprika	1 tsp. chat masala
1 tsp. black pepper	1 tsp. garam masala powder
1 tsp. salt	
3 tsp. ginger-garlic paste	1 tsp. red chili powder
2nd Marinade:	1 tsp. salt
1 cup yogurt	3 drops of red color

Directions:
Make the first marinade and soak the cut squab in it for four hours. While this is happening, make the second marinade and soak the squab in it overnight to let the flavors blend. Pre heat the Instant Vortex oven at 160 degrees Fahrenheit for 5 minutes.

Place the Oregano Fingers in the fry basket and close it. Let them cook at the same temperature for another 15 minutes or so. Toss the Oregano Fingers well so that they are cooked uniformly. Serve them with mint sauce.

---

677.   Chicken Rochambeau With Mushroom Sauce

Servings: 4   Cooking Time: 30 Minutes
Ingredients:

1 tablespoon melted butter	Cooking spray
	Mushroom Sauce:
¼ cup all-purpose flour	2 tablespoons butter
4 chicken tenders, cut in half crosswise	½ cup chopped mushrooms
4 slices ham, ¼-inch thick, large enough to cover an English muffin	½ cup chopped green onions
	2 tablespoons flour
	1 cup chicken broth
2 English muffins, split in halves	1½ teaspoons Worcestershire sauce
Salt and ground black pepper, to taste	¼ teaspoon garlic powder

Directions:
Put the butter in the baking pan. Combine the flour, salt, and ground black pepper in a shallow dish. Roll the chicken tenders over to coat well.   Arrange the chicken in the baking pan and flip to coat with the melted butter.   Slide the baking pan into Rack Position 2, select Convection Broil, set temperature to 390°F (199°C) and set time to 10 minutes.   Flip the tenders halfway through.   When cooking is complete, the juices of chicken tenders should run clear.   Meanwhile, make the mushroom sauce: melt 2 tablespoons of butter in a saucepan over medium-high heat.   Add the mushrooms and onions to the saucepan and sauté for 3 minutes or until the onions are translucent.   Gently mix in the flour, broth, Worcestershire sauce, and garlic powder until smooth.   Reduce the heat to low and simmer for 5 minutes or until it has a thick consistency. Set the sauce aside until ready to serve. When broiling is complete, remove the baking pan from the oven and set the ham slices into the basket. Put the air fryer basket on the baking pan and slide into Rack Position 2, select Air Fry, set time to 5 minutes.   Flip the ham slices halfway through. When cooking is complete, the ham slices should be heated through.   Remove the ham slices from the oven and set in the English muffin halves and warm for 1 minute.   Arrange each ham slice on top of each muffin half, then place each chicken tender over the ham slice.   Transfer to the oven and set time to 2 minutes on Air Fry.   Serve with the sauce on top.

---

678.   Amazing Bacon & Potato Platter

Servings: 4   Cooking Time: 40 Minutes
Ingredients:

4 potatoes, halved
6 garlic cloves, squashed

4 streaky cut rashers bacon
1 tbsp olive oil

Directions:
In a mixing bowl, mix garlic, bacon, potatoes, and olive oil; toss to coat. Place the mixture in the basket and fit in the baking tray; roast for 25-30 minutes at 400 F on Air Fry, shaking once.

679. Baked Chicken Noodle Casserole

Servings: 4   Cooking Time: 55 Minutes
Ingredients:

2 cups cooked chicken, diced
10.5 oz cream of chicken soup
2 cups dry egg noodles

3/4 cup frozen peas
1/2 cup milk
1/2 cup cheddar cheese, shredded
2 tbsp breadcrumbs
1 tbsp butter, melted

Directions:
Fit the Instant Vortex oven with the rack in position Cook noodles according to the packet instructions. Drain well.   Add cooked noodles, milk, soup, chicken, and peas into the greased casserole dish. Sprinkle with shredded cheese.   Mix melted butter and breadcrumbs and sprinkle over chicken noodle mixture.   Set to bake at 425 F for 60 minutes. After 5 minutes place the casserole dish in the preheated oven.   Serve and enjoy.

680.   Meatballs(12)

Servings: 6   Cooking Time: 25 Minutes
Ingredients:

1 lb ground turkey
1 egg, lightly beaten
2 tbsp basil, chopped
2 tbsp coconut flour

1 tsp olive oil
1/2 tsp ground ginger
1/2 tsp salt

Directions:
Fit the Instant Vortex oven with the rack in position In a bowl, mix turkey, basil, coconut flour, olive oil, ginger, egg, and salt until well combined.   Make small balls from the meat mixture and place it into the parchment-lined baking pan.   Set to bake at 375 F for 30 minutes. After 5 minutes place the baking pan in the preheated oven.   Serve and enjoy.

681.   Tuscan Air Fried Veal Loin

Servings: 3 Veal Chops   Cooking Time: 12 Minutes
Ingredients:

1½ teaspoons crushed fennel seeds
1 tablespoon minced fresh rosemary leaves
1 tablespoon minced garlic
1½ teaspoons lemon zest

1½ teaspoons salt
½ teaspoon red pepper flakes
2 tablespoons olive oil
3 (10-ounce / 284-g) bone-in veal loin, about ½ inch thick

Directions:

Combine all the ingredients, except for the veal loin, in a large bowl. Stir to mix well.   Dunk the loin in the mixture and press to submerge. Wrap the bowl in plastic and refrigerate for at least an hour to marinate.   Arrange the veal loin in the basket. Put the air fryer basket on the baking pan and slide into Rack Position 2, select Air Fry, set temperature to 400°F (205°C) and set time to 12 minutes.   Flip the veal halfway through.   When cooking is complete, the internal temperature of the veal should reach at least 145°F (63°C) for medium rare. Serve immediately.

682.   Apricot-glazed Chicken Drumsticks

Servings: 6 Drumsticks   Cooking Time: 30 Minutes
Ingredients:

For the Glaze:
½ cup apricot preserves
½ teaspoon tamari
¼ teaspoon chili powder
2 teaspoons Dijon mustard
For the Chicken:

6 chicken drumsticks
½ teaspoon seasoning salt
1 teaspoon salt
½ teaspoon ground black pepper
Cooking spray
Make the glaze:

Directions:
Combine the ingredients for the glaze in a saucepan, then heat over low heat for 10 minutes or until thickened.   Turn off the heat and sit until ready to use.   Make the Chicken: Spritz the air fryer basket with cooking spray.   Combine the seasoning salt, salt, and pepper in a small bowl. Stir to mix well.   Place the chicken drumsticks in the basket. Spritz with cooking spray and sprinkle with the salt mixture on both sides.   Put the air fryer basket on the baking pan and slide into Rack Position 2, select Air Fry, set temperature to 370°F (188°C) and set time to 20 minutes.   Flip the chicken halfway through.   When cooking is complete, the chicken should be well browned. Baste the chicken with the glaze and air fry for 2 more minutes or until the chicken tenderloin is glossy.   Serve immediately.

683.   Zucchini Chicken Meatballs

Servings: 6   Cooking Time: 18 Minutes
Ingredients:

1 lb ground chicken
1 tbsp basil, chopped
1/3 cup coconut flour
2 cups zucchini, grated
1 tsp dried oregano
1 tbsp nutritional yeast

1 tbsp garlic, minced
1 tsp cumin
1 tbsp dried onion flakes
2 eggs, lightly beaten
Pepper
Salt

Directions:
Fit the Instant Vortex oven with the rack in position Add all ingredients into the mixing bowl and mix until well combined.   Make small balls from the meat mixture and place them into the baking pan. Set to bake at 400 F for 23 minutes. After 5 minutes

place the baking pan in the preheated oven.   Serve and enjoy.

684.   Parmesan Chicken Cutlets

Servings: 4   Cooking Time: 30 Minutes

Ingredients:

¼ cup Parmesan cheese, grated	2 tbsp panko breadcrumbs
4 chicken cutlets	½ tbsp garlic powder
⅛ tbsp paprika	2 large eggs, beaten

Directions:

In a bowl, mix Parmesan cheese, breadcrumbs, garlic powder, and paprika. Add eggs to another bowl. Dip the chicken in eggs, dredge them in cheese mixture and place them in the basket and fit in the baking tray. Cook for 20-25 minutes on Air Fry function at 400 F.

685.   Juicy & Tender Chicken Breast

Servings: 4   Cooking Time: 20 Minutes

Ingredients:

4 chicken breasts, skinless & boneless	1 tsp Italian seasoning
1/4 tsp pepper	1 tbsp brown sugar
1/4 tsp onion powder	3 tbsp butter, melted
1/4 tsp garlic powder	1 tsp salt
1 tsp paprika	

Directions:

Fit the Instant Vortex oven with the rack in position In a small bowl, mix paprika, brown sugar, Italian seasoning, garlic powder, onion powder, pepper, and salt.   Brush chicken with melted butter and rub with spice mixture.   Place chicken into the baking dish.   Set to bake at 425 F for 25 minutes. After 5 minutes place the baking dish in the preheated oven.   Serve and enjoy.

686.   Barbecue Pork Club Sandwich With Mustard

Ingredients:

2 slices of white bread	½ cup water.
1 tbsp. softened butter	¼ tbsp. Worcestershire sauce
½ lb. cut pork (Get the meat cut into cubes)	½ tsp. olive oil
1 small capsicum	½ flake garlic crushed
¼ tbsp. red chili sauce	¼ cup chopped onion
1 tbsp. tomato ketchup	¼ tsp. mustard powder
	½ tbsp. sugar
	A pinch of salt and black pepper to taste

Directions:

Take the slices of bread and remove the edges. Now cut the slices horizontally. Cook the ingredients for the sauce and wait till it thickens. Now, add the pork to the sauce and stir till it obtains the flavors. Roast the capsicum and peel the skin off. Cut the capsicum into slices.   Mix the ingredients together and apply it to the bread slices.   Pre-heat the Instant Vortex oven for 5 minutes at 300 Fahrenheit. Open the basket of the Fryer and place the prepared Classic Sandwiches in it such that no two Classic Sandwiches are touching each other. Now keep the fryer at 250 degrees for around 15 minutes.   Turn the Classic Sandwiches in between the cooking process to cook both slices. Serve the Classic Sandwiches with tomato ketchup or mint sauce.

687.   Nice Goulash

Servings: 2   Cooking Time: 17 Minutes

Ingredients:

2 red bell peppers, chopped	2 medium tomatoes, diced
1 pound (454 g) ground chicken	Salt and ground black pepper, to taste
½ cup chicken broth	Cooking spray

Directions:

Spritz the baking pan with cooking spray.   Set the bell pepper in the baking pan.   Slide the baking pan into Rack Position 2, select Convection Broil, set temperature to 365°F (185°C) and set time to 5 minutes.   Stir the bell pepper halfway through. When broiling is complete, the bell pepper should be tender.   Add the ground chicken and diced tomatoes in the baking pan and stir to mix well. Set the time of oven to 12 minutes. Stir the mixture and mix in the chicken broth, salt and ground black pepper halfway through.   When cooking is complete, the chicken should be well browned. Serve immediately.

688.   Turkey Grandma's Easy To Cook Wontons

Ingredients:

1 ½ cup all-purpose flour	2 tbsp. oil
½ tsp. salt	2 tsp. ginger-garlic paste
5 tbsp. water	2 tsp. soya sauce
2 cups minced turkey	2 tsp. vinegar

Directions:

Squeeze the dough and cover it with plastic wrap and set aside. Next, cook the ingredients for the filling and try to ensure that the turkey is covered well with the sauce. Roll the dough and place the filling in the center. Now, wrap the dough to cover the filling and pinch the edges together. Pre heat the Instant Vortex oven at 200° F for 5 minutes. Place the wontons in the fry basket and close it. Let them cook at the same temperature for another 20 minutes. Recommended sides are chili sauce or ketchup.

689.   Flank Steak Fajitas

Ingredients:

3 cloves garlic	3 sprigs rosemary
½ cup soy sauce	2 limes, juiced
½ cup honey	2 medium onions,

Salt and pepper, to taste
3 bell peppers of various colors, washed, seeded and sliced
peeled and sliced into rings
10 Portobello mushrooms, washed and sliced
4 flour tortillas

Directions:
Combine garlic, soy sauce, honey, rosemary, salt, pepper and lime juice in a Ziploc bag. Add steak and marinate for 1-2 hours in the refrigerator. Remove meat from marinade and shake off excess liquid. Place Instant Vortex oven on the grill and heat until smoking. At this point, you can sear the meat in the pot or directly on the grill. If you cook meat directly on the grill, sear for 3-4 minutes on each side. While meat cooks on the grill, add 1 Tbsp oil to the Instant Vortex oven a add peppers, onions, mushrooms, salt and pepper. Allow vegetables to sear. Stir frequently for about 6 minutes. Meat and vegetables should be ready about the same time. Transfer both to a platter and place tortillas in Instant Vortex oven to toast, about 30 seconds. Allow meat to rest. Slice against the grain and serve along with vegetables.

---

690. Cheese-encrusted Chicken Tenderloins With Peanuts

Servings: 4   Cooking Time: 12 Minutes

Ingredients:
½ cup grated Parmesan cheese
½ teaspoon garlic powder
1 teaspoon red pepper flakes
Sea salt and ground black pepper, to taste
2 tablespoons peanut oil
1½ pounds (680 g) chicken tenderloins
2 tablespoons peanuts, roasted and roughly chopped
Cooking spray

Directions:
Spritz the air fryer basket with cooking spray. Combine the Parmesan cheese, garlic powder, red pepper flakes, salt, black pepper, and peanut oil in a large bow. Stir to mix well. Dip the chicken tenderloins in the cheese mixture, then press to coat well. Shake the excess off. Transfer the chicken tenderloins in the basket. Put the air fryer basket on the baking pan and slide into Rack Position 2, select Air Fry, set temperature to 360°F (182°C) and set time to 12 minutes. Flip the tenderloin halfway through. When cooking is complete, the tenderloin should be well browned. Transfer the chicken tenderloins on a large plate and top with roasted peanuts before serving.

Meatless Recipes

691. Spicy Thai-style Vegetables

Servings: 4   Cooking Time: 8 Minutes

Ingredients:

1 small head Napa cabbage, shredded, divided	1 red or green bell pepper, sliced into thin strips
1 medium carrot, cut into thin coins	2 tablespoons freshly squeezed lime juice
8 ounces (227 g) snow peas	2 teaspoons red or green Thai curry paste
1 tablespoon vegetable oil	1 serrano chile, deseeded and minced
2 tablespoons soy sauce	1 cup frozen mango slices, thawed
1 tablespoon sesame oil	½ cup chopped roasted peanuts or cashews
2 tablespoons brown sugar	

Directions:

Put half the Napa cabbage in a large bowl, along with the carrot, snow peas, and bell pepper. Drizzle with the vegetable oil and toss to coat. Spread them evenly in the air fryer basket.   Put the air fryer basket on the baking pan and slide into Rack Position 2, select Roast, set temperature to 375°F (190°C), and set time to 8 minutes.   Meanwhile, whisk together the soy sauce, sesame oil, brown sugar, lime juice, and curry paste in a small bowl. When done, the vegetables should be tender and crisp. Remove from the oven and put the vegetables back into the bowl. Add the chile, mango slices, and the remaining cabbage. Pour over the dressing and toss to coat. Top with the roasted nuts and serve.

692. Stuffed Mushrooms

Servings: 12   Cooking Time: 8 Minutes

Ingredients:

2 Rashers Bacon, Diced	½ Bell Pepper, Diced
½ Onion, Diced	1 Small Carrot, Diced
24 Medium Size Mushrooms (Separate the caps & stalks)	1 cup Shredded Cheddar Plus Extra for the Top
	½ cup Sour Cream

Directions:

Preparing the Ingredients. Chop the mushrooms stalks finely and fry them up with the bacon, onion, pepper and carrot at 350 ° for 8 minutes.   When the veggies are fairly tender, stir in the sour cream & the cheese. Keep on the heat until the cheese has melted and everything is mixed nicely.   Now grab the mushroom caps and heap a plop of filling on each one.   Place in the fryer basket and top with a little extra cheese.

693. Roasted Bell Peppers With Garlic

Servings: 4   Cooking Time: 22 Minutes

Ingredients:

1 green bell pepper, sliced into 1-inch strips	1 orange bell pepper, sliced into 1-inch strips
1 red bell pepper, sliced into 1-inch strips	1 yellow bell pepper, sliced into 1-inch strips
2 tablespoons olive oil, divided	Pinch salt
½ teaspoon dried marjoram	Freshly ground black pepper, to taste
	1 head garlic

Directions:

Toss the bell peppers with 1 tablespoon of olive oil in a large bowl until well coated. Season with the marjoram, salt, and pepper. Toss again and set aside. Cut off the top of a head of garlic. Place the garlic cloves on a large square of aluminum foil. Drizzle the top with the remaining 1 tablespoon of olive oil and wrap the garlic cloves in foil.   Transfer the garlic to the air fryer basket.   Put the air fryer basket on the baking pan and slide into Rack Position 2, select Roast, set temperature to 330°F (166°C) and set time to 15 minutes.   After 15 minutes, remove from the oven and add the bell peppers. Return to the oven and set time to 7 minutes.   When cooking is complete or until the garlic is soft and the bell peppers are tender.   Transfer the cooked bell peppers to a plate. Remove the garlic and unwrap the foil. Let the garlic rest for a few minutes. Once cooled, squeeze the roasted garlic cloves out of their skins and add them to the plate of bell peppers. Stir well and serve immediately.

694. Vegetable Pie

Ingredients:

2 cups roasted vegetables	1 tbsp. unsalted butter
2 tbsp. sugar	4tsp. powdered sugar
½ tsp. cinnamon	2 cups cold milk
2 tsp. lemon juice	½ cup roasted nuts
1 cup plain flour	

Directions:

In a large bowl, mix the flour, butter and sugar with your Oregano Fingers. The mixture should resemble breadcrumbs.   Squeeze the dough using the cold milk and wrap it and leave it to cool for ten minutes. Now, roll the dough out and cut into two circles. Press the dough into the pie tins and prick on all sides using a fork. Cook the ingredients for the filling on a low flame and pour into the tin. Cover the pie tin with the second round. Preheat the fryer to 300 Fahrenheit for five minutes.   You will need to place the tin in the basket and cover it. When the pastry has turned golden brown, you will need to remove the tin and let it cool. Cut into slices and serve with a dollop of cream.

695. Cheddar & Tempeh Stuffed Mushrooms

Servings: 3 To 4   Cooking Time: 20 Minutes

Ingredients:

1 clove garlic, minced	14 mushroom caps
Salt and pepper to taste	¼ cup grated Cheddar cheese
4 slices tempeh, chopped	1 tbsp olive oil
	1 tbsp chopped parsley

Directions:

Preheat on Air Fry function to 390 F. In a bowl, add olive oil, tempeh, cheddar cheese, parsley, salt, pepper, and garlic. Mix well with a spoon. Fill the mushroom caps with the tempeh mixture. Place the stuffed mushrooms in the basket and fit in the baking tray; cook for 8 minutes. Once golden and crispy, plate them and serve with green salad.

---

696. Mediterranean Baked Eggs With Spinach

Servings: 2   Cooking Time: 10 Minutes

Ingredients:

2 tablespoons olive oil	4 eggs, whisked
5 ounces (142 g) fresh spinach, chopped	½ teaspoon ground black pepper
1 medium-sized tomato, chopped	½ teaspoon coarse salt
1 teaspoon fresh lemon juice	½ cup roughly chopped fresh basil leaves, for garnish

Directions:

Generously grease the baking pan with olive oil. Stir together the remaining ingredients except the basil leaves in the greased baking pan until well incorporated. Slide the baking pan into Rack Position 1, select Convection Bake, set temperature to 280°F (137°C), and set time to 10 minutes. When cooking is complete, the eggs should be completely set and the vegetables should be tender. Remove from the oven and serve garnished with the fresh basil leaves.

---

697. Simple Ricotta & Spinach Balls

Servings: 4   Cooking Time: 20 Minutes

Ingredients:

14 oz store-bought crescent dough	1 cup steamed spinach
1 cup crumbled ricotta cheese	¼ tsp garlic powder
	1 tsp chopped oregano
	¼ tsp salt

Directions:

Preheat Instant Vortex on Air Fry function to 350 F. Roll the dough onto a lightly floured flat surface. Combine the ricotta cheese, spinach, oregano, salt, and garlic powder together in a bowl. Cut the dough into 4 equal pieces. Divide the spinach/feta mixture between the dough pieces. Make sure to place the filling in the center. Fold the dough and secure with a fork. Place onto a lined baking dish and

then in your Instant Vortex oven. Cook for 12 minutes until lightly browned. Serve.

---

698. Cottage Cheese Flat Cakes

Ingredients:

2 or 3 green chilies finely chopped	2 cups sliced cottage cheese
1 ½ tbsp. lemon juice	3 tsp. ginger finely chopped
Salt and pepper to taste	1-2 tbsp. fresh coriander leaves
2 tbsp. garam masala	

Directions:

Mix the ingredients in a clean bowl and add water to it. Make sure that the paste is not too watery but is enough to apply on the cottage cheese slices. Pre heat the Instant Vortex oven at 160 degrees Fahrenheit for 5 minutes. Place the French Cuisine Galettes in the fry basket and let them cook for another 25 minutes at the same temperature. Keep rolling them over to get a uniform cook. Serve either with mint sauce or ketchup.

---

699. Teriyaki Tofu

Servings: 3   Cooking Time: 15 Minutes

Ingredients:

Nonstick cooking spray	½ tsp salt
14 oz. firm or extra firm tofu, pressed & cut in 1-inch cubes	½ tsp ginger
	½ tsp white pepper
¼ cup cornstarch	3 tbsp. olive oil
	12 oz. bottle vegan teriyaki sauce

Directions:

Lightly spray baking pan with cooking spray. In a shallow dish, combine cornstarch, salt, ginger, and pepper. Heat oil in a large skillet over med-high heat. Toss tofu cubes in cornstarch mixture then add to skillet. Cook 5 minutes, turning over halfway through, until tofu is nicely seared. Transfer the tofu to the prepared baking pan. Set oven to convection bake on 350°F for 15 minutes. Pour all but ½ cup teriyaki sauce over tofu and stir to coat. After oven has preheated for 5 minutes, place the baking pan in position 2 and bake tofu 10 minutes. Turn tofu over, spoon the sauce in the pan over it and bake another 10 minutes. Serve with reserved sauce for dipping.

---

700. Gorgonzola Cheese & Pumpkin Salad

Servings: 2   Cooking Time: 30 Minutes + Chilling Time

Ingredients:

½ lb pumpkin	1 spring onion, sliced
2 oz gorgonzola cheese, crumbled	2 radishes, thinly sliced
2 tbsp pine nuts, toasted	1 tsp apple cider vinegar
1 tbsp olive oil	
½ cup baby spinach	

Directions:

Preheat Instant Vortex on Bake function to 360 F. Peel the pumpkin and chop it into small pieces. Place in a greased baking dish and bake for 20 minutes. Let cool.   Add baby spinach, radishes, and spring onion in a serving bowl and toss with olive oil and vinegar. Top with the pumpkin and gorgonzola cheese and sprinkle with the pine nuts to serve.

---

701.   Broccoli & Cheese Egg Ramekins

Servings: 4   Cooking Time: 25 Minutes

Ingredients:

1 lb broccoli	½ tsp ground nutmeg
4 eggs, beaten	
1 cup cheddar cheese, shredded	1 tsp ginger powder
1 cup heavy cream	Salt and black pepper to taste

Directions:

In boiling water, steam the broccoli for 5 minutes. Drain and place in a bowl to cool. Mix in the eggs, heavy cream, nutmeg, ginger, salt, and pepper. Divide the mixture between greased ramekins and sprinkle the cheddar cheese on top. Place in a baking tray and cook in your Instant Vortex for 10 minutes at 360 F on Bake function. Serve.

---

702.   Air Fried Carrots, Yellow Squash & Zucchini

Servings: 4   Cooking Time: 35 Minutes

Ingredients:

1 tbsp. chopped tarragon leaves	1 pound yellow squash
½ tsp. white pepper	1 pound zucchini
1 tsp. salt	6 tsp. olive oil
	½ pound carrots

Directions:

Preparing the Ingredients. Stem and root the end of squash and zucchini and cut in ¾-inch half-moons. Peel and cut carrots into 1-inch cubes   Combine carrot cubes with 2 teaspoons of olive oil, tossing to combine.   Air Frying. Pour into the Oven rack/basket. Place the Rack on the middle-shelf of the Instant Vortex air fryer oven. Set temperature to 400°F, and set time to 5 minutes.   As carrots cook, drizzle remaining olive oil over squash and zucchini pieces, then season with pepper and salt. Toss well to coat.   Add squash and zucchini when the timer for carrots goes off. Cook 30 minutes, making sure to toss 2-3 times during the cooking process. Once done, take out veggies and toss with tarragon. Serve up warm!

---

703.   Mint French Cuisine Galette

Ingredients:

1-2 tbsp. fresh coriander leaves	1 ½ tbsp. lemon juice
2 or 3 green chilies finely chopped	2 medium potatoes boiled and mashed
Salt and pepper to taste	1 ½ cup coarsely

2 cups mint leaves (Sliced fine)	crushed peanuts
	3 tsp. ginger finely chopped

Directions:

Mix the sliced mint leaves with the rest of the ingredients in a clean bowl.   Mold this mixture into round and flat French Cuisine Galettes.   Wet the French Cuisine Galettes slightly with water. Coat each French Cuisine Galette with the crushed peanuts.   Pre heat the Instant Vortex oven at 160 degrees Fahrenheit for 5 minutes. Place the French Cuisine Galettes in the fry basket and let them cook for another 25 minutes at the same temperature. Keep rolling them over to get a uniform cook. Serve either with mint sauce or ketchup.

---

704.   Air Fried Kale Chips

Servings: 6   Cooking Time: 10 Minutes

Ingredients:

¼ tsp. Himalayan salt	Avocado oil
3 tbsp. yeast	1 bunch of kale

Directions:

Preparing the Ingredients. Rinse kale and with paper towels, dry well.   Tear kale leaves into large pieces. Remember they will shrink as they cook so good sized pieces are necessary.   Place kale pieces in a bowl and spritz with avocado oil till shiny. Sprinkle with salt and yeast.   With your hands, toss kale leaves well to combine.   Air Frying. Pour half of the kale mixture into the Instant Vortex air fryer oven, set temperature to 350°F, and set time to 5 minutes. Remove and repeat with another half of kale.

---

705.   Crispy Tofu Sticks

Servings: 4   Cooking Time: 14 Minutes

Ingredients:

2 tablespoons olive oil, divided	Salt and black pepper, to taste
½ cup flour	14 ounces (397 g)
½ cup crushed cornflakes	firm tofu, cut into ½-inch-thick strips

Directions:

Grease the air fryer basket with 1 tablespoon of olive oil.   Combine the flour, cornflakes, salt, and pepper on a plate.   Dredge the tofu strips in the flour mixture until they are completely coated. Transfer the tofu strips to the greased basket. Drizzle the remaining 1 tablespoon of olive oil over the top of tofu strips.   Put the air fryer basket on the baking pan and slide into Rack Position 2, select Air Fry, set temperature to 360°F (182°C), and set time to 14 minutes.   Flip the tofu strips halfway through the cooking time.   When cooking is complete, the tofu strips should be crispy. Remove from the oven and serve warm.

---

706.   Green Chili Flat Cakes

Ingredients:

2 or 3 green chilies finely chopped
1 ½ tbsp. lemon juice
Salt and pepper to taste
2 tbsp. garam masala

10–12 green chilies
3 tsp. ginger finely chopped
1-2 tbsp. fresh coriander leaves

Directions:
Mix the ingredients in a clean bowl and add water to it. Make sure that the paste is not too watery but is enough to apply to the green chilies. Pre heat the Instant Vortex oven at 160 degrees Fahrenheit for 5 minutes. Place the French Cuisine Galettes in the fry basket and let them cook for another 25 minutes at the same temperature. Keep rolling them over to get a uniform cook. Serve either with mint sauce or ketchup.

707.	Simple Ratatouille

Servings: 2   Cooking Time: 16 Minutes
Ingredients:

2 Roma tomatoes, thinly sliced
1 zucchini, thinly sliced
2 yellow bell peppers, sliced
2 garlic cloves, minced

2 tablespoons olive oil
2 tablespoons herbes de Provence
1 tablespoon vinegar
Salt and black pepper, to taste

Directions:
Place the tomatoes, zucchini, bell peppers, garlic, olive oil, herbes de Provence, and vinegar in a large bowl and toss until the vegetables are evenly coated. Sprinkle with salt and pepper and toss again. Pour the vegetable mixture into the baking pan. Slide the baking pan into Rack Position 2, select Roast, set temperature to 390°F (199°C) and set time to 16 minutes. Stir the vegetables halfway through. When cooking is complete, the vegetables should be tender. Let the vegetable mixture stand for 5 minutes in the oven before removing and serving.

708.	Roasted Butternut Squash With Maple Syrup

Servings: 4   Cooking Time: 30 Minutes
Ingredients:

1 lb butternut squash
1 tsp dried rosemary

2 tbsp maple syrup
Salt to taste

Directions:
Place the squash on a cutting board and peel. Cut in half and remove the seeds and pulp. Slice into wedges and season with salt. Spray with cooking spray and sprinkle with rosemary. Preheat Instant Vortex on AirFry function to 350 F. Transfer the wedges to the greased basket without overlapping. Press Start and cook for 20 minutes. Serve drizzled with maple syrup.

709.	Roasted Brussels Sprouts With Parmesan

Servings: 4   Cooking Time: 20 Minutes
Ingredients:

1 pound (454 g) fresh Brussels sprouts, trimmed
1 tablespoon olive oil

½ teaspoon salt
⅛ teaspoon pepper
¼ cup grated Parmesan cheese

Directions:
In a large bowl, combine the Brussels sprouts with olive oil, salt, and pepper and toss until evenly coated. Spread the Brussels sprouts evenly in the air fryer basket. Put the air fryer basket on the baking pan and slide into Rack Position 2, select Air Fry, set temperature to 330°F (166°C), and set time to 20 minutes. Stir the Brussels sprouts twice during cooking. When cooking is complete, the Brussels sprouts should be golden brown and crisp. Sprinkle the grated Parmesan cheese on top and serve warm.

710.	Black Gram French Cuisine Galette

Ingredients:

2 or 3 green chilies finely chopped
1 ½ tbsp. lemon juice
Salt and pepper to taste
2 medium potatoes boiled and mashed

2 cup black gram
1 ½ cup coarsely crushed peanuts
3 tsp. ginger finely chopped
1-2 tbsp. fresh coriander leaves

Directions:
Mix the ingredients in a clean bowl. Mold this mixture into round and flat French Cuisine Galettes. Wet the French Cuisine Galettes slightly with water. Pre heat the Instant Vortex oven at 160 degrees Fahrenheit for 5 minutes. Place the French Cuisine Galettes in the fry basket and let them cook for another 25 minutes at the same temperature. Keep rolling them over to get a uniform cook. Serve either with mint sauce or ketchup.

711.	Potato Club Barbeque Sandwich

Ingredients:

½ flake garlic crushed
¼ cup chopped onion
¼ tbsp. red chili sauce
2 slices of white bread

1 tbsp. softened butter
1 cup boiled potato
1 small capsicum
¼ tbsp. Worcestershire sauce
½ tsp. olive oil

Directions:
Take the slices of bread and remove the edges. Now cut the slices horizontally. Cook the ingredients for the sauce and wait till it thickens. Now, add the potato to the sauce and stir till it obtains the flavors. Roast the capsicum and peel the skin off. Cut the capsicum into slices. Mix the ingredients together and apply it to the bread slices. Pre-heat the Instant Vortex oven for 5 minutes at 300 Fahrenheit. Open the basket of the Fryer and place the prepared Classic Sandwiches in it such that no two Classic Sandwiches are touching each other. Now keep the fryer at 250 degrees for around 15 minutes. Turn the

Classic Sandwiches in between the cooking process to cook both slices. Serve the Classic Sandwiches with tomato ketchup or mint sauce.

712. Cilantro Roasted Carrots With Cumin Seeds

Servings: 4   Cooking Time: 15 Minutes
Ingredients:

1 lb carrots, julienned	1 tsp cumin seeds
1 tbsp olive oil	2 tbsp fresh cilantro, chopped

Directions:
Preheat Instant Vortex on AirFry function to 350 F. In a bowl, mix oil, carrots, and cumin seeds. Gently stir to coat the carrots well. Place the carrots in a baking tray and press Star. Cook for 10 minutes. Scatter fresh coriander over the carrots and serve.

713. Cheesy Rice And Olives Stuffed Peppers

Servings: 4   Cooking Time: 16 To 17 Minutes
Ingredients:

4 red bell peppers, tops sliced off	¾ cup tomato sauce
2 cups cooked rice	1 tablespoon Greek seasoning
1 cup crumbled feta cheese	Salt and black pepper, to taste
1 onion, chopped	2 tablespoons chopped fresh dill, for serving
¼ cup sliced kalamata olives	

Directions:
Microwave the red bell peppers for 1 to 2 minutes until tender.   When ready, transfer the red bell peppers to a plate to cool.   Mix the cooked rice, feta cheese, onion, kalamata olives, tomato sauce, Greek seasoning, salt, and pepper in a medium bowl and stir until well combined.   Divide the rice mixture among the red bell peppers and transfer to a greased baking pan.   Slide the baking pan into Rack Position 1, select Convection Bake, set temperature to 360ºF (182ºC) and set time to 15 minutes.   When cooking is complete, the rice should be heated through and the vegetables should be soft.   Remove from the oven and serve with the dill sprinkled on top.

714. Feta & Scallion Triangles

Servings: 4   Cooking Time: 20 Minutes
Ingredients:

4 oz feta cheese, crumbled	1 scallion, finely chopped
2 sheets filo pastry	2 tbsp olive oil
1 egg yolk, beaten	Salt and black pepper to taste
2 tbsp fresh parsley, finely chopped	

Directions:
In a bowl, mix the yolk with the cheese, parsley, and scallion.   Season with salt and black pepper. Cut each filo sheet in 3 strips. Put a teaspoon of the feta mixture on the bottom. Roll the strip in a spinning spiral way until the filling of the inside mixture is completely wrapped in a triangle.   Preheat Instant

Vortex on Bake function to 360 F. Brush the surface of filo with olive oil. Place up to 5 triangles in the oven and press Start. Cook for 5 minutes. Lower the temperature to 330 F, cook for 3 more minutes or until golden brown.

715. Roasted Carrots

Servings: 4   Cooking Time: 15 Minutes
Ingredients:

20 oz carrots, julienned	1 tsp cumin seeds
1 tbsp olive oil	2 tbsp fresh cilantro, chopped

Directions:
In a bowl, mix olive oil, carrots, and cumin seeds; stir to coat. Place the carrots in a baking tray and cook in your Instant Vortex on Bake function at 300 F for 10 minutes. Scatter fresh coriander over the carrots and serve.

716. Beetroot Chips

Servings: 3   Cooking Time: 25 Minutes
Ingredients:

1lb golden beetroots, sliced	1 tbsp yeast flakes
2 tbsp olive oil	1 tsp vegan seasoning
	Salt to taste

Directions:
In a bowl, add the olive oil, beetroots, vegan seasoning, and yeast and mix well. Dump the coated chips in the basket.   Fit in the baking tray and cook in your Instant Vortex for 15 minutes at 370 F on Air Fry function, shaking once halfway through. Serve.

717. Amazing Macadamia Delight

Servings: 6   Cooking Time: 20 Minutes
Ingredients:

3 cups macadamia nuts	Salt to taste
3 tbsp liquid smoke	2 tbsp molasses

Directions:
Preheat Instant Vortex on Bake function to 360 F. In a bowl, add salt, liquid, molasses, and cashews and toss to coat. Place the cashews ina baking tray and press Start. Cook for 10 minutes, shaking the basket every 5 minutes. Serve.

718.   Masala Potato Wedges

Ingredients:

½ tsp. red chili flakes	1 tsp. mixed herbs
A pinch of salt to taste	1 tbsp. lemon juice
2 medium sized potatoes (Cut into wedges)	ingredients for the marinade:
	1 tbsp. olive oil
	1 tsp. garam masala

Directions:
Boil the potatoes and blanch them. Mix the ingredients for the marinade and add the potato Oregano Fingers to it making sure that they are coated well.   Pre heat the Instant Vortex oven for around 5 minutes at 300 Fahrenheit. Take out the basket of the fryer and place the potato Oregano Fingers in them. Close the basket.   Now keep the

fryer at 200 Fahrenheit for 20 or 25 minutes. In between the process, toss the fries twice or thrice so that they get cooked properly.

719.Balsamic Asparagus

Servings: 4   Cooking Time: 10 Minutes
Ingredients:

4 tablespoons olive oil, plus more for greasing
1½ pounds (680 g) asparagus spears, trimmed

4 tablespoons balsamic vinegar
Salt and freshly ground black pepper, to taste

Directions:
Grease the air fryer basket with olive oil.   In a shallow bowl, stir together the 4 tablespoons of olive oil and balsamic vinegar to make a marinade.   Put the asparagus spears in the bowl so they are thoroughly covered by the marinade and allow to marinate for 5 minutes.   Put the asparagus in the greased basket in a single layer and season with salt and pepper.   Put the air fryer basket on the baking pan and slide into Rack Position 2, select Air Fry, set temperature to 350°F (180°C), and set time to 10 minutes.   Flip the asparagus halfway through the cooking time.   When done, the asparagus should be tender and lightly browned. Cool for 5 minutes before serving.

720.   Parsley Hearty Carrots

Servings: 3   Cooking Time: 25 Minutes
Ingredients:

2 tsp olive oil
2 shallots, chopped
3 carrots, sliced
Salt to taste
¼ cup yogurt

2 garlic cloves, minced
3 tbsp parsley, chopped

Directions:
In a baking dish, mix olive oil, carrots, salt, garlic, shallots, parsley, and yogurt.   Place the dish in your Instant Vortex and cook for 15 minutes on Bake function at 370 F. Serve with garlic mayo.

721.Rosemary Roasted Squash With Cheese

Servings: 2   Cooking Time: 20 Minutes
Ingredients:

1 pound (454 g) butternut squash, cut into wedges
2 tablespoons olive oil
Salt, to salt

1 tablespoon dried rosemary
1 cup crumbled goat cheese
1 tablespoon maple syrup

Directions:
Toss the squash wedges with the olive oil, rosemary, and salt in a large bowl until well coated.   Transfer the squash wedges to the air fryer basket, spreading them out in as even a layer as possible.   Put the air fryer basket on the baking pan and slide into Rack Position 2, select Air Fry, set temperature to 350°F (180°C), and set time to 20 minutes.   After 10 minutes, remove from the oven and flip the squash.

Return the pan to the oven and continue cooking for 10 minutes.   When cooking is complete, the squash should be golden brown. Remove from the oven. Sprinkle the goat cheese on top and serve drizzled with the maple syrup.

722.   Amaranthus French Cuisine Galette

Ingredients:

Salt and pepper to taste
2 cups minced Amaranthus
3 tsp. ginger finely chopped

1 ½ tbsp. lemon juice
1-2 tbsp. fresh coriander leaves
2 or 3 green chilies finely chopped

Directions:
Mix the ingredients in a clean bowl.   Mold this mixture into round and flat French Cuisine Galettes. Wet the French Cuisine Galettes slightly with water. Pre heat the Instant Vortex oven at 160 degrees Fahrenheit for 5 minutes. Place the French Cuisine Galettes in the fry basket and let them cook for another 25 minutes at the same temperature. Keep rolling them over to get a uniform cook. Serve either with mint sauce or ketchup.

723.   Mom's Blooming Buttery Onion

Servings: 4   Cooking Time: 40 Minutes
Ingredients:

4 onions
2 tbsp butter, melted

1 tbsp olive oil

Directions:
Preheat Instant Vortex on Air Fry function to 350 F. Peel the onions and slice off the root bottom so it can sit well. Cut slices into the onion to make it look like a blooming flower, make sure not to go all the way through; four cuts will do.   Place the onions in a greased baking tray. Drizzle with olive oil and butter and cook for about 30 minutes. Serve with garlic mayo dip.

724.   Parmesan Breaded Zucchini Chips

Servings: 5   Cooking Time: 20 Minutes
Ingredients:

For the zucchini chips:
2 medium zucchini
2 eggs
⅓ cup bread crumbs
⅓ cup grated Parmesan cheese
Salt
Pepper
Cooking oil

For the lemon aioli:
½ cup mayonnaise
½ tablespoon olive oil
Juice of ½ lemon
1 teaspoon minced garlic
Salt
Pepper

Directions:
Preparing the Ingredients. To make the zucchini chips: Slice the zucchini into thin chips (about ⅛ inch thick) using a knife or mandoline.   In a small bowl, beat the eggs. In another small bowl, combine

the bread crumbs, Parmesan cheese, and salt and pepper to taste.   Spray the Oven rack/basket with cooking oil.   Dip the zucchini slices one at a time in the eggs and then the bread crumb mixture. You can also sprinkle the bread crumbs onto the zucchini slices with a spoon.   Place the zucchini chips in the Oven rack/basket, but do not stack.   Place the Rack on the middle-shelf of the Instant Vortex air fryer oven.   Air Frying.   Cook in batches. Spray the chips with cooking oil from a distance (otherwise, the breading may fly off). Cook for 10 minutes. Remove the cooked zucchini chips from the air fryer oven, then repeat step 5 with the remaining zucchini. To make the lemon aioli: While the zucchini is cooking, combine the mayonnaise, olive oil, lemon juice, and garlic in a small bowl, adding salt and pepper to taste. Mix well until fully combined. Cool the zucchini and serve alongside the aioli.

725.   Lemony Wax Beans

Servings: 4   Cooking Time: 12 Minutes
Ingredients:

2 pounds (907 g) wax beans	Salt and freshly ground black pepper, to taste
2 tablespoons extra-virgin olive oil	Juice of ½ lemon, for serving

Directions:
Line the air fryer basket with aluminum foil.   Toss the wax beans with the olive oil in a large bowl. Lightly season with salt and pepper.   Spread out the wax beans in the basket.   Put the air fryer basket on the baking pan and slide into Rack Position 2, select Roast, set temperature to 400°F (205°C), and set time to 12 minutes.   When done, the beans will be caramelized and tender. Remove from the oven to a plate and serve sprinkled with the lemon juice.

726.   Cinnamon Celery Roots

Servings: 4   Cooking Time: 20 Minutes
Ingredients:

2 celery roots, peeled and diced	1 teaspoon extra-virgin olive oil
1 teaspoon butter, melted	Sea salt and freshly ground black pepper, to taste
½ teaspoon ground cinnamon	

Directions:
Line the baking pan with aluminum foil.   Toss the celery roots with the olive oil in a large bowl until well coated. Transfer them to the prepared baking pan.   Slide the baking pan into Rack Position 2, select Roast, set temperature to 350°F (180°C), and set time to 20 minutes.   When done, the celery roots should be very tender. Remove from the oven to a serving bowl. Stir in the butter and cinnamon and mash them with a potato masher until fluffy. Season with salt and pepper to taste. Serve immediately.

727.   Korean Tempeh Steak With Broccoli

Servings: 4   Cooking Time: 15 Minutes + Marinating Time
Ingredients:

16 oz tempeh, cut into 1 cm thick pieces	⅓ cup sherry
1 pound broccoli, cut into florets	1 tsp soy sauce
	1 tsp white sugar
⅓ cup fermented soy sauce	1 tsp cornstarch
	1 tbsp olive oil
2 tbsp sesame oil	1 garlic clove, minced

Directions:
In a bowl, mix cornstarch, sherry, fermented soy sauce, sesame oil, soy sauce, sugar, and tempeh pieces. Marinate for 45 minutes.   Then, add in garlic, olive oil, and ginger. Place in the basket and fit in the baking tray; cook for 10 minutes at 390 F on Air Fry function, turning once halfway through. Serve.

728.   Yummy Chili Bean Burritos

Servings: 3   Cooking Time: 30 Minutes
Ingredients:

6 tortillas	1 can (8 oz) beans
1 cup grated cheddar cheese	1 tsp Italian seasoning

Directions:
Preheat Instant Vortex on Bake function to 350 F. Season the beans with the seasoning and divide them between the tortillas. Top with cheddar cheese. Roll the burritos and arrange them on a lined baking dish. Cook for 5 minutes. Serve.

729.   Mushrooms Stuffed With Tempeh & Cheddar

Servings: 4   Cooking Time: 20 Minutes
Ingredients:

14 small button mushrooms	4 slices tempeh, chopped
1 garlic clove, minced	¼ cup cheddar cheese, grated
Salt and black pepper to taste	
1 tbsp olive oil	1 tbsp fresh parsley, chopped

Directions:
Preheat on AirFry function to 390 F. In a bowl, mix the oil, tempeh, cheddar cheese, parsley, salt, pepper, and garlic. Cut the mushroom stalks off and fill them with the tempeh mixture. Place the stuffed mushrooms in the basket and press Start. Cook at 390 F for 8 minutes. Once golden and crispy, plate them and serve with a green salad.

730.   Tomato & Feta Bites With Pine Nuts

Servings: 2   Cooking Time: 25 Minutes
Ingredients:

1 heirloom tomato, sliced	1 clove garlic
1 (4- oz) block Feta cheese, sliced	1 ½ tbsp toasted pine nuts

1 small red onion, thinly sliced
2 tsp + ¼ cup olive oil

¼ cup fresh parsley, chopped
¼ cup grated Parmesan cheese
¼ cup chopped basil

Directions:
Add basil, pine nuts, garlic, and salt to a food processor. Process while slowly adding ¼ cup of olive oil. Once finished, pour basil pesto into a bowl and refrigerate for 30 minutes.   Preheat Instant Vortex oven on AirFry function to 390 F. Spread some pesto on each slice of tomato.   Top with feta cheese and onion and drizzle with the remaining olive oil. Place in the frying basket and press Start. Cook for 12 minutes. Top with the remaining pesto and serve.

731.Cheesy Broccoli Tots

Servings: 4   Cooking Time: 15 Minutes
Ingredients:

12 ounces (340 g) frozen broccoli, thawed, drained, and patted dry
½ cup seasoned whole-wheat bread crumbs
¼ cup shredded reduced-fat sharp Cheddar cheese

1 large egg, lightly beaten
¼ cup grated Parmesan cheese
1½ teaspoons minced garlic
Salt and freshly ground black pepper, to taste
Cooking spray

Directions:
Spritz the air fryer basket lightly with cooking spray. Place the remaining ingredients into a food processor and process until the mixture resembles a coarse meal. Transfer the mixture to a bowl. Using a tablespoon, scoop out the broccoli mixture and form into 24 oval "tater tot" shapes with your hands.   Put the tots in the prepared basket in a single layer, spacing them 1 inch apart. Mist the tots lightly with cooking spray.   Put the air fryer basket on the baking pan and slide into Rack Position 2, select Air Fry, set temperature to 375°F (190°C), and set time to 15 minutes.   Flip the tots halfway through the cooking time.   When done, the tots will be lightly browned and crispy. Remove from the oven and serve on a plate.

732.   Asparagus French Cuisine Galette

Ingredients:
Salt and pepper to taste
2 cups minced asparagus
3 tsp. ginger finely chopped

1 ½ tbsp. lemon juice
1-2 tbsp. fresh coriander leaves
2 or 3 green chilies finely chopped

Directions:
Mix the ingredients in a clean bowl.   Mold this mixture into round and flat French Cuisine Galettes. Wet the French Cuisine Galettes slightly with water.

Pre heat the Instant Vortex oven at 160 degrees Fahrenheit for 5 minutes. Place the French Cuisine Galettes in the fry basket and let them cook for another 25 minutes at the same temperature. Keep rolling them over to get a uniform cook. Serve either with mint sauce or ketchup.

733.   Nutmeg Broccoli With Eggs & Cheddar Cheese

Servings: 4   Cooking Time: 15 Minutes
Ingredients:
1 lb broccoli, cut into florets
1 cup cheddar cheese, shredded

4 eggs
1 cup heavy cream
1 pinch of nutmeg
1 tsp ginger powder

Directions:
In boiling water, steam the broccoli for 5 minutes. Drain and place in a bowl. Add in 1 egg, heavy cream, nutmeg, and ginger. Divide the mixture between greased ramekins and sprinkle the cheddar cheese on top. Cook for 10 minutes at 280 F on AirFry function.

734.   Classic Baked Potatoes

Servings: 4   Cooking Time: 30 Minutes
Ingredients:
2 garlic cloves, minced
Salt and black pepper to taste

1 lb potatoes
1 tsp rosemary
1 tsp butter, melted

Directions:
Preheat Instant Vortex oven to 360 F on AirFry function. Prick the potatoes with a fork. Place into frying basket and press Start. Cook for 25 minutes. Cut the potatoes in half and top with butter and rosemary. Season with salt and pepper and serve.

735.   Cottage Cheese Fingers

Ingredients:
2 tsp. salt
1 tsp. pepper powder
1 tsp. red chili powder
6 tbsp. corn flour
2 cups cottage cheese Oregano Fingers

4 eggs
2 cup dry breadcrumbs
2 tsp. oregano
1 ½ tbsp. ginger-garlic paste
4 tbsp. lemon juice

Directions:
Mix all the ingredients for the marinade and put the chicken Oregano Fingers inside and let it rest overnight.   Mix the breadcrumbs, oregano and red chili flakes well and place the marinated Oregano Fingers on this mixture. Cover it with plastic wrap and leave it till right before you serve to cook.   Pre heat the Instant Vortex oven at 160 degrees Fahrenheit for 5 minutes. Place the Oregano Fingers in the fry basket and close it. Let them cook at the same temperature for another 15 minutes or so. Toss the Oregano Fingers well so that they are cooked uniformly.

736.　French Bean Toast

Ingredients:

1 tsp. sugar for every 2 slices	Bread slices (brown or white)
Crushed cornflakes	1 egg white for every
2 cups baked beans	2 slices

Directions:

Put two slices together and cut them along the diagonal.　In a bowl, whisk the egg whites and add some sugar.　Dip the bread triangles into this mixture and then coat them with the crushed cornflakes.　Pre heat the Instant Vortex oven at 180° C for 4 minutes. Place the coated bread triangles in the fry basket and close it. Let them cook at the same temperature for another 20 minutes at least. Halfway through the process, turn the triangles over so that you get a uniform cook. Top with baked beans and serve.

737.　Asian-inspired Broccoli

Servings: 2　Cooking Time: 10 Minutes

Ingredients:

12 ounces (340 g) broccoli florets	2 tablespoons Asian hot chili oil
1 teaspoon ground Sichuan peppercorns (or black pepper)	2 garlic cloves, finely chopped
1 (2-inch) piece fresh ginger, peeled and finely chopped	Kosher salt and freshly ground black pepper

Directions:

Toss the broccoli florets with the chili oil, Sichuan peppercorns, garlic, ginger, salt, and pepper in a mixing bowl until thoroughly coated.　Transfer the broccoli florets to the air fryer basket.　Put the air fryer basket on the baking pan and slide into Rack Position 2, select Air Fry, set temperature to 375°F (190°C), and set time to 10 minutes.　Stir the broccoli florets halfway through the cooking time.　When cooking is complete, the broccoli florets should be lightly browned and tender. Remove the broccoli from the oven and serve on a plate.

738.　Chili Cottage Cheese

Ingredients:

2 tbsp. olive oil	1-2 tbsp. honey.
1 capsicum. Cut into thin and long pieces (lengthwise).	2 ½ tsp. ginger-garlic paste
2 small onions. Cut them into halves.	1 tsp. red chili sauce
1 ½ tsp. ginger garlic paste.	¼ tsp. salt
½ tbsp. red chili sauce.	¼ tsp. red chili powder/black pepper
2 tbsp. tomato ketchup.	A few drops of edible orange food coloring
1 ½ tbsp. sweet chili sauce.	¼ tsp. Ajinomoto.
2 tsp. vinegar.	A pinch of black pepper powder.
2 tsp. soya sauce.	1-2 tsp. red chili flakes.

A few drops of edible red food coloring.	For the garnish, use the greens of spring onions and sesame seeds.
2 cups cubed cottage cheese	

Directions:

Create the mix for the cottage cheese cubes and coat the chicken well with it.　Pre heat the Instant Vortex oven at 250 Fahrenheit for 5 minutes or so. Open the basket of the Fryer. Place the Oregano Fingers inside the basket. Now let the fryer stay at 290 Fahrenheit for another 20 minutes. Keep tossing the Oregano Fingers periodically through the cook to get a uniform cook.　Add the ingredients to the sauce and cook it with the vegetables till it thickens. Add the Oregano Fingers to the sauce and cook till the flavors have blended.

739.　Gherkins Flat Cakes

Ingredients:

2 or 3 green chilies finely chopped	2 cups sliced gherkins
1 ½ tbsp. lemon juice	3 tsp. ginger finely chopped
Salt and pepper to taste	1-2 tbsp. fresh coriander leaves
2 tbsp. garam masala	

Directions:

Mix the ingredients in a clean bowl and add water to it. Make sure that the paste is not too watery but is enough to apply on the gherkin.　Pre heat the Instant Vortex oven at 160 degrees Fahrenheit for 5 minutes. Place the French Cuisine Galettes in the fry basket and let them cook for another 25 minutes at the same temperature. Keep rolling them over to get a uniform cook. Serve either with mint sauce or ketchup.

740.　Bean, Salsa, And Cheese Tacos

Servings: 4　Cooking Time: 7 Minutes

Ingredients:

1 (15-ounce / 425-g) can black beans, drained and rinsed	½ cup prepared salsa
1½ teaspoons chili powder	8 (6-inch) flour tortillas
4 ounces (113 g) grated Monterey Jack cheese	2 tablespoons vegetable or extra-virgin olive oil
2 tablespoons minced onion	Shredded lettuce, for serving

Directions:

In a medium bowl, add the beans, salsa and chili powder. Coarsely mash them with a potato masher. Fold in the cheese and onion and stir until combined. Arrange the flour tortillas on a cutting board and spoon 2 to 3 tablespoons of the filling into each tortilla. Fold the tortillas over, pressing lightly to even out the filling. Brush the tacos on one side with half the olive oil and put them, oiled side down, in the air fryer basket. Brush the top side with the remaining olive oil.　Put the air fryer basket on the baking pan and slide into Rack Position 2, select Air Fry, set temperature to 400°F (205°C), and set time to 7 minutes. Flip the tacos halfway through the cooking time. Remove from the oven and allow to cool for 5 minutes. Serve with the shredded lettuce on the side.

741.Maple And Pecan Granola

Servings: 4   Cooking Time: 20 Minutes
Ingredients:
- 1½ cups rolled oats
- ¼ cup maple syrup
- 1 teaspoon vanilla extract
- ¼ cup pecan pieces
- ½ teaspoon ground cinnamon

Directions:
Line a baking sheet with parchment paper. Mix together the oats, maple syrup, pecan pieces, vanilla, and cinnamon in a large bowl and stir until the oats and pecan pieces are completely coated. Spread the mixture evenly in the baking pan. Slide the baking pan into Rack Position 1, select Convection Bake, set temperature to 300°F (150°C), and set time to 20 minutes. Stir once halfway through the cooking time. When done, remove from the oven and cool for 30 minutes before serving. The granola may still be a bit soft right after removing, but it will gradually firm up as it cools.

742.   Dill Baby Carrots With Honey

Servings: 4   Cooking Time: 20 Minutes
Ingredients:
- 1 lb baby carrots
- 1 tsp dried dill
- 1 tbsp olive oil
- 1 tbsp honey
- Salt and black pepper to taste

Directions:
Preheat Instant Vortex Oven to 360 F on AirFry function. In a bowl, mix oil, carrots, and honey; stir to coat. Season with dill, pepper, and salt. Place the carrots in the basket and cook for 15 minutes.

743.   Cottage Cheese Pops

Ingredients:
- 1 tsp. dry basil
- ½ cup hung curd
- 1 tsp. lemon juice
- 1 cup cottage cheese cut into 2" cubes
- 1 ½ tsp. garlic paste
- Salt and pepper to taste
- 1 tsp. dry oregano
- 1 tsp. red chili flakes

Directions:
Cut the cottage cheese into thick and long rectangular pieces. Add the rest of the ingredients into a separate bowl and mix them well to get a consistent mixture. Dip the cottage cheese pieces in the above mixture and leave them aside for some time. Pre heat the Instant Vortex oven at 180° C for around 5 minutes. Place the coated cottage cheese pieces in the fry basket and close it properly. Let them cook at the same temperature for 20 more minutes. Keep turning them over in the basket so that they are cooked properly. Serve with tomato ketchup.

744.   Lemony Brussels Sprouts And Tomatoes

Servings: 4   Cooking Time: 20 Minutes
Ingredients:
- 1 pound (454 g), Brussels sprouts, trimmed and halved
- ½ cup sun-dried tomatoes, chopped
- 2 tablespoons freshly squeezed lemon juice
- 1 tablespoon extra-virgin olive oil
- Sea Salt and freshly ground black pepper, to taste
- 1 teaspoon lemon zest

Directions:
Line the air fryer basket with aluminum foil. Toss the Brussels sprouts with the olive oil in a large bowl. Sprinkle with salt and black pepper. Spread the Brussels sprouts in a single layer in the basket. Put the air fryer basket on the baking pan and slide into Rack Position 2, select Roast, set temperature to 400°F (205°C), and set time to 20 minutes. When done, the Brussels sprouts should be caramelized. Remove from the oven to a serving bowl, along with the tomatoes, lemon juice, and lemon zest. Toss to combine. Serve immediately.

745.   Sweet-and-sour Brussels Sprouts

Servings: 2   Cooking Time: 20 Minutes
Ingredients:
- ¼ cup Thai sweet chili sauce
- 2 tablespoons black vinegar or balsamic vinegar
- ½ teaspoon hot sauce
- 8 ounces (227 g) Brussels sprouts, trimmed (large sprouts halved)
- 2 small shallots, cut into ¼-inch-thick slices
- Kosher salt and freshly ground black pepper, to taste
- 2 teaspoons lightly packed fresh cilantro leaves, for garnish

Directions:
Place the chili sauce, vinegar, and hot sauce in a large bowl and whisk to combine. Add the shallots and Brussels sprouts and toss to coat. Sprinkle with the salt and pepper. Transfer the Brussels sprouts and sauce to the baking pan. Slide the baking pan into Rack Position 2, select Roast, set temperature to 390°F (199°C), and set time to 20 minutes. Stir the Brussels sprouts twice during cooking. When cooking is complete, the Brussels sprouts should be crisp-tender. Remove from the oven. Sprinkle the cilantro on top for garnish and serve warm.

746.   Potato Flat Cakes

Ingredients:
- 2 or 3 green chilies finely chopped
- 1 ½ tbsp. lemon juice
- Salt and pepper to taste
- 2 tbsp. garam masala
- 2 cups sliced potato
- 3 tsp. ginger finely chopped
- 1-2 tbsp. fresh coriander leaves

Directions:

Mix the ingredients in a clean bowl and add water to it. Make sure that the paste is not too watery but is enough to apply on the potato slices.   Pre heat the Instant Vortex oven at 160 degrees Fahrenheit for 5 minutes. Place the French Cuisine Galettes in the fry basket and let them cook for another 25 minutes at the same temperature. Keep rolling them over to get a uniform cook. Serve either with mint sauce or ketchup.

747.   Jalapeño Cheese Balls

Servings: 12   Cooking Time: 8 Minutes

Ingredients:

4 ounces cream cheese	½ cup bread crumbs
⅓ cup shredded mozzarella cheese	2 eggs
⅓ cup shredded Cheddar cheese	½ cup all-purpose flour
2 jalapeños, finely chopped	Salt
	Pepper
	Cooking oil

Directions:
Preparing the Ingredients. In a medium bowl, combine the cream cheese, mozzarella, Cheddar, and jalapeños. Mix well.   Form the cheese mixture into balls about an inch thick. Using a small ice cream scoop works well.   Arrange the cheese balls on a sheet pan and place in the freezer for 15 minutes. This will help the cheese balls maintain their shape while frying.   Spray the Oven rack/basket with cooking oil. Place the bread crumbs in a small bowl. In another small bowl, beat the eggs. In a third small bowl, combine the flour with salt and pepper to taste, and mix well. Remove the cheese balls from the freezer. Dip the cheese balls in the flour, then the eggs, and then the bread crumbs.   Air Frying. Place the cheese balls in the Oven rack/basket.   Spray with cooking oil. Place the Rack on the middle-shelf of the Instant Vortex air fryer oven. Cook for 8 minutes.   Open the air fryer oven and flip the cheese balls. I recommend flipping them instead of shaking, so the balls maintain their form. Cook an additional 4 minutes. Cool before serving.

748.   Cottage Cheese Gnocchi's

Ingredients:

2 tsp. ginger-garlic paste	½ tsp. salt
2 tsp. soya sauce	5 tbsp. water
2 tsp. vinegar	2 cups grated cottage cheese
1 ½ cup all-purpose flour	2 tbsp. oil

Directions:
Squeeze the dough and cover it with plastic wrap and set aside. Next, cook the ingredients for the filling and try to ensure that the cottage cheese is covered well with the sauce.   Roll the dough and place the filling in the center. Now, wrap the dough to cover the filling and pinch the edges together. Pre heat the Instant Vortex oven at 200° F for 5 minutes. Place the gnocchi's in the fry basket and close it. Let them cook at the same temperature for

another 20 minutes. Recommended sides are chili sauce or ketchup.

749.   Zucchini Crisps

Servings: 4   Cooking Time: 25 Minutes

Ingredients:

4 small zucchinis, cut lengthwise	¼ cup fresh parsley, chopped
½ cup Parmesan cheese, grated	4 garlic cloves, minced
½ cup breadcrumbs	Salt and black pepper to taste
¼ cup butter, melted	

Directions:
Preheat Instant Vortex on AirFry function to 350 F. In a bowl, mix breadcrumbs, Parmesan cheese, garlic, and parsley. Season with salt and pepper and stir in the butter.   Arrange the zucchinis with the cut side up. Spread the cheese mixture onto the zucchini and place them in the basket. Press Start and cook for 14-16 minutes. Serve hot.

750.   Stuffed Peppers With Beans And Rice

Servings: 4   Cooking Time: 18 Minutes

Ingredients:

4 medium red, green, or yellow bell peppers, halved and deseeded	½ cup diced roasted red peppers
4 tablespoons extra-virgin olive oil, divided	¼ cup chopped parsley
½ teaspoon kosher salt, divided	½ small onion, finely chopped
1 (15-ounce / 425-g) can chickpeas	3 garlic cloves, minced
1½ cups cooked white rice	½ teaspoon cumin
	¼ teaspoon freshly ground black pepper
	¾ cup panko bread crumbs

Directions:
Brush the peppers inside and out with 1 tablespoon of olive oil. Season the insides with ¼ teaspoon of kosher salt. Arrange the peppers in the air fryer basket, cut side up.   Place the chickpeas with their liquid into a large bowl. Lightly mash the beans with a potato masher. Sprinkle with the remaining ¼ teaspoon of kosher salt and 1 tablespoon of olive oil. Add the rice, red peppers, parsley, onion, garlic, cumin, and black pepper to the bowl and stir to incorporate.   Divide the mixture among the bell pepper halves.   Stir together the remaining 2 tablespoons of olive oil and panko in a small bowl. Top the pepper halves with the panko mixture. Put the air fryer basket on the baking pan and slide into Rack Position 2, select Roast, set temperature to 375°F (190°C), and set time to 18 minutes. When done, the peppers should be slightly wrinkled, and the panko should be golden brown.   Remove from the oven and serve on a plate.

751. Barbeque Corn Sandwich

Ingredients:

½ flake garlic crushed	1 tbsp. softened butter
¼ cup chopped onion	1 cup sweet corn kernels
¼ tbsp. red chili sauce	1 small capsicum
½ cup water	¼ tbsp. Worcestershire sauce
2 slices of white bread	½ tsp. olive oil

Directions:
Take the slices of bread and remove the edges. Now cut the slices horizontally. Cook the ingredients for the sauce and wait till it thickens. Now, add the corn to the sauce and stir till it obtains the flavors. Roast the capsicum and peel the skin off. Cut the capsicum into slices. Apply the sauce on the slices. Pre-heat the Instant Vortex oven for 5 minutes at 300 Fahrenheit. Open the basket of the Fryer and place the prepared Classic Sandwiches in it such that no two Classic Sandwiches are touching each other. Now keep the fryer at 250 degrees for around 15 minutes. Turn the Classic Sandwiches in between the cooking process to cook both slices. Serve the Classic Sandwiches with tomato ketchup or mint sauce.

752. Chili Veggie Skewers

Servings: 4   Cooking Time: 20 Minutes

Ingredients:

2 tbsp cornflour	½ tsp garam masala powder
1 cup canned white beans, drained	½ cup paneer
⅓ cup grated carrots	1 green chili
2 boiled and mashed potatoes	1-inch piece of fresh ginger
¼ cup chopped fresh mint leaves	3 garlic cloves
	Salt to taste

Directions:
Preheat Instant Vortex on Air Fry function to 390 F. Place the beans, carrots, garlic, ginger, chili, paneer, and mint in a food processor; process until smooth. Transfer to a bowl. Add in the mashed potatoes, cornflour, salt, and garam masala powder and mix until fully incorporated. Divide the mixture into 12 equal pieces. Shape each of the pieces around a skewer. Cook in your Instant Vortex for 10 minutes, turning once. Serve.

753. Vegetable And Cheese Stuffed Tomatoes

Servings: 4   Cooking Time: 18 Minutes

Ingredients:

4 medium beefsteak tomatoes, rinsed	2 cups fresh baby spinach
½ cup grated carrot	¼ cup crumbled low-sodium feta cheese
1 medium onion, chopped	½ teaspoon dried basil
1 garlic clove, minced	
2 teaspoons olive oil	

Directions:
On your cutting board, cut a thin slice off the top of each tomato. Scoop out a ¼- to ½-inch-thick tomato pulp and place the tomatoes upside down on paper towels to drain. Set aside. Stir together the carrot, onion, garlic, and olive oil in the baking pan. Slide the baking pan into Rack Position 1, select Convection Bake, set temperature to 350°F (180°C) and set time to 5 minutes. Stir the vegetables halfway through. When cooking is complete, the carrot should be crisp-tender. Remove from the oven and stir in the spinach, feta cheese, and basil. Spoon ¼ of the vegetable mixture into each tomato and transfer the stuffed tomatoes to the oven. Set time to 13 minutes. When cooking is complete, the filling should be hot and the tomatoes should be lightly caramelized. Let the tomatoes cool for 5 minutes and serve.

754. Italian Baked Tofu

Servings: 2   Cooking Time: 10 Minutes

Ingredients:

1 tablespoon soy sauce	1 tablespoon water
⅓ teaspoon garlic powder	⅓ teaspoon dried basil
⅓ teaspoon onion powder	Black pepper, to taste
⅓ teaspoon dried oregano	6 ounces (170 g) extra firm tofu, pressed and cubed

Directions:
In a large mixing bowl, whisk together the soy sauce, water, garlic powder, onion powder, oregano, basil, and black pepper. Add the tofu cubes, stirring to coat, and let them marinate for 10 minutes. Arrange the tofu in the baking pan. Slide the baking pan into Rack Position 1, select Convection Bake, set temperature to 390°F (199°C) and set time to 10 minutes. Flip the tofu halfway through the cooking time. When cooking is complete, the tofu should be crisp. Remove from the oven to a plate and serve.

755. Cumin And Cayenne Spicy Sweet Potatoes

Servings: 4   Cooking Time: 30 Minutes

Ingredients:

½ tsp garlic powder	¼ tsp cumin
½ tsp cayenne pepper	3 tbsp olive oil
3 sweet potatoes, cut into ½-inch thick wedges	2 tbsp chopped fresh parsley
	Sea salt to taste

Directions:
In a bowl, mix olive oil, salt, garlic powder, chili powder, and cumin. Add in potatoes and toss to coat. Arrange them on the basket and fit in the baking tray. Cook in your Instant Vortex for 20 minutes at 380 F on Air Fry function. Toss every 5 minutes. Sprinkle with parsley and serve.

756. Cabbage Flat Cakes

Ingredients:

2 or 3 green chilies finely chopped	2 cups halved cabbage leaves
1 ½ tbsp. lemon juice	3 tsp. ginger finely chopped
Salt and pepper to taste	1-2 tbsp. fresh coriander leaves
2 tbsp. garam masala	

Directions:
Mix the ingredients in a clean bowl and add water to it. Make sure that the paste is not too watery but is enough to apply on the cabbage.   Pre heat the Instant Vortex oven at 160 degrees Fahrenheit for 5 minutes. Place the French Cuisine Galettes in the fry basket and let them cook for another 25 minutes at the same temperature. Keep rolling them over to get a uniform cook. Serve either with mint sauce or ketchup.

757. Hearty Roasted Veggie Salad

Servings: 2   Cooking Time: 20 Minutes

Ingredients:

1 potato, chopped	¼ teaspoon sea salt
1 carrot, sliced diagonally	A handful of arugula
1 cup cherry tomatoes	A handful of baby spinach
½ small beetroot, sliced	Juice of 1 lemon
¼ onion, sliced	3 tablespoons canned chickpeas, for serving
½ teaspoon turmeric	Parmesan shavings, for serving
½ teaspoon cumin	
2 tablespoons olive oil, divided	

Directions:
Combine the potato, carrot, cherry tomatoes, beetroot, onion, turmeric, cumin, salt, and 1 tablespoon of olive oil in a large bowl and toss until well coated.   Arrange the veggies in the air fryer basket.   Put the air fryer basket on the baking pan and slide into Rack Position 2, select Roast, set temperature to 370°F (188°C) and set time to 20 minutes.   Stir the vegetables halfway through. When cooking is complete, the potatoes should be golden brown.   Let the veggies cool for 5 to 10 minutes in the oven.   Put the arugula, baby spinach, lemon juice, and remaining 1 tablespoon of olive oil in a salad bowl and stir to combine. Mix in the roasted veggies and toss well.   Scatter the chickpeas and Parmesan shavings on top and serve immediately.

758. Pizza

Ingredients:

2 tomatoes that have been deseeded and chopped	Grated pizza cheese (mozzarella cheese preferably) for topping
1 tbsp. (optional) mushrooms/corns	Use cooking oil for brushing and topping purposes
2 tsp. pizza seasoning	ingredients for topping:
Some cottage cheese that has been cut into small cubes	

(optional)   2 onions chopped
One pizza base   2 capsicums chopped

Directions:
Put the pizza base in a pre-heated Instant Vortex oven for around 5 minutes. (Pre heated to 340 Fahrenheit). Take out the base.   Pour some pizza sauce on top of the base at the center. Using a spoon spread the sauce over the base making sure that you leave some gap around the circumference. Grate some mozzarella cheese and sprinkle it over the sauce layer. Take all the vegetables mentioned in the ingredient list above and mix them in a bowl.   Add some oil and seasoning. Also add some salt and pepper according to taste. Mix them properly. Put this topping over the layer of cheese on the pizza. Now sprinkle some more grated cheese and pizza seasoning on top of this layer.   Pre heat the Instant Vortex oven at 250 Fahrenheit for around 5 minutes. Open the fry basket and place the pizza inside. Close the basket and keep the fryer at 170 degrees for another 10 minutes. If you feel that it is undercooked you may put it at the same temperature for another 2 minutes or so.

759. Cheese French Fries

Ingredients:

2 medium sized potatoes peeled and cut into thick pieces lengthwise	1 tbsp. lemon juice
1 tsp. mixed herbs	1 cup melted cheddar cheese (You could put this into a piping bag and
½ tsp. red chili flakes	1 tbsp. olive oil
A pinch of salt to taste	create a pattern of it on the fries.)

Directions:
Take all the ingredients mentioned under the heading "For the marinade" and mix them well. Now pour into a container 3 cups of water.   Add a pinch of salt into this water. Bring it to the boil. Now blanch the pieces of potato for around 5 minutes. Drain the water using a sieve. Dry the potato pieces on a towel and then place them on another dry towel. Coat these potato Oregano Fingers with the marinade made in the previous step. Pre heat the Instant Vortex oven for around 5 minutes at 300 Fahrenheit. Take out the basket of the fryer and place the potato Oregano Fingers in them.   Close the basket. Now keep the fryer at 220 Fahrenheit for 20 or 25 minutes. In between the process, toss the fries twice or thrice so that they get cooked properly. Towards the end of the cooking process (the last 2 minutes or so), sprinkle the cut coriander leaves on the fries. Add the melted cheddar cheese over the fries and serve hot.

760. Cottage Cheese French Cuisine Galette

Ingredients:

1-2 tbsp. fresh coriander leaves	2 tbsp. garam masala
2 or 3 green chilies finely chopped	2 cups grated cottage cheese
1 ½ tbsp. lemon juice	1 ½ cup coarsely

| Salt and pepper to taste | crushed peanuts |
| | 3 tsp. ginger finely chopped |

Directions:
Mix the ingredients in a clean bowl. Mold this mixture into round and flat French Cuisine Galettes. Wet the French Cuisine Galettes slightly with water. Coat each French Cuisine Galette with the crushed peanuts. Pre heat the Instant Vortex oven at 160 degrees Fahrenheit for 5 minutes. Place the French Cuisine Galettes in the fry basket and let them cook for another 25 minutes at the same temperature. Keep rolling them over to get a uniform cook. Serve either with mint sauce or ketchup.

761. Vegetable Spring Rolls

Servings: 4   Cooking Time: 15 Minutes
Ingredients:

½ cabbage head, grated	1 tsp soy sauce
2 carrots, grated	1 tsp sesame seeds
1 tsp minced ginger	½ tsp salt
1 tsp minced garlic	1 tsp olive oil
1 tsp sesame oil	1 package spring roll wrappers

Directions:
Combine all ingredients except for the wrappers in a large bowl. Divide the mixture between the spring roll wrappers and roll them up. Arrange on a greased baking tray and cook in your Instant Vortex for 5 minutes on Bake function at 370 F. Serve.

762. Cottage Cheese Best Homemade Croquette(2)

Ingredients:

1 big capsicum (Cut this capsicum into big cubes)	4 tsp. fennel
	1 small onion
1 onion (Cut it into quarters. Now separate the layers carefully.)	2 tbsp. ginger-garlic paste
	6-7 garlic flakes (optional)
5 tbsp. gram flour	3 tbsp. lemon juice
A pinch of salt to taste	2 cups cottage cheese cut into slightly thick and long pieces (similar to French fries)
2 cup fresh green coriander	
½ cup mint leaves	Salt

Directions:
Take a clean and dry container. Put into it the coriander, mint, fennel, and ginger, onion/garlic, salt and lemon juice. Mix them. Pour the mixture into a grinder and blend until you get a thick paste. Now move on to the cottage cheese pieces. Slit these pieces almost till the end and leave them aside. Now stuff all the pieces with the paste that was obtained from the previous step. Now leave the stuffed cottage cheese aside. Take the sauce and add to it the gram flour and some salt. Mix them together properly. Rub this mixture all over the stuffed cottage cheese pieces. Now leave the cottage cheese aside. Now, to the leftover sauce, add the capsicum and onions. Apply the sauce generously on each of the pieces of capsicum and onion. Now take satay sticks and arrange the cottage cheese pieces and vegetables on separate sticks. Pre heat the Instant Vortex oven at 290 Fahrenheit for around 5 minutes. Open the basket. Arrange the satay sticks properly. Close the basket. Keep the sticks with the cottage cheese at 180 degrees for around half an hour while the sticks with the vegetables are to be kept at the same temperature for only 7 minutes. Turn the sticks in between so that one side does not get burnt and also to provide a uniform cook.

763. Cauliflower Gnocchi's

Ingredients:

2 tbsp. oil	2 tsp. vinegar
2 tsp. ginger-garlic paste	½ tsp. salt
2 tsp. soya sauce	5 tbsp. water
1 ½ cup all-purpose flour	2 cups grated cauliflower

Directions:
Squeeze the dough and cover it with plastic wrap and set aside. Next, cook the ingredients for the filling and try to ensure that the cauliflower is covered well with the sauce. Roll the dough and place the filling in the center. Now, wrap the dough to cover the filling and pinch the edges together. Pre heat the Instant Vortex oven at 200° F for 5 minutes. Place the gnocchi's in the fry basket and close it. Let them cook at the same temperature for another 20 minutes. Recommended sides are chili sauce or ketchup.

764. Carrots & Shallots With Yogurt

Servings: 4   Cooking Time: 25 Minutes
Ingredients:

2 tsp olive oil	2 garlic cloves, minced
2 shallots, chopped	
3 carrots, sliced	3 tbsp parsley, chopped
Salt to taste	
¼ cup yogurt	

Directions:
In a bowl, mix sliced carrots, salt, garlic, shallots, parsley, and yogurt. Sprinkle with oil. Place the veggies in the basket and press Start. Cook for 15 minutes on AirFry function at 370 F. Serve with basil and garlic mayo.

765. Okra Spicy Lemon Kebab

Ingredients:

3 tsp. lemon juice	5 green chilies- roughly chopped
2 tsp. garam masala	
4 tbsp. chopped coriander	1 ½ tbsp. ginger paste
3 tbsp. cream	
3 tbsp. chopped capsicum	1 ½ tsp. garlic paste
3 eggs	1 ½ tsp. salt
2 cups sliced okra	2 ½ tbsp. white sesame seeds
3 onions chopped	

Directions:

Grind the ingredients except for the egg and form a smooth paste. Coat the okra in the paste. Now, beat the eggs and add a little salt to it. Dip the coated vegetables in the egg mixture and then transfer to the sesame seeds and coat the okra well. Place the vegetables on a stick. Pre heat the Instant Vortex oven at 160 degrees Fahrenheit for around 5 minutes. Place the sticks in the basket and let them cook for another 25 minutes at the same temperature. Turn the sticks over in between the cooking process to get a uniform cook.

---

766. Sweet And Spicy Broccoli

Servings: 4   Cooking Time: 15 To 20 Minutes

Ingredients:

½ teaspoon olive oil, plus more for greasing	1½ tablespoons soy sauce
1 pound (454 g) fresh broccoli, cut into florets	2 teaspoons hot sauce or sriracha
½ tablespoon minced garlic	1½ teaspoons honey
Salt, to taste	1 teaspoon white vinegar
Sauce:	Freshly ground black pepper, to taste

Directions:

Grease the air fryer basket with olive oil. Add the broccoli florets, ½ teaspoon of olive oil, and garlic to a large bowl and toss well. Season with salt to taste. Put the broccoli in the basket in a single layer. Put the air fryer basket on the baking pan and slide into Rack Position 2, select Air Fry, set temperature to 400°F (205°C), and set time to 15 minutes. Stir the broccoli florets three times during cooking. Meanwhile, whisk together all the ingredients for the sauce in a small bowl until well incorporated. If the honey doesn't incorporate well, microwave the sauce for 10 to 20 seconds until the honey is melted. When cooking is complete, the broccoli should be lightly browned and crispy. Continue cooking for 5 minutes, if desired. Remove from the oven to a serving bowl. Pour over the sauce and toss to combine. Add more salt and pepper, if needed. Serve warm.

---

767. Stuffed Capsicum Baskets

Ingredients:

1 green chili finely chopped	For filling:
2 or 3 large potatoes boiled and mashed	1 medium onion finely chopped
1 ½ tbsp. chopped coriander leaves	1 tsp. cumin powder
1 tsp. fenugreek	Salt and pepper to taste
1 tsp. dried mango powder	3 tbsp. grated cheese
3-4 long capsicum	1 tsp. red chili flakes
½ tsp. salt	½ tsp. oregano
½ tsp. pepper powder	½ tsp. basil
	½ tsp. parsley

Directions:

Take all the ingredients under the heading "Filling" and mix them together in a bowl. Remove the stem of the capsicum. Cut off the caps. Remove the seeds as well. Sprinkle some salt and pepper on the inside of the capsicums. Leave them aside for some time. Now fill the hollowed-out capsicums with the filling prepared but leave a small space at the top. Sprinkle grated cheese and also add the seasoning. Pre heat the Instant Vortex oven at 140 degrees Fahrenheit for 5 minutes. Put the capsicums in the fry basket and close it. Let them cook at the same temperature for another 20 minutes. Turn them over in between to prevent over cooking.

---

768. Chinese Spring Rolls

Servings: 4   Cooking Time: 15 Minutes

Ingredients:

½ head cabbage, grated	1 tsp sesame oil
2 carrots, grated	1 tsp soy sauce
1 tsp fresh ginger, minced	1 tsp sesame seeds
1 garlic clove, minced	½ tsp salt
	1 tsp olive oil
	1 package spring roll wrappers

Directions:

Combine all ingredients in a bowl. Divide the mixture between the roll sheets and roll them up; arrange on a baking tray. Press Start and cook in the Instant Vortex for 5 minutes on Bake function at 370 F.

---

769. Radish Flat Cakes

Ingredients:

1-2 tbsp. fresh coriander leaves	1 ½ tbsp. lemon juice
2 or 3 green chilies finely chopped	2 tbsp. garam masala
Salt and pepper to taste	2 cups sliced radish
	3 tsp. ginger finely chopped

Directions:

Mix the ingredients in a clean bowl and add water to it. Make sure that the paste is not too watery but is enough to apply on the radish. Pre heat the Instant Vortex oven at 160 degrees Fahrenheit for 5 minutes. Place the French Cuisine Galettes in the fry basket and let them cook for another 25 minutes at the same temperature. Keep rolling them over to get a uniform cook. Serve either with mint sauce or ketchup.

---

770. Zucchini Fried Baked Pastry

Ingredients:

1 or 2 green chilies that are finely chopped or mashed	½ tsp. cumin
1 tsp. coarsely crushed coriander	1 ½ cup all-purpose flour
1 dry red chili broken into pieces	A pinch of salt to taste
A small amount of salt (to taste)	Add as much water as required to make the dough stiff and firm

½ tsp. dried mango powder
½ tsp. red chili power.
2 tbsp. unsalted butter

3 medium zucchinis (mashed)
¼ cup boiled peas
1 tsp. powdered ginger
1-2 tbsp. coriander.

Directions:
Mix the dough for the outer covering and make it stiff and smooth. Leave it to rest in a container while making the filling. Cook the ingredients in a pan and stir them well to make a thick paste. Roll the paste out. Roll the dough into balls and flatten them. Cut them in halves and add the filling. Use water to help you fold the edges to create the shape of a cone. Pre-heat the Instant Vortex oven for around 5 to 6 minutes at 300 Fahrenheit. Place all the samosas in the fry basket and close the basket properly. Keep the Instant Vortex oven at 200 degrees for another 20 to 25 minutes. Around the halfway point, open the basket and turn the samosas over for uniform cooking. After this, fry at 250 degrees for around 10 minutes in order to give them the desired golden-brown color. Serve hot. Recommended sides are tamarind or mint sauce.

771. Cottage Cheese And Mushroom Mexican Burritos

Ingredients:
½ cup mushrooms thinly sliced
1 cup cottage cheese cut in too long and slightly thick Oregano Fingers
A pinch of salt to taste
½ tsp. red chili flakes
1 tsp. freshly ground peppercorns
½ cup pickled jalapenos
1-2 lettuce leaves shredded.
½ cup red kidney beans (soaked overnight)
½ small onion chopped
1 tbsp. olive oil
2 tbsp. tomato puree

¼ tsp. red chili powder
1 tsp. of salt to taste
4-5 flour tortillas
1 or 2 spring onions chopped finely. Also cut the greens.
Take one tomato. Remove the seeds and chop it into small pieces.
1 green chili chopped.
1 cup of cheddar cheese grated.
1 cup boiled rice (not necessary).
A few flour tortillas to put the filing in.

Directions:
Cook the beans along with the onion and garlic and mash them finely. Now, make the sauce you will need for the burrito. Ensure that you create a slightly thick sauce. For the filling, you will need to cook the ingredients well in a pan and ensure that the vegetables have browned on the outside. To make the salad, toss the ingredients together. Place the tortilla and add a layer of sauce, followed by the beans and the filling at the center. Before you roll it, you will need to place the salad on top of the filling. Pre-heat the Instant Vortex oven for around 5 minutes at 200 Fahrenheit. Open the fry basket and

keep the burritos inside. Close the basket properly. Let the Air Fryer remain at 200 Fahrenheit for another 15 minutes or so. Halfway through, remove the basket and turn all the burritos over in order to get a uniform cook.

772. Ratatouille
Servings: 6   Cooking Time: 12 Minutes
Ingredients:
1 medium zucchini, sliced ½-inch thick
1 small eggplant, peeled and sliced ½-inch thick
2 teaspoons kosher salt, divided
4 tablespoons extra-virgin olive oil, divided
1 small red bell pepper, cut into ½-inch chunks
1 small green bell pepper, cut into ½-inch chunks

3 garlic cloves, minced
1 small onion, chopped
½ teaspoon dried oregano
¼ teaspoon freshly ground black pepper
1 pint cherry tomatoes
2 tablespoons minced fresh basil
1 cup panko bread crumbs
½ cup grated Parmesan cheese (optional)

Directions:
Season one side of the zucchini and eggplant slices with ¾ teaspoon of salt. Put the slices, salted side down, on a rack set over a baking sheet. Sprinkle the other sides with ¾ teaspoon of salt. Allow to sit for 10 minutes, or until the slices begin to exude water. When ready, rinse and dry them. Cut the zucchini slices into quarters and the eggplant slices into eighths. Pour the zucchini and eggplant into a large bowl, along with 2 tablespoons of olive oil, garlic, onion, bell peppers, oregano, and black pepper. Toss to coat well. Arrange the vegetables in the air fryer basket. Put the air fryer basket on the baking pan and slide into Rack Position 2, select Roast, set temperature to 375°F (190°C), and set time to 12 minutes. Meanwhile, add the tomatoes and basil to the large bowl. Sprinkle with the remaining ½ teaspoon of salt and 1 tablespoon of olive oil. Toss well and set aside. Stir together the remaining 1 tablespoon of olive oil, panko, and Parmesan cheese (if desired) in a small bowl. After 6 minutes, remove from the oven and add the tomato mixture and stir to mix well. Scatter the panko mixture on top. Return to the oven and continue cooking for 6 minutes, or until the vegetables are softened and the topping is golden brown. Cool for 5 minutes before serving.

773. Stuffed Portobello Mushrooms With Vegetables
Servings: 4   Cooking Time: 8 Minutes
Ingredients:
4 portobello mushrooms, stem removed

½ small red onion, diced

1 tablespoon olive oil
1 tomato, diced
½ green bell pepper, diced

½ teaspoon garlic powder
Salt and black pepper, to taste
½ cup grated Mozzarella cheese

Directions:

Using a spoon to scoop out the gills of the mushrooms and discard them. Brush the mushrooms with the olive oil. In a mixing bowl, stir together the remaining ingredients except the Mozzarella cheese. Using a spoon to stuff each mushroom with the filling and scatter the Mozzarella cheese on top. Arrange the mushrooms in the air fryer basket. Put the air fryer basket on the baking pan and slide into Rack Position 2, select Roast, set temperature to 330°F (166°C) and set time to 8 minutes. When cooking is complete, the cheese should be melted. Serve warm.

---

774.   Burger Cutlet

Ingredients:

1 tbsp. fresh coriander leaves. Chop them finely
¼ tsp. red chili powder
½ cup of boiled peas
¼ tsp. cumin powder
1 large potato boiled and mashed
½ cup breadcrumbs

A pinch of salt to taste
¼ tsp. ginger finely chopped
1 green chili finely chopped
1 tsp. lemon juice
¼ tsp. dried mango powder

Directions:

Mix the ingredients together and ensure that the flavors are right. You will now make round cutlets with the mixture and roll them out well. Pre heat the Instant Vortex oven at 250 Fahrenheit for 5 minutes. Open the basket of the Fryer and arrange the cutlets in the basket. Close it carefully. Keep the fryer at 150 degrees for around 10 or 12 minutes. In between the cooking process, turn the cutlets over to get a uniform cook. Serve hot with mint sauce.

---

775.   Cottage Cheese Best Homemade Croquette(1)

Ingredients:

2 tbsp. dry fenugreek leaves
1 tsp. black salt
1 tsp. chat masala
1 tsp. garam masala powder
1 tsp. red chili powder
1 tsp. salt
2 packets cottage cheese cubed

3 drops of red color
3 tbsp. vinegar or lemon juice
2 or 3 tsp. paprika
1 tsp. black pepper
1 tsp. salt
3 tsp. ginger-garlic paste
1 cup yogurt
4 tsp. tandoori masala

Directions:

Make the first marinade and soak the cubed cottage cheese in it for four hours. While this is happening, make the second marinade and soak the cottage

cheese in it overnight to let the flavors blend. Pre heat the Instant Vortex oven at 160 degrees Fahrenheit for 5 minutes. Place the Oregano Fingers in the fry basket and close it. Let them cook at the same temperature for another 15 minutes or so. Toss the Oregano Fingers well so that they are cooked uniformly. Serve them with mint sauce.

---

776.   Zucchini Parmesan Crisps

Servings: 4   Cooking Time: 25 Minutes
Ingredients:

4 small zucchini, cut lengthwise
½ cup Parmesan cheese, grated
½ cup breadcrumbs
¼ cup melted butter

¼ cup chopped parsley
4 garlic cloves, minced
Salt and black pepper to taste

Directions:

Preheat Instant Vortex on Air Fry function to 350 F. In a bowl, mix breadcrumbs, Parmesan cheese, garlic, parsley, salt, and pepper. Stir in butter. Place the zucchinis cut-side up in a baking tray. Spread the cheese mixture onto the zucchini evenly. Cook for 13 minutes. Increase the temperature to 370 F and cook for 3 more minutes for extra crunchiness. Serve hot.

---

777. Cottage Cheese Spicy Lemon Kebab

Ingredients:

3 tsp. lemon juice
2 tbsp. coriander powder
3 tbsp. chopped capsicum
2 tbsp. peanut flour
2 cups cubed cottage cheese
3 onions chopped

5 green chilies- roughly chopped
1 ½ tbsp. ginger paste
1 ½ tsp. garlic paste
1 ½ tsp. salt
3 eggs

Directions:

Coat the cottage cheese cubes with the corn flour and mix the other ingredients in a bowl. Make the mixture into a smooth paste and coat the cheese cubes with the mixture. Beat the eggs in a bowl and add a little salt to them. Dip the cubes in the egg mixture and coat them with sesame seeds and leave them in the refrigerator for an hour. Pre heat the Instant Vortex oven at 290 Fahrenheit for around 5 minutes. Place the kebabs in the basket and let them cook for another 25 minutes at the same temperature. Turn the kebabs over in between the cooking process to get a uniform cook. Serve the kebabs with mint sauce.

---

778.   Garlicky Sesame Carrots

Servings: 4 To 6   Cooking Time: 16 Minutes
Ingredients:

1 pound (454 g) baby carrots
1 tablespoon sesame oil

Freshly ground black pepper, to taste
6 cloves garlic, peeled
3 tablespoons sesame seeds

½ teaspoon dried dill
Pinch salt

Directions:

In a medium bowl, drizzle the baby carrots with the sesame oil. Sprinkle with the dill, salt, and pepper and toss to coat well. Place the baby carrots in the air fryer basket. Put the air fryer basket on the baking pan and slide into Rack Position 2, select Roast, set temperature to 380°F (193°C), and set time to 16 minutes. After 8 minutes, remove from the oven and stir in the garlic. Return the pan to the oven and continue roasting for 8 minutes more. When cooking is complete, the carrots should be lightly browned. Remove from the oven and serve sprinkled with the sesame seeds.

779. Herbed Broccoli With Cheese

Servings: 4   Cooking Time: 18 Minutes

Ingredients:

1 large-sized head broccoli, stemmed and cut into small florets	2 teaspoons dried rosemary
2½ tablespoons canola oil	Salt and ground black pepper, to taste
2 teaspoons dried basil	⅓ cup grated yellow cheese

Directions:

Bring a pot of lightly salted water to a boil. Add the broccoli florets to the boiling water and let boil for about 3 minutes. Drain the broccoli florets well and transfer to a large bowl. Add the canola oil, basil, rosemary, salt, and black pepper to the bowl and toss until the broccoli is fully coated. Place the broccoli in the air fryer basket. Put the air fryer basket on the baking pan and slide into Rack Position 2, select Air Fry, set temperature to 390°F (199°C), and set time to 15 minutes. Stir the broccoli halfway through the cooking time. When cooking is complete, the broccoli should be crisp. Serve the broccoli warm with grated cheese sprinkled on top.

780. Chickpea Fritters

Servings: 4   Cooking Time: 10 Minutes

Ingredients:

Nonstick cooking spray	¼ tsp salt
1 cup chickpeas, cooked	¼ tsp pepper
1 onion, chopped	¼ tsp turmeric
	¼ tsp coriander

Directions:

Place the baking pan in position 2. Lightly spray the fryer basket with cooking spray. Add the onion to a food processor and pulse until finely diced. Add remaining ingredients and pulse until combined but not pureed. Form the mixture into 8 patties and place them in the fryer basket, these may need to be cooked in two batches. Place the basket in the oven and set to air fry on 350°F for 10 minutes. Cook fritters until golden brown and crispy, turning over

halfway through cooking time. Serve with your favorite dipping sauce.

781. Roasted Vegetables With Rice

Servings: 4   Cooking Time: 12 Minutes

Ingredients:

2 teaspoons melted butter	1 garlic clove, minced
1 cup chopped mushrooms	Salt and black pepper, to taste
1 cup cooked rice	2 hard-boiled eggs, grated
1 cup peas	1 tablespoon soy sauce
1 carrot, chopped	
1 red onion, chopped	

Directions:

Coat the baking pan with melted butter. Stir together the mushrooms, cooked rice, peas, carrot, onion, garlic, salt, and pepper in a large bowl until well mixed. Pour the mixture into the prepared baking pan. Slide the baking pan into Rack Position 2, select Roast, set temperature to 380°F (193°C), and set time to 12 minutes. When cooking is complete, remove from the oven. Divide the mixture among four plates. Serve warm with a sprinkle of grated eggs and a drizzle of soy sauce.

782. Panko Green Beans

Servings: 4   Cooking Time: 15 Minutes

Ingredients:

½ cup flour	1 teaspoon cayenne pepper
2 eggs	Salt and black pepper, to taste
1 cup panko bread crumbs	
½ cup grated Parmesan cheese	1½ pounds (680 g) green beans

Directions:

In a bowl, place the flour. In a separate bowl, lightly beat the eggs. In a separate shallow bowl, thoroughly combine the bread crumbs, cheese, cayenne pepper, salt, and pepper. Dip the green beans in the flour, then in the beaten eggs, finally in the bread crumb mixture to coat well. Transfer the green beans to the air fryer basket. Put the air fryer basket on the baking pan and slide into Rack Position 2, select Air Fry, set temperature to 400°F (205°C), and set time to 15 minutes. Stir the green beans halfway through the cooking time. When cooking is complete, remove from the oven to a bowl and serve.

783. Honey Chili Potatoes

Ingredients:

1 capsicum, cut into thin and long pieces (lengthwise).	2 ½ tsp. ginger-garlic paste
2 tbsp. olive oil	¼ tsp. salt
2 onions. Cut them into halves.	1 tsp. red chili sauce
1 ½ tbsp. sweet chili sauce	¼ tsp. red chili powder/black pepper
1 ½ tsp. ginger garlic paste	A few drops of edible orange food coloring
½ tbsp. red chili	2 tsp. soya sauce

sauce.
2 tbsp. tomato ketchup
3 big potatoes (Cut into strips or cubes)
2 tsp. vinegar
A pinch of black pepper powder
1-2 tsp. red chili flakes

Directions:
Create the mix for the potato Oregano Fingers and coat the chicken well with it.   Pre heat the Instant Vortex oven at 250 Fahrenheit for 5 minutes or so. Open the basket of the Fryer. Place the Oregano Fingers inside the basket. Now let the fryer stay at 290 Fahrenheit for another 20 minutes. Keep tossing the Oregano Fingers periodically through the cook to get a uniform cook.   Add the ingredients to the sauce and cook it with the vegetables till it thickens. Add the Oregano Fingers to the sauce and cook till the flavors have blended.

784.   Masala French Cuisine Galette

Ingredients:
1 ½ tbsp. lemon juice
Salt and pepper to taste
1-2 tbsp. fresh coriander leaves
2 or 3 green chilies finely chopped
2 tbsp. garam masala
2 medium potatoes boiled and mashed
1 ½ cup coarsely crushed peanuts
3 tsp. ginger finely chopped

Directions:
Mix the ingredients in a clean bowl.   Mold this mixture into round and flat French Cuisine Galettes. Wet the French Cuisine Galettes slightly with water. Coat each French Cuisine Galette with the crushed peanuts.   Pre heat the Instant Vortex oven at 160 degrees Fahrenheit for 5 minutes. Place the French Cuisine Galettes in the fry basket and let them cook for another 25 minutes at the same temperature. Keep rolling them over to get a uniform cook. Serve either with mint sauce or ketchup.

785.   Cheese-walnut Stuffed Mushrooms

Servings: 4   Cooking Time: 10 Minutes
Ingredients:
4 large portobello mushrooms
1 tablespoon canola oil
½ cup shredded Mozzarella cheese
⅓ cup minced walnuts
2 tablespoons chopped fresh parsley
Cooking spray

Directions:
Spritz the air fryer basket with cooking spray.   On a clean work surface, remove the mushroom stems. Scoop out the gills with a spoon and discard. Coat the mushrooms with canola oil. Top each mushroom evenly with the shredded Mozzarella cheese, followed by the minced walnuts.   Arrange the mushrooms in the basket.   Put the air fryer basket on the baking pan and slide into Rack Position 2, select Roast, set temperature to 350°F (180°C) and set time to 10 minutes.   When cooking is complete, the mushroom should be golden brown.   Transfer the mushrooms to a plate and sprinkle the parsley on top for garnish before serving.

786.   Mushroom Marinade Cutlet

Ingredients:
2 cup fresh green coriander
½ cup mint leaves
4 tsp. fennel
2 tbsp. ginger-garlic paste
1 small onion
6-7 flakes garlic (optional)
Salt to taste
2 cups sliced mushrooms
1 big capsicum (Cut this capsicum into big cubes)
1 onion (Cut it into quarters. Now separate the layers carefully.)
5 tbsp. gram flour
A pinch of salt to taste
3 tbsp. lemon juice

Directions:
Take a clean and dry container. Put into it the coriander, mint, fennel, and ginger, onion/garlic, salt and lemon juice. Mix them.   Pour the mixture into a grinder and blend until you get a thick paste. Slit the mushroom almost till the end and leave them aside. Now stuff all the pieces with the paste and set aside. Take the sauce and add to it the gram flour and some salt. Mix them together properly. Rub this mixture all over the stuffed mushroom. Now, to the leftover sauce, add the capsicum and onions. Apply the sauce generously on each of the pieces of capsicum and onion. Now take satay sticks and arrange the cottage cheese pieces and vegetables on separate sticks.   Pre heat the Instant Vortex oven at 290 Fahrenheit for around 5 minutes. Open the basket. Arrange the satay sticks properly. Close the basket. Keep the sticks with the mushroom at 180 degrees for around half an hour while the sticks with the vegetables are to be kept at the same temperature for only 7 minutes. Turn the sticks in between so that one side does not get burnt and also to provide a uniform cook.

787.   Asparagus Flat Cakes

Ingredients:
2 or 3 green chilies finely chopped
1 ½ tbsp. lemon juice
Salt and pepper to taste
2 tbsp. garam masala
2 cups sliced asparagus
3 tsp. ginger finely chopped
1-2 tbsp. fresh coriander leaves

Directions:
Mix the ingredients in a clean bowl and add water to it. Make sure that the paste is not too watery but is enough to apply on the asparagus.   Pre heat the Instant Vortex oven at 160 degrees Fahrenheit for 5 minutes. Place the French Cuisine Galettes in the fry basket and let them cook for another 25 minutes at the same temperature. Keep rolling them over to get a uniform cook. Serve either with mint sauce or ketchup.

788.   Cheesy Cabbage Wedges

Servings: 4   Cooking Time: 25 Minutes

Ingredients:

½ head cabbage, cut into wedges
2 cups Parmesan cheese, chopped
4 tbsp melted butter

Salt and black pepper to taste
½ cup blue cheese sauce

Directions:
Brush the cabbage wedges with butter and coat with mozzarella cheese. Place the coated wedges in the greased basket and fit in the baking tray; cook for 20 minutes at 380 F on Air Fry setting. Serve with blue cheese sauce.

789.   Masala Vegetable Skewers

Servings: 4   Cooking Time: 20 Minutes

Ingredients:

2 tbsp cornflour
1 cup canned white beans, drained
⅓ cup carrots, grated
2 potatoes, boiled and mashed
¼ cup fresh mint leaves, chopped

½ tsp garam masala powder
½ cup paneer
1 green chili
1-inch piece of fresh ginger
3 garlic cloves
Salt to taste

Directions:
Preheat Instant Vortex on AirFry function to 390 F. Place the beans, carrots, garlic, ginger, chili, paneer, and mint in a food processor and blend until smooth. Transfer to a bowl.   Add in the mashed potatoes, cornflour, salt, and garam masala powder and mix until fully incorporated. Divide the mixture into 12 equal pieces. Thread each of the pieces onto a skewer. Press Start and cook skewers for 10 minutes. Serve.

790.   Cashew Cauliflower With Yogurt Sauce

Servings: 2   Cooking Time: 12 Minutes

Ingredients:

4 cups cauliflower florets (about half a large head)
1 tablespoon olive oil
1 teaspoon curry powder
Salt, to taste
½ cup toasted, chopped cashews, for garnish
Yogurt Sauce:

¼ cup plain yogurt
2 tablespoons sour cream
1 teaspoon honey
1 teaspoon lemon juice
Pinch cayenne pepper
Salt, to taste
1 tablespoon chopped fresh cilantro, plus leaves for garnish

Directions:
In a large mixing bowl, toss the cauliflower florets with the olive oil, curry powder, and salt.   Place the cauliflower florets in the air fryer basket.   Put the air fryer basket on the baking pan and slide into Rack Position 2, select Air Fry, set temperature to 400°F (205°C) and set time to 12 minutes.   Stir the cauliflower florets twice during cooking. When cooking is complete, the cauliflower should be golden brown.   Meanwhile, mix all the ingredients for the yogurt sauce in a small bowl and whisk to combine.   Remove the cauliflower from the oven and drizzle with the yogurt sauce. Scatter the toasted cashews and cilantro on top and serve immediately.

791. Portobello Steaks

Servings: 4   Cooking Time: 20 Minutes

Ingredients:

Nonstick cooking spray
¼ cup olive oil
2 tbsp. steak seasoning, unsalted

1 rosemary stem
4 Portobello mushrooms, large caps with stems removed

Directions:
Place baking pan in position 2 and spray with cooking spray.   In a large bowl, stir together oil, steak seasoning, and rosemary.   Add mushrooms and toss to coat all sides thoroughly.   Set oven to bake on 400°F for 25 minutes. After 5 minutes, place the mushrooms on the pan and bake 20 minutes, or until mushrooms are tender. Serve immediately.

792.   Spinach Enchiladas With Mozzarella

Servings: 4   Cooking Time: 20 Minutes

Ingredients:

8 corn tortillas, warm
2 cups mozzarella cheese, shredded
1 cup ricotta cheese, crumbled
½ cup sliced onions

1 package frozen spinach
1 garlic clove, minced
½ cup sour cream
1 tbsp butter
1 can enchilada sauce

Directions:
In a saucepan, heat oil and sauté garlic and onion for 3 minutes. Stir in the spinach and cook for 5 more minutes. Remove and stir in the ricotta cheese, sour cream and some mozzarella.   Spoon ¼ cup of spinach mixture in the middle of a tortilla. Roll up and place seam side down in the basket. Repeat the process with the remaining tortillas.   Pour the enchilada sauce all over and sprinkle with the remaining mozzarella. Cook for 15 minutes at 380 F on AirFry function.

793.   Asian Tofu "meatballs"

Servings: 4   Cooking Time: 10 Minutes

Ingredients:

3 dried shitake mushrooms
Nonstick cooking spray
14 oz. firm tofu, drained & pressed
¼ cup carrots, cooked
¼ cup bamboo shoots, sliced thin
½ cup Panko bread crumbs

2 tbsp. corn starch
3 ½ tablespoon soy sauce, divided
1 tsp garlic powder
¼ tsp salt
1/8 tsp pepper
1 tbsp. olive oil
2 tbsp. garlic, diced fine
2 tbsp. ketchup
2 tsp sugar

Directions:
Place the shitake mushrooms in a bowl and add just enough water to cover. Let soak 20 minutes until soft. Drain well and chop.   Place the baking pan in position   Lightly spray the fryer basket with cooking spray.   Place mushrooms, tofu, carrots, bamboo shoots, bread crumbs, corn starch, 1 ½ tablespoons soy sauce, and seasonings in a food processor. Pulse until thoroughly combined. Form mixture into 1-inch balls.   Place balls in fryer basket, these may need to be cooked in batches, and place in oven. Set to air fry on 380°F for 10 minutes.

Turn the balls around halfway through cooking time. Heat oil in a saucepan over medium heat. Add garlic and cook 1 minute. Stir in remaining soy sauce, ketchup, and sugar. Bring to a simmer and cook until sauce thickens, 3-5 minutes. When the meatballs are done, add them to sauce and stir to coat. Serve immediately.

794. Cabbage Fritters(1)

Ingredients:

1-2 tbsp. fresh coriander leaves	2 tbsp. garam masala
2 or 3 green chilies finely chopped	2 cups cabbage
1 ½ tbsp. lemon juice	1 ½ cup coarsely crushed peanuts
Salt and pepper to taste	3 tsp. ginger finely chopped

Directions:
Mix the ingredients in a clean bowl. Mold this mixture into round and flat fritters. Wet the fritters slightly with water. Coat each fritter with the crushed peanuts. Pre heat the Instant Vortex oven at 160 degrees Fahrenheit for 5 minutes. Place the fritters in the fry basket and let them cook for another 25 minutes at the same temperature. Keep rolling them over to get a uniform cook. Serve either with mint sauce or ketchup.

795. Masala French Fries

Ingredients:

2 medium sized potatoes peeled and cut into thick pieces lengthwise	1 tbsp. lemon juice
	½ tsp. red chili flakes
1 tbsp. olive oil	A pinch of salt to taste
1 tsp. mixed herbs	

Directions:
Boil the potatoes and blanch them. Cut the potato into Oregano Fingers. Mix the ingredients for the marinade and add the potato Oregano Fingers to it making sure that they are coated well. Pre heat the Instant Vortex oven for around 5 minutes at 300 Fahrenheit. Take out the basket of the fryer and place the potato Oregano Fingers in them. Close the basket. Now keep the fryer at 200 Fahrenheit for 20 or 25 minutes. In between the process, toss the fries twice or thrice so that they get cooked properly.

796. Yam Spicy Lemon Kebab

Ingredients:

2 tsp. garam masala	3 onions chopped
4 tbsp. chopped coriander	5 green chilies- roughly chopped
3 tbsp. cream	1 ½ tbsp. ginger paste
3 tbsp. chopped capsicum	
3 eggs	1 ½ tsp. garlic paste
2 ½ tbsp. white sesame seeds	1 ½ tsp. salt
2 cups sliced yam	3 tsp. lemon juice

Directions:
Grind the ingredients except for the egg and form a smooth paste. Coat the yam in the paste. Now, beat the eggs and add a little salt to it. Dip the coated vegetables in the egg mixture and then transfer to the sesame seeds and coat the yam well. Place the vegetables on a stick. Pre heat the Instant Vortex

oven at 160 degrees Fahrenheit for around 5 minutes. Place the sticks in the basket and let them cook for another 25 minutes at the same temperature. Turn the sticks over in between the cooking process to get a uniform cook.

797. Cheese & Vegetable Pizza

Servings: 1   Cooking Time: 15 Minutes
Ingredients:

1 tbsp tomato paste	4 red onion rings
¼ cup mozzarella cheese, grated	½ green bell pepper, chopped
1 tbsp sweet corn, cooked	3 cherry tomatoes, quartered
4 zucchini slices	1 tortilla
4 eggplant slices	¼ tsp oregano

Directions:
Preheat Instant Vortex on Pizza function to 350 F. Spread the tomato paste on the tortilla. Top with zucchini and eggplant slices first, then green peppers, and onion rings. Arrange the cherry tomatoes on top and scatter the corn. Sprinkle with oregano and top with mozzarella cheeses. Press Start and cook for 10-12 minutes. Serve warm.

798. Broccoli Momo's Recipe

Ingredients:

2 tbsp. oil	2 tsp. vinegar
2 tsp. ginger-garlic paste	½ tsp. salt
2 tsp. soya sauce	5 tbsp. water
1 ½ cup all-purpose flour	2 cups grated broccoli

Directions:
Squeeze the dough and cover it with plastic wrap and set aside. Next, cook the ingredients for the filling and try to ensure that the broccoli is covered well with the sauce. Roll the dough and cut it into a square. Place the filling in the center. Now, wrap the dough to cover the filling and pinch the edges together. Pre heat the Instant Vortex oven at 200° F for 5 minutes. Place the gnocchi's in the fry basket and close it. Let them cook at the same temperature for another 20 minutes. Recommended sides are chili sauce or ketchup.

799. Cauliflower French Cuisine Galette

Ingredients:

3 tsp. ginger finely chopped	Salt and pepper to taste
1-2 tbsp. fresh coriander leaves	2 tbsp. garam masala
2 or 3 green chilies finely chopped	2 cups cauliflower
1 ½ tbsp. lemon juice	1 ½ cup coarsely crushed peanuts

Directions:
Mix the ingredients in a clean bowl. Mold this mixture into round and flat French Cuisine Galettes. Wet the French Cuisine Galettes slightly with water. Coat each French Cuisine Galette with the crushed peanuts. Pre heat the Instant Vortex oven at 160 degrees Fahrenheit for 5 minutes. Place the French Cuisine Galettes in the fry basket and let them cook for another 25 minutes at the same temperature.

Keep rolling them over to get a uniform cook. Serve either with mint sauce or ketchup.

800. Garlicky Fennel Cabbage Steaks

Servings: 3   Cooking Time: 25 Minutes
Ingredients:

1 cabbage head	2 tbsp olive oil
1 tbsp garlic paste	½ tsp black pepper
1 tsp salt	2 tsp fennel seeds

Directions:
Preheat Instant Vortex on Air Fry function to 350 F. Slice the cabbage into 1 ½-inch slices. In a small bowl, combine all the other ingredients; brush cabbage with the mixture. Arrange the steaks on a greased baking dish and cook for 15 minutes, flipping once. Serve.

801. Vegan Meatloaf

Servings: 8   Cooking Time: 65 Minutes
Ingredients:

Nonstick cooking spray	3 tbsp. vegan Worcestershire sauce
3 1/3 cups chickpeas, cooked	3 tbsp. soy sauce, divided
1 onion, chopped fine	2 tbsp. olive oil
2 stalks celery, chopped	2 tbsp. flax seeds, ground
2 carrots, chopped fine	¼ cup + 2 tbsp. tomato paste
2 cloves garlic diced fine	1 tsp liquid smoke
2 cups panko bread crumbs	¼ tsp pepper
½ cup almond milk, unsweetened	2 tbsp. maple syrup
	2 tbsp. apple cider vinegar
	1 tsp paprika

Directions:
Place rack in position   Lightly spray a 9-inch loaf pan with cooking spray.   Place chickpeas, onion, celery, carrots, cloves, bread crumbs, milk, Worcestershire, 2 tablespoons soy sauce, oil, flax seeds, 2 tablespoons tomato paste, liquid smoke, and pepper in a food processor, you may need to do this in batches. Pulse until ingredients are combined but don't over blend. Transfer each batch to a large bowl, then mix together.   Set oven to bake on 375°F for 35 minutes.   Press mixture into the prepared pan. After the oven has preheated 5 minutes, add loaf pan to the oven and bake 30 minutes.   In a small bowl, whisk together remaining tomato paste and soy sauce, along with the syrup, vinegar, and paprika until smooth. When the timer goes off, remove the loaf from the oven. Spoon glaze over top and bake another 20-25 minutes. Let cool 10 minutes before slicing and serving.

802. Parmesan Coated Green Beans

Servings: 4   Cooking Time: 20 Minutes
Ingredients:

1 cup panko breadcrumbs	1 tsp cayenne pepper powder
2 whole eggs, beaten	1 ½ pounds green beans
½ cup Parmesan cheese, grated	Salt to taste
½ cup flour	

Directions:
Preheat Instant Vortex on AirFry function to 380 F. In a bowl, mix breadcrumbs, Parmesan cheese, cayenne pepper powder, salt, and pepper. Flour the green beans and dip them in eggs. Dredge beans in the Parmesan-panko mix. Place in the cooking basket and cook for 15 minutes Serve.

803. Mushroom Pops

Ingredients:

1 tsp. dry basil	1 ½ tsp. garlic paste
1 tsp. lemon juice	Salt and pepper to taste
1 tsp. red chili flakes	
1 cup whole mushrooms	1 tsp. dry oregano

Directions:
Add the ingredients into a separate bowl and mix them well to get a consistent mixture.   Dip the mushrooms in the above mixture and leave them aside for some time.   Pre heat the Instant Vortex oven at 180° C for around 5 minutes. Place the coated cottage cheese pieces in the fry basket and close it properly. Let them cook at the same temperature for 20 more minutes. Keep turning them over in the basket so that they are cooked properly. Serve with tomato ketchup.

804. Potato Fries With Ketchup

Servings: 2   Cooking Time: 20 Minutes
Ingredients:

2 potatoes	Salt and black pepper to taste
1 tbsp ketchup	
2 tbsp olive oil	

Directions:
Use a spiralizer to spiralize the potatoes. In a bowl, mix olive oil, salt, and pepper. Drizzle the potatoes with the oil mixture. Place them in the basket and press Start. Cook for 15 minutes on AirFry function at 360 F. Serve with ketchup or mayonnaise.

805. Palak French Cuisine Galette

Ingredients:

1-2 tbsp. fresh coriander leaves	2 tbsp. garam masala
2 or 3 green chilies finely chopped	2 cups Palak leaves
1 ½ tbsp. lemon juice	1 ½ cup coarsely crushed peanuts
Salt and pepper to taste	3 tsp. ginger finely chopped

Directions:
Mix the ingredients in a clean bowl.   Mold this mixture into round and flat French Cuisine Galettes. Wet the French Cuisine Galettes slightly with water. Coat each French Cuisine Galette with the crushed peanuts.   Pre heat the Instant Vortex oven at 160 degrees Fahrenheit for 5 minutes. Place the French Cuisine Galettes in the fry basket and let them cook for another 25 minutes at the same temperature. Keep rolling them over to get a uniform cook. Serve either with mint sauce or ketchup.

Snacks And Desserts Recipes

806. Baked Plums

Servings: 6   Cooking Time: 20 Minutes

Ingredients:

6 plums, cut into wedges	½ teaspoon cinnamon powder
1 teaspoon ginger, ground	Zest of 1 lemon, grated
2 tablespoons water	10 drops stevia

Directions:
In a pan that fits the air fryer, combine the plums with the rest of the ingredients, toss gently, put the pan in the air fryer and cook at 360 degrees F for 20 minutes.   Serve cold.

807. Orange Citrus Blend

Ingredients:

3 tbsp. powdered sugar	2 persimmons (sliced)
3 tbsp. unsalted butter	2 cups milk
2 oranges (sliced)	2 cups almond flour
	2 tbsp. custard powder

Directions:
Boil the milk and the sugar in a pan and add the custard powder followed by the almond flour and stir till you get a thick mixture. Add the sliced fruits to the mixture.   Preheat the fryer to 300 Fahrenheit for five minutes. Place the dish in the basket and reduce the temperature to 250 Fahrenheit. Cook for ten minutes and set aside to cool.

808. Autumn Walnut Crisp

Servings: 8   Cooking Time: 15 Minutes

Ingredients:

1 cup walnuts	½ cup swerve
1/2 cup swerve	
Topping:	½ teaspoon ground cardamom
1 ½ cups almond flour	A pinch of salt
1/2 cup coconut flour	1 stick butter, cut into pieces
1 teaspoon crystallized ginger	

Directions:
Place walnuts and 1/2 cup of swerve in a baking pan lightly greased with nonstick cooking spray.   In a mixing dish, thoroughly combine all the topping ingredients. Sprinkle the topping ingredients over the walnut layer.   Bake in the preheated Air Fryer at 330 degrees F for 35 minutes.

809. Tasty Pumpkin Cookies

Servings: 27   Cooking Time: 25 Minutes

Ingredients:

1 egg	1 tsp liquid stevia
2 cups almond flour	1/2 tsp pumpkin pie spice
1/2 tsp baking	

powder

1 tsp vanilla

1/2 cup butter

1/2 cup pumpkin puree

Directions:
Fit the Instant Vortex oven with the rack in position In a large bowl, add all ingredients and mix until well combined.   Make cookies from mixture and place onto a parchment-lined baking pan.   Set to bake at 300 F for 30 minutes. After 5 minutes place the baking dish in the preheated oven.   Serve and enjoy.

810. Coconut Chip Mixed Berry Crisp

Servings: 6   Cooking Time: 20 Minutes

Ingredients:

1 tablespoon butter, melted	½ teaspoon ground cinnamon
12 ounces (340 g) mixed berries	¼ teaspoon ground cloves
1/3 cup granulated Swerve	¼ teaspoon grated nutmeg
1 teaspoon pure vanilla extract	½ cup coconut chips, for garnish

Directions:
Coat the baking pan with melted butter.   Put the remaining ingredients except the coconut chips in the prepared baking pan.   Slide the baking pan into Rack Position 1, select Convection Bake, set temperature to 330°F (166°C), and set time to 20 minutes.   When cooking is complete, remove from the oven. Serve garnished with the coconut chips.

811. Yummy Scalloped Pineapple

Servings: 6   Cooking Time: 35 Minutes

Ingredients:

3 eggs, lightly beaten	4 cups of bread cubes
8 oz can crushed pineapple, un-drained	1/4 cup milk
	1/2 cup butter, melted
2 cups of sugar	

Directions:
Fit the Instant Vortex oven with the rack in position In a mixing bowl, whisk eggs with milk, butter, crushed pineapple, and sugar.   Add bread cubes and stir well to coat.   Transfer mixture to the greased baking dish.   Set to bake at 350 F for 40 minutes. After 5 minutes place the baking dish in the preheated oven.   Serve and enjoy.

812. Vanilla And Oats Pudding

Ingredients:

2 tbsp. custard powder	3 tbsp. unsalted butter
3 tbsp. powdered	2 cups milk
	1 cup oats

sugar
2 cups vanilla powder

Directions:
Boil the milk and the sugar in a pan and add the custard powder followed by the vanilla powder followed by the oats and stir till you get a thick mixture. Preheat the fryer to 300 Fahrenheit for five minutes. Place the dish in the basket and reduce the temperature to 250 Fahrenheit. Cook for ten minutes and set aside to cool.

813.   Caramel Apple Cake

Servings: 12   Cooking Time: 55 Minutes

Ingredients:

1 cup coconut oil, melted	1 tsp baking soda
2 cups sugar	3 cups apples, peeled & chopped
3 eggs	½ cup butter
1 ½ tsp vanilla	1 cup brown sugar
2 cups flour	¼ cup milk
1 tsp salt	

Directions:
Place rack in position   Spray an 8x11-inch pan with cooking spray.   In a large bowl, beat oil, sugar, eggs, and vanilla until smooth.   Add flour, salt, and baking soda and stir to combine. Fold in apples. Set oven to bake on 350°F for 60 minutes.   Pour batter in prepared pan. After oven has preheated for 5 minutes, put cake in oven and bake 55-60 minutes, or until it passes the toothpick test. Let cool completely.   In a saucepan, over medium heat, combine butter, brown sugar, and milk. Stirring constantly, bring to a boil. Let boil, without stirring, 3 minutes. Remove from heat and spread over top of cake. Let sit 1 hour before serving.

814.   Avocado Bites

Servings: 4   Cooking Time: 15 Minutes

Ingredients:

4 avocados, peeled, pitted and cut into wedges	1 egg; whisked
	A pinch of salt and black pepper
1 ½ cups almond meal	Cooking spray

Directions:
Put the egg in a bowl and the almond meal in another.   Season avocado wedges with salt and pepper, coat them in egg and then in meal almond Arrange the avocado bites in your air fryer's basket, grease them with cooking spray and cook at 400°F for 8 minutes. Serve as a snack right away

815.   Yogurt Pumpkin Bread

Servings: 4   Cooking Time: 15 Minutes

Ingredients:

2 large eggs	4 tablespoons honey
8 tablespoons pumpkin puree	2 tablespoons vanilla essence
6 tablespoons banana flour	Pinch of ground nutmeg 6
4 tablespoons plain Greek yogurt	tablespoons oats

Directions:
In a bowl, add in all the ingredients except oats and with a hand mixer, mix until smooth.   Add the oats and with a fork, mix well.   Grease and flour a loaf pan.   Place the mixture into the prepared loaf pan.   Press "Power Button" of Air Fry Oven and turn the dial to select the "Air Crisp" mode.   Press the Time button and again turn the dial to set the cooking time to 15 minutes.   Now push the Temp button and rotate the dial to set the temperature at 360 degrees F.   Press "Start/Pause" button to start.   When the unit beeps to show that it is preheated, open the lid.   Arrange the pan in "Air Fry Basket" and insert in the oven.   Carefully, invert the bread onto wire rack to cool completely before slicing.   Cut the bread into desired-sized slices and serve.

816.   Spicy Cauliflower Florets

Servings: 4   Cooking Time: 15 Minutes

Ingredients:

1 medium cauliflower head, cut into florets	1/4 tsp cayenne
	1/4 tsp chili powder
1/2 tsp old bay seasoning	1 tbsp garlic, minced
	3 tbsp olive oil
1/4 tsp paprika	Pepper
	Salt

Directions:
Fit the Instant Vortex oven with the rack in position 2.   In a bowl, toss cauliflower with remaining ingredients.   Add cauliflower florets in air fryer basket then place air fryer basket in baking pan. Place a baking pan on the oven rack. Set to air fry at 400 F for 15 minutes.   Serve and enjoy.

817.   Tapioca Pudding

Ingredients:

3 tbsp. powdered sugar	2 cups tapioca pearls
	2 cups milk
3 tbsp. unsalted butter	2 tbsp. custard powder

Directions:
Boil the milk and the sugar in a pan and add the custard powder followed by the tapioca pearls and stir till you get a thick mixture.   Preheat the fryer to 300 Fahrenheit for five minutes. Place the dish in the basket and reduce the temperature to 250 Fahrenheit. Cook for ten minutes and set aside to cool.

818.   Perfectly Puffy Coconut Cookies

Servings: 12   Cooking Time: 15 Minutes

Ingredients:

1 cup butter, melted	1 cup coconut flour
1 ¾ cups granulated swerve	1 ¼ cups almond flour
3 eggs	1/2 teaspoon baking powder
2 tablespoons coconut milk	1/2 teaspoon baking soda
1 teaspoon coconut extract	1/2 teaspoon fine

1 teaspoon vanilla extract

table salt

1/2 cups coconut chips, unsweetened

Directions:
Begin by preheating your Air Fryer to 350 degrees F. In the bowl of an electric mixer, beat the butter and swerve until well combined. Now, add the eggs one at a time, and mix well; add the coconut milk, coconut extract, and vanilla; beat until creamy and uniform. Mix the flour with baking powder, baking soda, and salt. Then, stir the flour mixture into the butter mixture and stir until everything is well incorporated. Finally, fold in the coconut chips and mix again. Scoop out 1 tablespoon size balls of the batter on a cookie pan, leaving 2 inches between each cookie. Bake for 10 minutes or until golden brown, rotating the pan once or twice through the cooking time. Let your cookies cool on wire racks.

819. Eggless Brownies

Servings: 8   Cooking Time: 40 Minutes
Ingredients:

1/4 cup walnuts, chopped

1/3 cup cocoa powder

2 tsp baking powder

1 cup all-purpose flour

1/2 cup chocolate chips

1 cup of sugar

2 tsp vanilla

1 tbsp milk

3/4 cup yogurt

1/2 cup butter, melted

1/4 tsp salt

Directions:
Fit the Instant Vortex oven with the rack in position In a large mixing bowl, sift flour, cocoa powder, baking powder, and salt. Mix well and set aside. In another bowl, add butter, vanilla, milk, and yogurt and whisk until well combined. Add flour mixture into the butter mixture and mix until just combined. Fold in walnuts and chocolate chips. Pour batter into the prepared baking dish. Set to bake at 350 F for 45 minutes. After 5 minutes place the baking dish in the preheated oven. Slice and serve.

820. Tasty Jalapeno Poppers

Servings: 4   Cooking Time: 13 Minutes
Ingredients:

4 jalapeno peppers, slice in half and deseeded

4 oz goat cheese, crumbled

1/4 tsp chili powder

2 tbsp chunky salsa

Pepper

Salt

Directions:
Fit the Instant Vortex oven with the rack in position 2. In a small bowl, mix together cheese, chunky salsa, chili powder, pepper, and salt. Stuff cheese mixture into each jalapeno half and place in the air fryer basket then place the air fryer basket in the baking pan. Place a baking pan on the oven rack. Set to air fry at 350 F for 13 minutes. Serve and enjoy.

821. Margherita Pizza

Servings: 4   Cooking Time: 18 Minutes
Ingredients:

1 whole-wheat pizza crust

1/2 cup mozzarella cheese, grated

1/2 cup can tomatoes

2 tbsp olive oil

3 Roma tomatoes, sliced

10 basil leaves

Directions:
Fit the Instant Vortex oven with the rack in position Roll out whole wheat pizza crust using a rolling pin. Make sure the crust is ½-inch thick. Sprinkle olive oil on top of pizza crust. Spread can tomatoes over pizza crust. Arrange sliced tomatoes and basil on pizza crust. Sprinkle grated cheese on top. Place pizza on top of the oven rack and set to bake at 425 F for 23 minutes. Slice and serve.

822. Tasty Potato Wedges

Servings: 4   Cooking Time: 15 Minutes
Ingredients:

2 medium potatoes, cut into wedges

1/4 tsp garlic powder

1/4 tsp pepper

1/2 tsp paprika

1 1/2 tbsp olive oil

1/8 tsp cayenne

1 tsp sea salt

Directions:
Fit the Instant Vortex oven with the rack in position 2. Soak potato wedges into the water for 30 minutes. Drain well and pat dry with a paper towel. In a bowl, toss potato wedges with remaining ingredients. Place potato wedges in the air fryer basket then place an air fryer basket in the baking pan. Place a baking pan on the oven rack. Set to air fry at 400 F for 15 minutes. Serve and enjoy.

823. Chocolate Ramekins

Servings: 4   Cooking Time: 12 Minutes
Ingredients:

½ cup butter

2/3 cup dark chocolate, chopped

2 teaspoons fresh orange rind, finely grated

¼ cup caster sugar

2 medium eggs

¼ cup fresh orange juice

2 tablespoons self-rising flour

Directions:
In a microwave-safe bowl, add the butter, and chocolate and microwave on high heat for about 2 minutes or until melted completely, stirring after every 30 seconds. Remove from microwave and stir the mixture until smooth. Add the sugar, and eggs and whisk until frothy. Add the orange rind and juice, followed by flour and mix until well combined. Divide mixture into 4 greased ramekins about ¾ full. Press "Power Button" of Air Fry Oven and turn the dial to select the "Air Fry" mode. Press the Time button and again turn the dial to set the cooking time to 12 minutes. Now push the Temp button and rotate the dial to set the temperature at 355 degrees F. Press "Start/Pause"

button to start. When the unit beeps to show that it is preheated, open the lid. Arrange the ramekins in "Air Fry Basket" and insert in the oven. Place the ramekins set aside to cool completely before serving.

824. Banana Butter Brownie

Servings: 4   Cooking Time: 16 Minutes
Ingredients:

1 scoop protein powder	2 tbsp cocoa powder
1 cup bananas, overripe	1/2 cup almond butter, melted

Directions:
Fit the Instant Vortex oven with the rack in position Add all ingredients into the blender and blend until smooth. Pour batter into the greased cake pan. Set to bake at 325 F for 21 minutes. After 5 minutes place the cake pan in the preheated oven. Serve and enjoy.

825. Mixed Berries With Pecan Streusel Topping

Servings: 3   Cooking Time: 17 Minutes
Ingredients:

½ cup mixed berries	1 egg, beaten
Cooking spray	3 tablespoons granulated Swerve
Topping:	2 tablespoons cold salted butter, cut into pieces
3 tablespoons almonds, slivered	
3 tablespoons chopped pecans	½ teaspoon ground cinnamon
2 tablespoons chopped walnuts	

Directions:
Lightly spray the baking pan with cooking spray. Make the topping: In a medium bowl, stir together the beaten egg, nuts, Swerve, butter, and cinnamon until well blended. Put the mixed berries in the bottom of the baking pan and spread the topping over the top. Slide the baking pan into Rack Position 1, select Convection Bake, set temperature to 340ºF (171ºC), and set time to 17 minutes. When cooking is complete, the fruit should be bubbly and topping should be golden brown. Allow to cool for 5 to 10 minutes before serving.

826. Delicious Jalapeno Poppers

Servings: 10   Cooking Time: 7 Minutes
Ingredients:

10 jalapeno peppers, cut in half, remove seeds & membranes	4 oz cream cheese
	1/4 tsp paprika
	1 tsp ground cumin
1/2 cup cheddar cheese, shredded	1 tsp salt

Directions:
Fit the Instant Vortex oven with the rack in position 2. In a small bowl, mix together cream cheese, cheddar cheese, cumin, paprika, and salt. Stuff cream cheese mixture into each jalapeno half. Place stuffed jalapeno peppers in air fryer basket then place air fryer basket in baking pan. Place a

baking pan on the oven rack. Set to air fry at 350 F for 7 minutes. Serve and enjoy.

827. Pancetta And Asparagus With Fried Egg

Ingredients:

½ lb. asparagus, tough ends broken off	1 Tbsp olive oil
Salt and pepper, to taste	¼ pound pancetta
	3 small shallots, sliced thin
2 eggs	

Directions:
Heat olive oil in Instant Vortex oven. Fry the pancetta, stirring frequently. Transfer to a plate. Add shallots and cook for 2 minutes. Add asparagus pieces and saute for several minutes. Sprinkle with salt and pepper and continue to watch closely that asparagus is browned and cooked through. Add pancetta back to the pan and stir together. Transfer to a plate. Add a little oil if necessary and fry an egg in pan. Top asparagus pancetta mixture with fried egg and season with salt and pepper.

828. Crispy Green Tomatoes With Horseradish

Servings: 4   Cooking Time: 13 Minutes
Ingredients:

2 eggs	¼ cup sour cream
¼ cup buttermilk	¼ cup mayonnaise
½ cup bread crumbs	2 teaspoons prepared horseradish
½ cup cornmeal	
¼ teaspoon salt	½ teaspoon lemon juice
1½ pounds (680 g) firm green tomatoes, cut into ¼-inch slices	
	½ teaspoon Worcestershire sauce
Cooking spray	
Horseradish Sauce:	⅛ teaspoon black pepper

Directions:
Spritz the air fryer basket with cooking spray. Set aside. In a small bowl, whisk together all the ingredients for the horseradish sauce until smooth. Set aside. In a shallow dish, beat the eggs and buttermilk. In a separate shallow dish, thoroughly combine the bread crumbs, cornmeal, and salt. Dredge the tomato slices, one at a time, in the egg mixture, then roll in the bread crumb mixture until evenly coated. Place the tomato slices in the basket in a single layer. Spray them with cooking spray. Put the air fryer basket on the baking pan and slide into Rack Position 2, select Air Fry, set temperature to 390ºF (199ºC), and set time to 13 minutes. Flip the tomato slices halfway through the cooking time. When cooking is complete, the tomato slices should be nicely browned and crisp. Remove from the oven to a platter and serve drizzled with the prepared horseradish sauce.

829. Fudgy Chocolate Brownies

Servings: 8   Cooking Time: 21 Minutes

Ingredients:

1 stick butter, melted
1 cup Swerve
2 eggs
1 cup coconut flour
½ cup unsweetened cocoa powder
2 tablespoons flaxseed meal
1 teaspoon baking powder
1 teaspoon vanilla essence
A pinch of salt
A pinch of ground cardamom
Cooking spray

Directions:

Spray the baking pan with cooking spray.   Beat together the melted butter and Swerve in a large mixing dish until fluffy. Whisk in the eggs.   Add the coconut flour, cocoa powder, flaxseed meal, baking powder, vanilla essence, salt, and cardamom and stir with a spatula until well incorporated. Spread the mixture evenly into the prepared baking pan.   Slide the baking pan into Rack Position 1, select Convection Bake, set temperature to 350°F (180°C), and set time to 21 minutes.   When cooking is complete, a toothpick inserted in the center should come out clean.   Remove from the oven and place on a wire rack to cool completely. Cut into squares and serve immediately.

830. Cheesy Zucchini Tots

Servings: 8   Cooking Time: 6 Minutes

Ingredients:

2 medium zucchini (about 12 ounces / 340 g), shredded
½ cup grated pecorino romano cheese
½ cup panko bread crumbs
1 large egg, whisked
¼ teaspoon black pepper
1 clove garlic, minced
Cooking spray

Directions:

Using your hands, squeeze out as much liquid from the zucchini as possible. In a large bowl, mix the zucchini with the remaining ingredients except the oil until well incorporated.   Make the zucchini tots: Use a spoon or cookie scoop to place tablespoonfuls of the zucchini mixture onto a lightly floured cutting board and form into 1-inch logs.   Spritz the air fryer basket with cooking spray. Place the zucchini tots in the pan.   Put the air fryer basket on the baking pan and slide into Rack Position 2, select Air Fry, set temperature to 375°F (190°C), and set time to 6 minutes.   When cooking is complete, the tots should be golden brown. Remove from the oven to a serving plate and serve warm.

831. Vanilla Chocolate Chip Cookies

Servings: 30 Cookies   Cooking Time: 22 Minutes

Ingredients:

⅓ cup (80g) organic brown sugar
⅓ cup (80g) organic cane sugar
½ cup coconut cream
1 teaspoon baking powder
4 ounces (112g) cashew-based vegan butter
1 teaspoon vanilla extract
2 tablespoons ground flaxseed
1 teaspoon baking soda
Pinch of salt
2¼ cups (220g) almond flour
½ cup (90g) dairy-free dark chocolate chips

Directions:

Line the baking pan with parchment paper.   Mix together the brown sugar, cane sugar, and butter in a medium bowl or the bowl of a stand mixer. Cream together with a mixer.   Fold in the coconut cream, vanilla, flaxseed, baking powder, baking soda, and salt. Stir well.   Add the almond flour, a little at a time, mixing after each addition until fully incorporated. Stir in the chocolate chips with a spatula.   Scoop the dough into the prepared baking pan.   Slide the baking pan into Rack Position 1, select Convection Bake, set temperature to 325°F (160°C), and set the time to 22 minutes. Bake until the cookies are golden brown.   When cooking is complete, transfer the baking pan onto a wire rack to cool completely before serving.

832. Breaded Bananas With Chocolate Sauce

Servings: 6   Cooking Time: 7 Minutes

Ingredients:

¼ cup cornstarch
¼ cup plain bread crumbs
3 bananas, halved crosswise
1 large egg, beaten
Cooking spray
Chocolate sauce, for serving

Directions:

Place the cornstarch, bread crumbs, and egg in three separate bowls.   Roll the bananas in the cornstarch, then in the beaten egg, and finally in the bread crumbs to coat well.   Spritz the air fryer basket with cooking spray.   Arrange the banana halves in the basket and mist them with cooking spray.   Put the air fryer basket on the baking pan and slide into Rack Position 2, select Air Fry, set temperature to 350°F (180°C), and set time to 7 minutes.   After about 5 minutes, flip the bananas and continue to air fry for another 2 minutes. When cooking is complete, remove the bananas from the oven to a serving plate. Serve with the chocolate sauce drizzled over the top.

833. Garlic Edamame

Servings: 4   Cooking Time: 9 Minutes

Ingredients:

1 (16-ounce / 454-g) bag frozen edamame in pods
2 tablespoon olive oil, divided
½ teaspoon salt
½ teaspoon garlic salt
¼ teaspoon freshly ground black pepper
½ teaspoon red pepper flakes (optional)

Directions:
Place the edamame in a medium bowl and drizzle with 1 tablespoon of olive oil. Toss to coat well. Stir together the garlic salt, salt, pepper, and red pepper flakes (if desired) in a small bowl. Pour the mixture into the bowl of edamame and toss until the edamame is fully coated. Grease the air fryer basket with the remaining 1 tablespoon of olive oil. Place the edamame in the greased basket. Put the air fryer basket on the baking pan and slide into Rack Position 2, select Air Fry, set temperature to 375°F (190°C), and set time to 9 minutes. Stir the edamame once halfway through the cooking time. When cooking is complete, the edamame should be crisp. Remove from the oven to a plate and serve warm.

834. Lemon Blackberries Cake(1)

Servings: 4   Cooking Time: 25 Minutes

Ingredients:

2 eggs, whisked	¼ cup almond milk
4 tablespoons swerve	
2 tablespoons ghee, melted	½ teaspoon baking powder
1 and ½ cups almond flour	1 teaspoon lemon zest, grated
1 cup blackberries, chopped	1 teaspoon lemon juice

Directions:
In a bowl, mix all the ingredients and whisk well. Pour this into a cake pan that fits the air fryer lined with parchment paper, put the pan in your air fryer and cook at 340 degrees F for 25 minutes. Cool the cake down, slice and serve.

835. Cranberry Scones

Servings: 4   Cooking Time: 10 Minutes

Ingredients:

1 cup of fresh cranberries	2 cups of flour
⅓ Cup of sugar	¼ teaspoon of salt
1 tablespoon of orange zest	¼ cup of butter, chilled and diced
¾ cup of half and half cream	¼ cup of brown sugar
¼ teaspoon of ground nutmeg	1 tablespoon of baking powder
	1 egg

Directions:
Set the Instant Vortex on Air fryer to 365 degrees F for 10 minutes. Strain nutmeg, flour, baking powder, salt, and sugar in a bowl. Blend in the cream and egg. Fold in the orange zest and cranberries to form a smooth dough. Roll the dough and cut into scones. Place the scones on the cooking tray. Insert the cooking tray in the Vortex when it displays "Add Food". Flip the sides when it displays "Turn Food". Remove from the oven when cooking time is complete. Serve warm.

836. Roasted Mixed Nuts

Servings: 6   Cooking Time: 20 Minutes

Ingredients:

2 cups mixed nuts (walnuts, pecans, and almonds)	2 tablespoons sugar
	1 teaspoon paprika
2 tablespoons egg white	1 teaspoon ground cinnamon
	Cooking spray

Directions:
Line the air fryer basket with parchment paper and spray with cooking spray. Stir together the mixed nuts, egg white, sugar, paprika, and cinnamon in a small bowl until the nuts are fully coated. Place the nuts in the basket. Put the air fryer basket on the baking pan and slide into Rack Position 2, select Roast, set temperature to 300°F (150°C), and set time to 20 minutes. Stir the nuts halfway through the cooking time. When cooking is complete, remove from the oven. Transfer the nuts to a bowl and serve warm.

837. Fried Bananas With Chocolate Sauce

Servings: 2   Cooking Time: 10 Minutes

Ingredients:

1 large egg	¼ cup cornstarch
¼ cup plain bread crumbs	Cooking oil
3 bananas, halved crosswise	Chocolate sauce (see Ingredient tip)

Directions:
Preparing the Ingredients. In a small bowl, beat the egg. In another bowl, place the cornstarch. Place the bread crumbs in a third bowl. Dip the bananas in the cornstarch, then the egg, and then the bread crumbs. Spray the air fryer rack/basket with cooking oil. Place the bananas in the basket and spray them with cooking oil. Air Frying. Cook for 5 minutes. Open the air fryer oven and flip the bananas. Cook for an additional 2 minutes. Transfer the bananas to plates. Drizzle the chocolate sauce over the bananas, and serve. You can make your own chocolate sauce using 2 tablespoons milk and ¼ cup chocolate chips. Heat a saucepan over medium-high heat. Add the milk and stir for 1 to 2 minutes. Add the chocolate chips. Stir for 2 minutes, or until the chocolate has melted.

838. Mini Crab Cakes

Ingredients:

½ cup dried bread crumbs	½ cup mayonnaise
¼ cup minced green onions	1 cup fresh cilantro leaves
3 tablespoons olive oil	½ cup chopped walnuts
1-pound canned lump crabmeat	½ cup grated Romano cheese
	2 tablespoons olive oil

Directions:
Drain crabmeat well and pick over to remove any cartilage. Set aside in large bowl. In food processor or blender, combine cilantro, walnuts, cheese, and 2

tablespoons olive oil (6 tablespoons for triple batch). Process or blend until mixture forms a paste. Stir into crabmeat.   Add bread crumbs, mayonnaise, and green onions to crab mixture. Stir to combine. Form into 2- inch patties about ½-inch thick. Flash freeze on baking sheet. When frozen solid, pack crab cakes in rigid containers, with waxed paper between the layers. Label crab cakes and freeze. Reserve remaining olive oil in pantry.   To thaw and reheat: Thaw crab cakes in refrigerator overnight. Heat 3 tablespoons olive oil (9 for triple batch) in large, heavy skillet over medium heat. Fry crab cakes until golden and hot, turning once, about 3 to 5 minutes on each side.

839.   Berry Crumble With Lemon

Servings: 6   Cooking Time: 30 Minutes
Ingredients:

12 oz fresh strawberries	5 tbsp cold butter
7 oz fresh raspberries	2 tbsp lemon juice
5 oz fresh blueberries	1 cup flour
	½ cup sugar
	1 tbsp water
	A pinch of salt

Directions:
Preheat Instant Vortex on Bake function to 360 F. Gently mash the berries, but make sure there are chunks left. Mix with the lemon juice and 2 tbsp of sugar. Place the berry mixture at the bottom of a greased cake pan. Combine the flour with salt and sugar in a bowl. Mix well.   Add the water and rub the butter with your fingers until the mixture becomes crumbled. Pour the batter over the berries. Press Start and cook for 20 minutes. Serve chilled.

840.   Olive Garlic Puffs

Ingredients:

¾ cup flour	5 tablespoons butter, softened
teaspoon pepper	
30 garlic-stuffed olives	1½ cups grated sharp Cheddar cheese
1 (3-ounce) package cream cheese, softened	1 teaspoon Worcestershire sauce

Directions:
In medium bowl, combine butter, cream cheese, and Cheddar cheese. Cream well until blended. Add Worcestershire sauce and mix until blended. Add flour and pepper and mix to form dough.   Form dough around each olive, covering olive completely. Flash freeze in single layer on baking sheets, then package in zipper-lock bags. Label bag and freeze. To reheat: Place frozen puffs on baking sheet. Bake at 400°F for 10 to 12 minutes or until hot, puffed, and golden brown.

841.   Strawberries Stew

Servings: 4   Cooking Time: 20 Minutes
Ingredients:

1-pound strawberries, halved	1 tablespoon lemon juice
4 tablespoons stevia	1 and ½ cups water

Directions:
In a pan that fits your air fryer, mix all the ingredients, toss, put it in the fryer and cook at 340 degrees F for 20 minutes.   Divide the stew into cups and serve cold.

842.   Flavorful Coconut Cake

Servings: 8   Cooking Time: 20 Minutes
Ingredients:

5 eggs, separated	1/2 tsp vanilla
1/2 cup erythritol	1/2 cup butter softened
1/4 cup coconut milk	
1/2 cup coconut flour	Pinch of salt
1/2 tsp baking powder	

Directions:
Fit the Instant Vortex oven with the rack in position Grease cake pan with butter and set aside.   In a bowl, beat sweetener and butter until combined. Add egg yolks, coconut milk, and vanilla and mix well.   Add baking powder, coconut flour, and salt and stir well.   In another bowl, beat egg whites until stiff peak forms.   Gently fold egg whites into the cake mixture.   Pour batter in a prepared cake pan.   Set to bake at 400 F for 25 minutes. After 5 minutes place the cake pan in the preheated oven. Slice and serve.

843.   Sausage And Mushroom Empanadas

Servings: 4   Cooking Time: 12 Minutes
Ingredients:

½ pound (227 g) Kielbasa smoked sausage, chopped	¼ teaspoon paprika
4 chopped canned mushrooms	Salt and black pepper, to taste
2 tablespoons chopped onion	½ package puff pastry dough, at room temperature
½ teaspoon ground cumin	1 egg, beaten
	Cooking spray

Directions:
Combine the sausage, mushrooms, onion, cumin, paprika, salt, and pepper in a bowl and stir to mix well.   Make the empanadas: Place the puff pastry dough on a lightly floured surface. Cut circles into the dough with a glass. Place 1 tablespoon of the sausage mixture into the center of each pastry circle. Fold each in half and pinch the edges to seal. Using a fork, crimp the edges. Brush them with the beaten egg and mist with cooking spray.   Spritz the air fryer basket with cooking spray.   Place the empanadas in the basket.   Put the air fryer basket on the baking pan and slide into Rack Position 2, select Air Fry, set temperature to 360°F (182°C), and set time to 12 minutes.   Flip the empanadas halfway through the cooking time.   When cooking is complete, the empanadas should be golden brown.

Remove from the oven. Allow them to cool for 5 minutes and serve hot.

844. Pita Bread Cheese Pizza

Servings: 4   Cooking Time: 6 Minutes
Ingredients:

- 1 pita bread
- ¼ cup Mozzarella cheese
- 7 slices pepperoni
- ¼ cup sausage
- 1 tablespoon yellow onion, sliced thinly
- 1 tablespoon pizza sauce
- 1 drizzle extra-virgin olive oil
- ½ teaspoon fresh garlic, minced

Directions:
Preheat the Air fryer to 350 degree F and grease an Air fryer basket.   Spread pizza sauce on the pita bread and add sausages, pepperoni, onions, garlic and cheese.   Drizzle with olive oil and place it in the Air fryer basket.   Cook for about 6 minutes and dish out to serve warm.

845. Chocolate Strawberry Cups

Servings: 8   Cooking Time: 15 Minutes
Ingredients:

- 16 strawberries; halved
- 2 tbsp. coconut oil
- 2 cups chocolate chips; melted

Directions:
In a pan that fits your air fryer, mix the strawberries with the oil and the melted chocolate chips, toss gently, put the pan in the air fryer and cook at 340°F for 10 minutes.   Divide into cups and serve cold

846. Shrimp Cheese Quiches

Ingredients:

- 1 (6-ounce) can tiny shrimp, drained
- ½ teaspoon dried marjoram leaves
- ½ teaspoon salt
- ½ teaspoon pepper
- ¾ cup shredded Havarti cheese
- 2 9-inch Pie Crusts
- ½ cup chopped leek, rinsed
- 1 tablespoon olive oil
- 2 eggs
- ½ cup cream

Directions:
Using a 2-inch cookie cutter, cut 36 rounds from pie crusts. Place each in a 1¾-inch mini muffin cup, pressing to bottom and sides. Set aside.   Sauté leek in olive oil until tender. Beat eggs with cream in medium bowl. Add drained shrimp, cooked leek, marjoram, salt, and pepper, and mix well. Sprinkle 1 teaspoon cheese into each muffin cup and fill cups with shrimp mixture. Bake at 375°F for 15 to 18 minutes or until pastry is golden and filling is set. Cool in refrigerator until cold, then freeze. Freeze in single layer on baking sheet. When frozen solid, pack in rigid containers, using waxed paper to separate layers. Label and freeze.   To reheat: Place frozen quiches on baking sheet and bake at 375°F for 8 to 11 minutes or until hot.

847. Flavorful Crab Dip

Servings: 6   Cooking Time: 15 Minutes

Ingredients:

- 6 oz crab lump meat
- 1 tbsp mayonnaise
- 1/8 tsp paprika
- 4 tsp bell pepper, diced
- 1 tbsp butter, softened
- 1 tsp parsley, chopped
- 1/4 cup sour cream
- 1 tbsp green onion, sliced
- 1/4 cup mozzarella cheese, shredded
- 4 tsp onion, chopped
- 2 oz cream cheese, softened
- 1/4 tsp salt

Directions:
Fit the Instant Vortex oven with the rack in position In a bowl, mix together cream cheese, butter, sour cream, and mayonnaise until smooth.   Add remaining ingredients and stir well.   Pour mixture into the greased baking dish.   Set to bake at 350 F for 20 minutes. After 5 minutes place the baking dish in the preheated oven.   Serve and enjoy.

848. Vanilla Brownies With Chocolate Chips

Servings: 2   Cooking Time: 25 Minutes
Ingredients:

- 1 whole egg, beaten
- ¼ cup chocolate chips
- 2 tbsp white sugar
- ⅓ cup flour
- 2 tbsp safflower oil
- 1 tsp vanilla
- ¼ cup cocoa powder

Directions:
Preheat Instant Vortex on Bake function to 320 F. In a bowl, mix the beaten egg, sugar, oil, and vanilla. In another bowl, mix cocoa powder and flour. Add in the egg mixture and stir until incorporated.   Pour the mixture into a greased baking pan and sprinkle chocolate chips on top. Press Start. Bake for 20 minutes. Chill and cut into squares to serve.

849. Arugula Artichoke Dip

Servings: 6   Cooking Time: 25 Minutes
Ingredients:

- 15 oz artichoke hearts, drained
- 1 cup cheddar cheese, shredded
- 1 tbsp onion, minced
- 1/2 cup mayonnaise
- 1 tsp Worcestershire sauce
- 3 cups arugula, chopped

Directions:
Fit the Instant Vortex oven with the rack in position Add all ingredients into the blender and blend until smooth.   Pour artichoke mixture into air fryer baking dish.   Set to bake at 400 F for 30 minutes. After 5 minutes place the baking dish in the preheated oven.   Serve and enjoy.

850. Air Fryer Pepperoni Chips

Servings: 6   Cooking Time: 8 Minutes
Ingredients:

- 6 oz pepperoni slices

Directions:
Fit the Instant Vortex oven with the rack in position 2.   Place pepperoni slices in an air fryer basket then place an air fryer basket in baking pan.   Place

a baking pan on the oven rack. Set to air fry at 360 F for 8 minutes.   Serve and enjoy.

851.   Lemon Cake Pudding With Blueberries

Ingredients:

6 Tbsp freshly squeezed lemon juice	3 eggs, separated
1 tsp grated lemon zest	3 Tbsp all-purpose flour
1¼ cups milk	1 cup sugar
Whipped cream, for garnish	1 Tbsp butter, melted
	Fresh blueberries, for garnish

Directions:
Preheat the oven to 350°F.   In a large bowl, beat the egg whites until stiff.   Beat the egg yolks in another large bowl, and add the flour and sugar. Add the butter, lemon juice, lemon zest, and milk. Fold in the egg whites.   Pour the mixture into a 2-quart Instant Vortex oven and bake, uncovered, for 40 minutes, or until the pudding is set.   Serve with whipped cream and blueberries.

852.   Raspberry-coco Desert

Servings: 12   Cooking Time: 20 Minutes
Ingredients:

Vanilla bean, 1 tsp.	Coconut milk, 1 cup
Pulsed raspberries, 1 cup	Coconut oil, ¼ cup
Desiccated coconut, 3 cup	Erythritol powder, 1/3 cup

Directions:
Preheat the air fryer for 5 minutes.   Combine all ingredients in a mixing bowl.   Pour into a greased baking dish.   Bake in the air fryer for 20 minutes at 375F.

853.   Raspberry Cream Rol-ups

Servings: 4   Cooking Time: 25 Minutes
Ingredients:

1 cup of fresh raspberries rinsed and patted dry	1 egg
½ cup of cream cheese softened to room temperature	6 spring roll wrappers (any brand will do, we like Blue Dragon or Tasty Joy, both available through Target or Walmart, or any large grocery chain)
¼ cup of brown sugar	
¼ cup of sweetened condensed milk	
1 teaspoon of corn starch	¼ cup of water

Directions:
Preparing the Ingredients. Cover the basket of the Instant Vortex air fryer oven with a lining of tin foil, leaving the edges uncovered to allow air to circulate through the basket. Preheat the Instant Vortex air fryer oven to 350 degrees.   In a mixing bowl, combine the cream cheese, brown sugar, condensed milk, cornstarch, and egg. Beat or whip thoroughly, until all ingredients are completely mixed and fluffy, thick and stiff.   Spoon even amounts of the creamy filling into each spring roll wrapper, then top each dollop of filling with several raspberries. Roll up the wraps around the creamy raspberry filling, and seal the seams with a few dabs of water. Place each roll on the foil-lined Oven rack/basket, seams facing down. Place the Rack on the middle-shelf of the Instant Vortex air fryer oven.   Air Frying. Set the Instant Vortex air fryer oven timer to 10 minutes. During cooking, shake the handle of the fryer basket to ensure a nice even surface crisp. After 10 minutes, when the Instant Vortex air fryer oven shuts off, the spring rolls should be golden brown and perfect on the outside, while the raspberries and cream filling will have cooked together in a glorious fusion. Remove with tongs and serve hot or cold.

854.   Famous New York Cheesecake

Servings: 8   Cooking Time: 15 Minutes
Ingredients:

1 ½ cups almond flour	1/2 cup heavy cream
3 ounces swerve	3 eggs, at room temperature
1/2 stick butter, melted	1 tablespoon vanilla essence
20 ounces full-fat cream cheese	1 teaspoon grated lemon zest
1 ¼ cups granulated swerve	

Directions:
Coat the sides and bottom of a baking pan with a little flour.   In a mixing bowl, combine the almond flour and swerve. Add the melted butter and mix until your mixture looks like breadcrumbs.   Press the mixture into the bottom of the prepared pan to form an even layer. Bake at 330 degrees F for 7 minutes until golden brown. Allow it to cool completely on a wire rack.   Meanwhile, in a mixer fitted with the paddle attachment, prepare the filling by mixing the soft cheese, heavy cream, and granulated swerve; beat until creamy and fluffy. Crack the eggs into the mixing bowl, one at a time; add the vanilla and lemon zest and continue to mix until fully combined.   Pour the prepared topping over the cooled crust and spread evenly.   Bake in the preheated Air Fryer at 330 degrees F for 25 to 30 minutes; leave it in the Air Fryer to keep warm for another 30 minutes.   Cover your cheesecake with plastic wrap. Place in your refrigerator and allow it to cool at least 6 hours or overnight. Serve well chilled.

855.   Air Fried Chicken Wings

Servings: 4   Cooking Time: 18 Minutes
Ingredients:

2 pounds (907 g) chicken wings	Cooking spray

Directions:
Marinade: cup buttermilk   ½ teaspoon salt
½ teaspoon black pepper   Coating: cup flour
cup panko bread crumbs   tablespoons poultry seasoning   teaspoons salt   Whisk together all

the ingredients for the marinade in a large bowl. Add the chicken wings to the marinade and toss well. Transfer to the refrigerator to marinate for at least an hour. Spritz the air fryer basket with cooking spray. Set aside. Thoroughly combine all the ingredients for the coating in a shallow bowl. Remove the chicken wings from the marinade and shake off any excess. Roll them in the coating mixture. Place the chicken wings in the basket in a single layer. Mist the wings with cooking spray. Put the air fryer basket on the baking pan and slide into Rack Position 2, select Air Fry, set temperature to 360°F (182°C), and set time to 18 minutes. Flip the wings halfway through the cooking time. When cooking is complete, the wings should be crisp and golden brown on the outside. Remove from the oven to a plate and serve hot.

856. Healthy Lemon Tofu

Servings: 4   Cooking Time: 15 Minutes

Ingredients:

1 lb tofu, drained and pressed	2 tsp arrowroot powder
1 tbsp tamari	1/3 cup lemon juice
1 tbsp arrowroot powder	1 tsp lemon zest
For sauce:	2 tbsp erythritol
	1/2 cup water

Directions:

Fit the Instant Vortex oven with the rack in position 2. Cut tofu into cubes. Add tofu and tamari into the zip-lock bag and shake well. Add 1 tbsp arrowroot into the bag and shake well to coat the tofu. Set aside for 15 minutes. Meanwhile, in a bowl, mix together all sauce ingredients and set aside. Add tofu to the air fryer basket then place an air fryer basket in the baking pan. Place a baking pan on the oven rack. Set to air fry at 390 F for 15 minutes. Serve and enjoy.

857. Herbed Focaccia Bread

Ingredients:

1 Tbsp prepared minced garlic	Salt and pepper, to taste
2 tsp chopped fresh rosemary	Flour for dusting
1 package pizza dough, defrosted if necessary	3 Tbsp extra virgin olive oil
	2 Tbsp grated Romano cheese

Directions:

Preheat your Instant Vortex oven to 400°F. Roll out pizza dough on floured surface. Stretch out to a 12-inch circle. Remove the pot from oven and coat with 1 Tbsp olive oil. Add dough to Instant Vortex oven and carefully stretch up the sides. Sprinkle with remaining olive oil, garlic, rosemary, salt, pepper and cheese. Bake until golden brown, about 30 minutes. Slice into wedges.

858. Classic Pound Cake

Servings: 8   Cooking Time: 30 Minutes

Ingredients:

1 stick butter, at room temperature	1/2 cup buttermilk
1 cup Swerve	1/4 teaspoon salt
4 eggs	1 teaspoon vanilla essence
1½ cups coconut flour	A pinch of ground star anise
1/2 teaspoon baking soda	A pinch of freshly grated nutmeg
1/2 teaspoon baking powder	Cooking spray

Directions:

Spray the baking pan with cooking spray. With an electric mixer or hand mixer, beat the butter and Swerve until creamy. One at a time, mix in the eggs and whisk until fluffy. Add the remaining ingredients and stir to combine. Transfer the batter to the prepared baking pan. Slide the baking pan into Rack Position 1, select Convection Bake, set temperature to 320°F (160°C), and set time to 30 minutes. When cooking is complete, the center of the cake should be springy. Allow the cake to cool in the pan for 10 minutes before removing and serving.

859. Chocolate Soufflé

Servings: 2   Cooking Time: 16 Minutes

Ingredients:

3 oz. semi-sweet chocolate, chopped	3 tablespoons sugar
1/4 cup butter	2 tablespoons all-purpose flour
2 eggs, yolks and whites separated	1 teaspoon powdered sugar plus extra for dusting
1/2 teaspoon pure vanilla extract	

Directions:

In a microwave-safe bowl, place the butter, and chocolate. Microwave on high heat for about 2 minutes or until melted completely, stirring after every 30 seconds. Remove from microwave and stir the mixture until smooth. In another bowl, add the egg yolks and whisk well. Add the sugar, and vanilla extract and whisk well. Add the chocolate mixture and mix until well combined. Add the flour and mix well. In a clean glass bowl, add the egg whites and whisk until soft peaks form. Fold the whipped egg whites in 3 portions into the chocolate mixture. Grease 2 ramekins and sprinkle each with a pinch of sugar. Place mixture into the prepared ramekins and with the back of a spoon, smooth the top surface. Press "Power Button" of Air Fry Oven and turn the dial to select the "Air Fry" mode. Press the Time button and again turn the dial to set the cooking time to 14 minutes. Now push the Temp button and rotate the dial to set the temperature at 330 degrees F. Press "Start/Pause" button to start. When the unit beeps to show that it is preheated, open the lid. Arrange the ramekins in "Air Fry Basket" and insert in the oven. Place the ramekins onto a wire rack to cool slightly. Sprinkle with the powdered sugar and serve warm.

860. Pork Taquitos

Servings: 4   Cooking Time: 10 Minutes

Ingredients:

Small whole-wheat tortillas, 10.
Shredded mozzarella cheese, 2 ½ cup
Cooked and shredded pork tenderloin, 30 oz.
Lime juice, 1 lime

Directions:

Preheat your air fryer to 380 degrees Fahrenheit. Stir the lime juice over the shredded pork tenderloins.   Soften the tortillas in your air fryer by microwaving it for 10 seconds.   For each tortilla, add 3-ounces of the shredded pork and ¼ cup of the mozzarella cheese.   Lightly roll up the tortillas.   Then spray a nonstick cooking spray over the tortillas and place it inside your air fryer. Cook it for 10 minutes or until it gets a golden brown color, as you flip after 5 minutes then serve and enjoy.

861. Zucchini Pancakes

Ingredients:

2 tsp. dried basil
2 tsp. dried parsley
Salt and Pepper to taste
3 tbsp. Butter
2 zucchinis (shredded)
1 ½ cups almond flour
3 eggs

Directions:

Preheat the air fryer to 250 Fahrenheit.   In a small bowl, mix the ingredients together. Ensure that the mixture is smooth and well balanced.   Take a pancake mold and grease it with butter. Add the batter to the mold and place it in the air fryer basket. Cook till both the sides of the pancake have browned on both sides and serve with maple syrup.

862. Seafood Turnovers

Ingredients:

½ teaspoon dried dill weed
1 sheet frozen puff pastry, thawed
1 egg yolk, beaten
1 (6-ounce) can small shrimp, drained
1 tablespoon water
½ cup ricotta cheese
3 green onions, finely chopped
1 cup shredded Havarti cheese

Directions:

In medium bowl, combine shrimp, ricotta, green onions, Havarti, and dill weed and mix well. Gently roll puff pastry into 12-inch by 18-inch rectangle. Cut into 24 3-inch squares. Place 2 teaspoons shrimp mixture in center of each square. Beat egg yolk with water in small bowl. Brush edges of pastry with egg yolk mixture. Fold puff pastry over filling, forming triangles; press edges with fork to seal.   Flash freeze turnovers in single layer on baking sheet. Then pack in rigid containers, with waxed paper separating the layers. Label containers and freeze.   To reheat: Preheat oven to 450°F. Place frozen turnovers on baking sheet. Bake at 450°F for 4 minutes; then turn oven down to 400°F and bake for 12 to 15 minutes longer or until pastry is golden and filling is hot.

863. Almond Pecan Cookies

Servings: 16   Cooking Time: 20 Minutes

Ingredients:

½ cup butter
1 tsp vanilla
2 tsp gelatin
2/3 cup Swerve
1 cup pecans
1/3 cup coconut flour
1 cup almond flour

Directions:

Fit the Instant Vortex oven with the rack in position Add butter, vanilla, gelatin, swerve, coconut flour, and almond flour into the food processor and process until crumbs form.   Add pecans and process until chopped.   Make cookies from prepared mixture and place onto a parchment-lined baking pan.   Set to bake at 350 F for 25 minutes. After 5 minutes place the baking pan in the preheated oven.   Serve and enjoy.

864. Preparation Time: 15 Minutes

Servings: 8   Cooking Time: 20 Minutes

Ingredients:

2 cups flour
½ teaspoon baking soda
½ teaspoon baking powder
½ teaspoon salt
1/3 cup butter, softened
¾ cup sugar
3 eggs
1 tablespoon vanilla extract
1 cup milk
½ cup bananas, peeled and mashed
1 cup chocolate chips

Directions:

In a bowl, mix together the flour, baking soda, baking powder, and salt.   In another large bowl, add the butter, and sugar and beat until light and fluffy.   Add the eggs, and vanilla extract and whisk until well combined.   Add the flour mixture and mix until well combined.   Add the milk, and mashed bananas and mix well.   Gently, fold in the chocolate chips.   Place the mixture into a lightly greased loaf pan.   Press "Power Button" of Air Fry Oven and turn the dial to select the "Air Crisp" mode. Press the Time button and again turn the dial to set the cooking time to 20 minutes.   Now push the Temp button and rotate the dial to set the temperature at 360 degrees F.   Press "Start/Pause" button to start.   When the unit beeps to show that it is preheated, open the lid.   Arrange the pan in "Air Fry Basket" and insert in the oven.   Place the pan onto a wire rack to cool for about 10 minutes. Carefully, invert the bread onto wire rack to cool completely before slicing.   Cut the bread into desired-sized slices and serve.

865. Ultimate Chocolate And Coconut Pudding

Servings: 10   Cooking Time: 15 Minutes

Ingredients:

1 stick butter
1 ¼ cups bakers' chocolate, unsweetened
2 tablespoons full fat coconut milk
2 eggs, beaten
1/3 cup coconut, shredded

1 teaspoon liquid
stevia

Directions:
Begin by preheating your Air Fryer to 330 degrees F. In a microwave-safe bowl, melt the butter, chocolate, andstevia. Allow it to cool to room temperature. Add the remaining ingredients to the chocolate mixture; stir to combine well. Scrape the batter into a lightly greased baking pan. Bake in the preheated Air Fryer for 15 minutes or until a toothpick comes out dry and clean. Enjoy!

866. Chocolate Pecan Pie

Servings: 8   Cooking Time: 25 Minutes
Ingredients:

1 (9-inch) unbaked pie crust	½ cup all-purpose flour
Filling:	1 cup milk chocolate chips
2 large eggs	
⅓ cup butter, melted	
1 cup sugar	1½ cups coarsely chopped pecans
	2 tablespoons bourbon

Directions:
Whisk the eggs and melted butter in a large bowl until creamy. Add the sugar and flour and stir to incorporate. Mix in the milk chocolate chips, pecans, and bourbon and stir until well combined. Use a fork to prick holes in the bottom and sides of the pie crust. Pour the prepared filling into the pie crust. Place the pie crust in the baking pan. Slide the baking pan into Rack Position 1, select Convection Bake, set temperature to 350°F (180°C), and set time to 25 minutes. When cooking is complete, a toothpick inserted in the center should come out clean. Allow the pie cool for 10 minutes in the pan before serving.

867. Perfect Chocolate Soufflé

Servings: 2   Cooking Time: 25 Minutes
Ingredients:

2 eggs, whites and yolks separated	3 tbsp sugar
¼ cup butter, melted	3 oz chocolate, melted
2 tbsp flour	½ tsp vanilla extract

Directions:
Beat the yolks along with the sugar and vanilla extract; stir in butter, chocolate, and flour. Preheat Instant Vortex on Bake function to 330 F. Whisk the whites until a stiff peak forms. Working in batches, gently combine the egg whites with the chocolate mixture. Divide the batter between two greased ramekins. Cook for 14-18 minutes. Serve.

868. Homemade Bbq Chicken Pizza

Servings: 1   Cooking Time: 8 Minutes
Ingredients:

1 piece naan bread	¼ cup Barbecue sauce
¼ cup shredded Monterrey Jack	

cheese
¼ cup shredded Mozzarella cheese
½ chicken herby sausage, sliced

2 tablespoons red onion, thinly sliced
Chopped cilantro or parsley, for garnish
Cooking spray

Directions:
Spritz the bottom of naan bread with cooking spray, then transfer to the air fryer basket. Brush with the Barbecue sauce. Top with the cheeses, sausage, and finish with the red onion. Put the air fryer basket on the baking pan and slide into Rack Position 2, select Air Fry, set temperature to 400°F (205°C), and set time to 8 minutes. When cooking is complete, the cheese should be melted. Remove from the oven. Garnish with the chopped cilantro or parsley before slicing to serve.

869. Sweet Potato Croquettes

Servings: 6   Cooking Time: 55 Minutes
Ingredients:

2 cups cooked quinoa	1 garlic clove, minced
1/4 cup parsley, chopped	1/4 cup celery, diced
1/4 cup flour	1/4 cup scallions, chopped
2 cups sweet potatoes, mashed	Pepper
2 tsp Italian seasoning	Salt

Directions:
Fit the Instant Vortex oven with the rack in position Add all ingredients into the mixing bowl and mix until well combined. Make 1-inch round croquettes from mixture and place in baking pan. Set to bake at 375 F for 60 minutes. After 5 minutes place the baking pan in the preheated oven. Serve and enjoy.

870. Ultimate Coconut Chocolate Cake

Servings: 10   Cooking Time: 15 Minutes
Ingredients:

1¼ cups unsweetened bakers' chocolate	1 stick butter
	2 tablespoons coconut milk
1 teaspoon liquid stevia	2 eggs, beaten
⅓ cup shredded coconut	Cooking spray

Directions:
Lightly spritz the baking pan with cooking spray. Place the chocolate, butter, and stevia in a microwave-safe bowl. Microwave for about 30 seconds until melted. Let the chocolate mixture cool to room temperature. Add the remaining ingredients to the chocolate mixture and stir until well incorporated. Pour the batter into the prepared baking pan. Slide the baking pan into Rack Position 1, select Convection Bake, set temperature to 330°F (166°C), and set time to 15 minutes. When cooking is complete, a toothpick inserted in the center should come out clean. Remove from the oven and allow to cool for about 10 minutes before serving.

871. Cookie Custards

Ingredients:

2 tbsp. margarine	1 cup all-purpose flour
A pinch of baking soda and baking powder	½ cup icing sugar
	½ cup custard powder

Directions:
Cream the margarine and sugar together. Add the remaining ingredients and fold them together. Prepare a baking tray by greasing it with butter. Make balls out of the dough, coat them with flour and place them in the tray.   Preheat the fryer to 300 Fahrenheit for five minutes. You will need to place the baking tray in the basket and cover it. Cook till you find that the balls have turned golden brown. Remove the tray and leave it to cool outside for half an hour. Store in an airtight container.

872. Summer Citrus Sponge Cake

Servings: 4   Cooking Time: 50 Minutes

Ingredients:

1 cup sugar	Frosting:
1 cup self-rising flour	4 egg whites
1 cup butter	1 orange, zested and juiced
3 eggs	
1 tsp baking powder	1 tsp orange food coloring
1 tsp vanilla extract	
Zest of 1 orange	1 cup superfine sugar

Directions:
Preheat Instant Vortex on Bake function to 350 F. Place all cake ingredients in a bowl and whisk with an electric mixer. Transfer half of the batter into a greased cake pan and bake for 15 minutes. Meanwhile, prepare the frosting by beating all frosting ingredients together. Spread the frosting mixture on top of the cake. Serve sliced.

873. Delicious Lemon Bars

Servings: 8   Cooking Time: 40 Minutes

Ingredients:

4 eggs	1 lemon zest
1/4 cup fresh lemon juice	1/2 cup sour cream
	1/3 cup erythritol
1/2 cup butter softened	2 tsp baking powder
	2 cups almond flour

Directions:
Fit the Instant Vortex oven with the rack in position In a bowl, beat eggs until frothy.   Add butter and sour cream and beat until well combined.   Add sweetener, lemon zest, and lemon juice and blend well.   Add baking powder and almond flour and mix until well combined.   Transfer batter in a greased baking pan and spread evenly.   Set to bake at 350 F for 45 minutes. After 5 minutes place the baking pan in the preheated oven.   Slice and serve.

874. Tuna Melts With Scallions

Servings: 6   Cooking Time: 6 Minutes

Ingredients:

2 (5- to 6-ounce / 142- to 170-g) cans oil-packed tuna, drained	1 tablespoon capers, drained
	¼ teaspoon celery salt
1 large scallion, chopped	12 slices cocktail rye bread
1 small stalk celery, chopped	2 tablespoons butter, melted
⅓ cup mayonnaise	6 slices sharp Cheddar cheese
1 tablespoon chopped fresh dill	

Directions:
In a medium bowl, stir together the tuna, scallion, celery, mayonnaise, dill, capers and celery salt. Brush one side of the bread slices with the butter. Arrange the bread slices in the baking pan, buttered-side down. Scoop a heaping tablespoon of the tuna mixture on each slice of bread, spreading it out evenly to the edges.   Cut the cheese slices to fit the dimensions of the bread and place a cheese slice on each piece.   Slide the baking pan into Rack Position 2, select Roast, set temperature to 375°F (190°C) and set time to 6 minutes.   After 4 minutes, remove from the oven and check the tuna melts. The tuna melts are done when the cheese has melted and the tuna is heated through. If needed, continue cooking.   When cooking is complete, remove from the oven. Use a spatula to transfer the tuna melts to a clean work surface and slice each one in half diagonally. Serve warm.

875. Moist Baked Donuts

Servings: 12   Cooking Time: 15 Minutes

Ingredients:

2 eggs	1/4 cup vegetable oil
3/4 cup sugar	1/2 tsp vanilla
1/2 cup buttermilk	1 tsp baking powder
1 cup all-purpose flour	1/2 tsp salt

Directions:
Fit the Instant Vortex oven with the rack in position Spray donut pan with cooking spray and set aside. In a bowl, mix together oil, vanilla, baking powder, sugar, eggs, buttermilk, and salt until well combined. Stir in flour and mix until smooth.   Pour batter into the prepared donut pan.   Set to bake at 350 F for 20 minutes. After 5 minutes place the donut pan in the preheated oven.   Serve and enjoy.

876. Almond Butter Cookies

Servings: 12   Cooking Time: 12 Minutes

Ingredients:

1 teaspoon vanilla extract	1 egg
	2 tablespoons erythritol
1 cup almond butter, soft	

Directions:
In a bowl, mix all the ingredients and whisk really well.   Spread this on a cookie sheet that fits the air fryer lined with parchment paper, introduce in the fryer and cook at 350 degrees F and bake for 12 minutes.   Cool down and serve.

877. Cheese And Ham Stuffed Baby Bella

Servings: 8   Cooking Time: 12 Minutes

Ingredients:

4 ounces (113 g) Mozzarella cheese, cut into pieces	¼ teaspoon ground oregano
½ cup diced ham	¼ teaspoon ground black pepper
2 green onions, chopped	1 to 2 teaspoons olive oil
2 tablespoons bread crumbs	16 fresh Baby Bella mushrooms, stemmed removed
½ teaspoon garlic powder	

Directions:

Process the cheese, ham, green onions, bread crumbs, garlic powder, oregano, and pepper in a food processor until finely chopped.   With the food processor running, slowly drizzle in 1 to 2 teaspoons olive oil until a thick paste has formed. Transfer the mixture to a bowl.   Evenly divide the mixture into the mushroom caps and lightly press down the mixture.   Lay the mushrooms in the air fryer basket in a single layer.   Put the air fryer basket on the baking pan and slide into Rack Position 2, select Roast, set temperature to 390°F (199°C), and set time to 12 minutes.   When cooking is complete, the mushrooms should be lightly browned and tender. Remove from the oven to a plate. Let the mushrooms cool for 5 minutes and serve warm.

878. Easy Egg Custard

Servings: 6   Cooking Time: 40 Minutes

Ingredients:

2 egg yolks	1/2 cup erythritol
1 tsp nutmeg	3 eggs
2 cups heavy whipping cream	1/2 tsp vanilla

Directions:

Fit the Instant Vortex oven with the rack in position Add all ingredients into the large mixing bowl and beat until just well combined.   Pour custard mixture into the greased pie dish.   Set to bake at 350 F for 40 minutes. After 5 minutes place the pie dish in the preheated oven.   Serve.

879. Simple Strawberry Cobbler

Servings: 4   Cooking Time: 25 Minutes

Ingredients:

Butter, 2 tsps.	Butter, 1 tbsp.
Hulled strawberries, 1 ½ cup	Heavy whipping cream, ¼ cup
White sugar, 1 ½ tsps.	Cornstarch, 1 ½ tsps.
Diced butter, 1 tbsp.	White sugar, ¼ cup
All-purpose flour, ½ cup	Water, ½ cup
	Salt, ¼ tsp.

Baking powder, ¾ tsp.

Directions:

Lightly grease a baking pan of air fryer with cooking spray. Add water, cornstarch, and sugar. Cook for 10 minutes 390F or until hot and thick. Add strawberries and mix well. Dot tops with 1 tablespoon butter.   In a bowl, mix well salt, baking powder, sugar, and flour. Cut in 1 tablespoon and 2 teaspoons butter. Mix in cream. Spoon on top of berries.   Cook for 15 minutes at 390F, until tops are lightly browned.   Serve and enjoy.

880. Yogurt Cake(1)

Servings: 12   Cooking Time: 15 Minutes

Ingredients:

6 eggs, whisked	1 tsp. vanilla extract
8 oz. Greek yogurt	1 tsp. baking powder
9 oz. coconut flour	
4 tbsp. stevia	

Directions:

Take a bowl and mix all the ingredients and whisk well.   Pour this into a cake pan that fits the air fryer lined with parchment paper.   Put the pan in the air fryer and cook at 330°F for 30 minutes

881. Easy Cheese Dip

Servings: 12   Cooking Time: 30 Minutes

Ingredients:

1/2 cup mayonnaise	4 oz cream cheese, cubed
1 small onion, diced	1 1/2 cups cheddar cheese, shredded
1 1/2 cups mozzarella cheese, shredded	

Directions:

Fit the Instant Vortex oven with the rack in position Add all ingredients into the mixing bowl and mix until well combined.   Pour mixture into the prepared baking dish.   Set to bake at 400 F for 35 minutes. After 5 minutes place the baking dish in the preheated oven.   Serve and enjoy.

882. Gooey Chocolate Fudge Cake

Ingredients:

3 Tbsp cocoa powder	1 cup flour
½ cup water	½ tsp baking soda
¼ cup whole milk	1 cup sugar
1 egg	Pinch of salt
1 tsp vanilla extract	½ cup vegetable oil

Directions:

Preheat the oven to 350°F.   In a large bowl, whisk flour, baking soda, sugar and salt.   Combine oil, cocoa powder and water in another bowl.   Whisk in flour mixture and pour into Instant Vortex oven. Incorporate milk, egg and vanilla into the batter. Bake for 25 minutes, or until edges are set and center is only slightly jiggly.

883. Strawberry Tart

Ingredients:

2 cups sliced strawberries	3 tbsp. unsalted butter
1 cup fresh cream	2 tbsp. powdered sugar
3 tbsp. butter	
1 ½ cup plain flour	2 cups cold water

Directions:
In a large bowl, mix the flour, cocoa powder, butter and sugar with your Oregano Fingers. The mixture should resemble breadcrumbs. Squeeze the dough using the cold milk and wrap it and leave it to cool for ten minutes. Roll the dough out into the pie and prick the sides of the pie.   Mix the ingredients for the filling in a bowl. Make sure that it is a little thick. Preheat the fryer to 300 Fahrenheit for five minutes. You will need to place the tin in the basket and cover it. When the pastry has turned golden brown, you will need to remove the tin and let it cool. Cut into slices and serve with a dollop of cream.

884.   Chocolate Cheesecake

Servings: 6   Cooking Time: 18 Minutes
Ingredients:

Crust:	Topping:
½ cup butter, melted	1 cup mascarpone cheese, at room temperature
½ cup coconut flour	
2 tablespoons stevia	
Cooking spray	1 teaspoon vanilla extract
4 ounces (113 g) unsweetened baker's chocolate	2 drops peppermint extract

Directions:
Lightly coat the baking pan with cooking spray. In a mixing bowl, whisk together the butter, flour, and stevia until well combined. Transfer the mixture to the prepared baking pan.   Slide the baking pan into Rack Position 1, select Convection Bake, set temperature to 350ºF (180ºC), and set time to 18 minutes.   When done, a toothpick inserted in the center should come out clean.   Remove the crust from the oven to a wire rack to cool.   Once cooled completely, place it in the freezer for 20 minutes. When ready, combine all the ingredients for the topping in a small bowl and stir to incorporate. Spread this topping over the crust and let it sit for another 15 minutes in the freezer.   Serve chilled.

885.   Bbq Pulled Mushrooms

Servings: 2   Cooking Time: 15 Minutes
Ingredients:

4 large portobello mushrooms	1 tbsp. salted butter; melted.
½ cup low-carb, sugar-free barbecue sauce	¼ tsp. onion powder.
1 tsp. paprika	¼ tsp. ground black pepper
	1 tsp. chili powder

Directions:
Remove stem and scoop out the underside of each mushroom. Brush the caps with butter and sprinkle with pepper, chili powder, paprika and onion powder.   Place mushrooms into the air fryer basket. Adjust the temperature to 400 Degrees F and set the timer for 8 minutes.   When the timer beeps, remove mushrooms from the basket and place on a cutting board or work surface. Using two forks, gently pull the mushrooms apart, creating strands.   Place mushroom strands into a 4-cup round baking dish with barbecue sauce. Place dish into the air fryer basket.   Adjust the temperature to 350 Degrees F and set the timer for 4 minutes. Stir halfway through the cooking time. Serve warm.

886.   Paprika Deviled Eggs

Servings: 12   Cooking Time: 16 Minutes
Ingredients:

3 cups ice	2 teaspoons salt
12 large eggs	2 teaspoons yellow mustard
½ cup mayonnaise	
10 hamburger dill pickle chips, diced	1 teaspoon freshly ground black pepper
¼ cup diced onion	½ teaspoon paprika

Directions:
Put the ice in a large bowl and set aside. Carefully place the eggs in the baking pan.   Slide the baking pan into Rack Position 1, select Convection Bake, set temperature to 250ºF (121ºC), and set time to 16 minutes.   When cooking is complete, transfer the eggs to the large bowl of ice to cool.   When cool enough to handle, peel the eggs. Slice them in half lengthwise and scoop out yolks into a small bowl. Stir in the mayonnaise, pickles, onion, salt, mustard, and pepper. Mash the mixture with a fork until well combined.   Fill each egg white half with 1 to 2 teaspoons of the egg yolk mixture.   Sprinkle the paprika on top and serve immediately.

887.   Bow Tie Pasta Chips

Servings: 6   Cooking Time: 10 Minutes
Ingredients:

2 cups white bow tie pasta	1 tablespoon nutritional yeast
1 tablespoon olive oil	1½ teaspoons Italian seasoning blend
½ teaspoon salt	

Directions:
Cook the pasta for 1/2 the time called for on the package. Toss the drained pasta   with the olive oil or aquafaba, nutritional yeast, Italian seasoning, and salt.   Place about half of the mixture in your air fryer basket if yours is small; larger ones may be able to do cook in one batch.   Cook on 390°F: 200°Cfor 5 minutes. Shake the basket and cook 3 to 5 minutes more or until crunchy.

888.   Air Fryer Mixed Nuts

Servings: 2   Cooking Time: 4 Minutes
Ingredients:

2 cup mixed nuts	1 tsp pepper
1 tbsp olive oil	1/4 tsp cayenne
1 tsp ground cumin	1 tsp salt

Directions:
Fit the Instant Vortex oven with the rack in position 2.   In a bowl, add all ingredients and toss well. Add the nuts mixture to the air fryer basket then place an air fryer basket in the baking pan.   Place

a baking pan on the oven rack. Set to air fry at 350 F for 4 minutes.   Serve and enjoy.

889.   Chestnuts Spinach Dip

Servings: 8   Cooking Time: 40 Minutes

Ingredients:

8 oz cream cheese, softened	1 cup mayonnaise
1 cup parmesan cheese, grated	1/4 tsp garlic powder
1 cup frozen spinach, thawed and squeeze out all liquid	1/2 cup onion, minced
	1/3 cup water chestnuts, drained and chopped
	1/2 tsp pepper

Directions:

Fit the Instant Vortex oven with the rack in position Spray air fryer baking dish with cooking spray. Add all ingredients into the bowl and mix until well combined.   Transfer bowl mixture into the baking dish.   Set to bake at 300 F for 45 minutes. After 5 minutes place the baking dish in the preheated oven. Serve and enjoy.

890.   Banana Brownies

Servings: 12   Cooking Time: 20 Minutes

Ingredients:

¼ cup butter, unsalted	½ cup sugar
4 oz. white chocolate, chopped	1 egg
2 bananas, mashed	¼ tsp salt
	1 tsp vanilla
	1 cup flour

Directions:

Place rack in position   In a microwave safe bowl, add butter and chocolate and microwave in 30 second intervals until melted, stirring after each cook time.   Stir in bananas, eggs, salt, and vanilla until combined. Stir in flour and mix well.   Set oven to bake on 350°F for 25 minutes.   Spread batter in prepared pan. After oven preheats for 5 minutes, place brownies in oven and bake 15-20 minutes or brownies pass the toothpick test.   Let cool 15 minutes before slicing.

891.   Sweet And Salty Snack Mix

Servings: About 10 Cups   Cooking Time: 10 Minutes

Ingredients:

3 tablespoons butter, melted	2 cups sesame sticks
½ cup honey	2 cups mini pretzel crisps
1 teaspoon salt	1 cup cashews
2 cups granola	1 cup pepitas
2 cups crispy corn puff cereal	1 cup dried cherries

Directions:

In a small mixing bowl, mix together the butter, honey, and salt until well incorporated.   In a large bowl, combine the granola, sesame sticks, corn puff cereal and pretzel crisps, cashews, and pepitas. Drizzle with the butter mixture and toss until evenly coated. Transfer the snack mix to the air fryer basket.

Put the air fryer basket on the baking pan and slide into Rack Position 2, select Air Fry, set temperature to 370°F (188°C), and set time to 10 minutes.   Stir the snack mix halfway through the cooking time. When cooking is complete, they should be lightly toasted. Remove from the oven and allow to cool completely. Scatter with the dried cherries and mix well. Serve immediately.

892.   Vanilla Soufflé

Servings: 6   Cooking Time: 23 Minutes

Ingredients:

¼ cup butter, softened	1 cup milk
¼ cup all-purpose flour	4 egg yolks
½ cup plus 2 tablespoons sugar, divided	5 egg whites
	1 teaspoon cream of tartar
3 teaspoons vanilla extract, divided	2 tablespoons powdered sugar plus extra for dusting

Directions:

In a bowl, add the butter, and flour and mix until a smooth paste forms.   In a medium pan, mix together ½ cup of sugar and milk over medium-low heat and cook for about 3 minutes or until the sugar is dissolved, stirring continuously.   Add the flour mixture, whisking continuously and simmer for about 3-4 minutes or until mixture becomes thick. Remove from the heat and stir in 1 teaspoon of vanilla extract.   Set aside for about 10 minutes to cool.   In a bowl, add the egg yolks and 1 teaspoon of vanilla extract and mix well.   Add the egg yolk mixture into milk mixture and mix until well combined.   In another bowl, add the egg whites, cream of tartar, remaining sugar, and vanilla extract and with a wire whisk, beat until stiff peaks form. Fold the egg whites mixture into milk mixture. Grease 6 ramekins and sprinkle each with a pinch of sugar.   Place mixture into the prepared ramekins and with the back of a spoon, smooth the top surface. Press "Power Button" of Air Fry Oven and turn the dial to select the "Air Fry" mode.   Press the Time button and again turn the dial to set the cooking time to 16 minutes.   Now push the Temp button and rotate the dial to set the temperature at 330 degrees F.   Press "Start/Pause" button to start. When the unit beeps to show that it is preheated, open the lid.   Arrange the ramekins in "Air Fry Basket" and insert in the oven.   Place the ramekins onto a wire rack to cool slightly. Sprinkle with the powdered sugar and serve warm.

893.   Mini Pancakes

Ingredients:

2 tsp. dried parsley	1 ½ cups almond flour
Salt and Pepper to taste	3 eggs
3 tbsp. Butter	2 tsp. dried basil

Directions:

Preheat the air fryer to 250 Fahrenheit.   In a small bowl, mix the ingredients together. Ensure that the mixture is smooth and well balanced.   Take a pancake mold and grease it with butter. Add the batter to the mold and place it in the air fryer basket. Cook till both the sides of the pancake have browned on both sides and serve with maple syrup.

894. Vanilla Almond Cookies

Servings: 4   Cooking Time: 45 Minutes + Cooling Time

Ingredients:

8 egg whites	1 ½ tsp vanilla extract
½ tsp almond extract	
1 ⅓ cups sugar	Melted dark chocolate to drizzle
2 tsp lemon juice	

Directions:

In a bowl, add egg whites and lemon juice. Beat using an electric mixer until foamy. Slowly add the sugar and continue beating until completely combined; stir in almond and vanilla extracts. Line the Air Fryer pan with parchment paper. Fill a piping bag with the meringue mixture and pipe as many mounds on the baking pan as you can leaving 2-inch spaces between each mound.   Cook at 350 F for 5 minutes on Bake function. Reduce the temperature to 320 F and bake for 15 more minutes. Then, reduce the heat to 190 F and cook for 15 minutes. Let cool for 2 hours. Drizzle with dark chocolate and serve.

895. Berry Tacos

Servings: 2   Cooking Time: 5 Minutes

Ingredients:

2 soft shell tortillas	¼ cup fresh raspberries
4 tablespoons strawberry jelly	
¼ cup fresh blueberries	2 tablespoons powdered sugar

Directions:

Spread 2 tablespoons of strawberry jelly over each tortilla   Top each with berries evenly and sprinkle with powdered sugar.   Press "Power Button" of Air Fry Oven and turn the dial to select the "Air Fry" mode.   Press the Time button and again turn the dial to set the cooking time to 5 minutes.   Now push the Temp button and rotate the dial to set the temperature at 300 degrees F.   Press "Start/Pause" button to start.   When the unit beeps to show that it is preheated, open the lid.   Arrange the tortillas in "Air Fry Basket" and insert in the oven.   Serve warm.

896. Tofu Steaks

Servings: 4   Cooking Time: 35 Minutes

Ingredients:

1 package tofu, press and remove excess liquid	1/4 cup olive oil
	1/4 tsp dried thyme
2 tbsp lemon zest	1/4 cup lemon juice
3 garlic cloves, minced	Pepper
	Salt

Directions:

Fit the Instant Vortex oven with the rack in position 2.   Cut tofu into eight pieces.   In a bowl, mix together olive oil, thyme, lemon juice, lemon zest, garlic, pepper, and salt.   Add tofu into the bowl and coat well and place it in the refrigerator overnight.   Place marinated tofu in an air fryer basket then places an air fryer basket in the baking pan.   Place a baking pan on the oven rack. Set to air fry at 350 F for 35 minutes.   Serve and enjoy.

897. Date Bread

Servings: 10   Cooking Time: 20 Minutes

Ingredients:

¼ cup of butter	½ teaspoon of salt
1½ cups of flour	1 cup of hot water
1 teaspoon of baking powder	½ cup of brown sugar
2½ cup of dates, pitted and chopped	1 teaspoon of baking soda
	1 egg

Directions:

Set the Instant Vortex on Air fryer to 340 degrees F for 20 minutes. Combine dates with butter and hot water in a bowl. Strain together brown sugar, flour, baking powder, baking soda, and salt in another bowl. Fold the brown sugar mixture and egg in the date's mixture. Place the mixture on the cooking tray. Insert the cooking tray in the Vortex when it displays "Add Food". Flip the sides when it displays "Turn Food". Remove from the oven when cooking time is complete. Slice into desired pieces to serve.

898. Delicious Raspberry Cobbler

Servings: 6   Cooking Time: 10 Minutes

Ingredients:

1 egg, lightly beaten	1/2 tsp vanilla
1 cup raspberries, sliced	1 tbsp butter, melted
	1 cup almond flour
2 tsp swerve	

Directions:

Fit the Instant Vortex oven with the rack in position Add raspberries into the baking dish.   Sprinkle sweetener over raspberries.   Mix together almond flour, vanilla, and butter in the bowl.   Add egg in almond flour mixture and stir well to combine. Spread almond flour mixture over sliced raspberries. Set to bake at 350 F for 15 minutes. After 5 minutes place the baking dish in the preheated oven. Serve and enjoy.

899. Cheesy Beef Dip

Servings: 12   Cooking Time: 25 Minutes

Ingredients:

1 lb corned beef, diced	8 oz Swiss cheese, shredded
¾ cup mayonnaise	Pepper
14 oz can sauerkraut, drained	Salt

Directions:

Fit the Instant Vortex oven with the rack in position Add all ingredients into the bowl and mix well and pour into the greased baking dish. Set to bake at 400 F for 30 minutes. After 5 minutes place the baking dish in the preheated oven. Serve and enjoy.

900. Bacon Wrapped Brie

Servings: 8   Cooking Time: 15 Minutes
Ingredients:
4 slices sugar-free bacon.   1 (8-oz.round Brie

Directions:
Place two slices of bacon to form an X. Place the third slice of bacon horizontally across the center of the X. Place the fourth slice of bacon vertically across the X. It should look like a plus sign (+on top of an X. Place the Brie in the center of the bacon Wrap the bacon around the Brie, securing with a few toothpicks. Cut a piece of parchment to fit your air fryer basket and place the bacon-wrapped Brie on top. Place inside the air fryer basket.   Adjust the temperature to 400 Degrees F and set the timer for 10 minutes. When 3 minutes remain on the timer, carefully flip Brie   When cooked, bacon will be crispy and cheese will be soft and melty. To serve; cut into eight slices.

901. Banana Clafouti

Ingredients:
1 tsp vanilla extract
2 Tbsp butter, melted
¼ tsp salt
½ cup all-purpose flour
2 bananas, peeled and thinly sliced

2 tsp fresh lemon juice
1 cup whole milk
¼ cup whipping cream
3 eggs
½ cup granulated sugar

Directions:
Preheat the oven to 350°F.   Whisk together milk, cream, eggs, sugar, extract, butter and salt.   Add the flour and whisk gently until incorporated. Place sliced bananas in a bowl with lemon juice. Lightly grease Instant Vortex oven and heat in oven for 5 minutes. Remove and pour in batter.   Scatter bananas over batter and bake until golden and puffed, about 35 minutes.

902. Apple-peach Crumble With Honey

Servings: 4   Cooking Time: 11 Minutes
Ingredients:
1 apple, peeled and chopped
2 peaches, peeled, pitted, and chopped
½ cup quick-cooking oatmeal
⅓ cup whole-wheat pastry flour

2 tablespoons honey
2 tablespoons unsalted butter, at room temperature
3 tablespoons packed brown sugar
½ teaspoon ground cinnamon

Directions:
Mix together the apple, peaches, and honey in the baking pan until well incorporated.   In a bowl,

combine the oatmeal, pastry flour, butter, brown sugar, and cinnamon and stir to mix well. Spread this mixture evenly over the fruit.   Slide the baking pan into Rack Position 1, select Convection Bake, set temperature to 380°F (193°C), and set time to 11 minutes.   When cooking is complete, the fruit should be bubbling around the edges and the topping should be golden brown.   Remove from the oven and serve warm.

903. Polenta Fries With Chili-lime Mayo

Servings: 4   Cooking Time: 28 Minutes
Ingredients:
Polenta Fries:
2 teaspoons vegetable or olive oil
¼ teaspoon paprika
1 pound (454 g) prepared polenta, cut into 3-inch × ½-inch strips
Salt and freshly ground black pepper, to taste
Chili-Lime Mayo:

½ cup mayonnaise
1 teaspoon chili powder
1 teaspoon chopped fresh cilantro
¼ teaspoon ground cumin
Juice of ½ lime
Salt and freshly ground black pepper, to taste

Directions:
Mix the oil and paprika in a bowl. Add the polenta strips and toss until evenly coated. Transfer the polenta strips to the air fryer basket.   Put the air fryer basket on the baking pan and slide into Rack Position 2, select Air Fry, set temperature to 400°F (205°C), and set time to 28 minutes.   Stir the polenta strips halfway through the cooking time. Meanwhile, whisk together all the ingredients for the chili-lime mayo in a small bowl.   When cooking is complete, remove the polenta fries from the oven to a plate. Season as desired with salt and pepper. Serve alongside the chili-lime mayo as a dipping sauce.

904. Shrimp And Artichoke Puffs

Ingredients:
1 (10-ounce) package frozen artichoke hearts, thawed
1 (3-ounce) package cream cheese, softened
1 cup shredded Coda cheese
1 tablespoon lemon juice

½ cup mayonnaise
1 teaspoon dried basil leaves
6 slices whole wheat bread
2 shallots, chopped
1 tablespoon olive oil
½ pound cooked shrimp

Directions:
Preheat oven to 300°F. Using a 2-inch cookie cutter, cut rounds from bread slices. Place rounds on a baking sheet and bake at 300°F for 7 to 9 minutes, or until crisp, turning once. Remove from oven and cool on wire racks.   In a heavy skillet, cook shallots in olive oil over medium heat until tender. Remove from heat. Chop shrimp and add to skillet along with thawed, drained, and chopped artichoke

hearts. Add both cheeses, mayonnaise, lemon juice, and basil; stir well to blend.   Spoon 1 tablespoon shrimp mixture onto each bread round, covering the top and mounding the filling. Flash freeze on baking sheets. When frozen solid, pack in rigid containers, with waxed paper between layers. Label puffs and freeze.   To reheat: Place frozen puffs on a baking sheet and bake at 400°F for 10 to 12 minutes or until topping is hot and bubbling.

905. Almond Flour Blackberry Muffins

Servings: 8   Cooking Time: 12 Minutes
Ingredients:

½ cup fresh blackberries	¼ teaspoon kosher salt
Dry Ingredients:	Wet Ingredients:
1½ cups almond flour	2 eggs
1 teaspoon baking powder	¼ cup coconut oil, melted
½ teaspoon baking soda	½ cup milk
½ cup Swerve	½ teaspoon vanilla paste

Directions:
Line an 8-cup muffin tin with paper liners. Thoroughly combine the almond flour, baking powder, baking soda, Swerve, and salt in a mixing bowl.   Whisk together the eggs, coconut oil, milk, and vanilla in a separate mixing bowl until smooth. Add the wet mixture to the dry and fold in the blackberries. Stir with a spatula just until well incorporated.   Spoon the batter into the prepared muffin cups, filling each about three-quarters full. Put the muffin tin into Rack Position 1, select Convection Bake, set temperature to 350°F (180°C), and set time to 12 minutes.   When done, the tops should be golden and a toothpick inserted in the middle should come out clean.   Allow the muffins to cool in the muffin tin for 10 minutes before removing and serving

906. Baked Apple Slices

Servings: 6   Cooking Time: 30 Minutes
Ingredients:

2 apples, peel, core, and slice	1/4 cup of sugar
1 tsp cinnamon	1/4 cup brown sugar
2 tbsp butter	1/4 tsp salt

Directions:
Fit the Instant Vortex oven with the rack in position Add cinnamon, sugar, brown sugar, and salt into the zip-lock bag and mix well.   Add apple slices into the bag and shake until well coated.   Add apple slices into the 9-inch greased baking dish.   Set to bake at 350 F for 35 minutes. After 5 minutes place the baking dish in the preheated oven.   Serve and enjoy.

907. Jalapeno Spinach Dip

Servings: 6   Cooking Time: 30 Minutes

Ingredients:

10 oz frozen spinach, thawed and drained	1/2 cup onion, diced
2 tsp jalapeno pepper, minced	2 tsp garlic, minced
	1/2 cup mozzarella cheese, shredded
1/2 cup cheddar cheese, shredded	1/2 cup Monterey jack cheese, shredded
8 oz cream cheese	1/2 tsp salt

Directions:
Fit the Instant Vortex oven with the rack in position Add all ingredients into the mixing bowl and mix until well combined.   Pour mixture into the 1-quart casserole dish.   Set to bake at 350 F for 35 minutes. After 5 minutes place the casserole dish in the preheated oven.   Serve and enjoy.

908. Peach-blueberry Tart

Servings: 6 To 8   Cooking Time: 30 Minutes
Ingredients:

4 peaches, pitted and sliced	3 tablespoons sugar
1 cup fresh blueberries	Cooking spray
2 tablespoons cornstarch	1 sheet frozen puff pastry, thawed
1 tablespoon freshly squeezed lemon juice	1 tablespoon nonfat or low-fat milk
	Confectioners' sugar, for dusting

Directions:
Add the peaches, blueberries, cornstarch, sugar, and lemon juice to a large bowl and toss to coat.   Spritz a round baking pan with cooking spray.   Unfold the pastry and put in the prepared baking pan. Lay the peach slices on the pan, slightly overlapping them. Scatter the blueberries over the peach. Drape the pastry over the outside of the fruit and press pleats firmly together. Brush the milk over the pastry.   Slide the baking pan into Rack Position 1, select Convection Bake, set temperature to 400°F (205°C), and set time to 30 minutes.   Bake until the crust is golden brown and the fruit is bubbling. When cooking is complete, remove from the oven and allow to cool for 10 minutes.   Serve the tart with the confectioners' sugar sprinkled on top.

909. Oaty Chocolate Chip Cookies

Servings: 4 Dozen (1-by-1½-inch) Bars   Cooking Time: 20 Minutes
Ingredients:

1 cup unsalted butter, at room temperature	2 cups old-fashioned rolled oats
1 cup dark brown sugar	1½ cups all-purpose flour
½ cup granulated sugar	1 teaspoon baking powder
2 large eggs	1 teaspoon baking soda
1 tablespoon vanilla extract	2 cups chocolate chips
Pinch salt	

Directions:
Stir together the butter, brown sugar, and granulated sugar in a large mixing bowl until smooth and light in color.   Crack the eggs into the

bowl, one at a time, mixing after each addition. Stir in the vanilla and salt. Mix together the oats, flour, baking powder, and baking soda in a separate bowl. Add the mixture to the butter mixture and stir until mixed. Stir in the chocolate chips. Spread the dough into the baking pan in an even layer. Slide the baking pan into Rack Position 1, select Convection Bake, set temperature to 350°F (180°C), and set time to 20 minutes. After 15 minutes, check the cookie. Continue cooking for a total of 18 to 20 minutes or until golden brown. When cooking is complete, remove from the oven and allow to cool completely before slicing and serving.

910. Easy Almond Butter Pumpkin Spice Cookies

Servings: 6   Cooking Time: 18 Minutes
Ingredients:

1/4 tsp pumpkin pie spice
1 tsp liquid Stevie
6 oz almond butter
1/3 cup pumpkin puree

Directions:
Fit the Instant Vortex oven with the rack in position Add all ingredients into the food processor and process until just combined. Drop spoonfuls of mixture onto the parchment-lined baking pan. Set to bake at 350 F for 23 minutes. After 5 minutes place the baking pan in the preheated oven. Serve and enjoy.

911. Easy Air Fryer Tofu

Servings: 4   Cooking Time: 15 Minutes
Ingredients:

16 oz extra firm tofu, cut into bite-sized pieces
1 tbsp olive oil
1 garlic clove, minced

Directions:
Fit the Instant Vortex oven with the rack in position 2. Add tofu, garlic, and oil in a mixing bowl and toss well. Let it sit for 15 minutes. Arrange tofu in the air fryer basket then place an air fryer basket in the baking pan. Place a baking pan on the oven rack. Set to air fry at 370 F for 15 minutes. Serve and enjoy.

912. Choco – Chip Muffins

Ingredients:

3 tsp. vinegar
½ tsp. vanilla essence
Muffin cups or butter paper cups
2 cups All-purpose flour
½ cup chocolate chips
1 ½ cup milk
½ tsp. baking powder
½ tsp. baking soda
2 tbsp. butter
1 cup sugar

Directions:
Mix the ingredients together and use your Oregano Fingers to get a crumbly mixture. Add the baking soda and the vinegar to the milk and mix continuously. Add this milk to the mixture and

create a batter, which you will need to transfer to the muffin cups. Preheat the fryer to 300 Fahrenheit for five minutes. You will need to place the muffin cups in the basket and cover it. Cook the muffins for fifteen minutes and check whether or not the muffins are cooked using a toothpick. Remove the cups and serve hot.

913. Tasty Gingersnap Cookies

Servings: 8   Cooking Time: 10 Minutes
Ingredients:

1 egg
1/2 tsp ground cinnamon
1/2 tsp ground ginger
1 tsp baking powder
3/4 cup erythritol
1/2 tsp vanilla
1/8 tsp ground cloves
1/4 tsp ground nutmeg
2/4 cup butter, melted
1 1/2 cups almond flour
Pinch of salt

Directions:
Fit the Instant Vortex oven with the rack in position In a mixing bowl, mix together all dry ingredients. In another bowl, mix together all wet ingredients. Add dry ingredients to the wet ingredients and mix until a dough-like mixture is formed. Cover and place in the refrigerator for 30 minutes. Make cookies from dough and place onto a parchment-lined baking pan. Set to bake at 350 F for 15 minutes. After 5 minutes place the baking pan in the preheated oven. Serve and enjoy.

914. Jalapeno Pops

Ingredients:

1 cup flour
½ teaspoon salt
1 egg, beaten
3 tablespoons cornstarch
24 small jalapeno peppers
cup ginger ale
2 cups grated Swiss cheese
1 (8-ounce) package cream cheese, softened

Directions:
Cut slit in side of peppers and gently remove seeds and membranes. Combine Swiss cheese and cream cheese in medium bowl and blend well. Stuff peppers with cheese mixture and press gently to seal. In a small bowl, combine flour, salt, egg, and ginger ale and mix until a thick batter form. Put cornstarch in another small bowl. Dip each stuffed pepper in cornstarch and shake off excess. Dip each pepper in batter and hold over bowl a few seconds for excess batter to drip off. Flash freeze peppers in single layer on baking sheet. When frozen solid, pack in rigid containers, with waxed paper separating layers. Label peppers and freeze. To reheat: Preheat oven to 400°F. Place frozen peppers on baking sheet and bake at 400°F for 20 to 30 minutes or until brown, crisp, and thoroughly heated.

915. Mixed Berry Compote With Coconut Chips

Servings: 6   Cooking Time: 15 Minutes
Ingredients:

1 tablespoon butter
12 ounces mixed berries
1/3 cup granulated swerve
1/4 teaspoon grated nutmeg

1/4 teaspoon ground cloves
1/2 teaspoon ground cinnamon
1 teaspoon pure vanilla extract
1/2 cup coconut chips

Directions:
Start by preheating your Air Fryer to 330 degrees F. Grease a baking pan with butter. Place all ingredients, except for the coconut chips, in a baking pan. Bake in the preheated Air Fryer for 20 minutes. Serve in individual bowls, garnished with coconut chips.

916. Toasted Coco Flakes

Servings: 4   Cooking Time: 15 Minutes
Ingredients:
1 cup unsweetened coconut flakes
2 tsp. coconut oil

¼ cup granular erythritol.
⅛ tsp. salt

Directions:
Toss coconut flakes and oil in a large bowl until coated. Sprinkle with erythritol and salt. Place coconut flakes into the air fryer basket. Adjust the temperature to 300 Degrees F and set the timer for 3 minutes. Toss the flakes when 1 minute remains. Add an extra minute if you would like a more golden coconut flake. Store in an airtight container up to 3 days.

917.Air Fryer Cabbage Chips

Servings: 6   Cooking Time: 25 Minutes
Ingredients:
1 large cabbage head, tear cabbage leaves into pieces
2 tbsp olive oil

1/4 cup parmesan cheese, grated
Pepper
Salt

Directions:
Fit the Instant Vortex oven with the rack in position 2. Add all ingredients into the large mixing bowl and toss well. Add cabbage pieces to the air fryer basket then place an air fryer basket in the baking pan. Place a baking pan on the oven rack. Set to air fry at 300 F for 25 minutes. Serve and enjoy.

918. Moist Pound Cake

Servings: 10   Cooking Time: 55 Minutes
Ingredients:
4 eggs
1 cup almond flour
1/2 cup sour cream
1 cup monk fruit sweetener

1 tsp vanilla
1/4 cup cream cheese
1/4 cup butter
1 tsp baking powder
1 tbsp coconut flour

Directions:
Fit the Instant Vortex oven with the rack in position In a large bowl, mix together almond flour, baking powder, and coconut flour. In a separate bowl, add cream cheese and butter and microwave for 30 seconds. Stir well and microwave for 30 seconds more. Stir in sour cream, vanilla, and sweetener. Stir well. Pour cream cheese mixture into the almond flour mixture and stir until just combined. Add eggs in batter one by one and stir until well combined. Pour batter into the prepared grease cake pan. Set to bake at 350 F for 60 minutes. After 5 minutes place the cake pan in the preheated oven. Slice and serve.

919. Almond Cherry Bars

Servings: 12   Cooking Time: 35 Minutes
Ingredients:
Xanthan gum, 1 tbsp.
Almond flour, 1 ½ cup
Pitted fresh cherries, 1 cup
Softened butter, ½ cup

Salt, ½ tsp.
Eggs, 2.
Water, ¼ cup
Vanilla, ½ tsp.
Erythritol, 1 cup

Directions:
Combine almond flour, softened butter, salt, vanilla, eggs, and erythritol in a large bowl until you form a dough. Press the dough in a baking dish that will fit in the air fryer. Set in the air fryer and bake for 10 minutes at 375F Meanwhile, mix the cherries, water, and xanthan gum in a bowl. Take the dough out and pour over the cherry mixture. Cook again for 25 minutes at 375F in the air fryer.

920. Baked Yoghurt

Ingredients:
1 cup blackberries
Handful of mint leaves
3 tsp. sugar
4 tsp. water
2 cups condensed milk

2 cups yoghurt
2 cups fresh cream
1 cup fresh strawberries
1 cup fresh blueberries

Directions:
Mix the ingredients together and create a thick mixture. Transfer this into baking bowls ensuring that you do not overfill. Preheat the fryer to 300 Fahrenheit for five minutes. You will need to place the bowls in the basket and cover it. Cook it for fifteen minutes. When you shake the bowls, the mixture should just shake but not break. Leave it in the refrigerator to set and then arrange the fruits, garnish and serve.

Other Favorite Recipes

921. Chocolate And Coconut Macaroons

Servings: 24 Macaroons   Cooking Time: 8 Minutes

Ingredients:

3 large egg whites, at room temperature
¼ teaspoon salt
¾ cup granulated white sugar

4½ tablespoons unsweetened cocoa powder
2¼ cups unsweetened shredded coconut

Directions:
Line the air fryer basket with parchment paper. Whisk the egg whites with salt in a large bowl with a hand mixer on high speed until stiff peaks form. Whisk in the sugar with the hand mixer on high speed until the mixture is thick. Mix in the cocoa powder and coconut.   Scoop 2 tablespoons of the mixture and shape the mixture in a ball. Repeat with remaining mixture to make 24 balls in total. Arrange the balls in a single layer in the basket and leave a little space between each two balls.   Put the air fryer basket on the baking pan and slide into Rack Position 2, select Air Fry, set temperature to 375°F (190°C) and set time to 8 minutes.   When cooking is complete, the balls should be golden brown.   Serve immediately.

922. Simple Air Fried Edamame

Servings: 6   Cooking Time: 7 Minutes

Ingredients:

1½ pounds (680 g) unshelled edamame
1 teaspoon sea salt

2 tablespoons olive oil

Directions:
Place the edamame in a large bowl, then drizzle with olive oil. Toss to coat well. Transfer the edamame to the air fryer basket.   Put the air fryer basket on the baking pan and slide into Rack Position 2, select Air Fry, set temperature to 400°F (205°C) and set time to 7 minutes.   Stir the edamame at least three times during cooking.   When done, the edamame will be tender and warmed through.   Transfer the cooked edamame onto a plate and sprinkle with salt. Toss to combine well and set aside for 3 minutes to infuse before serving.

923. Hillbilly Broccoli Cheese Casserole

Servings: 6   Cooking Time: 30 Minutes

Ingredients:

4 cups broccoli florets
¼ cup heavy whipping cream
¼ cup ranch dressing

½ cup sharp Cheddar cheese, shredded
Kosher salt and ground black pepper, to taste

Directions:
Combine all the ingredients in a large bowl. Toss to coat well broccoli well.   Pour the mixture into the baking pan.   Slide the baking pan into Rack Position 1, select Convection Bake, set temperature to 375°F (190°C) and set time to 30 minutes. When cooking is complete, the broccoli should be tender.   Remove the baking pan from the oven and serve immediately.

924. Banana Cake

Servings: 8   Cooking Time: 20 Minutes

Ingredients:

1 cup plus 1 tablespoon all-purpose flour
¼ teaspoon baking soda
¾ teaspoon baking powder
¼ teaspoon salt
9½ tablespoons granulated white sugar

5 tablespoons butter, at room temperature
2½ small ripe bananas, peeled
2 large eggs
5 tablespoons buttermilk
1 teaspoon vanilla extract
Cooking spray

Directions:
Spritz the baking pan with cooking spray. Combine the flour, baking soda, baking powder, and salt in a large bowl. Stir to mix well.   Beat the sugar and butter in a separate bowl with a hand mixer on medium speed for 3 minutes.   Beat in the bananas, eggs, buttermilk, and vanilla extract into the sugar and butter mix with a hand mixer. Pour in the flour mixture and whip with hand mixer until sanity and smooth.   Scrape the batter into the pan and level the batter with a spatula.   Slide the baking pan into Rack Position 1, select Convection Bake, set temperature to 325°F (163°C) and set time to 20 minutes.   After 15 minutes, remove the pan from the oven. Check the doneness. Return the pan to the oven and continue cooking. When done, a toothpick inserted in the center should come out clean.   Invert the cake on a cooling rack and allow to cool for 15 minutes before slicing to serve.

925. Teriyaki Shrimp Skewers

Servings: 12 Skewered Shrimp   Cooking Time: 6 Minutes

Ingredients:

1½ tablespoons mirin
1½ teaspoons ginger juice
12 large shrimp (about 20 shrimps per pound), peeled and deveined

1½ tablespoons soy sauce
1 large egg
¾ cup panko bread crumbs
Cooking spray

Directions:
Combine the mirin, ginger juice, and soy sauce in a large bowl. Stir to mix well.   Dunk the shrimp in

the bowl of mirin mixture, then wrap the bowl in plastic and refrigerate for 1 hour to marinate. Spritz the air fryer basket with cooking spray. Run twelve 4-inch skewers through each shrimp. Whisk the egg in the bowl of marinade to combine well. Pour the bread crumbs on a plate. Dredge the shrimp skewers in the egg mixture, then shake the excess off and roll over the bread crumbs to coat well. Arrange the shrimp skewers in the basket and spritz with cooking spray. Put the air fryer basket on the baking pan and slide into Rack Position 2, select Air Fry, set temperature to 400°F (205°C) and set time to 6 minutes. Flip the shrimp skewers halfway through the cooking time. When done, the shrimp will be opaque and firm. Serve immediately.

---

926. Greek Frittata

Servings: 2   Cooking Time: 8 Minutes

Ingredients:

1 cup chopped mushrooms	2 tablespoons heavy cream
2 cups spinach, chopped	A handful of fresh parsley, chopped
4 eggs, lightly beaten	Salt and ground black pepper, to taste
3 ounces (85 g) feta cheese, crumbled	Cooking spray

Directions:
Spritz the baking pan with cooking spray. Whisk together all the ingredients in a large bowl. Stir to mix well. Pour the mixture in the prepared baking pan. Slide the baking pan into Rack Position 1, select Convection Bake, set temperature to 350°F (180°C) and set time to 8 minutes. Stir the mixture halfway through. When cooking is complete, the eggs should be set. Serve immediately.

---

927. Sweet Air Fried Pecans

Servings: 4 Cups   Cooking Time: 10 Minutes

Ingredients:

2 egg whites	2 teaspoons kosher salt
1 tablespoon cumin	
2 teaspoons smoked paprika	1 pound (454 g) pecan halves
½ cup brown sugar	Cooking spray

Directions:
Spritz the air fryer basket with cooking spray. Combine the egg whites, cumin, paprika, sugar, and salt in a large bowl. Stir to mix well. Add the pecans to the bowl and toss to coat well. Transfer the pecans to the basket. Put the air fryer basket on the baking pan and slide into Rack Position 2, select Air Fry, set temperature to 300°F (150°C) and set time to 10 minutes. Stir the pecans at least two times during the cooking. When cooking is complete, the pecans should be lightly caramelized. Remove from the oven and serve immediately.

---

928. Apple Fritters With Sugary Glaze

Servings: 15 Fritters   Cooking Time: 8 Minutes

Ingredients:

Apple Fritters:	¼ cup milk
2 firm apples, peeled, cored, and diced	2 tablespoons unsalted butter, melted
½ teaspoon cinnamon	2 tablespoons granulated sugar
Juice of 1 lemon	Cooking spray
1 cup all-purpose flour	Glaze:
1½ teaspoons baking powder	½ teaspoon vanilla extract
½ teaspoon kosher salt	1¼ cups powdered sugar, sifted
2 eggs	¼ cup water

Directions:
Line the air fryer basket with parchment paper. Combine the apples with cinnamon and lemon juice in a small bowl. Toss to coat well. Combine the flour, baking powder, and salt in a large bowl. Stir to mix well. Whisk the egg, milk, butter, and sugar in a medium bowl. Stir to mix well. Make a well in the center of the flour mixture, then pour the egg mixture into the bowl and stir to mix well. Mix in the apple until a dough forms. Use an ice cream scoop to scoop 15 balls from the dough onto the pan. Spritz with cooking spray. Put the air fryer basket on the baking pan and slide into Rack Position 2, select Air Fry, set temperature to 360°F (182°C) and set time to 8 minutes. Flip the apple fritters halfway through the cooking time. Meanwhile, combine the ingredients for the glaze in a separate small bowl. Stir to mix well. When cooking is complete, the apple fritters will be golden brown. Serve the fritters with the glaze on top or use the glaze for dipping.

---

929. Baked Cherry Tomatoes With Basil

Servings: 2   Cooking Time: 5 Minutes

Ingredients:

2 cups cherry tomatoes	1 teaspoon olive oil
1 clove garlic, thinly sliced	1 tablespoon freshly chopped basil, for topping
⅛ teaspoon kosher salt	Cooking spray

Directions:
Spritz the baking pan with cooking spray and set aside. In a large bowl, toss together the cherry tomatoes, sliced garlic, olive oil, and kosher salt. Spread the mixture in an even layer in the prepared pan. Slide the baking pan into Rack Position 1, select Convection Bake, set temperature to 360°F (182°C) and set time to 5 minutes. When cooking is complete, the tomatoes should be the soft and wilted. Transfer to a bowl and rest for 5 minutes. Top with the chopped basil and serve warm.

---

930. Fast Cinnamon Toast

Servings: 6   Cooking Time: 5 Minutes

Ingredients:

1½ teaspoons cinnamon
1½ teaspoons vanilla extract
2 teaspoons ground black pepper

½ cup sugar
2 tablespoons melted coconut oil
12 slices whole wheat bread

Directions:
Combine all the ingredients, except for the bread, in a large bowl. Stir to mix well. Dunk the bread in the bowl of mixture gently to coat and infuse well. Shake the excess off. Arrange the bread slices in the air fryer basket. Put the air fryer basket on the baking pan and slide into Rack Position 2, select Air Fry, set temperature to 400°F (205°C) and set time to 5 minutes. Flip the bread halfway through. When cooking is complete, the bread should be golden brown. Remove the bread slices from the oven and slice to serve.

931. Dehydrated Vegetable Black Pepper Chips

Ingredients:

Spice mix for parsnip chips
½ teaspoon ground turmeric
1 teaspoon kosher salt
½ teaspoon ground white or black pepper
Red wine vinegar glaze for beet chips
2 tablespoons red wine vinegar
1 medium sweet potato
2 medium parsnips
Spice mix for sweet potato chips

2 medium beets
½ teaspoon dried thyme
½ teaspoon onion powder
½ teaspoon garlic powder
¼ teaspoon ground white pepper
1 teaspoon kosher salt
½ teaspoon kosher salt
½ teaspoon ground white or black pepper

Directions:
For the sweet potato chips, combine spice mix in a little bowl and set aside. Peel sweet curry then slice using a mandolin. Arrange slices in One coating on the dehydrate baskets. Gently and evenly sprinkle with the spice mixture. Place dehydrate baskets in rack positions 5 and 3 and press START. Assess on crispiness and rotate trays occasionally, every 4--5 hours. Chips should sense paper-dry and snap in half easily. For the parsnip chips, combine spice mix in a little bowl and set aside. Arrange pieces in a single layer on the dehydrate baskets. Lightly and evenly sprinkle with the spice mixture. Dehydrate chips as per step 3, altering the dehydrate period to 6 hours. For the beet chips, peel beets then thinly slice using a mandolin. Arrange slices in a single layer on the dehydrate baskets. Lightly brush with red wine vinegar then lightly and evenly sprinkle with pepper and salt. Dehydrate chips According to step 3.

932. Salty Tortilla Chips

Servings: 4   Cooking Time: 10 Minutes
Ingredients:

4 six-inch corn tortillas, cut in half and slice into thirds
Cooking spray

1 tablespoon canola oil
¼ teaspoon kosher salt

Directions:
Spritz the air fryer basket with cooking spray. On a clean work surface, brush the tortilla chips with canola oil, then transfer the chips to the basket. Put the air fryer basket on the baking pan and slide into Rack Position 2, select Air Fry, set temperature to 360°F (182°C) and set time to 10 minutes. Flip the chips and sprinkle with salt halfway through the cooking time. When cooked, the chips will be crunchy and lightly browned. Transfer the chips to a plate lined with paper towels. Serve immediately.

933. Cinnamon Rolls With Cream Glaze

Servings: 8   Cooking Time: 5 Minutes
Ingredients:

1 pound (454 g) frozen bread dough, thawed
2 tablespoons melted butter
1½ tablespoons cinnamon
¾ cup brown sugar
Cooking spray

Cream Glaze:
4 ounces (113 g) softened cream cheese
½ teaspoon vanilla extract
2 tablespoons melted butter
1¼ cups powdered erythritol

Directions:
Place the bread dough on a clean work surface, then roll the dough out into a rectangle with a rolling pin. Brush the top of the dough with melted butter and leave 1-inch edges uncovered. Combine the cinnamon and sugar in a small bowl, then sprinkle the dough with the cinnamon mixture. Roll the dough over tightly, then cut the dough log into 8 portions. Wrap the portions in plastic, better separately, and let sit to rise for 1 or 2 hours. Meanwhile, combine the ingredients for the glaze in a separate small bowl. Stir to mix well. Spritz the air fryer basket with cooking spray. Transfer the risen rolls to the basket. Put the air fryer basket on the baking pan and slide into Rack Position 2, select Air Fry, set temperature to 350°F (180°C) and set time to 5 minutes. Flip the rolls halfway through the cooking time. When cooking is complete, the rolls will be golden brown. Serve the rolls with the glaze.

934. Enchilada Sauce

Servings: 2 Cups   Cooking Time: 0 Minutes
Ingredients:

3 large ancho chiles, stems and seeds removed, torn into pieces
1½ cups very hot water
2 garlic cloves, peeled

2 tablespoons wine vinegar
½ teaspoon dried oregano
½ teaspoon ground cumin

and lightly smashed
1½ teaspoons sugar
2 teaspoons kosher salt or 1 teaspoon fine salt

Directions:
Mix together the chile pieces and hot water in a bowl and let stand for 10 to 15 minutes.   Pour the chiles and water into a blender jar. Fold in the garlic, vinegar, sugar, oregano, cumin, and salt and blend until smooth.   Use immediately.

---

935.   Shawarma Spice Mix

Servings: About 1 Tablespoon   Cooking Time: 0 Minutes

Ingredients:
1 teaspoon smoked paprika
1 teaspoon cumin
¼ teaspoon turmeric
¼ teaspoon kosher salt or ⅛ teaspoon fine salt
¼ teaspoon cinnamon
¼ teaspoon allspice
¼ teaspoon red pepper flakes
¼ teaspoon freshly ground black pepper

Directions:
Stir together all the ingredients in a small bowl. Use immediately or place in an airtight container in the pantry.

---

936.   Chocolate Buttermilk Cake

Servings: 8   Cooking Time: 20 Minutes

Ingredients:
1 cup all-purpose flour
⅔ cup granulated white sugar
¼ cup unsweetened cocoa powder
¾ teaspoon baking soda
¼ teaspoon salt
⅔ cup buttermilk
2 tablespoons plus 2 teaspoons vegetable oil
1 teaspoon vanilla extract
Cooking spray

Directions:
Spritz the baking pan with cooking spray. Combine the flour, cocoa powder, baking soda, sugar, and salt in a large bowl. Stir to mix well. Mix in the buttermilk, vanilla, and vegetable oil. Keep stirring until it forms a grainy and thick dough. Scrape the chocolate batter from the bowl and transfer to the pan, level the batter in an even layer with a spatula.   Slide the baking pan into Rack Position 1, select Convection Bake, set temperature to 325°F (163°C) and set time to 20 minutes. After 15 minutes, remove the pan from the oven. Check the doneness. Return the pan to the oven and continue cooking.   When done, a toothpick inserted in the center should come out clean. Invert the cake on a cooling rack and allow to cool for 15 minutes before slicing to serve.

---

937.   Shrimp Spinach Frittata

Servings: 4   Cooking Time: 14 Minutes

Ingredients:

4 whole eggs
1 teaspoon dried basil
½ cup shrimp, cooked and chopped
½ cup baby spinach
½ cup rice, cooked
½ cup Monterey Jack cheese, grated
Salt, to taste
Cooking spray

Directions:
Spritz the baking pan with cooking spray.   Whisk the eggs with basil and salt in a large bowl until bubbly, then mix in the shrimp, spinach, rice, and cheese.   Pour the mixture into the baking pan. Slide the baking pan into Rack Position 1, select Convection Bake, set temperature to 360°F (182°C) and set time to 14 minutes.   Stir the mixture halfway through.   When cooking is complete, the eggs should be set and the frittata should be golden brown.   Slice to serve.

---

938.   Cheddar Jalapeño Cornbread

Servings: 8   Cooking Time: 20 Minutes

Ingredients:
⅔ cup cornmeal
⅓ cup all-purpose flour
¾ teaspoon baking powder
2 tablespoons buttery spread, melted
½ teaspoon kosher salt
1 tablespoon granulated sugar
¾ cup whole milk
1 large egg, beaten
1 jalapeño pepper, thinly sliced
⅓ cup shredded sharp Cheddar cheese
Cooking spray

Directions:
Spritz the baking pan with cooking spray. Combine all the ingredients in a large bowl. Stir to mix well. Pour the mixture in the baking pan. Slide the baking pan into Rack Position 1, select Convection Bake, set temperature to 300°F (150°C) and set time to 20 minutes.   When the cooking is complete, a toothpick inserted in the center of the bread should come out clean.   Remove the baking pan from the oven and allow the bread to cool for 5 minutes before slicing to serve.

---

939.   Cheesy Green Bean Casserole

Servings: 4   Cooking Time: 6 Minutes

Ingredients:
1 tablespoon melted butter
1 cup green beans
6 ounces (170 g) Cheddar cheese, shredded
7 ounces (198 g) Parmesan cheese, shredded
¼ cup heavy cream
Sea salt, to taste

Directions:
Grease the baking pan with the melted butter. Add the green beans, Cheddar, salt, and black pepper to the prepared baking pan. Stir to mix well, then spread the Parmesan and cream on top. Slide the baking pan into Rack Position 1, select Convection Bake, set temperature to 400°F (205°C) and set time to 6 minutes.   When cooking is complete, the beans should be tender and the cheese should be melted.   Serve immediately.

940. Ritzy Chicken And Vegetable Casserole

Servings: 4   Cooking Time: 15 Minutes

Ingredients:

4 boneless and skinless chicken breasts, cut into cubes	1 teaspoon Sriracha
	3 tablespoons soy sauce
2 carrots, sliced	2 tablespoons oyster sauce
1 yellow bell pepper, cut into strips	1 tablespoon rice wine vinegar
1 red bell pepper, cut into strips	1 teaspoon cornstarch
15 ounces (425 g) broccoli florets	1 tablespoon grated ginger
1 cup snow peas	2 garlic cloves, minced
1 scallion, sliced	1 teaspoon sesame oil
Cooking spray	1 tablespoon brown sugar
Sauce:	

Directions:

Spritz the baking pan with cooking spray. Combine the chicken, carrot, and bell peppers in a large bowl. Stir to mix well.   Combine the ingredients for the sauce in a separate bowl. Stir to mix well.   Pour the chicken mixture into the baking pan, then pour the sauce over. Stir to coat well.   Slide the baking pan into Rack Position 1, select Convection Bake, set temperature to 370°F (188°C) and set time to 13 minutes.   Add the broccoli and snow peas to the pan halfway through. When cooking is complete, the vegetables should be tender.   Remove from the oven and sprinkle with sliced scallion before serving.

941. Crunchy Green Tomatoes Slices

Servings: 12 Slices   Cooking Time: 8 Minutes

Ingredients:

½ cup all-purpose flour	1 cup cornmeal
1 egg	1 cup panko
½ cup buttermilk	½ teaspoon salt
2 green tomatoes, cut into ¼-inch-thick slices, patted dry	½ teaspoon ground black pepper
	Cooking spray

Directions:

Spritz a baking sheet with cooking spray.   Pour the flour in a bowl. Whisk the egg and buttermilk in a second bowl. Combine the cornmeal and panko in a third bowl.   Dredge the tomato slices in the bowl of flour first, then into the egg mixture, and then dunk the slices into the cornmeal mixture. Shake the excess off.   Transfer the well-coated tomato slices in the baking sheet and sprinkle with salt and ground black pepper. Spritz the tomato slices with cooking spray.   Put the air fryer basket on the baking pan and slide into Rack Position 2, select Air Fry, set temperature to 400°F (205°C) and set time to 8 minutes.   Flip the slices halfway through the cooking time.   When cooking is complete, the tomato slices should be crispy and lightly browned. Remove the baking sheet from the oven.   Serve immediately.

942. Arancini

Servings: 10 Arancini   Cooking Time: 30 Minutes

Ingredients:

⅔ cup raw white Arborio rice	1¼ cups seasoned Italian-style dried bread crumbs
2 teaspoons butter	
½ teaspoon salt	
1⅓ cups water	10 ¾-inch semi-firm Mozzarella cubes
2 large eggs, well beaten	Cooking spray

Directions:

Pour the rice, butter, salt, and water in a pot. Stir to mix well and bring a boil over medium-high heat. Keep stirring.   Reduce the heat to low and cover the pot. Simmer for 20 minutes or until the rice is tender.   Turn off the heat and let sit, covered, for 10 minutes, then open the lid and fluffy the rice with a fork. Allow to cool for 10 more minutes.   Pour the beaten eggs in a bowl, then pour the bread crumbs in a separate bowl.   Scoop 2 tablespoons of the cooked rice up and form it into a ball, then press the Mozzarella into the ball and wrap. Dredge the ball in the eggs first, then shake the excess off the dunk the ball in the bread crumbs. Roll to coat evenly. Repeat to make 10 balls in total with remaining rice.   Transfer the balls in the air fryer basket and spritz with cooking spray.   Put the air fryer basket on the baking pan and slide into Rack Position 2, select Air Fry, set temperature to 375°F (190°C) and set time to 10 minutes.   When cooking is complete, the balls should be lightly browned and crispy.   Remove the balls from the oven and allow to cool before serving.

943. Dehydrated Honey-rosemary Roasted Almonds

Ingredients:

1 heaping tablespoon demerara sugar	8 ounces (225g) raw almonds
1 teaspoon finely chopped fresh rosemary	2 tablespoons kosher salt
1 teaspoon kosher salt	Honey-Rosemary glaze
	¼ cup (80g) honey

Directions:

Place almonds and salt in a bowl. Add cold tap water to cover the almonds by 1-inch   (2cm). Let soak at room temperature for 12 hours to activate.   Rinse almonds under cold running water, then drain. Spread in a single layer on the dehydrate basket. Dehydrate almonds for 24 hours or till tender and somewhat crispy but additionally spongy in the middle. Almonds may be eaten plain or roasted each the next recipe.   Put honey in a small saucepan and heat over Low heat. Put triggered nuts   At a medium bowl and then pour over warm honey. Stir To coat nuts equally. Add rosemary, sugar   And salt and stir to blend.   Spread Almonds in one layer on the skillet.   Insert cable rack into rack place   6.   Select   BAKE/350°F (175°C)/CONVECTION/10 moments and empower Rotate Remind.   Stirring almonds when Rotate

Remind signs.   Let cool completely before storing in an airtight container.

944.   Spicy Air Fried Old Bay Shrimp

Servings: 2 Cups   Cooking Time: 10 Minutes

Ingredients:

½ teaspoon Old Bay Seasoning

1 teaspoon ground cayenne pepper

1 tablespoon olive oil

½ teaspoon paprika

⅛ teaspoon salt

½ pound (227 g) shrimps, peeled and deveined

Juice of half a lemon

Directions:
Combine the Old Bay Seasoning, cayenne pepper, paprika, olive oil, and salt in a large bowl, then add the shrimps and toss to coat well.   Put the shrimps in the air fryer basket.   Put the air fryer basket on the baking pan and slide into Rack Position 2, select Air Fry, set temperature to 390°F (199°C) and set time to 10 minutes.   Flip the shrimps halfway through the cooking time.   When cooking is complete, the shrimps should be opaque. Serve the shrimps with lemon juice on top.

945.   Asian Dipping Sauce

Servings: About 1 Cup   Cooking Time: 0 Minutes

Ingredients:

¼ cup rice vinegar

¼ cup low-sodium chicken or vegetable stock

3 tablespoons soy sauce

1 tablespoon minced or grated ginger

¼ cup hoisin sauce

1 tablespoon minced or pressed garlic

1 teaspoon chili-garlic sauce or sriracha (or more to taste)

Directions:
Stir together all the ingredients in a small bowl, or place in a jar with a tight-fitting lid and shake until well mixed.   Use immediately.

946.   Cauliflower And Pumpkin Casserole

Servings: 6   Cooking Time: 50 Minutes

Ingredients:

1 cup chicken broth

2 cups cauliflower florets

1 cup canned pumpkin purée

¼ cup heavy cream

1 teaspoon vanilla extract

2 large eggs, beaten

⅓ cup unsalted butter, melted, plus more for greasing the pan

¼ cup sugar

1 teaspoon fine sea salt

Chopped fresh parsley leaves, for garnish

TOPPING:

½ cup blanched almond flour

1 cup chopped pecans

⅓ cup unsalted butter, melted

½ cup sugar

Directions:
Pour the chicken broth in the baking pan, then add the cauliflower.   Slide the baking pan into Rack Position 1, select Convection Bake, set temperature to 350°F (180°C) and set time to 20 minutes. When cooking is complete, the cauliflower should be soft.   Meanwhile, combine the ingredients for the topping in a large bowl. Stir to mix well.   Pat the cauliflower dry with paper towels, then place in a food processor and pulse with pumpkin purée, heavy cream, vanilla extract, eggs, butter, sugar, and salt until smooth.   Clean the baking pan and grease with more butter, then pour the purée mixture in the pan.   Spread the topping over the mixture.   Put the baking pan back to the oven. Select Bake and set time to 30 minutes.   When baking is complete, the topping of the casserole should be lightly browned.   Remove the casserole from the oven and serve with fresh parsley on top.

947.   Herbed Cheddar Frittata

Servings: 4   Cooking Time: 20 Minutes

Ingredients:

½ cup shredded Cheddar cheese

½ cup half-and-half

2 tablespoons chopped scallion greens

2 tablespoons chopped fresh parsley

4 large eggs

½ teaspoon kosher salt

½ teaspoon ground black pepper

Cooking spray

Directions:
Spritz the baking pan with cooking spray.   Whisk together all the ingredients in a large bowl, then pour the mixture into the prepared baking pan. Slide the baking pan into Rack Position 1, select Convection Bake, set temperature to 300°F (150°C) and set time to 20 minutes.   Stir the mixture halfway through.   When cooking is complete, the eggs should be set.   Serve immediately.

948.   Ritzy Pimento And Almond Turkey Casserole

Servings: 4   Cooking Time: 32 Minutes

Ingredients:

1 pound (454 g) turkey breasts

1 tablespoon olive oil

2 boiled eggs, chopped

2 tablespoons chopped pimentos

¼ cup slivered almonds, chopped

¼ cup mayonnaise

½ cup diced celery

2 tablespoons chopped green onion

¼ cup cream of chicken soup

¼ cup bread crumbs

Salt and ground black pepper, to taste

Directions:
Put the turkey breasts in a large bowl. Sprinkle with salt and ground black pepper and drizzle with olive oil. Toss to coat well.   Transfer the turkey to the air fryer basket.   Put the air fryer basket on the baking pan and slide into Rack Position 2, select Air Fry, set temperature to 390°F (199°C) and set time

to 12 minutes.   Flip the turkey halfway through. When cooking is complete, the turkey should be well browned.   Remove the turkey breasts from the oven and cut into cubes, then combine the chicken cubes with eggs, pimentos, almonds, mayo, celery, green onions, and chicken soup in a large bowl. Stir to mix.   Pour the mixture into the baking pan, then spread with bread crumbs.   Slide the baking pan into Rack Position 1, select Convection Bake, set time to 20 minutes.   When cooking is complete, the eggs should be set.   Remove from the oven and serve immediately.

949.   Sweet And Sour Peanuts

Servings: 9   Cooking Time: 5 Minutes
Ingredients:

3 cups shelled raw peanuts
1 tablespoon hot red pepper sauce

3 tablespoons granulated white sugar

Directions:
Put the peanuts in a large bowl, then drizzle with hot red pepper sauce and sprinkle with sugar. Toss to coat well.   Pour the peanuts in the air fryer basket. Put the air fryer basket on the baking pan and slide into Rack Position 2, select Air Fry, set temperature to 400°F (205°C) and set time to 5 minutes.   Stir the peanuts halfway through the cooking time. When cooking is complete, the peanuts will be crispy and browned. Remove from the oven and serve immediately.

950.   Garlicky Spiralized Zucchini And Squash

Servings: 4   Cooking Time: 10 Minutes
Ingredients:

2 large zucchini, peeled and spiralized
2 large yellow summer squash, peeled and spiralized
1 tablespoon olive oil, divided

½ teaspoon kosher salt
1 garlic clove, whole
2 tablespoons fresh basil, chopped
Cooking spray

Directions:
Spritz the air fryer basket with cooking spray. Combine the zucchini and summer squash with 1 teaspoon of the olive oil and salt in a large bowl. Toss to coat well.   Transfer the zucchini and summer squash to the basket and add the garlic.   Put the air fryer basket on the baking pan and slide into Rack Position 2, select Air Fry, set temperature to 360°F (182°C) and set time to 10 minutes.   Stir the zucchini and summer squash halfway through the cooking time.   When cooked, the zucchini and summer squash will be tender and fragrant. Transfer the cooked zucchini and summer squash onto a plate and set aside.   Remove the garlic from the oven and allow to cool for 5 minutes. Mince the garlic and combine with remaining olive oil in a small bowl. Stir to mix well.   Drizzle the spiralized zucchini and summer squash with garlic oil and sprinkle with basil. Toss to serve.

951.   Parsnip Fries With Garlic-yogurt Dip

Servings: 4   Cooking Time: 10 Minutes
Ingredients:

3 medium parsnips, peeled, cut into sticks
¼ teaspoon kosher salt
1 teaspoon olive oil
1 garlic clove, unpeeled
Cooking spray
Dip:

¼ cup plain Greek yogurt
⅛ teaspoon garlic powder
1 tablespoon sour cream
¼ teaspoon kosher salt
Freshly ground black pepper, to taste

Directions:
Spritz the air fryer basket with cooking spray.   Put the parsnip sticks in a large bowl, then sprinkle with salt and drizzle with olive oil.   Transfer the parsnip into the basket and add the garlic.   Put the air fryer basket on the baking pan and slide into Rack Position 2, select Air Fry, set temperature to 360°F (182°C) and set time to 10 minutes.   Stir the parsnip halfway through the cooking time. Meanwhile, peel the garlic and crush it. Combine the crushed garlic with the ingredients for the dip. Stir to mix well.   When cooked, the parsnip sticks should be crisp. Remove the parsnip fries from the oven and serve with the dipping sauce.

952.   Kale Chips With Soy Sauce

Servings: 2   Cooking Time: 5 Minutes
Ingredients:

4 medium kale leaves, about 1 ounce (28 g) each, stems removed, tear the leaves in thirds

2 teaspoons soy sauce
2 teaspoons olive oil

Directions:
Toss the kale leaves with soy sauce and olive oil in a large bowl to coat well. Place the leaves in the baking pan.   Put the air fryer basket on the baking pan and slide into Rack Position 2, select Air Fry, set temperature to 400°F (205°C) and set time to 5 minutes.   Flip the leaves with tongs gently halfway through.   When cooked, the kale leaves should be crispy. Remove from the oven and serve immediately.

953.   Corn On The Cob With Mayonnaise

Servings: 4   Cooking Time: 10 Minutes
Ingredients:

2 tablespoons mayonnaise
2 teaspoons minced garlic
1 cup panko bread crumbs

½ teaspoon sea salt
4 (4-inch length) ears corn on the cob, husk and silk removed
Cooking spray

Directions:

Spritz the air fryer basket with cooking spray. Combine the mayonnaise, garlic, and salt in a bowl. Stir to mix well. Pour the panko on a plate. Brush the corn on the cob with mayonnaise mixture, then roll the cob in the bread crumbs and press to coat well. Transfer the corn on the cob in the basket and spritz with cooking spray. Put the air fryer basket on the baking pan and slide into Rack Position 2, select Air Fry, set temperature to 400°F (205°C) and set time to 10 minutes. Flip the corn on the cob at least three times during the cooking. When cooked, the corn kernels on the cob should be almost browned. Remove from the oven and serve immediately.

954.	**Sumptuous Beef And Bean Chili Casserole**

Servings: 4   Cooking Time: 31 Minutes
Ingredients:

1 tablespoon olive oil	½ teaspoon parsley
½ cup finely chopped bell pepper	½ tablespoon chili powder
½ cup chopped celery	1 teaspoon chopped cilantro
1 onion, chopped	1½ cups vegetable broth
2 garlic cloves, minced	1 (8-ounce / 227-g) can cannellini beans
1 pound (454 g) ground beef	Salt and ground black pepper, to taste
1 can diced tomatoes	

Directions:
Heat the olive oil in a nonstick skillet over medium heat until shimmering. Add the bell pepper, celery, onion, and garlic to the skillet and sauté for 5 minutes or until the onion is translucent. Add the ground beef and sauté for an additional 6 minutes or until lightly browned. Mix in the tomatoes, parsley, chili powder, cilantro and vegetable broth, then cook for 10 more minutes. Stir constantly. Pour them in the baking pan, then mix in the beans and sprinkle with salt and ground black pepper. Slide the baking pan into Rack Position 1, select Convection Bake, set temperature to 350°F (180°C) and set time to 10 minutes. When cooking is complete, the vegetables should be tender and the beef should be well browned. Remove from the oven and serve immediately.

955.	**Simple Butter Cake**

Servings: 8   Cooking Time: 20 Minutes
Ingredients:

1 cup all-purpose flour	9½ tablespoons butter, at room temperature
1¼ teaspoons baking powder	2 large eggs
¼ teaspoon salt	1 large egg yolk
½ cup plus 1½ tablespoons granulated white sugar	2½ tablespoons milk
	1 teaspoon vanilla extract
	Cooking spray

Directions:
Spritz the baking pan with cooking spray. Combine the flour, baking powder, and salt in a large bowl. Stir to mix well. Whip the sugar and butter in a separate bowl with a hand mixer on medium speed for 3 minutes. Whip the eggs, egg yolk, milk, and vanilla extract into the sugar and butter mix with a hand mixer. Pour in the flour mixture and whip with hand mixer until sanity and smooth. Scrape the batter into the baking pan and level the batter with a spatula. Slide the baking pan into Rack Position 1, select Convection Bake, set temperature to 325°F (163°C) and set time to 20 minutes. After 15 minutes, remove the pan from the oven. Check the doneness. Return the pan to the oven and continue cooking. When done, a toothpick inserted in the center should come out clean. Invert the cake on a cooling rack and allow to cool for 15 minutes before slicing to serve.

956.	**Supplì Al Telefono (risotto Croquettes)**

Servings: 6   Cooking Time: 54 Minutes
Ingredients:

Risotto Croquettes:	Kosher salt and ground black pepper, to taste
4 tablespoons unsalted butter	Cooking spray
1 small yellow onion, minced	Tomato Sauce:
1 cup Arborio rice	2 tablespoons extra-virgin olive oil
3½ cups chicken stock	4 cloves garlic, minced
½ cup dry white wine	
3 eggs	¼ teaspoon red pepper flakes
Zest of 1 lemon	1 (28-ounce / 794-g) can crushed tomatoes
½ cup grated Parmesan cheese	2 teaspoons granulated sugar
2 ounces (57 g) fresh Mozzarella cheese	Kosher salt and ground black pepper, to taste
¼ cup peas	
2 tablespoons water	
½ cup all-purpose flour	
1½ cups panko bread crumbs	

Directions:
Melt the butter in a pot over medium heat, then add the onion and salt to taste. Sauté for 5 minutes or until the onion in translucent. Add the rice and stir to coat well. Cook for 3 minutes or until the rice is lightly browned. Pour in the chicken stock and wine. Bring to a boil. Then cook for 20 minutes or until the rice is tender and liquid is almost absorbed. Make the risotto: When the rice is cooked, break the egg into the pot. Add the lemon zest and Parmesan cheese. Sprinkle with salt and ground black pepper. Stir to mix well. Pour the risotto in a baking sheet, then level with a spatula to spread the risotto evenly. Wrap the baking sheet in plastic and refrigerate for1 hour. Meanwhile, heat the olive oil in a saucepan over medium heat until shimmering. Add the garlic and sprinkle with red pepper flakes. Sauté for a minute or until fragrant. Add the crushed

tomatoes and sprinkle with sugar. Stir to mix well. Bring to a boil. Reduce the heat to low and simmer for 15 minutes or until lightly thickened. Sprinkle with salt and pepper to taste. Set aside until ready to serve.   Remove the risotto from the refrigerator. Scoop the risotto into twelve 2-inch balls, then flatten the balls with your hands.   Arrange a about ½-inch piece of Mozzarella and 5 peas in the center of each flattened ball, then wrap them back into balls. Transfer the balls to a baking sheet lined with parchment paper, then refrigerate for 15 minutes or until firm.   Whisk the remaining 2 eggs with 2 tablespoons of water in a bowl. Pour the flour in a second bowl and pour the panko in a third bowl. Dredge the risotto balls in the bowl of flour first, then into the eggs, and then into the panko. Shake the excess off.   Transfer the balls to the baking pan and spritz with cooking spray.   Slide the baking pan into Rack Position 1, select Convection Bake, set temperature to 400°F (205°C) and set time to 10 minutes.   Flip the balls halfway through the cooking time.   When cooking is complete, the balls should be until golden brown.   Serve the risotto balls with the tomato sauce.

---

957.   Classic Churros

Servings: 12 Churros   Cooking Time: 10 Minutes

Ingredients:

4 tablespoons butter	2 teaspoons ground cinnamon
¼ teaspoon salt	
½ cup water	¼ cup granulated white sugar
½ cup all-purpose flour	
2 large eggs	Cooking spray

Directions:
Put the butter, salt, and water in a saucepan. Bring to a boil until the butter is melted on high heat. Keep stirring.   Reduce the heat to medium and fold in the flour to form a dough. Keep cooking and stirring until the dough is dried out and coat the pan with a crust.   Turn off the heat and scrape the dough in a large bowl. Allow to cool for 15 minutes.   Break and whisk the eggs into the dough with a hand mixer until the dough is sanity and firm enough to shape. Scoop up 1 tablespoon of the dough and roll it into a ½-inch-diameter and 2-inch-long cylinder. Repeat with remaining dough to make 12 cylinders in total. Combine the cinnamon and sugar in a large bowl and dunk the cylinders into the cinnamon mix to coat.   Arrange the cylinders on a plate and refrigerate for 20 minutes.   Spritz the air fryer basket with cooking spray. Place the cylinders in the basket and spritz with cooking spray.   Put the air fryer basket on the baking pan and slide into Rack Position 2, select Air Fry, set temperature to 375°F (190°C) and set time to 10 minutes.   Flip the cylinders halfway through the cooking time. When cooked, the cylinders should be golden brown and fluffy.   Serve immediately.

---

958.   Oven Grits

Servings: About 4 Cups   Cooking Time: 1 Hour 5 Minutes

Ingredients:

1 cup grits or polenta (not instant or quick cook)	2 tablespoons unsalted butter, cut into 4 pieces
2 cups chicken or vegetable stock	1 teaspoon kosher salt or ½ teaspoon fine salt
2 cups milk	

Directions:
Add the grits to the baking pan. Stir in the stock, milk, butter, and salt.   Select Bake, set the temperature to 325°F (163°C), and set the time for 1 hour and 5 minutes. Select Start to begin preheating. Once the unit has preheated, place the pan in the oven.   After 15 minutes, remove the pan from the oven and stir the polenta. Return the pan to the oven and continue cooking.   After 30 minutes, remove the pan again and stir the polenta again. Return the pan to the oven and continue cooking for 15 to 20 minutes, or until the polenta is soft and creamy and the liquid is absorbed.   When done, remove the pan from the oven.   Serve immediately.

---

959.   Creamy Pork Gratin

Servings: 4   Cooking Time: 21 Minutes

Ingredients:

2 tablespoons olive oil	1 teaspoon coarse sea salt
2 pounds (907 g) pork tenderloin, cut into serving-size pieces	½ teaspoon freshly ground black pepper
	1 cup Ricotta cheese
1 teaspoon dried marjoram	1½ cups chicken broth
¼ teaspoon chili powder	1 tablespoon mustard
	Cooking spray

Directions:
Spritz the baking pan with cooking spray.   Heat the olive oil in a nonstick skillet over medium-high heat until shimmering.   Add the pork and sauté for 6 minutes or until lightly browned.   Transfer the pork to the prepared baking pan and sprinkle with marjoram, chili powder, salt, and ground black pepper.   Combine the remaining ingredients in a large bowl. Stir to mix well. Pour the mixture over the pork in the pan.   Slide the baking pan into Rack Position 1, select Convection Bake, set temperature to 350°F (180°C) and set time to 15 minutes.   Stir the mixture halfway through. When cooking is complete, the mixture should be frothy and the cheese should be melted.   Serve immediately.

---

960.   Spanakopita

Servings: 6   Cooking Time: 8 Minutes

Ingredients:

½ (10-ounce / 284-g) package frozen spinach, thawed and squeezed dry	¾ cup crumbled feta cheese
1 egg, lightly beaten	⅛ teaspoon ground nutmeg
¼ cup pine nuts, toasted	½ teaspoon salt
	Freshly ground black

¼ cup grated Parmesan cheese

pepper, to taste

6 sheets phyllo dough

½ cup butter, melted

Directions:
Combine all the ingredients, except for the phyllo dough and butter, in a large bowl. Whisk to combine well. Set aside.   Place a sheet of phyllo dough on a clean work surface. Brush with butter then top with another layer sheet of phyllo. Brush with butter, then cut the layered sheets into six 3-inch-wide strips.   Top each strip with 1 tablespoon of the spinach mixture, then fold the bottom left corner over the mixture towards the right strip edge to make a triangle. Keep folding triangles until each strip is folded over.   Brush the triangles with butter and repeat with remaining strips and phyllo dough.   Place the triangles in the baking pan. Put the air fryer basket on the baking pan and slide into Rack Position 2, select Air Fry, set temperature to 350°F (180°C) and set time to 8 minutes.   Flip the triangles halfway through the cooking time. When cooking is complete, the triangles should be golden brown. Remove from the oven and serve immediately.

| **961.** | **Lush Seafood Casserole** |

Servings: 2   Cooking Time: 22 Minutes

Ingredients:

1 tablespoon olive oil

1 small yellow onion, chopped

2 garlic cloves, minced

4 ounces (113 g) tilapia pieces

4 ounces (113 g) rockfish pieces

½ teaspoon dried basil

Salt and ground white pepper, to taste

4 eggs, lightly beaten

1 tablespoon dry sherry

4 tablespoons cheese, shredded

Directions:
Heat the olive oil in a nonstick skillet over medium-high heat until shimmering.   Add the onion and garlic and sauté for 2 minutes or until fragrant. Add the tilapia, rockfish, basil, salt, and white pepper to the skillet. Sauté to combine well and transfer them into the baking pan.   Combine the eggs, sherry and cheese in a large bowl. Stir to mix well. Pour the mixture in the baking pan over the fish mixture.   Slide the baking pan into Rack Position 1, select Convection Bake, set temperature to 360°F (182°C) and set time to 20 minutes. When cooking is complete, the eggs should be set and the casserole edges should be lightly browned. Serve immediately.

| **962.** | **South Carolina Shrimp And Corn Bake** |

Servings: 2   Cooking Time: 18 Minutes

Ingredients:

1 ear corn, husk and silk removed, cut into 2-inch rounds

8 ounces (227 g) red potatoes, unpeeled,

2 teaspoons vegetable oil, divided

¼ teaspoon ground black pepper

cut into 1-inch pieces

2 teaspoons Old Bay Seasoning, divided

8 ounces (227 g) large shrimps (about 12 shrimps), deveined

6 ounces (170 g) andouille or chorizo sausage, cut into 1-inch pieces

2 garlic cloves, minced

1 tablespoon chopped fresh parsley

Directions:
Put the corn rounds and potatoes in a large bowl. Sprinkle with 1 teaspoon of Old Bay seasoning and drizzle with vegetable oil. Toss to coat well. Transfer the corn rounds and potatoes into the baking pan.   Slide the baking pan into Rack Position 1, select Convection Bake, set temperature to 400°F (205°C) and set time to 18 minutes. After 6 minutes, remove from the oven. Stir the corn rounds and potatoes. Return the pan to the oven and continue cooking.   Meanwhile, cut slits into the shrimps but be careful not to cut them through. Combine the shrimps, sausage, remaining Old Bay seasoning, and remaining vegetable oil in the large bowl. Toss to coat well.   After 6 minutes, remove the pan from the oven. Add the shrimps and sausage to the pan. Return the pan to the oven and continue cooking for 6 minutes. Stir the shrimp mixture halfway through the cooking time.   When done, the shrimps should be opaque. Transfer the dish to a plate and spread with parsley before serving.

| **963.** | **Shrimp With Sriracha And Worcestershire Sauce** |

Servings: 4   Cooking Time: 10 Minutes

Ingredients:

1 tablespoon Sriracha sauce

1 teaspoon Worcestershire sauce

2 tablespoons sweet chili sauce

¾ cup mayonnaise

1 cup panko bread crumbs

1 egg, beaten

1 pound (454 g) raw shrimp, shelled and deveined, rinsed and drained

Lime wedges, for serving

Cooking spray

Directions:
Spritz the air fryer basket with cooking spray. Combine the Sriracha sauce, Worcestershire sauce, chili sauce, and mayo in a bowl. Stir to mix well. Reserve ⅓ cup of the mixture as the dipping sauce. Combine the remaining sauce mixture with the beaten egg. Stir to mix well. Put the panko in a separate bowl.   Dredge the shrimp in the sauce mixture first, then into the panko. Roll the shrimp to coat well. Shake the excess off.   Place the shrimp in the basket, then spritz with cooking spray.   Put the air fryer basket on the baking pan and slide into Rack Position 2, select Air Fry, set temperature to 360°F (182°C) and set time to 10 minutes.   Flip the shrimp halfway through the cooking time. When cooking is complete, the shrimp should be opaque.   Remove the shrimp from the oven and serve with reserve sauce mixture and squeeze the lime wedges over.

964. Buttery Knots With Parsley

Servings: 8 Knots   Cooking Time: 5 Minutes

Ingredients:

1 teaspoon dried parsley

2 teaspoons garlic powder

¼ cup melted butter

Directions:

1 (11-ounce / 312-g) tube refrigerated French bread dough, cut into 8 slices   Combine the parsley, butter, and garlic powder in a bowl. Stir to mix well. Place the French bread dough slices on a clean work surface, then roll each slice into a 6-inch long rope. Tie the ropes into knots and arrange them on a plate. Transfer the knots into the baking pan. Brush the knots with butter mixture.   Put the air fryer basket on the baking pan and slide into Rack Position 2, select Air Fry, set temperature to 350°F (180°C) and set time to 5 minutes.   Flip the knots halfway through the cooking time.   When done, the knots should be golden brown. Remove from the oven and serve immediately.

965. Sausage And Colorful Peppers Casserole

Servings: 6   Cooking Time: 25 Minutes

Ingredients:

1 pound (454 g) minced breakfast sausage

2 cups Cheddar cheese, shredded

1 yellow pepper, diced

6 eggs

1 red pepper, diced

Salt and freshly ground black pepper, to taste

1 green pepper, diced

1 sweet onion, diced

Fresh parsley, for garnish

Directions:

Cook the sausage in a nonstick skillet over medium heat for 10 minutes or until well browned. Stir constantly.   When the cooking is finished, transfer the cooked sausage to the baking pan and add the peppers and onion. Scatter with Cheddar cheese.   Whisk the eggs with salt and ground black pepper in a large bowl, then pour the mixture into the baking pan.   Slide the baking pan into Rack Position 1, select Convection Bake, set temperature to 360°F (182°C) and set time to 15 minutes.   When cooking is complete, the egg should be set and the edges of the casserole should be lightly browned.   Remove from the oven and top with fresh parsley before serving.

966. Parmesan Cauliflower Fritters

Servings: 6   Cooking Time: 8 Minutes

Ingredients:

2 cups cooked cauliflower

1 large egg, beaten

1 cup panko bread crumbs

1 tablespoon chopped fresh chives Spritz the air fryer basket with cooking spray

½ cup grated Parmesan cheese

Cooking spray.

Directions:

Put the cauliflower, panko bread crumbs, egg, Parmesan, and chives in a food processor, then pulse to lightly mash and combine the mixture until chunky and thick.   Shape the mixture into 6 flat patties, then arrange them in the basket and spritz with cooking spray.   Put the air fryer basket on the baking pan and slide into Rack Position 2, select Air Fry, set temperature to 390°F (199°C) and set time to 8 minutes.   Flip the patties halfway through the cooking time.   When done, the patties should be crispy and golden brown. Remove from the oven and serve immediately.

967. Chicken Sausage And Broccoli Casserole

Servings: 8   Cooking Time: 20 Minutes

Ingredients:

10 eggs

1 cup broccoli, chopped

1 cup Cheddar cheese, shredded and divided

2 cloves garlic, minced

¾ cup heavy whipping cream

½ tablespoon salt

1 (12-ounce / 340-g) package cooked chicken sausage

¼ tablespoon ground black pepper

Cooking spray

Directions:

Spritz the baking pan with cooking spray.   Whisk the eggs with Cheddar and cream in a large bowl to mix well.   Combine the cooked sausage, broccoli, garlic, salt, and ground black pepper in a separate bowl. Stir to mix well.   Pour the sausage mixture into the baking pan, then spread the egg mixture over to cover.   Slide the baking pan into Rack Position 1, select Convection Bake, set temperature to 400°F (205°C) and set time to 20 minutes. When cooking is complete, the egg should be set and a toothpick inserted in the center should come out clean.   Serve immediately.

968. Chicken Divan

Servings: 4   Cooking Time: 24 Minutes

Ingredients:

Salt and ground black pepper, to taste

4 chicken breasts

1 head broccoli, cut into florets

1 cup shredded Cheddar cheese

½ cup cream of mushroom soup

½ cup croutons

Cooking spray

Directions:

Spritz the air fryer basket with cooking spray.   Put the chicken breasts in the basket and sprinkle with salt and ground black pepper.   Put the air fryer basket on the baking pan and slide into Rack Position 2, select Air Fry, set temperature to 390°F (199°C) and set time to 14 minutes.   Flip the breasts halfway through the cooking time.   When cooking is complete, the breasts should be well browned and tender.   Remove the breasts from the oven and allow to cool for a few minutes on a plate, then cut the breasts into bite-size pieces. Combine the chicken, broccoli, mushroom soup, and Cheddar cheese in a large bowl. Stir to mix well.

Spritz the baking pan with cooking spray. Pour the chicken mixture into the pan. Spread the croutons over the mixture. Slide the baking pan into Rack Position 1, select Convection Bake, set time to 10 minutes. When cooking is complete, the croutons should be lightly browned and the mixture should be set. Remove from the oven and serve immediately.

969.	Southwest Seasoning

Servings: About ¾ Cups   Cooking Time: 0 Minutes

Ingredients:

3 tablespoons ancho chile powder	2 teaspoons cayenne
3 tablespoons paprika	2 teaspoons cumin
	1 tablespoon granulated onion
2 tablespoons dried oregano	1 tablespoon granulated garlic
2 tablespoons freshly ground black pepper	

Directions:
Stir together all the ingredients in a small bowl. Use immediately or place in an airtight container in the pantry.

970.	Dehydrated Crackers With Oats

Ingredients:

3 tablespoons (20g) psyllium husk powder	¾ cup (50g) pumpkin seeds
2 teaspoons fine sea salt	¼ cup (35g) sesame seeds
1 teaspoon freshly ground black pepper	2 tablespoons (30g) chia seeds
2 teaspoons ground turmeric, divided	1½ cups (150g) rolled oats
3 tablespoons melted coconut oil	1½ cups (360ml) water
1 cup (125g) sunflower seeds	1 large parsnip (10 ounces/300g), finely Grated
½ cup (75g) flaxseeds	

Directions:
In a large bowl Blend All of the seeds, Oats, psyllium husk, pepper, salt and 1 teaspoon ground turmeric. Whisk coconut water and oil together in a measuring Cup. Add to the dry ingredients and blend well until all is totally saturated and dough becomes very thick. Mix grated parsnip using 1 tsp turmeric and stir to blend. Shape the first half to a disc and place it with a rolling pin, firmly roll dough to a thin sheet that the size of this dehydrate basket. Put dough and parchment paper at the dehydrate basket. Repeat steps 4 with remaining dough. Hours and allow Rotate Remind. Place dehydrate baskets in rack positions 5 and 3. Press START. Dehydrate crackers until tender. When prompted By Rotate Remind, rotate the baskets leading to back and change rack amounts. Eliminate baskets out of oven and let rest for 10 minutes. Split crackers into shards. Container for up to two months.

971.Sweet Cinnamon Chickpeas

Servings: 2   Cooking Time: 10 Minutes

Ingredients:

1 cup chickpeas, soaked in water overnight, rinsed and drained	1 tablespoon cinnamon
	1 tablespoon sugar

Directions:
Combine the cinnamon and sugar in a bowl. Stir to mix well. Add the chickpeas to the bowl, then toss to coat well. Pour the chickpeas in the air fryer basket. Put the air fryer basket on the baking pan and slide into Rack Position 2, select Air Fry, set temperature to 390°F (199°C) and set time to 10 minutes. Stir the chickpeas three times during cooking. When cooked, the chickpeas should be golden brown and crispy. Remove from the oven and serve immediately.

972.	Broccoli, Carrot, And Tomato Quiche

Servings: 4   Cooking Time: 14 Minutes

Ingredients:

4 eggs	¼ cup crumbled feta cheese
1 teaspoon dried thyme	1 cup grated Cheddar cheese
1 cup whole milk	
1 steamed carrots, diced	1 teaspoon chopped parsley
2 cups steamed broccoli florets	Salt and ground black pepper, to taste
2 medium tomatoes, diced	Cooking spray

Directions:
Spritz the baking pan with cooking spray. Whisk together the eggs, thyme, salt, and ground black pepper in a bowl and fold in the milk while mixing. Put the carrots, broccoli, and tomatoes in the prepared baking pan, then spread with feta cheese and ½ cup Cheddar cheese. Pour the egg mixture over, then scatter with remaining Cheddar on top. Slide the baking pan into Rack Position 1, select Convection Bake, set temperature to 350°F (180°C) and set time to 14 minutes. When cooking is complete, the egg should be set and the quiche should be puffed. Remove the quiche from the oven and top with chopped parsley, then slice to serve.

973.   Simple Cheesy Shrimps

Servings: 4 To 6   Cooking Time: 8 Minutes

Ingredients:

⅔ cup grated Parmesan cheese	1 teaspoon basil
4 minced garlic cloves	2 tablespoons olive oil
1 teaspoon onion powder	2 pounds (907 g) cooked large shrimps, peeled and deveined
½ teaspoon oregano	Lemon wedges, for topping
1 teaspoon ground black pepper	Cooking spray

Directions:

Spritz the air fryer basket with cooking spray. Combine all the ingredients, except for the shrimps, in a large bowl. Stir to mix well.   Dunk the shrimps in the mixture and toss to coat well. Shake the excess off. Arrange the shrimps in the basket.   Put the air fryer basket on the baking pan and slide into Rack Position 2, select Air Fry, set temperature to 350°F (180°C) and set time to 8 minutes.   Flip the shrimps halfway through the cooking time.   When cooking is complete, the shrimps should be opaque. Transfer the cooked shrimps onto a large plate and squeeze the lemon wedges over before serving.

974.   Air Fried Blistered Tomatoes

Servings: 4 To 6   Cooking Time: 10 Minutes
Ingredients:

2 pounds (907 g) cherry tomatoes	2 teaspoons balsamic vinegar
2 tablespoons olive oil	½ teaspoon ground black pepper
½ teaspoon salt	

Directions:
Toss the cherry tomatoes with olive oil in a large bowl to coat well. Pour the tomatoes in the baking pan.   Put the air fryer basket on the baking pan and slide into Rack Position 2, select Air Fry, set temperature to 400°F (205°C) and set time to 10 minutes.   Stir the tomatoes halfway through the cooking time.   When cooking is complete, the tomatoes will be blistered and lightly wilted. Transfer the blistered tomatoes to a large bowl and toss with balsamic vinegar, salt, and black pepper before serving.

975.   Chinese Pork And Mushroom Egg Rolls

Servings: 25 Egg Rolls   Cooking Time: 33 Minutes
Ingredients:

Egg Rolls:

1 tablespoon mirin	1 clove garlic, minced
3 tablespoons soy sauce, divided	¼ teaspoon cornstarch
1 pound (454 g) ground pork	1 (1-pound / 454-g) package frozen egg roll wrappers, thawed
3 tablespoons vegetable oil, plus more for brushing	Dipping Sauce:
5 ounces (142 g) shiitake mushrooms, minced	1 scallion, white and light green parts only, sliced
4 cups shredded Napa cabbage	¼ cup rice vinegar
¼ cup sliced scallions	¼ cup soy sauce
1 teaspoon grated fresh ginger	Pinch sesame seeds Pinch red pepper flakes
	1 teaspoon granulated sugar

Directions:
Line the air fryer basket with parchment paper. Set aside.   Combine the mirin and 1 tablespoon of soy sauce in a large bowl. Stir to mix well.   Dunk the ground pork in the mixture and stir to mix well.

Wrap the bowl in plastic and marinate in the refrigerator for at least 10 minutes.   Heat the vegetable oil in a nonstick skillet over medium-high heat until shimmering. Add the mushrooms, cabbage, and scallions and sauté for 5 minutes or until tender.   Add the marinated meat, ginger, garlic, and remaining 2 tablespoons of soy sauce. Sauté for 3 minutes or until the pork is lightly browned. Turn off the heat and allow to cool until ready to use.   Put the cornstarch in a small bowl and pour in enough water to dissolve the cornstarch. Put the bowl alongside a clean work surface.   Put the egg roll wrappers in the basket.   Put the air fryer basket on the baking pan and slide into Rack Position 2, select Air Fry, set temperature to 400°F (205°C) and set time to 15 minutes.   Flip the wrappers halfway through the cooking time. When cooked, the wrappers will be golden brown. Remove the egg roll wrappers from the oven and allow to cool for 10 minutes or until you can handle them with your hands.   Lay out one egg roll wrapper on the work surface with a corner pointed toward you. Place 2 tablespoons of the pork mixture on the egg roll wrapper and fold corner up over the mixture. Fold left and right corners toward the center and continue to roll. Brush a bit of the dissolved cornstarch on the last corner to help seal the egg wrapper. Repeat with remaining wrappers to make 25 egg rolls in total.   Arrange the rolls in the basket and brush the rolls with more vegetable oil. Select Air Fry and set time to 10 minutes. Return to the oven. When done, the rolls should be well browned and crispy.   Meanwhile, combine the ingredients for the dipping sauce in a small bowl. Stir to mix well.   Serve the rolls with the dipping sauce immediately.

976.   Keto Cheese Quiche

Servings: 8   Cooking Time: 1 Hour
Ingredients:

Crust:

1¼ cups blanched almond flour	⅓ cup minced leeks
1 large egg, beaten	4 large eggs, beaten
1¼ cups grated Parmesan cheese	½ cup chicken broth
¼ teaspoon fine sea salt	⅛ teaspoon cayenne pepper
Filling:	¾ teaspoon fine sea salt
4 ounces (113 g) cream cheese	1 tablespoon unsalted butter, melted
1 cup shredded Swiss cheese	Chopped green onions, for garnish
	Cooking spray

Directions:
Spritz the baking pan with cooking spray. Combine the flour, egg, Parmesan, and salt in a large bowl. Stir to mix until a satiny and firm dough forms. Arrange the dough between two grease parchment papers, then roll the dough into a 1⁄16-inch thick circle.   Make the crust: Transfer the dough into the prepared pan and press to coat the bottom. Slide the baking pan into Rack Position 1, select Convection Bake, set temperature to 325°F (163°C)

and set time to 12 minutes. When cooking is complete, the edges of the crust should be lightly browned. Meanwhile, combine the ingredient for the filling, except for the green onions in a large bowl. Pour the filling over the cooked crust and cover the edges of the crust with aluminum foil. Slide the baking pan into Rack Position 1, select Convection Bake, set time to 15 minutes. When cooking is complete, reduce the heat to 300°F (150°C) and set time to 30 minutes. When cooking is complete, a toothpick inserted in the center should come out clean. Remove from the oven and allow to cool for 10 minutes before serving.

---

977. Golden Salmon And Carrot Croquettes

Servings: 6   Cooking Time: 10 Minutes
Ingredients:

2 egg whites	1 cup almond flour
1 cup panko bread crumbs	2 tablespoons minced garlic cloves
1 pound (454 g) chopped salmon fillet	½ cup chopped onion
⅔ cup grated carrots	2 tablespoons chopped chives
	Cooking spray

Directions:
Spritz the air fryer basket with cooking spray. Whisk the egg whites in a bowl. Put the flour in a second bowl. Pour the bread crumbs in a third bowl. Set aside. Combine the salmon, carrots, garlic, onion, and chives in a large bowl. Stir to mix well. Form the mixture into balls with your hands. Dredge the balls into the flour, then egg, and then bread crumbs to coat well. Arrange the salmon balls on the basket and spritz with cooking spray. Put the air fryer basket on the baking pan and slide into Rack Position 2, select Air Fry, set temperature to 350°F (180°C) and set time to 10 minutes. Flip the salmon balls halfway through cooking. When cooking is complete, the salmon balls will be crispy and browned. Remove from the oven and serve immediately.

---

978. Goat Cheese And Asparagus Frittata

Servings: 2 To 4   Cooking Time: 25 Minutes
Ingredients:

1 cup asparagus spears, cut into 1-inch pieces	Kosher salt and pepper, to taste
1 teaspoon vegetable oil	Add the asparagus spears to a small bowl and drizzle with the vegetable oil. Toss until well coated and transfer to the air fryer basket.
1 tablespoon milk	
6 eggs, beaten	
2 ounces (57 g) goat cheese, crumbled	
1 tablespoon minced chives, optional	

Directions:
Put the air fryer basket on the baking pan and slide into Rack Position 2, select Air Fry, set temperature

to 400°F (205°C) and set time to 5 minutes. Flip the asparagus halfway through. When cooking is complete, the asparagus should be tender and slightly wilted. Remove from the oven to the baking pan. Stir together the milk and eggs in a medium bowl. Pour the mixture over the asparagus in the pan. Sprinkle with the goat cheese and the chives (if using) over the eggs. Season with salt and pepper. Slide the baking pan into Rack Position 1, select Convection Bake, set temperature to 320°F (160°C) and set time to 20 minutes. When cooking is complete, the top should be golden and the eggs should be set. Transfer to a serving dish. Slice and serve.

---

979. Taco Beef And Chile Casserole

Servings: 4   Cooking Time: 15 Minutes
Ingredients:

1 pound (454 g) 85% lean ground beef	2 large eggs
1 tablespoon taco seasoning	1 cup shredded Mexican cheese blend
1 (7-ounce / 198-g) can diced mild green chiles	2 tablespoons all-purpose flour
½ cup milk	½ teaspoon kosher salt
	Cooking spray

Directions:
Spritz the baking pan with cooking spray. Toss the ground beef with taco seasoning in a large bowl to mix well. Pour the seasoned ground beef in the prepared baking pan. Combing the remaining ingredients in a medium bowl. Whisk to mix well, then pour the mixture over the ground beef. Slide the baking pan into Rack Position 1, select Convection Bake, set temperature to 350°F (180°C) and set time to 15 minutes. When cooking is complete, a toothpick inserted in the center should come out clean. Remove the casserole from the oven and allow to cool for 5 minutes, then slice to serve.

---

980. Pastrami Casserole

Servings: 2   Cooking Time: 8 Minutes
Ingredients:

1 cup pastrami, sliced	½ cup Cheddar cheese, grated
1 bell pepper, chopped	4 eggs
¼ cup Greek yogurt	¼ teaspoon ground black pepper
2 spring onions, chopped	Sea salt, to taste
	Cooking spray

Directions:
Spritz the baking pan with cooking spray. Whisk together all the ingredients in a large bowl. Stir to mix well. Pour the mixture into the baking pan. Slide the baking pan into Rack Position 1, select Convection Bake, set temperature to 330°F (166°C) and set time to 8 minutes. When cooking is complete, the eggs should be set and the casserole edges should be lightly browned. Remove from

the oven and allow to cool for 10 minutes before serving.

981.   Chicken Ham Casserole

Servings: 4 To 6   Cooking Time: 15 Minutes

Ingredients:

2 cups diced cooked chicken	½ cup half-and-half
1 cup diced ham	½ teaspoon ground black pepper
¼ teaspoon ground nutmeg	6 slices Swiss cheese
	Cooking spray

Directions:
Spritz the baking pan with cooking spray. Combine the chicken, ham, nutmeg, half-and-half, and ground black pepper in a large bowl. Stir to mix well.   Pour half of the mixture into the baking pan, then top the mixture with 3 slices of Swiss cheese, then pour in the remaining mixture and top with remaining cheese slices.   Slide the baking pan into Rack Position 1, select Convection Bake, set temperature to 350°F (180°C) and set time to 15 minutes.   When cooking is complete, the egg should be set and the cheese should be melted. Serve immediately.

982.   Kale Salad Sushi Rolls With Sriracha Mayonnaise

Servings: 12   Cooking Time: 10 Minutes

Ingredients:

Kale Salad:	Sushi Rolls:
1½ cups chopped kale	3 sheets sushi nori
1 tablespoon sesame seeds	1 batch cauliflower rice
¾ teaspoon soy sauce	½ avocado, sliced
¾ teaspoon toasted sesame oil	Sriracha Mayonnaise:
½ teaspoon rice vinegar	¼ cup Sriracha sauce
¼ teaspoon ginger	¼ cup vegan mayonnaise
⅛ teaspoon garlic powder	Coating:
	½ cup panko bread crumbs

Directions:
In a medium bowl, toss all the ingredients for the salad together until well coated and set aside. Place a sheet of nori on a clean work surface and spread the cauliflower rice in an even layer on the nori. Scoop 2 to 3 tablespoon of kale salad on the rice and spread over. Place 1 or 2 avocado slices on top. Roll up the sushi, pressing gently to get a nice, tight roll. Repeat to make the remaining 2 rolls.   In a bowl, stir together the Sriracha sauce and mayonnaise until smooth. Add bread crumbs to a separate bowl.   Dredge the sushi rolls in Sriracha Mayonnaise, then roll in bread crumbs till well coated.   Place the coated sushi rolls in the air fryer basket.   Put the air fryer basket on the baking pan and slide into Rack Position 2, select Air Fry, set temperature to 390°F (199°C) and set time to 10 minutes.   Flip the sushi rolls halfway through the cooking time.   When cooking is complete, the sushi rolls will be golden brown and crispy. . Transfer to a platter and rest for 5 minutes before slicing each roll into 8 pieces. Serve warm.

983.   Oven Baked Rice

Servings: About 4 Cups   Cooking Time: 35 Minutes

Ingredients:

1 tablespoon unsalted butter, melted, or 1 tablespoon extra-virgin olive oil	1 cup long-grain white rice, rinsed and drained
2 cups water	1 teaspoon kosher salt or ½ teaspoon fine salt

Directions:
Add the butter and rice to the baking pan and stir to coat. Pour in the water and sprinkle with the salt. Stir until the salt is dissolved.   Select Bake, set the temperature to 325°F (163°C), and set the time for 35 minutes. Select Start to begin preheating. Once the unit has preheated, place the pan in the oven.   After 20 minutes, remove the pan from the oven. Stir the rice. Transfer the pan back to the oven and continue cooking for 10 to 15 minutes, or until the rice is mostly cooked through and the water is absorbed.   When done, remove the pan from the oven and cover with aluminum foil. Let stand for 10 minutes. Using a fork, gently fluff the rice.   Serve immediately.

984.   Air Fried Crispy Brussels Sprouts

Servings: 4   Cooking Time: 20 Minutes

Ingredients:

¼ teaspoon salt	1 pound (454 g) Brussels sprouts, trimmed and halved
⅛ teaspoon ground black pepper	
1 tablespoon extra-virgin olive oil	Lemon wedges, for garnish

Directions:
Combine the salt, black pepper, and olive oil in a large bowl. Stir to mix well.   Add the Brussels sprouts to the bowl of mixture and toss to coat well. Arrange the Brussels sprouts in the air fryer basket. Put the air fryer basket on the baking pan and slide into Rack Position 2, select Air Fry, set temperature to 350°F (180°C) and set time to 20 minutes.   Stir the Brussels sprouts two times during cooking. When cooked, the Brussels sprouts will be lightly browned and wilted. Transfer the cooked Brussels sprouts to a large plate and squeeze the lemon wedges on top to serve.

985.   Traditional Latkes

Servings: 4 Latkes   Cooking Time: 10 Minutes

Ingredients:

2 tablespoons all-purpose flour	1 egg
2 medium potatoes, peeled and shredded, rinsed and drained	¼ teaspoon granulated garlic
	½ teaspoon salt
	Cooking spray

197

Directions:
Spritz the air fryer basket with cooking spray. Whisk together the egg, flour, potatoes, garlic, and salt in a large bowl. Stir to mix well. Divide the mixture into four parts, then flatten them into four circles. Arrange the circles onto the basket and spritz with cooking spray. Put the air fryer basket on the baking pan and slide into Rack Position 2, select Air Fry, set temperature to 380°F (193°C) and set time to 10 minutes. Flip the latkes halfway through. When cooked, the latkes will be golden brown and crispy. Remove from the oven and serve immediately.

---

986. Citrus Avocado Wedge Fries

Servings: 12 Fries   Cooking Time: 8 Minutes
Ingredients:

1 cup all-purpose flour	1 cup yellow cornmeal
3 tablespoons lime juice	2 large Hass avocados, peeled, pitted, and cut into wedges
¾ cup orange juice	
1¼ cups plain dried bread crumbs	Coarse sea salt, to taste
1½ tablespoons chile powder	Cooking spray

Directions:
Spritz the air fryer basket with cooking spray. Pour the flour in a bowl. Mix the lime juice with orange juice in a second bowl. Combine the bread crumbs, cornmeal, and chile powder in a third bowl. Dip the avocado wedges in the bowl of flour to coat well, then dredge the wedges into the bowl of juice mixture, and then dunk the wedges in the bread crumbs mixture. Shake the excess off. Arrange the coated avocado wedges in a single layer in the basket. Spritz with cooking spray. Put the air fryer basket on the baking pan and slide into Rack Position 2, select Air Fry, set temperature to 400°F (205°C) and set time to 8 minutes. Stir the avocado wedges and sprinkle with salt halfway through the cooking time. When cooking is complete, the avocado wedges should be tender and crispy. Serve immediately.

---

987. Spinach And Chickpea Casserole

Servings: 4   Cooking Time: 21 To 22 Minutes
Ingredients:

2 tablespoons olive oil	1 onion, chopped
2 garlic cloves, minced	1 pound (454 g) spinach
1 tablespoon ginger, minced	1 can coconut milk
1 chili pepper, minced	½ cup dried tomatoes, chopped
Salt and ground black pepper, to taste	1 (14-ounce / 397-g) can chickpeas, drained

Directions:
Heat the olive oil in a saucepan over medium heat. Sauté the garlic and ginger in the olive oil for 1 minute, or until fragrant. Add the onion, chili pepper, salt and pepper to the saucepan. Sauté for 3 minutes. Mix in the spinach and sauté for 3 to 4 minutes or until the vegetables become soft. Remove from heat. Pour the vegetable mixture into the baking pan. Stir in coconut milk, dried tomatoes and chickpeas until well blended. Slide the baking pan into Rack Position 1, select Convection Bake, set temperature to 370°F (188°C) and set time to 15 minutes. When cooking is complete, transfer the casserole to a serving dish. Let cool for 5 minutes before serving.

---

988. Sumptuous Vegetable Frittata

Servings: 2   Cooking Time: 20 Minutes
Ingredients:

4 eggs	1 small red onion, sliced
⅓ cup milk	
2 teaspoons olive oil	⅓ cup crumbled feta cheese
1 large zucchini, sliced	
2 asparagus, sliced thinly	⅓ cup grated Cheddar cheese
⅓ cup sliced mushrooms	¼ cup chopped chives
1 cup baby spinach	Salt and ground black pepper, to taste

Directions:
Line the baking pan with parchment paper. Whisk together the eggs, milk, salt, and ground black pepper in a large bowl. Set aside. Heat the olive oil in a nonstick skillet over medium heat until shimmering. Add the zucchini, asparagus, mushrooms, spinach, and onion to the skillet and sauté for 5 minutes or until tender. Pour the sautéed vegetables into the prepared baking pan, then spread the egg mixture over and scatter with cheeses. Slide the baking pan into Rack Position 1, select Convection Bake, set temperature to 380°F (193°C) and set time to 15 minutes. Stir the mixture halfway through. When cooking is complete, the egg should be set and the edges should be lightly browned. Remove the frittata from the oven and sprinkle with chives before serving.

---

989. Roasted Mushrooms

Servings: About 1½ Cups   Cooking Time: 30 Minutes
Ingredients:

1 teaspoon kosher salt or ½ teaspoon fine salt	1 pound (454 g) button or cremini mushrooms, washed, stems trimmed, and cut into quarters or thick slices
3 tablespoons unsalted butter, cut into pieces, or extra-virgin olive oil	
	¼ cup water

Directions:
Place a large piece of aluminum foil on the sheet pan. Place the mushroom pieces in the middle of the foil. Spread them out into an even layer. Pour the water over them, season with the salt, and add the butter. Wrap the mushrooms in the foil. Select Roast, set the temperature to 325°F (163°C), and set the time

for 15 minutes. Select Start to begin preheating. Once the unit has preheated, place the pan in the oven. After 15 minutes, remove the pan from the oven. Transfer the foil packet to a cutting board and carefully unwrap it. Pour the mushrooms and cooking liquid from the foil onto the sheet pan. Select Roast, set the temperature to 350°F (180°C), and set the time for 15 minutes. Return the pan to the oven. Select Start to begin. After about 10 minutes, remove the pan from the oven and stir the mushrooms. Return the pan to the oven and continue cooking for anywhere from 5 to 15 more minutes, or until the liquid is mostly gone and the mushrooms start to brown. Serve immediately.

990.   Hot Wings

Servings: 16 Wings   Cooking Time: 15 Minutes
Ingredients:

3 tablespoons hot sauce	16 chicken wings
	Cooking spray

Directions:
Spritz the air fryer basket with cooking spray. Arrange the chicken wings in the basket. Put the air fryer basket on the baking pan and slide into Rack Position 2, select Air Fry, set temperature to 360°F (182°C) and set time to 15 minutes. Flip the wings at lease three times during cooking. When cooking is complete, the chicken wings will be well browned. Remove from the oven. Transfer the air fried wings to a plate and serve with hot sauce.

991.   Mediterranean Quiche

Servings: 4   Cooking Time: 30 Minutes
Ingredients:

4 eggs	½ cup milk
¼ cup chopped Kalamata olives	½ tablespoon chopped oregano
½ cup chopped tomatoes	½ tablespoon chopped basil
¼ cup chopped onion	Salt and ground black pepper, to taste
1 cup crumbled feta cheese	Cooking spray

Directions:
Spritz the baking pan with cooking spray. Whisk the eggs with remaining ingredients in a large bowl. Stir to mix well. Pour the mixture into the prepared baking pan. Slide the baking pan into Rack Position 1, select Convection Bake, set temperature to 340°F (171°C) and set time to 30 minutes. When cooking is complete, the eggs should be set and a toothpick inserted in the center should come out clean. Serve immediately.

992.   Potato Chips With Lemony Cream Dip

Servings: 2 To 4   Cooking Time: 15 Minutes
Ingredients:

2 large russet potatoes, sliced into ⅛-inch slices, rinsed	¼ teaspoon lemon juice
Sea salt and freshly ground black pepper, to taste	2 scallions, white part only, minced
Cooking spray	1 tablespoon olive oil
Lemony Cream Dip:	¼ teaspoon salt
½ cup sour cream	Freshly ground black pepper, to taste

Directions:
Soak the potato slices in water for 10 minutes, then pat dry with paper towels. Transfer the potato slices in the air fryer basket. Spritz the slices with cooking spray. Put the air fryer basket on the baking pan and slide into Rack Position 2, select Air Fry, set temperature to 300°F (150°C) and set time to 15 minutes. Stir the potato slices three times during cooking. Sprinkle with salt and ground black pepper in the last minute. Meanwhile, combine the ingredients for the dip in a small bowl. Stir to mix well. When cooking is complete, the potato slices will be crispy and golden brown. Remove from the oven and serve the potato chips immediately with the dip.

993.   Caesar Salad Dressing

Servings: About ⅔ Cup   Cooking Time: 0 Minutes
Ingredients:

½ cup extra-virgin olive oil	¼ teaspoon kosher salt or ⅛ teaspoon fine salt
2 tablespoons freshly squeezed lemon juice	1 egg, beaten
1 teaspoon anchovy paste	Add all the ingredients to a tall, narrow container.
¼ teaspoon minced or pressed garlic	

Directions:
Purée the mixture with an immersion blender until smooth. Use immediately.

994.   Crunchy And Beery Onion Rings

Servings: 2 To 4   Cooking Time: 16 Minutes
Ingredients:

⅔ cup all-purpose flour	¾ cup beer
1 teaspoon paprika	1½ cups bread crumbs
½ teaspoon baking soda	1 tablespoons olive oil
1 teaspoon salt	1 large Vidalia onion, peeled and sliced into ½-inch rings
½ teaspoon freshly ground black pepper	Cooking spray
1 egg, beaten	

Directions:
Spritz the air fryer basket with cooking spray. Combine the flour, paprika, baking soda, salt, and ground black pepper in a bowl. Stir to mix well. Combine the egg and beer in a separate bowl. Stir to mix well. Make a well in the center of the flour mixture, then pour the egg mixture in the well. Stir to mix everything well. Pour the bread crumbs and olive oil in a shallow plate. Stir to mix well. Dredge the onion rings gently into the flour and egg mixture, then shake the excess off and put into the plate of bread crumbs. Flip to coat the both sides

well. Arrange the onion rings in the basket.   Put the air fryer basket on the baking pan and slide into Rack Position 2, select Air Fry, set temperature to 360°F (182°C) and set time to 16 minutes.   Flip the rings and put the bottom rings to the top halfway through.   When cooked, the rings will be golden brown and crunchy. Remove from the oven and serve immediately.

995.   Bartlett Pears With Lemony Ricotta

Servings: 4   Cooking Time: 8 Minutes
Ingredients:

3 tablespoons melted butter	2 large Bartlett pears, peeled, cut in half, cored
½ teaspoon ground ginger	1 teaspoon pure lemon extract
¼ teaspoon ground cardamom	1 teaspoon pure almond extract
3 tablespoons brown sugar	1 tablespoon honey, plus additional for drizzling
½ cup whole-milk ricotta cheese	

Directions:
Toss the pears with butter, ginger, cardamom, and sugar in a large bowl. Toss to coat well. Arrange the pears in the baking pan, cut side down.   Put the air fryer basket on the baking pan and slide into Rack Position 2, select Air Fry, set temperature to 375°F (190°C) and set time to 8 minutes.   After 5 minutes, remove the pan and flip the pears. Return to the oven and continue cooking.   When cooking is complete, the pears should be soft and browned. Remove from the oven.   In the meantime, combine the remaining ingredients in a separate bowl. Whip for 1 minute with a hand mixer until the mixture is puffed.   Divide the mixture into four bowls, then put the pears over the mixture and drizzle with more honey to serve.

996.   Garlicky Olive Stromboli

Servings: 8   Cooking Time: 25 Minutes
Ingredients:

4 large cloves garlic, unpeeled	½ cup packed fresh basil leaves
3 tablespoons grated Parmesan cheese	¼ teaspoon crushed red pepper
½ cup marinated, pitted green and black olives	4 ounces (113 g) sliced provolone cheese (about 8 slices)
½ pound (227 g) pizza dough, at room temperature	Cooking spray

Directions:
Spritz the air fryer basket with cooking spray. Put the unpeeled garlic in the basket.   Put the air fryer basket on the baking pan and slide into Rack Position 2, select Air Fry, set temperature to 370°F (188°C) and set time to 10 minutes.   When cooked, the garlic will be softened completely. Remove from the oven and allow to cool until you can handle. Peel the garlic and place into a food processor with 2 tablespoons of Parmesan, basil, olives, and

crushed red pepper. Pulse to mix well. Set aside. Arrange the pizza dough on a clean work surface, then roll it out with a rolling pin into a rectangle. Cut the rectangle in half.   Sprinkle half of the garlic mixture over each rectangle half, and leave ½-inch edges uncover. Top them with the provolone cheese. Brush one long side of each rectangle half with water, then roll them up. Spritz the basket with cooking spray. Transfer the rolls to the basket. Spritz with cooking spray and scatter with remaining Parmesan. Select Air Fry and set time to 15 minutes.   Flip the rolls halfway through the cooking time. When done, the rolls should be golden brown.   Remove the rolls from the oven and allow to cool for a few minutes before serving.

997.   Butternut Squash With Hazelnuts

Servings: 3 Cups   Cooking Time: 23 Minutes
Ingredients:

2 tablespoons whole hazelnuts	3 cups butternut squash, peeled, deseeded and cubed
¼ teaspoon kosher salt	2 teaspoons olive oil
¼ teaspoon freshly ground black pepper	Cooking spray

Directions:
Spritz the air fryer basket with cooking spray. Spread the hazelnuts in the pan.   Put the air fryer basket on the baking pan and slide into Rack Position 2, select Air Fry, set temperature to 300°F (150°C) and set time to 3 minutes.   When done, the hazelnuts should be soft. Remove from the oven. Chopped the hazelnuts roughly and transfer to a small bowl. Set aside.   Put the butternut squash in a large bowl, then sprinkle with salt and pepper and drizzle with olive oil. Toss to coat well. Transfer the squash to the lightly greased basket.   Put the air fryer basket on the baking pan and slide into Rack Position 2, select Air Fry, set temperature to 360°F (182°C) and set time to 20 minutes.   Flip the squash halfway through the cooking time.   When cooking is complete, the squash will be soft. Transfer the squash to a plate and sprinkle with the chopped hazelnuts before serving.

998.   Lemony Shishito Peppers

Servings: 4   Cooking Time: 5 Minutes
Ingredients:

½ pound (227 g) shishito peppers (about 24)	Coarse sea salt, to taste
1 tablespoon olive oil	Lemon wedges, for serving
	Cooking spray

Directions:
Spritz the air fryer basket with cooking spray. Toss the peppers with olive oil in a large bowl to coat well.   Arrange the peppers in the basket.   Put the air fryer basket on the baking pan and slide into Rack Position 2, select Air Fry, set temperature to 400°F (205°C) and set time to 5 minutes.   Flip the peppers and sprinkle the peppers with salt halfway through the cooking time.   When cooked, the

peppers should be blistered and lightly charred. Transfer the peppers onto a plate and squeeze the lemon wedges on top before serving.

---

999. Golden Nuggets

Servings: 20 Nuggets   Cooking Time: 4 Minutes

Ingredients:

1 cup all-purpose flour, plus more for dusting

1 teaspoon baking powder

½ teaspoon butter, at room temperature, plus more for brushing

¼ teaspoon salt

¼ cup water

⅛ teaspoon onion powder

¼ teaspoon garlic powder

⅛ teaspoon seasoning salt

Cooking spray

Directions:
Line the air fryer basket with parchment paper. Mix the flour, baking powder, butter, and salt in a large bowl. Stir to mix well. Gradually whisk in the water until a sanity dough forms.   Put the dough on a lightly floured work surface, then roll it out into a ½-inch thick rectangle with a rolling pin.   Cut the dough into about twenty 1- or 2-inch squares, then arrange the squares in a single layer in the basket. Spritz with cooking spray.   Combine onion powder, garlic powder, and seasoning salt in a small bowl. Stir to mix well, then sprinkle the squares with the powder mixture.   Put the air fryer basket on the baking pan and slide into Rack Position 2, select Air Fry, set temperature to 370°F (188°C) and set time to 4 minutes.   Flip the squares halfway through the cooking time.   When cooked, the dough squares should be golden brown.   Remove the golden nuggets from the oven and brush with more butter immediately. Serve warm.

1000. Pão De Queijo

Servings: 12 Balls   Cooking Time: 12 Minutes

Ingredients:

2 tablespoons butter, plus more for greasing

½ cup milk

1½ cups tapioca flour

½ teaspoon salt

1 large egg

⅔ cup finely grated aged Asiago cheese

Directions:
Put the butter in a saucepan and pour in the milk, heat over medium heat until the liquid boils. Keep stirring.   Turn off the heat and mix in the tapioca flour and salt to form a soft dough. Transfer the dough in a large bowl, then wrap the bowl in plastic and let sit for 15 minutes.   Break the egg in the bowl of dough and whisk with a hand mixer for 2 minutes or until a sanity dough forms. Fold the cheese in the dough. Cover the bowl in plastic again and let sit for 10 more minutes.   Grease the baking pan with butter.   Scoop 2 tablespoons of the dough into the baking pan. Repeat with the remaining dough to make dough 12 balls. Keep a little distance between each two balls.   Slide the baking pan into Rack Position 1, select Convection Bake, set temperature to 375°F (190°C) and set time to 12 minutes.   Flip the balls halfway through the cooking time.   When cooking is complete, the balls should be golden brown and fluffy.   Remove the balls from the oven and allow to cool for 5 minutes before serving.

1001. Milky Pecan Tart

Servings: 8   Cooking Time: 26 Minutes

Ingredients:

Tart Crust:

¼ cup firmly packed brown sugar

⅓ cup butter, softened

1 cup all-purpose flour

¼ teaspoon kosher salt

Filling:

¼ cup whole milk

4 tablespoons butter, diced

½ cup packed brown sugar

¼ cup pure maple syrup

1½ cups finely chopped pecans

¼ teaspoon pure vanilla extract

¼ teaspoon sea salt

Directions:
Line the baking pan with aluminum foil, then spritz the pan with cooking spray.   Stir the brown sugar and butter in a bowl with a hand mixer until puffed, then add the flour and salt and stir until crumbled. Pour the mixture in the prepared baking pan and tilt the pan to coat the bottom evenly.   Slide the baking pan into Rack Position 1, select Convection Bake, set temperature to 350°F (180°C) and set time to 13 minutes.   When done, the crust will be golden brown.   Meanwhile, pour the milk, butter, sugar, and maple syrup in a saucepan. Stir to mix well. Bring to a simmer, then cook for 1 more minute. Stir constantly.   Turn off the heat and mix the pecans and vanilla into the filling mixture.   Pour the filling mixture over the golden crust and spread with a spatula to coat the crust evenly.   Select Bake and set time to 12 minutes. When cooked, the filling mixture should be set and frothy.   Remove the baking pan from the oven and sprinkle with salt. Allow to sit for 10 minutes or until cooled. Transfer the pan to the refrigerator to chill for at least 2 hours, then remove the aluminum foil and slice to serve.

Made in United States
Orlando, FL
16 December 2024

55716168R00111